-Rep) is
front
the
's donors.

Israeli government approaches SA to suggest a weapons-for-coal barter trade worth $300 million.

Georges Starckmann organises the purchase of 160 Soviet-built missiles for SA from East Germany. In 1986 Noriega seizes shipment in Panama.

ersonally
ment of
m China
adi in

Ton Vosloo confirms that Naspers makes R150,000 donation to the National Party.

US Senator Richard Stone proposes $50 million pro-apartheid propaganda plan to the South African Department of Foreign Affairs.

SA's embassy in Tel Aviv warns Pretoria that the presence of SA military officials is obvious due to the prevalence of Afrikaans spoken in schools and shops.

US company International Signal and Control (ISC), allegedly backed by the CIA, ships ballistic missile technology and equipment to SA... some of which were passed on to Beijing.

Tory MP Julian Amery visits Jonas Savimbi in Jamba. He is later chastised by the US ambassador to Oman for not helping set up a missile transaction with Savimbi.

Mid-1980s–mid-1990s:

$15 million passed through the Armscor bank accounts in Luxembourg weekly during this period.*

*According to an ex-Armscor employee in Paris,

d sets up
telligence
S missiles

International Freedom Foundation, a South African military front, funds Jack Kemp's unsuccessful campaign for Republican nominee.

s meeting
ation, Le
h. Repeat
s in 1988

Senior SADF and French officials meet in Paris. French offer spare parts for Mirage jets and to smuggle weapons via South America. Chirac asks Pretoria to delay release of French political prisoner Pierre-André Albertini.

First democratic election, Nelson Mandela elected president of Government of National Unity. The new South African Constitution adopted in 1996.

W Botha's
m prison.

State of Emergency declared. Hundreds of civilians are killed and thousands injured by police during protests.

F)   PW Botha delivers 'Rubicon' speech.

South African troops re-enter Angola, leading to the battle of Cuito Cuanavale.

ANC chief representative to France, Luxembourg and Switzerland, Dulcie September, is murdered in Paris.

FW de Klerk announces unbanning of liberation movements and release of Mandela. Negotiations take place during period of bloody conflict.

1960s–1990:

80,000 people detained without trial, many tortured and some disappeared.

Namibia gains independence.

| 1985 | 1986 | 1987 | 1988 | 1989 | 1990 | 1991 | 1992 | 1993 | 1994 |

se to roll over
SA, prompting
Swiss banker
r negotiates a
ill for Pretoria.

French Prime Minister Jacques Chirac elected (until 1988); Comprehensive Anti-Apartheid Act passed by US Congress.

US Congress starts hearings on Iran-Contra affair.

End of war in Angola. South African, Cuban and Russian troops agree to withdrawal, unlocking Namibian independence.

Arms and oil sanctions lifted.

er 100,000 Angolans
as a result of war-
ated famine.

Berlin Wall is torn down, Cold War ends

The Tale of Profit
in numbers

$36.8 billion

spent from the Special Defence Account on weapons and intelligence (1974–1994)*

*Current value

600:1

The size of the Special Defence Account versus the Information Scandal

76 Armscor front companies in Liberia

39 in Panama – linked to hundreds of bank accounts

30 the number of Armscor officials working on the top floor of South Africa's embassy in Paris, tasked with buying weapons and managing the money-laundering network.

844 bank accounts

in 196 banks across at least 27 countries helped Armscor move money around the globe to bust sanctions.

40 years

The legacy of economic crime from apartheid to contemporary state capture

'One of the most important global money-laundering schemes ever'

~Professor Mark Pieth.

The five permanent members

All five members of the UN Security Council – France, UK, USA, China and the Soviet Union – busting sanctions by selling weapons and/or technology to apartheid South Africa

$3.1+ million

in donations to the National Party from 48 individuals and companies revealed for the first time*

*Current value

47 countries identified as collaborating to bust arms, oil and trade sanctions for apartheid South Africa

APARTHEID GUNS AND MONEY

Apartheid Guns and Money

A tale of profit

Hennie van Vuuren

RESEARCH

Michael Marchant
with
Anine Kriegler & Murray Hunter

HURST & COMPANY, LONDON

First published in the United Kingdom in 2018 by
C. Hurst & Co. (Publishers) Ltd.,
41 Great Russell Street, London, WC1B 3PL

Printed in the United Kingdom by Bell & Bain Ltd, Glasgow

Distributed in the United States, Canada and Latin America by
Oxford University Press, 198 Madison Avenue, New York, NY 10016,
United States of America.

The right of Hennie van Vuuren to be identified as the author of this
publication is asserted by him in accordance with the Copyright, Designs
and Patents Act, 1988.

A Cataloguing-in-Publication data record for this book
is available from the British Library.

ISBN: 978-1-78738-097-4

www.hurstpublishers.com

Dedicated to friends and comrades who,
in seeking justice, demand the right to know,
live to tell the truth and love unconditionally

'*You follow drugs, you get drug addicts and drug dealers.*
But you start to follow the money, and you don't
know where the fuck it's gonna take you.'
– DETECTIVE LESTER FREAMON, *THE WIRE*, SEASON 1

This book is intended to be in the public interest. The public has a right to know. It is based on a vast body of information collected from numerous sources. These include archival records, declassified documents, academic literature such as books, and newspaper articles. Interviews with sources, both named and those who didn't want to reveal their identity, provide eye witness accounts. In addition, material was provided to me from confidential sources. I have endeavoured to verify information to the extent possible.

Subsequent to publication of this book, Open Secrets together with the South African History Archive will make available source documents for public scrutiny.

Contents

INTRODUCTION

On the Trail of Profit

'We are the liquidators of this firm,' the state president is reported to have said to one of his ministers in December 1989.[1] The two men stood on the stoep of the presidential home outside Durban overlooking the Indian Ocean. The humid air was almost certainly heavy with the smell of expensive liquor and acrid cigarette smoke. The Berlin Wall had fallen a month prior and the tide of politics seemed to be turning across the globe. FW de Klerk, the newly elected state president and leader of the National Party (NP), was the CEO of a regime at war with its people and running out of time. The death squads prowling the streets and the nuclear warheads in its bunker could hold the line, but for how much longer? A decade, perhaps; maybe two.

Three years later the trucks grumbled to a halt at a factory outside Pretoria. The final act of liquidation was about to begin. A former intelligence officer reports that after the shredders stopped working, millions of documents containing the intimate details of agents and citizens alike were torn up by hand, packed into standard, black refuse bags and fed to the roaring flames.[2] The heat was so intense that the bags sometimes bounced back before the fire caught them. The National Intelligence Agency (NIA) alone destroyed 44 tonnes of documents.[3]

1

With this, the written record of countless acts of individual culpability were destroyed. The memory of iniquity, injustice and oppression could not be erased as easily. It remains with those who carry that burden, physically, emotionally and materially. But could the last all-white government, through this final act of vengeance and self-preservation, leave enough blank spaces in history that future generations would forever fail to tell this country's story? Will this act condemn South Africans who outlived this regime to repeat its wicked ways?

There is little evidence to suggest that South Africa today, while still struggling to achieve the democratic heights envisioned by activists past and present, is threatened by a reintroduction of the system of apartheid. However, shades of that system, which continue to this day, do threaten our freedom. Inequality, poverty, insecurity, state surveillance, excessive police force, selective prosecutions and threats to media freedom form a good part of the post-apartheid political experience. Such practices strike a chord of anger among ordinary people precisely because this is familiar terrain. South Africans have good reason to demand that elites take their finger off the repeat button, not only because our Constitution is explicit about what our rights are, but because it is aspirational in how these rights should be advanced to the benefit of all.

An outlier in our understanding of apartheid practice has been the issue of corruption and economic crime in the post-apartheid period. It did not start to manifest the day that the Mandela administration was inaugurated. Our conception of South Africa as a 'new' nation was a helpful tool to build national unity at a key moment, but it has also meant that we have denied uncomfortable truths. When Nelson Mandela was elected president, his government had to craft a new administration from disparate authorities in former white-administered provinces and ethnic black homelands alike. He had to deal with the internal contradictions of a liberation movement that was home to all and inevitably counted crooks and opportunists among its ranks. Added to this was the existence of a powerful private sector, dominated by white business interests, that had a habit of betting on the short term.

The democratic elections in 1994 and the finalisation of the Constitution two years later signalled a commitment to integrity and to the creation of public institutions that sought to uphold these principles. With this, a message was sent that corruption at all levels would not be tolerated. But this important process had a caveat: corruption and economic crime in the past would be left to lie, like fat, rich sleeping dogs. To have looked backwards and prosecuted past crimes at that exact moment could have wrecked the peace-making process. The reason was the scope and scale of economic crimes. Thorough investigation would have touched powerful interest groups across the globe: bankers, arms dealers, political parties, foreign leaders, arms companies, oil traders, lobbyists, foreign intelligence agencies and the domestic military. They were all implicated in a largely criminal economy that was thought best left buried – even if we recognise, in hindsight, that this was folly.

The apartheid economy had, in the preceding 15 years, built a massive infrastructure to bust international sanctions. With the help of friends across the globe who smelt profit, a criminal economy was put in place to sustain white power. A highly secretive machinery was created to corrupt politicians, launder public and private funds, and break international sanctions. This effectively criminalised key institutions within the public and private sector. And it relied extensively on the support of right-wing business, political and intelligence networks across the globe.

This pervasive international system – a war machine, as I describe it – remains a largely hidden aspect of our past, and it is this that I attempt to piece together in this book. So, too, does the identity of the multitude of individuals who created and ran it. Nevertheless, there is no doubt that the war machine was an essential element of the survival of PW Botha's government and the political fortunes of his ministers such as De Klerk. The machinery funded war and violence in South Africa and elsewhere. NP politicians and their allies in business became enmeshed in a sinister world governed by the interests of right-wing forces, neoconservatives and anti-democratic regimes. Even the South African parliament, which existed for minorities only, was largely blind to the extent of these endeavours. These were deep state networks that operated outside the law in South Africa and other countries. Gallingly, as we will see repeatedly through this book, many of the countries that aided and abetted apartheid had officially supported sanctions against South Africa's racist regime and, in certain instances, openly funded the liberation movements.

All this came at great cost. It required money and a reliance on intelligence structures, particularly within the military, to manage these power networks. To bust sanctions, to buy guns and oil and other goods, required ideological affinity, race-based sympathy and money – in vast quantities.

The reason for forgetting is, also, deeply personal. It is undeniable that white South Africans in general benefited from apartheid – a form of corruption that looked after a small group at the expense of the majority. By the mid-1980s, the NP had begun to privatise state institutions, emulating Margaret Thatcher's Britain. It needed poorer white voters, and relied on beating the drum of communism, the *swart gevaar*, and the war on the 'border' to ensure that it retained its electoral majority. But at the same time this race-based oligarchy increasingly gave special attention to its richest and most powerful citizens and their international networks. They needed influence and access. The men who could guarantee this were kept close.

In February 1990, little over a month after De Klerk's seaside epiphany, he would set in motion the release of Nelson Mandela, the unbanning of liberation movements and the start of negotiations that led to South Africa's first democratic elections. Four years later, more than a decade of low-level conflict was ended and the system of apartheid was finally eradicated. It would be wrong, however, to succumb to De Klerk's post-apartheid predilection for playing up the altruism and humanity of his decision. He did help bring an end to apartheid. However, he was arguably as much motivated by self-preservation and the strategic realisation that further decades of apartheid would end up eroding the viability of the state and threaten the economic well-being of the businesses and white voters on which he based his support.

Today, many of those who supported apartheid and oppression in South Africa either deny or conceal their acts of past complicity. With the interests of the firm wound up, these men – and they were almost always men – assuage their conscience with random acts of charity or statements of exculpation. The messiness of undoing the damage is left to others.

The former state president's analogy of South Africa as a firm is a helpful one. The country has, for much of its past, been beholden to the interests of corporations that sought to extract its abundance to the detriment of most of its people. The fight for political control of South Africa has therefore inevitably involved powerful private interests. The first European settler community in the Cape did not serve a king but the Dutch East India Company, the world's first multinational corporation and one of the wealthiest corporations in human history, which made its fortune off the spice trade. Its settlement at the foot of Table Mountain was an important replenishment point for its ships that passed between Europe and Asia.

By the 19th century, the British Empire had gained control over a significant part of South Africa, apart from the two republics governed by the Boers. After the discovery of the largest deposits of gold on earth, shareholders in South African and British mining companies aimed their sights on controlling these areas, too, under the British flag. Businessmen such as Cecil John Rhodes fomented conflict that, to his personal advantage, led to war. The Empire prevailed, at great human cost, together with a small group of mining companies that reaped the economic benefit. It was all theirs. They were aided by the destructive 1913 Natives Land Act, which served to alienate black people from ancestral land, forcing men to seek employment as low-earning mine workers far from home.

The rise of Afrikaner nationalism in 1948 saw the cruel politics of apartheid become state policy. Black South Africans and dissenting voices were stripped of the little political power they had. With independence from the British Commonwealth in 1961, it was self-evident that English capital would need to accommodate the interests of new white Afrikaans corporations that had strong ties to the NP establishment. For decades, they supported the policies of apartheid while their opposition, when it registered, was more of a whisper than a shout of protest. By the late 1980s, following sustained internal resistance and external pressure, something had to give. Even the largest South African corporations, powerful shareholders in the NP's system of dominance, were willing to compromise if they could cash in their shares.

At the time of writing, South Africa is wrestling with how to dislodge the interests of firms that again threaten freedom. We now refer to this as 'state capture'. Despite universal suffrage and a Constitution that provides a powerful defence of personal and political freedoms, we see private interests enmeshed in our politics in a way that thwarts the realisation of the aspirational vision of the Constitution. This was evident in the murder in 2012 of Lonmin mine workers at Marikana by the police. It is also evident in alleged links between President Zuma and the Gupta family, as set out in the Public Protector's 2016 'State of Capture' report. The report, based on testimony by prominent public figures, exemplifies attempts by a small group of well-connected businessmen to capture politics and, ultimately, the Treasury, which the politicians control. The cry for economic justice is intensifying, exactly at the same time as integrity among those who have stewardship over the economy falters.

How then do we untangle this mess?

A first step is to understand the manner in which private interests have, over a long time, been complicit in acts of oppression. This is by no measure a uniquely South African experience. However, the question demands an answer if we are to address the inequality of economic power in South Africa, the seventh most unequal country in the world. Ahead in that poll are all four of the other BRICS member-states.[4] The global wealth pyramid is stubbornly geared towards the mega-rich. According to the anti-poverty group Oxfam, in 2017 only eight people own as much wealth as the poorest half of the population.[5] Post-apartheid South Africa, too, has shown the same trend of rising income and wealth inequality. Two South African families have assets equal to those of 50% of the country's poorest people.

The problems of inequality will, however, not be addressed by political leaders who have allowed themselves to be corrupted. It is therefore fundamental to understand both the nature of power in South Africa and the nature of elite criminality – the way in which corruption has become ingrained in the practice of our politics and business.

When attempting to understand the phenomenon of corruption, our recorded history suggests a trajectory that starts with relatively small crimes and mismanagement in the Mandela era (think of the speaker of parliament, Baleka Mbete, and her fake driver's licence). This was accelerated under the Mbeki administration with the post-apartheid multibillion-dollar arms deal with corrupt European arms companies. This was the first big scandal that rocked our politics. It has undermined the constitutional order as public institutions were weakened to protect the corporations, their middlemen and South African politicians from prosecution for their alleged crimes linked to the deal. This happened against the backdrop of narrow black economic empowerment and other types of collusive corporate behaviour, such as price fixing, that have damaged the economy at the expense of the poor. Jacob Zuma, a man implicated in over 783 acts of criminality linked to the arms deal, enters this timeline as proof of a country gone wrong, a politician allegedly steeped in the practice of corruption and patronage who now uses the might of state security to cling to power.

Missing from this analysis is an important prequel, an understanding of a crucial period in South Africa's history from the mid-1970s to the mid-1990s. During this 20-year period a mix of factors gave rise to a perfect storm that left an indelible impact on our history and society. It was a time of unparalleled abuse of power. When the struggle for South Africa's freedom was at its fiercest, economic crime not only festered, but became state policy. Corruption, money laundering, sanctions busting and organised crime, the elements of such economic crime, had become a necessity for the survival of the state.

This was not only a pattern of practice that would be inherited at the end of apartheid. Many of the actors that were corrupt under apartheid rapidly ingratiated themselves into the new order. This created a new elite pact based on criminality and corruption. The arms deal is the most potent example of the devastating impact this new criminal class had on the country's democratic institutions. The old and the new were quickly intertwined and found in each other partners and protectors.

In April 1961 Nelson Mandela wrote a final letter of ultimatum to NP Prime Minister Hendrik Verwoerd on behalf of the African National Congress (ANC). It requested the government to abandon plans of establishing a Republic that carried only the mandate of white South Africans, and instead called for a sovereign national convention to draw up a non-racial and democratic constitution. Failing this, Mandela and the ANC, in lucid tones, promised protest and resistance. Importantly, he also called for sanctions, which would become a pillar of resistance politics for the next decades: 'We call on democratic people the world over to refrain from any cooperation or dealings with the South African government, to impose economic and other sanctions against this country and to isolate in every possible way the minority Government whose continued disregard of all human rights and freedoms constitutes a threat to world peace.'[6]

Mandela would subsequently organise a strike as he had threatened, which led Verwoerd's government to imprison him on this and related charges. The United Nations (UN) General Assembly responded with a voluntary arms embargo in 1963. By 1964 Mandela and other ANC leaders were sentenced to life in prison. Following the Soweto uprisings of 1976 and the murder of Steve Biko in 1977, the UN Security Council imposed mandatory arms sanctions on South Africa. One of the longest-lasting sanctions in modern international politics, they would starve the South African war economy. Underpinning this was a 1973 decision by the UN General Assembly that declared apartheid a crime against humanity. It condemned not only racism in South Africa but all 'inhuman acts committed for the purpose of establishing and maintaining domination by one racial group of persons over any other racial group of persons and systematically oppressing them'.[7]

With a civil war in Angola raging and the securocrats under PW Botha in the ascendant, plans had to be made to circumvent these sanctions. Weapons were needed to make war and oil was needed to fuel an economy that had become part of the war effort. Such plans were devised by the securocrats under PW Botha, the influential bureaucrats in the security sector such as the military, the intelligence services and police who dominated government thinking at the time.

This book sets out the implementation of this plan.

Firstly, heightened state secrecy was key to the plan, criminalising any reporting – be it by journalists or nominally independent oversight mechanisms – that could undermine the anti-sanctions effort. The security state became a central tenet of PW Botha's administration. In the process the public were fooled into complacency after the apartheid-era Information Scandal of the late 1970s, which led to the promise of a new, cleaner and more ordered regime. In reality, a new, more sinister, secret, money-for-arms machine was developed by Botha's securocrats. It was far larger than the Information Scandal by an order of magnitude. All government departments were drawn into the anti-sanctions effort in different ways. Within the defence force, the establishment of Armscor as the state-owned arms company was a crucial element. It established an international network to procure weapons and technology, which were reproduced or improved at home, tested in battle in countries such as Angola, and then subsequently marketed overseas to foreign clients as a source of foreign revenue.

Secondly, a secret economy was required that bound the interests of domestic corporations into the 'anti-sanctions' campaign. Reliant on procurement by the state for its growing war economy, corporations were accomplices to the project of the NP: funding the party, defending the status quo and busting sanctions as required. A key element of the secret economy was the covert channelling of oil to South Africa from across the globe by supplier countries, traders and shipping companies that reaped the profits from the premiums they were able to charge.

Thirdly, trusted banking allies were called on to keep the lines of credit flowing in the face of growing calls from the anti-apartheid movement that apartheid should no longer have access to easy money on international capital markets. This was successful, thanks in part to the European lenders. However, the banks also played a far more sinister role. They acted as money launderers for tens of billions of rands (more than half a trillion rands in current values) used to purchase weapons on the international market. The 1980s, which ushered in electronic banking systems connected via primitive internet-like networks that made the large-scale, rapid movement of cash across the globe easy and instantaneous, could not have come sooner. Armscor, with requisite approval from the Reserve Bank and the executive, began to move cash between front companies in Panama and Liberia, with the complicity of one notable European bank in particular.

Fourthly, allies were called on to secretly lend a hand. The most important group were the Big Five permanent members of the UN Security Council, the most powerful nations on earth at the time and the biggest arms manufacturers. France was an old ally that looked the other way despite a socialist president. The United Kingdom and the United States were far safer bets with the emergence of the conservative governments of Ronald Reagan and Margaret Thatcher. Their brand of neoliberalism wanted apartheid 'reformed' without fundamentally challenging white rule. Within all these countries there is significant evidence of deep state networks at play – the confluence of interests between intelligence sectors, governments, corporations, arms producers and political parties. At the other end of the Cold War spectrum we can reveal that the liberation movement's traditional allies in the Eastern bloc, including Russia and China, were also finding ways to accommodate and trade weapons with the apartheid state.

Finally, we have found evidence of at least four dozen other countries that acted as proxies for the big powers in providing the apartheid state with weapons. They were located in Africa, Asia, Europe and the Americas. In turn, they were matched by the eager assistance provided by fellow pariah states such as Israel, Argentina and Chile, whose authoritarian regimes or domestic policies made them fellow outcasts and natural allies of the apartheid regime. Support for apartheid South Africa relied on more than just racial solidarity: by the 1980s money was driving covert politics across the globe.

This description of corruption, a secret economy and a network of international allies has for long been shielded and obscured by myths. These in turn have created a misleading narrative about the nature of apartheid and economic crime in that period. This book seeks to dispel those myths. It specifically aims to help the reader bust the following inventions.

11

Myth 1: Corruption is a racial phenomenon

A powerful misconception, fuelled both by former NP leaders and persistent racism, is that corruption in South Africa is a phenomenon that is intrinsic to majority rule. It is the subtext of some criticism of the post-apartheid state. It is made more obvious by the singular focus on contemporary corruption in government, with little reflection on the private sector where white South Africans are more prominent. As the book shows, the apartheid regime lied, bribed and broke every rule in the book to bust sanctions. The scale of these activities was so large that they should have been included in economic indicators at the time. These were not piecemeal activities. Instead, state capture was systemic. This is therefore not a study of what is incorrectly labelled 'white corruption'. To refer to white or black corruption is not only crude, but is simply incorrect: there is no basis in evidence to support a racial reading of corruption. Money does not know colour, as shown by the profile of people who assisted with arms sanctions-busting activities. While there was a predisposition to networks of white power, powerful people of all shades, religious beliefs and continents were drawn into aiding and abetting these crimes.

Our understanding of issues of economic crime the world over is still bedevilled by cultural relativism. The consequence of seeing such crimes, which are fundamentally crimes of human rights, as specific to cultural groups is that it shifts our attention away from powerful corrupt elite networks that claim a false cultural neutrality. The propensity for corruption relies on a mixture of secrecy and concentration of power. Apartheid is an excellent example of this. Nevertheless, countless other examples are evident, from New York's Wall Street to the Communist Party headquarters in Beijing.

One of the reasons that South Africa cannot afford to be caught in the trap of what the writer Songezo Zibi refers to as 'moral relativism' is that it entraps us. It leaves us unable to confront contemporary corruption because the practice was largely unchecked during apartheid.[8] Mobilising race when dealing with corruption is, when considered, merely an expedient argument best left to the paid Twitter followers of the corrupt.

Myth 2: Freedom signalled a clean break with the past

Everything did not change overnight in newly democratic South Africa. Consider how we continue to battle with the increasing problems of unemployment and inequality. The corporations, middlemen, politicians and intelligence agencies that assisted the apartheid state also did not disappear off the scene for good. This is most evident in the corrupt arms deal of the Mbeki era. A number of the leading arms, oil and commodity sanctions busters played a role in this. In some instances, tenders were incorrectly and corruptly awarded to the same companies that had kept apartheid alive. If we had investigated these issues at the time – or if intelligence authorities spent time in the state archives – they might have done more to insulate the state from doing business with such corrupt entities. Within the private sector, these tendencies to subvert and undermine the rule of law could be arrested by new corporate governance standards, but they could not be erased overnight.

There was therefore no clean break with our past after 1994: the corrupt networks would soon be back. On their return, they were more nuanced in their approach and deferential to the new elite, who rapidly welcomed them in with a familiar, warm South African embrace.

Myth 3: Apartheid South Africa was an isolated state

The sanctions period was known as 'isolation'. This was made tangible at the UN, in international forums and in areas such as sports and culture. Psychologically this was a powerful weapon that was used skilfully by the organised anti-apartheid movement across the globe. From Lagos to London and Washington DC, tens of thousands of activists organised themselves into local groups and rallied against apartheid. It was one of the most significant acts of international solidarity of the 20th century, driven by human rights groups, faith groups, trade unions and other structures. The notion of 'isolation' is now used as one of the primary reasons for the end of apartheid.

In reality, while it significantly contributed to the regime's economic woes, it did not provide an existential threat. The apartheid security state under PW Botha used the threat of 'isolation' to its own advantage. As Hannah Arendt has argued, isolationism is an intrinsic element of totalitarian regimes.[9] The NP could use this, through propaganda, to rally support while heaping on themselves the status of victim.

We need to separate reality from fiction. Isolation was the fiction, widely repeated for political ends. In reality, the apartheid state walked through open doors around the world, and had direct diplomatic and economic links behind closed doors. It bought, sold and bartered with the heads of corporations, governments and intelligence agencies. An army of crafty middlemen made a mint of money out of helping to cut such deals. This is a reflection not of how the anti-apartheid movement was defeated, but of how conservative political groupings and their financial interests collude to undermine the work of democrats. This book sets out to prove that point.

Economic and strategic sanctions did little to visibly alter the lives of the white minority: they simply paid more tax. The banks lent money, the oil tankers kept arriving, and weapons systems and associated technology, though more expensive to procure, remained in abundant supply.

Myth 4: Apartheid was self-sufficient
One of the myths of the late-apartheid period was that South Africa was a self-sufficient arms producer. It was not. It became expert at smuggling technology and expertise into the country and, in some instances, improving on this, before churning out the same goods under other names in its own factories. In other instances, container loads of key weapons were simply imported. This not only fuelled a war economy, but became the driver for a conflict in which the military–industrial complex was deeply invested.

Myth 5: Apartheid was unprofitable

The South African casino economy of the 1980s left a small elite group very wealthy. Money was extracted from the mines, the arms sector and state procurement. All were key to the fortunes made by a tiny elite within the golden circle. There were no doubt major factors which inhibited economic development. These included the debt crisis of the mid-1980s, political unrest, high public debt and spending on war, inflation and a host of other factors. However, for much of the 1980s big business made massive profits from apartheid. For the captains of industry to arrive, cap in hand, at the Truth and Reconciliation Commission (TRC) and argue, disingenuously, that they too were 'victims' of apartheid is an affront to the truth and an insult to the true victims of apartheid.

Myth 6: The defeat of apartheid was inevitable

An idea that has been popularised by some ANC leaders is that victory in 1994 was inevitable. Following this logic is that all concessions that were made were consciously done by the ANC as a calculated political choice. This has, in turn, led critics of the ANC to suggest that it sold out on the cheap to (white minority) capital.

This is a deeply ahistorical understanding of the country's recent history. The capitulation of the apartheid regime was by no means inevitable by the early 1990s. It was undoubtedly under immense internal and external pressure; however, the regime had developed a clandestine supply chain of weapons and was looking at going as far as building its own clandestine ports to deliver goods to foreign countries. We can speculate, but if the securocrats had prevailed, it is possible that the regime could have lasted for another ten or 20 years. It may have seen a much closer relationship with countries such as China, or isolationism protected by a nuclear shield as in the case of North Korea. However, the military could have very likely kept on fighting, resulting in the loss of tens of thousands more lives. This is not to detract from the struggle against apartheid but to recognise how powerful the military machinery was that these women and men confronted.

It was this power that helped to secure the survival of this elite and its perpetuation in the post-apartheid period. The negotiation process was not a process of surrender. It was a process of give and take. The power of these groups and the potential they had at the time to wreak havoc by using their military and economic might should not be underestimated.

Myth 7: We cannot undo this wrong

Truth telling and justice are essential components for lasting peace. It is crucial that we continue to unpick the open secrets of our recent past. They inevitably define part of who we are as a country and the factors that represent obstacles in any quest to achieve meaningful social justice. The crimes of profit, just like those of murder, deserve to be challenged, and as the last chapter suggests, we can use advocacy and the law to achieve this. There are opportunities in law that should allow us to address some of these issues if there is the political will to do so. South Africa is also not the only country attempting to clear up the legacy of economic crimes that are linked to human rights violations, and the experience of other countries shows that it is not only never too late, but it is possible.

The personal is inevitably political and this book, while evidence-based, is also deeply personal. As an African and a South African, the journey of researching this book was not only about finding the facts, but gaining a better understanding of the forces that shape our present and what that means for our future.

Under apartheid, my classification as white brought me spoken and unspoken privilege and, most importantly, the benefit of a solid public education. I am a product of state subsidies that saw me attend universities beyond the reach of my parents, neither of whom completed their schooling or lived a life of plenty. They worked the land. They are the children of concentration camp inmates and prisoners of war who had trekked to the highveld in the mid-19th century. It's an ancestry of both refugees who settled in the Cape in the 17th century and aristocrats who led the Dutch East India Company. It is a bloodline of peasants and scoundrels and of black and white.

I cannot forget the madness of apartheid even if it was intended for my benefit: the family members in the police; the indoctrination at school which demanded preparation for a war that I am happy I never had to fight; a system that controlled all aspects of life, including who we loved and how we did so.

I have a strong memory of being caught up in this as a ten-year-old. I was with hundreds of white primary school kids, on the field of the Harry Oppenheimer Stadium, not far from the country's biggest gold mines in the North West Province. Security was tight on this crisp highveld morning when the old apartheid Republic Day was to be celebrated. PW Botha landed next to the stadium in a helicopter and alighted into a black limousine that drove him slowly around the track. As he circled, he waved to the crowds of white folks. I saw his hand or his hat peeking out of a back window. He then gave a speech as we sweltered in the sun, after which he quickly took off in his helicopter. With this came the realisation that we were there merely to witness his presence. He had not come to see us, as had been drummed into our heads in dozens of hours of rehearsal at school. Without a crowd of applauding white people he was nothing, but with their support came his power. Complicity is not only about pulling the trigger, but requires ordinary people to acquiesce and agree to give power to those who use it against us.

PW Botha, unlike other authoritarian leaders, never took a bullet in a bunker. Instead he retired to a modest villa in the seaside resort town of Wilderness. He may never have had to account for his crimes, but the marvel of democracy unfolded despite his presence on our landscape.

I have had the privilege to work on this book with a small team of researchers for more than four years. They, together with the lawyers, archivists and friends who have supported this process, are the 'we' I refer to in this book, as it is a collective effort. They are individually acknowledged at the end of the book.

I first started looking at some of these issues almost ten years ago. At the time, leaders in civil society lobbied government to investigate what we referred to as 'apartheid grand corruption'. It was a no-brainer – a story of corruption that the 'new government' would surely want to deal with. However, I soon recognised that there was little appetite for the past. Friendly government officials told me that a report I wrote went to Cabinet and was manoeuvred into a bureaucratic dead end. I found myself in the company of leaders of business and civil society caught up in an exchange with the finance minister, Trevor Manuel, who, visibly irritated, remarked that he had fought these men but that we must nevertheless tread carefully when discussing these issues.

Since then, this question has always nagged. I was told we would never figure out the sanctions networks. I was also warned by old lefties with holiday villas by the sea that we shouldn't 'tamper with the compromise', as if it was a golden calf that demanded our adulation and not our questions. A multi-billionaire, a so-called proud South African, with a wine farm in Franschhoek berated me at our first meeting for using a few inches in a newspaper column to indirectly question the source of some of his wealth. Over the next two hours he proceeded to harangue me in front of his son. I was to serve as a lesson to the younger man. The bottom line of his rant was that he demanded both my pity and respect. He was the victim. It made no sense that a man with unimaginable wealth and power would spend over two hours trying to convince me of his struggle credentials, reading from a handwritten note of praise he had received from Nelson Mandela. I left with more questions.

As the scale of high-level corruption in successive democratic administrations became apparent, it seemed clear to me that we had to grapple with the longer-term question of elite corruption in South Africa. This is a missing piece of the puzzle.

The research process that has resulted in this book has been an arduous but ultimately rewarding one. We benefited from over 110 interviews with leaders in government, business and the security sector. Some of them were opponents of the regime. Many of these people gave of their time. While they may not all agree with the content of the book, their insights proved hugely important as they were eyewitnesses to many of these secrets.

A vast collection of apartheid-era material remains locked away in public and private archives. Much of it has been untouched by South African researchers. It's a rich vein of material that demands our attention as we come to understand our story. We worked through more than two million pages of documents. Many of these were secret government documents declassified in response to access to information requests using the Promotion of Access to Information Act (PAIA). We collected approximately 40,000 documents in 25 public archives, consulting numerous collections in seven countries including South Africa, Belgium, Germany, the Netherlands, Switzerland, the United Kingdom and the United States. In most instances, these documents have either only recently been declassified or received little attention from researchers given the dearth of investigative work undertaken in this field. All the documents collected will be handed to the South African History Archive (SAHA) to allow for consultation by other researchers.

In some instances, access to information requests made by SAHA, at our request, have been inexplicably denied. In mid-2013, 48 requests were lodged with state agencies in terms of PAIA. Most of these documents date from the period 1978–94 and also include TRC-related investigations (from the late 1990s). Most access to information requests have been ignored or refused on flimsy grounds. It was thanks to wise pro bono legal counsel that some departments finally relented. However, at the time of writing, SAHA has been forced to use the courts to challenge the Department of Defence and the

South African Reserve Bank. Both are obstinate in their refusal to grant access to apartheid-era records. Access to most public records remains a challenge in democratic South Africa.

This book is about a hidden past in a time of oppression. However, it is also a book about the present: about why open, honest government is worth fighting for on a daily basis and why the views of the powerful must never be accepted at face value. It also hopefully serves as a reminder of the destructive role that sinister conservative forces have played in world politics. As democracies lurch towards the right in Asia, Europe and the United States and we see foreign powers attempt to subvert democratic processes, we are reminded that democracy demands daily struggle.

This book is also a reminder to the powerful that the shame of the past will eventually haunt them and those that carry their name, even if they refuse to show contrition for profiting from injustice. We will never forget the names of those who died for freedom. Equally, we will never forget the names of the perpetrators of these crimes.

The Secret State

'As a nation, we would do well to examine
the taboos, the secrets and the disavowals at
the core of our collective memories.'
JACOB DLAMINI, *ASKARI*, 2015

CHAPTER 1

Securocrats, Sanctions and Assassinations

'Let me say, no attempt to overthrow our country by embargoes, subversion or revolution will succeed. Our security forces are trained to withstand revolution.'

– PW BOTHA, MINISTER OF DEFENCE,
23 AUGUST 1977

An obsession with secrecy

The apartheid regime, under the leadership of PW Botha, created an arms money-laundering machine to bust international sanctions. Before we delve into the murky international dimensions of this machinery, we need to understand how it was anchored in the deep state in South Africa. The central player was the military and, linked to it, the state-owned arms company, Armscor. From there the links flowed to Military Intelligence, business people and the international banking sector, whose absolute discretion, confidence and complicity were key requirements. The many thousands of people who worked for these organisations were sworn to secrecy and remained committed to that undertaking. If exposed, these deep state networks would have revealed an enormous criminal enterprise. This is not a tale of conventional corruption or theft, of which there was more than enough to go round. This was about something more sinister and central to the longevity of apartheid rule: the secret state.

To understand the legacy of apartheid-era secrecy, fast-forward to the present. In 2010, just as the world was gripped by World Cup soccer fever, the government of President Zuma was stealthily attempting to pass a new law – dubbed the 'Secrecy Bill' – that would criminalise the possession and dissemination of information that could expose the abuse of power. It was a law intended to strangle whistleblowers and investigative journalists. Its passage followed the decision to disband the Scorpions, the country's top anti-corruption agency. In a remarkable show of defiance, thousands of members of the public took to the streets across the country to protest against the Secrecy Bill, heralding the emergence of a broad new movement focusing on the nexus between political secrecy and the country's socio-economic malaise. Civil society leaders from all sectors organised under the banner of the Right2Know Campaign and were led in their marches by imams, bishops, rabbis, atheists, writers and recovering politicians.

This struggle shone the light on what has become a trend of growing malfeasance and political interference involving the State Security Agency. It was also a prescient reminder that many of today's leaders in politics, such as the president, who had been a spy chief in the ANC underground, remain enamoured of the politics of secrecy and security. Our current concern about contemporary acts of secrecy is born out of a healthy obsession with the abuse of power. The current administration is not immune to using the security services for its own political ends. It is precisely because we have seen the worst excesses of a secret state that this should never be allowed to be repeated.

The military take control

Behind the scenes: Brothers in arms

To understand the origins of the secret state, it is important to recognise that the National Party (NP) has a long association with the cult of secrecy. It was deeply ingrained in the NP way of thinking and informed the manner in which state and society would be organised. The invisible hand that directed the NP, and thus state policy, was the Broederbond (Brotherhood), an all-white patriarchal secret society established in 1918. It was originally intended as a society working for the economic, social and political upliftment of white Afrikaners following the end of the South African War. In time it grew to a membership of over 12,000 handpicked individuals organised in over 800 cells across the country.[1] It could count among its members every NP prime minister and president between 1948 and 1994, DF Malan to FW de Klerk. In addition, most cabinet members, military generals, heads of Afrikaans-speaking universities and the South African Broadcasting Corporation (SABC) were '*broeders*'. They were augmented by leaders in business, the clergy, teachers and other members of the new elite. What had started as a welfare organisation was, by the second half of the 20th century, the organisation at the centre of the apartheid machinery.

As Max du Preez notes, the Broederbond was obsessed with total secrecy. Members were required to swear a solemn oath to eternal secrecy, even if they were expelled or resigned.[2] The Broederbond used its influence, by the late-apartheid era, to drag the NP towards considering a new power-sharing arrangement. To ensure the survival of the Afrikaners it opened the way for real talks with the liberation movement.[3] However, like with many secretive societies, its influence was not benign. Some historians have argued that it was by the 1980s just a backroom reformist movement. This sidesteps the fact that it was responsible for developing some of the earliest thinking around the policy of apartheid. It normalised the practice of quashing the truth within the echelons of power. It should therefore be no surprise that its activities and modus operandi began to infect the rest of the white establishment.

BJ Vorster: Making war, losing battles

BJ Vorster, who had served as a hardline minister of justice, was elected as prime minister in 1966 in the immediate aftermath of the assassination of Hendrik Verwoerd. Two major events that occurred during Vorster's term of office changed the course of history in South Africa and in the region. One was the Soweto uprising, and the other was the war in Angola.[4]

To deal with internal opposition, Vorster significantly strengthened the role of the police in intelligence operations. In 1969 he set up the Bureau of State Security (BOSS), reporting directly to the prime minister, under General Hendrik van den Bergh, an old ally and friend, who is described by Dan O'Meara as personifying 'the most paranoid and most vicious tendencies in Afrikaner nationalism'.[5]

Vorster's style of managing his cabinet was fundamentally different from that of his predecessor and successor. He regarded himself as first among equals, allowing his ministers to fight over policy and pre-eminence. This pitted, for instance, the Department of Information, the country's propaganda unit, against the Ministry of Foreign Affairs. It equally meant that BOSS, which gathered intelligence both inside and outside the country, came into serious conflict with the military, which had regional ambitions of its own.[6]

In June 1975 the South African Defence Force (SADF), with authorisation from Vorster, began to arm the National Union for the Total Independance of Angola (UNITA) and the National Liberation Front of Angola (FNLA) rebels in Angola as part of a strategy to counter the left-leaning People's Movement for the Liberation of Angola (MPLA) government in Luanda. By August 1975, South African troops entered Angola in what would be an ill-considered conflict that saw them reach within spitting distance of Luanda before beating a hasty retreat in March 1976 as the campaign collapsed.[7]

The person held primarily responsible for this debacle was Van den

Bergh. As the primary source of intelligence to the military, BOSS had miscalculated the support the South Africans would receive from the Americans through their old friends at the Central Intelligence Agency (CIA).[8] BOSS had also misread a supposed verbal promise made by the US secretary of state, Henry Kissinger, that the United States had Pretoria's back.[9]

The war in Angola and the Soweto uprising led to a crisis of confidence in Vorster and his security apparatus. Most importantly, the military felt exposed by these conflicts. They did not have the requisite weaponry and, despite the influence of the defence minister, PW Botha, they felt overshadowed by Van den Bergh, the former policeman, who was effectively dictating military strategy.

Conjuring up the 'total onslaught'

Power started to tilt towards Botha and the military in 1977 when a new Defence White Paper was unveiled. This promised a far more strategic role for the military in future and envisioned the military as playing a far greater role in the affairs of the state. PW Botha famously defined the new logic of the state in 1978 as its preparedness for what he termed 'a psychological onslaught, an economic one, a diplomatic one, a military onslaught – a total onslaught'. The minister of defence imagined a situation of total war both at home and abroad that required a concomitant response. This was the 'total strategy' in which all sectors of society would become involved in the defence of the white state.

This new paradigm also placed the guarantee of 'free enterprise' at the core of its mission, ensuring that Botha had the support not only of the military but also the captains of industry.[10] These were the real beginnings of the military–industrial complex in South Africa and facilitated far more overt collaboration between government and business in the defence sector. The state also changed its discourse from favouring crude race-based policies to one of power sharing and economic growth as the panacea for all political and social woes.[11]

From the late 1970s an obsession developed within the state for technocratic, military-oriented solutions to political problems. This enabled the rise of the securocrats: technocrats who leaned heavily towards the narrow mindset of the military and state intelligence agencies and the police.

PW Botha: Imperial ambitions

Within a year of unveiling his new 'total strategy', Botha toppled Vorster and secured the leadership of the National Party and the country during heavy infighting within the NP in 1978.

As state president, he appointed General Magnus Malan as minister of defence, a political ally and loyal soldier with whom he had worked, while still himself minister of defence, as head of the army. Malan's rapid rise through the military, consistently being the youngest man in each of the senior positions he occupied, was in large part thanks to Botha's support. As Phillip Frankel points out, Botha nurtured a patron–client relationship with the military.[12] He listened to their leaders, promoted their interests, modernised their organisation and saw to their pre-eminence in both the intelligence and policy spheres.

Some of his colleagues still view Botha and the army of securocrats he employed to run the state as decisive leaders, tough men, like the Boer generals fighting the English empire, but with a soft heart and a love for the land. Such nostalgia is deceptive. Botha was a hard Cold War warrior who tended to view the world through the barrel of a gun. His ministers and supporters, happy to defer to his leadership, cheered him on.

As defence minister and later state president, Botha was credited with modernising the SADF, turning it from an army that operated with outdated equipment into the most potent military machine on the African continent by the late 1980s. All this came at massive human and financial cost. Botha's strategy for arming apartheid was based on the language of threat, total onslaught and resultant war. For this he needed an army of mostly white conscripts and a smaller number of coloured and black volunteers. In addition, the SADF had a permanent force of 85,000 and a further 10,000 men in the bantustan armies. Many of these men were left damaged and scarred for life by what they did and saw being done. In the event of war the defence force could muster between 500,000 and 1 million men.[13] Little wonder then why Abdul Minty, a leading voice in the Anti-Apartheid Movement's arms sanctions campaign, describes South Africa as a garrison state during the last years of PW Botha's rule.[14]

The primary area of deployment for the military was the occupation of Namibia and the war in Angola.[15] There was, to a lesser extent, some engagement in the proxy war in Mozambique. Between 1975 and 1988, with some intervals, the war in Angola was fought in support of Jonas Savimbi's UNITA movement and against the ruling MPLA in Luanda. It was also intended to weaken support for SWAPO resistance fighters and their call for the independence of Namibia, at that stage still under occupation by South Africa.[16]

The war in Angola recorded significant casualties. UNICEF estimated that between 1980 and 1985 over 100,000 Angolans died, largely as a result of war-related famine.[17] There is little doubt that the war would not have continued for as long as it did without its foreign backers – South Africa, the United States, Cuba, Russia and a host of other countries such as Zaire and China – which all gave covert support to the various warring parties.

In the environment of war, secrecy quickly became the default position for a government that gave priority to national security. Under the cloak of secrecy the abuse of power was tolerated and nurtured. People were murdered, detained and tortured within South Africa. Restrictions were regularly placed on the media, in particular during the 1970s and 1980s.[18] Cross-border raids on liberation movement bases saw people killed in countries such as Lesotho, Botswana and Swaziland. In maintaining the system that perpetuated such war and conflict, collaborators were important.[19] Firstly, they participated as bureaucrats, police officers and other functionaries. Secondly, the system relied on the soldiers, spies and sanctions busters in government and on the private sector for its defence needs.

The system also relied on politicians to manipulate the truth.PW Botha's National Party perfected the performance of white democracy. Much was invested in mechanisms intended to create the illusion of accountable governance.[20] Widespread corruption in government departments was dealt with by official commissions of inquiry, which in some rare instances saw senior ministers forced to resign in disgrace. But these mechanisms only served to distract from the key terrain of power, the 'deep state', where the decisions that really mattered were taken in secret, without accountability and with little consequence for criminal behaviour. The military, intelligence, foreign service, heads of corporations, the secretive Afrikaner Broederbond, police death squads and their various counterparts were all part of this deep state system.

Christi van der Westhuizen, in her book *White Power*,[21] describes this as a system of 'executive lawlessness', in which the excesses of the presidency and the securocrats were no longer beholden to justice. Through organs like the State Security Council (SSC), Botha's parallel secret cabinet, the security services increasingly directed public policy. They were intended to keep a lid on the growing calls for democratic government, which were crushed with overt force. From 1985 onwards, the few spaces that existed to move and organise were increasingly curtailed by successive states of emergency, which granted the executive even more power to suppress dissent and enforce NP rule.

To maintain its regime and wage its wars, South Africa needed arms, for which it was largely reliant on foreign imports. But its ability to procure weapons overseas was hampered by an arms embargo. In 1963 the UN imposed a voluntary arms embargo on South Africa. Rather optimistically, the embargo relied on 'the goodwill and integrity of member states' for its effective implementation.[22] Then, following years of lobbying by the Anti-Apartheid Movement, the UN passed a mandatory arms embargo in 1977. The groundwork for this was laid at an international conference earlier that year in Lagos,

Nigeria, attended by representatives from many countries.[23] A draft resolution, including economic and arms sanctions, was first blocked by the 'triple Western veto' by the United Kingdom, United States and France. But with pressure mounting – and after an agreement that economic sanctions would only be voluntary – the Security Council adopted Resolution 418. It made the arms embargo mandatory for all UN member states. UN members could no longer export weapons to South Africa, provide new licences to manufacture weapons, or assist in the development and manufacture of nuclear weapons.[24]

This was a victory for the Anti-Apartheid Movement with its tens of thousands of supporters across the globe. This broad coalition was one of the most effective social movements of the 20th century. Despite their idealism, courage and tenacity, they had a hard time challenging one of the most corrupt businesses on earth. Persuading the many government and private-sector interests tied to the murky world of the arms trade to abide by the arms embargo was an almost impossible task.

Abdul Minty served as the director of the World Campaign against Military and Nuclear Collaboration with South Africa from 1979. The World Campaign was established at the request of the UN in Norway under the patronage of luminaries of the left such as former Tanzanian President Julius Nyerere, Swedish Prime Minister Olof Palme (whose assassination remains unexplained), and the US human rights activist Coretta Scott King. When I met Minty, now a retired diplomat, in a Pretoria coffee shop, he set out the difficult circumstances in which he and his colleagues worked. Always wary of false flags, they had to take great care in verifying material. This was compounded by the politics of the time. Minty recalled, 'This was not just about scoring points but also about convincing people of our arguments. There was delicate diplomacy required throughout the process.'[25]

Much of Minty's material was open source. In most instances, weapons eventually make their way onto a battlefield and are reported on. However, he points out that they collaborated with journalists and activists who risked their lives to monitor the sale of weapons to South Africa. Given their formidable opponents, this small group was understandably unable to consistently pierce the veil of arms sanctions-busting networks. Searches through many archives, including that of the Anti-Apartheid Movement, show that there was little publicly accessible information about arms sanctions busting. The high-profile cases that were exposed, numbering two dozen at most, received extensive attention.

Despite this, South Africa's march to militarisation was unstoppable. It became both the moral justification for and the product of the country's growing isolation. In 1978, at the time that PW Botha was elected as prime minister, all defence production and procurement capacity was centralised under a new state-owned arms company, Armscor. By the mid-1980s, Armscor was one of the top 20 companies in South Africa in terms of its holdings. It operated its 11 manufacturing units, among other things, for aircraft (Atlas), guided missiles (Kentron), computer technology (Infoplan), heavy-calibre ammunition and bombs (Naschem), propellants and explosives (Somchem), satellites and long-distance missiles (Houwteq) and sight equipment (Eloptro). At its height Armscor employed 20,000 people directly and a further 100,000 indirectly, many of whom worked for its 3,000 subcontractors.[26] Several large private South African corporations, including Altron, Anglo American and Barlow Rand, were drawn into the arms industry, as we will see later in Chapter 2.

Armscor's mission was to procure, develop and produce weapons for domestic consumption by the SADF. By the late 1980s much of this newly acquired and developed technology became the basis for the export of weapons across the globe. This, too, was in contravention of the UN arms embargo. By that point Armscor, through massive public subsidy, had helped equip the most advanced military machine south of the Sahara. It was also one of the top arms exporters in the world, ranking behind Brazil and Israel among developing-country military suppliers and producers.[27]

Of course, Armscor's domestic manufacturing capacity required a network of international suppliers that provided the arms manufacturer with sophisticated technology to re-engineer as homegrown products. In other instances, the cargo holds of ships carried arms and ammunition to South Africa and its allies. As an officially authorised account of Armscor's history states,

> Successes achieved enabled Armscor to openly negotiate with most of the suppliers. Often the suppliers offered their assistance and advice regarding the creation of channels and the acquisition of end user certificates ... With the help and co-operation of a variety of friends from all over the world, Armscor succeeded in supplying the SADF and befriended countries with the necessary arms. All this was possible under the Armscor motto: 'A will to win'.[28]

Danie Steyn was a long-standing senior manager at Armscor before spending most of the 1980s as a minister in PW Botha's cabinet. He attributes much of Armscor's success to PW Botha and his will to get things done. In an interview, he described Botha's role in glowing terms: 'You know, Armscor was one of the most wonderful things that PW Botha established. We had no weapons when I arrived, just old stuff, but after PW left [as minister] we had weapons, equipment. It was definitely due to his leadership. I worked with him for eight years as minister of defence and then eight years as minister under him as president. He didn't struggle to give an answer. If he said no, you knew.'[29]

Revealingly, Steyn adds that he was able to travel around the world, although often covertly, concluding deals for secret defence projects with arms manufacturers and their agents during the 1970s: 'I was known in Europe as the man with a bag of gold, I got all the projects I needed. Nothing was turned down in France, the United Kingdom, Germany, anywhere.'[30]

Secret funds: The bag of gold

The massive arms procurement machine relied exclusively on state funding. Jacklyn Cock, a key writer on South Africa's militarisation, argues that at its peak the real defence budget was almost double the figure stated by Botha's government, accounting for 28% of state expenditure in 1988. To give a sense of contemporary scale: if one in every four rands from the national budget were to be spent on defence and war efforts today, it would consume over R250 billion, the amount spent on basic education, tertiary education and policing combined.[31]

An important channel for funding the military was the Special Defence Account (SDA), established in 1974 and intended to enable military procurement through Armscor. It did also, to a lesser extent, fund propaganda projects and sinister third-force activities that targeted civilians and political opponents in the late 1980s and early 1990s. It has also incorrectly, but rather appropriately, been labelled the Secret Defence Account. According to a report submitted by the auditor general's office to the Truth and Reconciliation Commission (and only recently declassified), from its inception in 1974 up to 1994 total expenditure from the account was a fraction shy of R50 billion.[32] In today's value, that amounts to R501 billion.

Expenditure on the account saw a general upward trend but it spiked in the mid-1980s, at the height of the civil revolt and the state of emergency. From 1985 to 1989, spending from the SDA more than doubled per year from R2.4 billion to R6 billion.[33] The auditor general's report provides an important record of this expenditure and was submitted on a voluntary basis to the TRC. Inexplicably, there was no examination of these records in any public hearings. By way of comparison, the National Intelligence Service (the civilian spooks), the South African Police (SAP) and the Department of Foreign Affairs were allocated a far smaller budget from the Secret Service Account. This amounted to little more than 2% of the funds allocated to the SDA between 1978 and 1994.[34]

The utilisation of SDA funds, as we will see, remains a matter largely of mystery. Some of it is pieced together in this book, but the extent of such expenditure and its utilisation are buried in tens of millions of classified pages of documents held in the Department of Defence archives. This is understandable as the system was designed to confound members of the public and oversight bodies alike.

Firstly, the public and the media were shut out by the secrecy provisions of the 1968 Armaments Act. The Act made any disclosure of Armscor imports, exports, acquisition, development and manufacture a crime punishable with a maximum 15-year jail term.[35] Secondly, according to the auditor general's report to the TRC, all reporting to oversight authorities on secret expenditure only required the relevant minister's signature as proof that all was above board. This changed following the Information Scandal in 1979, when the auditor general's office was accorded limited access. By 1981 an entirely unsatisfactory solution was found: the appointment of a retired SADF general who would have the right to review the content of projects and issue an audit certificate on behalf of the auditor general. This was clearly untenable. From the mid-1980s selected members of the auditor general's staff were allowed to audit ultra-sensitive portions of the SDA, but access to information about what they were auditing was still off limits.[36] However, in this period, the auditor general reported on these matters at the discretion of the state president. If he balked, access would be denied.

As the auditor general's office noted in its report to the TRC, 'Whilst Parliament required the Office to provide audit assurance, the Government begrudgingly provided access to information and the quality of some of the audit evidence produced was limited.'[37] To protect itself from being implicated in a cover-up, the auditor general's office went as far as seeking a legal opinion regarding its responsibilities.[38] A routine disclaimer on the audit of the SDA noted that 'the level of audit assurance that can be furnished will often be lower than is normally the case in ordinary audits'.[39] What this meant was that the qualified audited records complied with the legal requirements, but the auditor general's office couldn't confirm that goods had been delivered in terms of the law.[40]

Joop de Loor, the auditor general between 1985 and 1988, recalls in an interview that his office was not allowed to have any information on what he terms secret oil and arms procurement schemes: 'we only knew second-hand about what was going on'.[41] De Loor says that the lack of investigation by the auditor general into the Special Defence Account did not become a major issue in the white parliament as the minister of finance (especially Owen Horwood) would keep the chairperson of the Public Accounts Committee up to date and ensure that no questions would be put in parliament regarding 'sensitive' information. According to him, Harry Schwartz, who chaired the Public Accounts Committee, and others in the opposition benches 'knew what was going on'.[42] Helpfully, Schwartz, a leader in the opposition Progressive Federal Party (PFP) and the person responsible for ensuring oversight of public funds, was a military hawk, as his colleague Helen Suzman recognised.[43]

According to De Loor, the minister of finance had to take full responsibility for any secret accounts that were 'not available for auditing'.[44] On the other hand, the former finance minister Barend du Plessis, contrary to his auditor general, maintains that he knew very little about how the SDA worked. 'I was not informed of the details of the budget comprising the SDA. I didn't know anything about it. I didn't dare to ask, that was a military thing and that would have been inappropriate for me to ask. Once the budget is approved by parliament I had no say whatsoever or the right to be informed about anything.'[45] He did add that by the late 1980s, after De Loor had been succeeded by Peter Wronsley, they gained increasing insight into the books of the military. However, they were only informed 'about the objectives and we had to sign off that those objectives qualify to be included in terms of the relevant legislation. I got signing off powers. It would say: "cattle farming in Gabon, this was the amount, this was the major amounts that were spent." That was all done with the understanding that I was not to be privy to any information beyond the financing.'[46] This meant that the auditors were effectively flying blind; the books might balance, but they were prohibited from verifying much beyond that.

When pressed as to whether the lack of insight into the defence enclave was not disempowering as minister of finance, Du Plessis responds, 'That was reality. I could have thrown my toys out of the cot but that was the fact. PW Botha always thought of SA as being at war and we had an obligation to defend SA.'[47] He went on to add that he had full faith in Defence Minister Magnus Malan's use of state finances as he was 'patriotic and law abiding'.[48] But there is a caveat: Du Plessis argues that he didn't have power to change much and knew little. 'If I or my predecessor had been involved to the extent that we could veto something, then that would have been a very difficult position to retain … The secret thing was the head of state and his confidant, the minister of defence.'[49]

With this, Du Plessis sidesteps responsibility and passes the buck to Magnus Malan and PW Botha. However, Wally van Heerden, long-time senior official within the auditor general's office, has a different recollection. He was responsible for auditing secret projects during the 1980s to the extent that this was possible in terms of the law at the time. He recalls that when Du Plessis had to sign off on secret funding, he would 'hold his hands across a document so as to block out the text and ask "where must I sign?" We would say, no, Minister, you have to study the contents of the document as well.'[50] The diligent bureaucrats would not allow the minister to relinquish his responsibility. The minister of finance's signature was a requirement for expenditure from secret funds, including the SDA and such funding provided to the Department of Foreign Affairs, the police and intelligence.

The actual secret audit process was shared between nine people in total, all of whom had special security clearance. Van Heerden explained that 'you could not swap these people round. We had an audit team in each department and made one person responsible for heading up audits in each of the relevant departments such as Defence, Police and Foreign Affairs. Their role was not to ask what the money was used for. If one person had all that information they could be a vulnerable target.'[51] The auditors followed paper trails but stayed away from operational areas and foreign accounts such as Armscor's office in Paris. Van Heerden argues that there were real risks associated with this work that could endanger the auditors and that many were psychologically affected by it – 'That's why the AG decided that if we didn't get all the information required to undertake an audit, we would qualify the audit. That was probably a good thing. You hear about how these things affected people. An auditor is not able to get technically involved in all these issues.' Van Heerden, like many other people, argues that they did the best under the circumstances and that if there was massive abuse of the system, there ought to be far more obvious displays of ostentatious wealth among former officials. Crucially, he concedes that if someone from Armscor paid extra commission for himself or someone else in a foreign country, it would have been outside the control of the auditors.[52] It is staggering to hear a straight-talking official, who has a no-nonsense approach to corruption, admit that such a vast proportion of public expenditure had such poor oversight.

We found evidence in the Department of Defence archives that, in certain instances, private auditing firms were used to audit select secret projects. Jan van Schalkwyk, who joined the auditor general's office in 1997 and has risen to become one of its top managers, reflected on this in an interview. He observed that firms awarded such business during apartheid would almost inevitably have had strong Broederbond connections and therefore connections to the National Party. 'This is what the Broederbond was all about,' he added.[53]

Van Schalkwyk also makes some important observations about the legacy of past secrecy in state-owned corporations such as Armscor. 'We know much more about public sector irregularities now because the regulations demand greater disclosure and transparency. It may feel a lot worse because you see more.'[54] He argues, however, that many of the current problems faced by state-owned enterprises can be traced back to the apartheid era. 'Even when these places "transform", the company culture tends to stay, and this culture is one of a lack of control and management, and a fair amount of freedom around the rules, and not too much concern around what we would nowadays call corruption.'[55]

Armscor: Funny money and dirty secrets

Embargo busting required utmost secrecy. It also required money channels to buy the weapons and grease the wheels. We examine one of the most important Armscor constructions in Chapter 5. However, it is important to first recognise how Armscor managed its procurement, its propensity for off-the-book payments, and its appetite for criminal conduct.

The SADF organised its procurement, of either small individual items or new weapons systems, as projects. There is, based upon our research, no list of projects or their description to be found in any of the military archives. From what we have been able to ascertain from various former members of the military, the SADF and Armscor destroyed the lists of projects at some point in the early 1990s.

We have, over the past three years, constructed a list of arms procurement and propaganda projects and have identified some 500 projects ranging in alphabetical order from Project Aandblom to Zarki. As a rule, project names have no obvious association with the goods procured. They reflect the infantile humour of project managers who allocated these names. For example, Project Kerktoring (Church Tower) was the main project for nuclear weapons, and Project Kinky denoted SADF war games. To add to the confusion, each project often has more than one sub-project, and project names were changed or swapped from time to time for security reasons. In addition, Armscor would usually give projects its own name. These were often chosen directly by the project manager. This makes the lack of an index of projects all the more challenging.[56]

The activities undertaken for these projects were handled on a strictly need-to-know basis. This situation suited members of PW Botha's cabinet, who relied heavily on the excuse of plausible deniability to assuage their obvious culpability in terms of law and ethical conduct. At a cabinet meeting on 8 March 1989, when Botha's presidency was in the beginning of its terminal decline, the acting president, Chris Heunis, highlighted that 'the collective responsibility by members of Cabinet or State Security Council can only be decided on a case by case basis'.[57] The minutes of the cabinet meeting show that FW de Klerk added that projects (including clandestine projects) that a minister approved in terms of his own powers only became the collective responsibility of all cabinet members when it was approved by cabinet or subsequently sustained by cabinet. If not, the minister carried full responsibility for it.[58] As long as the SADF didn't involve anyone in their business, these powerful NP politicians could simply wash their hands of any responsibility.

This cabinet decision had the effect of covering the politicians from responsibility for human rights violations, such as those perpetrated by state-sponsored hit squads. It also insulated them in the event any secret projects were mired in scandal. As we will see later, there was scope for scandal even if it was not exposed at the time. Sanctions busting increases the opportunity for graft, as moneys have to be paid to middlemen who demand even heftier commissions to acquire weapons when the client is a 'rogue state'. In turn, the local officials entrusted with the task of procuring weapons have an almost unique opportunity to inflate the prices they have been quoted and keep the change or possibly split it with weapons suppliers, who inflate their prices accordingly. This murky world of the global arms trade is vividly described in Andrew Feinstein's book *The Shadow World*. 'The trade in weapons is a parallel world of money, corruption, deceit and death. It operates according to its own rules, largely unscrutinised, bringing enormous benefits to the chosen few, and suffering and immiseration to millions.'[59]

South Africa under apartheid was not immune to the worst excesses of the arms trade. Following an investigation into aspects of the South African arms trade in 1994, the commission of inquiry headed by Judge Edwin Cameron observed in its introduction that the world in which Armscor operated was characterised by 'freewheeling ... and subterfuge, of lucrative and often extravagant commissions ... of deliberately disguised conversations, of communications shrouded in complex documents and cryptic notes of deals structured to conceal their true nature, a world without rules and code of conduct, in which intimidation, threats and actual peril are ever present, a world also of unpredictable allegiances and loyalties, the world in short of arms dealers'.[60]

In his autobiography, Magnus Malan refused to reveal any detail of sanctions busting, 'because the sword of amnesty and punitive economic measures still hangs over the heads of those who helped South Africa in its struggle, these stories cannot be told. One also needs to take into account the effects such revelations could have on international relations with some other countries.'[61] This is an important consideration when asking why so little of this information has been made public since the transition to democracy. He admitted that truth telling about what he termed 'our struggle' could cause great embarrassment for former allies who were on the wrong side of history.

Those involved in the trade would be implicated not only in their support for apartheid but also potentially in criminal conduct. The success of Armscor in sanctions busting relied on a system built over a 20-year period that required a system of international money laundering and complicity by foreign governments, politicians, defence forces, intelligence agencies, arms companies and banks. The criminal nature of this system was largely lost on Malan, who drew attention to bribe payments in foreign countries, which he ascribed to 'different customs and value systems ... outside the limits of normal South African patterns of thinking and behaviour'.[62] There is little evidence of massive personal enrichment by any of the South African generals or politicians who held the purse strings over procurement budgets. However, Malan was not shy to personally authorise bribe payments, and so made his government complicit in such acts of corruption.[63]

Niël Barnard, PW Botha's trusted chief spook in the civilian National Intelligence Service (NIS), believes that the perceived threat of war and the interests of the military–industrial complex were intertwined. During his tenure as a securocrat, his agency was often at loggerheads with Military Intelligence as it battled over turf, budgets and the ear of PW Botha. Barnard argues that 'over time it became necessary to feed exaggerated information about the military threat from neighbouring states to the political leadership in order to justify Armscor's ambitious programme of weaponry development … At NIS we were convinced that the SADF strategy was not based on sound information.'[64]

This argument is backed up by the views of a former senior NIS agent with decades of experience to whom I spoke off the record. The wars on the country's borders became a means for military strongmen to amass ever-larger budgets and political power. This is not dissimilar to the argument that the US invasion of Iraq was in part a means of shoring up greater economic and political power for the US military–industrial complex allied to the government of George W Bush and Dick Cheney.

In researching this book, I attempted to interview more than a dozen former and current Armscor employees. These were men at the coalface of the organisation's embargo-busting activities in the 1970s and 1980s. More than any other group, they did not want to be interviewed. Most cited secrecy restrictions; a few did not respond or claimed ill health; and one current Armscor employee indicated through a third party that he didn't want to become embroiled in an investigation or commission of inquiry. The fear factor is still writ large. Of the five Armscor employees who agreed to an interview, all wanted anonymity or selective attribution.

The former Armscor officials I met live, for the most part, a relatively modest but comfortable existence. These are men who generally did not rock the boat and are genuinely critical of corruption in the democratic order. At least two wanted an opportunity to disavow any notion that the apartheid-era arms trade was mired in corruption. As one stated to me in an interview, 'There is a perception that Armscor is a nest for corruption, this was not the case when I was there. I want to change the perception that Armscor are collaborators [in corrupt acts].'[65] A second official argued in an interview that 'while there was corruption in the system, this was not a problem at

Armscor [during apartheid]'.[66] He went to great lengths to explain the separation between the SADF and Armscor in procurement processes. According to his version, the SADF would initiate requests for the type of systems they required and Armscor would respond by finding suitable bidders for the goods. The system had multiple checks and balances in-between.[67]

These discussions on procurement processes suggest to me that there were rigorous systems of control in place that might have prevented some of the corruption commonplace in the post-apartheid arms deal. However, this largely misses a crucial point. The system was designed to rely on criminal means to conduct business, even if officials were not pocketing the cash. As a result of, and as a response to, the arms embargo, Armscor's entire *raison d'être* was criminal.

Another Armscor official, who worked in the organisation for nearly a decade, was the most damning about his former employer and colleagues.[68] A former soldier, he is unapologetic about his role in the war but cusses repeatedly at the mention of Armscor. He now uses his logistics and engineering skills as part of a civil society initiative, led by a multiracial group of neighbours, to address infrastructure problems in his small town. It's hard to draw simple conclusions about the choices some of these people have made.

He describes a world of subterfuge and intrigue in which arms dealers made 'fat commissions'. He claims that 65% of the funds for some Armscor projects were effectively paid out as commission. He believes that these men and companies 'stole from us and used the cover of the embargo for this purpose'.[69] With such attractive money to be made, he believes that 'the war had become about money – it was dragged out because people could make money out of it. There was a manipulation of the system.'[70] The Armscor security intelligence department, responsible for counter-intelligence, drew his particular ire: he described it as a 'criminal nest' within Armscor.[71] The broad details he gives about this department's activities have proven difficult to verify because so few of the people who know about its activities are willing to talk.

◎

The exact nature of the utilisation of the Special Defence Account (SDA) during apartheid is a question whose answer continues to elude us. This information, together with that held by the South African Reserve Bank and the State Security Agency, is still treated like a holy of holies. Some of this has to do with the kind of material these institutions keep under lock and key. But it also reflects an institutional culture that shuns the constitutional right of citizens to access information.

In the case of Armscor, this is particularly troubling. Its records would reveal the most significant information about the utilisation of the SDA. Over the past four years, following dozens of emails and threatening legal letters from our colleagues at the South African History Archive (SAHA), assisted by Lawyers for Human Rights, we have managed to access some material at Armscor. According to one former Armscor employee, the corporation's archive was treated as a 'pariah' after 1994. At first the bookshelves of neatly ordered folders were shifted from the Armscor headquarters, a hulking presence perched above the N1 highway east of Pretoria, to a high-security storage facility at the Atomic Energy Corporation in Pelindaba, far west of the city.[72] It has, by one account, now found storage space in a large government archiving facility, away from the prying eyes of civilians.[73] This archive is treated like an item of inheritance that nobody wants, but does not have the heart or the legal right to destroy.

Attempts to access the records have proven frustratingly difficult. In some instances, we were told that documents have been destroyed or that software programs on which electronic documents were written can no longer be accessed. While Armscor has, surprisingly, released some records, they are heavily redacted by over-eager officials who are even more stringent than the Military Intelligence censors at the Department of Defence. While frustrating, this at least proves the existence of the records. They were not all destroyed by Armscor in Project Masada, a paper destruction exercise of allegedly biblical proportions at the end of apartheid.[74]

Armscor has retained its relevance in a democratic South Africa. In 1992 the state-owned enterprise was split in two, with Armscor retaining responsibility for procurement and the newly created Denel set up as the government's weapons sales arm. There can be no doubt that had there been a proper investigation and airing of Armscor's activities at the end of apartheid, it might have proved harder for the corrupt European corporations, middlemen and South African politicians to benefit from the post-apartheid arms deal. It would have exposed not only the criminal activities of the South African secret state during apartheid, but also the international network that collaborated and profited from it as a result. As we will see later, many of the companies that made hay from the post-apartheid arms deal had done extensive business with the apartheid state.

Such an investigation, if independent and well resourced, would also inevitably have stumbled on the trail of important unanswered questions concerning political intrigue and alleged murders. We turn to some of these next.

The deep state revealed

Muldergate: A coup by media

'Dr Connie Mulder has brought the greatest scandal the National Party has ever suffered. That is why he is where he is.'
– PRIME MINISTER PW BOTHA, 8 MARCH 1980

The Information Scandal, which was exposed in fits and starts from 1977, did not represent either a break with the past or the beginning of a new era of clean government. Rather, it marked the entrenchment of the status quo. The covert system of procurement and propaganda that PW Botha's regime implemented, using the cash-rich Special

Defence Account, subsequently made the Information Scandal look relatively benign. It helped usher in a new autocrat as head of state and cemented the influence of the military across the state. It is important to understand the Information Scandal not as an event of corruption exposed but as an issue that was instrumentalised to enable the military to take full control of the apartheid state. By design, the scandal ushered in PW Botha's presidency, thereby ensuring the supremacy of the military in the state.

The scandal implicated Vorster, his minister of finance, Nico Diederichs, the minister of information, Connie Mulder, and BOSS's Hendrik van den Bergh. They formed the cabinet committee that had authorised the expenditure on secret projects in Pretoria's propaganda war starting in the early 1970s.[75] Funds drawn from the Special Defence Account, over which PW Botha had ultimate authority as minister of defence, were used to purchase newspapers abroad, place pro-South Africa advertisements in various international newspapers and fund propaganda campaigns that look like a warm-up for the real covert action which was to follow in the 1980s. Attempts were made covertly to buy the *Washington Star* and various magazines in Europe. In South Africa, the secret funds were used to buy *The Citizen* newspaper, with the help of the South African businessman Louis Luyt, to give the regime an English-language mouthpiece. Ultimately, some of the money was simply wasted by this venal clique, who jetted around the world selling apartheid on the public's coin. The scandal, which we describe below, cost Vorster and his clique their jobs, not because they authorised it, but primarily because they covered it up and lied in doing so.

The one politician implicated in the scandal who escaped any political repercussion was Vorster's minister of defence, PW Botha. He would use this opportunity to defeat his political opponents and secure his election as prime minister in 1978. Botha steadfastly claimed ignorance as his defence. How he could make this claim is staggering. In his memoir, Eschel Rhoodie, one of the disgraced Department of Information officials, states that he briefed the head of

Military Intelligence, at Botha's request, about the exact nature of the Department of Information's activities in January 1975.[76] It is even suggested that some of the secret projects that were never exposed had direct ties to the defence ministry. Botha had direct responsibility for these funds and would sign off on the budgets. So how did he escape culpability?

The journalist

Mervyn Rees, the fearless *Rand Daily Mail* journalist, was central to exposing Muldergate. He was hailed at the time as one of South Africa's great investigative journalists. New evidence about his close, collegial contact with the Security Branch police during apartheid raises serious questions about his legacy and about the motives of his sources.

Rumours had circulated for some time in Pretoria about how the Department of Information was using its funds. However, the big breakthrough in the investigation was Rees's deep-throat source, nicknamed Myrtle. She led Rees to the evidence that exposed the jet-set lifestyle of the information department, and the holidays, at taxpayers' expense, for the officials to Seychelles, Europe, Canada and the United States. There was an apartment block in South Africa's most expensive real estate mile in Clifton, property in Plettenberg Bay and other luxury homes across the country. All were ostensibly bought for the purpose of entertaining influential guests who were lured to South Africa to do apartheid's bidding.[77]

According to Allister Sparks, Myrtle is an Afrikaner woman whom he last had contact with shortly before he published his final book in 2016.[78] He claims that Rees felt compassion for her and in return he was rewarded with a massive amount of information.[79] Her identity has never been revealed, except for Sparks's revelation shortly before his death that the source, always described in the masculine, was in fact a woman.

The Information Scandal attracted numerous covert operatives, conmen and bankers from countries such as the United States,

Switzerland and Israel. One was Arnon Milchan, the billionaire Hollywood producer behind blockbuster movies such as *The Revenant, The Big Short* and *12 Years a Slave*. A long-time close associate of Israeli politicians and intelligence agents, he was involved in the scandal as part of the Tel Aviv government's burgeoning relationship with Pretoria. In 2017 he was caught up in another political scandal following revelations that he was funding Prime Minister Benjamin Netanyahu's lavish lifestyle, thereby securing him access to the Israeli head of state.[80] Surprisingly, Milchan claims that he was in fact the 'deep throat' who led the *Rand Daily Mail* journalists to the exposure of the whole Muldergate scheme.[81]

Whether an honest bureaucrat leaked the information or it was part of internal National Party machinations is not known. It could well have involved third parties outside the country such as Milchan, whose close links to the apartheid regime as well as Mossad and the Israeli arms industry might have put him at the centre of a play to sink the career of politicians such as Vorster and secure the fortunes of PW Botha's clique. Either way, the evidence of the vast sums of money and the gilded lifestyle of members of the Department of Information had a devastating political impact, intended or otherwise, and eventually paved the way for PW Botha's path to the presidency.

I travelled to Amanzimtoti, the sleepy holiday town south of Durban, to interview Mervyn Rees in March 2013. Rees was ill and sat in his newly occupied apartment in a care facility. I could see unpacked boxes in his bedroom. Rees seemed to be in transit. Two piles of empty glass ashtrays were stacked together in the living room, a relic from a time when he used to smoke 60 cigarettes a day.[82] His wife had recently passed away and he would follow a month later.

It was by far the most melancholy interview I conducted for this book. It perplexed me that Muldergate was – bar his revelations concerning the arrest of South African naval officer turned KGB spy Dieter Gerhardt – his last big piece of investigative journalism. Why had he not investigated the far larger economic crimes of the 1980's? He was the perfect candidate and could surely be trusted by any deep throat. Instead, he had gone to spend some time on Fleet Street working for the *Mail on Sunday*.

When he tired of chequebook journalism, he returned to South Africa to start a private company that assisted international journalists to file their stories via telex. He also traded as a foreign correspondent.

The work undertaken by Rees in uncovering Muldergate is often compared with that of the *Washington Post*'s investigative journalists Bob Woodward and Howard Bernstein. Bernstein and Woodward broke the Watergate Scandal. It seems unimaginable that such journalistic luminaries would simply fade into the woodwork after an exposé of such proportions. Why had this happened to Rees? Was it simply a case of the soft-spoken reporter being sidelined while his editor, Allister Sparks, stole the show? While not critical of Sparks, Rees did describe him as a 'highlights guy'.[83]

When I asked Rees why he and colleagues had not investigated defence expenditure during the 1980s, especially given that he had secured a way into the workings of the Special Defence Account, he responded that he had no source; there was only one 'Myrtle'. According to Rees, 'as an investigative journalist my sole concentration was getting to the source and winning their confidence, this takes time, to find the right person and persuade them to share information. That's an aspect that people don't worry about so much. Without getting to people behind it. There is no longer trust and getting the right people.'[84]

As our research started to expose the extent of clandestine defence spending and the networks involved during the 1980s, I couldn't help wondering whether there wasn't more to Rees than met the eye.

Four sources suggest that Rees developed contact with the Security Branch. None of these sources could confirm if this predated Muldergate. But it is curious that someone who had peered into the heart of darkness would want to associate with its agents. One explanation is that journalists rely on all manner of informants working on all sides for information. Rees was no stranger to the police. He had worked the crime beat since the 1960s. His former editor Allister Sparks recalled: 'How Rees managed to hit it off with members of the South African Police always baffled me. But he did. His network of police contacts was unmatched, and he always seemed to know exactly who to call on any case he was investigating.'[85] His predecessor in that position was in fact the undercover police spy Gerald Ludi.[86]

I contacted Vic McPherson, who worked with the Security Branch and had testified before the TRC, naming contacts he had fostered among journalists. Mervyn Rees's name had never come up in his testimony or that of his police colleagues. At first McPherson said he had no recollection of who Rees was.[87] However, when I followed up with an email providing documentary evidence I had been handed, including a list of journalists' names which I was reliably told were his secret media contacts, he responded, 'Fine, Hennie, I remember now I know Mervyn Rees. Met him through Craig Williamson. Had regular contact. Was a casual friend, not working for me.'[88] He was referring to the notorious apartheid agent Craig Williamson.

When I pressed McPherson as to whether Rees worked for the security services or was just an informant, he responded, 'He was just a friend of the Security Branch. He said through his computer system he could assist us in communication overseas. We never used it.'[89] According to McPherson, Rees never received funding from the Security Branch for the wire service he had set up.

I followed the question up with Craig Williamson and asked him if he had any contact with Rees and what the nature of this contact was. Williamson sent me a response via WhatsApp shortly afterwards. 'I never knew him personally,' he said, contradicting McPherson.[90] He added, 'If he had been a source/asset/agent I probably would have known. My unit did some Intel work on Rhoodie etc. after the Info scandal.'[91] Williamson said, 'I think that his relationship with the SB [Security Branch] was probably more like Tertius Myburgh – close with key individuals but not under orders.' He added, 'Information is a commodity and was traded.'[92] Williamson was referring to the former editor of the *Sunday Times*, Tertius Myburgh, whose close relationship with the security establishment was revealed by the journalist John Matisonn in his 2016 book, *God, Spies and Lies*. These men weren't spies but traded on their access with the police at the time. It was a cozy relationship that inevitably demanded the type of bargaining that crosses every line of ethical journalism.

John Matisson is a veteran journalist who worked on the *Sunday Express* newspaper at the time of the Infogate scandal. His newspaper, together with the *Rand Daily Mail*, broke the Muldergate scandal, with the rest of the English- and Afrikaans-language press timidly reporting the details in their wake. He is also the only person to receive a jail sentence for reporting on the Information Scandal. He refused to name a source related to the Information Department's effort to undermine the anti-apartheid cleric Bishop Desmond Tutu and the South African Council of Churches. When I spoke with him, he said that while he wasn't aware of information that could confirm that Rees was connected to the Security Branch, he would think that Myburgh and Rees were in any event in a different category. He regarded Myburgh as far more political in his approach, in the sense that he actually believed in what he was doing. Nonetheless he never shared any information with Rees.[93]

It is important to recall that there were different levels of collaboration in the media during apartheid. John Horak, a former security operative who worked undercover as a journalist, revealed to the TRC that there were four categories of spies: agents who were professional police officers working undercover; informers who did it for ideology or money or to sabotage their colleagues who were viewed as competition; sources; and 'sleepers', who were long-term plants.[94] If Rees was a collaborator, he was possibly of a lower order.

I met with the veteran journalists Terry and Barbara Bell in January 2017 to ask them about Rees. Terry Bell had worked with Rees at the *Rand Daily Mail* in the 1960s, before he went into exile, and again after his return to the country in the 1990s. In 1993 he was employed by Rees as a contributor on a publication that Rees edited and co-owned called *African Exclusive*. They had stayed in contact and met in London from time to time in the 1980s.

Bell believes that Rees had links to the security establishment and he recounts his attempts to piece this together over many years.[95] Rees died just before Bell had planned to confront him with the information. Bell had successfully uncovered journalist Chris Olckers's covert association with the security sector during apartheid. When confronted with the evidence, Olckers admitted to Bell that he had been clandestinely linked to the spooks and added, 'Rees was a regular attendee at special braais organised by Police General Johann Coetzee. He said that invitations to these events were reserved for "only the trusted".'[96]

Bell recalls his first encounter with Rees at the *Rand Daily Mail* in 1964. As a young reporter he had looked after Rees's flat while he was out of town. That week, the police picked Bell up as part of a great sweep of anti-government activists. The police subsequently took him straight to the flat and gave it only a cursory search. Bell never told the police where he was living when they arrested him. They clearly knew already, and, with the benefit of hindsight, he believes that Rees had led the police to him that day.[97]

When Terry Bell was hired to work on Rees's publication *African Exclusive*, he says that he was struck by strange behaviour. Rees was obsessed with security, and doors and drawers in his office were all locked. When Bell noticed that Rees had copies of ANC members' ID cards in his office, alarm bells went off. There was no good reason for this.[98]

Mervyn Rees had a peculiar relationship with the security establishment. He was most likely an informal asset involved in the trade of information. When I first met him, a person I admired, I asked him to sign a copy of his book *Muldergate: The Story of the Info Scandal*, which he authored with fellow journalist Chris Day. The inscription reads, 'With best wishes and good hunting from one investigative journalist to another'. I never expected that the trail would lead back to the journalist.

The judges
The Infogate scandal sent shock waves through the South African political establishment, intensifying as opposition politicians called for a full investigation. One tool that governments have to assuage

an angry public and concurrently bury the truth is the appointment of a pliable commission of inquiry headed by a judge with one eye on the golf course. Judge Anton Mostert was not such a man. He was appointed in May 1978 to investigate exchange control violations but soon recognised the full importance of the Information Scandal. Mostert, a brave and honourable Afrikaner judge, resisted pressure from PW Botha, who had been appointed prime minister after Vorster resigned in disgrace. Botha wanted to suppress information revealed by the commission and prevent it from being revealed to the public. But Mostert 'decided to put his ethnic and political loyalties aside and to defy his Prime Minister in a matter he regarded as being in the national interest',[99] and published the transcripts of evidence given at his commission. He was fired by Botha in early November 1978 after an unsuccessful attempt to ban their release.[100] The information was damning as it confirmed the involvement of Vorster, Mulder and Van den Bergh in the scandal.

Botha was furious. The independent-minded Mostert had gone too far. He had not contained the problem and had caused further embarrassment for the National Party. However, Botha must have felt a sense of personal triumph in seeing all the men who could threaten his power eviscerated in one fell swoop. If Botha was involved behind the scenes in ensuring that he would benefit from the Information Scandal, his intention was to knock out the competition, not to destroy his party. Hence he handpicked Judge Rudolph Erasmus, a relatively junior provincial judge, to investigate the matter involving the executive in the same month that he fired Mostert. Judge Hiemstra would later describe his appointment as 'a means to remove the Information Scandal from the arena'.[101]

The findings of Judge Erasmus cleared PW Botha of any wrongdoing. He produced a total of three reports between December 1978 and June 1979. While the initial report cleared both Botha and Vorster, the third did an about-face and affirmed that 'Mr Vorster knew everything about the basic arrangement of the Department's funds'.[102] By this stage Vorster had been appointed to the largely honorary position of state president. The day after the report was released, Vorster resigned.

We found a copy of the first Erasmus report in Piet Koornhof's archive. One of the only sections highlighted by Koornhof is telling: 'the Commission finds that Mr Botha at all times acted honourably, in the best interests of the country, and that he had no other choice. He was never at any stage aware of any irregularity in the secret funds. His hands are clean in all aspects and his integrity remains unblemished in continuing his great task as Prime Minister.'[103] Erasmus had helped effect a cover up that ensured PW Botha's political survival. The manner in which the commission conducted itself would find a faint echo in the Seriti Commission of Inquiry into the post-apartheid arms deal, whose report was roundly rejected as a whitewash by civil society groups in 2016.

What has never been fully divulged until now is the direct contact and personal relationship between Erasmus, a sitting judge, and PW Botha, revealed in a string of correspondence located in Botha's archive. In March 1980, only nine months after his exoneration of Botha, Erasmus wrote to Botha on a Supreme Court letterhead in a fawning tone. He told Botha that he had recently heard from high-ranking friends of his in England 'that the world is saying good things about our honourable Prime Minister. It warmed my heart, because it was the first time in the four decades that have passed.'[104] In late February 1982, just as Botha faced a political rebellion within his party led by right-wing MPs who would soon break away to form the Conservative Party, he received a telegram of support from Erasmus. The telegram simply stated, 'Strength and onwards. Greetings, RPB Erasmus.'[105]

The coup

Was the Information Scandal really a coup by media? As we have seen, there is some evidence that Mervyn Rees, the investigative journalist on the *Rand Daily Mail*, who first exposed the scandal, may have been close to the security establishment and could have been fed information about the scandal from a source close to PW Botha.

However, we should not focus on Rees alone. Another compelling argument is that it was PW Botha's NP support base in the Cape Province that lay behind the leaks as a means of ensuring Botha's ascendancy to the party throne. This was a battle of South against North. The Cape Nationalists intended to politically neutralise Connie Mulder, who had the support of the powerful Transvaal wing of the party, and who was favoured to replace the ageing Vorster. The two men also represented different interest groups in the state. PW Botha had the support of the military as well as Military Intelligence, while Mulder, as head of the Information Department, relied on the police and BOSS for his security connections. It was no secret that Military Intelligence aspired to become the pre-eminent state intelligence agency, which was achieved when PW Botha disbanded BOSS in the wake of the Information Scandal.[106]

A further area of contestation between the Mulder and Botha camps lay in the Afrikaans media, which are thought to have been the initial source of the leaks, even if the exposé was left to the *Rand Daily Mail* and the *Sunday Express*. The Johannesburg-based Perskor newspaper group, headed by senior Broederbonder Marius Jooste, avidly supported Mulder. Botha, on the other hand, had a decades-long association with Naspers and sat on its board and relied on its support.[107] In backing the wrong candidate, Perskor would eventually lose all of its government printing contracts, which then went to the new dominant Afrikaans-language media player, Naspers.[108]

John Matisonn argues in his book that the *Sunday Express* source for Muldergate was the PW Botha faction. However, he subsequently made a startling new revelation to me. After his book was published in 2015, he was approached by a source, the journalist Alf Ries, who had worked at the *Die Burger*.[109] Ries had been a member of the Broederbond and a confidant of John Vorster and PW Botha.[110] He confirmed to Matisonn that their source was someone at the Naspers-controlled *Die Burger* newspaper. Matisonn explains the implication: 'So I'm now satisfied that both [English-language] papers – the only ones breaking the Muldergate stories – had PW Botha-related primary sources.'[111]

The Information Scandal ended as a controlled implosion of sorts, designed to instal a new leader and usher the military into every aspect of state function. As a by-product, it also helped create the fiction of democracy: a parliament that held the executive to account, a free press that exposed the scandal, and a judiciary that, with mixed success, investigated it.

The actions of the independent, conscientious Judge Mostert meant that Botha and his cronies could not control the leaks. Hence they focused on limiting the fallout. Most importantly, it meant that the far bigger scandal of money-laundering networks being set up across the world to circumvent the arms and oil embargoes would never be revealed. Consider for a moment that the total secret expenditure through the Special Defence Account between 1974 and 1994 was R50 billion. In comparison, R85 million was spent by the Department of Information on secret projects. This suggests that the total value of the Special Defence Account expenditure was almost 600 times higher than the Information Scandal. The Muldergate exposé was important in revealing corruption within the NP government, and its abuse of state resources for propaganda purposes. However, it was relatively small-fry. The big fish were left undisturbed.

The far larger economic crime scandal during apartheid was the use of the SDA in general. Placing the focus on the Information Scandal was a ruse. As the government's secretary of finance at the time, Joop de Loor, said to me in an interview, the SDA was a 'no-go area'.[112] De Loor felt that on many occasions this was abused for party political purposes, 'not to save the country, [but] to save the party', and this was why it was kept so secret.[113] He said that it would be fine to use this secrecy 'once or twice', but doing so for 'party political purposes' would run into trouble, suggesting that this approach was increasingly used after the Information Scandal.[114]

However, as the former *Rand Daily Mail* editor Allister Sparks argues, it was the outrageous freeloading and abuse of state funds that angered the white electorate at the time, far more than the idea of secret projects. As he points out in his book *The Sword and the*

Pen, 'To lie for one's country is okay, but to make free with the white taxpayer's money is certainly not.'[115]

Assassination: 'Monsters walking this land'

'Was the stabbing really necessary?' Liza Smit rhetorically asked of the TRC.[116] Her parents, Robert and Jean Cora Smit, were murdered at their home in November 1977. This was within a week of the parliamentary elections in which Robert Smit stood as a candidate for the National Party in the safe seat of Springs outside Johannesburg. She implored the TRC commissioners 'I don't understand how a person can push a 21cm long knife into a person, and 14 times in the case of my mother ... What type of monsters are walking this land?'[117]

The killers, according to the Police Investigative Diary, had stabbed Jean Smit and then shot her.[118] Robert Smit was shot three times in the head, neck and stomach before being stabbed once. The killers wanted both people dead, and no doubt intended that it should frighten others. Whatever Robert Smit, and possibly his wife, knew was not something that others should even contemplate talking about. This wasn't only murder, it was a message.

When we made an access to information request, through SAHA, to the police for information concerning the murder, they returned a redacted investigative diary. The police report notes, 'It appears that the person or persons spent a lengthy period in the house and that all cupboards and draws were searched and that everything was carefully repacked.'[119] Among the first journalists allowed into the house by the police was the crime reporter Mervyn Rees, who at that stage was investigating Muldergate.[120] Another journalist given access soon after the murder was the undercover spy Gordon Winter.[121] There would be no hiding the bodies, nor the bloodstains, nor the mysterious words RAU-TEM sprayed across a wall in the house. The security establishment never stopped the murders from making the news. It was the motive they showed less interest in.

The Smit murders rocked the South African establishment. This was the first time that a rising star of the NP, tipped to be a future minister of finance, was murdered. Robert Smit is reported to have whispered to a lover that he had ambitions to be prime minister or president someday.[122] He had all the right credentials as a loyal supporter of the NP who had ably represented the apartheid government at the International Monetary Fund (IMF) in Washington DC. An economist by training, he had received a PhD from Stellenbosch University and had been a Rhodes Scholar at Oxford University.[123]

This high-profile apartheid-era political assassination has remained unsolved for 40 years. I contacted the National Prosecutions Authority (NPA) in 2015 to ask about this and was informed in a voicemail by Advocate Torie Pretorius that he was still looking into the matter. From police correspondence it is apparent that Pretorius had written to the police in 2006 to request assistance in investigating the murders, suggesting a decade-long fruitless investigation.[124]

The TRC also investigated the murders and concluded that they were politically motivated, and not just a criminal act likely to have been perpetrated by members of the security forces. The commission also believed that 'explosive information' might have led to the assassination, which could have been linked to massive corruption in the government, the nuclear programme or the sanctions-busting programme of the state in which the TRC confirmed that Robert Smit had been involved.[125]

Robert Smit was part of the establishment and was no freedom fighter. However, the establishment froze when it came to providing answers to his murder. This had the potential to unlock too many truths. The Mandela administration was also reportedly reluctant to investigate the crime. According to Allister Sparks, he informed Dullah Omar, the first minister of justice in the Mandela administration, of a numbered Swiss bank account that he believed could lead to the identity of the killers. Sparks penned a brief for Mandela's attention. He claims that Omar eventually informed him there would be no investigation. 'I'm sorry but the old man doesn't want us to open up this thing. He doesn't want to stir up old conflict with the Afrikaners while he is working so hard to bring about racial reconciliation.'[126]

The investigation has attracted numerous theories over the years, from Cuban hit men to CIA involvement. Some of this seems merely speculative. One of the reasons for the controversy that surrounded the murder investigation was the often-repeated allegation that Smit intended to use his parliamentary seat to reveal large-scale financial malfeasance involving foreign bank accounts. One theory, proffered by Eschel Rhoodie shortly before his death in 1993, was that money was creamed off the Special Defence Account for this purpose.

It has proved difficult to answer this question conclusively. However, what is apparent is that far too few questions have been asked about Smit's role as a sanctions buster. If anything, this might have been an area of activity that gave him a unique insight into issues which led to the murders. Our focus is not on the killers or the so-called secret bank accounts. Rather, we look at Smit's connections to sanctions busting and the links he might have had with the security establishment at the time. It is the area about which the least is known.

The secret
Robert Smit was a sanctions buster. He saw this as his patriotic duty, and it paid his salary. In his election manifesto for the NP in Springs he undertook 'to reject unequivocally all outside interference in our affairs and to ... defeat any pressures, sanctions, or other unfriendly acts against the Republic'. He also supported a strong defence force, among other bread-and-butter issues of the day.[127]

Smit believed that the sanctions threat had to be vanquished. Speaking a month before his murder, he is reported as having said that 'Sanctions and boycotts will only succeed if we allow ourselves to be intimidated. Applying sanctions is against the interests of those countries ... my own experience is that all big international banks want to do business with South Africa as long as they are not legally prohibited from doing so by their governments.'[128] He added for good measure that 'it must be clear for countries that try and pressurize us with sanctions that they are busy with a dangerous game'.[129] This was not the voice of someone who doubted the regime. He was speaking as an insider to an international audience.

The police investigative diary into the murder shows that there was comparatively little investigation into Smit's line of work as a private actor engaged in sanctions busting for the government. A section of the diary that deals with this has been heavily redacted to the point of meaninglessness. There is, however, mention of a meeting between Smit and an old university friend (name redacted) from Oxford on two occasions in the month of the murders. During the first visit, Smit said that he had successfully developed plans to circumvent the oil sanctions against South Africa.[130] Another confidential source (name redacted) was a friend of Smit's and provided details of numbered Swiss bank accounts held by South Africans.[131] Smit is said to have met with Swiss bankers the day before his death.

The police also questioned a millionaire businessman (name redacted). He claimed that Smit and the NP had agreed to keep a certain scandal involving (name redacted) out of the media until after the elections.[132] He said that if Smit had come across another scandal or network, he would have also kept quiet until after the elections so as not to embarrass the NP. This meant that (name redacted) would have had a grace period in which to murder Smit before the elections.[133] There is little to suggest that the police ever conclusively investigated these claims, and their diary is silent on this and other issues.

The Smit children were under no illusion at the time of the TRC that their father was involved in sanctions-busting operations. They said that they had been informed that he had good relations with the Shah of Iran, the key oil supplier to apartheid South Africa, and according to a good family friend (who declined to be interviewed for this book) he regularly travelled to Iran via Turkey.[134] Most importantly, the Smit children drew the TRC's attention to a critical piece of information: their father was employed as the managing director of a shadowy sanctions-busting firm known as Santam International. This much detail is to be found in newspaper articles that canvassed Smit's opinion on the sanctions issue in the months before his murder.[135]

According to the Smit children, Smit wrote to Gerrit Viljoen saying that he wanted to return to South Africa after his stint at the IMF in Washington DC. Viljoen was a hugely influential NP politician and chairman of the Broederbond. Shortly after this, Smit flew to New York to meet the chairman of Santam International, Dr Carel van Aswegen. He was offered the job as the organisation's MD from January 1976.[136] On the day before his death, his secretary noticed a letter terminating his services. This was never made public.[137]

Santam International was a wholly private concern with links to the insurance giant Santam. Santam in turn was deeply enmeshed in the NP-linked group of corporations in the second half of the 20th century. Santam and its pension fund owned 46% of the shares in Santam International, Merca Bank owned 24% and the remaining 30% was divided up between Carel van Aswegen and Robert Smit.[138] Van Aswegen, to whom we return shortly, was the MD of Santam from the early 1960s.[139] He was later appointed chairman of Santam Bank, a post he held until 1994.[140] The board of Santam International was stacked with representatives of the same institutions as well as Smit and the NP-aligned Boland Bank. This was a tightly knit family affair.

Little is known of Merca Bank. However, reports of its oil-related sanctions-busting activities emerged in the early 1980s during the *Salem* oiltanker scandal. Merca is reported to have provided a letter of credit for $12 million to the oil trader Fred Soudan at the behest of Sasol and the Strategic Fuel Fund (SFF). The money was used to pay for oil that became the centre of an international scandal.[141] Smit is also reported to have worked from the offices of Merca Bank.

According to Liza Smit, she contacted Charles Ferreira, who represented Merca Bank on the board of Santam International, and quizzed him about her father's work. He would only say that Smit arranged lines of credit for South Africa. She would then meet the familiar refrain of denial. He had no idea what Robert Smit was working on.[142]

If Merca Bank represented a link to oil sanctions, then Carel van Aswegen was the link to the clandestine world of arms trading. He was a major shareholder and chairman of Santam International and also a senior member of the Broederbond and its executive committee. We have established that he also served on the board of Armscor.[143] Van Aswegen was appointed a member of the Armaments Board (precursor to Armscor) in 1968. In March 1977, eight months before the Smit murders, he was appointed to the four-person Armscor executive committee, a highly influential group tasked with dealing with top-secret orders.[144]

Van Aswegen was plugged into the most sensitive sanctions-busting projects. According to minutes of Armscor meetings, Van Aswegen was party to discussions concerning the procurement of nuclear components through Project Buzzard. At the same meeting, Armscor's relationship with various banks was discussed, including prominent creditors such as Kredietbank (Armscor's primary international money-laundering partner, to which we return in Chapter 5) and Santam Bank. From the minutes, it is apparent that he had an influential position in providing oversight over the investments and finances of Armscor.[145] Records found in the SADF archive show that Van Aswegen remained on the board of Armscor until at least the mid-1980s. In June 1982, he sent a letter to Magnus Malan on a Santam letterhead, thanking him for extending his term as director of Armscor for a further three years: 'I gratefully accept this nomination and am appreciative that you are of the opinion that my contribution in the past was of value.'[146]

Beyond Armscor's secrets, Van Aswegen was accustomed to moving in the shadows. In a letter to Anton Rupert, quoted by Rupert's biographer, Van Aswegen proposed to assist in creating a corporate vehicle to obscure Rupert's ownership of a bank he wanted to establish in Luxembourg in 1973. Van Aswegen offered to help Rupert in bending the truth: 'If any of the companies in your group should wish to form part of the proposed company situated in Luxembourg, we would gladly be of assistance by holding those shares in one of our nominee companies in our group so that it will not become known that you are participating in that Luxembourg enterprise.'[147] This was a man accustomed to the dark arts of finance.

When Liza Smit made telephonic contact with Van Aswegen in the mid-1990s, he came across as very nervous and eventually said that he had only a 'slight' memory of Robert Smit.[148] When asked what Robert Smit was doing at Santam International, he said, 'I don't know, I don't have the slightest clue about that. It will be impossible for me to help you.'[149] Van Aswegen, who had appointed Smit, chaired the company and was together with Smit the largest individual shareholder in Santam International, seemed to suffer a strange case of memory lapse. All investigations into Robert Smit's murder have given Santam International a wide berth.

The disquiet

> *'If I were to remain silent, I'd be guilty of complicity.'*
> – ALBERT EINSTEIN

Unsolved murders evoke a deep sense of unease, foreboding and vulnerability in the wider community. The Smit murders were no different. That the authoritarian government of PW Botha, with its well-oiled intelligence machinery and network of spies, could not solve this murder is telling. It is worth considering that it was never in the interests of the political establishment for the matter to be fully probed and exposed. Liza Smit recalls Pik Botha, the long-serving minister of foreign affairs, placing his hands on her shoulders at her parents' funeral and saying, 'I wish I could help you, but my hands are tied,' making a similar gesture with his hands. Years later, he told her that he meant that 'nothing he could do would bring them back'.[150] Pik Botha told us in an interview that he and Robert Smit were great friends. 'I have a suspicion but no evidence of why he was killed.'[151]

Joop de Loor, who replaced Smit as ambassador to the IMF and World Bank in 1975, had previously worked with Robert Smit at a time when they were both deputy secretaries of finance. In an interview, he recalls knowing him well. Smit told De Loor that he wanted to go into politics because 'he had a lot of information about money transfers ... that he thinks were untoward' and he felt he could do more as an MP.[152]

What was Smit investigating? In February 1979 the journalist Ken Owen told the Erasmus Commission that 'an official, a responsible man had said that ten days before the murders Smit had visited him. Smit had questioned him at length about the overseas activities of the Department of Information. They discussed nothing else.'[153] The official offered the police his co-operation but they simply ignored him.[154] There is no doubt that Smit was operating in the same orbit as the Department of Information, but what was he questioning? When author James Sanders questioned Deneys Rhoodie, the former deputy secretary of the Department of Information and Eschel Rhoodie's brother, about links between the murder and the Information Scandal, his hands started to shake and did not stop until they moved onto other matters.[155]

Liza Smit arranged to meet the former BOSS chief, General Hendrik van den Bergh, in December 1992. She looked him in the eyes and asked, 'What are those blue eyes of Uncle hiding away?' He responded, returning the gaze, 'That which I will take with me to my grave.'[156] Van den Bergh claimed that Smit had been one of his informers, reporting back to him on overseas trips that he made. This is not impossible given Smit's international contact base and his allegiance to the Vorster government and the NP. However, Van den Bergh added cryptically: 'When John Vorster asked me to start an intelligence network in South Africa I went to Allen Dulles [founder of the CIA] and I asked him how I should go about it. He said I would not have a problem gathering intelligence here, but that military intelligence would be my problem. They will also be your problem.'[157]

According to family members and friends, Robert Smit said shortly before his murder that once he was in parliament he would reveal a big scandal that 'will make Watergate look like a Sunday School picnic'.[158] What is almost certain is that the secret was related to his sanctions-busting work. Smit might have been about to reveal the massive abuse of the Special Defence Account, extending beyond the Information Scandal. As a banker, he would have had an insight into how new banking money-laundering networks were in the process of being established across the globe. (We return to these in Chapter 5.) If he did threaten to speak out, is it possible that the information he possessed could have threatened the interests of the military and their international network? All evidence suggests that the information he had at his disposal would have proven far more significant and difficult to contain than that volunteered by the Information Scandal informants. So the Smits had to be silenced and, with them, the prospect of any other whistleblowers of significance emerging from within the regime for years to come.

The heart of a criminal enterprise

The apartheid state was as its height an authoritarian regime which relied on high levels of secrecy to enforce the policies of apartheid. Who wielded the real power shifted from the 1970s, when the police and BOSS had the upper hand, to the 1980s, when PW Botha's military dominated.

Crucial to countering the massive international pressure on the apartheid regime was the sanctions-busting system. This relied on secret projects and secret funds available through the Special Defence Account. The intelligence agencies, the defence force and the state arms company, Armscor, were all important elements of this system. They were at the heart of a system of criminal enterprise that directed the state.

In later chapters we reveal the identities of the international networks that profited from sanctions busting. At the same time, we should not lose focus on the fact that the primary intended beneficiary was the National Party's militarised state.

'I was not informed of the details of the budget comprising the SDA. I didn't know anything about it. I didn't dare to ask, that was a military thing and that would have been inappropriate for me to ask.'

~ Barend du Plessis, Minister of Finance, 1984–1992

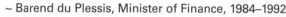

'We only knew second hand about what was going on… the SDA was a no-go area'

~ Joop de Loor, Auditor General, 1984–1992

'…the level of audit assurance that can be furnished will often be lower than is normally the case in ordinary audits.'

~ Disclaimer on all SDA audits
   by Auditor General

'One also needs to take into account the effects such revelations could have on international relations with some other countries'

~ Magnus Malan, Minister of Defence, 1981–1991

PW Botha's total strategy involved all sectors of society in his war effort.

Hidden from the public eye was the Special Defence Account (SDA), used to buy weapons across the world.

The Secret State
Secret money for guns

Hidden from the public:

Over R500 billion spent through the Special Defence Account in today's terms

A secret global money-laundering network set up to spend SDA funds

SDA funds used to bust the arms and oil embargo, and to pay middlemen hefty commissions

Auditor General forbidden to access any operational files in auditing the SDA

CUMULATIVE SPENDING FROM SDA

1974	R111 million
1975	R711 million
1976	R1.579 billion
1977	R2.577 billion
1978	R3.398 billion
1979	R4.587 billion
1980	R5.598 billion
1981	R6.859 billion
1982	R8.213 billion
1983	R9.745 billion
1984	R11.770 billion
1985	R14.191 billion
1986	R17.449 billion
1987	R21.587 billion
1988	R26.625 billion
1989	R32.580 billion
1990	R33.125 billion
1991	R38.404 billion
1992	R42.366 billion
1993	R46.454 billion
1994	R49.648 billion

CHAPTER 2

The Secret Economy

State capture

It remains stubbornly hard to have a reasonable conversation about the role of the private sector during apartheid. Criticism is disingenuously dismissed as 'anti-private sector'. Some go as far as to suggest that business was as much a victim as poor and working-class black people during apartheid. There is also ample evidence of business leaders who criticised Botha's government from the privileged position of their boardrooms. At the time of writing, with the threat of state capture posed by some of President Zuma's acolytes, even otherwise progressive folk stop such a conversation in its tracks for fear that it will play into an 'agenda'. The truth suffers when there is no room for nuanced conversations.

One of the many thorny issues facing the Truth and Reconciliation Commission (TRC) was how it should hold business to account for its collaboration and profit-making during apartheid. It is easy to forget just how high the stakes were for South Africa's big corporations and super-rich at the time. Much of their capital was still anchored in South Africa, given the strict exchange control regulations, which made the legal export of capital difficult. In 1997, ownership of the economy was still almost exclusively in the hands of white South Africans.

The focus on the private sector as one of six special 'institutional hearings' was relatively novel among truth commissions and provided a welcome opportunity to focus on corporate complicity. But the hearings, which took place over a three-day period, offered only a superficial examination of a subject that deserved far more careful attention. In total, the commission received 86 submissions, of which roughly a quarter stemmed from big business and state-owned corporations. Individual submissions were received from large companies such as Anglo American, Rembrandt, Sanlam, South African Breweries and Gencor, and from some business associations such as the Chamber of Mines and the Afrikaanse Handelsinstituut (AHI).

The submissions were breathtaking in their brevity. No doubt acting on legal advice, many of the corporations and wealthy individuals admitted that apartheid was a crime but neglected to include any significant details of their direct or indirect complicity with the apartheid state. Where detail was included, it erred towards demanding absolution. The industry bosses such as Johann Rupert who were bold enough to appear at the hearings tended to shift the focus to their humble efforts in opposing apartheid and their corporate charity programmes. As the journalist Max du Preez noted, 'Despite the many dark suits and striped shirts, one could at times be forgiven for thinking this was a meeting of Anti-Apartheid movements ... especially when powerful companies like Anglo and Barlow Rand claimed to have always opposed apartheid.'[1]

One of the factors that contributed to the relatively light examination of the evidence was the position the TRC took in approaching the role of business. This was, as Nicoli Nattrass argues, primarily focused on the systemic relationship between the private sector and the apartheid regime. This meant that all businesses, from corner stores to giant monopolies, were seen to be complicit in a similar manner. Such an approach informed the commission's important finding that 'business generally benefited financially and materially from apartheid'.[2] But it also meant that the commission focused little on specific acts of complicity, such as sanctions busting, by the most powerful corporations and business leaders.[3]

This chapter, like the previous one, is intended to provide context for the sanctions-busting system. The focus now shifts from the South African state to the private sector. It should be stressed that this is not an exhaustive account of private sector activities in the 'secret economy'. Rather, it is meant to be merely indicative of a practice that was pervasive at the time. A study of the role of the mining, banking or manufacturing sector is worthy of other books, some of which still demand writing. What we offer here is relatively brief insights, based on newly declassified or unearthed archival material, intended to illuminate this tale. In this chapter we focus on four aspects of the involvement of the domestic private sector in apartheid.

Firstly, we turn to the war economy and the role of the private sector in the defence sector. A little-reported aspect of the war economy was the special dispensation offered to corporations engaged in sanctions busting. They could, with government approval, withhold information from shareholders if this was in the, vaguely defined, 'national interest'. Secondly, we reveal for the first time details of some of the key corporate donors to the National Party (NP) during apartheid. This raises the question how these corporations and institutions benefited in turn. We have also uncovered the details of an NP-owned front company, intended to create distance between the party and key donors. Thirdly, the chapter contains revelations about the historical role that Naspers played in apartheid politics during the PW Botha era and the special access to power it was granted at the time. Fourthly, we examine the international anti-sanctions lobby groups established by the private sector, such as the South Africa Foundation, and how domestic business responded to sanctions through covert initiatives of their own.

An economy at war

Guns for hire

In the previous chapter, we focused on the role of the state, through Armscor, in domestic arms development and production. Although not in contravention of any sanction provisions, the role of the domestic private sector in arming apartheid during the sanctions period should also be considered.

From the late 1970s, as part of the government's 'total strategy' project, legislation was put in place to draw businesses into the militarisation of society, ensuring seamless 'co-operation' between the private sector and the defence industry.[4] The 1979 Carlton Conference was a meeting at a plush five-star Johannesburg hotel between business leaders and PW Botha's government. It introduced a new partnership between the two, and marked a new era in the expansion of South Africa's military industry. Botha told the room, filled with hand-picked industrialists, 'We have our differences, but we are creating reciprocal channels to plan strategy in South Africa as a team.'[5] The discussion in this first of three key meetings between government and business that stretched from 1979 to 1986 was broad-ranging but it had the desired effect of 'unit[ing] business leaders behind the SADF'.[6]

Another building block in the nascent military–industrial complex was the 1977 National Supplies Procurement Act, passed in direct response to the arms embargo. This Act empowered the minister of economic affairs to 'order the manufacture of goods without due process of public tender and to order persons capable of supplying such goods to the state to do so'.[7] Private sector industries were 'requested to produce items ranging from combat vehicles to warships and electronic equipment' as well as supply components and assemblies.[8] By the end of the 1970s, a total of 29,000 people were employed by Armscor and a further 71,000 worked in the private sector fulfilling Armscor contracts.[9]

As defence expenditure ballooned in the 1980s to well over 20%

of the annual budget, private sector contractors became important and highly profitable players in the siege economy. By the late 1980s, Armscor had around 3,000 private sector subcontractors.[10] The development of a 'mutually dependent relationship between business and the military, characterised by the infusion of the strategic concerns of the security establishment within the South African economy as a whole', was integral to the growth of the country's local production capabilities and to the government's goal of self-sufficiency.[11]

The extent of this corporate collusion was illustrated in the TRC report by the fact that business people were members of the Armscor board or even owners and managers of Armscor's numerous subsidiaries. These allegiances, as the commission stressed, involved the strategic and morally reproachable decision to 'collaborate actively' with and profiteer from the apartheid government's 'war machine'.[12] As the Centre for Conflict Resolution noted in its submission to the TRC, 'There was a high degree of integration between the public and private sectors ... Three industrial groups, namely Reunert, Altech and Grintek, dominated the private sector defence industry. These groups were in turn owned or controlled by one of the six large financial, mining and industrial conglomerates. Reunert was controlled by Old Mutual, Altech by Anglo American, and Grintek by Anglovaal.'[13]

This militarisation of the South African economy is an unsavoury, yet unsurprising, historical fact. Irrespective of many leading corporates' anti-apartheid rhetoric, it was in their interests to marry their manufacturing outputs to security priorities. South African corporates in many ways saw their involvement in the apartheid economy either as apolitical or as part of a deeply political and patriotic project of protecting South Africa against external aggression and the supposed impending 'total onslaught' of communism.[14]

As corporate activities were shrouded in secrecy and there was a reluctance to present submissions and testimonies to the TRC, the names of these businesses and their subsidiaries are largely unknown. Nonetheless, the security sector expert Graeme Simpson provides an exemplary case study of the 'Barlow Rand experience' to demonstrate the mutually beneficial relationship between private capital and military expansion.[15] While Barlow Rand (now trading as Barloworld), a leading electronics industrial corporate, presented itself as an 'enlightened opponent of apartheid', it was simultaneously 'a major contributor in the production of technology and armaments' and, as such, directly involved in the promotion of the regime and its wars.[16] In the 1960s, the Barlow Rand chairman, CS Barlow, was invited by the minister of defence, PW Botha, to sit on the Defence Advisory Board, and the company soon became the chief electrical supplier to the SADF.[17]

In the 1980s the Defence Advisory Board included '13 of the biggest names in South African industry'.[18] Among them were Barlow's chief executive, Richard 'Dick' Goss, the managing director of South African Breweries, and Frans Cronje, chairman of Nedbank.[19] Although Anton Rupert was initially invited by Botha to join the Defence Advisory Council, it seems that the prime minister subsequently let him off the hook, as membership might have imperilled his businesses overseas.[20] Rupert responded by thanking his 'dear friend' for this let-off, which he greatly appreciated.[21] Further correspondence suggests that Fred du Plessis, chairman of the insurance giant Sanlam, subsequently replaced Rupert.[22] Basil Hersov of Anglovaal, who was linked later on to allegations of corruption in the post-apartheid arms deal, which he flatly denies, was also a member of the Defence Advisory Council. Hersov said that the council was set up but that its members were never engaged – 'it was bullshit ... I don't think I was ever on it'. Pushed a little harder, Hersov said, 'I remember it, but it never met.'[23]

In his autobiography, Magnus Malan states that the development of the domestic arms-manufacturing capacity would have been impossible without the assistance of the South African private sector. According to the former minister of defence, 'we still owe these top businessmen and businesswomen our thanks for their selfless service'.[24] Even though the SADF's claims of military self-sufficiency were to a large extent overstated and very much part of Armscor's persuasive propaganda, domestic business was a key player in the war economy.

Corporate secrets and sanctions busters

Corporate reports and balance sheets can be deceptively boring at first glance. But sometimes they are meant to hide information from or else deceive oversight authorities, tax authorities and shareholders. During apartheid, the government made this far easier for corporations. They created a law that allowed large corporations simply to withhold crucial financial information. The reason cited was simple, to keep prying competitors guessing or to serve the 'national interest'. This fuzzy term was most likely a codeword for the government's business of sanctions busting.

How did it work? As a rule, large publicly listed companies are required to include a wide range of financial and ownership information in their company reports. Such reports can then be scrutinised by shareholders, analysts and the broader public to track performance, consider investments and ensure that management or directors are not pocketing the profits. Yet many of South Africa's large companies were given consent to bypass full financial reporting from 1973 until at least the mid-1990s. This was based on a little-known clause of the 1973 Companies Act.

According to Section 15A(1)(b) of the 1973 Companies Act (and Section 310 of the preceding Companies Act), companies could apply to the Registrar of Companies (in the Department of Trade and Industry) for certain disclosure exemptions. Specifically, the law stated that this included 'particular information or a particular fact concerning the affairs or business of the company, or that of any of its subsidiaries' that it would usually be required by the Act to disclose.[25] The precise conditions for such exemption were not clearly laid out in the Act. However, the effect was clear, for the exemption could obscure the movement of money, particularly as it related to subsidiaries. According to a circular from the South African

Association of Chartered Accountants in 1991, a request for an exemption by a company needed to demonstrate that the disclosure of financial information would 'result in the national interest being adversely affected'.[26] The national interest is a vague concept that could mean anything and is most often used by governments that wish to abuse power and entrench secrecy. Surprisingly, the former minister of finance, Barend du Plessis, argued, 'It's the first question I have received in my life about this [Section 15A] ... I never knew about this.'[27]

Why would the government build in such a broad 'national interest' exception to the regulations? Scouring press-clipping services from the period, we found slivers of reporting on this secret clause. One source is the New York-based Investor Responsibility Research Center, a pioneering not-for-profit organisation that provided re-search on social and corporate responsibility issues.[28] It argued that the law was a means of shielding from scrutiny companies that were assisting the state in sanctions busting.[29] In 1984, the deputy registrar of companies, Hans Coetzee, confirmed that at least 150 companies and a range of their subsidiaries were 'operating in secret'.[30] The companies exempted from disclosing information were in a range of sectors from arms to strategic minerals or were simply involved with 'sensitive trading partners'.[31] This last term has the ring of sanctions busting.

I set out to find details of the companies that were granted such exemptions. This process in itself was illuminating, as I was either denied access to old annual reports by large corporations or else these have been inexplicably destroyed or removed from public collections. I requested the Companies and Intellectual Property Commission (CIPC), through the South African History Archive, to provide us with a list of all the exemptions granted. On one of my visits I received a call on the office phone from an Afrikaans-speaking official whose name I do not have. She confirmed that a list did exist and was kept in a 'special safe' until 1998, well after the transition. Thereafter the list was, according to her, returned to the boxes containing company records. Having spent days working through these boxes, I could confirm to her that there was no such list, to which she responded, 'If the information is not in the files I don't know what happened.' Were the lists destroyed or simply 'lost', given the parlous state of some of the CIPC's records? Both are possible explanations.

Despite this, our searches were not in vain. We can reveal that some of the largest South African corporations used this shield to hide key details in their annual reports. CIPC records indicate that Bill Venter's Altech (Altron) Group used the exemption throughout the 1970s and 1980s. Altech had a long-standing association with the apartheid military in the development of missiles, military technology and dual-purpose technology. Another regular user of this secret veil was Anton Rupert's Rembrandt group.[32] An article in the *Financial Mail* in 1980 referred to Rembrandt's 'obsessive corporate camouflage' in order to protect its interests from sanctions and embargoes.[33] According to the article, Rembrandt had only very recently disclosed its revenue flows to its own shareholders, but still refused to list its associate and subsidiary companies in 1980.[34] The Anglo American Corporation similarly utilised Section 15A, withholding the names of its subsidiaries and associates, at least from 1984 to 1994.[35]

How did the exemptions work in practice? Exemption may well have been part of a larger sanctions-related give and take between government and business. Could this have been an opportunity for businesses that assisted in sanctions busting to be given a special dispensation to move cash offshore during a period of stringent exchange controls? We do not know, but the Section 15A exemptions could have served as a perfect cover for this kind of arrangement.

I asked the former auditor general Joop de Loor about how Section 15A was used. He admitted that this secrecy provision was used more and more in the late 1980s when foreign countries and individuals increasingly 'stirred the pot', as he expressed it in reference to sanctions pressure, and it became more difficult to 'manage the country'.[36] De Loor said he was 'aware of it [the provision in the Act] but was not aware of how much it was used'.[37] This was, after all, a smuggling operation that few people would know about. He did add, though, that in terms of companies approaching the Reserve Bank to take money out of the country, it would be 'dealt with by the president of the Reserve Bank personally ... with his personal assistant – those are the only people who would know'.[38]

Given that almost all evidence of the exemption has been destroyed or lost, it is almost impossible to identify the amount of money that was kept off the books as a result. This was nothing short of a failure of corporate governance, authorised by the National Party government. Shareholders were in effect kept in the dark about the secret movement of money. In addition, taxpayers, even through the limited public accountability mechanism of the white parliament, were unable to monitor the true income of some of the country's largest corporations and their ownership of subsidiaries. Without this information, how could the public be assured that the corporations were paying the requisite taxes and were not cut special deals by the government? An important segment of corporate South Africa embraced state secrecy, potentially for private gain. The exact extent of this collusion for now remains a mystery.

There is no doubt that it was helpful for any company assisting the government in busting sanctions. Basil Hersov, the former head of the Anglovaal mining group, told me in an interview that government would regularly approach private sector companies to assist in this manner. 'There were a lot of schemes to get around sanctions and they worked at a cost ... They might ask you to import a specific machine ... and you might say yes.'[39]

Tithing to the tyrant:
Who funded the National Party?

One of the greatest threats to democratic politics is the unregulated funding of political parties.[40] Central to this is, on one hand, a culture of expectation among politicians that wealthy interest groups, corporations and foreign governments will fund party politics. On the other hand, these powerful donors rely on a culture of secrecy to conceal their identity from ordinary voters, who might otherwise be outraged at the type of influence that such money can buy. For more than five decades, no regulation has existed to force the disclosure of political parties' private funding sources. In tolerating this, political parties have given a green light to an insidious form of corruption, which without access to information is almost impossible to detect. Since 1994, this has meant that the ANC has accepted cash from mega-corporations, rogue businesspeople and murderous politicians alike. This practice of cash-for-access has continued under the leadership of Jacob Zuma, who in 2015 addressed an ANC gala fundraising dinner at which he told business leaders that if they joined the ANC, their businesses would benefit as 'everything you touch will multiply'.[41]

Today we rely on investigative journalists and whistleblowers to expose important examples of these sources of funding. During apartheid, very little was publicly disclosed about how political parties raised their funds. Within the white parliament, it was an open secret that large Afrikaner businesses such as Sanlam and Gencor funded the National Party, and that Anglo American was an obvious supporter of the more liberal opposition. Yet the details behind this have been undisclosed until now.

Information found in the archival records of PW Botha, FW de Klerk and Danie Steyn reveals some important details of corporate funders of the NP. These are by no means complete accounts, as they reflect funding sources only in particular constituencies or provinces or at a national level for a limited period during the 1980s. The value lies in the fact that they provide inescapable evidence of collaboration with the NP.

NP funders revealed

Oppression delivers paperwork, and the NP political machinery was no different. We were speechless when the archivist at the University of the Free State delivered folders marked 'National Party donations'.

In these and other folders are letters of thanks, requests for anonymity, copies of cheques and carefully written receipts to NP donors. The story of party finance is often revealed only through whispers, but here we had found indisputable documentary evidence.

In total, we have identified approximately 70 individual donations to the NP between 1979 and 1989, ranging in value from R5,000 to R290,000 (between R40,000 and R2.4 million in 2017 terms). The sum of these donations is R4.5 million (R43 million today). An important caveat to note is that the list is not conclusive.[42] In addition, these figures are relative to the size of election expenditure at the time, which was minuscule in comparison with the money spent on elections today.[43]

In PW Botha's archive, we located a list of all the major contributors to the NP's 1987 electoral campaign. During that year, Botha's notes show that the cost of the campaign was approximately R2 million (R16 million today). This figure is likely to exclude expenditure at a provincial and constituency level, which could have trebled the cost. (In comparison, the ANC spent R429 million in the 2014 national and provincial elections.) Yet we should not miss the point that these relatively small amounts (by today's standards) were in fact highly significant to the NP machine at the time.[44]

The first noteworthy group of donors was corporations historically closest to the NP.[45] These included the insurance giant Sanlam, their investment arm Federale Volksbeleggings, and the Afrikaans mining group Gencor (today a significant part of BHP Billiton). Other donor companies traditionally aligned to the NP during apartheid were Volkskas (now part of ABSA) and the now defunct Saambou Bank.

We can also reveal evidence of funding provided by Naspers to the NP. Ton Vosloo, Naspers MD, confirmed in writing that the company had made a donation of R150,000 (approximately R1 million today) to the NP before the 1987 election.[46] The confirmation is contained in a letter to FW de Klerk at the time of his making a further donation shortly before the decisive white election in September 1989. Vosloo wrote two letters to De Klerk on 17 August, committing Naspers to provide funding to the NP to the value of R290,000 (approximately R2 million today). Vosloo noted that one of the donations to the Transvaal NP 'is a token of loyalty and friendship with the NP in the Transvaal'.[47] He added that 'our newspaper *Beeld* in the Transvaal is your ally and we trust that this formidable combination will wipe out the competition'.[48]

Johann Rupert, one of Africa's wealthiest men, also made at least one donation to the NP in 1989. In August 1989, former NP minister Hendrik Schoeman wrote a letter marked 'personal and confidential' to Rupert, at that stage the executive director of Rembrandt. The letter confirmed that following a meeting at which he had been asked for a financial donation to the NP, Rupert had handed R20,000 to FW de Klerk. He added, 'Please be assured that we place this delightful gesture in high regard. It is highly appreciated. We are aware that you do not wish to give any publicity to this donation and we will handle it in a confidential manner.'[49] We found no evidence of Rupert funding the NP prior to the emergence of the more reform-minded FW de Klerk as party leader.

Another noteworthy NP donor was Christo Wiese who, according to *Forbes*, occupies the fourth position jointly with Rupert on the list of the richest people in Africa.[50] In a letter to FW de Klerk in August 1989, Minister Kent Durr reported that 'on Saturday night I received a call from Mr Christo Wiese of Pepkor, an old friend and supporter of the National Party'.[51] Wiese offered the NP printing to the value of R25,000 from his company Printkor and assured that he would 'distribute a further R25,000 at his own discretion to individual candidates with whom he has a personal relationship and whom he would like to help'.[52] Wiese was apparently anxious that Durr should make this information known to FW de Klerk, who had been sworn in as president just ten days before. De Klerk sent Wiese a letter of thanks on an NP letterhead a few months later, following the NP's electoral victory. Thanking him for his generous donation, De Klerk noted, 'it is donors such as you which put the National Party in a position to win and to work resolutely on a new dispensation'.[53]

The letters from donors, understandably thought to be confidential, provide some insight into the thinking of the powerful men behind these companies. For example, the managing director of Federale Volksbeleggings, PT van der Merwe, opened a letter to Botha by reminiscing about a meeting they had both attended of the pro-Nazi Ossewa-Brandwag (OB) group in 1941 or 1942. At that time the Germans had achieved a devastating victory in Western Europe, much to the jubilation of the OB. He recalled Botha's remarks at the time, 'We don't know who is going to win the war ... but we can guess.'[54] One indication of the extent to which Botha's politics had shifted since the war was a letter he received in 1979 from the MP Jan Marais, with a subject line marked 'Jewish and English businessmen, a further contribution'. This detailed funds sought and obtained from prominent South African Jewish business people such as Isaac Kaye and Freddy Hirsch.[55] Kaye, a multi-millionaire, now resides in the UK, where he was caught up at one time in party-funding scandals linked to Tony Blair's Labour Party.[56]

At least six payments were made by the Sanlam group, totaling R220,000 (R3.7 million today). In 1983, the Sanlam chairman Fred du Plessis, who also served on PW Botha's Defence Advisory Council, wrote to Botha to assure him of his company's 'moral support in carrying out the demanding tasks which rest on his shoulders'.[57] For good measure, Du Plessis threw in a company-branded pocket diary. Botha responded to his friend and indicated that it had been brought to his attention that state-owned corporations were operating in a manner that discriminated against Sanlam. He intended to remedy this: 'I have now given orders that Sanlam and its affiliates are properly considered in the awarding of any business by State-Owned Enterprises.'[58]

Botha's correspondence with Sanlam's chairman was not without minor squabbles. Apparently Du Plessis had in October 1984 made a statement about the economy that irritated the short-tempered Botha and led him to tell Du Plessis that he 'thought he no longer wanted to be part of the team'.[59] Du Plessis responded to defend his comments, explaining that without exception he had raised any disagreements about government policy within what he referred to as the 'inner circle'. He also noted that over the previous few years, he had taken the unusual step to submit drafts of his chairman's address at Sanlam to PW for commentary.[60]

The mining conglomerate Gencor, represented by its chairman Tom de Beer, made at least four contributions to the NP between 1981[61] and 1988[62] to the value of R245,000 (R2.8 million today). Botha could also count on his friend Boet Troskie, owner of the Mimosa film group, which produced one of South Africa's highest-grossing movies, *The Gods Must Be Crazy*. Troskie's company donated R250,000 (R2 million today) in 1987.[63] As the former spy boss Niël Barnard has noted, Troskie was the only person present with Botha to give him advice on the evening before he resigned on 14 August 1989.[64] Troskie would also act as a conduit for other businesses that wished to remain anonymous, such as Comair and National Airways Corporation.[65]

Powerful companies involved in the arms trade and arms production also made sure to keep the NP sweet. Barlow Rand made two payments on 1987 and 1988 to the value of R100,000 (R800,000 today), duly acknowledged by FW de Klerk. He noted in correspondence with PW Botha that the company wished to keep the donations confidential. The donations were made by the Barlow chairman, Derek Cooper, who continued to play a prominent role in South African business until his retirement as Standard Bank chairman in 2010.[66] The arms trader Dan Maartens of the Intertechnic group and Giovanni Mario Ricci, an Italian fraudster and sanctions buster who worked closely with Craig Williamson, also made donations. Ricci, who relied heavily on the government's covert business, provided the NP with R250,000 in 1987 (R2 million today).[67]

Unsurprisingly, Bill Venter and his Altech (Altron) group, which developed important technology for the military, including missile systems, made a strong showing among the donors. As a sign of his appreciation, Venter made a down payment of R10,000 and promised to donate an amount of R150,000 in 1982.[68] Venter again contributed a generous R200,000 in 1985 (R2.2 million today) and again in 1989.[69]

Surprisingly, on the list of donors are numbers of prominent English-speaking business leaders, who are generally regarded as having held a position that was mildly critical of the NP. Bennie Slome, the founder of the Tedelex television rental company, made regular substantial donations between 1981[70] and 1984.[71] In a letter accompanying a donation in 1984, Slome congratulated PW Botha on a very successful overseas tour (which was in fact an unmitigated PR disaster), and committed himself to fund the NP, 'in desiring once again to express my appreciation for what is being done for the country'.[72] Eric Samson of Macsteel, one of South Africa's largest companies, was listed as a donor in 1987.[73] PW Botha also thanked Louis Shill, founder of the Sage financial group, which pioneered unit trusts in South Africa, for 'substantial personal donations' made between 1981 and 1983.[74] Bertie Lubner is on record as having made one donation to the NP of R20,000 in 1982. In a letter on his PG Glass letterhead, Lubner thanked Botha for 'a very wonderful evening that we spent with you, charming members of your family and other guests'. He also paid special tribute to Botha 'for your outstanding leadership of this country'.[75]

I asked Lubner about his support for the NP when I interviewed him in January 2016, a few months before his death. He said, 'Let me just get my position clear: I made it clear to any government minister, including De Klerk, when I was asked to join the National Party ... I indicated there were three reasons why not. One, the membership card said total national Christian education – how can I as a Jew? Secondly, the whole profile of apartheid is an enigma [anathema] to Jews who have suffered all around the world, particularly in the Holocaust, because of an idea that people are not equal, there is no way I could support that. Thirdly, we needed to start a programme of upliftment, in terms of employment, training, etc. in order to make people's lives better.'[76]

In a December 2015 interview with Basil Hersov, I asked him about funding of the NP. He answered with the simple word 'never',[77] although he was sure that some people did try to 'buy leverage' and encourage reform that way.[78] The archives reveal that Hersov did in fact make a payment to the NP in 1983, and sent a personal handwritten letter to PW Botha in October of that year. He indicated that he was prepared to make a donation in recognition of Botha's role in the 'further dismantling of the hurtful aspects of discrimination and segregation'.[79]

Projek Republiek: The NP's fundraising front

In 2006, investigative researchers revealed that the ANC had established a trust called Chancellor House (named after the building that housed the legal practice of Nelson Mandela and Walter Sisulu), which was doing business with the government and engaged in fundraising for the benefit of the governing party. Did the NP ever consider a similar scheme?

The NP had a secret front of its own, a company called Projek Republiek (ProRep), established in 1985 to hide the identities of NP donors. At a Transvaal NP meeting in 1984, chaired by FW de Klerk, the financial committee proposed 'that a company is registered with an eye to donations from corporations that do not want to directly fund the party'.[80] At a subsequent meeting it was resolved that the name of the company would be Natpro or Naspro, with Louis le Grange, minister of law and order, nominated as its director.[81] Such an obvious allusion to the NP was eventually abandoned in favour of ProRep or Project Republic.

The company was registered in February 1985, with a group of well-connected directors, including ministers Hendrik Schoeman,[82] Danie Steyn[83] and Org Marais, all old hands at NP fundraising.[84] According to company records, at least seven additional directors were appointed, most as late as 1992. These included Gerhardus Koornhof and Gerhardus Oosthuizen.[85] Both men, once NP MPs, are now firmly ensconced within the ANC caucus. Oosthuizen has been so successful at managing this transition that he has held the position of deputy minister of sport under three presidents, since his appointment by Thabo Mbeki in 2004. Koornhof, the son of long-time NP minister Piet Koornhof, was an NP member of parliament from 1994 before being appointed an ANC MP in 2001.[86]

Given the lack of information available, we know little else about the activities of ProRep. However, the NP had several other fundraising initiatives and investments. These included the so-called Club of 50 for the National Party, whose members, it was proposed, would be required to make a R2,000 annual contribution to the party.[87] This model is not dissimilar to the ANC's progressive business forum, which is used to court business. This ANC forum also has an interesting link to the NP leadership: one of its founders and co-conveners from 2006 to 2014 was Renier Schoeman, a former NP deputy minister before 1994.[88]

Naspers: 'A tap root of the National Party'

In 2015 the management of Africa's largest media and internet company, Naspers, finally apologised for supporting apartheid during its foundational years and acknowledged 'complicity in a morally indefensible political regime'.[89] The Naspers apology, made possible by the long-standing chairman Ton Vosloo's retirement the same year, is rightly considered to have come too late. The company had not only benefited politically from its close ties to the NP, but had also profited financially. During apartheid, this meant that its newspapers could rely on government advertising and its publishing houses on lucrative school textbook contracts. By the mid-1980s it was awarded the rights to start South Africa's first private television service, M-Net. This would become its cash cow, today broadcasting as DStv across the African continent. Thanks to an astute purchase of nearly 50% of stock in the Chinese internet company Tencent in 2001, Naspers is today worth more than R1 trillion and is one of the most important shares on the Johannesburg Stock Exchange.[90] Its outlook is now resolutely global, but is also unquestionably rooted in the apartheid economy.

Two decades previously, during the 1997 TRC media hearings, the Naspers management, under the leadership of Vosloo, refused to appear before the commission. This led the TRC chairperson, Archbishop Desmond Tutu, to ask, 'Is silence from that quarter to be construed as consent, conceding that it was a sycophantic handmaiden of the apartheid government?'[91] Instead it was left to a group of 127 conscientious journalists, who defied their management and made a submission to the TRC, to declare that 'a close relationship had developed between Nasionale Pers and the National Party, with our newspapers acting as NP mouthpieces'.[92] Vosloo shot back an angry, ill-considered defence in response to his journalists' apology: 'This document is in fact a repudiation of good and honourable names in Naspers's long and rich and proud journalistic tradition and is to be regretted.'[93]

During the apartheid era, the regime was relentless in its desire to control public opinion. It sought to do this through any means possible, from fake news to full-blown censorship. Much as with some streams within the ANC today, the ability to control the press was a prized goal of the NP leadership. With the SABC transmitting PW Botha's propaganda, the state broadcaster presented no threat to the NP government. Control over privately owned newspapers was therefore a coveted goal. Newsrooms were infiltrated with spies or, in the case of strong, independent critical newspapers, faced harsh censorship or the debilitating banning of both journalists and editions.

In the mainstream Afrikaans-language milieu, the newspaper owners were solid NP supporters. Cape Town-based Naspers and its northern rival, Perskor, showed their commitment to Afrikaner nationalism in their editorial content. Where the newspapers were critical of the regime, it was as a loyal opposition, favouring certain provincial branches of the NP over others (Cape vs Transvaal) or certain political streams within the NP (verligtes vs verkramptes). By the 1980s, with the accession to power of its favoured son, PW Botha, the fortunes of Naspers were on the rise. By the end of the decade Naspers would eliminate its Afrikaans rival, Perskor, and its three main titles, *Die Burger*, *Beeld* and *Rapport*, would dominate the Afrikaans media landscape.

Time spent in the NP archives provides a unique insight into the type of backroom conversations that were commonplace between senior NP politicians and Naspers. As we have already established, Naspers funded the NP. Also, as we saw in Chapter 1, Naspers was so close to the NP that PW Botha, leader of the Cape NP, was given a seat on the company's board from 1966 until his resignation around the time of his election as prime minister in 1978.[94] In addition, NP financial records we have accessed reveal that the NP owned 74,000 shares in Naspers (in 1984), further entrenching the conflicting interests between the party and its media organ.[95]

The influence that PW Botha exercised over the press was evident throughout the 1980s. There are many accounts of his calls to the SABC to complain about the evening's news. The NP archives reflect a similar relationship with the Naspers top brass. For example, the editor of the Cape Town daily, *Die Burger*, submitted a grovelling apology to Botha when he heard that Botha was unhappy with an article published the previous week. The editor, WD Beukes, reacting to rumour alone and anticipating Botha's wrath, wrote a letter to the state president replete with apologies, perhaps pre-empting the inevitable.[96] Botha wrote back two days later, acknowledging the letter but still expressing his regret at what he termed 'this blatant defiance of the good relations which have always existed between us'.[97]

Botha had a fragile ego which he made up for in bluster and threats. In 1981, he took time out from the war in Angola to write to the chairman of Naspers a letter, marked 'personal and confidential', concerning the 'leftist propaganda' published in the magazine *Fair Lady*, then edited by Jane Raphaely. Botha directed his attention to an article about Bishop Desmond Tutu and his wife Leah, which his government regarded as highly disappointing.[98] It was time, he stated, to 'put an end to Jane Raphaely's leftist politics'.[99] Cillié, the chairman of Naspers, wrote back to signal his agreement, noting that 'we are already dealing with this issue and I trust that in future there will be fewer reasons for disagreement'.[100] Such acquiescence continued throughout the 1980s. A subsequent editor of the *Fair Lady* (and, later, Democratic Alliance MP), Dene Smuts, resigned for similar reasons in 1986 after Botha expressed his displeasure that a magazine oriented towards female readers should report on the life of Winnie Mandela.[101]

Botha's archive shows that petulant complaints to media editors were commonplace. In 1985, in correspondence with Dr W van Heerden of Perskor, Botha complained about the preponderance of 'negative' articles in the weekly *Rapport*, suggesting that it was not fulfilling its political role.[102] At the time, Naspers and Perskor held joint ownership of *Rapport*. In response, Van Heerden apologised and promised Botha that he had warned the editor, Wimpie de Klerk, to avoid this in the future.[103] Surprisingly, the archive also includes deferential letters from Wimpie de Klerk, the brother of FW. In one instance, he asked Botha for permission to publish a right-wing conspiratorial letter doing the rounds in Pretoria that suggested that Botha was an agent of the US.[104] On other occasions, De Klerk apologised to Botha, and also sent him a letter of praise on his election as state president.[105] His chairman at Naspers, Piet Cillié, was prone to similar obsequiousness.[106]

With the closure of the *Rand Daily Mail* in 1985, the government got rid of its most influential English-language critic. PW Botha was eager to see a new English-language title emerge to fill this gap but one that would support the NP regime and have a wider reach than *The Citizen*, which he derided in private. Ton Vosloo, then Naspers MD, responded to a letter from PW Botha on this subject to say, 'The issue that you are advocating is also of concern to us. It is an order – that's what I wish to call it – that we cannot nor do we wish to avoid … If you can for one moment put on your hat as leader [*hoofleier*] of the NP, I want to suggest that the federal information service [the NP's propaganda unit] can play a role in this in which we can be of assistance. I will thus like to leave an idea with you that a small group of us can informally talk about how to tackle this issue.'[107]

At around this time, Naspers had its eye on the prize of a licence to start South Africa's first paid television service. Piet Cillié lobbied Botha in a flurry of correspondence starting in late 1984, asking him to keep Naspers in mind for a stake in what would become a lucrative new market. He reminded Botha that Naspers needed this contract because of dwindling newspaper sales, in order to remain 'one of the tap roots of National power, and Afrikaner leadership'.[108] Vosloo continued along the same vein in the first half of 1985 when writing to Botha about the pay television licence. On at least two occasions he forwarded to Botha copies of letters he had sent to Pik Botha, the minister in charge of the process. In April 1985 Vosloo sent PW Botha a briefing note, marked 'strictly confidential', in which he proposed scope for collaboration between Naspers and Perskor that would result in a new, revitalised version of *The Citizen*. However, Vosloo was clear that this was dependent on support for the award of a stake in the new TV licence.[109]

The lobbying seems to have had the desired impact, as on 4 July 1985 Vosloo wrote to Botha concerning plans to beef up the pro-government *Citizen*. Vosloo ended the letter to Botha: 'Thank you for your leadership on the TV matter and your quick decision. I appreciate it. The decision now places the matter in a more certain trajectory.'[110] As a result of the close relationship between Naspers and the NP, the former was awarded a 26% stake by the government in the country's first commercial pay TV service, M-Net.[111]

Vosloo had a particularly close relationship with Botha's administration. In June 1987 he was invited to give a briefing to Botha and five ministers on proposed changes in the media landscape. This was extraordinary privilege for any business leader, particularly in a sector that relied heavily on government contracts. The minutes of the meeting, marked secret, show the extent to which Vosloo and Naspers were able to shape government policy from the inside. The discussion even extended to school textbook policies, with PW Botha suggesting that the government could accommodate Naspers in lessening the impact of a decision to charge learners for textbooks.[112]

School textbooks have always been a lucrative and highly competitive market for publishers.

In 2015 at the time of his retirement as chairperson of Naspers, Vosloo is reported as having said, 'Journalism is the last line of opposition against the powerful [*oormag*], corruption and misdeeds [*wandadigheid*]. May our knees never weaken.'[113] Perhaps he should have added, 'again'.

Friends in faraway places

The private sector was an important lobbyist against sanctions on behalf of the South African government. All sanctions hurt their profitability. They hampered the export of goods ranging from coal to fruit. Conversely, the hiked price and premiums on imported goods from weapons to oil meant higher taxes and less consumer spending on the type of products these corporations produced.

The private sector also played the role of 'reasonable' voice when addressing international audiences and promoting less stringent sanctions in return for reform initiatives. One of the more peculiar arguments in favour of a better understanding of Pretoria's position was made by Anton Rupert, the billionaire who built his South African empire off the cigarette industry.[114] In an address to an influential Detroit business association in America's rust belt in the mid–1960s, Rupert called for solidarity with white South Africa. 'I implore you to listen to me because we may today indeed be the most important White men in the world, as the most important Coloureds in the world are the 20 million Coloureds in the United States of America.'[115] Rupert seemed to believe that white South Africans and African Americans required special treatment. 'No people of our numbers has ever before occupied such a place in the flood tide of history, for we are of two worlds – the old and the new. We alone are the hinge between the West and Africa, and upon us and your Coloureds may hang your destiny.'[116]

The South African private sector was generally well placed to use its contacts and overseas networks to discourage and, if necessary, evade sanctions. To achieve this, they organised their own structures to challenge sanctions. Although not universally supportive of government policy, they were also careful not to tread on any toes.

The 'petty crooks'

Three interviews with Basil Hersov, Bertie Lubner and Tony Bloom, all business luminaries in the 1980s, provided rare insight into the role that South African business played in busting sanctions.

I interviewed Lubner in January 2016 while he was undergoing dialysis treatment in a private Sandton clinic a few months before he passed away. When I walked into his private ward, the congenial man joked, 'So, have you come for me?'[117] He was lying on the hospital bed with arms outstretched, a Nelson Mandela 46664 bangle visible. The wealthy businessman had a disarming air of vulnerability. In our discussion, Lubner was concerned that he should not be portrayed only as a sanctions buster but as an outspoken proponent of the transition to democracy. He stressed, 'I played a very, very simple role that was good for the country, that was good for our business, and that was good for others.'[118] 'Obviously there were places like Switzerland and Luxembourg, where companies' names were set up. They were the trading companies, they bought the products, but they were just name plates, you just had the address and the people [often in Zug, Switzerland] who would run the accounts.'[119]

Lubner, together with his brother Ronnie, was the head of PG Glass and a timber empire in the 1980s. According to him, during that time 'we unfortunately had to undertake the breaking of sanctions because we were buying a lot of our timber products from countries like Malaysia, Indonesia, West Africa, Brazil, etc. and everyone was more than happy to supply us because they didn't care less'.[120] His company would obtain documentation showing another country as the destination of imports, and, while at sea, that documentation would be changed and the timber would be brought to South Africa.[121]

A poignant moment in the interview was not about sanctions busting but business complicity with the military. I asked Lubner about a document we had found in the SADF archive that suggested that he agreed to donate 'wreck benches' to the army. The equipment was intended for Jonas Savimbi's troops to process hardwood in southern Angola. Lubner suddenly looked a little startled, as he did not know what 'wreck benches' were. He asked, 'Are they for torture?'[122] We were silent for a brief moment before I clarified the point. In that instant there was the recognition that the 1980s was not just about business as usual. The unimaginable was possible: timber merchants might unwittingly have become accomplices to torture.

In comparison with Lubner, Basil Hersov was far more defensive of the former status quo and had a cynical perspective about the country's future that left a sad 'cut-and-run' air about him. He echoed this in statements like 'If my grandchildren say they want to leave the country, I am not going to dissuade them'.[123] A very affluent man by all accounts, Hersov was appointed CEO and chairman of his father's Anglovaal mining group from 1973 to 2001. He was also chairman of Barclays Bank South Africa from 1983 to 1991. Hersov argued, 'Broadly speaking we were against sanctions, although sanctions were very good for us and for the economy, as it forced South Africa to manufacture a lot of things and it expanded the manufacturing industry in a very big way.'[124] He added a caveat to this: 'It also turned most of us into petty crooks, because of getting round sanctions.'[125]

Hersov said that the business community opposed sanctions because they created conditions of 'economic warfare' and 'we did not want to see South Africa destroyed in any sense ... because whoever was going to run the country would need a vibrant and stable economy, which I think we produced.'[126] In my interview Hersov was far more evasive when it came to the detail. When asked about the relationship between government and business in driving anti-sanctions projects, he would only say that 'what business did individually, didn't involve government' but that 'government would often come to business and asked "Can you help with the import of this?", and business sometimes did and sometimes didn't'.[127]

The third business view on sanctions came from Tony Bloom, whom I interviewed in his home in Hanover Terrace in London opposite Regent's Park. The former head of the Premier Group (then one of the country's largest conglomerates), he left South Africa in the late 1980s after engaging in some of the first meetings between South African businessmen and the ANC in Lusaka. Like Lubner, he cut a more genuinely friendly liberal figure.

Life has been good to Bloom, who is now in the Cognac trade. Otto Dix and George Grosz paintings dot the walls. After a difficult start to the conversation in the formal lounge, we made our way to his small kitchen where he toasted us bagels and offered apricot jam and cheese, a staple from the old country. Bloom argued that sanctions were not a good thing for business. According to him, South African business got used to cutting deals and cutting corners in an unconventional way.[128] There was also the air of adventure about the practice: 'business got used to ducking and diving', he said, recalling the Costa Rican passport that enabled him to travel to places where his South African passport could create obstacles.[129]

Noteworthy about all three interviews is that these worldly individuals saw little wrong in their work in assisting with sanctions busting. I asked Bloom whether business didn't miss an important opportunity to help South Africans come clean with issues of economic crime by appearing before the TRC. He replied that the TRC had more important issues to deal with.[130] Though none of the men I interviewed suggested that they were completely blameless, they did give the impression that any blame is simply irrelevant.

The South Africa Foundation

The South Africa Foundation (SAF) was launched in December 1959, just one month after the British Anti-Apartheid Movement (AAM) formed a South African boycott committee. Established by prominent South African businessmen, including Harry Oppenheimer, the SAF was first led by Sir Francis de Guingand, a close friend of Franklin D Roosevelt and deeply embedded in the Washington establishment.[131] A member of the UK AAM recalls how the SAF was set up with capital of £260,000, a tidy sum at the time. In contrast, the AAM 'had no budget, not even of five or ten shillings'.[132]

The SAF's mandate was to provide 'objective information' about apartheid South Africa in order to counter what the business community saw as lies peddled by anti-apartheid activists around the world. The group used an extensive international network and their own vast financial resources to lobby against sanctions overseas.[133] According to Ron Nixon, in his book *Selling Apartheid*, the SAF 'received favourable reviews from apartheid officials. And in its annual reports, the foundation often noted its cooperation with the Department of Information and the South African embassies throughout the world, which assisted the group in the reception of foreign visitors.'[134]

Basil Hersov was chairman of the SAF from 1977 to 1993. He reflected on the leverage his organisation had: 'A lot of what we did was behind the scenes where we had access in many ways, that the government did not.'[135] 'Broadly, we started the foundation because we found that the press overseas was getting a very distorted view of South Africa.'[136] The SAF had a role in 'straightening this out, at which it was very successful'. The second goal was to invite prominent foreigners, on the advice of contact groups in various countries, to visit South Africa and 'see for themselves', ensuring 'a balanced view of South Africa'.[137] As a tool of soft diplomacy the SAF had access to some foreign ears that the South African government did not, as 'no one really believed what the government was saying anyway'.[138]

Bertie Lubner was also a member of the SAF. He spoke about the internal contradictions within the SAF: 'You must remember that the board members were very mixed in their opinions about apartheid.'[139] They were divided between the predominantly Afrikaans members and the 'verligte English people'. 'But the point was, you had to accept it – that's what the country's laws were and you either lived by it or you buggered off.'[140] Lubner argued that an important goal of the SAF was to persuade countries to abandon their boycotts 'because we felt that the boycotts would only make the PW Botha regime even more determined to maintain control and not have any sort of changes in the political world'.[141]

The balance sheet

This chapter has revealed three primary ways in which the private sector escaped any accountability for questionable actions it performed during apartheid. They were not all illegal, under South Africa law, but they were questionable practices that were normalised and have remained a stubborn characteristic of business practice to this day.

Firstly, there was overt collaboration. This we saw exemplified in the way in which business helped arm apartheid and became part of the war economy. Many corporations became fat off contracts selling everything from explosives to shoe polish that met the military's requirements. Then there was the South Africa Foundation, a nominally independent business association, working in tandem with government to counter sanctions overseas. Another example of overt collaboration was the nature of the relationship between Naspers and the government of PW Botha, which was deeply conflicted at every level. Naspers was not alone, and there are numerous examples of other corporations that enjoyed similar close ties to the NP.

Secondly, there was covert support. Secret funding to the NP provides a good example of this. By its very nature, secret funding of political parties, an insidious practice protected by most parties today, is intended to buy influence. Even so-called progressive NP donors suggested that they did so to shift government policy. The NP had many supporters across society, including in business. By the late 1990s, however, most had erased their association with the party of apartheid.

The third element was sanctions busting, both for private ends and to assist the apartheid state. Malfeasance involving the private sector is quickly reduced to acceptable tales of cunning business people who outsmart rivals. The truth is far less glamorous than this. These men were, through their actions, part of the system that supported apartheid and they profited thereby. Above all, these accounts are not a tale of petty crookery. They inform the very nature of economic crime that was common in the late-apartheid period and that stubbornly persists today.

CHAPTER 3

Oil and Other Foreign Affairs

*'I have told you about the power of money, you don't
understand it.'*

– PIK BOTHA, FORMER MINISTER OF FOREIGN AFFAIRS, ON
WHY INTERNATIONAL SANCTIONS FAILED[1]

In this chapter, we focus on networks of secret suppliers and intermediaries that were crucial to the South African economy during the last 15 years of apartheid. In addition to arms (the focus of later chapters), oil, computer technology and other strategic commodities were vulnerable to sanctions from the late 1970s. The voluntary oil embargo at first hit Pretoria hard. With no significant domestic reserves and only expensive coal-to-oil technology, covert networks had to be built to ensure that South Africa continued to receive oil. This trade made everyone rich other than the South African people. The traders made a killing, the shippers made a fortune, and the suppliers charged a premium. How this sanctions-busting system worked is the subject of this chapter.

Foreign affairs

In an attempt to co-ordinate and monitor efforts to counter sanctions, the government established a dedicated civilian ministerial committee on sanctions in the mid-1980s. Chaired by the minister of finance, it met regularly to fine-tune the sanctions-busting machine, with the Reserve Bank in attendance. The committee in turn provided President PW Botha with fortnightly updates on sanctions-busting projects, which he monitored closely.

Of the government departments supporting these initiatives, two are important. The first was the Unconventional Trade Unit within the Department of Trade and Industry. We describe its activities behind the Iron Curtain and in China later on. The second was the Department of Foreign Affairs under the leadership of Pik Botha. A career NP politician, he served uninterruptedly as a cabinet minister from the administration of John Vorster to that of Nelson Mandela. By the mid-1980s his department had extended its focus beyond bread-and-butter tasks of diplomacy and propaganda. In charge of the department's sanctions-busting operations was one of his officials, Marc Burger, an 'ambassador on special assignment'. Empowered by a cabinet decision, he was accountable directly to the president while the Department of Foreign Affairs controlled his budget.[2]

I spent a few hours interviewing Pik Botha in early 2016. He was not willing to share much insight into the who and how of sanctions busting. 'It is dangerous to name those companies. We cannot smear them now,' he said.[3] However, he spoke in glowing terms of his former colleague Marc Burger, who passed away in 2012. 'I had two dreams about Marc in recent months. We were in Switzerland, where the Rothschilds have their secret bank. We arrived at the door and it was locked. Marc turned to me and said, "Don't worry, I will climb through the window."'[4] In a similar vein, Burger's autobiography, *Not the Whole Truth*, published shortly after his death, leaves the reader with a sense that sanctions busting was a great adventure. It's a common thread with some of the people I interviewed, who see this as their own, rather mundane, James Bond moment.

Botha's wife Ina describes Burger as a 'funny little man in a pin-striped suit ... He was slightly chubby and liked good food, wine.'[5] The former auditor general Joop de Loor said in an interview that he remembers Burger well, 'his movements were always in the shadows ... but he had the knack of bragging about his prowess'.[6] Burger's autobiography unfortunately sheds little light on the names of people and institutions involved in sanctions-busting operations. He remained reticent in sharing the truth to the last. As one reviewer noted, 'Confidences kept make for good friends, but bad authors.'[7] However, we have, through access to declassified documents and helpful sources, been able to piece together the identity of some important covert operations.

A businessman and a bank

Burger, a diplomat first and foremost, needed an accomplice who understood international business. Both PW and Pik Botha asked the leading businessman Wim de Villiers, a member of the Defence Advisory Council, to pick a man for the job.[8] Burger gave his South African accomplice, a leading businessperson, the *nom de guerre* 'Owen'. As we will soon see, Owen was useful in opening doors for Burger across the globe. I interviewed Burger's daughter Alexandra, who would not reveal any of her father's secrets, but confirmed that this mysterious figure was a South African who died three or four years ago in his eighties.[9] None of the many people I interviewed could confirm the true identity of Owen.

Together Burger and Owen set up over 600 operations in a seven-year period.[10] Many of these included covert structures and companies that looked innocent from the outside. In some cases, even their fiercest corporate rivals did not suspect a South African connection. As Burger says, 'The best place to hide a tree is in the forest.'[11]

The next step was to ensure that funds could be moved clandestinely to conceal their South African identity. They turned to the wealthy tax haven of Liechtenstein, a sliver of a country nestled between Austria and Switzerland. In unpublished papers we found at Stellenbosch University, Burger gives the name of the front as the Taussig Family Trust.[12] He claims that only PW and Pik Botha knew the identity of the trust at the time. The trust had belonged to a German family whose patriarch had died on board the *Titanic*.[13] According to Burger, 'this fairly prominent Jewish family had suffered a variety of tragedies before Nazi Germany extinguished the last survivors in the Holocaust.'[14]

The Taussig Family Trust's existence was revealed in the Truth and Reconciliation Commission report but with little detail about who was behind it. A recently declassified report of the Khan Commission, which investigated the government's secret projects in 1991 at the request of FW de Klerk, noted that one of the trustees was Casimir Prince Wittgenstein.[15] A minor member of a European royal family, Casimir Johannes Prinz zu Sayn-Wittgenstein-Berleburg was a member of the European Parliament for the German Christian Democratic Union (CDU) in the 1980s. Deeply conservative politically, Wittgenstein was at the centre of a party-funding scandal in Germany in the 1990s. As treasurer of the CDU in Hesse, he was prosecuted for fraud linked to a CDU donation from an anonymous overseas funder paid into a Liechtenstein bank account.[16]

One of the projects Burger and Owen were involved in was a large computer data storage company based in Europe and the United States.[17] Sold off by a multinational corporation, the company was bought by the South African government as part of the secret Project Grail in the late 1980s. The purpose of the project was to ensure the supply of sophisticated computer technology to South Africa, whose import was threatened by the embargo. The required funds were channelled through the Taussig Family Trust. According to Burger, the front man for this operation was a South African living overseas, by the name of Barry, 'who was a rising star in computers'.[18] The company is said to have subsequently become a significant international player in the computer industry and attracted among its clients intelligence agencies, including one from what Burger termed a 'nuclear power' that was on friendly terms with South Africa – and that he claimed was unaware of the company's true owners. Alexandra Burger says that 'Barry' is still alive but declined to provide more details.[19]

Turkish delights

By the late 1980s the international boycott of coal was beginning to affect South Africa, one of the biggest exporters in the world. Burger and Owen went about acquiring 'control over a deep-water free port plus coal terminal facility cum industrial zone in a serious country which offered substantial domestic markets and re-export possibilities'.[20] Burger doesn't name the country but we can: it is Turkey.

Tom Wheeler, a retired diplomat, confirmed to me in an interview that plans were afoot to build the port in Turkey at Yumurtalik, east of the coastal city of Iskenderun.[21] Wheeler was only alerted to this in 1997 when meeting a member of the Turkish Chamber of Commerce, who asked when South Africa would at last build the planned deep-sea port.[22] Burger had met and managed to persuade the Turkish prime minister, Turgut Özal, to give the South Africans the opportunity to proceed with the scheme.[23] Özal regarded this as his pet project. The successful South African coal terminal at Richards Bay is said to have convinced him of the South Africans' credentials.[24]

According to Burger, they now had to find a way to pay for the project. With this in mind, all the country's top business leaders were assembled at a meeting hosted by Acting President Chris Heunis (shortly after PW Botha suffered a stroke in 1989) in Cape Town.[25] Burger and Owen briefed the businessmen and, despite initial interest, competition got the better of the big coal miners, who lost their appetite for co-operation.[26] However, Ankara remained committed and as late as 1992 communicated through Owen that they were still open for business.[27] The recently declassified Khan Commission report shows that the intention had been to build not only a port but also a coal-fired power station in southern Turkey as part of 'Project Six Pack', with financing from the World Bank and Taiwan.[28]

The Department of Foreign Affairs was not the only party interested in a port facility on the Mediterranean. Recently declassified SADF Military Intelligence documents show that the military was working with the Turkish government of Northern Cyprus, in 1985, on a project imaginatively named Tulband (Turbin). The intention was to set up a similar sanctions-busting cover on the Mediterranean island. A top-secret military document, dated May 1985, reported on special Military Intelligence projects and noted that 'Personal contact with the President [Rauf Denktaş] has been established and the biggest advantage is that the President has approved our use of the free port of Famagusta. Use of the port is dependent on co-operation with the South African private sector for the establishment of storage infrastructure in the harbour. Negotiations are currently underway and contact can possibly lead to direct contact with Turkey'.[29] The ancient port of Famagusta is the most important commercial harbour of Northern Cyprus and a gateway to trade with the Middle East.[30] A year later, in 1986, Military Intelligence reported that progress was being made and that a private front company had been established that could benefit both the SADF and Armscor. In addition, these efforts had been rewarded by a planned visit to South Africa by a cabinet-level representative from Turkey, which was seen as a step towards gaining 're-entry' into that country.[31]

In this clandestine world, government departments ran the risk of doubling efforts and wasting cash. However, they were clearly spoilt for choice among suitors who were ready to undertake secret deals with Pretoria.

Oiling apartheid

Like guns, oil was a major strategic weak point for the apartheid government, and the world knew it. Without oil, the economy and the military would grind to a halt.

Several Arab countries imposed an oil embargo on South Africa in 1973, but this only became an existential threat in 1977 following an endorsement by individual members of the Organisation of the Petroleum Exporting Countries (OPEC).[32] Stepping into the breach was the Shah of Iran, who continued to supply oil to South Africa throughout the 1970s. The Iranian Revolution of 1979 and further UN oil sanctions in the same year changed everything: South Africa's oil supply became imperilled.

Innovative alternative schemes like Sasol's oil-from-coal synthetic fuel process did make up part of the shortfall, but new 'unorthodox' importation tactics were clearly necessary. These would, as with weapons, require a mixture of secrecy and lots of cash to bust the embargo. In 1985 Minister Danie Steyn, responsible for the oil portfolio, said, 'We are receiving more offers because the oil is running out of the suppliers' ears and they do not know what to do with it. However, every offer contains the clause, "We will give you oil but nobody must know about it."'[33]

The public cost of such sanctions busting cannot be under-estimated. In 1986 PW Botha admitted that South Africa's need to buy oil on the black market had cost it an extra R22 billion (nearly R300 billion in 2017 value) over a ten-year period from the mid-1970s and that the country was being devastated as a result. 'There were times when it was reported to me that we had enough oil for only a week,' Botha said in a statement quoted in the *Windhoek Advertiser*.[34] 'Our economic life would have collapsed, so we paid a price, which we are still suffering from today.'[35]

The Shipping Research Bureau undertook to calculate the total cost of the embargo from 1979 to 1993, including the payment of exorbitant premiums to middlemen, maintenance of strategic stockpiles as well as costs of projects at Sasol and Mossgas related to tackling the embargo. They estimated that the additional cost to South Africa was $34.6 billion over this period. That is a staggering R500 billion in today's value.

The sanctions watchdogs

The most significant adversary that the apartheid regime faced in its bid to access oil in the face of sanctions was the small, dedicated group of researchers at the Shipping Research Bureau (SRB) in Amsterdam. Their work built on the mass-based campaign calling for Shell's withdrawal from South Africa.[36] With financial support from trade unions, churches and the governments of Norway, Sweden and Canada, the SRB became the intelligence centre for monitoring oil shipments from across the globe to South Africa.[37]

What the SRB achieved in the pre-internet era is nothing short of extraordinary. They relied on hard work and on informers and eyewitnesses across the globe. The second major source of data was reams of official paperwork, newspapers and insurance reports from the shipping company Lloyd's. Pieced together, these provided insight into the movement of ships and oil around the Cape.[38] Between 1979 and 1993, the SRB identified 865 cases of secret oil deliveries to South Africa.

To add to their difficulties, they had to deal with disinformation planted by the South African government and their agents. All of this meant that they erred on the side of caution when claiming to have identified illicit shipments. All the same, they earned the respect of many for their rigorous, detailed reports. These proved the most vital resource for activists, government officials and UN agencies that sought to expose oil embargo busting.

Embargo busters: The SFF

Crucial to embargo-busting efforts was the government's Strategic Fuel Fund (SFF). It operated as an affiliate of the state-owned Strategic Energy Fund (SEF) together with affiliates Soekor (the oil and exploration company) and Mossgas (which mined gas at massive cost off the coast of Mossel Bay). All these companies today form part of the state-owned enterprise PetroSA. The SFF operated as an autonomous unit within the state with the sole objective of oil procurement. All its international payments were made through the

South African Reserve Bank.[39] It also borrowed substantially in terms of trade finance from French, Swiss and German banks.[40]

I interviewed Kobus van Zyl, who was appointed the head of the SFF in 1989, on two occasions. Van Zyl is a straight talker who lives in a modest townhouse in Cape Town's northern suburbs. He believes that sanctions posed no threat, as the SFF paid a premium above the price of Brent Crude, thus ensuring supply. This premium and the need for camouflage were the only real consequences of sanctions. He is equally dismissive of the SRB, who he claims identified only 40% of oil shipments to South Africa.

By the late 1980s Van Zyl says that South Africa never had any problem obtaining oil. To underscore this, he claims that the SFF was even able to import 'carbon black oil' from the United States, which is used extensively in tyre and rubber production.[41] 'There was never anyone running around the corridors saying that the oil is finished ... We had a strategic reserve of 100,000 barrels, which was never used.' These reserves were stored in disused mine shafts at Ogies, and later in a massive underground tank farm at Saldanha Bay north of Cape Town. Van Zyl adds, 'We never had to tap this during the sanctions period because of a shortage.'[42]

There was indeed no noticeable shortage of oil during the 1980s, but it came with a heavy financial burden and attracted a fair share of conmen and crooks. One example of this was the *Salem*, a supertanker destined for South Africa that became embroiled in the greatest fraud in maritime history in 1980. At least 25 countries were touched by the case, setting off 13 separate investigations and legal proceedings in the United States, Greece, the Netherlands, Britain and Liberia. The only country in which no investigations or prosecutions took place was the beneficiary state, South Africa.

What happened was that the SFF supplied a cash advance that allowed oil traders to purchase a tanker (the *Salem*), a shipping company and the required insurance. The tanker docked in Kuwait and filled its tanks with oil owned by Shell. The oil was registered for delivery in France. However, en route to Europe from the Gulf, the tanker stopped in Durban and offloaded almost all its crude oil, nearly 180,000 tonnes. The South Africans paid the difference between the purchase price and the fees it had advanced for the purchase of the tanker.[43]

The *Salem* was then filled up with water in order to create the impression that it was still laden with oil. Off the coast of Senegal, at one of the deepest points of the Atlantic, the ship was scuttled and the crew, prepared in advance for the evacuation, were rescued. They had hoped to make an extra $24 million from the insurance claim for the lost oil. Following investigations by the insurance company, the main perpetrators were prosecuted. The biggest loser next to Shell was South Africa, as it agreed to pay the Dutch multinational $30 million in an out-of-court settlement. Shell was left to carry the remaining loss of $20 million. The use of corrupt middlemen had cost South Africa almost half a billion rand (in today's value), even though it clawed back some of the cash from Shell. There was no prosecution of the officials at the SFF who had authorised the procurement of a full tanker of oil from a small group of criminal entrepreneurs.

The suppliers: Breaking the rules

Despite the OPEC embargo, several major oil producers remained committed to providing oil to South Africa throughout the 1970s and 1980s. Of the various Middle Eastern suppliers, Iran was one of the most important throughout. Prior to 1979, Iran and South Africa had a long-standing relationship dating back to the Second World War, when the last Shah's father had sought refuge in South Africa, where he died and was buried as an 'honorary white' in Johannesburg in 1944. By the mid-1970s, South Africa was a prominent Iranian oil importer. In return, the Shah's government invested in South African uranium enrichment and secured a steady supply of uranium in the process.[44]

This should all have changed with the Iranian Revolution of 1979. Yet despite the strong anti-apartheid position of the government of Ayatollah Khomeini, oil continued to flow to the Cape. One of the reasons for this was that Iran was competing with Iraq for access to South African weapons during the protracted war between the two countries in the 1980s. These deals took different forms, including direct oil-for-arms bartering. For example, in 1985, the government of Iran agreed to purchase $750 million worth of South African weapons from Armscor in return for Iranian crude of equal value. The government of Iraq is said to have concluded a similar oil-for-arms deal in the same year to the value of $1 billion.[45]

Kobus van Zyl told me that although Oman offered oil, it was too expensive.[46] According to him, 'We lived off oil from Iran throughout the 1980s.' He points out that South African oil refineries were established to deal with Iranian oil, and that's what they primarily processed throughout the period. Today these facts have been conveniently swept under the carpet. Van Zyl recalls attending a dinner in the mid-1990s at which President Mandela and the Iranian minister of oil were present. 'They both spoke of how Iran had supported South Africa's liberation by observing the boycott. This was bullshit. They were lying through their arses.'[47] Van Zyl recalls three trips to Iran during the embargo period. He would first travel to Tehran to meet top officials and then on to Isfahan for sightseeing. 'These trips were goodwill trips, as I would travel to London to negotiate the offers by the Iranian Oil Company.'[48]

Van Zyl also recalls similar goodwill trips to the United Arab Emirates (UAE) cities of Dubai and Abu Dhabi.[49] From 1986, the UAE became an increasingly important supplier of oil to the apartheid regime. Dubai was rewarded not only in monetary terms. By 1990 it had become an eager buyer of sophisticated South African weaponry.[50]

According to the SRB, around 75% of oil shipments to South Africa that it was able to identify originated in the Middle East. The research showed that the main violators of the embargo from that region were the United Arab Emirates (UAE), Saudi Arabia, Iran and Oman. The incentive for this was a surcharge on every barrel of oil. In the case of Oman, in a deal for 44 million barrels of oil in 1979, the charge was stipulated in the contract at $4.50 per barrel. This meant that the oil was 18% more expensive than it should have been on the open market. The deal was struck by the oil trader John Deuss with Dr Omar Zawawi, a close adviser of Sultan Qaboos bin Said of Oman.[51] The incentives on both sides were glaringly obvious: there was a small fortune to be made out of Pretoria.

The Saudi government, official supporters of the embargo, also opened the taps to Pretoria, and supplied 2 million tonnes of oil per year in the 1980s at a similar premium to that of Oman. One of the reasons offered for Saudi sales of oil is that prominent members of the royal family directly benefited from this business. For example, the oil trader John Deuss, a leading South African supplier, maintained a business partnership with Prince Muhammad bin Fahd, second eldest son of the Saudi king.[52] In marked contrast, the neighbouring country of Kuwait adhered more strictly to the UN embargo and provided only a handful of clandestine deliveries to South Africa.[53]

The SRB also identified Egypt, Brunei, the Netherlands and the United Kingdom as important source countries for oil. When I interviewed the minister of minerals and energy in PW Botha's cabinet, Danie Steyn, he confirmed that other African options were also on the table. 'We thought about going to drill for oil in Sudan and I also thought about buying oil from Nigeria. However, back then the South African refineries couldn't handle such thick oil.'[54] Steyn went on to add that by 1984 his department had confirmation from Nigerian suppliers about their willingness to trade.

According to documents found in the Stasi archives, East German intelligence noted in mid-1989 that negotiations had taken place in Budapest to supply oil from Hungary to South Africa to the value of between $25 and $50 million. The source of this crude was possibly the Soviet Union. The deal would be concluded between a company called Universal Trade Consulting, based in Frankfurt, and a commercial counterpart in Pretoria. The Hungarian Ministry of Foreign Trade was represented in the negotiations by an official who was authorised to conclude unofficial 'three-way deals'.[55] Everyone was in on the game.

◎

We have already alluded to the procurement of oil through barter. It is possible, however, that oil intended for South Africa formed part of the sinister Iran–Contra scandal that rocked Ronald Reagan's government in the mid-1980s. In a remarkable scheme, apparently the work of the CIA chief Bill Casey, Saudi Arabia was approached, and may have assented to becoming an accomplice in the scheme. At the time, Saudi Arabia was exceeding its OPEC oil quota and part of this excess was covertly sold to South Africa at an inflated price, contrary to the embargo. According to the criminologist RT Naylor, some of the excessive profits from the South African sanctions premium were to be contributed to a secret fund run by American intelligence.[56] The CIA would then buy Soviet bloc-manufactured weapons, which couldn't be traced back to the United States, to arm anti-communist guerrilla forces around the world, including the Contras in Nicaragua.[57]

The *Boston Globe* provided some more detail on these dealings at the time. According to its reports, a US-based Saudi Arabian businessman, Sam Bamieh, said that he was asked by the Saudi ambassador to the US, Bandar bin Sultan, to set up a corporation for King Fahd.[58] This was supposed to funnel oil from Saudi Arabia to South Africa and in turn money, possibly from the oil profits, would be distributed to 'anticommunist movements in Angola and Nicaragua, all at the direction of Casey'.[59] Bamieh went on to add, 'I was told specifically that the plan had the approval of the US government', and that 'CIA director Casey was meeting with King Fahd to arrange the deal. Fahd wanted to enhance his image in the royal family that he could make deals with Uncle Sam, and this was a way to do it.'[60]

According to Bamieh, after his alleged meeting with King Fahd, Casey made a secret trip to South Africa to meet President PW Botha on 8 March 1986.[61] Bamieh claimed not to have set up the corporation because of its illegality, but thought that it was consummated all the same.[62] Around the same time this deal was taking place, according to the former US national security adviser Robert McFarlane, Ambassador Bandar told him that he would deposit $1 million a month into an account for the Contras.[63]

At the time of the *Boston Globe* story being published, the implicated parties provided little insight into these allegations. The CIA remained mum on all aspects of Iran–Contra, and Casey, who had been ill and would rather mysteriously die in 1987, took all the Iran–Contra secrets with him to his grave. The Saudi embassy in the US called the idea 'preposterous'.[64] A spokesperson for the South African embassy in the US denied any Contra links, but did venture to say that oil-for-arms deals were not impossible. 'In principle, it would be possible. We believe in capitalism in South Africa. We believe in trade in South Africa. We don't believe in sanctions in South Africa.'[65]

Another twist in the oil link was uncovered in 1987 when it was reported that US Federal investigators were probing whether Iran had purchased South African weapons, which were built in part from US designs, in exchange for huge amounts of oil.[66] Investigators said the reported deals raised the question whether a key element had been missing from the Iran–Contra story: the all-important role of oil.[67] We return in more detail to Pretoria's covert connection in the Iran–Contra affair in Chapter 8.

The traders: Making the money

As important as the source countries were the oil traders. The middlemen in particular are worth noting. According to official reports, South Africa paid them a fee of anything from $8 to $20 per barrel of oil in the period 1979 to 1980,[68] when the cost of a barrel fluctuated between $13 and $35.[69] Kobus van Zyl agrees that in the early years the traders made 'a lot of money off us', but by the end of the 1980s he claims that they only received 1c on every barrel.[70]

Chief among those who made fortunes out of the embargo were Marc Rich and John Deuss. But they were by no means the only traders eager to get a slice of the South African business. Some of these middlemen also had links to the arms trade, including the French businessman Jean-Yves Ollivier (see Chapter 6). According to Van Zyl, South Africa 'had a complicated contract with him', and he was mostly active in the Ivory Coast, Angola and francophone

West Africa.[71] Records from that time show that by 1991 Ollivier, who was close to the former French prime minister Jacques Chirac, had a contract to supply the SFF with 15,000 barrels per day.[72]

A covert conduit for oil was the Seychelles-based sanctions-busting operation GMR, named after its principal, Giovanni Mario Ricci. Ricci operated from 1986 with a South African partner, the former police spy Craig Williamson. According to the historian and expert on apartheid-era sanctions busting, Stephen Ellis, after Williamson's entry into GMR there were rumours that the government of Seychelles and its parastatal oil companies were being used as a cover for South Africa to import embargoed oil. Ellis clarifies: 'This has never been proven, and oil traders and shippers did not report any extraordinary tanker movements to Seychelles. Nevertheless, a senior Seychellois diplomat has confirmed that, within a couple of years of Williamson's entry into GMR, Seychelles had come to occupy a place in South African sanctions-busting networks, apparently using paper transactions rather than physical transhipment of oil.'[73]

To understand the extent of the oil trade we now turn to the two most important middlemen, Marc Rich and John Deuss.

Probably the most successful oil trader of all time, Marc Rich achieved true fame with his 1983 indictment in the United States on tax evasion charges, which led him to flee to Switzerland to avoid prosecution.[74] After 18 years in exile (during which time he was on the FBI's most wanted list), Rich was pardoned by Bill Clinton during the president's final hours in office. Rich's successes as a trader came primarily from oil, but also from metals and minerals. These he traded with Franco's Spain, apartheid South Africa, the Ayatollah's Iran and the Soviet Union, to name a few. His controversial methods of conducting business and his disregard for international sanctions became legendary.

While all of his obituaries mention his business links with apartheid in passing, the regime in Pretoria may have been the single greatest source of his wealth. In the years before his death, Rich admitted that busting oil sanctions for South Africa was his company's 'most important and most profitable' business.[75] Much of this was channelled through a front company called Minoil. Rich himself managed to achieve a remarkable cognitive dissonance on the question of his relationship with the apartheid state. He denied that his business had helped prolong apartheid, insisting: 'I was fundamentally against apartheid. We were all against apartheid. I just was doing normal business with South Africa.'[76] The definition of 'normal business' is, of course, flexible: it is an established fact that the first oil Rich sold to South Africa came from the Soviet Union, at the height of the Cold War. An early, critical biography of Rich raised the allegation, from an anonymous 'former shareholder', that 'We were selling Iranian and Soviet oil to South Africa in return for Namibian uranium we sold to the Soviets'.[77]

One of the most remarkable things about Marc Rich was his ability to make money talk louder than politics. For this reason, he was able to continue doing business with South Africa after 1994, despite his links to the apartheid regime. As *The Spectator* argues, 'his former protégés and apprentices now control, through his empire's successor companies Glencore Xstrata and Trafigura, the price of just about everything'.[78] They also control a substantial share of South African and global natural resources. One of Rich's protégés from that time is the secretive South African multi-billionaire, Ivan Glasenberg. Today one of the richest people in Switzerland with a fortune worth over $5 billion, Glasenberg cut his teeth working for Rich in the 1980s.

Another former Rich employee is Alan Duncan, who worked for Rich between 1982 and 1988, operating in both London and Singapore. Duncan, a Tory MP, became a minister in Theresa May's cabinet after having served a stint in David Cameron's cabinet as well. In 2001, *The Guardian* raised accusations from other oil traders (quoting documents in their possession) that Duncan had played a role in providing oil to South Africa, contrary to sanctions. He is alleged to have helped move oil from Brunei to Durban, which earned him approximately £100,000 per year at the time.[79]

Rich was not alone in making a fortune from the oil embargo. The Dutch businessman John Deuss, the second most important oil trader with apartheid South Africa, is said to have earned up to $500 million from his sanctions-busting exploits.[80] In his later life, Deuss was the chairman of a Bermuda bank alleged to have been involved in money laundering, a charge which he settled with a hefty fine in 2013.[81] He spent his fortune on estates in the Netherlands and Florida, and at one stage owned 170 champion jumping horses.[82] With a taste for champagne, cigars and yachts, accompanied by groups of young women and deckhands in white shorts, he is described by at least one colleague in the oil business as 'sleazy'.[83]

Deuss also kept a presence in South Africa. In 1982, it was revealed that he had bought the South African golfing legend Gary Player's Muldersdrift estate.[84] By this time, Deuss was well entrenched in the South African economy. According to SRB researchers, he 'had supplied South Africa with 8 million tonnes of oil per year, or 57% of the country's imports by 1981'.[85] Deuss maintained in a 1985 interview: 'I disagree with apartheid. At the same time, I maintain that a refusal to supply oil to South Africa is counterproductive to the socio-political problems of that country.' With this justification, he was able to leap to the conclusion that 'I don't regard the oil I send as embargoed oil … I don't do anything illegal.'[86]

Danie Steyn recalls Deuss. 'I thought he was a good man. Many people said to me he was a crook. I never experienced this; he was trustworthy.' He added, 'I wouldn't be surprised if we got all our oil through him.'[87]

The SRB believed that Deuss's supply of oil to South Africa started to taper off in the mid-1980s because of public pressure. However, according to a 1991 memo to the South African minister of minerals and energy affairs, John Deuss's company Transworld Oil had just signed a contract to supply 45,000 barrels per day. The contract started on 1 January 1991. It further stated that this was an increase from the 30,000 barrels per day that Deuss had been supplying the year before. The crude oil being supplied originated in Abu Dhabi.[88]

The shippers: In on the deal

The traders and suppliers never needed to set foot in South Africa. It was the companies that sent their ships laden with crude towards South African harbours that faced the practical challenge of avoiding detection by activists monitoring such movements.

The SFF encouraged the use of false names as one solution. In November 1992, at a secret pricing meeting at the SFF, attended by senior representatives from major oil companies, BP, Shell, Engen, Total, Caltex, Zenex and Sasol, it was noted: 'Some ship-owners have expressed concern about the tracking of vessels coming to RSA. Since the embargo is still in place, ship-owners wish to maintain secrecy.'[89] To camouflage these shipments, the SFF suggested that the names of scrapped ships or smaller vessels be used as codenames.[90]

Many of the shipping companies used flags of convenience such as Panama to obscure the true identity of the owners. According to the SRB, Norwegian ship owners remained in the forefront of oil deliveries until 1987, when banned by domestic law.[91] The Hong Kong-based World Wide Shipping Group benefited from this ban, together with their Greek competitors, and made at least 150 deliveries to South Africa after 1987. Other significant oil transporters included the large Danish shipping company AP Møller.[92]

One of the most significant suppliers of shipping services was the Greek businessman Tony Georgiadis. Georgiadis was from a wealthy Greek family, but grew up in Nairobi, was educated in England, and went on to study at Oxford and Columbia.[93] Throughout the 1980s, he and his brother Alex built up extensive business dealings in South Africa as well as globally. He was, by all accounts, well connected, an excellent business analyst, and an impressive golf and dinner-party companion.[94] Among others, Georgiadis would host FW de Klerk at his home in the grounds of Hampton Court Palace and on board his yacht in the Mediterranean until his wife Elita left him for De Klerk, whom she later married.[95] Georgiadis was an ally of the apartheid regime from the 1980s, and was a crucial campaigner in the battle against oil sanctions.[96] According to the SRB, roughly 50 shipments of crude oil to South Africa in the late 1980s could be linked to Alandis (London), a firm still headed by Tony Georgiadis and his brother.[97]

The *Mail & Guardian* reported that Alandis helped the apartheid government beat the oil embargo by managing both third-party shipments and a crude tanker, the *Pacificos*, owned by the SFF.[98] Kobus van Zyl confirmed this to me. He said that the *Pacificos* traded under a Panamanian or Liberian flag and was managed by Tony Georgiadis.[99] He recalls that the SFF sold the vessel at a significant profit in 1993–94. According to Van Zyl, the success of this operation is evident from the fact that when the *Pacificos* sprung a leak off the coast of Maputo, discharging 10,000 barrels of oil into the sea, the media reported on this without realising the true ownership of the vessel.[100]

Van Zyl describes Georgiadis as 'not very impressive'.[101] He recalls visiting Georgiadis at his Stud House; 'there were photos of him with every international politician that you can imagine. He had contacts with the Bush family. There were lots of big elephant tusks.' Van Zyl even remembers that he sat in his office with the Iranian deputy minister of energy to negotiate a deal.[102]

Georgiadis's political mastery seems to have consisted in how he managed the South African transition to democracy. Numerous reports suggest that Georgiadis cultivated his contacts with the ANC leadership from the early 1990s.[103] However, the most troubling revelation of his alleged covert dealings in South Africa emerged when his name was linked directly to the corrupt arms deal in 1999. A leaked compliance report conducted by the US-based legal firm Debevoise and Plimpton LLP, to review the German arms company Ferrostaal's potential criminal liability in the arms deal, is revealing.[104] It alleged that Ferrostaal had paid Georgiadis $20 million to help smooth the way for the German submarine consortium's bid. This was over and above an alleged $20 million paid to him by the German frigate consortium in which Ferrostaal also featured prominently.[105]

Oiling Apartheid
Greasy profits for some

Marc Rich

Marc Rich and Company AG formed in Switzerland.

Contract signed with Rich through Minoil for long-term supply of oil to SA government.

Rich indicted for tax evasion in US, flees to Switzerland.

Ivan Glasenberg starts working in coal division of Marc Rich and Company AG

26.2 million tonnes of oil shipped by Rich's companies to SA.

John Deuss

Deuss supplies 8 million tonnes of oil per year to SA.

Dutch activists fire-bomb Deuss's $6 million Dutch castle.

Up to $500 million made through oil trade with South Africa.

Deuss purchases Gary Player's Muldersdrift estate.

Tony Georgiadis

Alandis Shipping, Georgiadis's company, linked to nearly 50 oil shipments to South Africa

Georgiadis hosts Energy Minister Danie Steyn for dinner in London, and at Wimbledon.

THE CONTEXT

1970

1975

1980

1985

UN Security Council vetoes mandatory oil embargo against South Africa.

PW Botha claims R22 billion was spent above market price for oil. (historical value)

Voluntary oil embargo on South Africa adopted by UN General Assembly. UK, US, France and Germany vote against.

Arab countries impose oil embargo on South Africa.

All OPEC members endorse oil embargo.

The UAE becomes largest single oil supplier to South Africa.

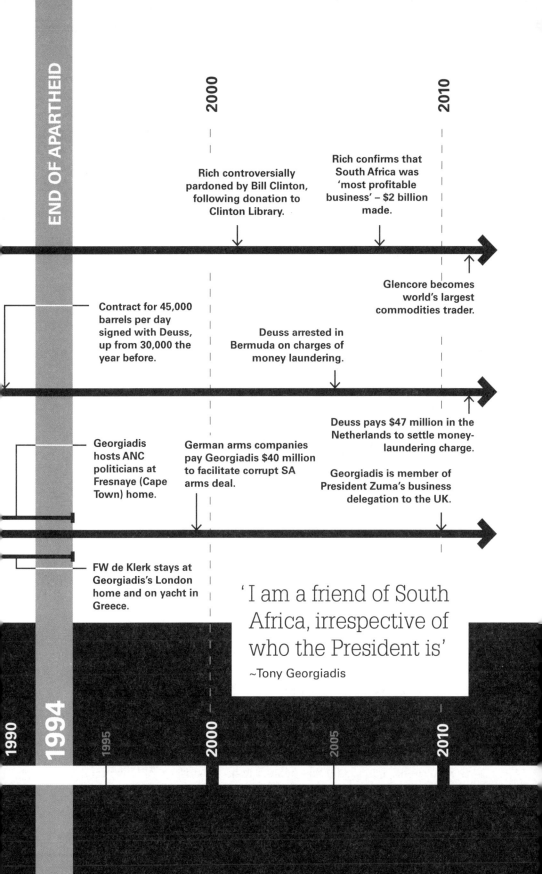

END OF APARTHEID

2000

2010

Rich controversially pardoned by Bill Clinton, following donation to Clinton Library.

Rich confirms that South Africa was 'most profitable business' – $2 billion made.

Glencore becomes world's largest commodities trader.

Contract for 45,000 barrels per day signed with Deuss, up from 30,000 the year before.

Deuss arrested in Bermuda on charges of money laundering.

Deuss pays $47 million in the Netherlands to settle money-laundering charge.

Georgiadis hosts ANC politicians at Fresnaye (Cape Town) home.

German arms companies pay Georgiadis $40 million to facilitate corrupt SA arms deal.

Georgiadis is member of President Zuma's business delegation to the UK.

FW de Klerk stays at Georgiadis's London home and on yacht in Greece.

'I am a friend of South Africa, irrespective of who the President is'
~Tony Georgiadis

1990

1994

1995

2000

2005

2010

It is hard to accuse many of the oil embargo busters with any ideological alignment with apartheid. This was purely business, and old friends would soon be forgotten when a new group of politicians came to control the National Treasury after 1994.

The Helderberg: A deadly cargo?

On 28 November 1987, the *Helderberg* aeroplane from the South African Airways (SAA) fleet crashed into the Indian Ocean off the coast of Mauritius. Travelling en route from Taiwan to South Africa, it was nine hours into its flight and just 45 minutes from a planned stopover in Mauritius. The tragedy, which claimed the lives of 159 people, was headline news across South Africa for weeks after the event. A forensic investigation took place, involving the reconstruction of the aircraft, whose remains were collected off the ocean floor. Vic McPherson, a Security Branch spy, recalls attending a meeting of the Broederbond just hours after the crash, at which PW Botha informed the gathering of the news and led them in prayer.[106]

The disaster has been the subject of a judicial investigation and subsequent probes by the TRC, the Scorpions and individual forensic investigators. There is consensus among them all that an in-flight fire caused the crash. However, what caused the fire remains in dispute. Is it possible that the flight was carrying smuggled weapons or components for the South African government? Much evidence points to that possibility. An examination of the cause of the *Helderberg* fire may shed light on sanctions-busting operations and the extent to which the national carrier was used for such purposes.

Inconclusive investigations
The first investigation into the crash was a commission of inquiry led by Judge Cecil Margo. The commission, appointed by PW Botha, considered evidence over a two–year period, much of which had to be recovered from 15,000 feet below the ocean surface.[107] This inquiry,

together with the participation of international experts, is often used to suggest that the apartheid government had nothing to hide.[108] However, the commission could only conclude that 'an intense fire … in the right-hand forward pallet' of the cargo area was responsible for the crash. It suggested that the cause of such an intense blaze could not be determined beyond the fact that the materials involved in combustion were cardboard and plastic.[109]

A glaring failure of the report was that there was seemingly little investigation into the obvious question whether the SAA flight might have been used to transport military materials for Armscor. Only one page out of 274 was dedicated to this question, and it simply stated that Taiwanese customs inspected the cargo before boarding and that both the SADF[110] and Armscor[111] confirmed in the briefest of notes that they had not used the flight to transfer weapons material.[112] There is also no indication that any Armscor officials were interviewed in any depth. Regarding Taiwanese customs, the inquiry relied on affidavits from SAA officials and the director of the Civil Aviation Administration.[113] These emphasised the high level of security checks for cargo and passengers at the Chiang Kai-shek airport in Taiwan, implying that smuggling military material would have been impossible. Again, the report failed to consider the close military and intelligence relationships between Taiwan and South Africa (see Chapter 12). As we will see, many such relationships across the world led officials to turn a blind eye to malfeasance.

The TRC conducted closed hearings into the *Helderberg* crash, but ultimately dedicated just over six pages to the case in its final report.[114] The TRC admitted that it was unable to determine the cause of the accident, but made several findings and recommendations with an eye to future investigations. Perhaps most importantly, the TRC suggested that the Margo inquiry was inadequate, not least because it failed to invite evidence from Armscor officials. It further argued that the evidence presented to the commission suggested that it was not unusual for Armscor to use SAA to transfer material, and that the cargo manifests in their possession could not be verified as authentic.[115]

One of the claims made at the TRC, by the forensic investigator David Klatzow, was that the flight was carrying highly combustible rocket fuel. He argued that Armscor's subsidiary Somchem was not able to keep up the production needed for the war in Angola owing to maintenance issues at its plant, and that 'it was brought in on SAA passenger planes as an integral part of the necessary deception'.[116] This is not as far-fetched as it might seem. Recently declassified Military Intelligence documents show that in 1984 Armscor, operating through a front company headed by an official named Stuart Pretorius, had established an office in Hong Kong, which was to be used as a base for trade in the region. In a letter to headquarters, Pretorius informed the SADF that Armscor units such as Somchem could import chemicals via his office.[117][118]

Following on the recommendation of the TRC, the minister of justice, Dullah Omar, asked the Scorpions unit within the National Prosecuting Authority to investigate the matter. Their investigation, led by Advocate Welch, found that there was no new evidence to justify reopening the inquiry. This was accepted by Omar in October 2002.[119] Once again, none of Armscor's operational personnel appear to have been interviewed.

However, the Scorpions did follow some important leads. The first was that of Johanna Uys, wife of the *Helderberg* pilot, Dawie Uys, who told the Scorpions that her husband had once complained about being forced to fly with ammunition aboard his plane from London. He had been so afraid that he had posted the cargo list to his home address as an insurance policy before the flight. Mrs Uys was terrified of losing her SAA pension and thus would not sign her statement.[120] Following the preliminary report, Uys refused to co-operate with the investigation any longer.[121] Secondly, Rennie van Zyl, who worked at the Directorate of Civil Aviation at the time of the crash, confirmed that a Safair flight left for Mauritius immediately after the crash with Armscor officials on board. Safair was used extensively by the military to transport weapons covertly during apartheid. The presence of Armscor officials on the island was confirmed by an interview with Schalk William Davel, who also informed investigators that he had heard that Dawie Uys (a close friend of his) had been reluctant to fly the plane because of the cargo on board.[122] The investigation also revealed that the original flight recording had been scrubbed to omit a discussion between the flight crew that carried the words 'we fly in their bomb'.[123]

If there was a cover-up, what was being hidden?

A man of mystery

Thomas Barry Osler was the head of the SFF and thus South Africa's chief oil sanctions buster. He also happened to be a passenger on board the *Heldeberg* and perished on that fateful day. According to Osler's son Geordie, his father had originally intended to travel home the following day.[124]

In addition to his SFF responsibilities, Osler was also a director of the Industrial Development Corporation and a prominent figure in the business world. The first substantive evidence we found of public acknowledgement of his links to sanctions-busting entities is in the now publically accessible 500-page transcript of the TRC's closed door hearings into the disaster. During examination, led by the investigators Debora Patta, Christelle Terreblanche and David Klatzow, Armscor's John Hare was asked about possible links between Osler and Armscor. Hare was a long-time director of Armscor and a senior manager in its finance department, who subsequently worked for SAA. Hare confirmed that Osler 'provided assistance to Armscor on a consultative basis, regarding a transaction that Armscor was interested in'.[125] Hare told the TRC that this was on a 'one-off basis' and was linked to the export of material by Armscor.

Importantly, this was the first time that Armscor publicly acknowledged that Osler had any dealings with it.[126] I contacted Hare via email to ask him about his knowledge of links between Armscor and Osler. Hare responded, 'The Armscor organisations were very well compartmentalised and very rarely was information between departments shared other than on a strictly need-to-know basis. I am not aware of any employment of Mr Osler by anyone within Armscor.'[127] He added, 'Any discussions I had with him would have been on a collegial basis between members of organisations that had difficult dealings in a sanction trading situation we were both experiencing.'[128]

Osler's death on board the *Helderberg* was revealed by the media in 2000 following a tip-off from a source within the TRC. *Beeld* newspaper described Osler as an Armscor agent, which Armscor immediately denied. According to *Beeld*'s sources, also from within the TRC, Osler had travelled to China, Vietnam and Singapore in the days before his death. They claim that on the morning of the day that he boarded the *Helderberg* he was flown from Singapore to Taipei on board a Taiwanese military aircraft.[129] As we reveal in later chapters, the South African military and Armscor were involved in weapons exchanges with both China and Singapore at the time. I asked Kobus van Zyl, who succeeded Osler as head of the SFF in 1989, whether he knew of any oil dealings with China. 'I don't know what Osler might have been doing there. I never even heard rumours about what he was involved in.'[130]

Geordie Osler's memories of his father are of a compassionate man who didn't subscribe to apartheid. He also doesn't believe that his father had any dealings with Armscor; 'that wasn't his thing'. All the same, his work at the SFF brought him into contact with known sanctions busters such as Tony Georgiadis and associates of Marc Rich.[131] In an interview with me, he also recalled that his father had a telephone scrambler at home (to encrypt his phone calls) and that he would receive confidential written briefings at home. I asked Van Zyl, as his successor, if such measures were standard practice. As MD of the SFF, he says that he never had a secure telephone at home nor did he ever receive documents there.[132] 'You worked only at the SFF and never used home telephones; this was part of the security requirements.'[133]

We can only speculate whether Osler, who was connected to a

number of government institutions at the time, was in Asia for any business related to Armscor. Once again, the various state-funded inquiries failed to probe this question sufficiently. Yet, even if Armscor was smuggling weapons on the *Helderberg*, is there any evidence to suggest that its use of civilian aircraft in this manner might have been standard practice?

Guns in the hold?

In September 2014, ex-SAA employee Willem Bothma compiled an affidavit about the events in the days after the *Helderberg* crash. He was in Taiwan after the crash and claims that the fire had in fact started soon after take-off from Taiwan, but that, contrary to procedure, Uys had been told to continue to Mauritius and not to turn around or land anywhere else. Bothma, who worked as cabin crew for SAA for over a decade, also claims that he saw pallets of missiles being loaded onto SAA planes at Israel's Ben Gurion airport on 'two or three occasions'.[134]

At around the same time, another former SAA official, Allan Dexter, who was battling terminal cancer, signed an affidavit that supports the claim that there was a dangerous substance on board the *Helderberg*, and that Captain Dawie Uys knew about it. Dexter alleged that the presence of a type of rocket fuel and ammunition was confirmed to him by an SAA official in Taiwan at the time, and subsequently by another 'top official'.[135]

In 2000, a former SAA avionics engineer, Johan Meyer, told *Rapport* that it had been 'general practice' for SAA to transport weapons during the 1980s. He claimed to have witnessed how ammunition for the powerful G5 cannon was placed in the hold during those years.[136] Other anecdotal evidence strongly suggests that civilian aircraft were used to transport weapons. For example, in a secret cable from the military attaché in Brussels to Armscor in 1977, coded reference was made to the shipment of 'Twenty S plus W' (thought to be from the gun manufacturer Smith and Weston). The cryptic message said, 'Shipment per SAA.'[137]

Further evidence can be found in the minutes of a 1987 State Security Council (SSC) meeting, chaired by PW Botha. The SSC resolved that given the US decision to deny SAA landing rights in the States, Pik Botha should request the Americans to provide landing rights for South African military flights to the US on a quid pro quo basis in the first few months of 1987.[138] From this we can infer that SAA was probably used to transport military equipment when its passenger and cargo flights had landing rights in the US, and that what Botha was requesting was an extension of an existing transport route.

Finally, as late as 1998, *The Star's* Business Report noted that airport authorities in Buenos Aires had seized a cargo of 25,000 grenades and 365 grenade launchers which Denel (Armscor's former export unit) had shipped to Peru on board an SAA passenger flight. An SAA spokesperson subsequently confirmed that the airline had been given a signed declaration stating that there was no hazardous material in Denel's consignment.[139]

If the allegations are true that the *Helderberg* was carrying weapons, which the evidence suggests would not have been a complete anomaly, the consequences were fatal and the cover-up complete. Thirty years after the *Helderberg* crash, we are still no closer to the truth. The obvious missed opportunity is that Armscor was never put in the dock and made to answer difficult questions about its trading activities in Asia. To do so would no doubt have opened a can of worms. This may have been a powerful disincentive to arrive at a closer understanding of the truth.

Grease is the word

South Africa has always been a trading nation. Despite official claims that the apartheid economy was self-sufficient, it is patently obvious that this was never the case. New covert networks had to be created to export goods such as coal and import strategic goods such as oil and computers. There was undeniably a large network of businesspeople across the globe ready to step into the breach regardless of sanctions provisions. There was, after all, enormous profit to be made. This came at great financial cost and contributed to the apartheid debt, which in turn placed a burden on the first years of the post-apartheid economy. The fabulous profits made by oil traders and suppliers had a deep knock-on impact on social upliftment in South Africa, something for which these businessmen should have been forced to account. Instead, as we have seen, they were either accommodated in the post-1994 democratic South Africa or were even allowed to feast yet further on corruption in the arms deal of the late 1990s.

The deeply fraudulent nature of these schemes also raises the question about the extent to which the apartheid state was integrated into an international criminal economy by the 1980s. When we turn in the next chapters to arms smuggling, this viewpoint is again reinforced.

Banking on Apartheid

*'It may be that apartheid brings such stupendous economic
advantages to countries that they would sooner have
apartheid than permit its destruction.'*

– OLIVER TAMBO

*'People who supported South Africa made a profit.
You will be surprised how many people of note at that time
offered their services because of some belief in
South Africa and affection.'*

– BAREND DU PLESSIS

CHAPTER 4

Bunkers, Bankers and Gold

Of the international banks, Swiss commercial banks were among the most significant and long-standing supporters of Pretoria. They pumped money into South Africa to provide credit that would keep the country afloat. They benefited, at least until the mid-1980s, from a borrower who paid its debt on time and at a premium. Apartheid was a safe bet. It was backed by gold, as abundant in supply as the labour of poorly paid black miners, without whom South Africa could not provide the commodity that became the international reserve currency.

The banking establishment in all the Western world's largest economies wanted a stake in the South African game, from the United States to France, West Germany, Italy, Belgium and Luxembourg. Over the next two chapters we focus on three safe havens for bespoke banking operations that served the regime in a very particular manner, and formed apartheid's major banking jurisdictions: Switzerland, Belgium and Luxembourg. Each country is home to banking institutions that appear to provide legitimate banking services but, in fact, operate in the shadows as the cash conduits for many criminal enterprises, including the criminal arms trade. The banks, with support from politicians and corporations, have set in place complex mechanisms to evade the curiosity of outsiders. In this chapter we focus on Switzerland, one of the most secretive banking jurisdictions.

To understand the connection between international finance and apartheid we have to follow the money trail. It leads us to a network of bankers driven by ego, racism and ideology. Many no doubt saw themselves as functionaries, committed to civic duty. These men of standing in their societies learned far too little from the European genocide and the totalitarian states that enabled it in the 20th century. In denying the crime of apartheid they also failed to acknowledge the role that commercial banks in Switzerland and elsewhere had played as functionaries in the Nazi machinery. In turn, the men who shaped the thinking of these institutions in the second half of the 20th century have bequeathed a legacy that remains fiercely protected by the institutions they left behind.

To be clear at the outset, the Swiss connection is not a tale of money laundering. We turn to that in Chapter 5. Instead, Switzerland acted as the gateway to European capital for the apartheid regime, though it was not the only source of such funding. Its example helps us understand how influential international banks related to the apartheid regime.

The relations between South Africa and Switzerland were based on commercial, largely non-sanctions-related business. This formed the foundation for a shared interest in the well-being of each country. For its part, Switzerland mostly provided 'legitimate' banking services, including acting as the gold market and the loan market, in a way that did not rely primarily on banking secrecy or subterfuge. The provision of those services may have been unethical, but from what we have been able to ascertain it was not obviously criminal.

The business with the banks had the support of some of the most powerful Swiss businessmen. They continued to shield South Africa from Swiss sanctions and pressure by lobbying their government and through their active support for Pretoria. The value of these networks cannot be underestimated. We now turn to explore this in more detail.

Swiss secrets

'Secrecy is as vital as the air we breathe.'

– THE SWISS BANKING ASSOCIATION IN RESPONSE TO REVELATIONS
OF SWISS INVOLVEMENT IN THE NAZI GOLD SCANDAL[1]

Understanding the relationships between powerful political and business figures requires knowledge and information. The Swiss government has for many years blocked access to material detailing its economic ties with the apartheid regime: ties that hypocritically existed at the same time as the country repeatedly condemned Pretoria from the late 1960s, supported the arms embargo from 1963 and attempted to limit investment from 1974.[2] Indeed, in 2002 the Swiss government took the unique step of imposing an embargo on any Swiss records created after 1 January 1960 that contained information on Swiss companies that had any business relationship with apartheid South Africa.[3] This is contrary to the general Swiss rule governing the release of documents after 30 years. This deplorably secretive initiative by Swiss politicians has been successful in bedevilling research into Swiss–South African relationships in the first two decades after the end of apartheid.

Even the parliamentary-sanctioned Swiss National Science Foundation's National Research Project into Swiss–South African relations between 1945 and 1990 suffered the consequences of this decision.[4] Formally commissioned in 2000, the project was officially regarded as a means of analysing past policy with an eye to future policy design. However, the researchers engaged in the project acknowledge that the political motive for the project stemmed from ongoing attention to the 'murky areas' of the relationship, including sanctions busting. Representatives of the Green Party in the Swiss parliament were particularly supportive in ensuring that this initiative got off the ground. The researchers faced officials who withheld records, a situation that was exacerbated from 2002 when the Nazi-era claims against Swiss banks were launched in the United States.

The Swiss researcher Peter Hug, who has undertaken detailed research as part of the parliamentary-backed project, confirmed to me in an interview that the embargo decision was made following intensive lobbying by Swiss banks.[5] He believes that they feared that by opening the door to South African secrets, a precedent could be set that would endanger the secrecy on which the Swiss financial system trades.[6] Alexander Karrer, from the Swiss Ministry of Finance, was the official who was central to the decision to embargo and hide records. He is renowned in Swiss political circles for being a 'puppet of the Zurich financial sector'.[7] Hug believes that the Swiss government, which was complicit in the financial sector's relationship with apartheid, shared the banks' fear.[8]

The ban was eventually lifted in June 2014, following renewed calls by left-wing Swiss politicians for the records to be released in the wake of Nelson Mandela's death. The Swiss government then explained that the measures 'were introduced in 2003 to prevent Swiss firms involved in apartheid class actions in the US from being in a worse position procedurally than foreign companies' and that 'the government decided to lift the measure following "extensive clarifications" by federal departments and the Swiss National Bank that showed that the risks for Swiss companies had declined considerably'.[9] As this suggests, the trigger for the release was not Mandela's death, but rather the news in December 2013 that a class action lawsuit, brought by the Khulumani Support Group, a national membership organisation of victims and survivors of apartheid human rights violations, had been dismissed by the New York Appeals Court. The case had originally involved the Swiss banks UBS (Union Bank of Switzerland) and Credit Suisse, and a host of other multinationals from Ford and Daimler to IBM and Rheinmetall, for their alleged role in aiding and abetting gross human rights violations during apartheid.[10]

While the New York Appeals Court judgment was considered a major blow to attempts to hold transnational corporations to account for human rights violations, the Swiss government was clearly pleased, for it was now 'quite unlikely that Swiss companies will be involved in these class actions again'.[11] The cynical Swiss establishment had thus both weathered the storm of corporate accountability and, together with officials in Pretoria, simultaneously wrecked efforts at truth telling. Indeed, the voluminous Swiss research report notes: 'Research was seriously affected in both its form and content by the particular conditions under which it was carried out. We were given extremely limited access in both Switzerland and South Africa to archive material from 1970 onwards, in particular that of a financial nature.'[12]

I have visited the Swiss Federal Archives in Bern on one occasion before, and once since the decision to lift the embargo was made in 2014. Unfortunately, there has been no deluge of new material: the 30-year rule of limiting access still applies. While such rules have become the norm in archival practice across the world, they have the effect of stifling access to the truth and testing the resolve of the handful of people who continue the struggle for accountability decades later.

Swiss secrecy made it nearly impossible to hold the financial institutions and politicians to account in the first two decades of South Africa's freedom, arguably when it mattered the most. What it couldn't whitewash, however, was the fiction of Switzerland's status as a 'neutral' country during the apartheid period. The men with true power, who manage the country's banks, corporations and arms companies, sided with apartheid. They may have escaped accountability for their complicity in upholding a criminal enterprise, but they are nonetheless tainted by it. 'Neutrality is no guarantee against radioactivity,' warned a Swiss government public service announcement about the threat of nuclear fallout during the Cold War.[13] As we will see, Swiss bankers did not exercise the same caution when it came to apartheid. Their reasons were entirely selfish.

Love in the time of the bomb

Switzerland has been a safe haven for other people's money for almost two centuries. The meticulous discretion of Swiss bankers has provided a secure stronghold for the profits of luck, plunder and pain from elsewhere. As institutions in a small country at a crossroad between the great trading nations of Western Europe, enjoying a stable political system, Swiss banks provide certainty to both borrowers and lenders. During the Second World War, Switzerland escaped Nazi occupation as a result of its policy of 'neutrality'. This malleable cornerstone of its foreign affairs was also the basis for the 'don't ask, don't tell' policy when it came to the bags of money or bars of gold that arrived on its bankers' doorsteps.

During the Cold War, the Swiss authorities were wary of Soviet expansionism and the threat of nuclear war, and were also fiercely anti-Soviet. At the same time Switzerland was a predominantly Christian country whose population had strong agrarian roots, and had carved out a very high standard of living from its manufacturing sector and financial institutions.

Switzerland has a long-standing reputation as a haven for dirty money, and investigative journalists have unsuccessfully tried to find accounts stashed full of apartheid loot. However, a more whimsical question is whether Switzerland might have imagined a similar role, though under different circumstances, for South Africa. A file accessed in the Swiss Federal Archives, entitled '*Sitzenverlegung*' (head office relocation), provides insight into the 'South Africa option'. In the 1950s the Swiss government was considering a safe haven for its corporations and its politicians in the case of a third world war. Seemingly, South Africa was one of the best options available. Far from the centre of a nuclear war, South Africa promised good weather, mountains, wine, gold and perpetual white Christian nationalist rule. The information contained in the file is rather patchy, but is sufficient to reveal that South Africa, Canada and New Zealand were all considered as destinations to relocate the Swiss government and corporations in an imagined dystopian future.

In 1960 the Swiss ambassador in Pretoria presented a six-page memorandum to South Africa's secretary for foreign affairs.[14] The memorandum laid out a proposal for relocating the registered head offices of the major Swiss corporations to the Union of South Africa 'for the duration of an international crisis' (but only in the case of an 'imminent international danger') and made several requests regarding the easing of visa regulations and the avoidance of any double taxation.[15] The tax issue was soon the subject of a bilateral agreement, thereby also smoothing the way for further negotiations. These were standard considerations that the Swiss had also raised with the Canadian government as part of a parallel process: Canada had been approved as a suitable exile destination by the Swiss cabinet in 1959. These negotiations were characterised by great secrecy; none of the potential host governments was to be informed of negotiations with the others.[16]

The Swiss secretary of foreign affairs was upbeat about South Africa's prospects in 1960, given 'that it is relatively liberal, welcoming of investment by foreign corporations, and geographically located far away from the likely main theatre of war'.[17] The Swiss were eager to negotiate a favourable deal with South Africa. The ambassador was advised to draw the South African official's attention to the fact that the Central American state of Panama had created regulations that would allow foreign firms to register themselves in Panama and, at the same time, keep their headquarters in their home country. Panama's regulation was described as 'remarkable' by Swiss officials.[18] This crafty scheme by the Panamanian government, drawing on the Swiss model, was exposed in 2016 when a consortium of investigative journalists from across the globe released the Panama Papers. These show how wealthy individuals and corporations who continue to use Panamanian shell companies avoid tax and stash away stolen wealth.

Reporting back to Bern from a meeting with the foreign affairs secretary in February 1960, the Swiss ambassador indicated that there was support from the South Africans for the proposal to grant 'asylum' to Swiss companies and that they could retain their Swiss identity when based in South Africa. What is particularly notable in the correspondence was the Swiss official's insensitivity and lack of judgement when it came to apartheid and its violent application. Writing to his minister in the wake of the Sharpeville Massacre, in which 69 protesters were shot dead by the police, the ambassador remarked: 'There is no doubt that the South African government is committed to ensuring peace and order and security under all circumstances. We can also expect positive efforts to be made to maintain good relations between the races. Under these circumstances, it appears justified to continue the discussions with the South African officials.'[19] Just a few weeks prior to the writing of this letter, the South African government had declared a state of emergency, banned the ANC and PAC, and imprisoned 18,000 people, many of whom were kept in solitary confinement. His was surely a curious interpretation of 'ensuring peace', given that the South African government had opened a new front line of attack on its inhabitants.

The Swiss files do not, for unknown reasons, contain an official agreement between the countries on the granting of asylum to Swiss firms. However, subsequent correspondence confirms that an agreement was reached and entered into. Countries with whom asylum agreements were concluded had to be approved by the Swiss cabinet. Thereafter, companies could register an intention with the Swiss Federal Trade Registry to relocate to one of what were probably not more than a handful of countries.

One significant corporation that did consider relocation to South Africa was the Union Bank of Switzerland (UBS), one of the three most powerful Swiss banks. This is revealed in a confidential November 1982 memorandum reporting on a meeting that had taken place between the Swiss Ministry of Foreign Affairs, Dr FG Gygax, head of UBS, and representatives of Intrag AG, the UBS fund management company. The purpose of the meeting was to finalise an 'emergency agreement' for the South African Trust Fund (SAFIT).[20]

SAFIT was an investment fund in South Africa set up by UBS

in 1948, and was central to the sale of South African gold through Switzerland. It was agreed that UBS would delegate all management functions to the Swiss Union Trust for South Africa in the event of a crisis, an arrangement that had the stamp of approval of the South African authorities.[21] This agreement would come into force in the event of war through the communication of a secret codeword, preferably sent by telex. In December 1982, the manager of UBS in Johannesburg wrote to the Swiss ambassador, thanking him for the opportunity to meet at the embassy. He cryptically concluded by saying, 'We do hope that the agreement which we discussed with you will never be put into force.'[22] This suggests that UBS, which today employs 60,000 people to look after approximately R30 trillion in assets, may have considered relocating its headquarters to the highveld.

When I quizzed PW Botha's minister of finance, Barend du Plessis, about this possible arrangement, he said he had never heard of it but struggled to curb his enthusiasm, 'My goodness, this is very good news. It underscores what I told you … the century-long association with South Africa [with the Swiss] financing a great number of projects. I think that's one of the greatest compliments I have heard for the previous government.'[23] When I put the same question to the former secretary of the Department of Finance and auditor general in the 1980s, Joop de Loor, he also claimed not to have heard about these plans, but said it was possible because UBS was very active in South Africa.[24]

As we will see, UBS's activities relied on personal relationships that may also have enabled Swiss bankers to imagine a post-apocalyptic Helvetic banking system operating from under the highveld sun.

All that is gold does not glitter

Gold has made almost every fortune in South Africa for the past 150 years. While gold mining is today a minor contributor to export earnings, every plutocrat from the Randlords to the Oppenheimers, Ruperts and, more recently, Patrice Motsepe has built his empire in part on the back of gold. For long periods, South Africa produced over half of the world's gold. This was not only a major foreign currency earner, but also a safety buffer against the loss of investment and increased isolation that became a threat in the later apartheid years.[25] During the 1960s and 1970s South Africa found itself in the midst of a currency conflict. The international order established at Bretton Woods, which was based on the convertibility of dollars to gold, with the gold price fixed at $35 an ounce, started to come under strain. Japan and a number of continental European countries begrudged the way in which the United States used its artificially inflated dollar to run vast balance of payments deficits.[26] What this meant was that the US was importing more than it was exporting but still managed to strengthen the value of its own currency. Foremost in the 'war against the dollar' was France, which, under the leadership of Charles de Gaulle, supported closer relations with South Africa.[27] This came to a head in the early 1970s, when South Africa started to withhold gold from the market, placing increasing pressure on the dollar. In return France, which supported efforts to challenge US hegemony, made assurances to South Africa that it would limit obstacles to access its weapons market and bank loans.[28] Ultimately, the United States was forced to cede control of the gold price in 1974. The result was an economic boom in South Africa as the gold price rose from $35 to $197.50 per ounce.[29] This illustrates the centrality of gold to the economic order during this period, and the manner in which it inflated South Africa's political and economic importance at the time.

Given the value of gold, Swiss banks saw an enormous financial opportunity in becoming one of the world's primary gold salesmen. They may not have controlled the mines, but instead would seek to direct the flow of gold into Swiss vaults from where easy money was to be made by selling the precious metal to central banks and corporations across the globe. The Swiss banks, having seen an opportunity, were eager by the late 1940s to establish a free market for gold, requiring them to woo the South Africans.[30] The Zurich gold market, established by the Swiss banks, would eventually become a cornerstone of the Swiss–South African relationship. The anti-apartheid World Gold Commission, established in 1988, regarded Swiss banks as the central provider of South African gold to the international market.[31] How did this relationship come about?

Swiss banks take a shine to gold

The London gold market, traditionally the sole market for South African gold, closed at the beginning of the Second World War and only reopened 15 years later.[32] During this period the Bank of England exercised strict control on the sale of gold at the agreed price of $35 per ounce. This led to the creation of a parallel market, in which Swiss banks were very active, in which gold was traded away from prying central bankers but in which significant profits (in some instances, double the official price) could be achieved.[33] The motive for the Swiss banks was both profit and a strategic hope that this market would expand their global network and operations and develop the Swiss banking sector beyond its Alpine enclave into becoming a world player.[34]

With this in mind, two of the big three Swiss banks, UBS and the Swiss Bank Corporation (SBC), sought to entice South Africa to use the Zurich market and sell its gold to the banks instead of to London. In 1952, the SBC director general, Albert-Charles Nussbaumer, approached the South African Finance Ministry and Chamber of Mines to try to obtain a commitment for the regular supply of gold to the bank.[35] Nussbaumer was willing to return the favour and in 1961 wrote to Prime Minister Hendrik Verwoerd to say: 'I would be delighted to do anything in Europe that could be of indirect assistance and help to you, because I fully agree with you that people do simply not seem to understand your position and problems which are basically only for the defence of the white race in your continent.'[36] Similar to that of UBS, SBC's strategy to supply capital loans to South Africa from the 1950s should be seen as part of a package of inducements on offer.[37] This strategy was partly successful, but when the London gold market reopened in 1954, South African gold largely moved back to the United Kingdom.[38] But Swiss banks now had a taste for gold – and they were not ready to give up the chase quite so easily.

In 1968, responding to pressure on the dollar, South Africa shifted its gold sales to Zurich, and the big three Swiss banks (UBS, Credit Suisse and SBC) agreed to establish a 'buyer's pool' (the Zurich gold pool).[39] From then onwards, Swiss bankers would be the safe hands that managed South African gold sales, particularly since the Zurich market offered a higher price than London.[40] The Swiss researcher Sandra Bott, who has undertaken extensive research on South African gold sales to Switzerland during apartheid, shows that there were various reasons for this.[41] Firstly, acting in alliance, the Swiss banks faced no constraints in purchasing vast quantities of gold from South Africa. Secondly, the Swiss banks provided crucial loans to South Africa, particularly from this time. Thirdly, the Swiss market offered an anonymity that was not possible in London or elsewhere. In fact, the Zurich gold pool was primed for apartheid and was deliberately set up so that not even the banks in the pool knew who each other's clients were. Lastly, following the UK decision not to relax its arms embargo in 1968, Swiss support for a more limited sanctions regime was proof of their dependability as an ally.[42]

Switzerland, with its exclusive gold pipeline to Pretoria, became the centre of the world gold market between 1968 and 1990, importing two-thirds of the new gold supply. In certain years, Switzerland absorbed and marketed up to 80% of South Africa's output.[43] Unsurprisingly, some of the largest Swiss purchases of gold occurred during some of the apartheid regime's most severe crises; the 1976 Soweto uprising, the need for enriched uranium in 1981, the debt rescheduling in 1985 and the liquidity crises in 1983 and 1988.[44] There was a fortune to be made in misery. This situation was likely the result of South Africa dipping into its reserves to turn them into cash. However, there was also an element of 'help from an ally', particularly because after 1983 the purchases of gold were coupled with increases in much-needed short-term bank credits.[45]

However, it wasn't just the sale and purchase of gold that was so beneficial to both countries. The South African government also used gold swaps to obtain numerous short-term loans from Swiss banks. Unlike ordinary commercial loans, the gold swaps did not require authorisation and therefore were not identifiable. The total number of swaps amounted to over $2 billion between 1985 and 1989. These swaps were used to protect South Africa at times of liquidity crisis in the 1980s, as well as to shield it from scrutiny by the Anti-Apartheid Movement and other critics of the regime.[46]

When I asked the former senior government finance official Joop de Loor if the Swiss banks' financial commitment to South was ideological or personal, he responded that 'they don't do it for the love of it'.[47] Their role in holding the monopoly on South African gold sales, combined with the trustworthy payment record by the South African Treasury, meant 'there was never a question of not rolling over the credit'.[48] Additionally, these loans were proportionally small on the banks' balance sheets, allowing them to absorb some of the risk.

The Union Bank of Switzerland (UBS)

*'The South African native is still absolutely raw ... In short
he is half child, half animal ... Is apartheid necessary, or
desirable? Hardly necessary, but certainly desirable.'*
– UBS MANAGING DIRECTOR, JOHANNESBURG BRANCH, 1963[49]

The big three banks in Switzerland until the late 1990s were UBS, the SBC and Credit Suisse. In 1998 SBC merged with UBS, becoming the largest bank in Switzerland and one of the most influential in the world. Before the merger, UBS was the smallest of the big three, but it had the closest relationship with apartheid's political and economic elite.[50]

It is worth noting that all three banks were part of an overall trend that saw Swiss banks dramatically increase direct and indirect financing to the apartheid regime from 1968 onwards, which coincided with the move of the South African gold market to Zurich.[51] At the same time, the assets of Swiss banks in South Africa tripled between 1979 and 1993.[52] It was for this reason that the apartheid victims rights group Khulumani, ultimately unsuccessfully, sought a reparations claim against UBS and Credit Suisse.

Although a relatively small contributor to the total capital inflow to South Africa in this period, Switzerland was a key financier of South African public authorities and parastatals, and one of the four central contributors to South Africa's long-term debt by the 1990s.[53] In 1979–80, the big three Swiss banks (each with a representative office in South Africa) were committed to 32% of total loans to South Africa raised on the international market, and this does not include their contributions to loans by banking syndicates, which was a common practice.[54] These loans were to large public entities such as the government and Eskom.[55] The Swiss Anti-Apartheid Movement labelled UBS as the central player in this regard, as UBS participated, usually as 'lead manager', in numerous large loans in the early 1980s.[56] In 1985 UBS's Nikolaus Senn negotiated a $75 million loan directly with the South African finance minister, Barend du Plessis; the loan was not earmarked for any particular project, meaning that it could be used to reinforce the army and police.[57] Such loans, which could be used to fund weapons projects or police batons and boots, were in line with the role that Swiss industry played in South Africa's atomic weapons programme, the sale of weapons and the ongoing close collaboration between Swiss and South African intelligences services, to which we return in Chapter 11.[58]

In conversation with Barend du Plessis, I asked him what was in this for the Swiss banks: Did it also help them internationalise their business, as some studies suggest? From his vantage point, this was a very obvious decision based on good business, without a hint of the handsome profits or dehumanising apartheid politics: 'In terms of the wealth and the massive capital that the Swiss handled, they had a lot of money to invest. In terms of that scale of things, I wouldn't say that South Africa was an important percentage. But to the extent that they did business here, that was safe, it was pleasant, it was nice to come here, they liked the people and they liked the business that they did. Don't forget in the days before the sanctions the Americans did whatever they could to do business here – you could get a good deal here. Your money would be repaid and this was a good investment.'[59]

Despite Du Plessis's positive spin, there is no doubt that the Swiss banks and politicians granted the apartheid regime significant favours. This was despite calls for banking sanctions, which led the World Council of Churches and other members of the Anti-Apartheid Movement to withdraw all their deposits from UBS. In August 1984, the South African embassy in Bern revealed that Switzerland's ceiling on financing to South Africa was widely and intentionally publicised, but it noted:

> Secret agreements have been made to provide the most favourable conditions to South Africa. Switzerland's 'neutral' position on SA is largely a result of the influence that bankers have on politics, and the social relations that SA ambassadors have with Swiss bankers are thus vital. Understandably, details on this are not given. This situation was not raised in the recent general meeting between SA and Swiss government representatives and officials, but instead raised in private between the PM [PW Botha] and [Swiss] President Schlumpf. The President of the Swiss National Bank [the Swiss central bank], the President as well as the Chairman of the Board of Directors of the Bank for International Settlements, and the General Manager of the Union Bank of Switzerland are in on it, among others.[60]

The memo was in fact a motivation for an experienced new ambassador to be appointed because of the importance of a Bern posting. It added that the embassy needed a strong leader given the unusually broad scope of propaganda services they were managing in Switzerland.

Thus, while the interests of the elites were clearly aligned, it was essential that the rest of the Swiss population were kept firmly supportive of South Africa.

This memo provides insight into the extraordinary role played by the personalities who ran the banks. A common mistake is that because large institutions such as banks are faceless, they are not really controlled by anybody. Hence it follows the logic that nobody can be held to account for misdeeds other than hapless small depositors, who are usually left to clean up the mess, as was the case during the 2008 banking crisis. The memo quoted above shows just how untrue this trope really is.

A further handwritten secret memo from the South African embassy to the Department of Foreign Affairs underscores the importance of these personal relationships. It stated:

> There would be intensive interest among certain institutions ... such as the Swiss Parliament ... in the fact that the South African Ambassador through ongoing lobbying has succeeded to get the Swiss government to agree to let Swiss Banks provide South Africa with the most preferential loan conditions that are possible given the circumstances ... It would therefore be appreciated why detailed information is not provided in this report ... In this scenario, the South African Ambassador enjoys the trust and good will of among others the President of the Swiss National Bank (Edmund Wyss), the Chairperson and President of the Bank for International Settlements (Fritz Leutwiler), and the General Manager of UBS (Nikolaus Senn).[61]

Fritz Leutwiler, to whom we turn in the next section, also chaired the Swiss National Bank, and was a key figure in the relationship between the two countries. However, it is striking that the two memos single out links to UBS in particular. It should therefore come as no surprise that PW Botha, on a short visit to Switzerland in October 1988, conferred the Order of Good Hope on Georges Meyer, then president of the Swiss–South African Association (SSAA) and vice-president of UBS.[62] Meyer is described as having a long-standing relationship with South Africa.[63] Botha also used the opportunity to meet senior members of the Swiss business and banking sector in order to confirm certain commitments made by Barend du Plessis, so as to secure further loans for South Africa.[64]

Meyer wasn't the only senior UBS official to befriend the regime. In fact, there were two particularly important UBS officials who became regime allies: UBS director general, Bruno Saager, and long-time UBS chief executive, Nikolaus Senn. Their relationship with South Africa was deeply personal, and their support for the apartheid regime was unwavering. Both men were also very close to the wealthy, politically influential Afrikaner businessman Anton Rupert.[65]

The vanguard: Bruno Saager

When Bruno Saager retired from UBS in 1979 after more than three decades in leadership positions, he could look back at a career that helped shape the dependable Swiss bank into a global financial institution. As with most successful bankers, personal contacts beyond the Alps were key. In North America he had, for example, advised US President John F Kennedy on the role of gold in the US balance of payments concerns in the 1960s.[66] However, one constant throughout his professional career was his deep and abiding relationship with apartheid South Africa.

Saager first visited South Africa in 1948, just as the National Party came to power, in his capacity as a 40-year-old vice-director general of UBS, to offer the South African government public sector bonds.[67] UBS was seen at the time as the 'vanguard of involvement in South Africa' among Swiss banks, with Saager central to this strategy. This was followed up by a visit in 1950 to meet with top management of the country's biggest gold and diamond mining houses: Anglo American and De Beers.[68] Saager continued to broker loans from Swiss and German banks to the South African government for several decades, including several secretive loans to the state power utility, Eskom, in 1965.[69] In 1975 Saager was among a small group of prominent international bankers invited as guests for the inauguration as state president of Nico Diederichs, illustrating his closeness to the South African establishment.[70] Saager described Diederichs, who had been minister of finance for many years, as 'a personal friend of mine'.[71]

Diederichs, nicknamed 'Dr Gold', was often linked at the time to unproven rumours of financial impropriety. In 1980, Judge Joe Ludolf informed the *Rand Daily Mail* of a R28 million secret UBS bank account held in Switzerland with links to Diederichs.[72] This was allegedly a kickback for the Swiss gold pool agreement, with money going either to Diederichs or to fund a white South African government in exile. The *Rand Daily Mail* editor, Allister Sparks, travelled to Switzerland soon afterwards, where he successfully deposited cash into the account at UBS – proof that it existed. Diederichs was eventually cleared of wrongdoing by a government investigation, but not before it had been revealed that the bank account in fact belonged to another friend of his.[73] When Saager was asked to comment, in view of the UBS link, he remained steadfastly loyal: 'I will not do anything that will raise matters again that will harm him.'[74]

This was not to be the only brush that Saager and UBS had with the apartheid regime's funny money scandals of the late 1970s. In fact, Saager retired from UBS just as the Information Scandal began to break in 1979. This might have been a coincidence, but it proved fortunate for UBS, as it was revealed that a wholly owned UBS company, Thesaurus Continental Securities Corporation, had been used to channel funds central to the Information Scandal. The use of Thesaurus, in turn, was based on an agreement between Saager and Diederichs.[75] Saager was also involved in the cover-up: he reportedly signed a letter containing false information, helping the Information Department's Eschel Rhoodie to conceal its secret funding of *The Citizen* newspaper, which had been set up as a government mouthpiece.[76]

Saager's relationship with the apartheid government was matched by friendships in the private sector, including the billionaire businessman Anton Rupert.[77] Rupert long had a knack for internationalising the board membership of his various companies by carefully selecting influential men who would provide access to the high table in Europe and North America.[78] When the Rupert tobacco interests in Rembrandt and Carreras merged in 1972 to form Rothmans International, Bruno Saager, along with the banker Edmund L de Rothschild, were on the first board of directors.[79] In the same year, Saager and Rupert established the Development Bank for Equatorial and Southern Africa, to provide 'capital for private enterprise, particularly in Southern Africa'.[80] The failed venture, described by Rupert as one of his career low lights, was, unsurprisingly, headed by another former UBS man, René Gerber.[81]

Saager and UBS clearly had an uncomplicated relationship with the South African elite. Joop de Loor argued that this was 'largely because of the personalities involved – [the finance minister] Owen Horwood [Barend du Plessis's predecessor] and Bruno Saager were buddies basically, and on every visit to Europe we would first go to Saager to find out about the European banking situation. Saager would advise how to structure the loans, who to approach and how to ensure that the loans fit into both their portfolios and the South African portfolio.'[82] In reference to President Zuma's decision to hire and fire his acolyte Des van Rooyen as minister of finance in the timespan of less than a week in December 2015, with disastrous consequences for the economy, De Loor pointed out that the nature of the game hasn't changed when it comes to the markets. It is 'not a question of being bright, it's about longstanding relationships'.[83]

Barend du Plessis recalls from his period as minister of finance that the Swiss held South Africa in confidence because it met all its commitments without fail: 'they were relaxed ... there was literally no risk for those banks to come and do business in South Africa. In the process of visiting South Africa they obviously fell in love with it. One Swiss banking family had residences in SA, they had farms.'[84] When I interrupted to ask him if he was referring to the Saager family wine farm at Eikendal outside Cape Town, which was bought in 1981, he responded, 'That's absolutely right, I opened [inaugurated] that one – Eikendal ... It would not be strange to hear that Swiss businessmen, not only bankers, would invest in property in South Africa and do the swallow thing – follow the sun.'[85] Though Bruno Saager is long dead, the old family relationships persist in the new South Africa. His son Hansjürg Saager, until recently one of the 600 wealthiest Swiss, reportedly spends much of the year at Eikendal still.[86]

The defender: Nikolaus Senn

Dr Nikolaus Senn, a generation younger than Saager, picked up the mantle as new UBS chief in the 1980s. His four-decade-long UBS career culminated in his position as CEO from 1980 to 1988 in a period of aggressive expansion, and subsequently as UBS chairman from 1988 to 1996.[87]

Senn had been a supporter of UBS's South African business from well before the 1980s, when he battled calls for the bank to sever its commercial ties with the pariah government. In a letter to the South African minister of finance, Nico Diederichs, in 1970, Senn bemoaned 'agitators' (referring to the Anti-Apartheid Movement) who were making it more difficult for UBS to continue to provide loans to South Africa, adding: 'your country is a highly valued trading partner of Switzerland and the banks are anxious to offer you any facility to take recourse to our capital market.'[88] This relationship extended well into the 1980s, when Senn would visit South Africa annually. Barend du Plessis recalls that 'Dr Senn always used to come and see me at my office and I would ensure that special coffee was brewed for him. He said to me so many times that there are so many opportunities for my bank in South Africa but I can't help you.'[89]

Like Saager, Senn was close friends with Anton Rupert and was drawn into his group of companies. The Ruperts retreated to the Swiss Alpine enclave of Zug in 1988, as monopoly capital feared expropriation as the prospect of regime change loomed in South Africa. The Ruperts transferred their company Rembrandt's foreign interests into the leading luxury goods company, Richemont.[90] This was not dissimilar to the manner in which the Oppenheimer clan at Anglo saw the creation of Minorco as a vehicle for its offshore portfolio. Rupert approached Senn, while hosting him and his wife at the Salzburg festival, to act as chairman of the dynasty's flagship company, Richemont, which Senn agreed to do, serving for the following 14 years.[91]

Senn's views about doing business with apartheid South Africa are instructive, and reflective of the sentiment expressed by several Swiss individuals and institutions at the time. At a UBS shareholders' meeting in 1989, Senn shut down pleas by the Anti-Apartheid Movement's patron, Bishop Trevor Huddleston, not to do business with apartheid. Senn explained that 'we do not like you to attack a government with which we have normal diplomatic relations'.[92] When questioned about his thoughts at the time of civil unrest in South Africa in the 1980s, Senn was quoted as saying that 'domestic politics are not our thing ... We judge countries by economic criteria ... We supported neither the regime nor the government who ran it, we simply maintained normal relations with South Africa.'[93]

Senn was another in a long line of men with short memories who profited from but claimed never to support corrupt, oppressive regimes the world over. In fact, the record shows that Senn brazenly defended white minority rule as late as 1985. 'If I lived in South Africa, I also would not be prepared to relinquish the reins ... For me, "one man-one vote" is not a world religion,' Senn was reported to have said.[94] Why would it not apply in South Africa? Senn suggested that although he was at first shocked by the 'system' in South Africa, he started to see it as unavoidable because of the lower education of 'the blacks'.[95]

Entirely 'unavoidable' is the basic fact that Saager, Senn and UBS, which they led, made huge profits from their support for apartheid and their links to South African elites. They knew this, their board of directors knew this, as did their subordinates and the politicians who regulated their activities. Everyone was in on the game. No wonder they have never been held responsible for this.

Without the investigative weight of the US Department of Justice, there seems to be no institution that can hold Swiss banks to account for past crimes.

The debt collector

> *'Out of the mist of the Swiss mountains came Dr Leutwiler.*
> *What a man. He said, I can't allow you guys to go into that*
> *lion's den, I'll help you.'*
>
> — BAREND DU PLESSIS, FORMER FINANCE MINISTER[96]

Dr Fritz Leutwiler, the éminence grise of Swiss banking, came knocking on the South African Treasury's door in 1985. The emissary of 29 international banks was an old friend of apartheid South Africa and therefore Pretoria's ideal man with whom to negotiate a debt standstill.

By 1985 South Africa faced a significant debt crisis. Between 1980 and 1984, South African external debt had escalated by nearly 50% to $24.3 billion.[97] Crucially, two-thirds of the money was owed in short-term debt to external creditors who could demand full repayment in less than a year.[98] In addition, 80% of this debt was owed to commercial banks, which could prove either cunning allies or ruthless creditors once they smelt any blood in the water that could endanger their investment.[99] When the first banks in the United States indicated that they would not roll over South Africa's debts (driven in part by pressure from the US Anti-Apartheid Movement), and instead demanded repayment, South Africa faced a liquidity crisis and called for a moratorium on repayment.

Barend du Plessis recalls the financial crisis, still the worst in the country's history. It was further exacerbated at the time by PW Botha's Rubicon speech, in which he signalled to the world that there would be no significant change to apartheid rule:

I don't think PW Botha understood what it meant to cross the Rubicon. We declared a debt standstill. How do we deal with this? Chris Stals [the director general of finance] said we only have dollars for a few weeks, who is going to help us? ... Some of the banks immediately retaliated. One of our SAA [South African Airways] Boeings landed in Switzerland with gold. A very small bank that was a creditor wanted to confiscate the airplane with the bullion on board. During the course of that day Dr Senn of UBS, who was a great friend of SA, bought the bank. He never told me the name of the bank as it was confidential at the time – and he fired the very brave CEO.[100]

While the government could rely on a Band-Aid provided by the aggressive Dr Senn and the South African private sector, this was unsustainable. What was needed, and fast, was a solution to the crisis. Without bridging finance, the South African economy would spin further into a downward cycle. To fight a war in Angola and Namibia and face off popular uprisings at home, money was needed. It was also a time of potentially enormous leverage for the anti-apartheid movement: this was a rare opportunity to force massive concessions from a cash-starved regime. Even a moody old warmonger like PW Botha could be tamed by the fact that he could not simply print US dollars to repay the banks. No repayment meant no new debt. As the rand went into free fall, the government would have little choice but to lay off a large chunk of its voting fodder, white conservative voters. The crisis could have sunk the National Party government.

To its rescue, 'out of the mist of the Swiss mountains', came Fritz Leutwiler, calming the markets as only a conservative Swiss banker of pedigree can. Barend du Plessis recalls: 'The team of Leutwiler, [Chris] Stals and another chap then went from bank to bank to convince them. However, Leutwiler never wanted a cent, I don't think he ever wanted a refund on his travelling expenses, that kind of Prussian honour.'[101]

Before we turn to Leutwiler's role in South Africa, it is useful to reflect briefly on his pedigree, as that explains the nature of his influence. With a freshly minted PhD, the 24-year-old Leutwiler began his nearly four-decade-long association with banking in 1948. An avid bookbinder, he was also a general in the Swiss Home Guard.[102] Following a four-year stint at the private Swiss Bank Corporation (now part of UBS), he joined the Swiss National Bank and rose to the rank of its president in 1974, continuing there until 1984.[103] Shortly before the South African debt crisis, he was appointed president of the Basel-based Bank of International Settlements (BIS) in 1982 for a two-year period.[104] The BIS, owned at the time by approximately 30 of the world's central banks, is essentially the bank of all central banks, from the mighty US Federal Reserve to its counterparts in Switzerland, the United Kingdom and the South African Reserve Bank. Leutwiler, described by colleagues as 'a crafty old fox', was a popular choice for this prominent international position. He was known as a hard man and no push-over, who ruthlessly took the scalpel to treat a problem he didn't like. For example, when he sought to quell inflation in Switzerland in the 1970s, he cut money supply to the extent that Switzerland suffered a 7% negative growth rate in one year.[105]

Leutwiler also befriended politicians with whom he shared a similar worldview.[106] A notable example was British Prime Minister Margaret Thatcher, an ally of Pretoria during apartheid, with whom he dined when she holidayed in Switzerland. When Mexico faced a debt crisis in 1982, he was one of the first people to whom the head of the US Federal Reserve, Paul Volcker, turned for help.[107] Leutwiler subsequently encouraged central bankers to contribute money to stave off disaster in Mexico, just as he had led efforts that ultimately raised $50 billion to support the US dollar in 1978.[108]

Leutwiler's international standing was essential to alleviating the South African situation. While it was by no means the only country that faced a debt crisis during this period, it did, however, receive unique treatment from international creditors, especially compared with other countries in similar crises like Peru.[109] The South African exceptionalism lay in part in the high-profile support that the country enjoyed with the appointment of Leutwiler to personally manage and negotiate a solution to South Africa's debt crisis, indicating enviable international political support.[110]

According to the South African diplomat André Brink, Leutwiler jumped at the appointment when he was approached in his office by the South African ambassador to Bern. He was handed a memorandum written by Barend du Plessis, formally requesting Leutwiler to manage the negotiation of the debt standstill. After reading it, Leutwiler made one phone call and agreed within five minutes to take on the role.[111] Leutwiler's account of the story suggests that he was approached by the governor of the South African Reserve Bank, a politically more palatable suitor, upon which he phoned his personal friend, the president of the Swiss Confederation, and asked whether it would damage Switzerland in any way should he take the role.[112] Leutwiler, who was at this stage chairman of the Swiss engineering firm Brown Boveri & Cie, then conferred with colleagues before accepting the position.[113]

While he held numerous other prominent board appointments, including with Nestlé, his association with Brown Boveri is of particular interest.[114] Leutwiler was responsible for ushering in a new era after the merger of the Swiss firm with the Swedish group ASEA in 1988 to form ABB. Leutwiler was chairman of Brown Boveri from 1985 and continued in that position at ABB until 1992. ABB also had extensive interests and operations in South Africa and was the primary supplier of generators for several of Eskom's coal-fired power stations. ABB was also awarded the important contract to provide the 'switchyard' for the Koeberg nuclear power station.[115] The most vocal criticism from within Swiss banking circles of his position in negotiating the South African debt crisis appears to have been based on a fear that the extensive interests of Brown Boveri in South Africa would compromise his objectivity in this new role.[116]

Despite his personal and professional links to apartheid, he was cast in the international press as scrupulously principled. The *Wall Street Journal* and the *New York Times* in September 1985 spoke of his 'personal revulsion at the system of apartheid', which apparently would not cloud what must have been an already hazy sense of judgement.[117] In reality, Leutwiler, a vehement anti-communist, did not shy away from criticising the ANC and other opposition groups, and argued that South Africa's problem was one of inadequate public relations rather than anything else.[118]

In a 1986 interview with South African *Leadership* magazine, Leutwiler also described his attempts to use his influence at the Swiss National Bank to aid South Africa long before this particular crisis. 'I have been interested in South Africa for a long time. I first went there as the guest of the Governor of the Reserve Bank seven years ago. I was on very good terms with the former finance minister Horwood. I tried to help South Africa while I was still at the Swiss National Bank when the country had difficulties raising international capital because there was a ceiling on South African borrowings, even in Switzerland. You could call me a friend of the country – not of any particular regime.'[119] Leutwiler was of course being modest. He was not just a friend but an ally, and he supported the big three Swiss private banks in their opposition to any credit limit or restrictions placed on exporting capital to South Africa.[120]

A preliminary agreement to resolve the South African debt crisis was eventually concluded in February 1986 in London. It set a framework for resolving outstanding issues. This included an agreement to suspend payment on $10 billion of debt for a year, subject to a South African down payment of $500 million in April 1986.[121] *Business Day* argued that Pretoria would be delighted at the terms of the deal.[122] Leutwiler later admitted that he gave the commercial banks a 'take it or leave it ultimatum' to pressure them into accepting the deal.[123] His pro-Pretoria negotiating style drew sharp criticism from the Anti-Apartheid Movement, which lambasted him for missing an opportunity to push for greater political and social reforms, and labelled him a 'mouthpiece for PW Botha'.[124]

With the crisis having subsided in favour of South Africa, Leutwiler returned to tend his interests in Brown Boveri.[125] Nonetheless, his association with South Africa was far from over, even though we may know little about the detail. The South African chief sanctions-busting diplomat, Marc Burger, suggests that the Swiss banker may have helped shape some of his department's thinking about how it should counter sanctions: 'Although default was averted when Herr Leutwiler … succeeded in rescheduling our debt repayments to foreign creditors, South Africa's vulnerability was exposed. Sanctions threats became realities … An immediate consequence was a rearrangement of certain priorities and responsibilities. Significantly, Leutwiler was brought to a working lunch by [the governor of the Reserve Bank Gerhard] De Kock and [finance official Chris] Stals, to agree the "go ahead" with the minister of foreign affairs – not finance.'[126] While Burger provides little detail, his autobiography describes the meeting as seminal in kick-starting his new role as sanctions buster-in-chief for foreign affairs.

Brown Boveri also continued its engagement with South Africa, including the SADF, despite the arms embargo. Records in the SADF archives reveal that the Swiss corporation had set up a South African subsidiary company, Brown Boveri Pty (Ltd), which was a 50/50 partnership with Bill Venter's Powertech group.[127] Venter had a long association with the apartheid military–industrial complex. In a letter written in 1988 to the SADF, Armscor complained of the growing problem of acquiring infrared, radar and microwave technology for physical security systems from their traditional suppliers in the United States because of sanctions. According to the letter, Brown Boveri agreed to set up a local production facility to meet this demand.[128] In addition, Armscor and the SADF project officers accompanied a Mr Brian Tucker (who was the contact with the Brown Boveri director) to Switzerland and Germany, where Brown Boveri organised visits to various nuclear and NATO facilities to observe the physical security systems at these installations.[129] This trip was planned for August 1988, the first year of ABB's existence.

ABB would be implicated in the late 1990s in bribe payments in one of the biggest construction projects in southern Africa, the

Lesotho Highlands Water Scheme. The overall project financing was described as a way of breaking financial sanctions against apartheid. It provided a cover for capital to flow to South Africa, the real borrower and beneficiary of the water scheme, via a trust fund in London to launder the contributions of various financiers for the project.[130] ABB was awarded several contracts to supply generators for the Muela dam project and was prosecuted for bribing Lesotho officials to obtain the contracts.[131] The company CEO admitted in 1999 that the company had been aware of 'issues' with its involvement with the project from 1987, and that at least one official had been fired as a result.[132]

Fritz Leutwiler negotiated an important lifeline for the apartheid regime. He claimed he was opposed to apartheid but he used a position of extraordinary influence, first at the Swiss National Bank and later as a mediator, to favour the apartheid government. While he may never have received any direct payment as thanks, the Swiss banks and his company ABB benefited handsomely from doing business with Pretoria. Not only was South Africa a diligent debtor but, given the right circumstances, it would return favours to its friends.

The bankers' circle

The Swiss gnomes and the Belgian bankers (see Chapter 5) are worthy of singling out in view of their importance in propping up the South African economy. However, for many other bankers the business of loans to the apartheid state continued as usual. Among these, British, German and French banks were probably the biggest culprits. It is worth remembering that everyone was involved. The banks included Hill Samuel and Barclays in the United Kingdom; Deutsche Bank, Dresdner Bank, Commerzbank and all the major German banks; and the Parisian banks Société Générale, Paribas and Suez.[133] US banks, including Citibank and Chase Manhattan, also did business with Pretoria until they felt the heat from the active US anti-apartheid movement. This list excludes many other banks, large and small, in countries across the globe. When pressure was placed on the money supply, fronts were created, the bantustans were used as a conduit, or some of South Africa's private banks raised capital on the government's behalf.

In 1994, South Africa was heavily indebted to these financial institutions, which had continued to lend to the apartheid regime right up until the brink of financial crisis. By this time, and with a new government in place, this debt and the significant repayments required formed a major diversion of funds from vital domestic spending. The 'odious debt doctrine' suggests that states should be allowed unilaterally to repudiate the debts of a previous regime when they did not have the consent of the people, when they were not used for the benefit of the people, and when the lenders knew this was the case.[134] It is clear that the vast majority of South Africans neither consented to nor benefited from these loans. In fact the opposite was true, considering the role of this capital in financing oppression and in prolonging a system that was a crime against humanity. Given that it is also true that the lenders were acutely aware of the state of South Africa under apartheid and of the actions of the regime, the third condition is also met.

The democratic South African government never pressed the issue regarding apartheid debt, and it is not the only one not to have done so.[135] The power of international capital markets and the need to access future capital ensure that many new governments prefer to take on crippling debt rather than fight for its repudiation. Unfortunately, this means that banks knowingly and recklessly lend vast sums of money to violent and repressive governments and enjoy not only impunity, but the guarantee of a return.

The South African government and private sector developed a heavy reliance on private loan capital from bond issues and syndicated loans in the Euromarket in the 1970s; this became 'an orgy of borrowing from private international banks' in the early 1980s.[136] Despite the warning signs of an impending debt crisis, in 1984 the magazine *Euromoney* noted that South African borrowers 'have never been more welcome in the Euromarkets than they are at present'.[137] In fact, loans to South African public borrowers were very often oversubscribed. The rush to these markets for finance was led by large state-owned enterprises and public entities, particularly Eskom, and the government itself.[138] The largest transnational banks, acting in syndicate with numerous other partner banks, underwrote the loans.

Swiss politicians, too, were planning for all eventualities and very quickly attempted to cosy up to both Nelson Mandela and Thabo Mbeki after 1994. To their advantage, they had also played the long game. In 1977, when the relationship with apartheid was the most resolute, the Swiss minister of foreign affairs, Pierre Graber, wrote to the Swiss federal president, Kurt Furgler, to persuade him to evade a meeting with the South African state president, Nico Diederichs, who was on holiday in Switzerland. He went on to note: 'for your personal and confidential information, we wish to add that the political department (foreign affairs) has established its first contact with the African National Congress (exile organization of the Blacks in South Africa). As a result of this we are considering providing the ANC with limited humanitarian assistance (medicine to the value of ±SFR50,000 and two scholarships).'[139] The Swiss were starting to court future players in South African politics discreetly.

Large Swiss banks supported apartheid. They may not have broken the rules, but they made significant riches from their relations with their South African friends. Legal business in an abnormal society is no doubt profitable. Banking institutions across the globe, including Switzerland, were fundamental in propping up the apartheid regime. Their relationship was based on the gold markets and the provision of loans to the South African government and corporations. The relationship was so steadfast that Swiss institutions, including possibly one of its biggest banks, considered relocating to South Africa if ever another war threatened Europe. South Africa had the added benefit of being plugged into the financial system in a manner that belied its distance from all major financial trading hubs.

To cement these ties, both countries counted on close contact between their business and political elites. Within the Swiss banking community there is undeniable evidence that some of the very top bankers were well disposed to South Africa despite apartheid. In some instances they may well have been well disposed because of apartheid.

The value of such networks cannot be underestimated. They facilitated legal connections, as we have just seen. However, as we will see in the next chapter, they had an even more sinister aspect. We next turn to a scandal within the larger scandal of apartheid-era sanctions busting, and discover how a small European bank in Belgium, through its subsidiaries in Luxembourg and Switzerland, became rich off the back of racism. In doing so, we reveal an international money-laundering network that was apartheid's arms money machine.

CHAPTER 5

The Arms Money Machine

'It is not in the weapons trade that one finds the worst crooks
... It is in the world of banking. There, gentlemen of the most
honourable appearance benefit with absolute impunity from
every kind of trafficking.'

– Georges Starckmann, veteran French arms trader
and apartheid sanctions buster

How do you smuggle half a trillion rand across the globe without anyone noticing?

In 1977, with the prospect of international arms sanctions looming, the securocrats in Pretoria needed a plan. The clichéd brown envelopes and duffle bags of cash were not going to cut it. Not only did they have to move large volumes of money between thousands of people and entities, but they needed to do so in absolute secrecy. They needed banks that could keep secrets. They needed bankers who wanted to make money and maintain white supremacy – bankers who could help design and maintain one of the largest and most complex sanctions-busting operations the world has known. Not only were the bankers central to prolonging the crime of apartheid, but some actively participated in the conspiracy of money laundering. Despite this, both bank and bankers remain today as feted models of success. The public remains oblivious of the role they played at the time.

This is their story. It has remained largely unexposed since the end of apartheid. It winds through front companies in Liberia and Panama, and bank accounts across the globe, to bespoke banks in Belgium and Luxembourg that were at the centre of an international criminal enterprise. This was one of the most serious and sophisticated examples of sanctions busting the world has ever seen. A system of hundreds of front companies supported a grand conspiracy, which for 20 years was the conduit for 70% of the cash used by South Africa to buy weapons illegally. This was the arms money machine, one of the most sinister pieces of secretive corporate and banking architecture constructed during apartheid. Its scale has for decades been covered with a blanket of secrecy, in this way hiding a history of collaboration, profit and repression. Only now are we able to reveal the scale of this crime and the people who inspired it and we turn our attention to the Kredietbank of Belgium and its subsidiary in Luxembourg..

The Kredietbank: 'A Flemish fairytale'

'The driver of everything is self-interest,
the rest is self-deception.'

– FERNAND COLLIN, CHAIRMAN OF
KREDIETBANK (1938–1973)[1]

A Flemish affair

Kredietbank, now known as KBC Bank, is the 18th largest bank in Europe and employs 51,000 people, serving 11 million customers across the globe. KBC survived the 2008 banking crisis thanks to a Belgian government bailout. It staved off the wolves through taxpayers' money and the sale of its prized asset, the private banking subsidiary Kredietbank Luxembourg (KBL), to the Qatari investment fund Precision Capital for over €1 billion (approximately R15 billion).

Kredietbank's fortunes mirrored the rise in prosperity of Belgium's Flemish speakers in the 20th century. The economic clout of the Flemish, relative to their political power, is not dissimilar to that of the now relatively prosperous middle–class white Afrikaners. There is also a hint of similarity between Kredietbank and Volkskas Bank, today ABSA. Volkskas was established in 1934 and would eventually become the primary bank of not only Afrikaner industrialists, but also Afrikaner Christian nationalists and the apartheid state. Similarly, Kredietbank was the bank of choice for the Flemish elite.

When the Kredietbank was set up in 1935, a holding company, Almanij, was established to house the interests of the bank and other investments in the financial sector and large industries. Almanij was led by two large clans: the Collin and Vlerick families.[2] The busy port city of Antwerp was chosen as its base and the bank was housed in one of Europe's first skyscrapers.[3]

Fernand Collin chaired the bank for 35 years from 1938 to 1973.[4] His life philosophy, in his own words, was that 'the driver of everything is self-interest, the rest is self-deception'.[5] Entrenched as a member of the Belgian power elite for decades, he had little care for those whom society left behind. Collin travelled to South Africa on numerous occasions, heading trade delegations, and showed great empathy for the apartheid regime. 'What happens there I cannot explain in a positive light, but I understand their situation, the whites established something that is exceptional,' he commented. 'And everywhere where blacks have become boss, everything disappears. Zimbabwe is a typical example. What has become of the riches of English colonial Rhodesia? It was an empire with mines and mighty agriculture. There were also many rich farmers. But go and have a look now – terrible!'[6]

André Vlerick: Banker, Belgian and bigot

The other important figure in Kredietbank who became central to the South African money-laundering scheme was André Vlerick. For over two decades, he filled several senior management positions at the bank, first as deputy chairman from 1974 to 1980 and then as chairman of the board from 1980 to 1989.[7] Shortly before his death in 1990 he was appointed honorary chairman. In the 1960s Vlerick had begun a career as an academic, becoming something of a guru in the new science of executive management, and he set up the Vlerick School of Management, now one of Europe's top business schools with over 20,000 alumni, at the University of Ghent.[8] The business school's fortunes and that of its founder are closely tied. In 2006 Vlerick's widow bequeathed the school €50 million.[9]

Vlerick came from a wealthy family of Flemish Belgians, a group who had been sidelined historically by the French-speaking commercial and political class in Belgium. The similarity of their struggle against a dominant commercial and cultural class to that of the Afrikaners in South Africa helps to explain the admiration Vlerick developed for white Afrikaner nationalism and the policy of apartheid. His defence of apartheid as a model for peaceful coexistence was tied to his deeply Flemish nationalistic identity. On one occasion he praised the way 'Afrikaners have fought for the right of their nation and to remain as they are ... If we in Belgium had established parallel development we would not be sitting with the well-known problems we have.'[10]

To promote his views, in 1977 Vlerick helped found a powerful lobby in Belgium called Protea, after the iconic South African flower, whose members were described as existing in an orbit around the country's two largest banking institutions, Kredietbank and Banque Paribas.[11] According to the Belgian newspaper *De Morgen*, 'in reality, the Protea club operates as a propaganda organ, behind which significant Flemish South African business interests shelter, which for their own interests defend the racist minority government in Pretoria'.[12] André Vlerick had his own view of the aim of his pro-Pretoria group, which he chaired for 13 years: 'Protea does not turn the clock back, but turns it in a good direction.'[13]

The 142 founding members of Protea all had political clout; 46 of them were mostly centre-right members of the Belgian parliament.[14] Although attempts to recruit members of the judiciary to their ranks were stymied by the Ministry of Justice, numerous prominent bankers and business people joined in droves.[15] As the authors of an investigative book said at the time, 'Many of them are plain racists, others are naïve, motivated by sentiments such as tribal and language ties. Many others know exactly what this is all about. They are the investors and the bankers, all of whom wish for no fundamental change to happen in Southern Africa.'[16]

There is evidence that illicit funds from the Information Scandal were used to finance Protea. Former BOSS agent Gordon Winter told the Belgian magazine *Knack*, 'Protea does not need to know where the money comes from. It is sufficient that one or two men know.'[17] Protea published crude propaganda in its rag *Zuid-Afrika*. In 1987 it featured an article on Archbishop Desmond Tutu, titled 'Angel of peace or wolf in sheep's clothing?', accompanied by a drawing showing Tutu holding a cross-shaped wooden box, which, when opened, revealed a dagger.[18]

Protea did not exist in isolation. It was one of nine national bodies operating as 'sister organisations' throughout Europe in Austria, Belgium, Britain, Denmark, France, Italy, the Netherlands, Switzerland and West Germany.[19] With funding from Pretoria, these associations were organised in 1979 under an umbrella group called Eurosa, the Union of Associations of Southern Africa. Headquartered in Brussels, this pro-apartheid federation had over 10,000 members across Western Europe.[20] Eurosa acted as a relatively loose association of pro-Pretoria groups, and Vlerick proposed a most unlikely role model for the organisation: 'we must use the example set by the professional conduct of the Anti-Apartheid Movement'.[21] We have established from numerous documents in Vlerick's archive that Eurosa received funding from the apartheid government, which was channelled through a Kredietbank account.[22] In one instance Vlerick wrote to the South African ambassador in Brussels: 'My colleagues and I of the executive council of Eurosa would be very grateful if you could, in the near future, let us know if this budget has been approved by Pretoria. Thereafter, we would like to speak with you about the manner in which the funds can be transferred to Eurosa.'[23] The salary of the secretary and treasurer of Eurosa, Albert van Oppens, a member of the South Africa Foundation's board of trustees, was also paid for by Pretoria through its embassy in Paris.[24]

Vlerick's links with South Africa were strengthened by numerous visits he paid to the country. These reveal the extent to which he was integrated into the apartheid political and business elite.[25] In 1975 he attended the presidential inauguration of Dr Nico Diederichs,[26] whom he had first met in the 1960s when Diederichs was minister of finance and Vlerick a globe-trotting business guru.[27] Among many other visits, he met PW Botha in 1983 and discussed with him the philosophy of apartheid. Afterwards, the South African ambassador to Belgium wrote to Botha to thank him for meeting Vlerick:

> For him this was certainly the high point of his visit to South Africa. He told me about the solution to our colour problem as he proposed to you, that the Afrikaners and Coloureds must integrate because they speak the same language, and he believes that language signifies a nation. I personally can't help but smile when you consider how naïve the Europeans are with their solutions for our problems. In answer to his proposed solution, I said to him, 'firstly the motto (language is the whole nation) can be applied to the Flemish with ease as they are still a homogenous nation with no other people of colour. Secondly he must remember that politics is the art of the possible and what does he think would become of the National Party if you had to implement such an integration policy.' In reply Vlerick admitted that he had not thought of that. However, we should not judge him too harshly, he does very good work for South Africa here [in Belgium] and is prepared to stand up and step into the breach for us.[28]

The Belgian king conferred the title of Baron on Vlerick in 1985.[29] For his efforts the South African government awarded him the Order of Good Hope in 1987. The citation read, 'Professor Vlerick is invaluable to the relationship between the Republic and Belgium, as well as in world fora.'[30] The South African ambassador added, 'The

Protea on the insignia of Baron André Vlerick is perhaps the most visible symbol of the close ties of one of Flanders' greatest sons with South Africa.'[31]

Boom time and political connections

Kredietbank was not only the home of the politically ignorant and racist like Vlerick and Collin. Part of its success can be attributed to the fact that Kredietbank was home to politically well-connected men who benefited from the revolving door between political office and the bank, including Vlerick, who became Belgian minister of finance in 1972 and was closely associated with the Flemish Christian People's Party. Another prominent example is Eric Van Rompuy, ex-minister in the Flemish government and brother of the Flemish prime minister, and president of the European Council, Herman Van Rompuy, who also started his career at the bank.[32]

Political connections in a Belgian province with a booming economy helped drive the bank's growth, and the future heralded new opportunities.[33] Kredietbank grew faster than the Belgian economy between 1945 and 1984, with its balance sheet leaping from 5.8 to 730 billion Belgian francs (R294 billion in 2017 values).[34] By 1984, Kredietbank was the fastest-growing bank in Western Europe, the third-largest retail bank in Belgium, and it contributed three-quarters of Almanij's profits. As a result, Almanij became one of the biggest holding companies in Belgium.[35] A key to its success was its offshore subsidiaries, the most important of which was in Luxembourg.

KBL/Kredietbank Luxembourg: 'The most important link'

A defining moment in Kredietbank's history was the establishment of the Kredietbank Luxembourg (KBL) in 1949. As the two neighbouring states of Belgium and the smaller principality of Luxembourg were in a monetary union at the time, this ensured a relatively seamless connection across an almost transparent border. As we will see, KBL was crucial to the South African story, as the evidence presented in this chapter shows the bank was utilised for covert sanctions-busting operations. Luxembourg's status as a tax haven that vigorously protects its clients' information is well known. As Joop de Loor, former head of the South African Treasury in the 1980s, recalls in reference to Kredietbank, 'Yes, we did a little of our borrowing from the Belgians ... Interestingly enough, if they didn't want to supply the money directly to us so that it was open, they sent it via a bank in Luxembourg.'[36]

KBL, one of the first banks created after the Second World War in Luxembourg, played an important role in implementing the Marshall Plan. It also had ties to big US businesses such as Goodyear and, later, Monsanto.[37] The investigative journalist Ludwig Verduyn believes that banks such as KBL, in addition to their day-to-day activities, may have distributed covert money to American allies in Europe, including the centre-right Christian Democratic trade unions in Belgium, France and Italy.[38]

From an American intelligence perspective, the political model best suited to Western Europe was conservative, Catholic and anti-communist, and the CIA worked hard to facilitate this new democratic post-war order as a bulwark against Soviet influence. They intended to isolate communism in the East while at the same time covertly taking the wind out of the sails of popular socialist parties in the West with the support of top CIA men.[39]

Banks such as KBL, at the crossroads of international capital transfers, may also have become an important node in the collection of intelligence on international money flows. Following the money can be immensely revealing. Verduyn, who has undertaken extensive research into international money laundering, argues that US intelligence would routinely follow clandestine money flows around the world, and the SWIFT international money exchange system was infiltrated for this purpose.[40] A reasonable question worth asking is whether intelligence agencies of the major Western powers picked up on questionable transactions involving banks such as KBL. We do know that at the height of the Cold War the intelligence agencies were intensely interested in covert activities in their own backyard. If they did pick up on such patterns of malfeasance and never acted upon them, it raises the question why this was tolerated.

André Vlerick, who was in senior management at Kredietbank from the 1950s, brought his own men into KBL, such as his assistant at the University of Ghent, Jean Blondeel, who helped establish KBL. Blondeel served as its first CEO and later made a significant contribution to the development of a European network of Catholic-inspired banks.[41]

By the 1970s, the role of KBL within the Kredietbank structure shifted towards growing the global market and engaging in international investment banking.[42] This included a KBL subsidiary in Switzerland, the Kredietbank Suisse. The Swiss subsidiary was also run by Vlerick's friend Jean Blondeel.[43] KBL soon rose to prominence in a time of crisis in the context of Luxembourg's development. One of the most important victims of the 1970s oil crisis was Luxembourg's once-powerful steel industry. As a result of its demise, the GDP of Luxembourg sank by almost 25%. The Luxembourg government consequently decided to speed up its focus on new forms of income, and Luxembourg became a fully fledged offshore financing centre and tax haven.[44] In 1975, 60% of Luxembourg's economic activity was in the steel industry. By the 1990s, almost 60% of economic activity was a result of banking; the contribution of the steel industry had shrunk to 4.3%.[45]

Over the years KBL grew into 'the most important link in Kredietbank's international network'.[46] Given a more restrictive taxation environment in Belgium, many large and small investors – seeking to escape their tax obligations – started moving their money to Luxembourg, and a number of large international banks were invited to participate in capitalising the bank.[47] Trading at arm's length from Belgian authorities, the banks drew benefit from a less restrictive regulatory environment in Luxembourg. In this environment, without the pesky handbrake of strict oversight, corporations flourished.

Luxembourg's official position against apartheid was characterised by hypocrisy. This contrasted with its informal relations with Pretoria through its embassy from the 1980s onwards. A confidential report from the South African ambassador about his arrival in Luxembourg in 1982 provides insight into the relationship between the two countries. The secretary-general of the Luxembourg Foreign Ministry met him on his arrival and stressed 'the good relations between the two countries ... He also referred to the importance of commercial ties with South Africa'.[48] This was echoed by the chief of protocol at the Foreign Ministry, who 'referred to the present economic problems besetting Luxembourg and the need therefore to maintain and strengthen commercial ties with South Africa'.[49]

Ambassador Dempsey, accompanied by the military attaché, Captain Penning, presented his credentials to the principality's Grand Duke Jean in October 1982. The grand duke extended the time allocated to accepting the ambassador's credentials to discuss South African affairs. He remarked 'how saddened he had been when we [South Africa] had been ousted from the International Olympic Movement. The Grand Duke said he would like ties strengthened with South Africa on different levels, including sport.' Turning to the military attaché, he questioned Captain Penning about the capability of the South African Navy and agreed that 'South Africa in monitoring the movement of Soviet war ships is being of great assistance to the Western Alliance'.[50] As this suggests, even if the Luxembourg authorities caught wind of the role of KBL in Armscor's arms sanctions-busting machine, it is unlikely that the country's political leadership at the time would have lifted a finger.

In 1996, KBL was confronted with a potentially catastrophic problem. A large number of internal dossiers had been leaked from the bank to officials in the Belgian capital. These allegedly revealed widespread, almost daily construction of entities in Luxembourg to bypass the laws of European countries.[51] The leaked documents suggested that in the absence of effective regulation and enforcement, Kredietbank had created its own fiscal 'paradise' in Luxembourg.[52]

In the wake of the explosive information in the KBL dossiers, it is perplexing that the Belgian prosecutors commenced an investigation into Kredietbank, but not into KBL. This strategy protected KBL from Belgian investigators and meant that the mighty Kredietbank would bear the brunt of the scrutiny.[53] The investigation dragged on for years without any successful prosecution. It seems that both Luxembourg and Kredietbank were almost untouchable at this time: the tiny European country and the mighty Belgian bank serviced a powerful network of political and private interests across the globe.

Kredietbank's South African business

Deeply politicised institutions are usually the first to bang on about their impartiality. During apartheid, fair-minded and non-judgemental impartiality was touted as some kind of escape clause from culpability for those that aligned themselves with the regime, from institutions of faith to institutions of money. In contrast, the popular British band Dire Straits donated their profits from record sales in South Africa to Amnesty International in 1982. 'You can't ignore the fact that when you're working in rock & roll, you're working in a political framework. You have to stand up and say, "We don't like what's going on over there." … You have to put your money where your mouth is.'[54] Kredietbank, along with many other banks, put its money where its mouth was and bet in favour of apartheid.

The bank's financial interests in South Africa date to at least 1960. An examination of documents from André Vlerick's archive reveals the bank's extensive investments in the country, particularly focused on gold and diamond mining. And they were planning for the long haul. Their 7% holding in the Western Reefs mines at Klerksdorp, for example, was seen as a good 30-year life cycle investment in good-quality gold.[55] In addition to investments in South Africa, Kredietbank was an important lender to South African state entities from the 1960s, and at least to the end of the 1980s it provided many such loans. A 1974 annual report, for example, details major loans to South African state-owned corporations, including Eskom, Iscor and the government itself, totalling $624 million in the period 1967–74. This constituted approximately 13% of the bank's loans for the entire period from 1961 to 1975.[56] Even the nuclear power station at Koeberg was co-financed by KBL.[57]

Throughout the 1970s and 1980s, at the height of apartheid repression and military activity, Kredietbank and its various subsidiaries were deeply engaged as participants and lead agents in organising credit lines for the regime in Pretoria and its various state-owned entities. A study commissioned by the World Council of Churches identified 17 loans to South African state entities between 1982 and 1984.[58] These totalled more than R36 billion in 2017 value, with KBL appearing most frequently as a creditor.

The role of Belgian banks in aiding apartheid was further confirmed by the United Nations Centre Against Apartheid in 1984. Their research listed the top 30 lenders to South Africa, given the catchy name the 'dirty thirty'.[59] Belgium was the sixth-largest source of loans to South Africa, and Kredietbank was among the most important of the Belgian banks.[60] The top four lenders to Pretoria at the time were identified as UBS (Switzerland), Citicorp (USA), Kredietbank (Belgium) and Dresdner Bank (West Germany).[61]

The banks were also eager to do business with the bantustans, which for ideological reasons Vlerick had personally committed to 'assist'. In June 1982, Bophuthatswana raised $10 million under the lead management of Kredietbank International Group.[62] The credit crisis facing Pretoria in 1986 meant that there was a lull in new loans during this period. Despite this, according to the Belgian Banking Commission, Kredietbank loans to South Africa still amounted to 20.9 billion Belgian francs in 1985 and 12.2 billion in 1986.[63]

As we saw earlier, another bank in Kredietbank's stable, Kredietbank Suisse, was run by one of Vlerick's long-standing associates, his former assistant at the University of Ghent, Jean Blondeel, who was also a director of KBL and a member of Protea. In the Swiss capital of Bern, I found copies of the annual financial statements of this bank. They reveal that the Swiss Banking Supervisory Authority took a special interest in Kredietbank Suisse because 20% of its loan portfolio was destined for South Africa. Swiss oversight authorities noted hefty loans, such as R175 million to Volkskas Bank (with all its ties to the apartheid regime).[64] In 1982, South Africa was the second-largest recipient of loans from Kredietbank Suisse at 7 million Swiss francs, which included participation in a $250 million loan to the South African government and loans to the Bophuthatswana National Development Corporation. By 1983, South Africa constituted approximately 10% of loans by geographic area made by Kredietbank Suisse. By 1987, approximately 20% of loans made by Kredietbank Suisse were intended for South African public institutions, including to Volkskas and the governments of South Africa and Transkei.[65]

The extent of support from Belgian banks to the apartheid regime did not go unnoticed or unchallenged. The World Council of Churches, which had published the 'dirty thirty' list, was particularly vocal in its criticism of banks that provided credit to Pretoria. They organised a Commission on Justice and Peace, part of whose investigations involved discussions with four Belgian banks regarding the impact of their investments in South Africa.[66] The discussions were described as 'mostly polite but not positive discussions. The main sticking point was the so-called "efficiency principle" of the banks, the problem of banking secrecy and the almost uncontrollable power concentration within the banking sector.'[67] A few banks were responsive. The Amsterdam–Rotterdam bank WMRO announced in 1977 that they would no longer loan money to the South African government or state-owned enterprises.[68] The AMRO bank also called for fundamental changes and an end to legislation supporting racism. These banks were, however, in the minority and most did little to alter their behaviour. Other banks, such as Kredietbank, instead chose to ramp up their assistance to South Africa after sanctions were introduced.

Kredietbank and Armscor: Inside the arms money machine

*'This represents one of the most important global
money laundering schemes ever.'*
– PROFESSOR MARK PIETH, LAW FACULTY,
UNIVERSITY OF BASEL[69]

How do you build an international money-laundering network?

Armscor fostered a network of individuals and organisations around the world that all became links in a chain of weapons supply and covert cash flow. But there were significant obstacles Armscor faced on three fronts: the global anti-apartheid movement was gaining traction in many countries; governments and arms dealers could 'leak' such information as a way of damaging rivals in third companies or countries; and investigative journalists were eager to expose what was a crime and a violation of the UN embargo. Another weakness was that, despite a massive economic commitment to domestic weapons development, the regime also needed to buy new technology, equipment and expertise from abroad. Armscor would never have been able to build its arsenal of weapons without external intervention, regardless of what reams of propaganda suggested at the time.

How did the South African regime respond? It did so in five different, mutually supporting ways.

Firstly, it made laws that criminalised any reporting of weapons procurement and aspects of sanctions busting.[70] This protected local arms manufacturers, Armscor, domestic banks and the South African Reserve Bank in equal measure. Consequently, as we will show, orders for weapons could be placed by Armscor from South Africa, and cash channelled through commercial banks such as Volkskas, with the requisite oversight by the Reserve Bank in absolute secrecy. One such law was the Special Defence Account Act. The Act gave the government the right to classify the auditor general's reports that dealt with the Special Defence Account, a secret account that did not need to disclose item-by-item expenditure to the public. The Act, distressingly, remains in place today, and was one of the means by which malfeasance in the 1999 post-apartheid arms deal was covered up.

Secondly, Armscor put in place a system of front companies across the world that could act as a camouflage for such transactions. This was made possible by the emergence of offshore tax havens, first in Europe and European dependencies, and eventually in countries across the globe. Two small countries in particular, Panama in Central America and the West African state of Liberia, were and remain almost impenetrable to outsiders trying to sniff around the complex fronts operating from these jurisdictions. The Panama Papers have revealed that, just by scratching the surface regarding the role of one law firm, a treasure trove of secrets can come tumbling out.

This was not Pretoria's first attempt at creating such an elaborate scheme. The Information Scandal that was exposed in 1978 used a similar, albeit less sophisticated, web of front companies to generate propaganda across the globe. Officially these fronts were shut down by PW Botha's government. Secretly, however, PW Botha's military created a new money-laundering scheme of a magnitude that dwarfed the Information Scandal as we shall show. The new scheme was more sophisticated, secretive and global in reach.

Thirdly, the way money moved around the world began to change. By the late 1970s business had started moving into a rapid phase of integration, with the beginnings of an accelerated process of financial globalisation. One of the greatest enablers and beneficiaries of this system has been international banks. For the first time, they could almost seamlessly shift cash between people, corporations and countries by means of electronic transactions. Where limited controls were in place, it made the business of crime far easier. Despite attempts at regulation over the past 20 years, the sheer volume of transactions makes it nearly impossible to police – unless you have the capacity of an intelligence agency.

Fourthly, the apartheid scheme required the tacit support of foreign intelligence agencies, which expend a great amount of resources following such money trails. Many of the most well-resourced intelligence agencies in the world must at some stage have had an inkling of the scheme, to which they turned a blind eye. There are numerous reasons for this. Some are commercial and in the interests of their domestic defence sector. Another is that they regarded the apartheid regime as a covert ally or simply, cynically, monitored the operation in the hope that it would lead them to an even bigger fish involving their real 'enemy'. Whatever the reasons, their silence was an act of complicity. An outspoken South African anti-apartheid activist, with intimate knowledge of the security sector, and who was imprisoned for years by the apartheid regime, said to me: 'They knew, the Americans and the British intelligence. If they didn't they were wilfully negligent. If they did, they were knowingly complicit.' At a function hosted by one of these governments, I asked the distinguished man, with little to fear, whether I could attribute this quote to him. He bit into his canapé and mumbled emphatically 'No, absolutely not!' before walking away. Fear still lurks.

Fifthly, apartheid could rely on complicit banks that had made it their business to provide secretive banking services to the rich and criminal around the world. It should be clear from the outset that there were dozens of banks that played such a role. However, only one bank, according to the evidence we collected for this book, actively helped establish the architecture of front accounts and front companies in Panama and Liberia without which the scheme would never have worked. This was Kredietbank and its subsidiary, Kredietbank Luxembourg.

How then do you crack open such an enterprise more than two decades after the end of apartheid?

The origin of this investigation was fortuitous, but required much perseverance. It started with a Portuguese arms dealer, Jorge Pinhol. Pinhol has, for nearly 30 years, been fighting a claim for a sizeable commission he believes Armscor owes him for sanctions busting in the acquisition of helicopters for the SADF.[71] The size of the potential payout – up to R5 billion – has meant that he has pursued his fortune relentlessly from courts in South Africa to France, Portugal and Belgium. It is worth noting that while Pinhol's claim has been vigorously contested by Armscor, Kredietbank and the French arms company Aérospatiale, the existence of the alleged sanctions-busting network (involving Armscor, KBL and the arms companies) has not been challenged by any of these parties. In fact, Armscor has noted the dispute in a number of its annual reports over the past 20 years but never argued that the underlying structure alleged by Pinhol might be a fiction.

The court cases, in turn, have left a scattering of court papers which can be pieced together. In addition, two sources provided substantial documentary evidence showing bank account information, details of front companies, transactions and witness statements that form the basis of the findings below. The material in this chapter draws primarily from affidavits from former Armscor officials and international banking and money-laundering experts. The witness statements, mostly signed and certified, in particular provide a rich vein of the material.

Colleagues and I spent many weeks poring over spreadsheets to try to verify some of the information contained in these documents. They include lists of bank names, account numbers and specific transactions. Some of the material is a forensic investigator's dream, even if at least one accountant pushed the material back to me, indicating that the stuff was far too dense. We will save you the overwhelming detail.

The hundreds of pages reveal staggering evidence gleaned from Armscor's electronic database for the years 1990–95. This data, while not exhaustive, includes details of Armscor bank accounts that were closed before 1990. One explanation for why the data covers only this period is that the Armscor financial system was only computerised in the late 1980s. The documents show that Armscor had 844 bank accounts in 196 banks across at least 27 countries, with most of these domiciled in Europe. The lion's share of the accounts were in Luxembourg (349), followed by Switzerland (186) and France (80), the United Kingdom (43), Germany (26), and the United States and Canada (16). Other countries on the list stretch from Zimbabwe to Iraq, Colombia and South Korea. In this global enterprise, 487 were Armscor's own main bank accounts. The remaining 357 bank accounts were in the name of beneficiaries who received payments from Armscor.

In the process of working through the documents, we have identified the account numbers of a total of 67 Armscor main accounts. Of these, 25 were held by KBL, 7 by Kredietbank (we have the account numbers for three of these) and a further 25 with the Banque Continentale du Luxembourg. The remainder are in banks in Luxembourg as well as Banque Paribas, Banque Cantrade and the Guernsey-based Rea Brothers.

In addition, we have identified bank officers who managed the Armscor main accounts and serviced the needs of their cash-flush clients. Some of the names listed include Dr Gerard Mergen and Germain 'Dick' Menager, both of Kredietbank, and J de Greef of Banque Continentale. These are far from faceless corporations. These men would, we assume, process payments for Armscor to buy weapons at least once a week for many years.

The final piece of the puzzle is the front companies, their purpose and the Armscor bank account associated with each of them. Armscor set up 76 front companies in Liberia, which in turned operated a total of 198 Kredietbank accounts. A further 39 front companies were set up in Panama. Using these secret jurisdictions as a base, they were able to throw nosey investigators off the scent. This was because the purchaser of weapons wasn't Armscor, but a secret company in tropical jurisdictions that didn't care much for transparency or the rule of law. The real identity of the front companies was a secret closely guarded by Armscor, the banks and, in some instances, the arms dealers who relied on their custom.

With this information in mind we scoured archives across the globe for four years for any material on defence procurement. In the millions of pages consulted we were able to verify some of the source material and also gained a deeper understanding of Kredietbank's role in providing loans to Armscor and its involvement in clandestine transactions. Many of the people we identified in these documents have declined to be interviewed – even with their identities withheld. Armscor has, with the exception of some information, been unyielding in releasing documents that could shed real light on these relations. It is as if the securocrats and the old men who used to work the system fear the money secrets the most.

However, every now and then in the millions of pages consulted a sliver of information is revealed. A real gem is an Armscor top management report from 1980 which reveals that its accounts at KBL were being used to such an extent to make payments to suppliers that Armscor was worried it was becoming over-reliant on Kredietbank Luxembourg. It noted: 'As a result of circumstances, the [Armscor] Paris office made significant use of the services of Kredietbank Luxembourg to make payments. The high concentration of payments through this channel is regarded as risky in the event that the implicated individuals at the bank should be identified.'[72]

During the process of this research I approached most of the men whose affidavits I quote from, with little success. Daniel Loubser, through his lawyer, denied a request. Martin Steynberg did not respond to repeated phone calls. Tonie de Klerk's wife indicated that her husband was not well and enquiries by another party had upset him so much that he slept with a gun under his pillow. Raymond Pretorius, an alert and defensive-sounding man, declined an interview, as he could no longer recall what happened 22 years ago. John Hare indicated by email that he would need formal authorisation to participate in an interview, given the classified nature of Armscor's work. This cast of Armscor characters is introduced in more detail in what follows.

Finally, I contacted Kredietbank's archive on the recommendation of the Belgian National Archive before a trip to Brussels. I requested access to any records concerning the bank's dealings with South Africa and was informed by email that 'our archives are private and the period you are doing research on is too recent to be public. I can't help you in this matter.'[73] Despite this long list of refusals, the documents nevertheless still shed much light and reveal information that has never been disclosed publicly before in any great detail.

Armscor in Paris: The paymasters

From 1977, Armscor put in place a scheme to actively combat sanctions. When the SADF placed orders for weapons, its arms corporation would either manufacture them or secretly procure them (or the necessary technology) abroad. The Armscor headquarters in Pretoria ensured the release of cash from Volkskas bank accounts, through the South African Reserve Bank, and then for onward disbursement through a money-laundering scheme that boggles the mind.

However, possibly the most important and sensitive node in the Armscor network was located in Paris, which we will discuss in much more detail in Chapter 6. This was the largest Armscor office outside South Africa, known as the Technical Council. It consisted of up to 30 Armscor staff members, housed in a secret floor of the South African embassy. It placed orders for weapons across Europe and much of the world, working in tandem with an office in Tel Aviv and project offices and smaller offices across the globe.

Daniel Loubser, judging by his WhatsApp photo, is a man who likes to braai in short pants and crocs. Loubser was, for many years, a guardian of Armscor's financial secrets during postings to Paris between 1981 and 1985 and again from 1987 to 1990. He argues that the French government was in the know about sanctions violations undertaken from Paris.

> Pressure built up after the embargo, and things became tighter on the
> political side. The Armscor management team in Paris had a clear
> indication from the French government along the lines of 'do what
> you want to do, but do not embarrass us'. The suppliers remained
> willing to trade with Armscor despite the sanctions, they would

however always set the price higher than normal ... In other words, the suppliers were willing to take the risk of dealing with the Republic of South Africa despite the sanctions.[74]

Former Armscor employee Martin Steynberg is the CEO of Titan Helicopters, based in George, South Africa, where he operates a fleet of aircraft. Steynberg was transferred to the Armscor office in Paris in 1986.[75] Working as a contracts administrator for Armscor gave him unique insight into the operations at Armscor's head office in Europe.[76] According to him, employees of the Technical Council, about 25 at any given time, were allocated various tasks, ranging from weapons procurement, sales and logistics to the more mundane tasks of financial management.[77] Steynberg claims that Armscor operated from the embassy with the knowledge of the French government and with the support of the Mitterrand and Chirac administrations in the 1980s, which 'acknowledged our diplomatic status and gave us work permits to fulfil our duties. Our work was classified as top secret, and our cover was secure. Our projects were given codenames, as well as for our agents.'[78]

With the guarantee of a secure cover and a host government active in busting the arms embargo, regardless of its obligations as a UN Security Council member, the Armscor officials could discreetly get on with their work unhindered. According to Steynberg, the weapons procurement projects were set up so that, if Armscor headquarters needed a product, they would inform their office in Paris, which would in turn identify and negotiate with an appropriate supplier. Once the Pretoria Armscor office gave a green light, 'the Paris financial section would get involved and establish and implement a suitable channel for payments'.[79]

These 'channels', run by the Technical Council, consisted of a series of bank accounts and front companies established with the assistance of Kredietbank Luxembourg for Armscor. According to Loubser, 'from 1977 onwards, the [Armscor] top management was looking for new ways to make payments, and he understood that top management of KBL and other banks (in Luxembourg, Switzerland, Singapore, UK, etc.) had agreed to help Armscor'.[80] Steynberg claims that the relationship with KBL was originally established in 1977 – at the time of a compulsory UN arms embargo against South Africa. He further suggests that the relationship was critical 'to South Africa having any prospect of circumventing the influence of the sanctions'.[81]

According to Loubser, Armscor's banking relationship with KBL was set up initially by senior management in Armscor Pretoria, as with other banks in Luxembourg. He suggests that Armscor's head of finance, John Hare, or someone on his behalf from that office, would have gone to the bank to open the original accounts. Once the banking relationships had been established in Luxembourg, the day-to-day operations were controlled out of Armscor's Paris office.[82] Loubser concedes that the Armscor office in Tel Aviv might have had its own bank accounts with KBL, but these would have been outside his purview at the time.[83]

Tonie de Klerk, Armscor's manager of foreign procurement in Paris during the 1980s, confirms that the Paris office

> was used by Armscor for the clandestine procurement of weapons, equipment and spare parts originating in the United Kingdom, Western Europe and certain Eastern Bloc countries which were required by the SADF. As a result of the embargo on the supply of weapons and related items, it was my function to develop structures in terms of which the required items could be purchased without identifying the Republic of South Africa as end-user. These structures were generally described as so-called channels within the Armscor organisation.[84]

What did the top NP politicians and government officials know about the money-laundering system? Steynberg believes that, while the day-to-day running of the complex network of shell companies and numbered accounts was left to Kredietbank Luxembourg and the Technical Council, there can be no doubt that knowledge of the system stretched to the very highest levels of government in Pretoria. In describing the sensitivity of his work, he says that 'the trading activities for which I had responsibility required very discreet handling indeed and in the event of any problems arising, like other members of Armscor Paris, we had a special South African Intelligence squad to call upon, they being the notorious CCB [Civil Co-operation Bureau] who were answerable only to PW Botha, the President of South Africa'.[85]

The minister of defence sat at the helm of a chain of command within the embargo-busting system. According to Steynberg, the Paris office was subjected to an annual internal audit undertaken by personnel from Armscor's head office in Pretoria and a team of auditors led by two senior partners from the large UK auditing firm Coopers Lybrand, today trading as PwC. He explains that the chain of accountability stretched to the top echelons of government, to the minister of defence.[86] This reveals that PW Botha and Magnus Malan were almost certainly aware of and involved in this scheme. In addition, this covert structure relied on the auditing services of one of the world's leading auditing firms.

PW Botha's secret scheme no doubt necessitated that bribes were paid to ensure that politicians, officials and the media in Europe, Israel and elsewhere turned a blind eye to these operations. According to Steynberg,

> Armscor was allowed considerable discretion in the application of financial resources. In the operating climate that prevailed, apart from suppliers of sensitive items requiring substantial premiums to normal market rates, considerable largess had to be expanded to promote goodwill amongst the international media to keep a lid on our activities and to ensure that the case for South Africa's political agenda was aired. Such largess also found its way to famous politicians and their parties whose co-operation in allowing activities in their countries was vital. Similar activities and operational methods as deployed by Armscor Paris were also undertaken by a much larger Armscor set-up established at Tel Aviv in Israel.[87]

Steynberg notes, 'Quite often, almost as often as the normal payments, we received orders from head office, in South Africa, to execute payments without referring to any specific projects. These mysterious payment instructions came quite regularly and were substantial.'[88] He goes on to add that 'for reasons beyond my knowledge, throughout the years, billions of US dollars were transferred from Luxembourg to secret numbered accounts all over the world, to individuals and companies without reference to any specific project or contract. Funds were transferred regularly to accounts in Luxembourg, Switzerland, London, Hong Kong, Germany and the USA. All US dollar transfers were executed and cleared through American banks in New York City.'[89]

'We will need him later on': Armscor's man joins Kredietbank

While we know that Armscor had men and women in Paris who worked with Kredietbank in obtaining cash to procure weapons, did Kredietbank have a man in Pretoria? A faint trail in PW Botha's archive in the Free State, the SADF archive in Pretoria and André Vlerick's archive in Belgium leads us to Leendert Dekker. Dekker, a chartered accountant by profession, was first appointed as an Armscor director by PW Botha in 1968. He was subsequently promoted to senior general manager and effectively ran Armscor as its CEO from 1977 until 1979.[90] For his efforts at Armscor he was awarded the Order of the Star of South Africa (civilian section) in 1979.[91] Dekker was without doubt a man that Botha trusted and relied upon. Apart from his senior management positions in Armscor, he was appointed in late 1977 to a small team working in the Department of Commerce that was tasked with dealing with the sanctions problem.[92] In this role Dekker was active in helping to reshape Pretoria's arms relations in a clandestine manner. In June 1977 he joined a high-level Armscor delegation travelling to Paris to meet Armscor's government counterpart in France and discuss possible new arms contracts with France, despite the implementation of the arms embargo.[93]

Dekker was also involved in guiding Armscor's new procurement practices as sanctions took hold. In November 1977 he co-signed a letter from Armscor to the chief of the SADF setting out the options for ensuring the continuation of the French supply of weapons to South Africa. This included clandestine methods to fulfil contracts and the identification of sources and channels for future SADF requirements. Dekker was confident that South Africa would soon attract the interest of prominent, reliable weapons smugglers. He advised that these transactions should maintain a low profile, emphasising their clandestine nature.[94] This was all part of the sobering process of accepting that the arms embargo would never be lifted: 'It has come to stay and we must learn to live with it.'[95]

Shortly after Dekker resigned from Armscor, PW Botha sent him a letter expressing his appreciation for his service. 'You have made a great contribution to your country and more specifically Armscor, there is great appreciation for this. Your goodwill towards me will always remain a pleasant memory.'[96] Dekker responded, expressing his appreciation to PW Botha for his support and interest in his work over many years at Armscor. While he was leaving Armscor with some nostalgia, he saw his reward in his modest success and the friends he left behind in Armscor and the SADF. Regarding future plans, Dekker informed Botha that he had established a consultancy, Leendert Dekker Partners. It was based in the Volkskas Centre (today the imposing ABSA building in the centre of Pretoria, close to the Reserve Bank), and specialised in the representation of foreign commercial and financial institutions.[97]

Dekker also thanked Botha for his appointment to the State Trust Board,[98] a body set up in June 1979 to wind up the affairs of the scandal-ridden Department of Information, which he regarded as an important 'moral contribution'.[99] PW Botha made a note on the letter in pencil predicting Dekker's continued importance, saying 'NB: remember him. We will need him later on.'[100] With the Information Scandal out of the way and the Armscor money-laundering scheme being implemented without detection in South Africa, Dekker would certainly have been an ideal candidate for Botha's new venture.

Shortly thereafter, Dekker assumed the position of representative for none other than Kredietbank Luxembourg in Johannesburg and Pretoria. According to our records, he fulfilled this role for nearly two decades between 1982 and 2001.[101] André Vlerick's travel diary to South Africa in 1982 reveals Dekker's role as his chaperon on his visit to South Africa and as the bank's representative in Pretoria. Dekker, who was an Armscor blue-blood and close to Botha, was the ideal candidate to help smooth things over on the South African end of this international operation.

When I contacted the 83-year-old Dekker by phone in mid-2016 to request an interview, he politely declined. He claimed that, as everything he did at Armscor was governed by secrecy laws, he had never granted an interview to anyone about it. He also claimed to be of ill health. We did have an opportunity for a brief exchange in which Dekker confirmed that he had worked for both Armscor and Kredietbank and its subsidiaries.[102] However, he flatly denied that Kredietbank assisted Armscor in obtaining loans, despite the Armscor records which show the contrary. He also denied that Kredietbank was in any way involved in providing foreign banking services for the SADF's foreign weapons procurement. 'No, never, I can assure you that neither Kredietbank or any of the Nordic banks I represented were involved in this.'[103] When I pressed him as to whether this included KBL, he responded without hesitation: 'Yes, not KBL nor KB Suisse or Kredietbank were involved in this or with Armscor in any way.'[104] When I told him about the declassified documents and other Armscor source material which painted a different picture, his denial remained steadfast: 'I have no idea where you found such information; however, my work with Armscor came to an end when I left there [1979]. I had no further dealings with them through any of the banks I represented.'[105]

Kredietbank: The willing executioners?

> '*In the business which he conducted on Armscor's behalf with*
> *KBL that bank knew that all the front companies,*
> *as established by the bank for Armscor, were beneficially*
> *owned entirely by Armscor.*'[106]
>
> – MARTIN STEYNBERG

Financial institutions often escape accountability for their illicit actions by arguing that they were unwitting conduits who were hoodwinked by criminals. However, in this case, the evidence of ex-Armscor officials suggest that Kredietbank Luxembourg was easily the most important bank and willing accomplice in Armscor's money-laundering machine. Perhaps the most damning claim in this regard comes from the ex-Armscor official Martin Steynberg, who notes that 'KBL with its core financial role in the receipt and distribution of funds through a whole network of accounts handled about 70% of all our activities'.[107]

Steynberg is unequivocal about how much Kredietbank Luxembourg's senior management knew of this clandestine network. 'All bank accounts were opened with the knowledge, assistance and counsel of the bank's top administration and employees, according to the planning of the channel, and it was structure[d] in such a way that if something went wrong with one channel, other payment channels were not affected.'[108] This damning statement indicates that officials at Kredietbank and KredietTrust not only had full knowledge of Armscor's activities, but were essential in facilitating the structure that had been created.

What does this mean in terms of the volume of money? Steynberg says that approximately $15 million passed through the Armscor bank accounts in Luxembourg every week from the mid-1980s to the mid-1990s. They were closed in 1998. 'I estimate that from 1980 to 1996, our accounts in Luxembourg had a turnover of about $7 billion. A lot of money, if you consider that the SADF did not possess sophisticated and expensive equipment … One does not have to be a top military analyst to see that our defence force did not have the equipment that justified the amount of funds spent overseas.'[109] Once again, Steynberg suggests overpayment, which may have benefited unnamed third parties.

Nicolaas Palm, an Armscor programme manager, who later gained some notoriety for his work in private security operations, was at Armscor from 1983 until 1992. He also supports the suggestion of overpayment: 'as project manager, I had insight into classified top secret documentation. This bank [KBL] was one of Armscor's main banks in Europe … Due to the special circumstances … on all foreign procurement acquisitions, a premium of 25–30% was common practice.'[110]

The cloak-and-dagger nature of arms dealing also meant that a lot of cash was passing hands at any given time, with limited oversight. Daniel Loubser recalls that on one occasion he flew to Luxembourg to withdraw $500,000 in cash from KBL and then flew to Geneva where he met another Armscor agent and handed the cash over to him. The agent in question simply thanked him, took the black case and left without counting it.[111] Perhaps there is indeed honour among thieves?

One of the reasons for choosing KBL, aside from the ideological and business ties, was its discretion. Steynberg recalled the following interaction with a senior manager at KBL and official in the Armscor money machine, Germain Menager:

When the Armscor top management were considering how best to assure the full and completely [complete] confidentiality of its procurement project payments and all associated payments, Germain Menager reassured Steynberg as he understood it, that this had previously been done amongst the more senior management of both organisations and that Luxembourg had 'better banking secrecy' than did Switzerland or other countries. This was stressed as a reason to make the transfers through KBL. In particular, he was told that in Luxembourg there was no required disclosure of the beneficial owner of the account which was required elsewhere.[112]

Indicative of the trust between Armscor and KBL managers, the latter were privy to other banks in the Armscor network. If this information leaked out, it could have stopped all arms transfers in the middle of a war. Loubser says:

> prior to 1981, Banque Paribas was still used by Armscor as the major bank for paying French suppliers. But due to the political pressure, some of the payments started to go through KBL. It became clear that it was smart for Armscor to have discrete backup systems for payments and not put all its eggs in one basket. A reliable and working back up was needed, in case any payment channel were to cease working for any reason. In this respect, Germain Menager knew about Armscor's other banks in Luxembourg and in Switzerland but to his knowledge, there were no direct contacts between the various bank managers for Armscor accounts in Luxembourg.[113]

Steynberg records:

> Once a week mainly myself but sometime my colleagues would visit KBL in Luxembourg to hand written instructions to their officials and to receive paperwork from those officials covering our activities with the Bank. The Bank would acquire for us off shore companies that would be used as 'front companies' to mask our trading activities and would open bank accounts at KBL for those companies. The front companies secured by the Banks from company formation agents with whom they dealt were in the main companies incorporated in Panama and Liberia, and apart from supplying us with such companies they also arranged for such companies to have Directors and any other Company Officers based in the countries of incorporation and who would execute documentation and do all that was required of them by the Bank.[114]

Armscor was a privileged client of KBL and was known by the name '*le group special*' by personnel working in the bank. Travelling from Paris, Loubser enjoyed lunches at the bankers' club in Luxembourg with KBL's Germain Menager. It appeared to him that 'KBL's management would go out of their way to do our bidding'. Loubser never met any of the top directors or managers at KBL other than Menager and, occasionally, his colleague Anton Gaton. He was, however, aware that some of the Armscor top brass, such as Raymond Pretorius, visited KBL about twice a year.[115] He drives home the point that 'the business which Armscor did with KBL, and the other banks in Luxembourg … could not have been done without the full knowledge and blessing of the very top managements of both Armscor and the banks involved. This was due to the volumes of money being channelled and the sensitivity of the activities associated with the transfers.'[116]

Steynberg adds that he had 'developed a good relationship with Germain Menager who was known to all of us at Armscor Paris as Dick. Dick's response sought to relieve me of my concern, he saying in so many words that I should not worry as the powers that be had everything under control, both of us recognising that such powers involved his top Management and very Senior Politicians.'[117]

The secret money-laundering system

The arms money machine was a massive operation, moving billions of dollars over almost two decades through approximately 850 bank accounts at KBL set up for this purpose. The sheer scale meant that its existence was undeniable, as was the nature of the money-laundering operation. Steynberg says that 'the reducing of fund movements into less conspicuous sums and the regular drawing of large cash sums were methods typically utilized in money laundering which indeed was the case here given that the channelling of the funds was directly linked with activities illegal at the times in question by reason of being sanctions busting'.[118]

In his Paris office Daniel Loubser meticulously tracked Armscor's foreign procurement programme by a handwritten accounting system.[119] However, by the late 1980s the scale of the operation required a computer program to keep track of the scheme, given its scale and complexity. Loubser helped design such a system: 'My computer system's network was programmed and used systematically to make payments of several billions of dollars, French francs and other currencies, to our front companies and ultimately to our suppliers.'[120] Loubser describes the system set up to achieve this in the following way:

> We incorporated front companies and opened bank accounts in their names. These bank accounts and companies were structured in such a way that different payment channels would not compromise each other if something went wrong. At that time, we handled more or less 200 different accounts of approximately 120 different front companies. A front company is a company incorporated for a specific purpose to mislead anyone that may inquire about what a certain payment is all about, the real participants in the contract or payments are therefore totally disguised.[121]

The 850 or more accounts at KBL were, according to Steynberg, either in the name of front companies or in numbered accounts as facilitated by KBL. There were certain accounts that tended to be main accounts for receiving funds or holding funds.[122] The majority of the funds originated from Armscor's bank in Pretoria, specifically the Volkskas Bank (today ABSA) branch in Van der Walt Street.[123] Steynberg refers to Volkskas as a 'correspondent bank of KBL'.[124] 'The funds that originated from Pretoria were routed to Luxembourg via a trail of accounts maintained at a number of international Banks around the world, including banks in New York and Singapore.'[125]

In a further affidavit, Steynberg describes the money flow as including the use of 'dark zones' and 'jump accounts', the purpose of which was primarily to break up the money trail and obscure its origin. Because secrecy was paramount, the Paris officials would often not have knowledge of the route that the money had taken from

Volkskas in Pretoria to the accounts they managed and controlled at Kredietbank Luxembourg.[126] Steynberg states that for sensitive procurement, payments might well arrive at the jump account from a bank outside South Africa, as arranged by the Armscor finance division in Pretoria, suggesting that much was done to camouflage such transactions.[127]

Philippe Mortge, a Swiss forensic accountant with twenty years' professional experience, has examined the complexity of the payments made and the invention of shell companies in the payment system. After considering over 4,000 transactions involving over $300 million, he concluded: 'This type of operation is found in the classical cases of money laundering where shell companies are used to "mask" the real purpose relating to the movement of funds. This obscure end trail is illustrative of many "dark zones" where, in effect, the audit trail stops so that you cannot see the ultimate beneficiaries.'[128]

In addition to the multiple numbered accounts and front companies, Steynberg confirms that an important method was to make

> regular drawings of cash designed to break the trail of fund movements. This happened on average once a month and utilizing a code which Dick [Menager] and I had developed for discussing cash requirements on the telephone, I would subsequently provide Dick with written instructions to cover the cash withdrawals which ranged in size from 10,000 USD to as much as 500,000 USD. Apart from the cash withdrawals being used to break fund movements trails, sometimes it was necessary as some suppliers and agents would only deal in cash because of the sensitive nature of the activities involved. When I drew cash, often I would go across the street in Luxembourg and deposit the same in accounts that we maintained in other Luxembourg Banks. On other occasions the cash would not actually leave the Bank and in such instances, Dick would in effect take the cash out of accounts maintained at KBL and deposit the same in other accounts that we had at KBL.[129]

To make such a system work, it was necessary to travel to the European banks on a regular basis. Steynberg goes on to say:

> My department was responsible for the final authorisation, supervision and execution of all the payments, which means we had to travel to the respective countries, mainly Luxembourg and Switzerland, to visit banks and personally give the payment instructions to the bank officials. These payment instructions and documents were highly classified and always sealed in special envelopes until we reached the bank. We were given diplomatic courier envelopes and courier letters which gave us immunity at border posts in the case of a customs search. Instructions from Armscor head office in Pretoria was sent to Armscor in Paris by diplomatic bag every Sunday. We would spend Monday processing and updating project files, and making all necessary arrangements and appointments with the respective bank officials for meetings on Wednesday in Luxembourg and other places.[130]

These weekly meetings with their bankers were made in addition to visits to Luxembourg by staff from the Armscor finance division headquarters.[131]

This was another reason why the route of the Luxembourg carrier Luxavia between the principality and Jan Smuts Airport in Johannesburg was key to the operation. A further factor was the good relations between the governments of the two countries, which did away with the need for visas or public record of frequent visits to the tax haven by Armscor personnel. During one meeting with the South African ambassador to Luxembourg and officials in the government, thought was given to how visas could be issued on board Luxavia flights from Johannesburg to Luxembourg. This would satisfy new stipulations set by the Netherlands encumbering the travel of South Africans overseas.[132]

Loubser says that to preserve confidentiality, no phone calls were made about the payments to or from the bank. Matters were handled strictly on a 'need to know' basis:

All communications, both ways, were handled through the diplomatic pouches we carried to/from the Wednesday meetings. These carried the fully completed instructions to the bank for the week in question. They seldom signed anything at the bank during the visit, other than the small receipt document to acknowledge receipt of the various account statements. Later on a structure was set up for urgent papers using faxes, containing an agreed code which was on the same basis as that used with Armscor Pretoria, which was a coded telex.[133]

When instructions had to be given to the bank, the signed documents were sent to the South African embassy in a diplomatic bag.[134] Presumably someone like the military attaché working in the embassy would then carry the documents over to KBL for processing, or bank officials would collect these from their South African clients.

Kredietbank did not only play a role as banker in the traditional sense of holding and managing accounts for Armscor. It went a step further in assisting in obtaining nominee directors for the purpose of setting up front companies and providing 'tame directors' – straw men who asked few questions. Steynberg reveals the real power that KBL wielded:

Armscor personnel, including myself, merely became signatories under the terms of the Bank, which created Power of Attorney with its incorporated delegated mandate powers. The prime corporate responsibilities remained with the Directors and other Company Officers who were offshore officials provided for such roles by the company formation agents used by the Bank [KBL] and if necessary for security reasons, they could liquidate the companies and lose trace thereof 'at the drop of a hat'.[135]

KredietTrust, a KBL affiliate based in Luxembourg, was also said to help with the construction of money-laundering systems and the provision of 'straw directors'. (Dick Menager worked for them.) KredietTrust would cut and paste directors using copies of passports supplied by these straw men, many of whom were Armscor officials who had worked in Paris. Far from turning a blind eye to malfeasance, the bank was the creator of the architecture. Steynberg says that 'tame directors were supplied by offshore brokers to KB Trust ... KBL had already taken copies of the relevant passports and had no problem in putting these directors onto the account documents without more than the Paris office request that they do so.'[136]

Follow the front companies to find the money

Armscor required a fiction: it needed to fabricate dozens of front companies that could order weapons and, if probed, would lead to a dead end in secret off-shore jurisdictions, particularly in Panama and Liberia. Both countries have, for much of the second half of the 20th century, specialised in providing a variety of services that enable tax evasion and the clouding of criminal enterprises. Panama, because of its proximity to the United States and as a link between North and South America, provides a full house of services ranging from corrupt lawyers and accountants to officials who are willing to turn a blind eye. The West African state of Liberia, which like Panama has historic links to the United States, has seen more than its fair share of war and suffering. However, throughout this period it retained its position as provider of flags of convenience to some of the world's largest shipping companies. Both Panama and Liberia are also good places to register front companies, with the assistance of a nominee director, who may run hundreds of these 'enterprises' for shadowy clients. Because the share registries are largely secret, there is little risk of the true owners ever being revealed.

Let's first focus on Liberia, where in sifting through the documents provided by former Armscor employees we have identified a total of 76 front companies established by Armscor, which in turn had 198 bank accounts with Kredietbank (predominantly KBL). The name of the bank's official Dr Gerard Mergen features prominently. The bank accounts were opened between 1980 and 1992, which ties in neatly with the embargo period. In some instances, accounts appear to have been established for a single procurement; an important example of this was a Kredietbank Luxembourg account linked to Cedon Inc. for the purposes of obtaining sophisticated French Mistral missiles via the Congo (see Chapter 6). This account was opened in November 1988 and closed in March 1989, which fits neatly into the timeline of the deal.

Also indentified in the documents are a host of companies with innocuous-sounding names that were used by Armscor to purchase everything from nuclear weapons components to AK-47s. A few of the examples include Space Holdings NV, utilised as a holding company for Project Austin, which involved the procurement of electronic warfare and 155 mm guns; Aero Afrique Incorporated, for acquiring C13 transport plane engines from South Korea; Colet Trading EST Ltd, utilised for Project Buzzard, involving the acquisition of nuclear components; Valro Trading Ltd, for RPG launchers; Passerines International Ltd, for obtaining fraudulent end-user certificates from Zaire; Nimrod International Ltd, used by Armscor for marketing weapons internationally; Ironside Metal Pressings Ltd, Sinotana and Birolo Engineering, all with the purpose listed as 'Lanvin', the codename for Israel; Slingsby Trading Co. Ltd, for the supply of 140 mm howitzer cannons and parts from Clement Shaw Ltd, a UK company found to have supplied these weapons by UK customs but never prosecuted; Artifix Financing Ltd, for the supply of weapons from the French state-owned arms company OFEMA, via Israel; IPTN, for obtaining letters of credit for Project Natural, involving submarines; and Commodities International Incorporated (with bank accounts at KBL and Kredietbank Hong Kong), for the purpose of Project Hansa, involving the supply of weapons from the Chinese state-owned arms company Norinco, via Zaire.

We have also identified 39 front companies registered in Panama, for which there is significantly less data available. However, through searches of the Panama company register, we have been able to establish that the companies were all formed between 1978 and 1991 and dissolved between 1984 and 1999. The majority of the companies were closed around the time of South Africa's first democratic elections in 1994. Paul Holden has undertaken extensive research on corruption in the global arms trade. He has analysed these records and argues that 'this strongly suggests the companies, as a totality, were specifically established to undertake secret transactions, and were universally closed down, either due to necessity or as a method of evading detection, once the apartheid regime was overthrown'.[137]

Holden believes that the evidence suggests that most of the companies, with one exception, were formed by using well-known company formation agents as their nominee directors. Company formation agents typically act as the 'cover' for individuals looking to establish companies without leaving registration fingerprints, and often offer a package of company management services ranging from formation to submitting annual financial returns. The agents will most often also serve as nominee directors, with the powers associated with directors in that given jurisdiction. This prevents the 'true' owner from having to be associated with directorial decisions. However, as nominee directors, the individuals appointed would typically be held to a legal agreement signed in the jurisdiction in which the company formation agent operated (usually different from the offshore country in which the companies are formed). The agreement typically provides that nominee directors can only perform functions with the express instruction of the 'true' owners and clients of the agents. This can be supplemented by power-of-attorney documents that give banking facility access to non-directors in a manner that hides their involvement in the company in its filings.

Based on the documents perused, Holden believes that Armscor made extensive use of company formation agents, in particular four based in Luxembourg.

It is unclear whether the agents formed the companies associated with Armscor as shelf companies to be sold to the first bidder, or were set up at Armscor's behest as was needed (some agents keep rosters of companies on their books that can be quickly sold to new clients).

Considering that the companies were formed in batches, but not in batches significant enough to generate any practicable savings, the safest inference would be that they were formed at Armscor's behest and potentially for very specific transactions.[138]

A large number of the companies were formed by the directors Fernando Dondelinger, Edmond Ries and Marc Mackel and, when Dondelinger retired, Marc Lamesch. All four directors appear in hundreds of companies registered in Luxembourg, Panama and other secrecy jurisdictions. They also all provide the same physical address in the company formation and closure documents: 11 boulevard du Prince Henri, Luxembourg. This is also the listed address of Fiduciaire Montbrun, a company linked to a host of other dubious transactions, in Europe and elsewhere.[139]

Holden concludes that as a result of the wide use of nominee directors, it is not possible to extract any useful company information regarding true ownership, and especially any connection to Armscor. However, the widespread use of company formation agents, and in particular one set of agents based in Luxembourg (where Armscor conducted the majority of its sanctions-busting banking), reflects a pattern of behaviour designed to achieve the greatest level of secrecy in corporate affairs, as well as a highly organised and systematic approach to achieving this aim.

How did this work in practice?

An instructive case study was uncovered in the SADF archives involving a large consignment of weapons that South Africa bought directly from a major Chinese state-owned weapons company (codenamed Hansa). We explain this in detail in Chapter 10. Conveniently, and with approval from the Zairean head of state, Mobutu Sese Seko, the communist Chinese and South Africans (officially enemies) used false end-user certificates from Zaire (now the Democratic Republic of Congo). Zaire would also serve as a point of transhipment as the goods made their way from Shanghai to Durban. In February 1983 SADF officials visited Zaire to obtain letters of appointment or accreditation from Zaire. With these in hand, the SADF officials 'Col. Pretorius and Mr Otter ... will be appointed in writing to conclude the contract with Norinco [the Chinese state-owned arms company] on behalf of Zaire, by means of the company Adam Export'.[140]

In the SADF archive we found two invoices, for $2 million and $567,500, to be paid to Adam Export for the fraudulent end-user certificates.[141] According to the invoice, dated nearly one year later, payment was to be made to accounts with KBL. The purchase of the weapons from the state-owned China North Industries Corporation (Norinco) included small arms, ammunition, rocket launchers, grenades, mortars, mines, missiles, explosives and bombs.[142]

Banking records obtained in the course of this investigation reveal further links between Armscor and the company Adam Export. In records that describe the system of front companies and bank accounts to cover payments made by Armscor, there is an innocuous-looking entry for a company called Geuther Sales Inc. This company is registered in Panama, and its purpose is listed as 'Director from Adam Export'.[143]

Loans to Armscor

In addition to the money-laundering system, Armscor had links to banks that provided the arms manufacturer with loans that have, until now, been shrouded in absolute secrecy. This contradicts the conventional wisdom that all Armscor financing was made directly by the SADF from its Special Defence Account. A declassified secret Armscor report from 1980 shows that Armscor was itself an active player in international credit markets, obtaining significant amounts of credit from various private international banks.[144] These loans were anything but ordinary financial transactions, because loaning money to Armscor effectively made the banks complicit in busting the arms embargo. If this had been made public at the time, it is likely that public outcry would have led to government intervention to stop the practice. The total value of the revolving credit loans we were able to identify was R57 million (over R1.1 billion in 2017 value). Some of these loans were for a period of up to five years, suggesting that the creditors were committed to financing the South African war effort for at least half a decade.[145] Declassified, heavily redacted documents released by Armscor show that the practice of undertaking loans continued until at least 1987.

A key creditor in this market in the early 1980s was KBL, with most of its loans managed by its South African agent, Volkskas. Kredietbank made up 25% of Armscor's foreign loan portfolio as at 20 September 1980, being the single biggest source of loans to Armscor in this period.[146] Financing arms development seems to have been part of Kredietbank business at the time. Records show that its Luxembourg subsidiary managed a $60 million syndicated bond facility for the US Lockheed Corporation at about the same time.[147] It is not inconceivable that the secretive loans to Armscor could have been used as conduits for all manner of clandestine payments to Kredietbank.

A former top Treasury official from the 1980s, Joop de Loor, confirms that such loans could not have been entered into by Armscor without the approval of the South African ministers of defence and finance and, ultimately, the state president. This suggests that complicity in such loans did not only involve the top officials in the bank but also the South African head of state and two of his most trusted ministers.[148]

The motive is profit

The affidavits and leaked financial documents that inform our story have also been examined and considered by several experts in the European banking community. These experts, from varied backgrounds, all concur that the system put in place and maintained by Kredietbank was a typical, albeit egregious, form of money laundering. They further agree that the bank had explicit knowledge of the system's construction, and that the behaviour was unambiguously in violation of international law and contrary to banking best practice. It was done in the interests of profit for the bank and its senior executives.

Swiss forensic accountant Philippe Mortge argues: 'my analysis of the documents supports [my] conclusion that KBL had a detailed insight into all Armscor operations'. In reference to the 40 front companies he was able to identify, he adds, 'Each of these companies have been supplied by KBL and KredietTrust and were operated through KBL for Armscor's account, having tame (nominee) directors with no awareness whatsoever about the purchase made by Armscor, whose personnel were mandated to have total control of the accounts under powers of attorney.'[149]

This is corroborated by the independent expert testimony of Christian Weyer, who has over 35 years of banking experience, including as president of Banque Paribas (Suisse) in Geneva. Weyer had this to say after considering the evidence provided to him: 'Having reviewed the file documents, it is my opinion that in light of the continuing nature, the size and the sensitivity of these Armscor payments, they would have certainly been known to the Senior Management of KBL, including the President or Chief Executive Officer.' This is particularly likely given Luxembourg's 1978 commitment to the Security Council that it would adhere to the mandatory arms embargo against South Africa.[150]

Weyer argues that the senior executives at the bank no doubt supported the activities of Armscor out of self-interest, having recognised how profitable this business could be for the bank and for themselves.[151] But this was arguably not the only factor at play. Weyer suggests that it is equally important to note that the behaviour of KBL is typical of small to mid-sized banks engaged in generating profit aggressively. It is not a sufficient argument to suggest that the behaviour of the bank was standard practice for the time, as there was growing awareness of issues around this kind of criminality during this period in the banking world.

> In my professional experience, small and mid-sized banks would often
> attempt to grow by engaging in sensitive or marginal business areas,

where the possibility of gain for the bank was greater. Such smaller banks did not have the opportunity or capacity to undertake substantial wealth management activities nor important trade financing work ... Such small and mid-sized bank could also grow by accepting more sensitive types of business. It was recognized that assisting clients to achieve certain corporate endeavours, including for example tax reduction or avoidance of currency exchange restrictions, could carry risks for the bank and its officers as well as for the clients.[152]

He goes on to add that while anti-money laundering laws were playing catch-up with illicit practice during this period, 'international banks in Europe were [from] the early 1980s aware of serious concerns relating to laundering of criminal proceeds, especially those from drug-related crimes, arms trades, and were establishing internal controls to avoid any participation in such matters'.[153]

A violation of international law

Professor Mark Pieth of Basel University is an international expert in economic crime. He has served as chairman of the OECD's Working Group on Bribery in International Business Transactions for almost two decades and was appointed by the UN secretary general to act as a member of the Independent Inquiry Committee into the Oil-for-Food Program of the UN in Iraq together with Paul Volcker and Richard Goldstone in the mid-2000s.[154]

Pieth considers the evidence of Kredietbank's involvement in the arms money machine to be damning:

If it were true, as the former employees of Armscor suggest, that KBL served as a deliberate conduit for 70% of the clandestine trade conducted by the European central [office] of Armscor, hidden in its Paris embassy, opening and using up to 850 shell corporations, this would be one of the most serious forms of sanctions violation registered so far: together with those selling the goods and those serving as clandestine routes for the goods, the financial channel is a fundamental part of the conspiracy to subvert the UN Security Council Resolution 418 ... For a bank to be one of the cornerstones of undermining the sanctions against an entire country is a very serious matter.[155]

Pieth argues that such behaviour is tantamount to the sale of weapons and would have been stopped by the regulators at the time had they detected this offence. He believes that in evaluating the system, judgement cannot be based on a narrow, technical definition of the law, focusing on which anti-money laundering provisions were in place at the time. 'A bank that deliberately channels billions of dollars of then undoubtedly illegal payments through its system does not offer the requirements of an "honorable" and "experienced" professional. This is an obvious offence against the rule of "fit and proper conduct". Exactly this type of conduct was meant, when the first prudential instruments asked financial centers to prevent the abuse of its financial institutions for the transfer of funds of criminal origin.'[156] In a very serious instance like this, it could have led regulators to revoke the banks operating license – which, of course, never happened.[157]

Former Swiss banker Christian Weyer agrees that the consequences for KBL would have been dire had this alleged scheme been exposed. He argues that the CEO and president of the bank would have to have known, and reported, such practice. He adds that others, such as the board of directors, internal and external auditors, and compliance officers, would have been privy to such behaviour, and should have reported it to top management.[158] It is of course inconceivable that the pro-apartheid bankers would blow the whistle. Complicity is often richly rewarded.

Weyer sums up the practice stating, 'It is not difficult for me to conclude, based on my years of international banking experience, that the conduct of KBL in respect of its clients Armscor and BSL does not come even close to meeting the minimum legal and good practice standards of a major international European bank.'[159]

There can be little doubt that the arms money machine, with its many moving parts, facilitated sanctions busting on a massive scale.

This was in violation of international law, purposely undermining the UN arms embargo and making such banks complicit in an international violation of human rights. The evidence of Kredietbank's history, its ideological support for the apartheid regime and its crucial role in allegedly hiding up to 70% of Armscor's cash over a number of years suggests that the bank and its subsidiaries need to be held accountable for these actions.

Such systems ultimately rely on people who make them work. The effectiveness of this criminal enterprise relied heavily on André Vlerick and the pro-apartheid networks he fostered through Protea and other similar organisations across Europe. These men were central to this conspiracy. Vlerick is feted today, and students who graduate with 'his' degree go on to lead private and public institutions across Europe and the world. The Vlerick family remain influential and André's nephew, Philippe Vlerick, continues the legacy of his uncle as a director at Vlerick Business School, Almanij and the Kredietbank (KBC) Group.[160] Belgian students and leaders should do the correct thing and ensure that the family name is no longer recognised as part of a public institution in this way.

Kredietbank and KBL, with little doubt, made money from racial oppression and war in southern Africa. They actively supported, aided and abetted apartheid. Accountability for these crimes is vital: not only to force contrition, but to ensure that these and other banks never fuel conflict in the same way again.

That said, the banks were not the only collaborators. Their complicity was never exposed, because the apartheid regime was reliant on other accomplices in intelligence agencies, arms companies, political parties and thousands of other influential supporters. They were driven by a mix of profit and ideology, supporting the regime with varying degrees of discretion. These allies were to be found across the globe. We start with the secret Armscor office in Paris – and an unsolved murder.

The Arms Money Machine

A tale of banks and front companies

(3) Paris Embassy: Armscor's secret hub responsible for all weapons trade with France and Europe. They managed 487 Armscor bank accounts, mostly with Kredietbank.

Kredietbank Belgium: The bank's senior managers included pro-apartheid lobbyists. They owned KBL – the primary conduit for Armscor's money-laundering network.

Kredietbank Luxembourg (KBL): Armscor's main bank in Europe provided hundreds of untraceable accounts. KBL officials assisted in the formation of Armscor's front companies.

At least 39 Armscor front companies were set up in Panama between 1978 and 1991.

Front companies registered here were used to hide payments made to bank accounts controlled by Armscor in Europe.

USA

(2) Panama

Chile

'One of the most important global money-laundering schemes ever'

~ Professor Mark Pieth

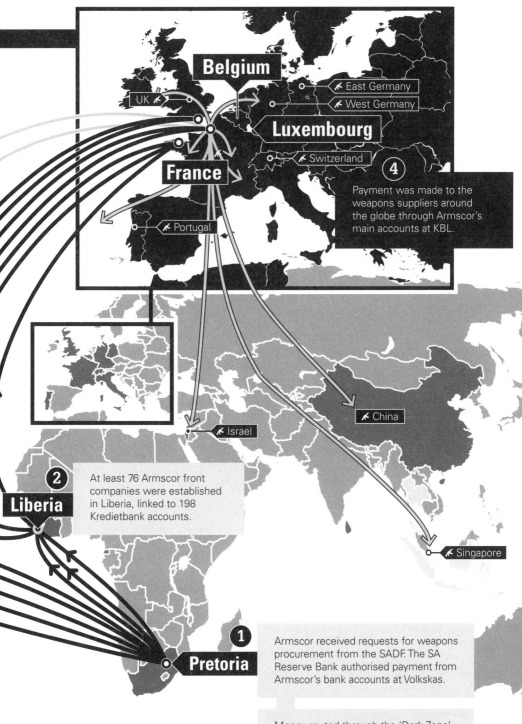

Belgium

UK ✈

✈ East Germany

✈ West Germany

Luxembourg

France

✈ Switzerland

④

Payment was made to the weapons suppliers around the globe through Armscor's main accounts at KBL.

✈ Portugal

✈ China

✈ Israel

②

Liberia

At least 76 Armscor front companies were established in Liberia, linked to 198 Kredietbank accounts.

✈ Singapore

①

Pretoria

Armscor received requests for weapons procurement from the SADF. The SA Reserve Bank authorised payment from Armscor's bank accounts at Volkskas.

Money routed through the 'Dark Zone', a trail of secret international bank accounts.

The Big Five

*'Lies written in ink cannot disguise
facts written in blood.'*

– Lu Xun

CHAPTER 6

France

*'One does not export democracy in
an armoured vehicle.'*

– Jacques Chirac[1]

Dulcie September

Dulcie September was not just murdered: she was erased. There would be no prolonged torture and interrogation followed by a murder in the veld. No braai and beer in celebration for the security men and secret handshakes by generals and knowing nods from the politicians; no need to try to cover up the chain of command. September was to be erased in such a way as to suggest that she had never lived. It was March 1988, Mandela would be a free man in less than two years, and secret negotiations towards a political settlement were well under way inside and outside South Africa. What was to be gained from her murder?

Who killed Dulcie September?

Dulcie September was born in the Cape Town suburb of Athlone in 1935. As a teenager she was kicked out of her home by an autocratic father and forced to make her own way. September, with other coloured

South African activists, was soon active in the resistance movement and was eventually detained without trial in 1963. After being found guilty, she was imprisoned by the state and moved from Cape Town to Kroonstad as a punishment for her 'influence over illiterate prisoners' whom she was teaching to read and write.[2] Following her release from prison in 1969, she faced a highly restrictive banning order.[3] Her liberty imperilled, and the prospects for freedom bleak, she applied for and was given an exit permit from South Africa in 1973.[4] The magistrate ordered her to take 'the shortest direct route to the harbour', from where she sailed to the UK.[5]

In London she came into contact with the UK Anti-Apartheid Movement (AAM). She first joined the International Defence and Aid Fund (IDAF) and eventually the ANC. She then moved to the ANC head office in Lusaka, working closely with the ANC treasurer general, Thomas Nkobi. Here she enjoyed a reputation as a hard-working, no-nonsense activist, alert to sexism, which she described as a pattern of behaviour within the ANC. 'We must seriously examine our atrocious methods of work and our attitude towards people,' she warned.[6]

Dulcie September was appointed to the position of the ANC's chief representative for France, Switzerland and Luxembourg, based in Paris, in 1983. Although that year saw the election of a socialist government under President François Mitterrand, France's relations with the apartheid regime did not seem to alter much as a result. If anything, this strengthened September's resolve to isolate South Africa, by calling on the French government for the imposition of full economic and military sanctions.[7]

Jacqueline Derens, one of her closest friends, described her comrade's resolve when we met in Paris. Dulcie had a manner of keeping secrets even from those she trusted, as if she knew she was dealing with a 'hot potato'.[8] Recently released records confirm that her concern for confidentiality was not paranoid, as the French AAM was the subject of interest by the South African government. From as early as 1982, 'friendly sources' had provided the South African embassy with internal documents from the French AAM.[9]

The scant records available in the ANC archives at Fort Hare University suggest that September undertook extensive investigation into the illicit arms trade with South Africa and delved deeply into the clandestine aspects of South African–French relations. In the process she must have developed an insight into the extent of French circumvention of the arms embargo.[10] In a speech she wrote in 1987, she said: 'in the sale of arms to the Pretoria regime, France is the second most important collaborator [after Israel] ... This collaboration in the military and nuclear fields poses a threat to peace in the African continent.'[11]

Given her outspokenness, it is hardly surprising that she was met with threats and intimidation. In 1985 she wrote a detailed memo, probably for the ANC office in London, in which she reported: 'it is quite obvious that the telephone both in my apartment and office are tapped'.[12] She also mentioned numerous mysterious calls to her apartment, including an instance when she lifted her phone to make a call and found other people speaking on the line. She listened to their conversation and when this ended, 'a telephone rang and a woman answered and said "Thomson and Cie" [referring to the French arms company Thomson-CSF]. I was so shocked that I replaced my receiver.'[13] A month before her murder she reported: 'office entered during night on a number of occasions. Lights left on. Once electric meter turned off. Nothing disturbed or stolen.'[14] The rising star of the French right-wing Front National, Jean-Marie Le Pen, publicised September's address in what was a veiled threat to the representative of what he regarded as a terrorist organisation.[15]

Then, on 29 March 1988 she was killed by a gunman as she was entering the small ANC office in the heart of Paris. There was a powerful popular response to her murder in Paris, which brought together over 20,000 mourning Parisians in a sea of banners proclaiming, 'Dulcie was our friend'.[16]

The ANC's Solly Smith (aka Samuel Khanyile) was appointed September's successor. The choice could not have been worse. Smith was later revealed to have been recruited by the South African Police

Special Branch.[17] Craig Williamson, an ex-security policeman, told me that he had been Smith's handler.[18] Smith gained access to September's flat and helped co-ordinate the funeral arrangements. In this way he was able to ask probing questions, cast his eyes over her documents and rummage through her personal belongings. The ANC Paris office was now in the hands of a Security Branch double agent with a weakness for alcohol.[19]

At the time of the assassination, President Mitterrand did not respond to public calls to break off diplomatic relations with South Africa. When drawn on the possible perpetrators, he is reported to have remarked, 'I can't say anything, even if I have an intuition.'[20] Even the British prime minister, Margaret Thatcher, is said to have responded by sending to the South African government 'the clearest possible warning that any such action would attract a strong reaction from us [the British government] ... This included telling them that we had received information that South African military agents were planning such action and this must be terminated immediately.'[21]

The identity of the person who murdered Dulcie September still remains a mystery. A judicial investigation by a French judge and an inquiry by the Truth and Reconciliation Commission produced no conclusive findings. We obtained a copy of the TRC investigation unit's report into September's murder. It had been kept under lock and key for 20 years by Department of Justice officials, and it took enormous effort by a team of lawyers and the South African History Archive to make public the contents. It provides surprisingly little new evidence, focusing on the so-called apartheid death squad theory. Importantly, the report does claim that the 'answer probably related to military links between France and RSA (Armscor particularly). France illicit supplier of essential parts and materials to Armscor ... September was an effective ANC rep and there were signs that she was putting together an effective Anti-Apartheid lobby. Thus a threat, thus a hit.'[22]

The TRC also drew on the testimony of Christo Nel, a former member of the Civil Cooperation Bureau (CCB), a covert SADF unit, who stated that 'from the general atmosphere at the CCB head office whenever reference was made to Dulcie September's death I had never any doubt in my mind that it was a CCB operation'.[23] Despite this evidence being hearsay, the TRC was inclined to believe that September was 'a victim of a CCB operation involving the contracting of a private intelligence organization, which, in turn, contracted out the killing'.[24]

As part of the TRC's investigation, the Swedish Police officer Jan-Åke Kjellberg was tasked with investigating September's murder, together with the former South African policeman Wilson Magadla. When I spoke with the Swede, he sounded frustrated that the investigation was never properly followed up. As a general point he argued, 'We failed on arms deals.'[25] This was of course not helped by the fact that he was one of the only people tasked with examining international operations. He adds, 'I and other foreign investigators were frustrated that there wasn't time and resources to investigate. We felt that there was a political agenda that maybe didn't want to get at the truth ... What the TRC got from the Defence Force in terms of information was limited. There must have been an agenda.'[26]

A seasoned former military official, who wishes to remain anonymous, followed my line of questioning with his head in his hands. It was a contemplative, prayer-like gesture which I at first mistook for lack of interest. Is it possible, I probed, that the French intelligence had instigated September's murder? I had become somewhat convinced of this hypothesis given that Pretoria would have much to lose. As the obvious assailants, they could expect a public backlash that would endanger other sensitive operations.

He moved his hands away to reveal his face and murmured, 'But unfortunately it was the South Africans ...' At best I had thought that this retired military commander would duck and weave this question but he chose to speak his truth.[27] According to him, Dulcie September 'was identified as the number one person in Paris operationally speaking, in terms of spying on South Africa, that was her only job. It was hard to tell what she knew, in a case like that you say "let's expect the worst" and cut off her oxygen.'[28] He added that she had information about the extensive military relationship between South Africa and France, and that there was a risk of her 'blowing this open'. Thus 'the evidence that she had, had to be removed, and she had to be taken out of the equation'.[29]

Regarding the trigger man in her murder, the source said he did not 'know who pulled the trigger, but it was linked to the old security police'. According to him, the gun that was used was smuggled in 'piece by piece by piece to avoid detection' in an operation that required detailed long-term planning.[30] The matter was handled as a need-to-know operation and carried State Security Council approval, which would implicate PW Botha and one or more of his cabinet members. Not even Military Intelligence knew of the specifics of the operation: 'we only knew "she is a target" and it is only a matter of time', the source claimed.[31] Self-confessed assassin Craig Williamson also confirmed that September was on a kill list, which he likened to those used by the US administration that have been leaked by Wikileaks. He remarked, matter-of-factly, that if the [South African] war had 'gone on long enough they would have killed more of them'.[32]

I pushed my source as to who could have been involved in the murder. He said it was a man 'who could take equipment apart, and get it overseas in pieces and even produce a bomb … and then go over and reconstruct it … To put it in military terms, you know, he's fucked up, but if you get him sober …'[33]

The man's name? I ask. Colonel Vic McPherson.

McPherson agreed to meet at his neat suburban home. His face lit up when I asked him about work he had undertaken in Paris. He claims that he had no agents there but 'I was often in Paris and at times would ask my contacts to meet me there'.

I asked McPherson if September was ever on any kill list. He denied this was the case. I then asked him if he or one of his agents were involved, as had been suggested to me. He paused and responded, 'I would have known if one of our agents were involved. We didn't have people in Europe that could kill someone, she was walking in the passage and she was shot directly in the head. I didn't have people who could have shot her. I think it was the army – CCB, it's their stories. It had nothing to do with the police.' He took a sip from his drink. 'I can't remember.'[34] The detail about the murder, unprompted by me, is surprising. For a man who claimed innocence, he had an astonishingly clear recollection of how it took place almost three decades ago.

However, McPherson did very soon lead me back to the French intelligence. 'You see, the thing is, the French secret service would have been interested in the ANC, given the close link to the communists in Paris and the links to the Kremlin.'[35] Craig Williamson, also speculating, says it is entirely possible that the DGSE would help South Africa in this plan. 'France is not the UK, the French secret service is similar to [the Israeli secret service] Mossad, they are not shy of "direct action".'[36] This is high praise from a man who killed women and children with letter bombs. Breyten Breytenbach also believes that that French intelligence collaboration in her murder is plausible, not least because, according to him, local French intelligence cleared out all of her documents after her murder.[37]

What response, if any, has there been from quarters close to French intelligence? Maurice Dufresse, a former senior member of the French foreign intelligence service DGSE, gave some insight in a 2011 interview in the French documentary television programme *Special Investigation*.[38] Dufresse claimed that his superiors in the French secret service had asked him not to follow the information he had collected about Richard Rouget, whose name has been speculatively linked to the murders over the years, a contact of French intelligence.[39]

Because of the inconclusive nature of the official findings, it has been left to a handful of journalists and researchers to return to the scene of the crime and sift through the evidence. Their conclusion points in the direction of two probable instigators: South African security services and French intelligence. The person who pulled the trigger, we are led to believe, may have had links to the French right wing, the Foreign Legion or one of the third-force units in the South African security structure. Their involvement would have the advantage of giving their commanders and senior politicians a means to claim plausible deniability should the truth ever be revealed.

What all the evidence we have collected suggests is that it is necessary to look far deeper at the motives of the people who had the most to lose if the identity of September's murderer was uncovered. It is not enough to find the man who pulled the trigger. This has, after all, proven fiendishly difficult for a range of investigators over the past three decades. We should focus our energies instead on the motive, as this could expose a far greater conspiracy. As much as Dulcie September's life was a struggle to uncover this conspiracy, her death gives us important clues.

As Vic McPherson explained to me: 'You must understand that the French wanted to sell weapons, it meant billions of dollars for the French arms industry, but it was a state secret, and if this woman wants to expose this, it is better that she disappears. They could have used a South African connection to do the dirty work. They would also cover up the investigation. The guy who killed her has disappeared, nobody knows who that guy is, and they will never know.'[40]

The French arms bazaar

'I see the Eiffel Tower lights are shining today.'
– CODEWORDS ATTRIBUTED TO JACOB ZUMA[41]

'I see the Eiffel Tower lights are shining today.' With these words Jacob Zuma is alleged to have confirmed acceptance of an alleged bribe of R500,000 from the French arms company Thales (formerly Thomson-

CSF).[42] The money apparently bought Zuma's silence concerning the corrupt role of Thales in the multibillion-dollar post-apartheid arms deal. A statement by the former Thales fixer Ajay Sooklal, made under oath before a judge in 2014, alleged that not only did Zuma accept his offer of a bribe, but the ANC as a party benefited from the €1 million paid to its treasurer general, Mendi Msimang. Equally damning is the allegation that President Thabo Mbeki was lobbied by French President Jacques Chirac to drop bribery charges against the local Thales subsidiary, Thint. According to Sooklal, Mbeki then instructed his compliant minister of justice, Penuell Maduna, to help make the charges disappear.[43]

The arms deal and the South African protagonists involved in the deal have fundamentally weakened South Africa's democratic project. However, far less is spoken about the arms dealers who fuelled it. The profits of this corrupt venture have all flowed to Europe, leaving the South African public victim to a predatory elite class which this deal emboldened and enriched. The stereotype of corrupt African leaders usefully deflects attention from the co-conspirators. During apartheid, these corporations and their political allies dealt with the devil; with the prospect of non-racial democracy, they would poison the well of hope.

Corrupt corporations generally rely on politicians as accomplices to their crimes. Thales allegedly relied on the help of President Chirac in 2003 to ensure that its officials were never prosecuted in South Africa.[44] However, this triangular relationship between French arms companies, French politicians and the South African government predates the acquiescent attitude of the ANC administration. During apartheid all three were, as we shall see, as thick as thieves.

With the end of apartheid Chirac, in particular, has done much to try to ensure that these facts are conveniently forgotten. In his autobiography he recounts meeting President Nelson Mandela at the Union Buildings in 1998: 'it was with infinite joy and emotion that I met him in Pretoria on my first official visit to South Africa, where I had refused to go as long as racial segregation held sway.'[45] Not only had he not supported apartheid, his sanitised version of events would want us to believe that he was all along an ANC supporter: 'I had worked on his behalf in the early 1970s by participating in the financing of his political organisation, the ANC, at the request of the King of Morocco.'[46] How would Dulcie September view such a statement were she alive?

Chirac fails to mention that he had no need to travel to apartheid South Africa. He and a host of other French politicians provided the South Africans with a base in Paris instead. It was a covert alliance that would benefit both parties. This was not a relationship between equals: France was a democratic state and a member of the UN Security Council; South Africa was a 'pariah' with a state policy that had been declared a crime against humanity. Why and how did their interests overlap?

A beehive on the Seine

The South African embassy in Paris could be mistaken for a beehive; it's a glass box covered in an aluminium diaphragm.[47] Openings between the protective layers of aluminium are intended to provide a look-out while protecting those on the inside from rocks and bombs. Built in 1974, it overlooks the river Seine on the prestigious Quai d'Orsay and it projects both prosperous modernity and sinister insularity. It is located only three short blocks from the French Ministry of Foreign Affairs, in the heart of the city. From here the South Africans could do business and broker deals unhindered, with the tacit understanding that the beekeeper, the secretive branches of the French state, would harvest their share of honey.

The building of ten storeys, three of which are set underground, is at its base surrounded by massive panels of black and white marble, the fruits of the international gold boom of the early 1970s. The first two floors above ground are meant to receive visitors and the remaining five floors house embassy personnel. The most well-guarded secret was that one floor of the embassy housed more than two dozen Armscor officials from the late 1970s to the early 1990s. This was the base from which they brokered illegal arms deals. Its existence was so secretive that, according to the longstanding head of the anti-apartheid movement's campaign for arms sanctions, Abdul Minty, none of the anti-apartheid groups, including the ANC, had much knowledge of it. Minty became aware of an Armscor team in Paris in the mid–1980s (shortly before Dulcie September was murdered) but had no idea that it was located in the embassy.[48]

Glenn Babb, a diplomat who worked in the South African embassy in Paris from 1975 to 1978, confirms the presence of approximately 20 Armscor officials there during that time. According to Babb, an Armscor office was established in Paris in 1969 in the rue de Bassano, a few hundred metres from the Arc de Triomphe, and was later moved to the diplomatic mission in the 1970s to secure an effective cover. The establishment of the office also coincided with a major missile development project between Armscor and the French company Thompson-CSF (later Thales). Babb recalls meeting officials from Thompson-CSF at the embassy. He notes that 'the French couldn't care a stuff about the arms embargo and gave lip service to the sanctions campaign'.[49]

An authorised volume on Armscor's history, titled *The Leading Edge*, provides some insight into the Paris operation. It is not to be found in any library collection and doesn't appear in any public or university library indexes despite the fact that research for the book was paid for with public funds. We tracked down a copy from an Armscor official who asked to remain nameless. This, he said, was *the* history. The manuscript is revealing even if it is omits key details.

The book was first given the title *The Will to Win*, but at the time of publication in 1997 the post-apartheid Armscor board of directors understandably felt some discomfort with this and it was retitled *The Leading Edge*. The new title was simply pasted over the old. While at least appearing less like a victory lap for Armscor's apartheid-era craftiness, it was nevertheless quietly shelved and only printed privately. The volume records the repercussions of new French laws that formally complied with the 1977 arms embargo. As a result, the number of naval and Armscor personnel in Paris was reduced from over 200 during the early 1970s to 20 within the last few months of 1977.[50]

Despite this setback, the Paris office subsequently became the centre of Armscor's trading activities, serving as a thoroughfare for all trade with France and other Western European countries. The office grew in importance as the arms embargo kicked in though the personnel were reduced to those officials with responsibility for procurement and the management of secret channels. At the same time the nature of the operation changed: it became more clandestine, more secretive and more significant given its role in sanctions busting and money laundering.

The overall result, the book argues, was that the South African government was able to obtain a wide variety of main weapons systems as well as extensive co-operation and support in developing a domestic armaments industry. Over the years, it received enthusiastic assistance from Western companies keen to profit from new ventures.[51] According to top-secret SADF documents, it was named the Armscor Technical Council and was officially established between 1976 and 1977.[52] By 1986 the office recorded contact with more than 50 European suppliers, although the process of acquisition had become more difficult, as complicated channels had to be devised for the clandestine transportation of arms from France to South Africa.[53]

Few people know or are willing to confirm the existence of the Armscor Technical Council. It is as if many simply wish to erase these memories. However, dozens of people passed through its doors on the way to conclude arms deals or returned from forays to the banks in Luxembourg or elsewhere in Europe where contracts were recorded and transactions completed. Many lived ordinary lives in Paris.

Approximately a year into researching this book, I was invited along with a SAHA archivist to meet Armscor officials to discuss a long-pending access-to-information request. We faced an icy stand-off with a senior Armscor manager who insisted that the records we wished to see had all been destroyed. While we tried to establish facts, I noticed a collage of photographs on the wall. They appeared to be from an Armscor end-of-year staff function from the 1980s. The function had a bizarrely apt Asterix and Obelix theme. Keeping it light and cheerful, the arms peddlers dressed up as characters from the comic, impersonating the small, fearless warring Gaul and his friends. The village of white women and men of whom I catch a glimpse seem purposely oblivious to the rest of the world. Perhaps this is what it felt like to work in Paris for Armscor.

Documents found in the Foreign Affairs archives provide an insight into the personnel appointments in Paris. This unexpected trove of documents, a relic of dutiful inter-departmental bureaucracy, is a record of Armscor's requests to transfer personnel to and from Paris. It also reveals that Foreign Affairs officials, including the minister, were far less ignorant of the activities of the military than they would sometimes suggest. It appears that the Armscor Paris office had a staff complement of approximately 30 officials at any time throughout the 1980s.

A 1985 letter from the manager of Armscor's personnel division to the director general of foreign affairs requested permission to fill vacant posts at the Technical Council in order to bring it to its approved capacity of 29 posts, of which only two were locally employed.[54] There is no suggestion that the department questioned the wisdom of housing arms dealers, equivalent in number to a full field of rugby players, within a diplomatic mission. They were, after all, part of the same 'team'.[55]

The size of the Armscor contingent appears to have been consistent throughout the 1980s. When Marc Burger took up his appointment as ambassador in 1991, he noted that he had 200 people on staff, of which 29 were in the Armscor Technical Council. The veteran sanctions buster later verbalised the thoughts of many who knew what was happening at the time: 'I question whether there was an arms embargo,' he claimed in 2011.[56]

In 1985 the South African embassy in Paris, in response to a transfer request for two officials from Armscor, indicated that the French authorities must have known about the existence of the Armscor

Technical Council and its purpose.[57] While this is obvious, given the interaction between the South African arms dealers and their French counterparts, it is at the same time extraordinary because it suggests that French authorities tolerated the entire operation, including the diplomatic status of some of the staff, despite the illegality involved. The short report states: 'Notwithstanding the tense state of relations and the possibility that South African military attachés in France may have their accreditation withdrawn, we have, at present, no indication that any action is envisaged vis-à-vis the technical section. Although there is always the possibility that the Foreign Ministry, when we apply for registration and identity documents, may refuse to do so, we would advise that, for the moment, transfers of Armscor personnel proceed as usual.'[58]

The head of the Technical Council enjoyed full diplomatic status, granted by the French government from as early as 1981.[59] This continued for the remainder of the decade.[60] Not even the election of a socialist government under François Mitterrand in 1981 seemed to present an obstacle. When Armscor requested the transfer of an official in that year, a query was made regarding whether South Africa could expect any objections from the French authorities at a political level. The response from the embassy read: 'No indication has been received to date from the French government which could, from a political point of view, impact the embassy's current personnel composition. Therefore, there is no reason for objection against the customary replacement of personnel.'[61]

Each of the Armscor transfer requests would include standard personnel information. Of the dozen or so we have seen, many are for younger unmarried women and men. All the officials had either secret or top-secret security clearance, providing insight into the type of work they would be exposed to.[62] By day the officials were organising the clandestine purchase of guns, bombs and other munitions, and yet their personnel files suggest very ordinary bureaucrats who indulged in their prosaic hobbies when they went home at night. Such is the banality of evil.

Yet the activity at the embassy was far from pedestrian. It was a hive of clandestine activity, teeming with women and men trained in spycraft and, in some instances, combat. In addition to military and air force attachés, Military Intelligence would second its own agents to the Paris embassy with top-secret security clearance. An indication of the scale of the military presence in Paris can be found in a 1989 budget which allocated R430,000 (over R2.6 million in 2017) for the fees of the children of defence personnel attending school in the French capital.[63] The embassy also played host to National Intelligence agents.

State power is at times schizophrenic. On the top floor of the South African embassy there existed a central cog in the confident apartheid war machine, while paranoia prevailed elsewhere in the embassy. Headed by Hendrik Geldenhuys from late 1987, the embassy had come under pressure following protest action by young communist demonstrators, who at one time managed to enter the lower floor of the chancery. Marc Burger, who succeeded Geldenhuys, described him as being terrified of assassination attempts. 'He bullet-proofed the place from A to Z ... Whenever he travelled he had a French police car with armed cops in front, a South African bodyguard in his car, and a car behind him with French police.'[64]

With so many officials in the embassy, it raises the question: who were they doing business with?

Forging a new alliance

'France was built with swords. The fleur-de-lis, symbol of national unity, is only the image of a spear with three pikes.'
– CHARLES DE GAULLE[65]

On Monday morning, 9 June 1969, Defence Minister PW Botha woke up in room 7 of the Hôtel La Reserve just outside the French city of Bordeaux.[66] Soon to emerge from the bedrooms around him were his 14 fellow travellers, including ambassadors, generals, French officials, and the top brass of the French arms company Thomson-CSF, led by its chairman, Mr P Richard.[67] They had all arrived the previous night from Paris by two private planes and were in Bordeaux for missile testing and wine tasting. It was a year since the French student-led social revolution of May 1968. The old strongmen were still in power even if the world was changing around them. On that morning, Thomson-CSF would test-fire one of the Cactus missiles it had developed and produced in collaboration with South Africa. We can imagine the whoosh of the missile over PW Botha's fedora hat, its thunderous impact, the studious gaze of men with binoculars surveying little more than devastation, and the handshakes and backslapping that followed. By the evening, the men would be sipping the region's famed Château Haut-Brion and toasting their collaboration in French, Afrikaans and English.[68]

The apartheid government needed guns and the French arms industry needed money. Thus an alliance was cast. It was to be an enduring relationship, as the director of Thomson-CSF, Gérald Cauvin, remarked in a letter to PW Botha just weeks after the 1976 Soweto uprising about the 'long road travelled together by our company and your country'.[69]

Beyond money and pragmatism, this relationship was also based on long-standing ties between the two states.[70] It was the conservative French statesman Charles de Gaulle, a giant in his country's political life, who came to redefine the relationship between the two countries during the Cold War. By the 1950s France was looking for new markets and South Africa, with its rich supply of raw materials and 'cheap' labour, was of obvious interest. During this period a number of French multinational corporations such as Air Liquide, Total and Peugeot established themselves in South Africa.[71]

The UN voluntary arms embargo of 1963 saw sales of weapons from South Africa's former colonising power, the United Kingdom, taper off dramatically. Within five years, France replaced Britain as the major supplier of submarines, missiles, radar, helicopters and fighter planes to South Africa.[72] Helpfully for Pretoria, de Gaulle had little respect for the United Nations, which he regarded as a puppet of the United States. South Africa offered the largest, most easily accessible supply of gold and uranium, which was appealing to France's nuclear weapons ambitions. The collaboration was quickly cemented and by the mid-1960s South African scientists, together with their British counterparts, were invited by French authorities to monitor atmospheric nuclear tests in the Pacific Ocean.[73] France also helped to train SADF Military Intelligence officers. One of the South African officers seconded to the French forces in Algeria was Magnus Malan, later minister of defence throughout the 1980s, who was attached to General André Beaufre's forces in Algeria during the independence war in the early 1960s.[74]

In the wake of the 1963 UN arms embargo, France's policy in relation to South Africa was summed up by the French minister of defence, Pierre Messmer: 'France will obviously have to take them [UN Resolutions] into account but ... France had never distinguished itself by its obedience to, or high respect for, the resolutions of the UN. In broad terms, it would be French policy to supply any materials required by South Africa for its external defence, but not to supply materials required for the maintenance of internal order.'[75] Messmer, who had spent many years in France's West African colonies, sympathised with the policy of apartheid and was instrumental in building the flourishing arms trade between the two countries in the 1960s. Reflecting on the long-running relationship with France in 1989, PW Botha ascribed the French willingness to trade to the special bond of friendship between himself and Messmer, as well as de Gaulle's affection for the [white] Afrikaner nation.[76] The head of Armscor, HJ Samuels, more soberly remarked that financial gain from the transactions carried the most weight with the French.[77]

Stephen Ellis suggests that de Gaulle was also looking to build a relationship with a group of emerging middle powers, with dubious human rights records and in need of friends, including South Africa, Brazil and Israel.[78] They could be relied upon to support France and in turn become a market for French weapons. According to

Ellis, this was also a way to disarm his domestic right-wing lobby. The South African diplomat Glenn Babb believes that the Nigerian Civil War of 1967–70 also played an important role. While the United Kingdom supported the Nigerian government, France and the Ivory Coast supported the leader of the breakaway Biafran Republic, Chief Ojukwu. Moreover, the Biafran leader counted on France to organise covert support from South Africa and Israel. This was probably the first time that South African and British forces were involved in an indirect conflict on African soil since the South African War of 1899–1902. Babb also regards de Gaulle's establishment of an African agency based in the Elysée Palace, to manage affairs with friendly African nations, as being 'good for South Africa as it lubricated the relationship'.[79]

According to General Pierre Steyn, the military relationship with France was more open and 'business oriented' than that with the British. 'They are not embarrassed by South Africa and hypocritical like the British.'[80] The relationship did indeed flourish, very openly, throughout the 1960s, 1970s and 1980s. In addition to the joint Cactus/Crotale missile development, South Africa bought three Daphne-class submarines, one of which was launched by PW Botha's wife in Nantes in 1969.[81]

In the 1960s France rapidly developed into South Africa's primary weapons supplier. This would not change when de Gaulle's long-serving prime minister, Georges Pompidou, was elected French president in 1969. The relationship was lucrative and, at that point, worth more than R170 million (R10 billion in 2017 value).[82]

In 1970 and 1971 at least three teams of Thomson-CSF officials visited South Africa, meeting with Botha and other Armscor officials before the delivery of the Cactus/Crotale missile system to South Africa, which had financed 85% of the costs.[83] The development of this missile system was a three-way collaboration between two French arms companies, Thomson and Matra, and the South African government. While both companies shared an interest in marketing the missiles, they also found use for them at home. In France they were included in the country's long-term defence plan – where they are still in deployment today – and have since been sold to more than a dozen countries. In South Africa they were not only deployed in combat in Angola, but they later formed the basis for developing local missile design and production expertise, culminating in the establishment of a South African missile industry led by the Armscor subsidiary Kentron in the late 1970s.[84]

The relationship between South Africa and Thomson–CSF remained unbroken throughout the apartheid period even though Thomson–CSF was nationalised by President Mitterrand in 1982, and therefore should have actively enforced the arms embargo. Records show that the chief executive of Thomson, Alain Gomez, visited South Africa in 1987 to meet the minister of economic affairs, Danie Steyn. An old Armscor employee, Steyn also co-ordinated part of the government's sanctions-busting enterprise at this stage. In a letter to Steyn, Gomez was effusive, thanking Steyn for 'the marvellous friendly welcome you extended to us. We are very touched by your hospitality as much as we loved your great and beautiful country.' He went on to add, 'I told G Gauvin [long-time Thomson–CSF director] of your project of sending a small qualified team on a European high technology scanning mission. We are ready to welcome this team in Thomson when they come … He would be in charge of the organization of the visit which I shall personally monitor.'[85] In an interview with the *Harvard Business Review* in 1990, Alain Gomez spoke of his appointment as CEO of Thomson–CSF in 1981, and the decision to focus on military goods and adopt a 'flexibility to use whatever options come to hand' to make the company profitable.[86] Seemingly his approach to apartheid South Africa was informed by this strategy.

In 1988 the SADF was looking to update its Cactus missile system with the latest technology available in the French Crotale system. Given that some of the direct procurement channels were compromised, an alternative route had been found to procure the goods. According to declassified SADF documents, Chile agreed to sell the weapons directly to South Africa and a three-way negotiation then got under way with Thomson-CSF in France. We can only assume that the French well knew who the intended end-user would be. The Chilean defence force was clear that it would only work directly with the SADF, given that they anticipated collaboration with Armscor would result in a cost escalation of $2 million.[87] No reason is given for this projected increase though one suspects some Armscor officials may have been corruptly inflating prices.

A final twist in the Crotale/Cactus missile saga emerged in the early 2000s, with a strong whiff of involvement by Bill Venter's Altech group of companies. Fritz Louw, a former employee of the Altech subsidiary African Defence Systems, told me that he was involved as an engineer in upgrading the Cactus missile system in 1992.[88] Louw was aware that the French were supplying the various technical specifications or codes in contravention of the arms embargo. The upgrade was subsidised by Armscor – and therefore at the public's cost – and the technology was sold on the international market. The South African public had effectively subsidised the development of the technology without seeing any profit from the sale.[89]

In addition to missile technology, France was South Africa's largest supplier of military aircraft. In 1968 contracts were signed for an order of 32 helicopters.[90] The Mirage IIIB and Mirage F1 jet fighters were built in South Africa, which became only the third country in the world to build the Mirage aircraft under licence, after Switzerland and Australia.[91] A former Armscor employee, who asked for his identity to be kept anonymous, describes visiting France in the early 1970s while the aircraft were being built. According to him, the South African and French engineers worked well together, with a mix of 'can do' attitude and a dislike of paperwork.[92] At the time that the South Africans were in France, there were also many Israelis working with the French in developing their jet systems, which relied on Mirage technology. By the mid-1980s Israel would replace France as South Africa's primary fighter jet collaborator.

Show me the money

In May 1974, Valéry Giscard d'Estaing was elected the new French president. During his inaugural speech before parliament, he proclaimed that France would stop supplying military material to South Africa.[93] Unlike the Gaullists, his party hoped to broaden its relations in southern Africa to other states.[94] Following the Soweto uprisings, he said that France would accept no new military contracts with South Africa and that the only deliveries would be to complete existing contracts.[95]

Despite – or possibly because of – the threat of embargo, the French private sector consortium of Framatome–Spie Batignolles–Alsthom was awarded a lucrative $1 billion contract to build South Africa's nuclear power station at Koeberg, just outside Cape Town.[96] Until a few days before the official announcement in 1976, it was considered a certainty that the consortium headed by General Electric would receive the sought-after contract.[97] As far as we know, French–South African nuclear collaboration was limited to the energy sector.

While travelling in Mali in February 1977, Giscard d'Estaing declared that France would implement a total ban on sales or transfers of ground or air equipment of a military character to South Africa.[98] However, instructions to implement the embargo were temporarily withheld by the reliable French prime minister, Jacques Chirac, who did not see eye to eye with his president on this issue.[99] Finally, on 9 August 1977, France declared a total arms embargo on South Africa, but agreed to sneak through the sale of two submarines and two destroyers in order to honour existing contracts.[100] Pretoria was quick to seek new channels to lobby the French administration, and within three months the brother of the French president, Olivier Giscard d'Estaing, travelled to southern Africa. It is not known in what capacity he came, but his visit attracted the interest of apartheid politicians, given his family ties as well as his role as founding dean of the renowned French business school INSEAD, where he was influential among the French business elite. Piet Koornhof, minister in charge of forced removals, travelled together with d'Estaing, his wife and the South African businessman Basil Landau to Botswana on 29 and 30 October 1977. Following a weekend tour, Koornhof wrote to thank Olivier d'Estaing for an enjoyable weekend.[101]

Had France forsaken Pretoria? In the wake of sanctions in 1977, Armscor's chairman, Commander Marais, and its CEO, Leendert Dekker (later the long-standing representative of Kredietbank Luxembourg in South Africa), travelled to Paris for meetings with senior personnel in the DGA (Directorate General of Armaments, the equivalent of Armscor in France) led by General Martre.[102] Their mission was to salvage existing weapons orders. While the South Africans were frustrated by the seemingly immovable political obstacles they confronted, the DGA officials had a solution in mind already. Would South Africa be prepared to acquire equipment through a third country such as Argentina or Brazil?[103] The French on their part promised to 'do their best to help South Africa in a clandestine manner'.[104]

Yet while officials were becoming increasingly wary of direct contact, French arms companies were less coy. SADF Lieutenant General Dutton, who had accompanied the Armscor officials to France, used the trip to meet with corporations at the French Air Show and subsequently visited French and South African naval officials stationed in Nantes. Following a viewing of submarines that were being constructed for the South African Navy, Dutton met the navy's project officer, Commodore Mathers. Mathers would later be involved in the 1999 arms deal scandal; he was involved in recommending technical specifications for the submarines the government wanted to acquire, soon after which he became a consultant to the German company Ferrostaal, which won the bid to supply submarines to South Africa along with its other German partners.[105] Waiting for Dutton on the runway at Nantes was a Falcon 20 private jet belonging to Marcel Dassault, the founder of one of France's most important arms producers. The aircraft had been sent specially from Paris by the company to collect him.[106]

Despite the new French laws, OFEMA, the French state-owned

arms company responsible for managing sales from private arms companies in France, approved FFR13.2 million (R66 million in 2017 value) worth of orders through the Armscor office in Paris in the last few months of 1979.[107] The sanctions no doubt also had an impact on the cost of the equipment. A 1977 report from PW Botha's archive with his handwritten notes indicates the increase in cost of various aircraft spare parts between the early and mid-1970s. A number of items supplied by OFEMA had, in the short space of between one and five years, increased in price anywhere between 428% and 15,000%.[108] Clearly the French arms industry was raking in the cash.[109]

According to Chris Thirion, a former high-ranking Military Intelligence officer in the SADF, 'the French were always willing to do a deal, but at a very high price'.[110] He describes the more general agreement as being that France would ignore the extensive South African operation in France during the 1980s as long as South Africa kept a suitably 'low profile'.[111]

The Socialists take charge: Talk left, walk right

With the election of the Socialist Party and its leader, François Mitterrand, as president in 1981, the South African government was concerned about the possible ramifications of the new government. For the first time in nearly a quarter of a century they would need to deal with a socialist, who would eventually become the longest-serving president in French history. Mitterrand, who was in power until 1995, came to define French politics in this period in the same way that Thatcher, Reagan and Botha did for their countries through most of the 1980s. As an elected president he had significant executive powers. However, this was tempered by the fact that the conservative Rassemblement pour la République (RPR) party, led by Jacques Chirac, held control of the Assembly between March 1986 and May 1988.

There was no doubt shock in the ranks of the apartheid government at the election of the Socialist Party in France. This seemed to buck what they saw as a positive trend in the United Kingdom, United States and West Germany, where voters empowered conservative politicians with a willingness – at the very least – to give the apartheid government some breathing room. The first reaction from Pretoria was to approach France with new caution. In a cabinet meeting on 12 May 1981, two days after the French elections that had swept the Socialists to power, it was agreed that no minister would visit France in the near future, nor publish any statement about the presidential election and relations with France.[112] At a meeting two weeks later, the cabinet was so worried about a planned international conference about sanctions against South Africa in Paris that it proposed various counter-measures, one of which was to turn up the volume of the apartheid propaganda machinery. Accordingly, the Orwellian-sounding 'Inter-departmental Psychological Action Committee' was tasked with contacting the media in South Africa and motivating them to react in an appropriate editorial manner against calls for sanctions.[113] PW Botha's friends, expecting the worst, were preparing for an offensive of sanctions by the new French government.

While the new government and its foreign minister, Claude Cheysson, called for strict sanctions in public, he was far more amenable to accommodating South African interests in private. Only two months before he banned weapon sales to South Africa, he met with members of an international advisory committee to the French industrial gas giant Air Liquide at the home of the corporation's chairperson in Paris. The company also had a presence in South Africa, which was important as the oil sanctions impacted on South Africa's access to gas. One of the guests at the dinner was Etienne Rousseau, chairman of the National Party-aligned Federale Volksbeleggings, who dutifully reported the dinner table chatter to Foreign Minister Pik Botha in Pretoria.[114] According to Rousseau, Cheysson had declared sanctions to be ineffective and saw them as an emotional issue which he did not support. He also indicated that he would not take any steps to prevent Air Liquide from extending its investments in South Africa. Despite this, Rousseau regarded Cheysson as potentially very dangerous, given his willingness to change his opinion in order to achieve his personal ambition. What possibly weighed more on

Rousseau's mind was Cheysson's views about nationalisation and greater taxation of the rich. After supper, he and Cheysson retired to the lounge to drink coffee, and Cheysson asked him not to make public his comments but to feel free to communicate his views to the South African government.[115]

The other important contact that Rousseau established on his trip to Paris was with Robert Mitterrand, the elder brother of the French president, with whom he had met the evening before. With regard to southern Africa, he reported him to be 'conservative and appears to have great influence over his brother, the President'.[116] Robert Mitterrand, who was also a consultant to Air Liquide, visited South Africa in 1982, together with the vice-chairman of the company and another director. The group was hosted at a dinner by the deputy chairman of the South African subsidiary of Air Liquide, Basil Landau. Landau was a supporter of the National Party government and friend of the cabinet minister Piet Koornhof. Landau, as we saw with the Giscard d'Estaing family, had a knack for being in the company of French presidents and apartheid ministers. He invited Koornhof and his wife to dinner in Pretoria, noting, 'I am sure that Mr Mitterrand will find it interesting to be able to speak to you.'[117] With partners in business, access to foreign corporations and the ear of the French president's brother, the regime was eager to find ways to chip away at the official rejection of apartheid by the French government before it contaminated lucrative illicit ventures.

It appears that even French ministers were aware of the use of fraudulent end-user certificates to supply arms to South Africa. In 1981, the South African ambassador met with a former cabinet minister, Philippe Malaud, who reported on a conversation he had had a few days before with an old friend, Michel Jobert, a left-wing politician who was appointed minister of external commerce by François Mitterrand. With reference to South Africa, Jobert is reported to have said that 'they have no intention to take steps to rein in the trade relations, although it would sometimes have to take place discreetly and even covertly. It appears that Mr Jobert is fully informed about the fact that for practical reasons trade with South Africa takes place through certificates issued by third countries.'[118]

Efforts to nurture new allies was not limited to meetings with individuals but required the development of a pro-apartheid lobby presence in France. The lobby rested on three pillars: big business with interests in South Africa, French military and intelligence links to South Africa, and political support largely from the right, influenced in turn by French big business and securocrats. Central to co-ordinating much of the lobby work was the South African embassy and its four diplomatic missions in France. As in other major capitals, South African propaganda included films, glossy magazines and newsletters, which were distributed free of charge to schools, business associations and politicians. The South Africa Foundation, funded by South African business, would back-stop these activities with its own initiatives. Full-page adverts were bought by the South African embassy in major publications such as *Le Figaro* and *Paris Match*.[119] In order to influence editorial content, journalists from *Paris Match* were invited on a tour of southern Africa and given access to secret South African military bases and high-ranking officials, which in turn led to news articles displaying the prowess of the South African military.[120]

Within the French parliament, pro-South African initiatives were organised by the Franco-South African Parliamentary Group. The group enjoyed support from Jacques Chirac and other right-wing politicians, and was most effective when the Gaullist network was close to power in the 1980s, under the leadership of influential men like Charles Pasqua and Jacques Foccart, who in turn had strong relations with most African presidents.[121] Chirac, in turn, received President Lucas Mangope of Pretoria's proxy state Bophuthatswana on three occasions in Paris in the 1980s.[122]

Plus ça change

Upon taking office, the socialist government of François Mitterrand signalled in public a hard-line position banning the sale of weapons to South Africa. The French foreign minister, Claude Cheysson, declared within months of taking office that 'not one pistol, not one rifle, not one part of a rifle, will be sent to South Africa'.[123] While the policy made the open sale of military equipment impossible, in practice the sale of weapons was simply pushed further towards the deep state. There it relied on the collaboration of arms companies, intelligence agencies, and corrupt politicians and their middlemen. Very little has ever been made public about the nature of military ties between France and South Africa during the 1980s. Although the Israeli defence industry had become an important ally of and collaborator with the apartheid military machine from the mid-1970s, it wasn't the only ally. South Africa remained dependent on France for missile technology and spare parts and hardware for its air force, which was active in conflict throughout southern Africa.

Declassified SADF documents provide insights into this relationship. An important platform for deal-making was the Paris Air Show, attracting the world's most important arms merchants and their customers, including General Denis Earp and his South African Air Force delegation in 1985. He had a full schedule over three days, meeting with the top management of various arms corporations. This included a presentation by the president of Israeli Aircraft Industries (IAI) to showcase its advanced technology,[124] and presentations by various American and French firms including OFEMA, Snecma and Aérospatiale.[125] Despite South Africa's debt standstill and crippling domestic interest rates, the military remained cash flush and were looking for all manner of hardware during this period. An important example was the secret project, codenamed Adenia, to purchase 66 Super Puma S2 helicopters from the French aviation company Aérospatiale, which were originally intended for battle in Angola. They are believed to have been delivered clandestinely before the end of the Angolan War. Once converted into the 'home-grown' Oryx helicopter, they would feature prominently in sea rescue operations. Most notably, four helicopters were used to carry the new South African flag over the Union Buildings moments after Nelson Mandela was sworn in as first state president of democratic South Africa.

The procurement of these helicopters was one of the most lucrative sanctions-busting deals undertaken by the military and is thought to have cost as much as $3 billion at the time. This type of operation required a high degree of co-ordination between Armscor, which ordered the helicopters on behalf of the SADF, and management at Aérospatiale. Secret minutes of a meeting between the two parties in April 1986 reveal that their conversations extended well beyond the exchange of technical information.[126] Aérospatiale was represented by Jean-Marc Thomas (who went on to become the vice-president of Airbus France and later held a senior position at Rothschild Private Bank) and Jean-Claude Pascalucci from the helicopter division. The Armscor team included Tony de Klerk and Eric Bestbier from its Technical Council at the Paris embassy.

Aérospatiale reported at this meeting that, following the election of Jacques Chirac's right-wing government in 1986, 'there was an indication of a more relaxed policy towards South Africa in the future'.[127] They pointed out 'two excellent contacts at government level', one of whom was Jean Picq, defence adviser to Jacques Chirac and former financial director at Aérospatiale. Picq's functions included 'all defence budgets, political aspects in respect of armament exportation, [and] defence activities'.[128] According to this document, only five members of Aérospatiale management, including Picq, were aware of all the company's projects with South Africa. The Aérospatiale team also revealed the names of a number of current and former employees who would be made available on a full- or part-time basis to assist the South Africans. The meeting also discussed practical arrangements such as security concerns and the delivery of a prototype via Zaire as well as spares kits. These would be shipped through the Singapore state-owned company Unicorn, whose sanctions-busting activities are discussed further in Chapter 11. Armscor officials, always eager to trade, in turn offered Aérospatiale South African-manufactured anti-tank missiles.[129]

According to a CIA report declassified in 2017, Chirac did not make a secret of this 'more relaxed policy' towards South Africa. The report indicates that Chirac had informed the United States ambassador just prior to his election that his government planned to 'turn around 180 degrees on South Africa', and that he would 'favour dialogue over sanctions'.[130]

By late 1988 the battle-weary South African Air Force was in need of high-quality spare parts for their aircrafts. A decision was taken to send a delegation of senior management and operational officials from the air force and Armscor to France and Germany, where they were to be joined by officials from the Armscor office in Paris. The companies to be visited included the French aircraft and rocket manufacturer, Snecma (today operating as the multinational Safran). The chief of the SAAF argued that such visits had produced results in the past, opening doors and leading to the eventual delivery of embargoed equipment. It is apparent that approaches such as this were not piecemeal solutions but rather part of an ongoing relationship. In motivating for the financial allocation for the trip, he added that 'the inability to produce all the items locally, as well as the massive cost implication of large scale industrialization necessitates the RSA to remain reliant on the clandestine co-operation of manufacturers and producers in these countries'.[131]

Intelligence liaisons

'France has no friends, only interests.'
– CHARLES DE GAULLE[132]

The French intelligence services in France have long been the source of controversy. As in many democratic states, they have been vulnerable to subversion by narrow interests. An example is the Françafrique clique that was assembled around Jacques Foccart under de Gaulle, which ruthlessly asserted French influence over newly independent African nations from the 1960s. In the mid-1980s tensions developed into open hostility between the domestic (DST) and foreign services

(DGSE), and a third cell within the president's office at the Elysée. The split was described at the time as an 'implacable struggle' in which each side 'jealously keeps its information to itself, manipulates the other's services and practises disinformation'.[133]

The South African secret service, which was also accustomed to a fair amount of rivalry during the apartheid period, found itself in good company among some of the more conservative spies in Paris. Records that we accessed in the SADF archives provide an important perspective on the secret ties that existed between the powerful South African Military Intelligence and its counterparts in the French foreign spy agency (first known as the SDECE and later renamed the DGSE). One example of this is that routine annual intelligence conferences took place between the French and South African military intelligence services for much of the 1980s, with the venue rotating between the two countries.[134] The SADF went as far as to budget for the costs of flight and accommodation of three intelligence officials from Paris during that period.[135]

How this collaboration worked in practice has long remained secret.[136] Extensive archival research illustrates, for the first time, the deep complicity of French intelligence in undermining the arms embargo, and the manner in which this benefited French politicians. The arms embargo meant that Paris and Pretoria were supposed to halt the co-development and production of missile systems. The first clear indication to the contrary is found in secret defence force documents from 1980 that suggest that the French intelligence services would be the lead facilitator for future collaboration in missile development. In March that year, South Africa's chief of staff intelligence and other senior officers met the head of French External Intelligence Services (SDECE), Alexandre de Marenches, at the SDECE headquarters in Paris.[137] The party was warmly received by de Marenches, a tall, heavily built man who had headed the SDECE since 1970. This virulent anti-communist would, after leaving the French secret service, become an adviser to Ronald Reagan on American policy in Afghanistan.

De Marenches had a concrete proposal for the South Africans:

would they be willing to co-produce a 'carbon copy' of the Soviet-made SAM-7 missiles, with Russian serial numbers and markings?[138] The weapons were intended for Jonas Savimbi's UNITA, which French intelligence was clandestinely supporting at that stage. The use of 'Soviet' goods would hide the fingerprints of both the French and South Africans once they were deployed in Angola. In an internal memo, the South African officials revealed they had in fact already acquired the latest-model Soviet SAM-7 missile, manufactured in Poland and Bulgaria.[139] A subsequent secret internal memo from 1984 confirms that French intelligence, in likely collaboration with the South Africans, successfully acquired the SAM-7 for Savimbi from behind the Iron Curtain in Czechoslovakia.[140] In addition, a facility was established in Egypt for the production of SAM-7s, modified with Soviet markings, thus obscuring their origin.[141] If forces of the Angolan government captured this equipment from UNITA, it would undoubtedly serve to cause mistrust, given that the Soviet Union was one of Angola's closest allies.[142]

The top-secret SADF records of meetings between intelligence officials from France and South Africa from 22 to 24 July 1987 provide significant fresh insight into the nature of the close and clandestine collaboration between the two countries at the highest level. The chief of the SADF, General Jannie Geldenhuys, and the head of defence intelligence operations, Neels van Tonder, travelled to Paris to undertake important negotiations with a number of officials. At play were prisoner exchanges, weapons deals and mutual support during the last stages of the Angolan War. They were joined in the meetings by General Marius Oelschig, the military attaché in Paris. Oelschig was a long-time military operator who worked closely with UNITA at the height of the Angolan War. After his posting in Paris, he would lead the Ciskei Defence Force, giving the order to shoot during the bloody Bisho Massacre, which left over 30 people dead.[143] During meetings with General René Imbot, head of the DGSE, and one of his senior officials, Pierre Lethier, the French made an extraordinary offer to the South Africans.[144]

They would provide South Africa with three or four test models of the state-of-the-art French anti-aircraft missile Mistral. While details of the deal subsequently became known in a massive scandal that threatened to topple the French government, there has never been substantial proof of the meeting at which French intelligence initiated the deal by making the offer to the South Africans. The French officials expected the Mistrals to perform better than American Stinger missiles and proposed that they could be tested in 'operational areas', most likely referring to Angola. They added that they planned to make 20 missiles from their first production phase available to UNITA to use against MPLA forces the following year. This method of supplying sophisticated technology is a well-worn ploy by arms companies and governments, which fuel far-off conflicts by providing new technology that can be 'tested' on a live battlefield. As the casualties and destruction mount, the suppliers not only build up political credit with their partners (in this case, UNITA and South Africa), but can boast in secret to other militaries interested in the same technology that it has been 'battlefield-tested'.[145]

The DGSE, in a clear nod to the obstacle created by the arms embargo, went as far as proposing that the UN embargo could be circumvented 'in the event that a third country such as Zaire would place an order and provide end user certificates'.[146] There was no illusion that this was fraud requiring the bribery of officials, and hence that South Africa should 'expect to pay 10% commission to President Mobutu [Sese Seko] personally, or to the Zairean Minister of Defence, Likulia [Bolongo]'.[147]

The revelation contained in this document is extraordinary. It shows, first, that French intelligence was willing to provide the South Africans with cutting-edge military technology, even before it had been made available to French forces. Secondly, it shows that the war in Angola, in which South Africa was involved, continued to provide a testing ground for new weaponry in a combat situation. This is not dissimilar to the way in which new Israeli drones were tested in Angola shortly before their deployment in southern Lebanon by Israeli forces in 1982. Lastly, the French were prepared to co-manufacture a fiction, using their network and influence elsewhere in Africa, when illegally supplying South Africa with such weapons.

While the South Africans may have received this first batch of weapons, a much larger Mistral deal would be concluded a year later when, in August 1988, the French arms company Matra struck a deal with the Republic of Congo-Brazzaville for the sale of 50 Mistral missiles. This relied on the complicity of two Congolese officials – a Commandant Jacques Ongotto, from the embassy in Paris, and Colonel Lucien Gouegel, 'number two' in the Congolese intelligence services.

The transaction immediately raised eyebrows. Why was the relatively ill-equipped Congolese military dishing out cash for one of the most sophisticated missile systems in the world? It soon became apparent that the weapons' final destination was not the Congo, but South Africa or Angola. The Congolese claimed that they had nothing to do with the deal and that the official who signed the end-user certificates, Colonel N'Gouelondelé, insisted his signature had been forged.[148] French researchers Stephen Smith and Antoine Glaser reveal that 'Matra knew everything about the real addressee: a deposit of 15 million francs, one third of the amount of the contract, had been transferred via the Kredietbank Luxembourg. The origin of these funds, already cashed by the French firm: South Africa.'[149] Once again, the money trail leads us back to Kredietbank and its Luxembourg subsidiary. Professor Stephen Smith of Duke University and co-author Antoine Glaser revealed the involvement of Kredietbank in their book *Ces Messieurs Afrique: Le Paris-Village du Continent Noir*. Smith has confirmed via email that the arms company Matra challenged this account in a French court but that the authors prevailed.[150] In addition to this evidence, leaked records of Armscor's web of international front companies reveal that a company called Cedon Inc. was registered in Liberia for the sole purpose of obtaining the sophisticated Mistral missiles from France via the Congo. Linked to a Kredietbank Luxembourg bank account, it was opened in

November 1988 and closed in March 1989, by which time the deal had been concluded.

The Mistral affair caused serious embarrassment for President Mitterrand, not least because of the involvement of his son, Jean-Christophe. In March 1989, as French newspapers started to reveal the extent of the affair, the South African military's man in Paris, Oelschig, provided an update to Pretoria. He believed that South Africa's involvement might be revealed in further investigations. He also predicted that an Armscor official by the name of Wilmot and the South African National Intelligence agent Louis Steyn would be 'kicked out' of France because of their close association with Thierry Miallier, the middleman who was later imprisoned for two months for his role in the scandal.[151] Oelschig noted that there was no reason that Miallier would not speak the truth, particularly if he received a lesser sentence. He went on to add that Emmanuel N'Gouelondelé, of the Congo, 'probably also spoke the truth, under duress naturally'.[152] Pretoria initially denied any involvement in the deal, but by early February 1989 General 'Witkop' Badenhorst of Military Intelligence confirmed to Jacque Chirac's fixer, Jean-Yves Ollivier, that South Africa was involved.[153]

Miallier, the scapegoat, still retained enormous leverage because of the insider details he could reveal. Frustrated by an investigation which led to his personal bank accounts being frozen for more than two years after his release from prison, he re-established contact with the DGSE in 1991 and, according to a confidential report, provided them with a thinly veiled threat: 'I have written a complete account of this case with all the names, amounts and dates, and which is intended to unpack the mechanism of this operation with all its implications, especially at the political and diplomatic levels. I am considering whether to submit this document to court, but in that case, there will be no choice but to open up the affair again, with media impact that can easily be imagined.'[154] What Miallier might reveal could have had far-reaching implications across Europe, including for Kredietbank and France, as the FRF15 million payment via Kredietbank Luxembourg was only the tip of the iceberg. He stated that 'during the investigation, the Judge (Marie-Paule Moracchini) also ascertained that the French Office for the Export of Aeronautical Material (OFEMA) had received some thirty payments from this [Kredietbank Luxembourg] account. This fact would come out if the case proceeded to trial.'[155]

By implication, the French authorities and Kredietbank Luxembourg were involved in systemic criminal conduct. As if this was not enough, Miallier possessed another equally damning secret, which he revealed to the DGSE: 'part of the commissions he had received had been paid to a French political party ... The transaction had been filed by representatives of the South African Embassy in Paris; the tape is kept in a safe place but it would be produced in the case of a trial.'[156] Smith and Glaser argue that a low-level South African embassy employee, 'Nicolas Nvolk', who left Paris shortly after the affair broke, was denied permission to take up his post because he had facilitated the cash payment to an unnamed political party. 'He allegedly appears with his French partners on the famous video cassette filmed in the act of conducting business, complete with attaché cases and banknotes in their hands.'[157] The authors, writing in French, may well have misspelt the name of the official. A document from the South African Foreign Affairs archive reveals that Armscor had proposed the transfer of a man by the name of Nicolaas Vlok in September 1985 to join the Armscor Paris section.[158]

It is common cause that French political parties were kept afloat, particularly in the 1980s, by African governments. Part of such politics of patronage meant that French politicians protected the interests of their African counterparts, even when this was directly counter to the interests of the vast majority of those countries' inhabitants. A possible candidate for such funding was Jacques Chirac's Rassemblement pour la République (RPR). The RPR party was established in 1976 in the Gaullist tradition under the leadership of Chirac, and would assist Chirac in his election as prime minister from 1986 to 1988 and later as president during the 1990s.[159]

The DGSE report concluded: 'Until now, Miallier asserts that he has remained silent, refraining from any statement to the press because of the interests of the people involved, but that, should he be made to appear, he intends to call as a witness the French President's adviser on African and Malagasy affairs [his son, Jean-Christophe Mitterrand].'[160] Jean-Christophe is one of two French figures who escaped any responsibility for the deal. The other was Jean-Yves Ollivier, who negotiated the import of hundreds of thousands of tonnes of South African coal for French industry from 1986–87 (in violation of the embargo), and who was awarded the Order of Good Hope by the South African government in December 1987.[161] Ollivier was the CEO of the oil trader COMOIL,[162] and is described as having been 'of great use to the South Africans because of his participation in negotiations over an arms for oil deal between Pretoria and Iran via the Comoros'.[163] He later worked for the French arms company Thomson-CSF as their representative in South Africa. Ollivier insists that he helped blow the whistle on the affair, despite his close relations with all implicated parties: South African Military Intelligence, the Congolese president, French intelligence, and Jacques Chirac.[164] Ollivier, referred to as *missus dominicus* (envoy of the king) by Smith and Glaser, was also close to Jean-Christophe Mitterrand.[165] Jean-Christophe, an ambitious man, was later convicted in the Angolagate weapons scandal, in which he facilitated the supply of weapons to the government of Angola in return for $2 million. In selling arms to Savimbi's nemesis, the MPLA government, he had shifted sides, just as French arms companies would rush to offer weapons to the ANC government after the end of apartheid.

Soon after the Mistral affair broke, Jean-Christophe attempted to distance himself from the deal and said that exporting Mistrals to the Congo was as absurd as delivering aircraft carriers to Burkina Faso.[166] When the Elysée ordered an investigation, Jean-Christophe is reported to have said that the Mistral affair was explosive both for him and his father, and all but 'blew up in his face'.[167] These close familial ties in the Elysée once led the visionary president of Burkina Faso, Thomas Sankara, with a smile on his face, to quip to President Mitterrand that 'the father can advise the son, but it becomes interesting when the son can advise the father'.[168]

The Mistral affair ultimately produced a single token prosecution, that of the middleman Miallier, but with little consequence for the powerful players who had directed the deal. If it had been fully investigated and prosecuted, the consequences would have been dire for President Mitterrand, given the involvement of his son. Nor would the direct involvement of the DGSE and securocrats close to Chirac have left the right wing untarnished, and it could well have endangered Chirac's successful presidential campaign in 1995. And if the matter had been fully investigated, the exact role of Kredietbank in assisting with the sanctions busting would also have been exposed. Finally, it could have revealed the exact nature of the deep state networks assisting the apartheid regime at the highest level in France.

Instead, the affair became wrapped up in public perceptions of the role of Congo–Brazzaville, a small, 'corrupt' Central African state. There is no doubt that Congo–Brazzaville, under the leadership of President Sassou Nguesso, still in power today almost three decades later, was realigning towards South Africa at that stage. His country's involvement was therefore crucial to the success of the illegal transaction.[169] The Congo subsequently claimed and obtained restitution for payment advanced.

In the 1987 meeting between the DGSE and senior South African officials, where the first offer of Mistral missiles was made, the DGSE was in the mood to do business. The menu handed to the South Africans was for a veritable feast of weapons. They offered to provide 100 Apila armour-piercing anti-tank missiles, produced by the French arms company GIAT. In return, they required of the SADF the test results from a first batch of weapons that had already been supplied. In addition, the DGSE undertook to obtain SAM-9 missiles from West Germany. The final missiles on offer were newly manufactured Milan anti-tank missiles, which Savimbi had requested the DGSE to procure for him.[170] As Savimbi claimed that he had no money, French intelligence proposed that the South Africans provide the cash for 120 missiles and 30 launchers to the value of R17 million (R135 million in 2017 values). But the DGSE not only promised missiles; it was agreed that four members of the SADF's notorious Special Forces unit could visit France in the first half of September 1987 for training. They were regarded at the time as among the most skilled operatives in the world in covert military activity. Later in the year they would be followed by a team from the SADF's counter-intelligence unit, which planned to visit the DGSE to discuss enemy electronic equipment, as well as surveillance equipment that could be used in embassies.[171]

The Paris trip was not only about the procurement of missiles. Newly declassified documents show that the chief of the SADF and his colleagues also held meetings with influential politicians that would have far-reaching consequences for southern Africa. The first such meeting was with Jacques Foccart, the initiator of Françafrique. With decades of experience of linking African politics to French interests under his belt, Foccart was brought back into the inner circle of politics when Jacques Chirac appointed him as his adviser for African affairs between 1985 and 1987. Foccart was keen to help the apartheid state improve its relations with Africa, as 'there are only two countries with whom South Africa can conduct a fruitful bilateral relationship at this stage; Gabon and Ivory Coast'. He undertook to supply African ambassadors in Paris with publicly available summaries of reforms being undertaken in South Africa.[172]

Foccart had another far more sinister issue to discuss with the chief of the SADF. He wanted his assistance in ensuring that a French civilian, Pierre-André Albertini, would remain imprisoned by Pretoria's puppet regime in the Ciskei. The 27-year-old Albertini had been arrested in March 1987 in Ciskei on terrorism charges.[173] The Parisian was an academic at the University of Fort Hare and was close to the ANC-aligned United Democratic Front (UDF) and some of its leaders, such as Arnold Stofile (who would later become premier of the Eastern Cape). His crime was that he had refused to testify against five people accused of terrorism for assisting the ANC.[174] His imprisonment had led to tension between the French government and

Pretoria. Calls for his immediate release by the French government were met with the usual response from PW Botha's government that the Ciskei was an independent country and South Africa thus had no control over its government. As the French did not recognise the apartheid bantustan, it instead retaliated by refusing to recognise the new South African ambassador in Paris, Hendrik Geldenhuys. Given the importance of Paris as the primary nodal point for the procurement of weapons in Europe, the South Africans needed the situation urgently resolved. As the financiers and political masters of the Ciskei regime, it would take little more than a telephone call to release Albertini.

However, Foccart saw political advantage in his countryman's imprisonment at the hands of an illegitimate regime. He requested that South Africa should not release Albertini at that stage, given that 'in the event that Albertini is released now, President Mitterrand will receive credit for this. Prime Minister Chirac is eager to prevent this.'[175] Both Foccart and the prime minister of France were eager to assist in prolonging Albertini's imprisonment, despite the protestation by French officials, echoed by the French public, who called on Pretoria to release him. While these newly established facts may appear astonishing, this was not an isolated instance of French civilians' human rights being undermined for narrow political gain. It closely mirrors the revelation of the French newspaper *Le Matin* that just days before Chirac's election as prime minister in March 1986 he had sabotaged the release of French hostages in Tehran by promising the Iranian authorities a better deal should he be elected.[176]

In addition, Foccart believed that the release of Albertini had to be linked to a quid pro quo, including the recognition of the new South African ambassador and the release of a South African soldier, Wynand du Toit, who had been captured by the MPLA in Angola. If not, it would negatively impact on the image of the Frenchmen who were assisting the negotiations for Du Toit's release.[177]

On the same day, General Geldenhuys met Chirac's chief of staff, Michel Roussin, who was also a veteran of the French intelligence services. Roussin was joined by Chirac's other envoy, Jean-Yves Ollivier. Roussin turned the conversation to the Albertini matter. His position was unequivocal: 'he asked on behalf of Prime Minister Chirac that Albertini should not be released. Instead, the impression should be created that Mitterrand's actions had imperilled Albertini's release. The reasons he provided were that President Mitterrand would receive recognition for Albertini's release, and this is not beneficial for Chirac's image, and secondly the impression is created that the South African government reacts when put under pressure.'[178] Albertini's liberty had become caught up in Chirac's aspiration for the French presidency, and it appears that no price was too high for the former mayor of Paris. If these facts had become public at the time, this might have imperilled his election as president in 1995.

At the meeting, Roussin set out his plan: a representative of Chirac, possibly Fernand Wibeaux, a trusted adviser and part of Françafrique, would travel to Ciskei at the end of August 1987 and meet with President Lennox Sebe to 'negotiate' Albertini's release.[179] He insisted that communication concerning this charade should be handled only between himself and the chief of the SADF, as 'Chirac is afraid that in the event that the French Ministry of Foreign Affairs are used as a channel, this matter could be leaked to Mitterrand.'[180] Roussin felt that Albertini's release would force Mitterrand's hand to recognise the South African ambassador in Paris, and that 'Chirac can get credit for his release while Mitterrand is forced to accept the Ambassador's letter of accreditation'.[181]

General Jannie Geldenhuys went away to consider the matter, and met again with Roussin on 24 July with news that the South Africans were in agreement with the proposed time frames and methods to secure Albertini's release. However, in return they required the French government to secure the release of Wynand du Toit. Roussin communicated this to Chirac and, according to Ollivier, who was present at the discussions, the prime minister responded positively and was considering sending his adviser to meet President dos Santos to ensure Du Toit's release.[182] The records provide no further details, but on 7 September 1987 a complex prisoner exchange took place which saw the release of Albertini, Wynand du Toit and over 130 Angolan prisoners.[183]

The prisoner exchange was directed from the airport tarmac in Maputo by Jean-Yves Ollivier, who would eventually be mistakenly left behind as the various aircraft took off. Ollivier has been tremendously successful at cultivating his profile as a negotiator in unlocking the release of the prisoners, which in turn led to the eventual negotiations for Namibia's independence. His 2013 hagiography, *Plot for Peace*, directed by South African filmmaker Mandy Jacobson, suggests that it was Ollivier who secured the freedom of the prisoners and thereby was instrumental in the eventual release of Nelson Mandela.[184] There is no doubt that the former apartheid sanctions buster and arms trader had first-hand insight into the events that unfolded. However, as the documents reveal, the driving force behind the prisoner exchange was first and foremost the interests of Jacques Chirac and his clique in the intelligence community. All else was of secondary interest.

Apart from the prisoner exchange, Michel Roussin, the head of Jacques Chirac's office at the time, had more to offer his South African counterparts. In the meetings from 22 to 24 July 1987 he made offers to the South Africans that were in direct contravention of UN sanctions. He reported that he and the chief of Prime Minister Chirac's military cabinet, General Norlain, had had discussions about providing Mirage fighter jet spare parts directly to Pretoria; at the time these were being obtained via third parties. The directive that prohibited the sale of spare parts to South Africa gave the prime minister discretion in interpreting how the spares were to be classified. Roussin believed that should Chirac be convinced, he could give the orders to the French customs department to reinterpret the policy. Remarkably, the chief of the SADF indicated that there was no requirement for spare parts at the time. It is possible that he was wary of Roussin wanting something in return for this favour. Nevertheless, Roussin 'assured the Chief of the SADF that should such a requirement develop, they would be prepared to help'.[185]

On the following day, Roussin made an additional proposal concerning weapons smuggling. The French had received intelligence that French Mirage fighter planes would be provided to South Africa via Peru and Argentina. The Peruvians had ordered 16 Mirages, for which they were unable to pay. Peru planned to sell these to Argentina, which was prepared in turn to sell them to South Africa. According to Roussin, the Argentinians had already approached the French to ensure that there was no objection. 'Mr Roussin personally and the advisors to Chirac would do their best to ensure the successful implementation of such a scheme should South Africa be interested.'[186]

Roussin and Ollivier also had contact with other South African officials. Just two weeks before Dulcie September was murdered in March 1988, they met with Pik Botha when he made a stop at Roissy Airport.[187]

The new administration of FW de Klerk continued to value the influence of the network of French allies. In May 1990, De Klerk paid a visit to France as part of an attempt to shore up support in the wake of Nelson Mandela's release from prison. He spent one and a half days in Paris, which included a late-night discussion in the office of the mayor of Paris, Jacques Chirac, accompanied by his trusted lieutenant, Michel Roussin. In addition, a dinner hosted by a socialist member of parliament brought together a high-powered delegation of ministers, senior bureaucrats and politicians from both countries. Unsurprisingly, among the guests, seats at the dinner table were reserved for Jean-Christophe Mitterrand, Jean-Yves Ollivier and a man described as his 'associate', Pierre Lethier.[188]

The murder of Dulcie September in March 1988 appears to have had little impact on the unshakeable relationship between French and South African intelligence, raising the question whether this might have been the reason for her murder. An August 1988 top-secret report details a meeting between the SADF military attaché, General Marius Oelschig, and General René Imbot, now chief of staff of the French Army.[189] Fluent in French, Oelschig was invited to dinner at Imbot's home, together with Pierre Lethier, a senior officer at the

DGSE. The three discussed a range of issues concerning conflict around the world, with the focus on southern Africa. Oelschig placed emphasis on South Africa's future weapons requirements, given the need for the modernisation of its weapons systems. He emphasised that countries which had been loyal to the apartheid regime would be first in line for lucrative contracts. Imbot undertook to test the sentiment of French political and business leaders about the level of South African political reform that would be required to unlock the legitimate sale of arms to South Africa. He furthermore volunteered to brief the South African military about any progress he made, and would provide a full report during a trip he planned to make to South Africa in November that year.[190]

In 1989, the head of the DGSE, General Mermet, was fired at the insistence of President Mitterrand. This was a blow to the South Africans, who described their recent relations with the French secret services as 'excellent'.[191] Mermet's term in office had lasted little over a year, but it crucially coincided with the murder of Dulcie September. Oelschig, who had met Mermet on two or three occasions, described him as 'light-weight'. While he had a friendly meeting with the SADF head of intelligence operations in 1988, he was not prepared to work with the South Africans on the Angolan situation or commit to a visit to Pretoria. Despite this, there was a continuous flow of intelligence communication between the two services, thanks to what was regarded as a good long-standing relationship between the DGSE and South Africa.[192]

Dulcie September was killed by forces close to French–South African arms deals during apartheid. We do not know who pulled the trigger. Most likely, he was an official in South African Military Intelligence. Perhaps he worked for the DGSE. He could have worked for Armscor or a French arms manufacturer.

There was ample motive to murder her. If she had discovered

only the tip of the iceberg of French–South African intelligence and arms dealings during apartheid, it would have been cause enough for a bullet to find its way to her as she opened her office door that March morning.

A likely scenario is that Dulcie September was killed by a South African assassin with either the participation of French security services or at least their tacit approval. The arms deals at the time were not only a South African affair. The trail of profit-making led to Paris, where it benefited politicians, corporations and spies. If any of this was revealed, it might have endangered the continued existence of the Armscor office in Paris and, with that, the entire arms money-laundering machine. Those with power simply had too much to lose by her living. They continue to have as much to lose by the identity of her killer being revealed and held to account.

Why the continued cover-up so many years later? One reason is no doubt that the motive for the cover-up has additional layers of complexity. Some of the same players implicated in her murder engaged in cutting deals in the post-apartheid arms deal. These may have included French arms corporations and very powerful politicians in Paris. If they were exposed, it would harm this trade and their careers. It might also harm powerful politicians in post-apartheid South Africa who corruptly benefited from the arms deal. Hence the silence.

The past and the present are inextricably entangled. All this is too difficult to untangle, some argue. But judging from the manner in which she lived her life, Dulcie September would have insisted on the right to truth. Justice for her was not a luxury to be traded as a political good. It is the only weapon we have against future abuse by the powerful and corrupt.

Thomson-CSF headquarters, La Défense

Thomson-CSF was a leading supplier of weapons technology to Pretoria before and throughout the sanctions period.

Home to François Mitterrand (socialist) from 1981 to 1995. Though Mitterrand talked left, the French establishment walked right.

The Élysée: French Presidential residence

PARIS

South African Embassy

Inside:
Secret home to dozens of Armscor officials, the embassy in Paris controlled arms procurement throughout Europe and managed the money laundering it required.

Outside:
It was the centre of Anti-Apartheid protests, many organised by Dulcie September.

Quai d'Orsay: French Ministry of Foreign Affairs

Jacques Foccart, close to Chirac, influential creator of Françafrique, used his network in West Africa to assist the apartheid regime.

French intelligence, the DGSE, were close allies of Pretoria and ensured a continuous supply of weapons and intelligence.

La Piscine (The Swimming Pool): DGSE headquarters

ANC office

Dulcie September was murdered opening the door to the ANC office on 29 March 1988. She had worked there for five years.

Hotel Matignon: French Prime Minister's residence

Home to Jacques Chirac (conservative) from 1986 to 1988. Chirac's election was welcomed by French arms companies wanting to sell to apartheid South Africa.

EUROPE

Paris

France

The Paris Arms Bazaar
The French connection

CHAPTER 7

The Soviet Union and Eastern Europe

'It is a psychological onslaught, an economic one, a diplomatic one, a military onslaught – a total onslaught.'
– PW BOTHA, DESCRIBING THE SOVIET-BACKED 'ONSLAUGHT'[1]

'We did business with everyone – including the Russians.'
ARMSCOR OFFICIAL[2]

Behind the Iron Curtain

By the late 1970s apartheid could better be defined by what it stood against than what it stood for. With DF Malan and Hendrik Verwoerd long buried, the crude outright racism of this vision was quietly abandoned among apartheid's defenders, within and without the country, and instead integrated into the rhetoric of a global struggle against communism. The energy and purpose of continued white domination would be focused squarely on the bogeyman of communism. While communist literature and organisations had been banned for decades and the threat of Soviet Union highlighted, PW

Botha's 'total onslaught' was designed to up the ante.

The communist threat would no longer be countered by nasty police-state McCarthyism. Instead Botha's state policy would be governed by a total national strategy that was intended to counter the total national onslaught. Botha and his defence minister, Magnus Malan, believed that any form of black (and white) resistance to repression only served to reveal the sinister hand of the 'anti-Christian, anti-capitalist' Soviet state. The airwaves were filled with propaganda broadcast by the SABC playing up this threat. Many journalists took the red bait, as did thousands of school teachers and religious leaders. This threat, not dissimilar to the perpetual state of war in which the United States finds itself, ensured domestic support among whites for Botha's ideology.

Across the globe, lobbyists for the apartheid state drummed up the same message: the Eastern bloc had its eye on the South African prize. While it is correct that Angolan government forces were heavily reliant on Cuban, Soviet and East German support, it is equally true that they were up against the UNITA guerrilla army supported by the CIA, the South African military and various other groupings. Additionally, the Soviets had other more important terrains of struggle, such as the bloody losing battle in Afghanistan. The Angolan conflict, while significant in terms of the suffering it caused, was minor in terms of the greater game of global politics.

As the Russian historians Irina Filatova and Apollon Davidson point out:

> the fears of South Africa's ruling circles were not baseless, they were indeed the object of an onslaught, but from their own population not the Soviet Union ... What for the USSR would be yet another victory for progressive forces was for South Africa yet further proof of a total onslaught. The difference was that for the USSR, South Africa was just one of many fronts in the anti-Imperialist struggle, while the USSR, in the eyes of the South African government, was the centre and creator of a world conspiracy and onslaught aimed specifically at their country.[3]

As far back as 1980, the British government of Margaret Thatcher, itself prone to talk up the communist threat in southern Africa, noted in a secret Foreign and Commonwealth Office briefing that 'we do not believe that Southern Africa is central to the USSR's foreign policy. The Russians are simply exploiting the unresolved conflict in the region to embarrass the West.'[4]

Apartheid leaders cheered when the Cold War warrior Ronald Reagan coined the term 'the Evil Empire' when referring to the Soviet Union. However, the South African regime developed in secret an opportunistic relationship with its nemesis and with allied states in Eastern Europe. At the same time as it cried bloody murder in public at the sight of the hammer and sickle, it covertly handed over cash to the same governments for guns and other supplies. Sometimes it did so directly. Mostly, such deals were concluded with the connivance of shady middlemen whom we shall soon meet. Although this trade was small in comparison with that with countries such as France, it presented one of many contradictions that pointed towards the inevitable demise of the regime. And it needed to be hidden, a sentiment no doubt shared by the anti-apartheid liberation forces that relied on the same governments for a significant amount of their support.

A double cross on the high seas

A few dozen metres below the azure waters of the Caribbean, just off the coast of Venezuela, lies what at a distance appears to be an ominous shadow. Divers who plunge into the warm waters in Guabina Bay come here to swim around one of the country's most visited artificial reefs teeming with tropical fish and coral. The reef is a sunken ship, the *Pia Vesta*. There is little clue as one peers through its rusted hull that it was once at the centre of one of the greatest arms heists of the 1980s involving socialist East Germany, South Africa, Peru, Panama, probably the CIA and a crafty French arms dealer by the name of Georges Starckmann.

I first came across the name Georges Starckmann in a top-secret minute of a 1986 meeting between the chief of the French intelligence service (DGSE), one of his officers, Colonel Pierre Lethier, the chief of the SADF, General Jannie Geldenhuys, and his head of defence intelligence operations, Neels van Tonder. Tucked between arms and intelligence exchanges is a reference to the innocuous-sounding military operation codenamed 'Daisy'. The paragraph of information in Afrikaans provided us with some clues to start with. The DGSE reported that it had located a man by the name of Starckmann in Switzerland. He had sufficiently angered the South Africans that they turned to the French intelligence to help deliver this French national to them. The memo goes on to state that the DGSE, through Lethier, 'will work on a possible plan to entice Starckman[n] to Morocco with a "new transaction". The RSA will be responsible for the further handling of Starckmann in order to reclaim the $20 million that the RSA was swindled out of. This matter is being handled very delicately and very sensitively between Mr Lethier and the Chief of South Africa Defence Intelligence Operations.'[5]

Such intriguing material could only lead me to ask: who was Starckmann, and what had he done?

The former South African Military Intelligence boss Chris Thirion says he doesn't recall Starckmann, but acknowledges that covert procurement of weapons was open to abuse by middlemen.[6] When probed about how one dealt with such situations, he responded that while this was a price one had to accept in order to engage in these kinds of activities, one also had to kill those who double-crossed one. Doing so sent the message that one would not tolerate betrayal.[7] He went on to add that many people the South Africans dealt with were killed by other governments first – 'they did get killed, not by us, but they did get killed'.[8] Given that Starckmann, aged 88, is still alive, the SADF and DGSE seem to have come to an amicable arrangement with the wily arms dealer, who has survived almost five decades in his treacherous trade throughout Africa.

Depending on whom you believe, Starckmann has at various times had connections with French and American intelligence services and might even have been an agent at some point. According to reports in the *New York Times*, he had a reputation of swindling clients. It was reported that, in 1976, Starckmann had bilked the Libyan government for $15 million by shipping cheap field glasses under the ruse that they were sophisticated and highly secret military night-vision bino-culars.[9] When approached by the *Wall Street Journal*, he denied that either he or his associate, Patrice Genty de la Sagne, had ever sold arms. His cover? According to Starckmann, he and his associate were linked to a company unimaginatively called Star Productions which, among other pieces of media fluff, produced a French made-for-TV children's cartoon about a little bird called 'Wattoo/Wattoo'.[10]

I tracked Starckmann down in Paris, where he had agreed to meet for an interview. At his insistence, this was a loose arrangement: I was to call him after I arrived by train from London. Pacing a friend's apartment for a day and night, I left without meeting him, as he never took any of my calls or answered my emails. While I couldn't meet Starckmann, I managed to find a copy of his 1992 autobiography, *Noir Canon* (Black Cannon), published in French. The cover photograph of a rusty tank turret pointed at the reader leaves little to the imagination.[11] Most remarkable is his account of a covert weapons purchase he brokered from East Berlin, intended for apartheid South Africa.[12] Much of my account here is based on information from his book, with supplementary material we have managed to locate.

In 1985 Starckmann received a visit from an old associate, Gabriel Cheboub. The Egyptian-born arms dealer had just returned from South Africa and was in the market for 160 Soviet-built Gaskin SA-9 missiles and 20 missile launch vehicles on behalf of his new clients. They were both well aware that the Soviet Union would not sell this type of equipment directly to South Africa, and so Cheboub, aided by Starckmann, had to create a channel for the goods to be delivered.[13] This tallies with a reference in the authorised publication of Armscor's history to a contract for $20 million (the same amount with which the SADF wanted to lure Starckmann to Morocco) concluded 'for the purchase of SA-9 Gaskin type vehicles used to launch missiles with Poland and East Germany by means of a mediator'.[14]

Cheboub was a known arms trader for the apartheid regime. From documents in the South African Foreign Affairs archive we have established that he was offering wares to the South African embassy in Paris in 1977, just as the arms sanctions began to pinch. According to the ambassador to Brussels, he could procure items such as bombs, rockets and cartridges for Armscor with a commission that the diplomat balked at, given that it constituted almost a third of the price of the arms: 12% for Cheboub, 10% for the middleman, and 10% for a fraudulent end-user certificate from Ethiopia.[15] Cheboub again emerges in SADF documents from 1984 when he undertook to introduce South African Military Intelligence to the deputy prime minister of Mauritius, Gaëten Duval, in order to facilitate the supply of oil to South Africa from Saudi Arabia, greased by the supply of South African patrol boats to Mauritius in turn.[16]

Starckmann, an old hand at the trade, flew to West Berlin. Crossing through the Berlin Wall at Checkpoint Charlie, he was met by an official from IMES. This little-known East German state company was run by East Germany's deputy foreign trade minister, Alexander Schalck-Golodkowski. Its employees were all from the feared East German state security service known as the Stasi. The company had been a key part of an international smuggling network, with secret bank accounts and shell companies in West Germany, Switzerland and Liechtenstein. It was believed that some of its clients might well have included players in US intelligence that organised the Iran–Contra scandal.[17] The IMES official helped Starckmann clear customs with a visa stamped on a loose sheet of white paper, after which he proceeded to the IMES head office on Friedrichstrasse.[18] Starckmann claims not to have declared the identity of the client: it seems that the cash-hungry enterprise, organised along criminal lines, was persuaded not to ask too many questions by the initial offer of $10 million.[19]

Despite the allure of money, it is unlikely that functionaries of the

Stasi would walk blind into a major deal of this nature which could get them into trouble, not least with Moscow. From documents we managed to access in the Stasi archive, we have reason to believe that the Stasi and probably their agents in IMES either knew of or suspected the direct involvement of the South Africans. The clue is the ship that Starckmann used to transport the weapons, the *Pia Vesta*, now submerged as a coral reef in the Caribbean. Stasi records, predating the conclusion of the deal, note that Danish security services had since January 1985 been investigating a Danish and a Swedish citizen on suspicion of arms smuggling to South Africa.[20]

One of the people implicated is a Dane whose name has been blocked out, but whose date of birth is helpfully identified as 1920, the same year of birth as the Danish ship owner, Jørgen Jensen, who owned the *Pia Vesta*.[21] The Danish merchant fleet, despite Denmark's adherence to the embargo, was used to transport up to 60 shipments of weapons to South Africa during apartheid.[22] The Stasi documents note that Danish authorities were investigating a company by the name of Tinmar Shipping, based in Monrovia, Liberia.[23] While we could find no trace of Tinmar Shipping, it is surely more than coincidental that it mirrors the name of Jensen's ship the *Tinemaru*, which we have been able to link positively to the shipment of Chinese-manufactured arms for South Africa (more about that in Chapter 10).

It is highly unlikely that the Stasi did not make the rather obvious South African connection. They did, after all, manage one of the world's largest domestic spy programmes, with notes on every whisper heard in a Berlin bar. A far more probable explanation is that they simply chose to turn a blind eye. After all, Starckmann and his Egyptian sidekick not only provided some helpful distance from the source, but, according to Starckmann, the Stasi insisted that he produce a Peruvian end-user certificate. If asked any questions, they could plausibly deny knowledge of the South African link, given the certificate from the South American country. Starckmann worked his contacts in Lima and was issued a certificate by the Peruvian naval attaché and head of mission to Washington. The end-user certificate, dated 18 November 1985, fraudulently stated that the arms would not be re-exported.[24]

According to Starckmann, they eventually agreed to a price of $11 million, with the shipment costing an extra $460,000. A letter of credit was arranged in the name of the IMES through the Deutsche Handelsbank in Berlin.[25] After all the commissions were paid in this $21 million deal, including Cheboub's $2 million, this should have left Starckmann with a neat profit of over $5 million. However, the East Germans came with a rider to the agreement. Given that the ship was destined for Peru, or so the End User Certificate said, they wanted to piggyback a 'small' delivery of 1,400 anti-tank missiles, 1,500 AK-47s and 12 all-terrain trucks to the Peruvian government forces.[26] The East Germans wished to covertly supply unnamed leftist groups in the Americas with the help of the Peruvian military.[27] The crafty East Germans had cornered Starckmann: refuse the offer and this would raise uncomfortable questions he was unable to answer. Thus, he declares, he agreed to take the circuitous route from the Baltic port of Rostock, via the Panama Canal and Peru, to South Africa. The East Germans in turn provided him with cover documentation from a Peruvian vice-admiral which described the equipment on board as vehicles equipped for geophysical and seismic oil research.[28]

Starckmann now had to break the news to the South Africans whom he had not yet met. What followed was a number of meetings in Geneva between Starckmann, as well as probably Cheboub, and his South African clients. A team of six white, apparently dyed-in-the-wool Afrikaners presented themselves. Geneva, as we have seen, was one of the cities in which arms deals would frequently be brokered by Armscor and its agents. Starckmann can only recall the names of the two people leading the delegation – 'Toni and Basil'.[29] From what we have been able to establish, he most likely met with Tony de Klerk, the Armscor group manager for foreign procurement, and Basil Baker, the head of Armscor finance, both working from the Technical Council in the South African embassy in Paris. The deal was eventually concluded through a front company in Liberia which, as we have seen in Chapter 5, was standard Armscor operating procedure. Starckmann set up a front company to protect his identity, which he says was registered as TIT in the UK tax haven of Jersey. While we were unable to find a record of such a company in Jersey, there was a TIT domiciled in Guernsey, another UK tax haven, from 1985 to 1987, which matches Starckmann's account.[30] According to Starckmann, payment was made by the South Africans via 'a large bank in Luxembourg with a serious bank in Brussels'[31] and from there it would go to a bank account in Spain for transfer to IMES.

The crew of the *Pia Vesta*, captained by Johannes Christensen, were to be given scant details of their real destination. After offloading in the Peruvian port of Callao, Armscor had insisted that the crew only then be informed of their onward journey to Durban.[32] The name of the ship would be changed before reaching South African waters, and documents would show that the cargo was in fact intended for Maputo in Mozambique. The ship would be met at the dock by a group of men who would ask no questions when offloading the material.[33] This was all standard procedure for masking the identity of such arms shipments. The cargo was readied at the port of Rostock and inspected by an Armscor representative before the East German officials signed the necessary documentation.

At this point in the story, Starckmann travelled to Miami to meet an old friend by the name of David Duncan and discuss the *Pia Vesta* shipment.[34] Duncan is described by the *Wall Street Journal* in a 1988 story on the *Pia Vesta* as a 'thin, excitable, red-haired man in his 40s who uses a lot of cologne and boasts of his connections to U.S. intelligence agencies'.[35] If Starckmann is to be believed, Duncan saw a political opportunity for the Reagan administration in exposing the deal to show that Peruvian President Alan García was buying weapons from East Germany for the benefit of leftist 'guerrillas' in the Americas.[36] In this way Starckmann and Duncan could add value to the deal through a political dimension that would benefit Washington. The plan they hatched was complex and linked to the covert arms support supplied by US intelligence to the conservative

Contras groups in Nicaragua or to El Salvador – one side of the Iran–Contra affair.[37] The weapons intended for the 'communists' in Peru were to be 'liberated' and sent to the Contras instead. As for the arms for apartheid, the Frenchman and his shady friend in Miami agreed they should proceed to Durban. Apartheid was less obnoxious than the 'communists'.[38]

The *Pia Vesta* arrived at the port of Callao on 9 June and, with Duncan's intervention, all the equipment was offloaded, checked and then reloaded onto the boat. With the assistance of bribes, all the necessary documentation was signed and the port officials turned a blind eye to the fact that the cargo had mysteriously made its way back onto the ship. The ship left back up the Pacific Coast, destined for the repressive US-backed junta in El Salvador, after transhipment in Panama.[39] Starckmann contends that Panama's ruler, General Noriega, had given the green light for this operation but reneged on the deal when the ship arrived in Panama on 14 June 1986, when he had the crew arrested and impounded the weapons. This may well have been a trigger for Reagan's acolytes to turn on Noriega, who was eventually deposed and arrested by US forces in 1989. The Peruvians were angry and recalled their ambassador from East Berlin. The East German Stasi officials in the IMES feigned ignorance and the right-wing government in El Salvador lost out on a windfall.[40] But perhaps the biggest loser was the apartheid government, which had entrusted a network of swindlers with $20 million to buy weapons from a country that it wished the world to believe was its 'enemy'.

This scandal received no coverage in South Africa, not least because any unauthorised reporting on arms purchases carried a jail sentence. When Chris Streeter, a spokesperson at the South African embassy in Washington DC, was asked about the deal, he was reported by *Newsday* to have responded, 'Goodness, that's news to me,' and categorically denied that the deal had occurred.[41] Duncan claimed afterwards that he was owed 5% commission on the deal, and alleged to *Newsday* that the South Africans kept the deal secret because one of its officials had received a $2 million bribe, which could blow up in the

Behind the Iron Curtain

Double-cross on the high seas

The SADF needs 160 Soviet-built Gaskin missiles and 20 launchers, likely for use in Angola. Armscor's office in the Paris embassy is given instructions to find and buy the weapons.

Starckmann informs David Duncan of the shipment. Duncan has ties to US intelligence and approaches the CIA. He hatches a plan to divert the Peruvian weapons to the pro-CIA rebel Contras in El Salvador, before the ship proceeds to Durban.

The *Pia Vesta* ship leaves East Germany's largest shipping port in Rostock.

7 Rostock

6 Miami

9 Panama

President Noriega impounds the ship and the weapons, arresting the *Pia Vesta* crew.

8 Peru

The weapons are unloaded and reloaded onto the *Pia Vesta* at the Callao harbour. The ship departs bound for El Salvador, via Panama.

Venezuela 11

In 2000 the *Pia Vesta* is scuttled and becomes an artificial reef, popular with divers and snorkelers.

1 **Paris**

Armscor officials instruct Egyptian arms dealer and middleman, Gabriel Cheboub, who visits Georges Starckmann with a request for the weapons.

2 **Berlin**

Starckmann travels to East Berlin and meets with officials from East German arms company IMES. The East Germans approve the transaction.

Moscow **3**

Stasi secret police officials (East Germany) likely confer with Moscow. They confirm with Starckmann they will supply the missiles. However, they insist on a Peruvian end-user certificate and demand to add small-arms weapons to offload for leftists in Peru.

Switzerland **4**

Starckmann meets Armscor officials in Geneva to finalise the deal; agreement is reached.

Luxembourg **5**

SA makes the full payment of $21 million via a bank in Luxembourg. This may well have been KBL.

Morocco **10**

Despite payment of $20 million, the weapons never reach South Africa. SA military and French intelligence co-operate to lure Starckmann to Morocco and attempt to recover the funds.

face of the National Party.[42] While this is possible, it is far more likely that the government didn't want to admit to their electorate or friends in Western intelligence agencies that they were buying weapons from the 'enemy'. Duncan would later claim that European arms dealers had all taken an intense interest in the scam and that 'everybody in Geneva talks about it because this one is the jackpot ... Everybody was interested to find out what really happened.'[43]

The Peruvian government investigated the deal, 'chasing dozens of paper trails littered with nonexistent companies and forged documents'. It concluded that the 'Pia Vesta was the work of U.S. and other intelligence organisations routing arms to Central America'.[44] They believed their own country's involvement was a red herring.[45] While the Peruvians appear to have ignored the crucial role of South Africa, they may well have been onto something concerning links to the United States. According to the *Wall Street Journal*, Robert Owen, a courier for Colonel Oliver North, the man who headed US intelligence's Iran–Contra operation in Central America, 'mentioned Starckmann, Genty de la Sagne and Star Productions in a memo to the colonel. In the memo, Mr Owen associated Mr Duncan and the two Frenchmen with the secret Contra arms operation.'[46]

My final stop to try to verify this information was to check declassified documents related to the Iran–Contra affair, accessed at the National Security Archive in Washington DC. Here I found a National Security Council (NSC) memorandum to Oliver North, in which NSC official David Laux reported on contacts he had had with David Duncan. This was almost six weeks after the *Pia Vesta* was impounded by Panamanian authorities and publicly linked to Oliver North's Iran–Contra dealings. The document is heavily redacted, which likely includes much of the relevant information regarding the South African arms deal. According to Laux, he first met Duncan in July 1986 following an introduction from US Senator Glenn's office, which informed him that David Duncan was 'an arms merchant from Miami, Florida who had some information on illicit arms shipments in several areas of the world'. However, according to the CIA's assessment, 'Duncan was a wild man, unreliable, that they [the CIA] didn't want to talk to him, particularly with the story in today's Washington Post [about the *Pia Vesta*] and advised me to stay away from him too.'[47]

Needless to say, the *Pia Vesta* deal was, and remains, shrouded in mystery, raising any number of problems. But for all the smoke and mirrors, one thing is as clear as day: there is more than sufficient evidence that Armscor bought arms from IMES, a Stasi-run East German company operating behind the Iron Curtain. During the Cold War, much was not as it seemed.

Soviet-aligned Eastern Europe

The involvement of the Eastern bloc in this sort of sanctions-busting activity added an entirely new layer of secrecy to apartheid's covert operations. Unlike the case of France, whose complicity was widely suspected and where lips were somewhat looser, the threat of discovery carried even greater consequences for both parties. The Eastern bloc powers would no doubt be hugely embarrassed to be shown as doing business with the apartheid government when they were very publicly aligned with, and funding, the ANC. The South African government, for its part, would have to try to explain away a relationship with their mortal enemy, upon whose enmity the 'total strategy' and the survival of the apartheid state were based.

The result is that the record of the relations between apartheid South Africa, the Soviet Union and its satellite states is patchy and disparate. To use standard discursive archival phraseology, what we can now access is only a 'sliver' of a deeper reality: scraps of documents and fragments of stories that hint at a more complete narrative. What follows, here, is a sampling of those fragments that have squirrelled their way through the veil of secrecy to emerge briefly into view. While individually they may seem to be slight and disconnected vignettes, taken together I believe that they start to paint a compelling picture

– a picture that shows that the apartheid government could, and did, establish cordial relationships and pragmatic trading arrangements, in violation of sanctions, with the very governments it claimed were trying to destroy the bastion of Western capitalism at the bottom of the African continent.

As the sanctions noose threatened to tighten and include not only arms but also commercial goods, such as military electronics, from the West during the latter part of the 1980s, PW Botha's government and various state entities sought new trade contracts in 'enemy states' in Eastern Europe and the Soviet Union. While they still supported the ANC and its armed struggle, these countries were undergoing changes of their own from the mid-1980s, given the Soviet thaw and the more outward-looking policy of perestroika. They were also desperately in search of new markets, supplies and hard currency, which the Treasury in Pretoria seemed to have in ample supply.

Armscor concluded a number of weapons transactions with un-named countries in what it referred to as the 'East bloc' (primarily Eastern Europe and possibly the Soviet Union). An example of a direct contract was the purchase of 1,000 Belgian MAG machine guns and 4,500 FAL rifles and other material, facilitated by an Eastern European mediator. A number of other transactions took place with assistance from third countries that acted as transhipment points, including Oman and an unnamed North African country (likely Morocco). Sources in Eastern Europe also provided Armscor with a full manufacturing data package for AK-47s, enabling Armscor to produce Soviet-designed weapons in South Africa.[48]

The Iron Curtain did not prove to be an obstacle for the South African Department of Foreign Affairs covert sanctions-busting unit headed by Marc Burger. Minister of Foreign Affairs Pik Botha, quick to claim credit, boasted to his biographer about these operations: 'I gave the orders. The money came out of my budget.'[49] Botha, a man who prefers the big picture to details, confirmed that his people used front companies to gain access to Cuba, Eastern Europe and the Far East (probably referring to China). 'In Eastern Europe we had a company with the President's wife on the board of Directors! A number of cabinet ministers also sat on the board. We did a few things I really can't reveal, not even now.'[50] According to the former South African diplomat Johan Maré, who was tasked with setting up a new mission for South Africa in Budapest in 1990, he came across covert ties with various Eastern European countries in the 1980s. These 'contacts had been primarily with Russia but also with Poland and apparently Romania, the latter involving the relatives of high-positioned NP politicians, with a large focus on military equipment'.[51]

Pik Botha's department was not the only one in the fraudulent sanctions-busting business. In a letter marked 'top secret', the minister for economic affairs and technology as well as trade and industry, Danie Steyn, wrote to inform the state president of a visit by an East German middleman to South Africa in June 1988 and 'of the success that was achieved through this'. According to the documents located in PW Botha's archive at the University of the Free State, a Dr Leonhard Mehlber of the company Zekom AG in Augsburg acted as an 'agent, principal, partner in trade and official representative of certain East European countries and the Soviet Union as well as African countries and countries in the Middle and Far East'.[52] Mehlber, who was reported to 'control' 138 international companies, paid a secret visit to South Africa at the request of the East German government. He was accompanied at almost 30 meetings in Johannesburg and Cape Town by a government official working with the Department of Trade and Industry's 'Unconventional Trade Division', tasked with busting sanctions. According to the report, his visit had resulted in potential deals, some of which were at advanced stages of negotiation, that were valued at $1 billion. The most important deal – worth $700 million – involved the potential export of between 1 and 2 million tonnes of South African iron ore to East Germany and Russia, and 1 million tonnes of coal to Soviet-aligned states. It also included the potential for clandestine investment of $150 million in a South African mine in exchange for the annual export of 300,000 tonnes of a particular mineral to an Eastern bloc state to the value of R150 million.[53]

Mehlber also offered to assist South Africa with some of its other sanctions-busting initiatives. These opportunities were communicated to South African private sector corporations. Mehlber was politically well connected and plans were afoot for him to accompany the East German deputy minister of trade to South Africa in July 1988. In addition, he had already secured a meeting within a week of his visit to South Africa with the Russian minister of foreign trade and a senior member of the Soviet Union's Politburo, to discuss possible co-operation in the international marketing of certain minerals. A visit by officials of both countries was planned for the near future.[54]

The archives do not provide further information about which of these contracts were fulfilled. The intention, however, was clear, and was supported at cabinet level in South Africa, East Germany and possibly the Soviet Union. Little record can be found of Mehlber's company Zekom AG, except for the principality of Lichtenstein's company registry, which shows that a firm with the name Zekom AG was, after 21 years of trade, removed from the registry on 8 November 1989.[55] The following day, the Berlin Wall came tumbling down under the weight of popular protest across East Germany.

The Stasi is watching

The East German Ministry for State Security (Stasi) was one of the most pervasive and effective intelligence agencies in the world. By 1989 it employed 274,000 people, of whom approximately 175,000 were so-called unofficial informants, whose job was to engage in part-time spying.[56] Some estimates suggest that as many as 500,000 were in fact employed in this manner, but many of their records may have been among the almost one billion pages of documents destroyed by the repressive regime shortly before the fall of the Berlin Wall.[57] We submitted a request for information regarding South Africa and sanctions-related issues to the German state archives. While authorities give limited access to such records to researchers and journalists, which are mostly heavily redacted, a vast volume of records remains strictly off bounds. These are all the records collected outside East Germany by its agents and through its various embassies, which were seized by US intelligence after the fall of the Berlin Wall, and have not been returned despite repeated requests by the unified German state. The Stasi documents I consulted in Berlin, not far from its landmark television tower on the Alexanderplatz, nonetheless proved illuminating. The Stasi was always watching, even if it seldom proposed how to intervene in sanctions busting that involved South Africa.

Candy from the 'communists'

A Stasi report dated June 1988 suggested that East Germany had more than once been used to launder unknown goods as part of efforts to bust the embargo (as much as it existed) between the United States and South Africa.[58] The report, together with supporting cargo manifests, was based on reports from a Stasi informer named 'Peter', possibly from the West German port city of Hamburg. The process was relatively simple, although almost unthinkable given the Cold War mutual antagonism. Goods from either South Africa or the United States would be offloaded in Hamburg. From there, they would be transferred to new containers and relabelled as medical equipment or, on one occasion, as 'mint drops'. A major East German transport company called Deutrans would truck the goods across the East German border, and at one of the first truck stops turn around, heading back to West Germany. The goods, now with paperwork which presumably showed East Germany as the country of origin (still labelled as 'mint drops'), would then be offloaded in Hamburg, ready for shipment to South Africa or the United States. From the report it is clear that West German harbour workers were aware that this was a sanctions-busting operation, and had accused the truck driver on at least one occasion of East German complicity in the scheme. The report ends with a proposal to investigate whether this sort of practice by Deutrans was officially sanctioned and politically defensible. The report gives an indication that, if needed, officials could give further information about similar shipments.[59]

Broederbond in Leipzig

In 1984 a Stasi informer reported on a conversation with three people at East Germany's biggest annual trade fair held in Leipzig.[60] The three included a member of the South African trade council in Austria, an Austrian businessman and a representative of a London bank that had interests in South Africa. All three indicated that they were not in Leipzig in their private capacity, but were there to represent the South African government. They expressed frustration with the difficulty they were having in establishing trade links. They argued that East Germany shouldn't take a narrow view of South Africa, as there were traditionally good links with East Germany in the trade of industrial diamonds. They also said that Hungary purchased almost all of its uranium from South Africa and that trade flows with the Soviet Union currently stood at $20 million in a variety of areas, although made through third parties. In turn, they expressed an interest in purchasing mechanical equipment from East Germany.[61]

In 1989 the Stasi took special note of a South African businessman among the southern African delegation to the Leipzig Trade Show that year.[62] Interested in the purchase of East German computers, he had evidently far more influence than his role within the trade delegation suggested. What followed was a number of discussions with Stasi informers and agents concerning East German equipment, much of which took place in code and in English if any third person was close by. The East Germans were able to establish through various informants that the businessman, who represented a company called Transworld Technology, was acting as a front for the South African company National Panasonic (which in turn was owned by the South African company Nashua).[63] We were able to learn, from leaked documents that originate from the Armscor Paris office, that

Transworld Technology was a company registered in Liberia. It had been incorporated by Kredietbank by Dr G Mergen, who provided a similar service to a number of Armscor front companies. Its purpose was listed as 'Marketing Far East'.

The South African businessman (whose name has been redacted) is said to have been born in Stellenbosch, represented the interests of the South African government and was acting as their representative at the highest level in trade negotiations with East Germany. He was described as a Stellenbosch graduate who was a member of the NP's secretive controlling clique, the Broederbond. His father, a senior member of the Broederbond, was a clergyman and part of FW de Klerk's inner circle. The Stasi undertook further research through a number of its agents and confirmed his credentials and business contacts in South Africa and Germany, including the managing director of National Panasonic.

Besides an interest in East German computer technology, the businessman offered to establish co-operation with East Germany in the field of digital intelligence technology and satellite communication. He indicated that he was in the process of procuring documentation concerning the US Cray super-computer, and undertook his activities in close collaboration with Israeli intelligence. He specifically asked the Stasi informant 'Henry' to establish contact with the East German security services in July 1989. He was described as a supporter of apartheid but understood that the policy had brought about South Africa's isolation.[64]

Robert Mugabe and Robotron

A March 1989 Stasi memo concerns the sale of East German computers from the state firm Robotron to the Harare-based company ZCT. The East Germans had tried to establish this link because they knew that ZCT worked very closely with the company ZIDCO, owned by the ruling Zanu-PF party.[65] ZIDCO was similar to the Chancellor House, a trust alleged to kick back profits from sweetheart deals to the ANC.

The Stasi informant 'Phillip' reported that ZCT had an office in South Africa and its three directors were strongly suspected of belonging 'to the mafia and having interesting contacts in Zimbabwe'. The ZCT was apparently established by Robert Mugabe with the purpose of facilitating deals in southern Africa, including South Africa, and managed its relationship with South Africa through a subsidiary in Gaborone, Botswana. The South Africans were particularly interested in personal and large computers that they could purchase from Robotron, via ZCT. The East Germans had already started to test the export of equipment to South Africa, and noted 'the business in South Africa must be organised in such a manner that East Germany is not immediately identified as the direct partner in the production of these products'. The cover was provided by working through ZCT and Robotron as intermediaries. The deal was viewed as not being without risk and was described as a 'complicated, politically sensitive business'.[66] It is very likely, given these circumstances, that Mugabe and Zanu-PF would have benefited from a scheme intended to violate the embargo against South Africa.

However, the South Africans did not always feel the need to work through cumbersome schemes such as this. A May 1989 Stasi intelligence report summarised the South African interest in East German high-tech equipment.[67] This included computers and electro-technical equipment from the East German company AHB Robotron, as well as night-vision and other optical equipment from the renowned Carl Zeiss of Jena. In return, South Africa had promised the delivery of raw materials to East Germany and assistance with its own embargo-busting activities. East German intelligence sources indicated that South Africa was interested not only in technical and commercial equipment and information, but also political and economic information from East Germany. In one instance they had offered an East German official a new start in South Africa in return for them assisting to develop commercial activities between the two countries over a four- to five-year period.[68] Pretoria was starting to think long term and was cultivating a relationship with the men who held power behind the Berlin Wall. As two countries that had surrounded their people with fences, they had much in common.

Bombs from Bulgaria

A 1980 investigation by the German magazine *Der Spiegel* revealed that between 1976 and 1980 the Bulgarian secret service had assisted in supplying South Africa with weapons, which were to be used by the 'anti-communist' UNITA forces in Angola. According to the report, Bulgaria as well as, to a lesser extent, Poland provided war material to the value of approximately DM150 million, including AK-47s and RPG-7 rocket-propelled grenades. The chief buyer was Armscor's Charles Canfield, described as a smart young English speaker with 'Gucci looks' who operated with a network of arms dealers from the Armscor office in Paris. Armscor worked closely with the mother-and-daughter team of Maria and Vera Kelermer, arms brokers in Vienna, who helped facilitate contact with one Ivan Slavkov. Slavkov was the director general of the Bulgarian Television Services – a well-connected official whose father-in-law happened to be the head of state, Todor Zhivkov. *Der Spiegel* suggested that Slavkov might have been induced to co-operate by a love affair with Vera Kelmer, for whom he bought fur coats, a ring and a sports car.[69]

If so, it would have been a risky relationship given that his father-in-law ruled Bulgaria with an iron grip for 35 years until 1989. He was eventually found guilty of corruption and plundering state resources. The choice of Bulgaria as potential supplier to Armscor was additionally unexpected in view of the fact that Zhivkov was described by the writer and regime critic Georgi Markov as someone who 'served the Soviet Union more ardently than the Soviet leaders themselves did'.[70] Zhivkov would later have Markov, then living in exile in London, assassinated on Waterloo Bridge by a poison-tipped umbrella carried by an agent of the Bulgarian secret service, Darschawna Sugurnost.

The two Viennese arms brokers, using their political connections in Sofia, would turn to Darschawna Sugurnost to conclude a deal with Armscor's agent, the 'Gucci man' Canfield.[71] Within weeks of the first contact, weapons were loaded in the Bulgarian Black Sea port of Burgas with a fraudulent end-user certificate indicating Nigeria as the destination, which was provided by a Nigerian consular official. Payment was made in advance by Armscor through banks in Brussels and Luxembourg, possibly Kredietbank. Both the Western arms brokers and the Bulgarian secret service received a 15% commission. The shipment of the weapons relied on the Danish shipping company Trigon. Over a two-year period Trigon would collect its cargoes of weapons, set sail for a neutral country, and, when on the high seas hundreds of miles south of the Canary Islands off the coast of West Africa, change the flag and the name of the vessel using a fresh can of paint. This operation would take a mariner tied to the side of the vessel, paintbrush in hand, two hours to complete. Two of the ships concerned were the *Alice Trigon* and *Sarah Poulsen*.

The vessel would then set sail for Cape Town, from where weapons would be shipped to UNITA forces in Angola. The head of the shipping company, Anders Jensen, and his crew were awarded bonus payments from their South African paymasters, which included a risk premium paid to the captain for his role in falsifying his logbook to change the destination of the ship. The matter was contested by Jensen (a controversial figure to whom we will shortly return) and investigated by Danish officials. This resulted in the exposure of a second supply line involving the Copenhagen-based cargo ship *Romeo*, which for a fee of $130,000 shipped Czechoslovakian handguns from the Polish harbour of Gdynia to Durban. In response to the interest shown by the Danish police, the Bulgarian–South African arms deal found a new shipment point in Hamburg. From here, at least two cargo loads of weapons were delivered to Cape Town and Durban, including rockets, anti-tank missiles and AK-47s.[72]

Anders Jensen fled Denmark in 1983 and settled in South Africa, evading Danish justice for many years. In 1996 the Danish embassy in Pretoria confirmed that its attorney general in Copenhagen was considering charges against Jensen, as it had recently reinstated full diplomatic ties with the Mandela government. According to the Danish seamen's union, 60 illegal shipments were brought to South Africa on board Danish vessels from 1978 onwards. Jensen's company Trigon was responsible for 25 of these. In response to questions from the *Mail & Guardian*, Jensen commented: 'I don't regard myself as a criminal. If I am one, there are many other people who belong in jail, that's for sure.'[73] The Danish media reported in 2004 that Jensen, whose passport had been revoked by the Danish authorities, had given up hope of ever returning to Denmark. The 83-year-old believed he would die at his home in the exclusive Cape Town suburb of Oranjezicht.[74]

A document found in the South African Foreign Affairs archive in Pretoria, sent from the South African embassy in Brussels to the secretary of foreign affairs in Pretoria, dated March 1977, confirms the shipment of various goods and machinery from the Bulgarian capital of Sofia. A proposal was made that a South African naval ship be ready to provide assistance to the shipment on the high seas approximately 600 to 1,000 miles south of the Canary Islands, and offer a shadow convoy for two shipments. It was also requested that the secretive SADF listening station at Silvermine just outside Cape Town should monitor the ships' radio frequencies. This correlates with the modus operandi described in *Der Spiegel*'s investigation.[75]

The Bulgarian government, at least officially, denied any knowledge of involvement in arms deals with South Africa. Robert Hughes MP, chairman of the Anti-Apartheid Movement in the United Kingdom, wrote a letter to the Bulgarian ambassador to London, Kiril Shterev. Hughes expressed concern about Bulgaria's role in arming the apartheid state. Shterev responded in a letter dated 5 June 1984, stating that 'these reports are slanderous and markedly anti-Bulgarian. They have been fabricated by certain Western intelligence services and their aim is to disinform the world public opinion on the role played by my country in the struggle against Apartheid ... I wish to assure you ... that the government of the People's Republic of Bulgaria has never sold any weapons to countries with reactionary regimes, let alone to the racist Republic of South Africa.'[76]

The Soviet Union

When I interviewed an Armscor official in 2014, he leaned back in his chair as he explained away the contradiction of buying weapons from the '*rooi gevaar*' (red peril) in the 1980s.[77] According to him, Armscor did business with everyone, including the Soviets in the 1980s. He recalled how this fact had shaken the world of a young student intern working with him at Armscor in the 1980s. The young man was loyal to the NP and the ideals of Christian nationalism. Going through old typewriter lint, he had stumbled upon the text from a secret letter sent to Soviet counterparts confirming the purchase of equipment. The young man was perplexed: 'He wanted to find a way to do something about it because he said we are doing business with the anti-Christs, but of course he couldn't do anything. Yes, we were anti-communist but would buy weapons from the Russians.'[78]

Little is known about clandestine Soviet engagement with the apartheid regime precisely because neither party had any advantage in the material being disclosed. The Soviet intelligence archives, which could be helpful, are closed to researchers, as are their South African counterparts. It is worth noting that while we have found evidence of some clandestine contact, it was not on the scale of that with countries in the West, such as France or the United States. However, given more than three decades of simmering hostility between Pretoria and Moscow, this collaboration – along with that of China – is perhaps the most surprising.

The retired diplomat Tom Wheeler believes that what assisted the development of relations between the Soviet Union and South Africa was that government departments in Pretoria often worked in silos on a need-to-know basis. This, in turn, helped minimise the risk of news of the relationship spreading outside a tight circle.[79] While a trade in weapons appears to have taken place in violation of the UN arms embargo, it is useful to first examine the aspects of trade and collaboration between the two countries that could act as a shaky foundation on which more sensitive deals could be built. What mutual interest could reconcile these apparent arch-enemies?

Enter the Oppenheimers

According to the Russian historians Irina Filatova and Apollon Davidson, the Moscow theatre-going public was convinced they had caught sight of Harry Oppenheimer, head of South Africa's mining giants De Beers and Anglo American, at the Bolshoi theatre.[80] Is it conceivable that the old plutocrat, an institution among Western business moguls and politicians, had trekked behind the Iron Curtain at the height of apartheid and the Cold War?

The Soviet Union had called for a world trade boycott of apartheid in 1963 and had maintained no official diplomatic, trade or economic links with Pretoria since 1956. David Pallister, award-winning investigative journalist who has written extensively on the Oppenheimer empire, argues that this mattered little in practice when it came to the business of earning foreign exchange.[81] Apparently, co-operation between Moscow and De Beers had a long history dating back to the 1950s, just after the closure of Moscow's diplomatic mission in South Africa. 'According to some estimates, the funds that the USSR received from De Beers for their diamonds were the third largest source of hard currency for the country. At first relations were direct and straight forward, but after the ANC protested, they continued through a British company acting as a front.'[82] The London firm City and West-East, a subsidiary of the Hambros banking group, managed the movement of rough diamonds destined for the De Beers diamond monopoly, the Central Selling Organisation (CSO).[83] *Africa Confidential* reported in 1987 on the little-publicised relationship between Soviet Mineral Export Enterprises and the South African multinational De Beers, which controlled the world's diamond market at the time.[84] According to the article, Soviet representatives frequently met with senior De Beers executives, usually in London, to discuss diamond pricing and to sell Soviet gems.[85] The director of the Africa Institute, Anatoliy Gromyko, son of former Soviet foreign minister Andrei Gromyko, made a convenient distinction at the time, saying that 'the Soviet Union has contacts with the cartel that deals in diamonds, which is not to be confused with official government ties with South Africa'.[86] The private (sector) was apparently not political.

While we cannot confirm that Oppenheimer attended the Bolshoi theatre, the BBC correspondent John Osman was surprised to find one of Oppenheimer's most trusted lieutenants, Gordon Waddell, standing at the bar of the Bolshoi during the interval of a performance of the opera *Boris Godunov* in November 1980.[87] Waddell, a former British Lions rugby player and white MP in Helen Suzman's Progressive Federal Party, was executive director of Anglo American between 1971 and 1987 and chairman of the mining company Johannesburg Consolidated Investments and of Rustenburg Platinum Mines at the time.[88] According to Osman, Waddell was in the company of an Anglo man and two Soviet officials but said that there was no story: he was just passing through. Upon enquiries the following day, Waddell had vacated his hotel and none of his Soviet contacts knew or were willing to say anything about the matter.[89] It is highly unlikely that the Soviets would have given a visa to a white South African unless there was a more official reason for the visit. As David Pallister argues, 'the self-styled champion of black African nationalism has been trading and dealing with South Africa for years through price-fixing "understandings" on gold and platinum, and the sale of Russian diamonds by De Beers'.[90]

While Anglo American and the Soviets agreed on aspects of the gold trade, South Africa and the Soviet Union, as the world's biggest platinum producers, had more difficulty in coming to an under-standing on platinum pricing during the 1970s and 1980s, despite meetings between 'representatives of the two countries … in distant places far removed from either, such as Oslo and Hong Kong'.[91] However, by the 1980s Soviet representatives were travelling to South Africa regularly to discuss the sale of minerals such as platinum.[92]

Trading places

The trade between the Soviet Union and South Africa was monitored closely by the CIA director of economic research. The CIA noted, as far back as 1970, that while no exports from South Africa to the USSR had been reported, they believed that some flows took place through third countries, and that the Soviet Union exported between $500,000 and $700,000 worth of products to South Africa. South Africa also registered trade with six Eastern European countries, including East Germany, Bulgaria, Poland and Romania. In 1969 the total value of imports from these countries was approximately $6.9 million.[93]

The trading relationship between the two countries, despite an official cut in economic ties, began slowly to pick up in the 1980s. By way of example, in the 1980s and early 1990s South Africa sold the USSR a sixth of all Soviet mohair imports (3,000 tonnes), according to Konstantin Razumeev, director of Moscow's Central Research Institute of Wool Industry.[94] Much of this was the result of ongoing covert diplomacy led by the Ministry of Foreign Affairs sanctions-busting supremo, Marc Burger. Burger claims that numerous discreet, fruitful meetings took place between South African and Soviet heavyweights in both countries.[95] He recalls that one of the Soviet officials he dealt with in Leningrad had been born in Pretoria before his father was expelled by the South Africans on allegations of espionage in 1956. Thirty years later, the father was the KGB's second-in-command and the son was involved in secret trade talks with Burger and his colleagues from Pretoria.[96]

Some of the overtures were crude and ineffective, such as when Pik Botha was reported to have sent a message to Soviet officials who were in South Africa investigating the plane crash that killed Mozambican President Samora Machel. Botha proposed increased trade in return for South African neutrality.[97] Vladimir Shubin and Marina Traikova also provide details of similar attempts by Giovanni Mario Ricci, the shady Italian sanctions-buster stationed in the Seychelles, who was a close associate of the apartheid spy Craig Williamson.[98] Ricci had tried in vain to insert himself as an intermediary between Pretoria and the Soviet embassy in the Seychelles.[99]

By 1988, Pik Botha started to call publicly for the opening of trade relations with the Soviet Union. By 1989, the issue was the subject of debate in the white parliament – as always in the context of a grudge against the Americans and British.[100] The gist of the argument was expressed by an NP MP, who stated: 'If Russia can give us an opportunity or can help us to ward off the international economic war against South Africa … they must make use of the opportunity.'[101]

From Russia, with love?

Against this background, the thought of direct military trade between the two countries appears less far-fetched. Important to bear in mind, in this regard, is the fact that the Soviet perceptions of the ANC weren't static or necessarily uniformly held by Soviet decision-makers. There was apparently a divergence of views between the political leaders in the Central Committee and the Soviet Defence Ministry about the chance of success of the ANC's armed wing, Umkhonto we Sizwe. The Soviet soldiers had battled the SADF in Angola and were less optimistic about the liberation group's chances.[102] The former senior Military Intelligence officer Chris Thirion believes that South African efforts to try to isolate the ANC from their foreign support groups were successful, to an extent. According to him, the SADF had intelligence that the Russians were telling the ANC in the mid-1980s that they needed to engage with the Afrikaners, because the apartheid state was telling the Soviets that 'we are not going anywhere'.[103]

The Archive for Contemporary Affairs in Bloemfontein reveals over a hundred pages of Magnus Malan's handwritten notes in a South African Ministry of Defence folder marked 'Notes of discussions, Minister of Defence and Prime Minister'. This record of the SADF chief's meetings with PW Botha from the early 1980s includes details of the need to write a concept paper about the 'total onslaught' against South Africa, as well as the communist threat. Somewhat cryptically, marked in red pen, are notes of a meeting with PW Botha on 13 November 1982. In these Malan records that 'KBG prisoner/wants to buy mielies [maize]. White R[ussians] are minority group … They do not want to see Whites perish. Want an understanding/create situation that we will play into the hands of the West – they need Chrome from us. Chief Staff Intelligence discussion with Nel about mielies R[ussia] trade (top management thereof) (following discussion with PM).' Further reference is also made to enriched uranium, in reference to the Soviets.

Both Magnus Malan and PW Botha, the only participants in these meetings, have died, taking many of this country's secrets with them to the grave. We can read much into these notes, but one possible interpretation is that they record an early clandestine exchange of views between representatives from both sides, just at the time that Pretoria was about to turn its anti-communist rhetoric to fever pitch.[104]

A former senior Armscor official, who asked for his identity not to be disclosed, confirmed that not only were there talks between the parties, but that it had developed to such an extent by the late 1980s that Armscor had achieved the unthinkable.[105] Armscor had a team of military experts working from within the Soviet Union, including an office in Leningrad. Moreover, a team of Armscor officials, who we should recall received their funding from the Department of Defence, also operated from the Siberian city of Omsk, home to a squadron of MiG-23 and MiG-31 aircraft during the Cold War.[106] According to the source, the background to this is that a South African medical team, mostly from Wits University, responded to a call for volunteers to assist in the wake of the 1986 Chernobyl nuclear disaster. Although this team had no military ties, the Russians apparently developed a great affinity for South Africans as a result. I asked Dr Max Price about this, but neither he nor any of the former staff at Wits Medical School at the time could recollect this.

The Armscor team in Siberia were involved in jet engine development intended to improve the design of the French-manufactured aircraft which the South African Air Force possessed.[107] In return, the Armscor team taught the Russians how to develop single crystal blade technology for jet engines.

The relationship between the Soviets and the South African military could have had one positive impact, in making redundant the need for new fighter jets in the post-apartheid arms deal. As the book *Devil in the Detail* revealed, the Russian arms dealer Mark Voloshin entered into a deal with the apartheid state during the arms embargo to lease MiG-29 engines to the South Africans for testing so they could upgrade their Mirage and Cheetah fleet.[108] The deal had the alleged blessing of the Soviet state at the time, and approximately $18 million worth of technology and equipment was shipped to South Africa. However, instead of bench-testing the engines, Voloshin had the engines fitted directly to the planes. 'South Africa fitted the engines at the expense of the Russians, and refused to pay, while Voloshin moved from Russia to his new home in South Africa. As the Russians were reluctant to acknowledge that they had broken the arms embargo, no action was taken.'[109] The upgrades would have given the Cheetahs and Mirages a new lease on life and saved South Africa from a costly upgrade of new fighter jets.[110]

The record of Armscor's Siberian outpost is an extraordinary revelation of the manner in which the apartheid regime was continuously adapting its practice, even when this contradicted its own policy and politics. As Soviet politics themselves changed, so too did South Africa's covert approaches. This underscores the very apartheid-like discrepancy between publicly stated virtue and ideological purity, on the one hand, and private pragmatism and greed on the other. During the Cold War, nothing was quite what it seemed.

CHAPTER 8

The United States of America

'We must stay and work, not cut and run. It should be our policy to build in South Africa, not to bring down.'
– RONALD REAGAN, 1986[1]

'[Ronald Reagan] will always be remembered by South Africa for having preached good sense and tried to maintain it.'
– PW BOTHA, 1987[2]

For most American Republicans, Ronald Reagan was the ultimate politician – a guiding light to whom they have turned for decades since his presidency. Reagan and his coterie were phenomenally successful in creating the image of a president who was at once avuncular and a powerful, uncompromising foe of the dreaded 'Russkies'. It was, of course, an elaborate deception. In lockstep with his spiritual partner, Margaret Thatcher, Reagan introduced the extreme supply-side capitalism that has dominated the world for the last 30 years, and which has arguably culminated in the extreme inequalities and democratic deficits that saw the election of another entertainer with tyrannical impulses: Donald Trump.

But it was in Reagan's foreign policy that the disjuncture between his wholesome image and the painful reality became clear. His coterie of conservative extremists – George HW Bush, Alexander Haig and Dick Cheney – would lead the resurgence of neoconservative thinking. Their preferred tactics were to secretly fund and arm right-wing groups around the world, and insert themselves in covert military activities to undermine leftist governments, regardless of the will of the affected country's populace. This was often done in secret and in open defiance of the US constitutional order, which usually required at least some sort of congressional oversight. Nowhere was this clearer than in the Iran–Contra scandal, in which the Reagan White House used connections with arms dealers and crooks across the world to effectively create a secret foreign policy and covert action unit run on black money, outside government oversight and directly under the control of Reagan's White House staff.

It was in this noxious atmosphere of hyper-capitalism, contempt for democracy and appetite for covert action that the apartheid regime could make hay. Apartheid's operatives, its arms dealers and spies, were to work with conservative groups, comfortable with backroom wheeling and dealing, shaping American foreign policy in sub-Saharan Africa and beyond with remarkable ease. As cash became king in Washington in the 1970s and 1980s, apartheid's generosity allowed the regime to secretly buy politicians and secure the services of top lobbyists. When it came to the peculiarly American game of talking one way, acting another and cashing dirty cheques without guilt, Pretoria was only too eager to be a player.

Despite the aspirations of some conservatives, the United States is no monolith. For a right-wing government like that in Pretoria, this presented a profound obstacle. The president may have supported the South African government but the US Congress and Senate had both pro- and anti-sanctions voices that protested the issues loudly at the time. The CIA and other intelligence structures provided covert support to Pretoria, but the FBI investigated sanctions busters and the judiciary prosecuted them. This required South African spies and lobbyists to work selectively and mostly covertly while evading the law. Their favoured target was conservative groups that bought Pretoria's 'total strategy' argument, of a total war against communism, hook, line and sinker. The Christian nationalist state threw in pro-Christian policies and a commitment to free enterprise for good measure. For some conservatives the burgeoning ties between Pretoria and Tel Aviv were another tick. For other 'good ol' boys', South Africa at the time was a nostalgic throwback to a world they had left behind with the rise of the civil rights movement.

Above all, ordinary citizens in the United States, from college campuses to civil rights organisations and faith groups, organised on a massive scale to counter apartheid. They made the issue of disinvestment and sanctions an important one, to the extent that even presidential debates at the time featured discussions of South Africa and the sanctions question. This was done in the teeth of fierce opposition from many of Reagan's supporters. These feisty activists ensured that no corporate executive or banker or politician with any progressive merit could afford not to consider their position on South Africa. Pretoria, mostly covertly, worked tirelessly to counter this.

Money can buy you love?

The apartheid government actively sought to influence international public opinion in its favour. Covert contacts were always helpful, but as we have seen these came with risk, intrigue and costly premiums paid to middlemen. Shaping public opinion in your favour was an elusive goal given the growing antipathy towards the apartheid regime. However, this didn't stop the regime from lining the pockets of apartheid's silver-tongued lobbyists. Some were crackpot racists who were useful, but not the type of people you wanted to show off among establishment allies in New York or Washington DC. Here the South African government leaned on insiders and operators – guns for hire. These lobbyists came with a network that could be liberal or conservative, but fundamentally their 'causes' were interchangeable: tobacco, pharmaceuticals, arms and apartheid. If you had money, they promised to work their networks in your favour. Like many other snake-oil salesmen, they promised more than they could deliver, yet sometimes even a placebo is an effective elixir.

Not all the lobbyists in the US were Americans. Indeed, by the mid-1980s South African business people were equally important. The South African conglomerate Anglo American was the biggest foreign investor in the US at this time and, together with a number of other wealthy South African businessmen, it had associates and friends who could be leaned on for support. While they may now deny their support for apartheid, it was a system in which they reaped mega-profits and, as a result, they too were ready to do the government's bidding when asked.

Senator Richard Stone: 'Tricky Dicky' and his South African associates

Lying undisturbed for decades in South African archives is the story of Richard (Dick) Stone, a Democratic senator for Florida from 1975 to 1980 who made an extraordinary bid for what would have been one of the biggest pro-apartheid lobby deals of the 1980s.

Stone was a hawk who appealed to the Reagan White House. His track record as senator was vehemently pro-Israel, anti-Castro and in support of the neutron bomb, a favourite Reaganite project aimed at killing humans while not damaging property.[3] From 1981 to 1982 Stone worked as a paid lobbyist for the right-wing Guatemalan government of Fernando Lucas García, who came to power through a coup in 1978. He was responsible for the deaths of tens of thousands of Guatemalans, predominantly indigenous Maya people, during his rule.[4] In 1983, Stone was appointed by Ronald Reagan as ambassador at large and special envoy to Central America, at a time when the United States was actively supporting right-wing governments guilty of human rights abuses and rebel groups looking to overthrow democratically elected leftist governments in the region.

In October 1985 Stone, now back in the private sector, approached the South African embassy in Washington with a propaganda proposal dressed up as public diplomacy 'to refocus media attention on the positive nature of government reform initiatives in South Africa'.[5] He wanted to focus media attention on what he regarded as the violent and radical nature of the ANC, which would facilitate sympathy for their exclusion from any negotiation process.[6] Stone proposed the establishment of an organisation known as the 'Coalition for Reform in South Africa', headquartered in Washington DC, and 'funded by a Trust established in South Africa organized after confidential consultation between the South African government and several prominent, trustworthy South African business leaders'.[7] This would create some distance between him and the South African government and allow for the innocuous-sounding body to be registered in terms of the 1938 Foreign Agents Registration Act (FARA).[8]

The view of the South African embassy was that Stone offered proven success in altering media perceptions of events in Central America. The South African government then approved a proposal that Stone should visit South Africa on an 'orientation visit' in order to meet with selected government and business leaders and discuss the feasibility of his proposal.[9] One of Stone's unique selling points, which he did not hesitate to bring to the attention of the South African embassy, was the programme of public diplomacy he had led on behalf of the repressive regime in El Salvador.[10]

The initial cost proposed by Stone for this venture was a staggering $50 million, to be provided in secret by the friendly South African business community.[11] Fortuitously, in October 1985, a group of prominent South African industrialists travelled to Washington DC and expressed 'interest in contributing to an independent pro-South African lobbying group' such as that envisaged by Stone.[12] The prominent businessmen included Bertie and Ronnie Lubner (founders of what is now PG Glass), Eric Samson (Macsteel), Bennie Slome (Tedelex Group) and Graham Beck (who had interests in coal mines and is better known for a wine label that carries his name).[13] Despite their interest, Marc Burger and his colleagues at the Department of Foreign Affairs found it difficult to persuade South African business to participate in this exercise, and it was decided to negotiate Stone down to a more modest proposal of $1 million, to be borne by government and business.[14]

By April 1986 Stone had agreed to reduce his fee to $1.2 million. Yet the massive discrepancy between this and his original proposal of $50 million generated scepticism in the minds of both government and business. Ronnie and Bertie Lubner and some of their associates had indicated that they were willing to contribute up to $15 million for various projects to improve South Africa's image abroad. However, these funds would not be specifically earmarked for Stone's proposal. A top-secret memo went on to add that the possibility of obtaining such order of funds was largely down to the personal commitment and initiative of the Lubners, Gerry Muller (the CEO of Nedbank) and a circle of their close friends and associates. Attempts to contact over 200 domestic and foreign companies had proved futile, and the Lubners were said to be the best bet to raise sufficient funds for a project of this nature.[15]

Embassy officials stressed the importance of ensuring that Stone met with a broad spectrum of Afrikaans, English and Jewish businessmen in South Africa.[16] The possibility of including black, Indian and coloured businessmen at a later stage was regarded as a necessity.[17] Stone was slated to meet with the minister of foreign affairs, Pik Botha, Bertie Lubner and a select group of five to ten top businessmen. A guest list included Harry Oppenheimer, Basil Hersov, Donald Gordon (Liberty Life), Albert Wessels (Toyota) and Johann Rupert. The urgency of the initiative was due to imminent anti-sanctions legislation in the US. The initiative was likened to the intervention of the Swiss banker Fritz Leutwiler, who had played a central role as intermediary between the South African government and Swiss banks.[18] Stone would be his American equivalent in this unique public–private partnership. South African officials felt that Stone's 'heart is in it' and that 'there are political risks associated with this for Stone ... and there are risks even if agreement cannot be reached with him – leaks of this could be very damaging for him'.[19]

It was agreed that Stone would visit South Africa as a state guest in 1986, and contact would be made with local businessmen to discuss the initiative with them in preparation for his visit.[20] In February 1986 plans were made in a top-secret memo for 'S' to visit South Africa at the cost of the South African government but under the cover of the Lubners' US-based firm Solaglas International. The string of top-secret correspondence provides no insight into the actual meetings scheduled in South Africa. However, a comment from Foreign Affairs officials in Pretoria following a meeting with Stone in Johannesburg raised the concern that he demonstrated a 'serious lack of understanding of the situation on the ground in South Africa'. Bizarrely, Stone had suggested that the unbanning of Winnie Mandela should have been conveyed to her by PW Botha's wife as some sort of cold comfort.[21]

While I was in the US in May 2014, I attempted to meet Senator Richard Stone, now retired after a stint as US ambassador to Denmark in the early 1990s. I soon realised that I was dealing with a man who had over many years mastered the art of evasion. Each question was deftly deflected. It was not that he could not recall anything; it just seemed he could recall nothing about his connections with South Africa. When provided about details of his trip he responded, 'I recall going to South Africa and looking at a lot of wild animals. It was an impressive sight.'[22] Stone could not recall whom he had met, and when I asked if he was introduced to any South African ministers or State President PW Botha during his trip, he politely rounded the question by saying, 'I met with many heads of state during my time – I don't recall meeting the South African head of state. I might have.'[23] He said there was no value in my trying to come and meet him as he could help me no further.[24]

The South African businessman Basil Hersov told me that he did not recall a Senator Stone and added that the South Africa Foundation 'would not have supported the idea of a private agent acting on behalf of the government' even if some companies might have supported it individually.[25] He also said that he was never aware of any attempts by the Department of Foreign Affairs to approach the private sector to raise money to fund projects, though 'they may have approached individual companies'.[26]

Bertie Lubner, whom we met shortly before he passed away in 2016, recalled a trip that was organised for Stone to meet the Jewish community in South Africa. 'He [Stone] was an advocate for change in South Africa but also to … lessen the severity of sanctions.'[27] Lubner went on to add that Stone's proposal 'was a well-received programme but I don't think anything really came of it in any tangible form'.[28] The businessman remembered Richard Stone better than Stone cared to remember his association with South Africa during apartheid.

Paid to climb the greasy pole

By the mid-1970s apartheid propaganda in the US was in full swing and led by the shadowy Information Department. When the Information Scandal broke, it became apparent that not only had run-of-the-mill funding been provided to prominent lobbying firms such as Sydney Barron in New York, but clandestine money had been channelled to fund the election campaigns of pro-South African US politicians.[29] In both California and Iowa, South African funds, channelled via public relations executive Sydney Baron, reportedly helped beat Democratic senators John V Tunney and Dick Clarke respectively, both of whom were vocal critics of apartheid.[30]

In addition to funding politicians, South African assistance through the Department of Information also allowed the publisher John McGoff to try to buy two newspapers which faced financial difficulties, the *Washington Star* and the *Sacramento Union*.[31] McGoff's association with South Africa and other right-wing causes had made him wealthy; he sailed a 100-foot yacht and owned a luxury house in Miami which he purchased through a South African front company.[32] A South African front man in the international arena, McGoff had ties to the National Party elite independently of the Department of Information. A 1974 letter from McGoff to Jan Marais, founder and chairman of Trust Bank (now part of ABSA), reveals that he had visited South Africa and met with RSF McDonald, executive chairman of the National Coal Association. According to McGoff, McDonald and his associates were intent on establishing an English-language newspaper, and McGoff had indicated an interest in not only investing in but operating such a facility.[33] He hoped to conclude this transaction in 1975.[34]

As anti-Pretoria sentiment grew in Washington, the South African embassy came to rely on its paid lobbyists to act as a go-between with US lawmakers who were not eager to meet directly with South African officials. The embassy would provide the arguments and the lobbyists would deliver them into the ears of willing politicians.[35] In this sense, the practice that had started as part of the Information Scandal was normalised and budgeted for by the Department of Foreign Affairs. Propaganda became a necessary part of its DNA. By our calculation, between 1977 and 1991 a total of $105 million (over R2.5 billion in today's terms) was paid by the South African government and the private sector to US-based lobbyists. These figures were arrived at by searching the records of the US Department of Justice's Foreign Agents Register and collating individual filings over the 14-year period. While the figures are instructive, they are only indicative of the recorded expenditure. The true figure may have been far higher given the use of covert fronts operating across the world, including the United States.

One of the reasons for not disclosing the source of funding was that the lobbying firms often came under intense pressure from the US Anti-Apartheid Movement to drop their South African clients. In terms of overall expenditure, the South African government contributed only a third of the total. The majority of the expenditure came from the private sector in the form of the International Gold Corporation (Intergold), which lobbied to ensure that South Africa's primary export commodity could be traded with the US. The South Africa Foundation, a government-friendly corporate lobby group, contributed a modest 2% of the total sum, despite the fact that its members were among the primary beneficiaries of the government's lobbying efforts.[36]

South Africa was not alone in attempts to buy influence with US elected representatives through lobbying firms. To put South Africa's lobbying expenditure in context, it is useful to compare it with that of its ally Israel, which was also leading a propaganda war. During the period from 1980 to 1987 (for which comparative information is available), South Africa spent $90 million while Israel spent $120 million.[37] However, according to Tom Wheeler, a South African diplomat who worked in the US mission at the time, Israeli contacts would act as conduits for South African cash.[38] If the South Africans passed the cash to the Israeli government or to Israeli business, they could effectively, and fraudulently, bypass the FARA restrictions.

Craig Williamson believes that another channel for funding politicians, outside FARA, involved the use of corporations and trusts to camouflage the source of the funds.[39] One example of a politician who received such funding, according to Williamson, was the conservative Southern Democrat and congressman Larry McDonald, who was killed in a plane crash in 1983.[40] Williamson wistfully described him as 'pro-South Africa and going places, very high places'. Given his voting record as the second most conservative congressman in history, he would have made a fine ally.

The most comprehensive written record of the work of Pretoria's lobbyists is to be found in the South African Department of International Relations and Co-operation archives. It is in large part a treasure trove of material, including reports from the lobbyists to their paymasters in Pretoria on the 'progress' they were making.

While some may have questioned the value of lobbyists at the time, a 1987 classified memo from the South African ambassador in Washington DC proposed the extension of contracts for US-based lobbyists, with increased provision for expenses. The ambassador viewed the firms as serving an 'integral part of the embassy's political programme, and they provide us with valuable information, insights into the workings of the American political system, access to all levels of American political life and general guidance and assistance'.[41] The ambassador underscored the role of consultants in supporting general anti-sanctions activities, and described them as being 'fully integrated with the activities of the embassy's political and information sections. This is done by way of a joint weekly meeting with all consultant firms and then individual project meetings and activities with the separate firms.'[42]

In the shadow of the Information Scandal exposé, identifying a suitable US lobbying partner proved difficult. Many of the large firms flatly refused to deal with South Africa and those that did were only interested in the money – few were true believers in the mould of Richard Stone.[43] Eventually the embassy concluded a contract in 1980 with the firm of Smathers, Symington and Herlong.[44] Both Smathers and Symington had been long-term Democratic Party congressmen and had excellent ties to the Democratic Party opinion-makers who then controlled the White House.[45] In correspondence regarding the performance of the firm, there were misgivings about the effectiveness of their activities.[46] These were quashed first by Ambassador Donald Sole in Washington and then by Pik Botha, who remarked in a memorandum that 'it is difficult to express the true value of these services in money terms'.[47] But the bureaucrats may have had a point. Even a cursory reading of the firm's quarterly reports suggests that they did little else than attend meetings and monitor the passage of sanctions-related legislation.[48]

The election of Reagan as president meant that lobbyists had to be found within his fold. This was achieved through the longest-running and highest-paying contract that Pretoria entered into, with the lobbying firm of John P Sears between 1980 and 1992. Sears, a former Reagan campaign manager, brought with him a network of influential conservatives and provided access to senior administration officials and the Republican hierarchy. A report of his activities to the Department of Foreign Affairs from October 1985 to February 1986 provides insight into the role of his firm in drafting speeches, op-eds, letters to the editor of the *New York Times*, and press statements on behalf of the South African ambassador. Even a birthday message for Ronald Reagan was drafted for PW Botha's signature. In addition, meetings were arranged, including a lunch at the White House between the ambassador and Reagan's communications director, Pat Buchanan, a staunch conservative and Holocaust denialist. Meetings were also arranged between the deputy minister of foreign affairs and senators such as John McCain, the US presidential candidate in 2008.

Sears reported that he was present at many of the meetings, including one between the South African ambassador and General Alexander Haig (who was linked to the US sanctions-busting arms company ISC).[49] Sears was also a ghostwriter for the ambassador's articles in US media, and he revealed in reports his propaganda repertoire, including the headlines of two articles written in 1985: 'Racial apartheid is no longer the issue' and 'The USA expects too much for blacks'.[50]

African American lobbyists for apartheid

The most unexpected of the lobbyists who worked for the regime were not the opportunists or the right-wingers but black lobbyists, who made the argument for the white regime from the mid-1980s. One of these was International Public Affairs Consultants (IPAC), led by William A Keyes. While financially rewarding, supporting Pretoria did not come without drawbacks. A top-secret memo in 1986 indicated that IPAC employees and their families had received threatening letters and phone calls and that their work was undertaken 'in a hostile environment'.[51] James A Kendrick, also an African American, joined IPAC to assist the South African consulate in Beverly Hills, providing access to prominent African American politicians and businessmen.

Following SADF cross-border raids that resulted in the death of ANC activists and civilians in 1986 as well as the state of emergency, the US Senate and Congress considered a slew of anti-apartheid legislation. The South African embassy, with the assistance of its consultants, lobbied hard to limit the impact of any moves towards sanctions. As part of its outreach to African Americans it decided to employ Don Johnson, an African American who had formerly worked as an investment consultant for the Ciskei government, to mobilise grassroots responses for action in the Senate.[52]

The *New York Times* correspondent Ron Nixon reveals details of lobbying undertaken by another African American, Robert Brown, in his book *Selling Apartheid*. Brown had visited South Africa in the early 1980s and was at one point a potential candidate for the post of US ambassador to South Africa under the Reagan administration. Brown was also said to have a close relationship with Winnie Madikizela Mandela and gained the right to visit Nelson Mandela in prison in July 1988 with the assistance of the South African government. He would later become involved in a legal tussle with the ANC, as he believed he had been given power of attorney by the Mandela family to represent their interests. He also paid for the construction of Winnie Mandela's home in Soweto and for two of her children to attend college in the US. Brown was associated with the Coalition on Southern Africa, with its strong South African government connections. Brown later informed Ron Nixon that 'all I want people to do with me is judge me for what I did. I did a lot of good and I did not lobby for the South African government.'[53]

It was not for want of trying, according to an internal January 1988 Department of Foreign Affairs memo marked 'top secret'. The memo records that the South African embassy in Washington DC proposed to appoint Brown as part of a six-member black public affairs partnership to lobby for Pretoria.[54] The memo noted his relationship with the Mandela family, which was assumed to be an advantage. Brown and his associates had suggested an annual fee of $580,000, which would be managed by an 'offshore consultancy arrangement with the South African government'.[55] He would be appointed covertly to counter and modify proposals on US foreign policy that had been developed by progressive African American organisations, including the Congressional Black Caucus, the Martin Luther King Centre, the NAACP and the anti-apartheid group Transafrica. The Department of Foreign Affairs, after studying the proposal, noted that they 'very much doubt that Mr Brown and his associates would be able to counter the black policy proposals. The offshore consultancy arrangement also poses certain problems.'[56] In turning down Brown's proposal, the officials suggested that efforts be directed towards Jessie Jackson and possibly one or two other African American leaders.[57] While Brown is correct in saying that he was never appointed as a lobbyist for the apartheid government, official documents show that he actively sought such a position.

Reaching out to the base

As part of a new strategy from 1985 to counter the call for a comprehensive boycott of South Africa, the embassy in Washington recognised the difficulty of making direct inroads into the US business and political establishment, particularly in cities such as New York, which wanted little to do with South Africa. One of the responses was to develop a 'grassroots operation' to counter negative sentiment towards apartheid. In a top-secret memo, a proposal was made to pilot a three-month trial programme 'to recruit constituency support in the districts and states of those Representatives and Senators serving on House and Senate committees dealing with anti-South African legislation. The longer term goal would involve a similar programme throughout the whole country.'[58] In reaching out to the base, the officials hoped to put pressure on the politicians whom they were no longer able to influence from above.

Influencing the media was an important element of this strategy and included *Parade* magazine, a feature of US media culture for over 70 years. This weekly publication was inserted in over 50 million copies of major US Sunday newspapers in the 1980s. In early 1986, the journalist Jonathan Braun approached the South African embassy in Washington with an offer to implement a media strategy.[59]

Braun was the former editor of the *New York Jewish Week*, the largest-circulation Jewish newspaper in the United States, and was described as prominent in conservative Jewish circles. The strategy that Braun proposed would culminate in interviews with black South Africans opposed to disinvestment, such as the KwaZulu politician Mangosuthu Buthelezi. Braun was described in a letter from the South African ambassador as having 'approached us some months ago expressing his concern about the "extremely bad press" South Africa has been receiving and proposed to us that he assist with the "generation of positive news about South Africa"'.[60]

The first stage of his proposed strategy was to commission one of his media contacts in Israel, who wrote syndicated columns for the American press, to compare the South African situation with the 'Arab boycott against Israel'. Thereafter focus would shift to discussing disinvestment with prominent Jewish leaders in South Africa such as Pick n Pay's founder, Raymond Ackerman. The third leg of the strategy would focus on interviews with black South Africans.[61] The project, signed and approved on 24 March 1986, carried a budget of $17,800 (nearly R300,000 in today's terms), including a $5,000 fee for the journalist. It was considered to be 'a modest pilot undertaking which could lay the foundation for further more ambitious projects'.[62] Efforts to access the archive of *Parade* did not prove successful. However, this vignette illustrates the willingness on the part of apartheid's mandarins to use popular media; and of journalists to approach the apartheid cash cow for money in return for puff pieces.

Not all lobbying work was about subtlety. In January 1987 Oliver Tambo travelled to Washington for a high-profile meeting with the US administration, including US Secretary of State George Shultz. On the back of sanctions legislation in 1986, the South African Department of Foreign Affairs sprang into action to develop a propaganda strategy for the visit. The so-called communication plan, approved by Pretoria, had a number of elements, ranging from the crude to the sinister.[63] A copy of a video cassette detailing ANC links with the SACP and Moscow and activities such as 'necklacing' was provided by the South Africans to a contact for the National Religious Broadcasting Corporation, an international association of Christian broadcasters.[64] They would screen the video, followed by panel discussions and phone-in programmes. Copies of the video would also be distributed afterwards. Questions with which to confront Shultz about his meeting with Tambo were communicated to senators well disposed to South Africa. Media contacts were also provided with questions that sought to challenge Tambo at a meeting of the Washington Press Club on 22 January. The influential US right-wing Heritage Foundation was to be roped in to promote the video and generate unease among the American public 'given the presence of an official representative of the "necklacers" in the US'. Radio call-in programmes would be used to discredit Tambo and the ANC.[65]

The South African embassy in Washington also received approval to undertake a number of shady lobbying actions together with the Genesis Group, a firm of US consultants. They agreed to provide non-financial support to public demonstrations against the Shultz–Tambo meeting. Pro-Contra propagandists, linked to Genesis, were mobilised to write anti-ANC pieces, while the influential American Conservative Union (ACU) would be used as a vehicle to publish research in order to target prominent conservative politicians, at a cost of $15,000. The Genesis Group would also arrange to help sponsor the 1987 Conservative Political Action Committee (CPAC) meeting, the most high-profile annual gathering of American Republicans, from where they could positively influence opinion towards South Africa.[66]

There was no guarantee, of course, that the money spent on these exercises would actually be beneficial to the South African government. A 1985 memorandum from the South African consul general in Chicago expressed concern about a scheme proposed by Joe Batten, author of self-help books that sold over a million copies in the US.[67] Batten, chairman of the firm Batten, Batten, Hudson & Swab, wanted to bring 'opinion formers' to South Africa to see the country first hand. These types of public diplomacy efforts were nothing new and proved popular among foreign businesspeople and politicians, who got a free holiday as long as they could grin and bear the tune of the organ grinder. The consul general warned, however, that such efforts had mostly 'proved disappointing as the opportunity was misused to build a base for the "agent" involved and not for South Africa'.[68]

The loony lobby

The tongue-in-cheek online *Encyclopedia of American Loons* lists the author and producer David W Balsiger's professional interests as being 'into virtually anything as long as it has no foundation in reality. Bizarre, but probably harmless.'[69] Balsiger might be described as a loon, but he was far from harmless. In 1989, as the apartheid regime was running out of friends, Pik Botha directed his colleagues at the Department of Foreign Affairs to support a proposal by Balsiger's National Citizens Action Committee to counter sanctions.[70] A handwritten memo on a Military Intelligence letterhead shows that the proposal carried the support of the head of South African Military Intelligence.[71] However, they felt it wise for Botha to speak to their political head, Defence Minister Magnus Malan, to obtain his support. This would in turn give Military Intelligence the backing to 'find the funds somewhere'.[72]

The fact that the proposal had passed through so many hands is an indication of how out of touch the securocrats and their allies in Foreign Affairs actually were. Nevertheless, Pik Botha, a politician who could always be relied upon to tell a tall tale, saw merit in the proposal. Balsiger's previous activities in countering sanctions are well documented in a December 1988 report by the Africa Fund, *Apartheid Whitewash*. The report details anti-sanctions activities undertaken under different guises, both by the National Citizens Action Committee and the Biblical News Service.[73] In 1989, Balsiger set his sights on US Secretary of State Shultz and his 'anti-freedom allies', including American politicians he described as cowards. He opined that 'a good broadside of truth on South Africa would be refreshing'. His rhetoric no doubt resonated with Military

Intelligence: 'Let's get off the defense and on to the attack the next time the enemy shows itself on the battlefield.'[74]

The strategy proposed to focus on the suffering caused by sanctions and kicked off with a $5,000 fee for Balsiger to develop a 'masterplan'. He included a menu of 22 items that Pretoria could support, no doubt hoping that they would take the entire package for $646,000. This included a special edition of his right-wing *Christian Family Protection Scoreboard* magazine ($170,000); organising a Black Pastors Letter Writing campaign against sanctions ($25,000); overt monitoring and intelligence gathering by attending meetings of anti-South African groups ($15,000); countering the anti-apartheid lobby with counter-demonstrations, as they 'should never feel like they can act with impunity' ($24,000); promoting conservative Catholics to counter the progressive Catholic Bishops Conference in South Africa ($10,000); and a 'black front' for which Balsiger proposed to provide behind-the-scenes direction ($50,000).[75] There is no record of Balsiger or his organisation on the US Department of Justice's Foreign Agents Register, which raises the question: if the programme went ahead, could this have been an off-the-books arrangement?

The International Freedom Foundation

Another of apartheid's friends was the International Freedom Foundation (IFF). Operating from 1986 to 1993, it was, on the surface, a typical Washington DC policy think tank with an advisory board made up of a who's who of American conservatives, including leading right-wing figures like Dan Burton, who was the ranking Republican on the House of Representatives Foreign Affairs Committee's subcommittee on Africa; Alan Keyes, a black American conservative who had sought the Republican presidential nomination in 1996, 2000 and 2008; and Jack Abramoff, the Washington lobbyist who would later serve time in prison in one of America's biggest lobbying scandals.[76] The money behind the IFF came from Pretoria, specifically a secret military account that paid up to R20 million to the IFF in 1991–92 alone (R100 million in 2017 values).

Dubbed 'Operation Pacman' by the South Africans, the IFF oversaw two central tasks from its offices in Johannesburg, Washington, London, Brussels and Bonn. The first was to publish and promote as much propaganda as possible to counter sanctions against South Africa, support Savimbi and UNITA in Angola, and target and discredit the ANC and its leadership, including Mandela and Tambo. The IFF was successful in getting the city of Miami to cancel an event on Mandela's first visit to the US, by flooding newspapers with stories about Mandela's support for Fidel Castro. Its second role was as an intelligence-gathering operation for Military Intelligence. The apartheid spy Craig Williamson helped establish the IFF and confirmed that it was an elaborate intelligence-gathering operation that would be used to wage 'political warfare'. All information on political opponents gathered by the IFF offices was fed back to Williamson and his front company, Long Reach.[77] While Williamson would work the backroom, the US operation was run by Jack Abramoff, a vocal supporter of the Iran–Contra operation. In South Africa the IFF could rely on, among others, the leadership of Russel Crystal, who acted as IFF executive director. Crystal was rehabilitated by Democratic Alliance leader Tony Leon in 1999 to play a major role in his party's election campaign.

The IFF's work also extended beyond Washington and was particularly active in London, where it had the support of another core group of conservative figures. Co-founder of the London office was Dr David Hoile, who has been a remarkably consistent supporter of violent right-wing regimes across the world. Rhodesian-born, Hoile was a member of the Federation of Conservative Students in the UK and was subject to controversy when he wore a 'Hang Mandela' sticker at a march.[78] Hoile was also a vocal supporter of the Contras in Nicaragua, and authored several reports on Nicaragua for the IFF in addition to papers arguing vehemently against sanctions on South Africa. Today, Hoile is a lobbyist for the government of Sudanese President Omar al-Bashir and uses his well-honed propaganda skills to defend al-Bashir following his indictment by the International

Criminal Court.[79] The IFF's activities in the UK included publishing advertisements that criticised the international solidarity work of the respected anti-poverty campaigners, Oxfam. It also hosted two fringe meetings at Conservative Party conferences in Brighton, providing a platform for the IFP leader Mangosuthu Buthelezi in 1989 at buffet and wine functions.[80]

Howard Phillips: 'Evil, pure and simple'

The purchase of influence requires the funnelling of cash to political allies. An August 1985 letter from Howard Phillips, chairman of the Conservative Caucus, to Nico van Rensburg, of the South African firm Van Rensburg and Du Toit, stressed that if the South Africans wished to get their desired results from US Congress, the Conservative Caucus would need to see some money. 'We are at a crucial point in the Congressional decision-making process. No final action has been taken on the question of sanctions against South Africa ... The purpose of this letter is ... to determine whether you will send a generous contribution to support the work of The Conservative Caucus at this crucial moment ... This battle can be won. But only if we have the dollars to do the job.'[81] Phillips added a handwritten note at the bottom of the letter, appealing to the South Africans in the midst of the US sanctions debate that 'we need 34 senators to sustain a Reagan *veto*. Can you help?'[82]

Phillips was an arch-conservative and the Conservative Caucus was a lobby group founded and led by him for almost three decades before his death in 2013. Its policies were to the right even of Reagan's administration.[83] Appointed as head of the US Office of Economic Opportunity by President Nixon, his first act was to dismantle the anti-poverty programme, which he described as 'evil, pure and simple'.

Propaganda created by the Conservative Caucus was 'designed to build grass roots opposition' and included lists and headshots of 56 Republican congressmen who voted for 'the anti-South Africa legislation promoted by the extreme left'. Phillips visited South

Africa in 1985 as a guest of the South Africa Foundation, and spoke passionately about the need to support South Africa's anti-communist stance. On South African–US relations, Phillips added that 'few countries are more pro-US than South Africa. They sing our songs, eat our Kentucky Fried Chicken, watch our movies, use our products. They like us.'[84]

While Phillips was an unabashed supporter of Pretoria, he may also have proved a useful conduit to fund trips to South Africa for senators, congressmen and their staffers, who were otherwise prohibited from accepting foreign-sponsored travel. In February 1986, a letter was addressed from the Washington DC embassy to Marc Burger at Foreign Affairs. It was suggested that on Phillips's upcoming trip to South Africa, together with a group of his 'better-heeled' supporters, the South African government could cover the cost of all expenses and Phillips could use the trip as a fundraising initiative for his own purposes. The letter proposed that 'this may be a way in which to get the Conservative Caucus to sponsor trips to South Africa for Congressional visitors in future. I explored this possibility with him [Phillips], and he responded enthusiastically.'[85] Burger undertook to discuss the matter with Phillips at a meeting a few weeks later. The trip included a meeting with Mangosuthu Buthelezi on the Durban beachfront and with Major General Groenewald at the South African Military Intelligence HQ in Pretoria.[86]

Why was Phillips meeting with Groenewald? Craig Williamson might provide a clue. He claims that Phillips was involved in getting Stinger missiles to Angola and also played a part in the Russian Hind helicopter project, which was aimed at getting a Soviet aircraft captured in Angola to the United States.[87]

The relationship between South Africa and the United States in the 1980s benefited greatly from a conservative administration which favoured business. Wherever possible, the role of government was limited, including clandestine deal-making that benefited politically connected intelligence operatives. This shift to the right was contagious.

Buying the US presidency: The apartheid connection

*'When you open your heart to patriotism, there is no
room for prejudice.'*
– DONALD TRUMP, INAUGURAL ADDRESS, 20 JANUARY 2017[88]

The political agenda of President Donald Trump leans towards anti-science, and favours greater reliance on American police at home and on its military abroad. Above all, it is a throwback to a type of nationalism that never ends well. South Africa under Afrikaner nationalist rule is a prescient reminder that misplaced patriotism is the oxygen of prejudice.

A powerful link to US–South African relations of the 1980s is provided by Trump's adviser for the past 30 years, Roger Stone, and Trump's campaign manager during his 2016 presidential campaign, Paul Manafort.[89] Just as Trump was sworn in at the White House in January 2017, the media revealed that the FBI, CIA and other law enforcement agencies were investigating both men for their alleged ties to the Russian government during the US election race.[90]

Neither is a stranger to controversy, having been paid guns for hire by dubious corporations, conservative politicians and foreign governments. It's an agenda that favours powerful corporations, a big military and reduced social spending. Lobbyists such as Manafort and Stone play two roles. They lead non-fact-based attacks on figures such as Hillary Clinton whom they demonise through any media available. At the same time, these trusted old boys work the backroom to raise cash for and from their favourite causes. This has undeniably made these men wealthy and influential in shaping the new right-wing populist politics in the United States.

Roger Stone's reputation precedes him. Journalist Jacob Weisberg described Stone in 1985 as the 'state-of-the-art Washington sleaze-ball'.[91] Sporting what the *New Yorker* describes as 'prohibition-era mobster' outfits, Stone identifies as a libertarian.[92] Between his shoulder blades nestles a tattoo of scandal-ridden Richard Nixon's face, complete with a broad smile.

During the 1980s Stone and Manafort were partners in the lobbying firm Black, Manafort, Stone & Kelly. They kept a client base that included two of the most infamous kleptocrats of the 20th century, Ferdinand Marcos, the president of the Philippines,[93] and Mobutu Sese Seko, the president of Zaire.[94] Both regimes also enjoyed the support of the Reagan and Bush administrations. Stone is reported to have remarked about these relationships, 'If you look at all of our clients, they were all pro-Western, they were all pro-United States. They all had good relationships with Ronald Reagan and his administration.'[95]

Another well-paying client of the lobby firm was the UNITA rebel group of Jonas Savimbi. UNITA paid Black, Manafort, Stone & Kelly $600,000 in 1987 to represent the group in Washington DC. However, as Ron Nixon contends, 'it is likely that the money actually came from Pretoria'.[96] This was money well spent and in return the firm set up an audience with Reagan for Savimbi in 1988 and again in 1989.[97] According to Nixon, the firm lobbied US Congress members hard, setting up 500 meetings. They reportedly contributed to a decision by Reagan to turn on the taps of covert funding for Savimbi that had been shut by the Clark Amendment of the late 1970s.[98] Jardo Muekalia, a former UNITA fighter who now lives in the United States, told *The Guardian* in 2016 that the rebel fighters profited handsomely from their payment to the firm of lobbyists: 'we ended up getting up $40m over a period over four years, so it was a pretty good return on that investment'.[99]

An indirect and little understood link between Stone and the apartheid regime lies in one of the last big plays by Pretoria to influence US politics. In 1988 PW Botha's government had hoped to buy itself a US president in Jack Kemp, the former professional gridiron footballer and congressman. Kemp would eventually lose the nomination, which went in favour of George Bush. Bush nevertheless appointed Kemp to his cabinet a year later as the secretary of housing and urban development. Kemp was later on Bob Dole's ticket as vice-president as part of Dole's unsuccessful bid for the White House in 1996.

Stone was Kemp's senior adviser during his 1987–8 campaign and, since at least 1985, had been his 'principal political adviser', according to Kemp's press secretary at the time.[100] At one point in the 1980s, Kemp was Stone's biggest client and his fortunes were said to be closely linked to those of Kemp. At that time, Kemp received covert funding from the apartheid regime. In 1996 the *Mail & Guardian* reported that the apartheid front organisation the International Freedom Foundation (IFF) had planned to buy Kemp a jet worth $450,000 using Military Intelligence funds in 1987.[101] One of the backers of this scheme was the IFF South African operative Russel Crystal.[102] Former apartheid spy Craig Williamson confirmed that in 1986 'the South African intelligence agents who ran the IFF from Johannesburg had expected automatic membership in Kemp's "kitchen cabinet" and hoped to name an assistant secretary of state for Africa in a future Kemp administration as a reward for providing the Republican senator's campaign committee with a jet'.[103]

After a WhatsApp inquiry to Williamson in January 2017, he told me that 'there was talk of whether purchasing or leasing an aircraft was most effective. My objection to a purchase or lease was due to my doubt that the costs could be effectively hidden.'[104] This much has been known for some time. At the time Kemp, who is now deceased, denied having received any advantage from the IFF. When asked for comment by the journalist Dele Olojede from *Newsday* he said, 'I've made a lot of mistakes in my life, but that's not one of them, tying myself to South African intelligence.'[105]

Williamson now says that Kemp's campaign was indeed assisted by South African Military Intelligence through the IFF: 'Chartering on a when-required basis seemed a better way to go. I believe that some costs were covered.'[106] This is an extraordinary admission and suggests that Kemp's campaign did receive undeclared illicit funding from South Africa. When I asked Williamson if he knew of Stone or Manafort he indicated that he knew of neither nor had any links with them.[107] However, this raises the question: is it possible that Roger Stone, President Trump's trusted adviser, knew about support from apartheid South Africa for Jack Kemp? Given his closeness to both Kemp and to Pretoria through the work he was being paid to do for its ally UNITA, it would be surprising if he didn't.

Stone and Manafort arguably represent continuity between the deep state networks that seek to subvert the US democratic process. They also represent the continuity of the political culture from Reagan to Trump. These are men who favour the interests of the rich and the type of clandestine conservative politics that threatens to engulf a democratic system in a swamp of insider dealing. It is often men who are most eager to swear allegiance to a flag who are easy picking as potential guns for hire by foreign, anti-democratic powers.

A shadowy government

'There exists a shadowy Government with its own Air Force,
its own Navy, its own fundraising mechanism, and the ability
to pursue its own ideas of the national interest, free from all
checks and balances, and free from the law itself.'[108]
– US Senator Daniel Inouye, commenting on the
Iran–Contra Scandal (1987)

Collaboration between the United States and the South African government was based on shared economic, strategic and ideological interests. The clandestine collaboration between the countries' intelligence agencies has been the subject of much speculation and far less proof.

In August 1962, before a bullet would claim the life of President John F Kennedy, the CIA shopped Nelson Mandela.[109] According to a statement made by the former CIA agent Donald Rickard shortly before his death in 2016, he had provided South African authorities with the intelligence that directly led to Mandela's arrest in Howick on 5 August 1962. The leader of South Africa's liberation movement was sentenced to life imprisonment. He would only be freed after six other American presidents had been elected to office. Rickard, who was also working as a diplomat in Durban, said he believed at the time that Mandela 'was completely under the control of the Soviet Union' and 'would have incited war in South Africa'.[110]

While relations between the South African and US intelligence agencies were generally close throughout the 1960s and 1970s, the election of Ronald Reagan and the appointment of William (Bill) Casey as CIA chief proved particularly positive for Pretoria. Reagan's two terms in office in the 1980s came at an opportune moment for the regime. As important as having an ally in the White House was the appointment of Bill Casey as head of the CIA in 1981. This came at a time when the regime was feeling the pressure of sanctions and the effects of fighting a war at home in the townships and a conventional war in the region. Casey 'enjoyed the unusual status for a Director of Central Intelligence of having cabinet rank and, in the opinion of some, he was to become the most important figure in the Reagan administration second only to the President himself'.[111] Casey had worked for US intelligence since the Second World War and has been described by Stephen Ellis as a 'visceral anti-communist'. 'He took up the post of CIA chief determined to restore America's capacity to fight its foes around the world which, in his opinion ... had been undermined by misguided efforts, particularly under President Jimmy Carter, a Democrat, to impose restrictions on the Agency.'[112]

Casey's vision of fighting the Cold War was to 'develop an array of informal contacts [and] build a private-sector network which could deliver help to America's friends and allies around the world, including South Africa'.[113] This modus operandi was revealed in the Iran–Contra affair, which would eventually expose the secret wars fought by Casey. 'The South African government clearly came into the Cold War category of friends of America. It was a bastion of anti-Communism in Africa and it was the main conduit to the UNITA organization in Angola,' Ellis noted.[114] Casey's visits to South Africa included secret meetings with Prime Minister PW Botha, who described Casey as 'a good friend and a gentleman'.[115] He also maintained a good relationship with PW van der Westhuizen, head of South African Military Intelligence from 1978 to 1985.[116]

The apartheid spy Craig Williamson, who said in an interview that he met Bill Casey on two occasions, provides an account of how these contacts played out.[117] Representing the South African Police at the time, he recounts how he met with a US intelligence counterpart at a helipad south of Johannesburg in about 1984. The CIA agent asked to look in the helicopter cockpit, which featured GPS, considered very sophisticated technology at that stage. He turned to Williamson and sardonically remarked, 'I am glad to see that the arms sanctions are working so well.'[118]

From SADF records we gain an additional small window into the relationship between South African Military Intelligence and the local CIA representative, given the codename Citric at the time.[119] In March 1983 Citric (thought to be a CIA agent by the name of J Kelly) informed Military Intelligence that two members of the CIA psychological warfare department were eager to visit South Africa. They were described as 'highly skilled, intelligent and specialists on Cuba'. This would come in handy for the SADF, which was battling Cuban forces in Angola. The CIA felt that between its two officials and South African intelligence, the best plan had to be arrived at to beat the Cubans on the terrain of psychological warfare.[120] They would share methods that had proven effective and in return would require information they could use in their broadcasts to Cuba to demoralise the populace. The two men would be available to Military Intelligence for as long as was required.[121]

In turn, it was reported that PW van der Westhuizen was planning a visit to the United States, hoping to arrange a meeting with Bill Casey, in March 1983.[122] The same memo mentions training opportunities offered by Citric to the SADF, and it was agreed that it was advisable to organise a meeting between the SADF chief of counter-intelligence and the CIA.[123] The CIA also advised that their involvement in the affair surrounding the arrest of the KGB spy Dieter Gerhardt, who as a senior navy officer had passed

South African and NATO material to Moscow, should be treated as 'highly sensitive'.[124] Unfortunately, no further details are furnished as to what this points towards, other than collaboration.

The CIA also shared intelligence with the SADF. In March 1983, Military Intelligence registered nine pieces of intelligence-related material that they had received from the CIA (codenamed Citric). This concerned diverse matters such as relations between the Soviet Union, Libya and Syria, violence in the West Bank, and relations between Pakistan and Afghanistan. Another memorandum suggests the value of intelligence shared by the CIA with the South African military: they informed South African intelligence about the type of surface-to-air missiles held by the Angolan government in the cities of Lubango and Namibe.[125] A note in the margin of this document indicates that the CIA station chief called South African Military Intelligence three days later to inform them that there were at least eight of these missiles in both Angolan towns, and that they had been delivered a month previously. Such information was vital to South African intelligence and military strategists, who also worked closely with the UNITA rebels.

The exchange of information with US intelligence did not always take place in South Africa. Sometimes third countries provided a more discreet cover for interaction. In February 1988, a South African Military Intelligence official stationed in Lisbon, codenamed Thema, informed Pretoria that a South African military attaché had been approached by the US assistant army attaché, Lieutenant Colonel Padgett, at a Portuguese army function. Padgett had a proposal from Washington to discuss an exchange of South African 'human intelligence' (Humint) for US technical intelligence (reference was made to satellite technology). Humint is generally the type of information collected by spies or informers, and US technical intelligence was, and still is, the collection of satellite photographs or the interception of electronic communication. According to the memo, Padgett was a member of the highly secretive US Defence Intelligence Agency (DIA), and the recommendation from the agent in Portugal was that 'in the event that they are serious this time, we can possibly finally obtain valuable technical intelligence via this circuitous route'.[126]

The 1980s was a period in which states began to outsource some of their activities. This neoliberal model of Reaganomics, which sought to fundamentally alter the social contract by profiting the few, also crept into the manner in which other arms of the state, such as intelligence agencies, operated. The use of private contractors, now commonplace in US military and intelligence-gathering operations, has its roots in this period. One aspect of this was the use of quasi-state organisations to create a comfortable distance between the intelligence services and unlawful activities such as killings. This model has largely served to privatise military activity in the 21st century.

This type of activity, too, became standard practice in the late-apartheid period, with the establishment of the Directorate of Covert Collection (DCC). This secretive SADF unit, which operated through a number of quasi-private front companies such as Long Reach, controlled by Craig Williamson, was used in apartheid sanctions busting and other illegal activities. The DCC was also in the business of collecting intelligence and it budgeted for funds in 1988–9 to pay for four intelligence visits from the US to South Africa, as well as three visits to the US to make contact with intelligence sources (no names or organisations are provided).[127] Thus not only was the SADF sending its officers and agents to the United States, it was paying the cost of its counterparts' visits to South Africa.

From the US side, similar middlemen were put into play. This became the norm under the leadership of Bill Casey in the 1980s. One of the more notorious men in these circles was Ted Shackley. Formerly a CIA agent, he was described by his associates as 'cold, calculating, almost bloodless – weird'.[128] Shackley served with the CIA from 1951 to 1979, whereafter he established Research Associates International, through which he would later be directly linked to the Iran–Contra scandal.[129] Shackley was also head of a company called TGS International. In January 1982, the vice-president of TGS

International, Vernon Gillespie, travelled to South Africa, where he met with SADF Colonel Rick May of the Directorate of Special Tasks, a clandestine group which provided assistance for pro-South African groups in South Africa's neighbouring states. Gillespie was a former American army and intelligence officer with a long history in southern Africa, who lived in the States.[130] He came to South Africa to develop and deepen contact with South African intelligence and swap details of sanctions busting.[131]

The most tantalising prospect for Military Intelligence was that Gillespie had set up a safe house of sorts in the South African golfing champion Gary Player's former mansion, which they could use for clandestine meetings. Some of these meetings would almost certainly include sanctions-busting discussions. Gillespie explained:

> his organisation had recently purchased the Gary Player estate [in Johannesburg] and intended using it for hosting personages of importance from the United States, the Middle East and other parts of the world for meetings with members of the SA government and business, to the advantage of all parties concerned. The estate is to be fitted with the most modern anti-intrusion devices and will be patrolled by guard dogs as ... VIPS who stayed at the estate could be targets for international terrorists.[132]

The Iran–Contra scandal: South African links

The growing use of intelligence services for quasi-legal activities in the United States set the stage for the Iran–Contra affair, perhaps the defining scandal of the Reagan administration in the mid-1980s. It involved top US politicians and securocrats, who developed a complex scheme to sell weapons to Iran in violation of a US embargo against that country. The proceeds of the Iranian sales were used to supply weapons to the CIA-backed anti-government Contra rebels in Nicaragua.

The Iran–Contra scandal was investigated by the presidential-appointed Tower Commission as well as the US Congress. Reagan and his vice-president, George HW Bush, were largely cleared of direct involvement in the affair, although Reagan's complicity and that of other individuals and fronts were no doubt obscured by the fact that many of the intelligence documents linked to the deal were never released. Crucially, CIA chief Bill Casey died from a stroke the day before he was to appear at the congressional hearing into the matter. Rubbing salt in the wounds, many of those who were convicted of malfeasance were later granted a pardon by President Bush. Even the fall guy, Colonel Oliver North, who was a member of the US National Security Council, would be granted immunity by Bush.

One of the links that was never fully explored in the final reports of investigations into the deal by Congress was the role of South Africa. While much is known about the links to Israel, Iran, Saudi Arabia and Nicaragua, little has been written about the involvement of Casey and the US security establishment's old friends in Pretoria. One of the allegations that surfaced at the time, although denied by all parties, was that Saudi Arabia was covertly exceeding its OPEC oil quota and selling this at a premium to South Africa, which, according to RT Naylor, contributed to a secret fund run by American intelligence.[133]

When we turn to arms links, there is a view that South Africa was courted but a deal was never struck. According to this view, the CIA gained the promise of assistance for the Contras from South Africa in 1984, but balked when it learned that the South Africans expected payment from the United States.[134] According to Theodore Draper, author of a book on the scandal, 'the CIA backed out altogether ... as a CIA message put it because it did not wish to add a South African entanglement to the existing imbroglio. Despite his qualms, US Secretary of State Shultz was reported in a CIA cable to have approved of the "initiative".'[135]

A contrary view is provided by Craig Williamson, who confirms the South African arms link as part of South Africa's grand international 'anti-communist' alliance. 'You have to get into the context of the time. The Contras are fighting the Sandinistas. Russian weapons captured by UNITA in Angola would be passed to the SADF, who would pass it to the Contras. We were not feeling alone at the time.'[136]

Stephen Ellis, who investigated these types of clandestine Cold War links over a number of decades, believed that the South Africans saw Iran–Contra as an opportunity to cement its relationship with the United States and gain access to strategic resources.[137]

In 1988 the investigative journalist Steven Emerson[138] found evidence of Chinese and South African involvement, even though the Iran–Contra report made no mention of this.[139] According to him, Colonel Oliver North's notebooks reveal:

> on January 5, 1985, CIA official Dewey Clarridge called North to tell him that 200 tonnes of arms were being shipped from South Africa to Costa Rica. North wrote: '200 T of arms en route from South Africa to CR.' Soon afterwards he travelled to Central America and met with CIA and local senior government officials. In a meeting with Vince Shields, the CIA chief of station in Honduras, North was told that the Costa Rica-based Contra group ARDE (the Spanish acronym for Revolutionary Democratic Alliance) did not have the ability to resupply its forces in Nicaragua. After the meeting, North scribbled in his notebook: 'move S/A delivery from ARD to FDN' – the Honduras-based Contra group that had a much more developed infrastructure. The notebooks further disclose that in late 1984, a high-ranking South African official offered North free shipment of RPG grenade launchers if North arranged payment of the transportation costs. Clarridge, who was in charge of covert operations in Latin America, denied under oath to the Congressional committee that South Africa provided any assistance for the Contras, although he admitted that the Reagan administration had contemplated the idea.[140]

Another avenue for South African involvement in the Iran–Contra affair was the use of the SADF front company Safair to transport weapons. Safair is today one of South Africa's leading low-cost airlines, which describes its mission as being to 'unite people with who and what they love'.[141] At the height of the Iran–Contra affair, the airline allegedly carried payloads of misery for its paymasters.

Their activities included an agreement to lease planes to a company called Southern Air Transport, which flew Contra-supply missions in Central America.[142] At the time, Southern Air and Safair denied to the *Boston Globe* that South Africa in any way supported the arrangement, or that South Africa supplied planes, pilots or crew members.[143] This is disputed by a statement made by the Contra fundraiser and US presidential candidate, Pat Robertson. According to this right-winger, 'one helping hand for the Contra rebels came from South Africa. For example, some of the planes that supplied the Contras were made available by a South African air freight company [Safair], apparently after the head of the CIA's Latin America division took a secret trip to South Africa in early 1985 to solicit aid for the pro-Contra cause'.[144] According to news reports, at least 15 pilots and cargo handlers were based in Honduras to deliver supplies to the Contras.[145]

Another indirect South African link to the Iran-Contra affair is through Kredietbank Luxembourg (KBL), which reportedly provided banking services to one of the companies at the genesis of the affair. GeoMiliTech Consultants (GMT), a Delaware firm, actively sought either to sell or to exchange weapons with Iran, as well as to supply the Contras. GMT was established by Barbara F Studley, a former beauty queen from Miami and later conservative radio talk-show host in South Florida, who claimed to have years of experience working with the Pentagon.[146] The company was clearly well connected and employed consultants with links to US intelligence and the Reagan administration, including the former head of US Air Force intelligence.[147]

In supplying weapons to Iran in 1984, GMT was involved in negotiations with a company called Scandinavian Commodity (Scancom), headed by the renowned apartheid sanctions buster, Karl-Erik Schmitz. The arrangement was for a dizzying amount of weapons material, including 2,000 metric tonnes of propellant for 155 mm howitzers as well as 3,000 tonnes of TNT, fuses, mortar shells and two types of howitzer shells. Barbara Studley confirmed the smooth operation with a telex stating 'happy days'.[148] The cash payment for the deal was reportedly made 'against presentation of documents with Kredietbank, Luxembourg, against irrevocable letter of credit opened by Bank Melli [an Iranian state-owned bank] London in buyer's favour'.[149]

Armscor, get your gun

The US had an ambivalent relationship with South Africa in the 1980s. While the neocon networks regarded it as an ally, many other people did not condone apartheid. The apartheid government had to evade those state departments that were against it while collaborating with those departments that were for it.

While covert relations were often fruitful, the US Department of Justice and the FBI were less likely than their defence and intelligence counterparts to turn a blind eye to UN embargo busting. In July 1982 Justice Gabrielle McDonald, the third African American woman federal judge in the United States, fined two British arms smugglers who pleaded guilty to shipping weapons to South Africa. The weapons, found on board a chartered Austrian jetliner in May 1981 at Houston's Intercontinental Airport, included 1,000 fully automatic M16 rifles, grenade launchers and pistols valued at $1.2 million. A federal agent described the cache as 'enough weapons to fight a war' and it was said to have originated from an arms manufacturing plant in Connecticut.[150] A report in the *Financial Mail* suggested that the weapons were intended for use by either UNITA or a rebel group in Chad.[151] Three days before judgment was passed, the chairman of Armscor, PG Marais, wrote to Defence Minister Magnus Malan. He alerted him to the possibility of South Africa being implicated, particularly because the judge concerned was an African American appointed by Carter, and informed him that Armscor was preparing a media strategy to deal with the fallout.[152]

This meant that any mutual interests in issues of weapons had to be dealt with delicately. The official policy, when it came to the sales of weapons to South Africa, was to turn a blind eye or, if necessary, to facilitate the illicit transfer of weapons covertly. An example of this is a record of a meeting between President Reagan and Minister of Foreign Affairs Pik Botha at the White House in May 1981. If the record of Ambassador Donald Sole is accurate, it suggests that both sides danced delicately around the truth, including the subject of South Africa's growing nuclear weapons arsenal.[153] Once the two men had dispensed with the pleasantries, they got down to business, including the issue of nuclear weapons.[154] Botha argued that should South Africa sign the Non-Proliferation Treaty (NPT), 'it would terminate the speculation of South Africa's possession of the bomb. This would mean that South Africa would be deprived of an important deterrent of major psychological value. South Africa ... could not afford publicly to surrender this option.'[155] Reagan didn't see the need to ask an obvious question, whether Botha's government did in fact possess weapons that were regarded as a threat to world peace by the UN and both his own Senate and Congress. Instead, he 'indicated that he was particularly struck by this last argument which had not occurred to him before', and reiterated support for South Africa's nuclear power programme.[156]

What did this mean practically? According to the minutes of an Armscor management meeting, the victory of the Republicans in 1981 created an environment more favourable for weapons sales to South Africa. 'In order to exploit this expectation, points of contact on a low diplomatic level were sought, especially by making advisors, influential businessmen and militarists aware of common interests ... It was evident that there was indeed a change in America's attitude towards South Africa.'[157] By way of example, a request for know-how regarding a missile system was 'used by Armscor and the Minister of Defence as a starting point for high level negotiations on future cooperation with the USA'.[158]

This is supported by disclosures made under the US Freedom of Information Act in November 1983, which showed that

the State Department has authorised commercial sales of more than $28.3 million worth of military equipment to South Africa

> during fiscal years 1981–1983 (through 29 different export licenses)
> … During the last year of the democratic Carter administration in
> 1980, there were no licenses granted for sale of military equipment to
> Pretoria … US companies sold South Africa more than $556 million
> in aircraft and related parts in 1980–1982.[159]

An access-to-information request to Armscor, made by the South
African History Archive with our collaboration, provided a list
of approximately 1,200 contracts between Armscor and foreign
suppliers for which payments were made between 1990 and 1995,
that is, while the US arms embargo was still in place against South
Africa. The list includes contracts that came into force in the 1980s.[160]
The information is revealing as it provides evidence of at least 172
contracts between US entities and Armscor in the 1980s and early
1990s.[161] In addition, on at least four occasions in the 1980s, weapons
such as aircraft were sold to Pretoria's puppet defence forces in the
'homelands' of Ciskei and Bophuthatswana. This included the sale of
a C-212 transport craft for 'one of the homelands' in 1986.[162]

Much of this trade took place with the tacit approval of the White
House. Ambassador Donald Sole reports that 'under the Reagan
Administration, our relations with the Pentagon steadily improved
and there was an increasingly useful exchange of military intelligence,
which was perhaps facilitated by the fact that I was known to be on
excellent terms with Secretary of Defence Caspar Weinberger and
National Security Adviser William Clark.'[163]

These were not South Africa's only supporters. In February
1981, the South African military attaché in Paris passed on a secret
message from Arnaud de Borchgrave, an American journalist and
Belgian aristocrat by birth. The message read that US Secretary
of State Alexander Haig was against sanctions and embargoes that
targeted South Africa. 'General Haig stated to him unequivocally
that the USA will, during his tenure, neither implement nor support
sanctions/embargoes against South Africa.'[164] The cable also suggests
that de Borchgrave believed he had an influence on the former head

of NATO's foreign policy and thereby on US attitudes to South Africa.[165] De Borchgrave, who would become editor of the *Washington Times* in 1985, was not considered a lightweight. When he travelled to South Africa in May 1984, according to a top-secret memorandum, de Borchgrave met with the head of Military Intelligence and senior officers, as well as with PW Botha and Defence Minister Magnus Malan.[166] Upon his departure, de Borchgrave is reported to have told Military Intelligence that he wished to stay in close contact with them and wanted to know whom he could 'confide in' in Washington, or whether he should contact the SADF military attaché.[167] This is extraordinary evidence of an editor of a major Washington newspaper, which influenced US politics and had incredible access, reaching out to help apartheid South Africa.[168]

Quid pro quo

The arms trade between South Africa and the United States went both ways. Indeed, Craig Williamson claims that it was not unheard of that 'the US would have a list of priority items it required [from South Africa]. They would come to us and say they need a [Soviet] Hind gunship.[169] We delivered one of the first, if not the first, to them from Angola.'[170] The presence of Cuban forces and Russian weaponry in Angola's 'hot war' made it an ideal terrain to capture Russian weapons or intelligence about its systems, which could then be pored over by analysts in Pretoria, Paris or Washington DC.

On 9 August 1982, a secret memorandum was sent by Colonel David M Parker, the US defence attaché, to the SADF attaching a list of almost 100 types of items 'desired by the US Department of Defense for detailed technical exploitation in the United States'.[171] As a proposed counter-trade, Parker, without providing detail, indicated that 'information which the US Department of Defense is prepared to provide the SADF will be the subject of a separate memorandum'.[172] Further correspondence in 1982 relates to the proposed exchange with the US Army. Soviet equipment seized by the SADF in Angola would be swapped for intelligence from the Americans on the technology involved and on other Soviet and communist weaponry. The list of items offered included radio equipment, anti-tank mines, hand grenades and 12 different types of ammunition. The correspondence also indicated that certain captured Soviet radios would be loaned to the US for a period of between 12 and 15 months. These interactions underscore the mutual benefit that existed between Pretoria and the US military in sharing weapons technology.

Spy games

The South Africans were not above stealing weapons secrets from the United States if the situation demanded it. The former Security Branch colonel Vic McPherson believes that his old friend and former boss, Craig Williamson, ran one such illegal operation in the United States.[173] According to him, Williamson sent an 'illegal, undercover agent who worked in a computer company to the USA' in the late 1980s.[174] Williamson bought the man, a former policeman who had joined the SADF, a double-storey house with a view of the US defence headquarters at the Pentagon, of which McPherson claims to have seen a photo. From here, the secret agent 'handled someone, a young guy, who had access to US military intelligence at the Pentagon. Craig placed him there. He had a computer business with offices – but he was a handler.'[175] McPherson claims that the South African agent returned to Pretoria, and the US officials were never the wiser.

The spy games were not limited to South African intelligence. Armscor was willing to get in on the act too. Some of these activities required smoke and mirrors to ensure that it could not be accused of spying by the Americans if caught. One example of this is provided by an internal memorandum in August 1989 from Swartklip Products, an Armscor subsidiary, to Armscor Security. The memo gives details of a visit by one John Crewe to the United States to collect software for Armscor, which was to be given to him by a South African scientist completing his PhD at the Massachusetts Institute of Technology (MIT) in Boston.[176] It is believed that the scientist in question is Marthinus van Schoor (he is given the name MV van Schoor in the documents), founder and CEO of a company called Midé, formed in 1989, which works on sophisticated aerospace and naval products in the United States.[177]

A follow-up memorandum in August 1989 dealt with the security arrangement with Van Schoor, who was expected to supply South Africa with technology to use the Euler equation for the aerodynamics of Mirage III aircraft. Van Schoor would not buy the technology, which was deemed sensitive, but rather buy consultation from the creator of a programme to enable him to learn the Euler codes, which was regarded as an 'acceptable activity' under US sanctions law.[178] This use of middlemen and consultants skilfully circumvented sanctions, while simultaneously leaving little evidence should suspicions be aroused.

The final imbroglio: International Signal and Control

The US arms embargo against South Africa was officially lifted in 1997, three years after the country's first democratic elections and the UN's decision to lift the embargo. The reason for the delay was the almost decade-long investigation and prosecution of a US-based company by the name of International Signal and Control (ISC). ISC had been involved in the sale of missile technology to South Africa. We can now confirm the technology was in some form passed on to Beijing. And when the lifting of sanctions came, they were the result of three years of intense negotiations between President Mandela, President Clinton and their vice-presidents, Mbeki and Gore.[179] The negotiations were racked with tension and marred, at times, by conflicting interests. South African Ambassador Franklin Sonn bizarrely called on Louis Farrakhan and African Americans for support in lifting arms sanctions and proposed a 'million-man march' in Washington, effectively in defence of Armscor and its record as a sanctions buster.[180]

The United States, for its part, had a commercial interest in maintaining sanctions. The South African-manufactured Rooivalk attack helicopter presented potential competition in international markets and a US boycott could scuttle sales of its own product in many countries. The US in turn wanted to use its dominance to crush a potential competitor, no matter how unlikely it was that the Rooivalk would displace the US-manufactured Apache attack helicopter.

US federal prosecutors had a number of targets for prosecution, including sales by South Africa to Iraq in the late 1980s – which is ironic, considering that the US was secretly supplying dual-use items to Iraq's Saddam Hussein over the same period. The primary US investigations, however, were focused on seven Armscor officials linked to the procurement of weapons technology from a US corporation, including sophisticated missile technology, for South Africa. The US concerns also extended to the supply of arms to third countries such as Iraq and possibly China, and to the use of US technology in South Africa's nascent intercontinental ballistic missile programme.[181] The company at the centre of the scandal, ISC, a legitimate arms dealer, was alleged to have strong CIA links, and was ultimately at the centre of one of the most significant frauds in the international arms trade. It is possible that all these roles were reconcilable and often even mutually beneficial.

On 18 April 1994, Armscor sent the seven officials to the United States to provide information on the transaction in the hope that they would be indemnified from all further prosecution. The company feared that an ANC government would do little to protect apartheid's sanctions busters.[182] In fact, not only did the South African president, deputy president and minister of defence (all members of the ANC) argue Armscor's case in bilateral negotiations with their US counterparts, but in what appeared to be a tit-for-tat process, US companies were frozen out of bidding in the corruption-riddled post-apartheid arms deal in 1999. For its crimes, Armscor was fined in the US courts but was not required to pay the money to the United States. Instead, the funds were kept in trust in South Africa, to help assist South Africa in establishing a capacity to monitor future arms exports and ensure these were not in contravention of the law.[183]

At the helm of ISC was James H Guerin, a former CIA agent who eventually pleaded guilty in 1991 to an eight-count indictment, and was sentenced to 15 years in prison. 'The indictment also charged that Mr Guerin laundered more than $950 million to help cover up fictitious contracts, and illegally exported some $50 million of arms to South Africa.'[184] According to the *Wall Street Journal*, this pillar of his small Pennsylvania pacifist community 'built his backyard business in little more than a decade into a conglomerate selling military equipment around the world'.[185]

In 1994 Richard Knight, of the US Anti-Apartheid Movement, wrote in the *New York Times* that he believed there were many un-answered questions 'involving our own Government, its intelligence agencies and United States implementation of the United Nations arms embargo against South Africa'.[186] Giving credence to this claim was the fact that the ISC and the South African military establishment had ties that dated back to the 1970s; these continued despite the arms embargo and allowed the ISC and Guerin to make millions out of illegal weapons sales to South Africa. The question that Knight believed needed answering was whether the US intelligence agencies allowed the ISC to continue its illegal operations in exchange for intelligence on South Africa's nuclear and other military programmes, or to support South Africa's military for other reasons?[187]

The US National Security Agency (NSA) director, Vice-Admiral Bobby Ray Inman, reportedly acknowledged that, as director of Naval Intelligence in the mid-1970s, he knew of the first ISC contract and was aware of later information supplied by the company on South Africa's nuclear programme.[188] The Swiss researcher Peter Hug argues that Inman, who was associated with the ISC, was a supporter of military ties with apartheid: 'When NSA Director Vice-Admiral Bobby Ray Inman moved to the CIA in 1981, he continued to provide military equipment such as highly developed radar controlled air defence equipment to South Africa.'[189] According to Inman, who would rise to the rank of deputy director of the CIA in the 1980s, the ISC was an important conduit in the establishment of the secret South African naval 'listening station' at Silvermine near Cape Town. This had the capacity, from the 1970s, to monitor most shipping activity in the world's southern oceans. As the United States wanted to spy on Soviet ships off South Africa's coast, it began a secret programme to set up 'an ocean surveillance system for South Africa. In return for providing such a system [to South Africa], information would flow to the U.S.'[190] When the Carter administration introduced restrictions on the supply of material to South Africa, German corporations and the South African conglomerate Barlow stepped into the breach after the ISC stopped its collaboration with South Africa on the Silvermine project.[191]

Despite tight new controls under the Carter administration, shipments continued through a front company, Gamma Systems Associates, located at New York's John F Kennedy Airport, which Guerin repeatedly said 'is approved by Washington'.[192] According to a former ISC executive, they included 'military technology, missile technology, computer technology ... A truck went to JFK every Friday and loaded out onto a South African 747, and there was never a question.'[193]

While we cannot verify that the CIA assisted the ISC in busting sanctions, Richard M Moose, the US assistant secretary of state for African affairs under Jimmy Carter, believed so. Moose was quoted in an article in the *Philadelphia Inquirer* from 1991 as stating that 'I didn't trust our own agencies any more than I trusted the South Africans ... As it turned out, that was not unjustified ... Responsible officials of the Agency sat in my office and lied to me about what they were doing in Africa.'[194] Moose, who wrote the 1977 presidential order banning intelligence co-operation with South Africa, said that, despite the ban, the 'CIA felt their interests were best served by a collaborative relationship with South Africa ... People who believe they are above the law will make those kinds of arrangements.'[195] This underscores how the outright illegality of the US intelligence and military intelligence arms undermined attempts at democratic control and how this allowed apartheid to thrive through its US connections.

The most important aspect of an investigation by the UK and

US authorities into the ISC focused on whether 'US ballistic missile technology and military equipment was shipped illegally to South Africa between 1984 and 1986 with the full knowledge of the Central Intelligence Agency'.[196] A joint *Financial Times* and ABC News Nightline investigation was informed by US federal law enforcement officials that the illegal shipments to South Africa included equipment which could be used to develop a missile capable of carrying nuclear warheads.[197] While some sources suggested to the *Financial Times* that this was all part of an elaborate CIA plan to infiltrate South Africa's missile programme, it required notification to the Congressional Intelligence Committee. The relevant official in the CIA, Robert Gates, failed to do so.[198] These facts emerged shortly after Gates was confirmed as the new director of the CIA in 1991. It did little to impede a career that saw him appointed US Secretary of Defense between 2006 and 2011.[199]

The ISC, which traded some of the nastiest weapons in the world, including cluster ammunition, also traded with China. In 1984 it became the first US arms company to legally sell technology to China, a deal that was allegedly sealed with the help of the former US secretary of state Alexander Haig, for which he was paid $600,000 according to court documents.[200]

The Chinese connection is important. According to declassified SADF documents, we can confirm that Armscor sold ISC technology onwards to China. In March 1990, the head of Armscor's security department wrote to the head of SADF counter-intelligence, attaching an internal investigation into the ISC matter and various security recommendations that required implementation. This secret document listed individuals, projects and procurement channels that could be compromised by ongoing investigations by the US Department of Justice and US Customs. It confirmed the procurement of equipment by Armscor from the United States and revealingly showed that Armscor, through its Kentron subsidiary, was selling its newly developed, state-of-the-art ZT3 laser-guided anti-tank missiles to China. The technology from the missiles was listed as being sourced from the United States (most likely via the ISC). The channel for selling the missiles appears from various charts to have been an Armscor front company by the name of African Technical Systems, which sold the weapons to ISC Technology Inc., an ISC-owned cut-out firm.[201] This suggests that the ISC sourced the material, gave it to Armscor, and Armscor then used it to make weapons, and recouped some of its costs by selling the new weapons to ISC to sell on to China.

From 1987, communication between Kentron and ISC Technology was channelled covertly through Italy and Armscor's Hong Kong regional office. One of the people listed as being compromised by investigations was Herb Liu, the representative of the ISC in Hong Kong.[202] While no paperwork exists to show how China utilised this technology, one of the two major state-owned Chinese arms companies, Norinco, developed the Hong-Jian 9 or Red Arrow missile system in 1990. It is described as similar to the ZT3. Like its counterpart, it is still in use today. This suggests that South Africa not only covertly imported missile technology from the United States via the ISC, but could also have sold the modified technology via the ISC to China. If this was the case, then the ISC was able to extract profits at both ends of the deal, while the SADF received new technology that it could share with a new partner in 'communist China'.

It is largely due to the tenacity of activists and uncorrupted elements in US law enforcement that the ISC story came to light. But many questions remain. How did US intelligence benefit from the ISC story, for example? There is little doubt that some US officials were at the centre of South African sanctions-busting efforts, but did they place themselves there entirely for personal pecuniary gain, or were they given the nod by those higher up pursuing opaque strategic and ideological agendas? These, and other secrets, remain locked up in the CIA's archives. Indeed, it is perhaps because of how many secrets there remain to be uncovered that the CIA's archives are likely to remain shut for decades to come.

The best democracy money can buy

The 1980s represented an important point in US politics when new right-wing forces began to shape American politics. In starting the process of limiting oversight over the financial sector and giving a leg-up to Wall Street, it set the scene for the financial crisis of 2008. Politically, it was an important moment as many of the young neoconservatives cut their teeth, only to find appointment later in the governments of George W Bush and Donald Trump.

Fast-forward to the present and consider the alleged sinister influence that the Russian government of Vladimir Putin is said to have over US politics. It would be helpful to recall how easy it was for a relatively small, if cunning, power like South Africa to influence US policy in its favour. Russia with its extensive oil reserves, KGB-trained president and global intelligence network is a far more formidable opponent.

In the United States, as we have seen, democracy was literally for sale. All kinds of shady politicians and lobbyists were happy to undertake covert business with the apartheid state. They ranged from the avaricious to the loony right wing. However, in the middle were powerful men who could help influence the way US politics functioned to favour Pretoria and the anti-sanctions narrative.

This rightward drift that infected US politics afflicted the United Kingdom in a similar manner under Margaret Thatcher's leadership, albeit in a very British way. Here was another useful opportunity for Pretoria, as we shall see in the next chapter.

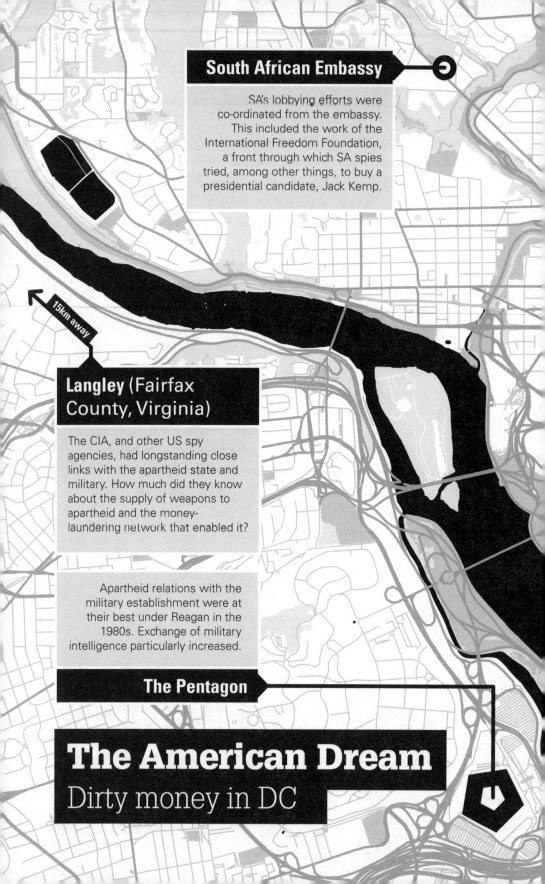

South African Embassy

SA's lobbying efforts were co-ordinated from the embassy. This included the work of the International Freedom Foundation, a front through which SA spies tried, among other things, to buy a presidential candidate, Jack Kemp.

15km away

Langley (Fairfax County, Virginia)

The CIA, and other US spy agencies, had longstanding close links with the apartheid state and military. How much did they know about the supply of weapons to apartheid and the money-laundering network that enabled it?

Apartheid relations with the military establishment were at their best under Reagan in the 1980s. Exchange of military intelligence particularly increased.

The Pentagon

The American Dream
Dirty money in DC

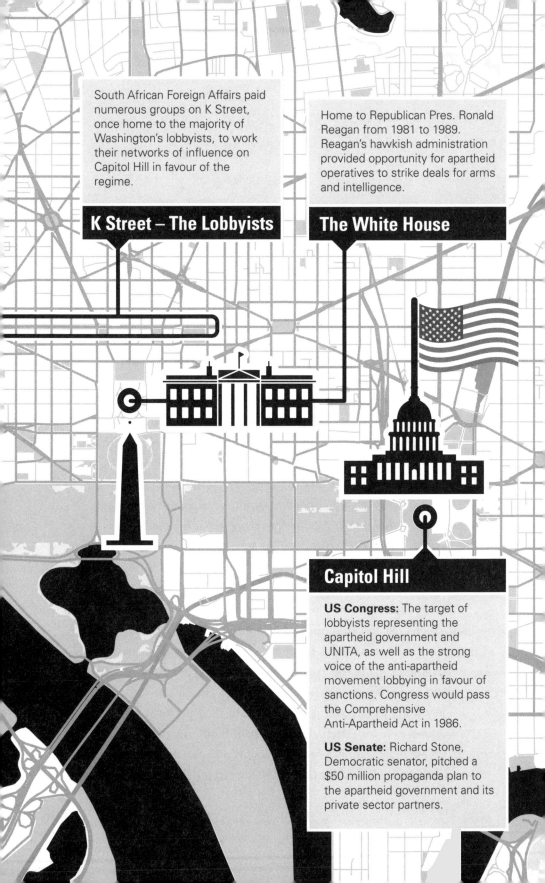

South African Foreign Affairs paid numerous groups on K Street, once home to the majority of Washington's lobbyists, to work their networks of influence on Capitol Hill in favour of the regime.

K Street – The Lobbyists

Home to Republican Pres. Ronald Reagan from 1981 to 1989. Reagan's hawkish administration provided opportunity for apartheid operatives to strike deals for arms and intelligence.

The White House

Capitol Hill

US Congress: The target of lobbyists representing the apartheid government and UNITA, as well as the strong voice of the anti-apartheid movement lobbying in favour of sanctions. Congress would pass the Comprehensive Anti-Apartheid Act in 1986.

US Senate: Richard Stone, Democratic senator, pitched a $50 million propaganda plan to the apartheid government and its private sector partners.

CHAPTER 9

The United Kingdom

Julian Amery: In defence of the realm

*'The prosperity of our people rests really on the oil in
the Persian Gulf, the rubber and tin of Malaya, and
the gold, copper and precious metals of South and Central Africa.
As long as we have access to these; as long as we can realise the
investments we have there; as long as we trade with this part of
the world, we shall be prosperous. If the communists [or anyone
else] were to take them over, we would lose the lot.'*

– JULIAN AMERY[1]

The hidden hand of the aristocratic Amery family has made its presence felt in European and African politics throughout the 20th century. They publicly promoted the British empire and Anglo-Saxon interests to the exclusion of all other. They were particularly adept at working in the shadows through elite secret organisations. They were fiercely anti-communist, and their personal and political fortunes were intimately tied to those of South Africa.

The Amery family's first interaction with South Africa dates back to the South African War (1899–1902) when the Oxford-educated Leo

Amery, who worked as a war correspondent for *The Times*, travelled to South Africa and later wrote that newspaper's history of the war. He was closely associated with important British political figures such as Alfred Milner, Joseph Chamberlain and Winston Churchill. In the 1920s he held the cabinet position of colonial secretary.[2]

His son Julian trod the establishment path with the ease of his father, holding a number of senior positions in government and serving as a Conservative Party MP for nearly four decades before his appointment as a life peer in 1992. A devotee of empire, he doted on the last white-controlled governments in Africa: Southern Rhodesia and South Africa. His domestic politics, particularly on issues of immigration, showed him to be an unreconstructed racist.

One of his abiding legacies would be the role he played as chairman of the secretive Le Cercle organisation, an important conservative and, later, neoconservative talk shop that focused on shaping the West's security policies in the later 20th century. Le Cercle also had direct links with South African business, diplomatic and military sectors from the 1970s to the 1990s, at the height of the sanctions period.

Julian Amery did not limit his skills or use of his networks to politics alone: he applied them with equal vigour in nurturing his own business interests. In South Africa he was a director of Vaal Reefs, one of the largest gold mines in the world at the time. The notorious Bank of Credit and Commerce International (BCCI) in London also employed Amery as a consultant. The BCCI, given the moniker Bank of Crooks and Criminals International by police and investigators, was said to be one of the most important banks for laundering the proceeds of arms and drugs sales in the 1970s and 1980s. In 1991, when BCCI collapsed, it was one of the biggest bank failures in history. The *New York Times* described it as a 'stateless bank that operated in the United States and about 70 other countries, chartered in Luxembourg, run by Pakistanis, owned by Arabs, headquartered in Britain and serviced by outposts in the Cayman Islands'.[3] The BCCI was a prime example of a major bank associated with corruption, bribery and capital flight, but whose activities were not denounced by major Western intelligence agencies despite being under observation.[4] In 2016 a former undercover US Internal Revenue Service (IRS) agent confirmed that the BCCI was extensively used to launder the drug money of Pablo Escobar's Medellin cartel.[5] For his services as 'adviser on international affairs' to the BCCI, Amery was paid what appears to be a regular amount of £20,000 per year.[6] While his appointment letter gives no indication of what he did to deserve this well-paid consultancy position, it seems that Amery may have been a useful political fixer for the bank in view of his political and intelligence connections.

Kith, kin and kindred spirits

Amery revealed his political colours through his long-term association with the Conservative Party pressure group, the Monday Club. Founded in 1961, the Monday Club sought to counter the decolonisation policies of Harold Macmillan's government.[7] It was vehemently supportive of white Rhodesia and apartheid South Africa and was a forerunner of the UK Independence Party (UKIP) in terms of its anti-immigration policies. From within the British establishment, the Monday Club advocated the 'complete cessation of "coloured" immigration into this country'.[8] Up to 35 British Conservative MPs were members of this strongly pro-Thatcher group during the 1980s.

Within six months of Ian Smith's government declaring unilateral independence in 1965, Amery pledged his allegiance to the Rhodesian government at a Monday Club rally to thunderous applause, calling for sanctions to be relaxed and proclaiming his allegiance to those in southern Africa 'whom we should never be ashamed to acknowledge as our kith and kin'.[9] Like his father, Rhodes and Milner, he wrote in 1974, 'The British nation is not confined to these islands. Canada, Australia, New Zealand and South Africa are all extensions of our country. This "British Overseas" is part of us.'[10]

Amery believed as much in the greatness of Britain as he did in the need for white men to hold the monopoly of power over large parts of Africa. In early 1988 Amery travelled to UNITA's headquarters at Jamba in southern Angola, where he met Jonas Savimbi.[11] Amery was clearly enamoured of both his host and the rondavel in which he overnighted. Such trips were clearly also important intelligence-gathering opportunities. Within months of his return he received a letter from the British secretary of state for defence, George Younger, concerning his discussions with Savimbi: 'I am grateful to you for keeping in touch with me in connection with your visit of this nature. I particularly noted your reference to military equipment captured from the MPLA and the Cubans, and I would indeed be interested in any additional information you may have on the subject.' As if to underscore the fact that Amery had his ear, he added, 'a copy of this letter goes to the Prime Minister and Geoffrey Howe [Foreign Secretary]'.[12]

A role not often ascribed to Amery is that of arms merchant. However, an extraordinary letter found in his archive suggests that governments were keen to seek his assistance in what may have been off-the-book weapons deals. In a handwritten letter dated 11 May 1988, the US ambassador to Oman, George Cranwell Montgomery (known as Cran), wrote to Amery, ostensibly requesting his assistance in the covert acquisition of Stinger missiles from UNITA. The recipients were unnamed parties in Oman or possibly in the Gulf.[13] Cran Montgomery wrote to Amery following Amery's 'recent trip to Africa', where he had met Savimbi. Reflecting on the Clark Amendment of the 1970s, in which the US Congress prohibited the provision of weapons to Angola, Montgomery lamented that 'I am struggling with a similar bit of foolishness. The Congress in its wisdom forbade the transfer of Stingers – hand-held anti-aircraft missiles – to GCC [Gulf Cooperation Community] countries, ostensibly to keep them out of the hands of terrorists. Since those who want them already have them, the only real effect is to keep them out of the hands of our friends'.[14] He added, 'I think I will be able to overcome this problem somewhat more quickly than Savimbi did his, but had I known that you were going to visit with him I might have asked you to borrow a few from him to get us by in the interim.'[15]

Amery had a long-standing association with Oman dating back to the 1950s when, as British undersecretary of war, he had sent in aircraft to quell an uprising against the kingdom's sultan.[16] For decades, the Omani government was engaged in low-intensity conflict against a popular insurgency, which was brutally crushed by Oman's despotic leader, causing thousands of deaths. None of this would have been possible without the intimate assistance of British intelligence and the free flow of British arms.[17]

Cran's proposition came only six months after the US Congress had finalised its report on the Iran–Contra scandal. What Montgomery was suggesting was an enterprise that mirrored aspects of the scandal, and would have earned him severe censure if this correspondence had been made public at the time. What is equally damning is that Montgomery's former boss in all of his political postings between 1976 and 1985, Senator Howard Baker, was Ronald Reagan's chief of staff at that time. Both Baker and Montgomery[18] were participants in the secretive Le Cercle's meetings under the chairmanship of Amery.[19]

South Africa: 'Quite a stimulating experience'

Amery was warmly welcomed into the bosom of apartheid political and economic power. From the late 1970s, he corresponded with leaders in South African politics, including Prime Minister John Vorster, Defence Minister PW Botha, Foreign Affairs Minister Pik Botha and Finance Minister Owen Horwood. Vorster emphasised the need to lift sanctions as soon as possible, 'otherwise it might be found that whatever settlement is arrived at will be too late to save the country from chaos'.[20] Amery also supported the reformist policies undertaken by PW Botha 'on behalf of' black South Africa in the early 1980s, while calling for an end to arms sanctions to South Africa.[21]

He regularly corresponded with the anti-sanctions business lobby group, the South Africa Foundation, as well as with Harry and Nicky Oppenheimer, with whom he was on first-name terms.[22] By 1989, Magnus Malan, then defence minister, addressed a letter to Amery as

'Dear friend', thanking him for his good wishes on his re-election.[23] When FW de Klerk undertook his first visit to the UK after the release of Mandela in 1990, Amery lunched with him as Thatcher's guest at Chequers and again at the South African embassy.[24]

Amery travelled to South Africa on at least five separate occasions between 1978 and 1991, meeting business leaders and senior politicians. In 1981 he managed to fit in a white rhino hunt, described in a letter to Harry Oppenheimer as 'quite a stimulating experience'.[25] The hunt took place between meetings with the ministers of defence and finance, meetings he subsequently briefed Margaret Thatcher about.[26]

Amery's diary provides important insight into his travels to South Africa and the network of business and political leaders that he nurtured, as well as the support he gave to the National Party government.[27] In January 1986 he met with officials at the Foreign and Commonwealth Office and the foreign secretary, Geoffrey Howe, before departing for South Africa. Amery considered the demands placed on Botha's government unreasonable: 'Botha was Mandela's prisoner just as much as Mandela was Botha's prisoner. How could he possibly release him without knowing what would happen? What would he do if he began to incite people to revolt? … Mandela probably didn't want to be released. He was more powerful in prison than out.'[28]

The prime minister, through her foreign affairs private secretary, also put points to Amery in preparation for his visit. He was informed that 'she wonders what are the possibilities of the South African government putting together an alternative black grouping to the ANC, including of course, Buthelezi … She regards it as something important, something that could be added to the coloured and Indian elements already cooperating with the government.'[29]

Amery arrived in Durban on 9 January 1986, where he was a guest at the Oppenheimer's Milkwood mansion, set in vast tropical gardens on the Umhlanga beachfront north of Durban. It was midsummer and others enjoying the Oppenheimer hospitality at the time included

Gordon Richardson, the former governor of the Bank of England, and Victor Rothschild, chairman of the bank NM Rothschild and Sons, who had a close relationship with both British prime ministers and their intelligence services. On his first day of holiday in Durban, Amery slept late, swam in the warm waters of the Indian Ocean and read Thomas Hardy's *Tess of the d'Urbervilles*.[30] Later in the day, the leader of the opposition Progressive Federal Party, Frederick van Zyl Slabbert, came to meet him. Amery unfairly dismissed Slabbert because of his progressive belief in universal suffrage, describing him as a 'fine looking fellow with remarkable blue eyes, but I am not at all sure how much there is up top'.[31]

By the next day he was on board Harry Oppenheimer's private plane to Johannesburg, where he attended a supper with the Swiss banker Fritz Leutwiler, who was in the country to negotiate South Africa's debt crisis.[32] Others in attendance included the chiefs of Anglo American, the Reserve Bank, the minister of finance, and the business luminary Anton Rupert. He was also invited to a braai by the exiled Albanian 'king', Leka; they discussed South African politics and Leka's financial problems before Amery retired to the five-star Carlton Hotel.[33] We return to Leka in Chapter 12.

Over the next few days Amery met with bankers and businessmen, discussing politics with senior executives at Anglo American over lunches and dinners of 'excellent crayfish and superb millet, topped up at the end with a sweet Nederburg'.[34] According to him, the De Beers chairman, Julian Ogilvie Thompson, who had frequently travelled to Brazil, was 'much impressed by how the Brazilians had retained power in white hands in a multi-racial system. He accepted that this had been possible hitherto by virtual military dictatorship.'[35]

Amery travelled to Cape Town to meet with Defence Minister General Magnus Malan, who he thought might end up running South Africa as a military dictatorship in which blacks could be promoted to key positions and whites could maintain real power. Amery's intimacy with power is reflected in his opening remarks in a meeting with PW Botha: 'I started by congratulating the State President on his seventieth birthday and remarking that though he hadn't had his face lifted and wasn't wearing a wig, he nevertheless looked younger than President Reagan.' His meetings with both Botha and Malan covered similar issues: Reagan and Thatcher could be trusted, Chester Crocker and Howe less so; the importance of Inkatha and the Zion Christian Church in countering the ANC's influence; and the future of Angola and Namibia.[36] From there he went to meet Pik Botha and then on to lunch with Anton Rupert at his estate just outside Stellenbosch: 'Anton was in a Calvinistic mood of repentance. He said he never believed in Apartheid but it was now necessary for the Government to admit their mistake.'[37]

Following his trip to South Africa in early 1986, Julian Amery wrote to PW Botha thanking him for meeting him in Cape Town and the confidence with which he spoke to him. 'Mrs Thatcher and Sir Geoffrey Howe both showed a keen interest in the account I gave them of our talk and, I think, a genuine understanding. My impression is that the tide is turning against the anti-apartheid movement though not yet strongly enough.' Amery added a postscript at the end of the letter: 'You may like to know that my old friend Woodrow Wyatt was deeply and favourably impressed with you and has been writing accordingly in the *News of the World* and *The Times*.' Wyatt, a British politician and journalist who was close to Thatcher and the Queen Mother, campaigned against Nelson Mandela and the ANC, which he accused of trying to establish a 'Communist-style black dictatorship'.[38] During a visit to South Africa in January 1987, Amery met Magnus Malan again and discussed the state of emergency with him. Malan envisaged it continuing for at least two years. 'He said the ANC had no proper organisation on the ground in the townships. In a way he wished they had as he would have a clear target to go for.'[39] Thereafter, the British MP was briefed by Malan's chief of staff, General Jannie Geldenhuys, on the situation in Angola.[40] Amery wished to linger for a 'much longer talk with the General who was engagingly frank', but he had a plane to catch. He arrived that evening in Durban just in time to join the Oppenheimers at their second course of dinner.

He briefed the clan about his 'tour' in South Africa and remarked: 'The great thing about talking to Harry is that it puts into perspective the views that I have been forming in the rest of the tour. Bridget [Oppenheimer] is much more left wing than he is nowadays. He remains extremely balanced. Strongly opposed to sanctions of any sort. Critical of the Government but well aware of the difficulties that PW Botha faces.'[41] Amery noted that he did not have an opportunity to visit any townships. As an interloper, he restricted his views on black opinion to a short paragraph reflecting on his conversation with 'our black drivers at Anglo American'.[42]

Le Cercle: 'In principle the group does not exist'

Tucked away in a report of the Khan Committee, declassified in 2016, are details of links between the apartheid regime and a shadowy secret international organisation, Le Cercle, chaired by Amery for many years. The Khan Committee was appointed by FW de Klerk in 1991 to investigate active secret state projects following media reports of 'third force' activities linked to the government. In its third report, reference was made to Le Cercle, which it described as an 'informal forum of influential representatives of a "conservative cast of mind" from Britain, France, Germany, Italy, Oman, the USA and South Africa. Annual meetings consider political, economic and military developments. SA contributes R33,000 plus donations to the secretariat. Valuable source of advice and friendship.'[43] At around this time, Le Cercle's chairman, Julian Amery, estimated that hosting its meetings cost about $50,000 per year (excluding flights). This suggests that South Africa was contributing a quarter of the secret society's budget just before the end of apartheid.[44] This generous South African funding, funnelled through the Department of Foreign Affairs, is believed to have been discontinued after almost two decades in late 1992.[45]

The existence of Le Cercle, as well as its potential influence, has long been the subject of speculation. Its membership and meeting venues are secret. Le Cercle wields potentially significant influence on political affairs through its convening power, information sharing and what amounted to quasi-intelligence activity during the Cold War. In internal documents the group describes its practice of meeting twice yearly, alternating between Washington and a European city. South Africa and Oman were the only exceptions in hosting this transatlantic affair. Amery said of the secret club: 'There is … no membership. Members are invited, the organization is completely flexible. In principle, the Group does not exist, it reaches no conclusions and no conclusions are thus made public.'[46] Our first clue to the existence of Le Cercle was found in a file in the South African Department of Foreign Affairs archives carrying the same name. The significance of these documents, when read together with papers subsequently located in Julian Amery's archive at Cambridge, is that they clarify the important role played by the apartheid state in Le Cercle's affairs as financier, host and beneficiary of intelligence.

Le Cercle was founded in the early 1950s, to facilitate the first secret talks between French and German heads of state after the Second World War, with a vision of integrating Christian Catholic Western Europe. For much of the next 50 years their politics veered between conservative and hard right-wing. Its Catholic membership showed a strong bias towards authoritarian orders such as Opus Dei and the Knights of Malta, which placed much value on secret networks, conservative politics and the money required to support both.[47] Operating in the shadows was a network of participants drawn from within the intelligence sector and with close association to the arms industry.

What started as an association of regular meetings between leaders of six Christian Democratic countries in the 1960s had, by the 1970s, morphed into a biannual secretive gathering for conservatives from both North America and Western Europe.[48] This signalled a change in focus to anti-communism, strengthened by the arrival of participants such as Henry Kissinger and David Rockefeller. Le Cercle thus evolved into a 'confidential forum for influential personalities and the policy advisors of the heads of state, rather than the heads of state themselves, to hold off the record discussions on current affairs and the desired action to be taken. The high-level discussion of policy would then be implemented by individual Le Cercle members working in their governments, legislatures, parties and public opinion.'[49]

From talk shop to intelligence outfit

Amery, who joined Le Cercle in the 1970s, had risen to the position of chairman by the 1980s. He provided an important link between the organisation, the United Kingdom and South Africa. The club, which had an 'invited members only' policy, was made up almost exclusively of old white influential and conservative men, and the countries that participated most actively were Britain, France, Germany, the United States and South Africa.[50]

A key Le Cercle member was the rabid anti-communist Brian Crozier, who played an important behind-the-scenes role during the 1980s. Crozier wrote numerous publications praising right-wing regimes, including a favourable biography of the Spanish dictator Franco.[51] He also worked closely with the CIA and met its head, Bill Casey, as well as President Ronald Reagan, with whom he would correspond through secret letters sent via Nancy Reagan.[52] Crozier saw South Africa as the West's mineral warehouse: it required little urgent change, Crozier noting only 'anomalies in its treatment of the black and coloured populations'.[53]

Crozier's ties to the CIA and British intelligence took on various practical dimensions in the form of think tanks and associations which operated in the same orbit as Le Cercle. The first of these was the Forum World Features, a CIA front 'news agency' based in London, which enabled Crozier to grow his network of international contacts to the point that it earned him the distinction in the *Guinness Book of World Records* of having interviewed the most heads of state or government, 58 in all.[54] By 1975 the link between Forum World Features and the CIA was blown open by British and American media. Crozier, however, had moved on to establish the Institute for the Study of Conflict (ISC).[55] He used this new vehicle, together with his contacts at Le Cercle, to establish a pro–South Africa propaganda organisation, the Foreign Affairs Research Institute (FARI) in the UK, which was heavily funded by the apartheid state.[56]

According to the researcher David Teacher, Crozier's ISC, with funding from South Africa's Department of Information, also established a pro-Pretoria propaganda unit in Paris.[57] Some of the activities of the ISC and its connections to Le Cercle were revealed in 1982, when the news magazine *Der Spiegel*, one of the few publications to report on Le Cercle's existence, exposed the links between Crozier and the Bavarian politician Franz Josef Strauss.[58] The source for this information was Dr Hans Langemann, an employee in the Bavarian Ministry of the Interior, who would eventually be sentenced to imprisonment for leaking details about intelligence interference in West German politics. The 'Langemann Papers' revealed that Crozier had actively worked within an intelligence network that unsuccessfully sought to deliver the German chancellorship in 1979 to the right-wing Strauss. This was hot on the heels of the successful election of Margaret Thatcher in Britain. Crozier claimed to have played a similar and central role in Britain, where he and a small insider group had set up a secret committee called Shield, which served to provide security and intelligence advice to Thatcher and her aides during her first campaign for prime minister.[59]

Le Cercle: South Africa takes its seat

A major emphasis of Le Cercle's strategy was to roll back communism in certain key countries. Le Cercle viewed the expansion of communism as a virtual World War Three being waged against the so-called Free World.[60] One of the countries that deserved particular attention was Angola, where Le Cercle liaised directly with UNITA leadership and argued against Namibian independence. In Mozambique it supported RENAMO and in Afghanistan the Mujahideen.[61]

According to Adrian Hänni, Le Cercle depended on funding from four sources: the South African government, conservative German party political foundations, European corporations, and its individual members.[62] The South African Department of Foreign Affairs not only financed but also hosted meetings of Le Cercle in January 1984 (at the Lanzerac Hotel in Stellenbosch), March 1988 (at the Mount Nelson Hotel in Cape Town), and March 1991 (at the Lord Charles Hotel, Somerset West).[63] The South African government's participation in Le Cercle can be traced as far back as 1974 when Harold Taswell, the ambassador to the UN in Geneva, attended meetings on a regular basis.[64] South Africa was equally useful to Le Cercle, and it was proposed that the initial contribution of R5,000 in 1974 would be increased to R7,500 in 1975 (over R300,000 today), with payment to be made through a bank account in Liechtenstein in favour of the innocuously named Institute for Research and Development.[65] The source of the funds was the Special Defence Account (SDA), which was the primary source of funding for covert arms purchases and clandestine projects for the apartheid regime.[66] South Africa got a good return on its investment. Taswell reported that at a meeting of Le Cercle a number of participants had remarked to him that 'you must be surprised to be at a meeting like this and to find a group of people so well disposed to you in South Africa'.[67]

Another example of the usefulness of these meetings was the exchange of informal intelligence. In a letter to his superior, Taswell informed him of arms sanctions issues. A German member of Le Cercle had learnt from the Siemens office in South Africa that the South African Post Office had ended its telephone contract with Siemens in favour of a French company as a quid pro quo for France's willingness to sell Mirage jets to South Africa.[68]

The South African diplomat Donald Sole attended meetings of Le Cercle in 1978, and noted an impressive presentation by Richard Perle, who was US Senator Jackson's adviser on strategic arms affairs.[69] Perle, a self-described neoconservative known in Washington circles as the 'Prince of Darkness', would become Ronald Reagan's assistant secretary for defence in the 1980s. He was also an outspoken proponent of the US invasion of Iraq in 2003. Other participants at this meeting in Washington included the former head of the US Defence Intelligence Agency and a member of the US National Security Council.[70]

With the election of Ronald Reagan in November 1980, the network of Le Cercle contacts in Washington grew in importance. Later that same month, the South African ambassador to Madrid sent a secret memo to his director general following a meeting with the Le Cercle member Sanchez Bella,[71] a diplomat and minister during the Franco dictatorship.[72] Bella stressed that it was important for the South Africans to send a delegation to a meeting of Le Cercle in December 1980 given that two or three of Reagan's close aides from California would attend the meeting and that any discussions with them 'would be as good as discussions with the President himself'.[73]

Always concerned with the communist threat, the Le Cercle meeting in 1984 addressed the serious threat of 'infiltration of Socialist parties of Europe and elsewhere by Communist agents'.[74] The meeting was hosted by the conservative Hanns Seidel Foundation, which was linked to Franz Josef Strauss's Christian Social Union (CSU). According to the South African ambassador who attended the meeting in Munich, the meeting cited the spillover effect of the alleged infiltration by socialist parties, by referring to 'Swedish Prime Minister Olof Palme, whose political views are on the extreme left, has for years been the foreign policy mentor of [Democratic Party presidential candidate] Walter Mondale, whose Scandinavian origins are well known. The SPD [Social Democrats] in Germany is especially heavily infiltrated.'[75] These views were stated 18 months before Palme was assassinated by an unknown gunman.

Le Cercle gatherings also attracted disreputable guest speakers such as Imelda Marcos,[76] the wife of the corrupt Filipino president. Another attendee was Richard Nixon, who resigned his presidency amid the notorious Watergate scandal, of which he was the primary architect.[77]

The first meeting of Le Cercle to take place in South Africa was from 12 to 15 January 1984 in Stellenbosch. Le Cercle wanted to create some distance from its South African backers, who were not the official hosts of the meeting. It was thus hosted by the Le Cercle member General CA Fraser, the head of the South African Army.[78] The Department of Foreign Affairs still assisted in numerous ways. The first was to ensure that the state-owned South African Airways (SAA) guaranteed the lowest-priced fares for participants and to up-grade tickets at no cost.[79] Thirty participants from the seven Western European countries and the United States attended the meeting, which included former French ministers, German MPs, UK politicians and US securocrats. The VIPs were accommodated at the Rupert-owned Fleur du Cap residence in Somerset West.[80] Documents accessed in the Foreign Affairs archive reveal that attempts were made to ensure the presence of State President PW Botha and Harry Oppenheimer at the meeting, although the files contain no further details to confirm this.

Two leading South African businessmen, Gavin Relly, the chair of Anglo American, and Basil Hersov of Barclays Bank, received personal invitations to Le Cercle's next secret gathering in Bavaria in July 1984. The invitation, delivered through the South African Department of Foreign Affairs, was signed by the Bavarian premier, Franz Josef Strauss.[81] Both Relly and Hersov would thereafter regularly appear on the list of Le Cercle invitees, suggesting that their membership had been secured.[82] When I asked Basil Hersov about these meetings, he had only a vague recollection of Le Cercle and described his only memory of Amery as one of 'general geniality'.[83] Anton Rupert of the Rembrandt Group and Julian Ogilvie Thompson of De Beers were also regular invitees and could therefore be considered members.[84] Ogilvie Thompson did not respond to repeated requests for an interview.

A further meeting of Le Cercle is reported to have taken place in Cape Town in March 1988.[85] Attendees were invited to a dinner at the Mount Nelson Hotel hosted by the National Party minister George Bartlett, and on the first day of the meeting subjected themselves to the usual range of government-aligned views by Pik Botha. His director general, Neil van Heerden, also delivered an address that summed up the position Pik Botha took in conversation with heads of state at the time. It was a title that appeared to suggest its own racist answer: 'Will black Africa die in misery?'[86] The third and last Le Cercle meeting to be hosted in South Africa took place in March 1991 at the Lord Charles Hotel in Somerset West. Prominent South African businessmen such as Basil Hersov and the Anglo American Minorco chief executive, Hank Slack, were invited to the secret gathering. The one surprising speaker at the meeting was South African writer and anti-apartheid activist, Fatima Meer, who had been banned and detained for her links to the Black Consciousness movement.[87]

With the election of Nelson Mandela as president in 1994, it is believed that South Africa discontinued its participation in Le Cercle activities. In tandem, the focus of Le Cercle shifted dramatically away from the southern African and Cold War terrains. New frontiers awaited, including the Balkans, Eastern Europe, the Middle East, North Korea and China. By 1995 the list of invitees had been extended to include representatives from arms companies Aérospatiale and British Aerospace, as well as Jonathan Aitken, the former UK defence minister who would become chair of Le Cercle in that year.[88]

Amery died in 1996 a few years after relinquishing his chairmanship of this secret society, a life's work made irrelevant by the end of the Cold War and white minority rule in southern Africa. He and others had ensured that South Africa was brought into the fold of this secret gathering to benefit from contact with like-minded elites. In return for gossip, intelligence and a seat at one of the high tables of anti-communism, South Africa would dutifully pick up the tab.

While Le Cercle does not represent a classic sanctions-busting operation, its importance lies in the creation of a platform that welcomed participants to cut deals away from the public eye. The apartheid regime was not the only rogue to benefit from this, and it will likely not be the last. Somewhere in the world this club no doubt still meets, having long shifted its attention to the opportunity that another nation's misery represents. Amery's legacy, unlike his British empire, has endured.

Margaret Thatcher and the Conservative Party

*'We don't just talk to you as businessmen, but as human
beings. Can you continue to allow such suffering?'*
– Oliver Tambo, ANC leader, addressing
UK business leaders[89]

'A typical terrorist organisation'
– Margaret Thatcher on the ANC[90]

I asked the former South African minister of foreign affairs Pik Botha about his meetings with Margaret Thatcher. He veered from the factual to his own personal impressions.

I am the only foreign dignitary to have [had] a private one-to-one meeting with her – without any of her staff present. My friends would joke, now what did the two of you do? It's strange how often other women don't seem to like her. She had very beautiful breasts. She couldn't sit still for a minute, the one leg over the other leg, to the sides the hands kept moving. I will never forget to this day that night in London, they had a tremendous dinner with all the important ones and the women dressed up, I am telling you. She was dressed up in a beautiful blue dress with her collar and her head like a flower emerging out of it. When I entered the meeting the following morning I said, 'Pardon, would you allow me to tell you how charming you looked last night? I would have given anything to be your partner.' Hell, for the first time she blushed. We remained very great friends despite difficult times. She was the one that was never in favour of sanctions.[91]

While Botha was thin on the detail of his actual discussion with the head of state of one of South Africa's most important trading partners, declassified minutes detail two separate meetings he had with Thatcher[92] and her foreign secretary Lord Carrington[93] in

1980. The focus of the discussions was on the peace talks concerning Namibia. Botha spoke to the British as if he was briefing a junior US Republican congressman on his first visit to Africa, but they seemed to tolerate this. He made repeated references to the fact that 'Africa was dying' and was beset by plague, locusts, rinderpest and poor infrastructure, with South Africa being the shining light in an otherwise dark continent. Botha wailed at the fact that African countries increased their trade with South Africa while calling on Britain for sanctions, telling Carrington, 'I cannot go on like this'. According to him, African countries were keeping people hungry in order to get more money for arms. This was rich coming from Africa's largest arms exporter, which spent up to 30% of its GDP on the war economy during the 1980s. When his arguments failed him, Botha, not unlike Donald Trump, said that perhaps it would suit South Africa to 'drag the region into a conventional war'.[94]

Margaret Thatcher led the Conservative Party between 1975 and 1990, and was prime minister between 1979 and 1990. These were critical years during the sanctions period, and for the South African government. While Thatcher never came out publicly in support of apartheid, she often tolerated governments that denied the majority of people the franchise. Thatcher, like Reagan, was committed to crushing trade unions and cutting social spending. She favoured the interests of the private sector and, given the extent of trade between the United Kingdom and South Africa, there were many private interests that required her protection.

While Conservative MPs like Julian Amery would frequently whisper into Thatcher's ear of the need for the UK to remain steadfast in its support of Pretoria, the anti-communist prime minister needed little convincing. As a woman she may always have been treated as an outsider, but ideologically she was on the inside of right-wing opinion that sought to gently criticise apartheid without threatening its enforcers with any serious consequence.

Thatcher was no stranger to South Africa. She and her family had longstanding ties with the country. Her first recorded visit to South

Africa was in 1973 as secretary of state for education and science. The first UK minister to visit South Africa since Harold Macmillan came to make his famous 'winds of change' speech in 1960, she would make no grand statement on the need for reform. Instead, records in the UK National Archives show that she was briefed by Prime Minister Vorster on 'the great differences … between the ways of thinking of the Africans and Europeans' and attended a 'multiracial lunch' given by the UK consul general in Johannesburg, before spending her last evening in the exclusive Mala Mala game park, courtesy of helicopter transport provided by the South African Air Force.[95]

Her son, Mark Thatcher, who had been sent by his parents to spend a year working in South Africa in 1972, lived in the leafy suburbs of Cape Town before his arrest and guilty plea for his role in an attempted coup in Equatorial Guinea in 2004. Her husband, Denis Thatcher, whom the prime minister regarded as an important behind-the-scenes adviser, travelled to South Africa on business on a number of occasions.[96] His racist and bigoted utterances were notorious: in 1984 he told the Swiss president at a dinner to 'keep Switzerland white', referred to black Britons as 'fuzzy wuzzies in Brixton' and lamented that India was 'high on the buggeration factor'.[97]

PW Botha took office as prime minister of South Africa shortly before Thatcher, and was eager to meet with his new counterpart. British diplomats described 'an organized campaign' of approaches by Harry Oppenheimer as well as hints by Pik Botha concerning the proposed visit.[98] Following a request by Botha, Margaret Thatcher decided to send Lord Hunt of Tanworth (formerly John Hunt, secretary to the cabinet) to meet Botha in April 1980. Hunt was instructed to act as Thatcher's emissary, even though 'the ostensible purpose of his visit will be to visit personal friends and to have meetings in connection with his directorship of the Prudential Assurance company'.[99] In his briefing notes Hunt was told that, while there could be no relaxation of the UN arms embargo, consideration was being made to improve the access and facilities given to South African military attachés in London, and that political reform would be rewarded with an upgrade in the volume and sensitivity of shared intelligence material.[100]

Hunt met with Margaret Thatcher on 31 March 1980 to discuss his mission. At the meeting, the Foreign and Commonwealth Office stressed that it wanted to 'avoid having to choose between Black and White Africa ... If faced with a choice we would almost certainly have to choose South Africa, i.e. we would have to veto a resolution imposing sanctions on South Africa (the Prime Minister agreed).' However, the sobering report reads that 'it was difficult to see how the problem of race relations in South Africa would ever be solved: the end result would probably be a blood bath'.[101] While the meetings with Botha, his minister of defence, Magnus Malan, and Pik Botha delivered little results, the UK side believed it could form the basis for continuing conversation with South Africa, which they feared risked becoming isolated in the same manner as East Germany.[102]

PW Botha, according to private correspondence from 1983, seemed to have little faith in Thatcher: 'since the mess the British Government under her leadership made of the Rhodesian question I have very little confidence in her'.[103] He would eventually meet with her on an ill-fated European tour in 1984. And while the two tolerated one another, she never befriended him as she did the Chilean dictator Augusto Pinochet.

Thatcher and the Conservative Party were, throughout most of this period, staunch supporters of Mangosuthu Buthelezi and the Inkatha Freedom Party. His moderate politics and status as a princeling in the Zulu kingdom made him a safe bet for the British. One anecdotal example of this was that the Foreign and Commonwealth Office allowed repeated use of its diplomatic bag by the IFP to ferry messages to the ANC leadership in London. As one official noted in relation to this, 'Our relations with them [the IFP] are, given the general political situation in South Africa, likely to become of increasing importance.'[104] The archives also show that Conservative politicians were frequent guests in South Africa. One such luminary was the future prime minister David Cameron, who visited in 1989 'when he was 23, on an all-expenses-paid "fact-finding mission" funded by Strategy Network International, a lobbying group seeking to lift sanctions'.[105] As leader of the Conservatives, David Cameron broke with his party's policy more than a dozen years after South Africa's first democratic elections when he finally conceded in *The Observer* in 2006 (after meeting Mandela) that 'the mistakes my party made in the past with respect to relations with the ANC and sanctions on South Africa make it all the more important to listen now'.[106]

Trade sanctions: 'A very difficult position'

Margaret Thatcher was an important ally in the anti-sanctions campaign, officially because it would harm black workers and privately because it would harm the UK economy. The call for sanctions in the UK only grew louder as she took office, backed by church groups, trade unions, and many liberal and left-inclined groups across Britain that formed the support base of the Anti-Apartheid Movement. In response, the UK government archives are peppered with correspondence between diplomats reporting their concerns and that of British corporations reporting potential commercial losses that would be suffered as a result of sanctions.

At a meeting of the cabinet ministerial group on southern Africa in April 1978, there was general agreement that

> the United Kingdom could not afford a trade embargo against South Africa and that we should be ready to use our veto in the Security Council to prevent one. In the meantime, although it would be a long process, it was essential to begin to take steps to reduce our economic dependence on South Africa. It was however important to understand clearly the nature of our dependence ... What was vital to us at present was the supply of South African raw materials: without these, important sections of British industry could be ruined ... In the mean-time we should remain within the convoy of the five [UN Security Council members], we are bound to be the slowest ship.[107]

At the third meeting of the cabinet ministerial group, the secretary of state reported on the 'very difficult position we are in'.[108] This would include massive job losses should sanctions be fully implemented: 'some 80,000 jobs were dependent on exports to South Africa, and in 1975 £250 million was remitted from South Africa'. Large UK corporations such as the chemical giant ICL and General Electric relied on South Africa for between 10% and 15% of their overall profit.[109] The report also stressed measures that could cautiously wean the UK off South African minerals. To deal with any sudden cessation of these supplies, it was proposed that 'we should stockpile the main strategic minerals we obtained from South Africa and we might add to these two or three minerals not specifically of South African origin so as to present our action as being intended as insurance against developments in East/West relations'.[110] South Africa was by far the most important single trading partner with the UK in Africa and contributed significantly to the UK's service economy, providing 20% of its total income by 1978.[111]

By their own admission, the UK argument against sanctions required a healthy dollop of sophistry. For example, British diplomats feared that proposed UN Security Council economic sanctions against the Iranian government of the Ayatollah Khomeini in 1980 would make the case for lifting South African sanctions so much harder.

> After all if economic sanctions can be urged against Iran for the sake of 50 (and those all white, with the release of the coloured and female hostages) Americans, it will need all the sophistry at the FCO's disposal to resist the political case, on human rights grounds, against South Africa for their continued political and social ill-treatment of 19 million non-whites. The attitude of the US towards sanctions against South Africa was, until recently, at best ambivalent. With an Iranian precedent, the US attitude must now be taken as settled in favour of imposing sanctions against South Africa if a suitable opportunity should offer itself ... I suggest that it behoves us to be on our guard.[112]

Robin Renwick, who was Thatcher's high commissioner in Pretoria from 1987 to 1991, argued that Thatcher was interested only in selective sanctions that would not harm black South Africans, such as the 500,000 jobs he claims were lost in the agricultural sector. When pushed that it was also about British jobs, he claimed, 'Mrs Thatcher wouldn't duck the question of protecting British jobs. She wouldn't pretend that she wasn't protecting British interests.'[113] Renwick retains a personal interest in South Africa as a member of the board of Johann Rupert's offshore luxury goods company Richemont. He is also director of Stonehage Fleming, one of the UK's leading private asset management companies with a reputation for discreetly assisting South Africa's super-rich to manage their extensive offshore wealth.

An example of the benefit to the UK of strong relations with Pretoria was the very lucrative public sector contracts for Eskom's fleet of coal and nuclear power stations built during apartheid. Today the big players are Chinese, American and French. However, in September 1980 the UK was first in line to win a large contract. Pik Botha informally addressed the matter with the UK consul general. According to archival records, he expressed disappointment at Britain's abstention in a recent Security Council vote on the South African Army's incursion into Angola.[114] Botha said that at least South Africa knew where they stood with the French and illustrated the benefits of this relationship given 'several contracts we have given them lately'. When pressed on whether public contracts would be awarded on grounds other than commercial considerations alone, Botha replied, 'I cannot say what the position will be next week.' In his briefing about the meeting to 10 Downing Street the consul general added, 'I hope that the importance to British industry of future power station business in South Africa will be borne in mind when tactics for the General Assembly debate are being decided.'[115]

The City of London also had substantial interests in South Africa. According to a secret report authored by the Bank of England, London remained the main financing centre for South Africa in 1980, despite its growing links with Germany and Switzerland. British banks with subsidiaries in South Africa profited hugely from this situation. 'The investments of three of these banks (Barclays, Standard and Hill Samuel) represents a significant proportion of the total capital of their parent group, ranging from 11%–23%, and the contribution to group profits from operations in South Africa are substantial.'[116]

However, the banks also played both sides. One example is Barclays Bank, which eventually withdrew from South Africa in 1986.[117] Shortly before Barclays' disinvestment, Gordon Adams, Barclays director for Africa, wrote to Minister Piet Koornhof to thank him 'for your sumptuous hospitality over luncheon and personally conducted tour of the office of the State President afterwards'.[118] Adams and Koornhof, both Oxbridge-educated, engaged in privileged schoolboy banter about their alma maters.[119] Just six months earlier, Adams was one of ten top British business leaders who met with the ANC leader Oliver Tambo at a secret meeting in London, organised by the former *Drum* editor and author Anthony Sampson. Tambo implored the gathering, 'We don't just talk to you as businessmen, but as human beings. Can you continue to allow such suffering?'[120] Other participants included Sir Alastair Frame (chairman of mining giant Rio Tinto), David Sainsbury (director of the Sainsbury's supermarket chain), Patrick Gillam (chairman of BP South Africa) and Michael Young (director of Consolidated Goldfields). In Sampson's notes from the meeting the Barclays director is recorded as saying, 'You [Tambo] may not realise how much pressure we exert behind the scenes. British are foreigners, we can't press too hard or they chuck us out. Different for SA companies. And remember we're not politicians – we're not good at it.'[121] The historical record confirms that the Barclays man was being economical with the truth.

Other British corporations were also starting to hedge their bets by the mid-1980s, such as mining giant Rio Tinto Zinc, which owned Rössing Uranium in Namibia, one of the world's largest open-pit uranium mines. According to a top-secret SADF memo, the company had, by 1983, started to meet with the liberation movement SWAPO to ensure that board member appointments were acceptable to them.[122] RTZ saw the 'SWAPO dealings [as] an insurance policy and as standard business practice'. The SADF was concerned about the risk of RTZ becoming co-opted by SWAPO for subversive ends. It also noted that the RTZ policy was unlikely to protect it from nationalisation upon SWAPO takeover, given the experience elsewhere in Africa.[123] History has proved that SADF wrongly predicted RTZ's demise in Namibia: the British multinational has increased its share in the mine from just over 50% to 69% over the past three decades. The Namibian government, far from nationalising the asset, has been accommodated through a puny 3% shareholding.

The British tax-haven islands of Jersey, Guernsey and the Isle of Man have long attracted a particular type of well-heeled South African clientele who wish to move their cash offshore while keeping it within reach of their London pads. The South African cabinet explored an idea of using the Isle of Man, a UK Crown dependency in the Irish Sea, as a potential free trade zone for the purpose of busting sanctions. Referred to as the 'Isle of Man opportunity', a decision was taken to inquire into if and how private sector sanctions-busting activities should be co-ordinated.[124] The South African Department of Trade and Industry liaised with a company called Street Financial of London, which acted as marketing agent for a free trade zone that the Isle of Man was setting up. The involvement of the South African government was welcomed and Dawie de Villiers, the South African minister of trade and industry, visited the island in September 1985. He was joined by senior bureaucrats including the chairman of the Industrial Development Corporation. It was later concluded that it would be uneconomical to make use of the island for trade purposes and a cabinet committee on sanctions eventually shelved the plan.[125]

Dirty tricks

From the late 1960s the apartheid government actively engaged in disinformation, eavesdropping, dirty tricks, front organisations and acts of terror in the United Kingdom. They were intended to de-stabilise the UK Anti-Apartheid Movement and build support for its own anti-sanctions campaign. In the 1970s, this included the Information Department's intention to purchase the *Guardian* and *Observer* newspapers, and its success in procuring a 30% stake in the international news company UPITN, which produced news footage for the prominent British broadcaster ITV.[126] This link, and the use of the station to broadcast a hammed interview with John Vorster, led to an embarrassed ITV buying out Pretoria's shares.[127]

The early 1980s saw burglaries at liberation movement offices and the bombing of the ANC's office in London in 1982, for which the Security Branch operatives Craig Williamson, Eugene de Kock and Vic McPherson, among others, took responsibility at the Truth and Reconciliation Commission. When I interviewed McPherson in Pretoria in 2016, he revealed that UK intelligence as well as Scotland Yard also bugged the phones of the ANC and the South African Communist Party in London.[128] He said this came to light when he and his colleagues planned to murder the leader of the SACP, Joe Slovo (McPherson's good friend Craig Williamson was responsible for the murder of Slovo's wife, Ruth First). At about this time, the head of the National Intelligence Service, Dr Niël Barnard, travelled to London. After his return McPherson was called in for a meeting with the head of the police, General van der Merwe. McPherson was told:

> the head of MI5 and MI6 said that they know that we planned to kill Joe Slovo, but we were told that if we plan to do so, we must just not do it in Great Britain because they know we are monitoring the ANC offices, they know who my people [agents] are in London and if we kill Slovo they will have to arrest all of my people as well, which they didn't want to have to do – so that means that MI6 were monitoring the ANC as well.[129]

British eavesdropping seems to have saved the day.

McPherson also spoke of a man 'working for him' but not for any payment: his fight was ideological. McPherson identified him as Andrew Hunter, a Conservative MP from 1983 to 2005. Like Julian Amery,

Hunter was closely associated with the Monday Club. According to McPherson, Hunter approached him in 1984 or 1985, as he was writing a book about the connections between the IRA and ANC, which he, like Thatcher, regarded as terrorist organisations. 'Thereafter I regularly met him every four or five months in Botswana.'[130] His usefulness apparently lay in the fact that he was a confidant of Thatcher, and that Hunter could pass information both ways:

> I also gave him information that he directly gave to Margaret Thatcher. He and Thatcher were close, they were buddies, I could give him information and write reports if there was terror, bombs, people killed by the ANC, keep him updated. I wrote reports about the safety situation in SA. This would go to Thatcher directly. This would be classified information, which I shared after clearing with my bosses, the generals. He was unpopular amongst MI5. He attacked MI5 in his book because the ANC as terrorists were based in London.[131]

In 2002 Hunter admitted to the BBC that he had handed an intelligence file, titled *Twilight and Terror*, detailing contact between the ANC and IRA, in 1992 to Thatcher's office. 'I was under the impression that the only people who ever saw that were the prime minister and the security service and perhaps the intelligence service MI6,' he said.[132]

I contacted Hunter in January 2017. He has since retired from active politics. The conversation was surprisingly easygoing and he struck me as candid in his response. He denied that he and McPherson shared an ideological fight but rather a 'shared strong opposition to ANC within a Cold War context given its link to terrorist activities and the IRA'.[133] He confirms that he approached McPherson but puts the date later, perhaps 1988, and that they met regularly after that. Hunter also confirms that he would pass on to Margaret Thatcher intelligence he received from McPherson. 'I did give her information that McPherson gave me.'[134] He hastily added, 'He wasn't my only source. On one instance he was my only source concerning a white cell, pro-ANC in Broederstroom.'[135] This was presumably a reference to the ANC MK operatives who were prosecuted by the South African state in 1989 – Damien de Lange, Ian Robertson and Susan Westcott. Importantly, Hunter confirmed that his activities were unpopular among UK intelligence agencies at the time.[136]

I asked McPherson if his activities led to co-ordination problems, given the close relationship between South African National Intelligence and MI6. He responded:

> NI would give info to the MI6 agent at the UK embassy [in Pretoria] – but they didn't put pressure on the British as it had to be handled diplomatically. We gave Hunter raw intelligence; it could have contradicted MI6 reports. She [Thatcher] could then confront them [MI6] directly about this and say 'you are not telling us the full truth'. It was a direct manner of accessing Thatcher and angered MI5 and MI6. It was a 'positive' way for South Africa to influence Thatcher.[137]

The South Africans were sometimes the beneficiaries of unexpected assistance. On the evening of 27 May 1987, Oliver Tambo was scheduled to appear as a guest speaker at a private function in the Crystal Room at the Mayfair InterContinental Hotel. According to the South African military attaché in London, it had a man on the inside: the chief security official of the InterContinental Hotel Group, who offered his services to the South Africans. As he would have to hire additional security, he could also place people as desired by the South African military. The military attaché noted that upon his departure he would hand such contact over to the South African National Intelligence officials, who, unlike Military Intelligence, had no way to access such meetings.[138]

Arms: From BAE to Blowpipe

The British government was a reluctant supporter of the arms embargo, as a concession in a bigger battle about not cutting off other trade links. A 1977 British cabinet meeting chaired by Prime Minister James Callaghan accepted a proposal by the foreign secretary that a UN mandatory arms embargo was a necessary compromise position.

> If however, a resolution regarding mandatory economic sanctions was put forward, he would recommend that we should use our veto. If it came to this, he was fairly confident that we should have unanimous support from other Western members from the Security Council and that the Americans would also veto. We should however be in a stronger position to resist going further if we had agreed to a mandatory arms embargo. This would not change South African policies, although he hoped that after the elections the South African government would relax their present hard line.[139]

In a 1978 briefing note for the UK defence secretary from the cabinet ministerial group on southern Africa, possible arms and economic sanctions against South Africa were discussed. The foreign secretary noted that 'preserving our vital interests in Black Africa and in South Africa is becoming impossible to achieve'. He proposed that the UK should disengage from all government involvement with South Africa in the economic and military fields, but he added that the British government should only act 'when our main trading partners act, and should delay action where possible'. Other officials argued against the proposed removal of defence attachés from South Africa in view of South Africa's military importance in the region and the information provided by the attachés about South Africa's military capacity. This included important intelligence such as naval photo reconnaissance provided directly by the South African Navy, and the 'requirement to obtain intelligence on the nationalist organisations, their influence in the country and the degree of support which they receive from external and in particular Sino/Soviet sources'.[140] In the end, the hawks held sway and a decision was taken only to reduce the number of attachés from three to two.[141]

The United Kingdom implemented an arms embargo against

South Africa from 1964. Despite this, a steady flow of spare parts continued and the UK remained a key supplier of defence equipment to South Africa.[142] According to the retired South African Air Force general Pierre Steyn, the UK's behaviour towards South Africa was hypocritical: 'They were publicly anti-apartheid, but showed a willingness to supply the SADF with various things, at least up to the late 1970s – and possibly later as well.'[143]

Officially at least, much changed after the UN mandatory arms embargo imposed in 1977. In April 1978 UK defence officials met with Mr Jordaan, the technical councillor to the South African embassy in Paris – an Armscor front – to confirm that the British government would no longer supply arms or spares to South Africa.[144] However, information obtained from Armscor by means of an access-to-information request by SAHA suggests that the implementation of the arms embargo was not as thorough as has long been supposed. Armscor provided us with a list of 553 foreign contracts, which were all in violation of international sanctions (this list excluded Israel). The contracts do not contain the names of companies, but do supply the project name (in most cases), some descriptions of the material, and the supplying country's name. There is no indication of the value of any of the contracts. However, 87 of the contracts were with UK companies – the third highest country on the list after the United States and Germany. In addition, Armscor provided a 'contract register' that listed 610 contracts, consisting of both foreign and domestic contracts entered into between 1979 and 1999. This register did not include any values, but it did indicate with whom the contract was signed, the subject of the contract (material purchased) and the date. We analysed this register and extracted those contracts that were clearly made with foreign companies between 1979 and 1990. This allowed us to identify 65 foreign contracts of which three were with Marconi (UK) and six with Plessey, both prominent British arms companies.

According to an authorised Armscor history, many suppliers were unwilling to render direct assistance to Armscor after the implementation of the UN mandatory arms embargo:

> In an effort to solve these problems, an officer of Armscor acted
> undercover in Britain effecting a slight improvement ... Orders
> were handled by front or befriended companies ... The necessary
> channel for the acquisition of the [aircraft] components, with a few
> exceptions, were successfully established. Contact and cooperation
> with the Rolls Royce organization provided substantial assistance ...
> Internal political goodwill towards South Africa in certain political
> party circles in Britain enabled South Africa to benefit from sporadic
> success in procuring weaponry and especially components from that
> country.[145]

The South African military did not always require direct access to
hardware. Sometimes secret documents, unethical British military
personnel and a photocopy machine would suffice. According to
James Sanders in his book *Apartheid's Friends*, the senior Military
Intelligence official General Tienie Groenewald told him in 1999 that

> the exchange of military information and designs for weapons
> systems with the British armed forces was a long standing tradition.
> He said that, in his experience, a party would be organized at a
> British military base and, at a certain point during the evening the
> British officers would withdraw, leaving the South Africans alone
> with a photocopying machine and whichever documents or plans
> were required. In that way the British officers would not, technically,
> have given their South African friends the information.[146]

South Africa's desire for trading British weapons was also matched by
that of British companies, who were persistent in attempts to supply
the South African military. In September 1980, for example, Sir
Denis Smallwood, a military adviser to British Aerospace (BAE) and
former commander of the UK Air Forces (until 1976), approached
the undersecretary for South Africa to ask informally if BAE could
sell between eight and 20 coastguard aircraft to the SADF for
maritime patrol work. According to Smallwood, the South Africans

provided an attractive offer, which included a 50% down payment in gold. In addition, the contract would provide much-needed work for the BAE factory in Manchester. The proposal was turned down and Smallwood 'admitted that he had not expected any other answer, but thought it was worth a try'.[147]

BAE would later be implicated in bribe payments in the post-apartheid arms deal. In plea deals, particularly with US authorities, the company acknowledged payments of hundreds of millions of dollars to agents to influence contract decisions across the world, including South Africa. According to a former Armscor employee, BAE's representative in the corrupt arms deal, Richard Charter, was also a sanctions buster and swindler.[148] He said that Armscor spent R8 million in 1989 buying data packs for fighter aircraft from a company owned by Charter in Midrand. The data packs were not delivered and, when confronted, Charter went white as a sheet. He had never procured the data packs and had intended to pocket the cash. The day was apparently saved by a more scrupulous sanctions buster, the UK company Martin Baker, led by Sir Dennis Burrell, which delivered the goods.[149]

Robin Renwick somewhat naïvely believes that the arms embargo actually worked. When I put it to him that Armscor might have had ways and means, he responded brusquely, 'Bollocks! Armscor was not able to buy heavy munitions, tanks, radar systems.'[150] He added, 'While there were connections in Israel and France, the USA and Britain did not provide any military supplies to South Africa.' According to him, 'this was the difference between the rule-abiding northern European states and the temperamental southern European states who do what they want.'[151]

In February 1981 Conservative Party MPs Jim Spicer and John Peyton, later Baron Peyton of Yeovil and a member of the Monday Club, approached Thatcher's office for a meeting to discuss the strategic and commercial reasons for selling weapons to South Africa. In a note to Thatcher's office, Spicer reiterated issues he had raised with Thatcher previously. 'The Prime Minister will know only too well the grievous state of our current naval order book, and will also know that unless some action is taken in the fairly near future, [naval] yards like Vospers will face closure.'[152]

At a meeting with Thatcher in February 1981, Spicer and Peyton complained that British arms companies were losing business and could be driven to bankruptcy: 'potentially their most promising market was the South African government. The difficulty was of course, the arms embargo. Unfortunately, HMG were the only government which "played it straight".' They reported on the use of French and Italian helicopters against SWAPO resistance fighters and frigates originally bought from the UK being openly re-equipped in Simonstown with French radar and French guns. 'All this equipment appeared to be supplied by third parties. Why could we here not act in the same way?'

Thatcher responded that she 'found it unacceptable that the French and Italians would apparently be able, with impunity, to supply South Africa with military equipment through third parties ... She would consider the implications for our own trading relations with South Africa.'[153] The Foreign Office reported back to Thatcher that it advised no relaxation in the arms embargo other than the 'existing permissive view' that allowed the sale of dual-purpose equipment. They were particularly worried about the interest of parliament and the press in any contravention of the arms embargo, which was in contrast to 'French public and parliamentary opinion [which] is remarkably indifferent'.[154]

Defence companies that covertly supplied weapons to Armscor could also prove a useful source of intelligence, given their contact with other defence forces. An example of this involved officials at Fairey Engineering, today rebranded as WFEL, which had contracts valued at millions of rand to supply military bridges to the SADF in the 1980s. Much of what they supplied was almost certainly in contravention of the arms embargo. According to a top–secret note from the South African military attaché in London to Military Intelligence, the senior management of the company was well disposed towards South Africa and frequently made contact to discuss security concerns. The company offered to provide and collect intelligence for the SADF when supplying training to other militaries in the region. One of the officials of the company had agreed to travel to South Africa from Zambia for a day and provide a briefing on the equipment provided to other countries along with his operational observations. According to the note, Armscor kept track of the movement of the company's personnel and the use of this source was very strongly recommended.[155]

Despite all this covert activity, there were two high-profile instances of arms sanctions busters being caught and exposed in the 1980s by UK authorities: the Coventry Four and the men involved in the so-called Blowpipe affair.

In 1984, four South Africans employed by the Armscor subsidiary Kentron were arrested and charged in a court in Coventry on counts relating to the acquisition of missile components, spare parts for Buccaneer bombers, and other military equipment. They became known as the Coventry Four. While out on bail, paid by the South African embassy, the Coventry Four returned to South Africa to await trial, only subsequently to refuse to return to the UK. A political hot potato had been neutralised for both Thatcher's and Botha's governments. The judge in the case described the original conspiracy as 'an extensive, profitable and well organized undercover operation'.[156] In a letter from the four fugitives, written on a Kentron letterhead to the executive director of Armscor, they thanked the government for providing them with support and gave their assurance that 'this incident has positively motivated and inspired us and we humbly wish to provide our services to turn these negative events, with their associated costs, into a positive dividend for the government and the organisations that we serve'.[157] The letter was subsequently shared by Defence Minister Magnus Malan with both PW Botha and Pik Botha.[158]

According to Armscor's authorised history,

this chain of events had a marked influence on Armscor's procurement and marketing transactions ... Armscor management was compelled to enforce a temporary embargo on all visits of the Armscor group to Britain as customs control, in particular, had been made more stringent. This negatively influenced further acquisition from Britain. This setback did not however cause a total stagnation of trade with Britain, only the method of acquisition was changed.[159]

The second exposure was known as the Blowpipe affair. In 1989 a South African, Daniel Storm, was arrested by French police in a hotel room while examining the motor unit of a stolen British Blowpipe missile. Storm was briefly interrogated by French counter-intelligence before falsely claiming diplomatic immunity.[160] It turned out he was acting at the behest of the South African government in procuring Blowpipe missiles from Protestant loyalists in Northern Ireland. The sting was most likely a joint operation between British and French intelligence services, and the source of great embarrassment for Pretoria – it led to a strain in relations with both London and Paris and the expulsion of South African diplomats from both countries. The apartheid regime wanted to use the parts in upgrading its own missile for use in Angola, where its ground forces were vulnerable to attack by Cuban-piloted MiG fighter jets.[161] One of the other South African envoys expelled from France together with Storm was Louis Steyn, a National Intelligence agent described as a 'rotund charming man who boasted that he could shoot a dog at 500 metres'.[162]

This raises the obvious question: why would UK and French authorities set up a sting operation to catch an embargo buster while, at the same time, they were busting sanctions willy-nilly themselves? The contradictions in the way that governments acted again suggest that they were not monolithic in their approach but shifted depending on the political streams of the time. Another possible reason is that any proposed deal with Protestant loyalists, on British soil, would have been a step too far for British authorities.

Following a report to the State Security Council by the minister of defence, President Botha indicated to his cabinet that he intended to write a letter to Margaret Thatcher. Botha would use the letter to confirm that South Africa did not train or arm terror organisations, and that what had happened was against state policy and appropriate measures would be taken against the implicated persons.[163]

Reports in the South African media argued that as Armscor had sufficient domestic weapons production capacity, it did not need the outdated British Blowpipe missile.[164] They were wrong. The Blowpipe affair also contaminated attempts by the South Africans to buy Blowpipe missiles from Chile at the same time. A secret Military Intelligence memo reveals that an Armscor team was in Chile in May 1989, weeks after the expulsion of the South African diplomats from the UK.[165] The memo indicates that they were in conversation with top Chilean generals, who had agreed to sell the South Africans 50 UK-manufactured Blowpipe missiles. Coincidentally, they believed that the British ambassador to Chile met with General Matthei of Chile, on the day of their arrival to negotiate a contract, to warn the Chileans against any sale of Blowpipe missiles to South Africa. In a friendly conversation between Armscor and General Vega of Chile, it was made clear that the deal was off, even though Vega believed the British had no specific information about this transaction and were rather taking preventive action after the Blowpipe affair in Paris. Given that the British wished to inspect Chile's missiles, the best an apologetic Vega could offer was to allow the South African team to undertake research on the missiles and take the intelligence home with them.[166]

Lonrho and Tiny Rowland

Peering through the window of his Gulfstream at an
African landscape, Tiny Rowland remarked to the
Zambian Foreign Minister: 'There is not a
president down there whom I cannot buy.'[167]

When the dust settled around the koppie at Marikana on 16 August 2012, 34 mineworkers lay dead and a further 78 injured. This was the single largest use of deadly force by the police in South Africa since the Sharpeville Massacre and an indictment of President Jacob Zuma's administration. Most of the civilians were shot in the back. The perpetrators, the South African Police Service, were responsible for a massacre of mine workers who were struggling for a living wage. The focus of their anger and frustration was not the state but, rather, the mine owners, Lonmin. Far from being blameless, this British platinum giant used its shareholder, the ANC heavyweight and, currently, South African deputy president, Cyril Ramaphosa, to call for what was termed 'concomitant action' against the workers. At stake was the continued supply of cheap labour required to maximise profit from the mine.

The struggle of these mineworkers was against a 110-year-old corporation which, for almost 90 years of its existence, was known as the London and Rhodesian Mining and Land Company (Lonrho). By the late 1980s Lonrho was active in 80 countries, employing over 140,000 workers in over 800 related subsidiary companies. Lonrho's interests in apartheid South Africa ranged from the distribution of Mercedes-Benz cars to ownership of the country's third largest platinum mine, Western Platinum, which it acquired in 1987.[168]

Lonrho shed its Rhodesian roots under the leadership of Tiny Rowland, who controlled the company for almost 30 years from 1962 onwards. Rowland was born in India to a British mother and German father. Both had been interned in a camp during the First

World War because of their German links. Rowland would spend part of the Second World War in a detention camp on the Isle of Man. During the 1930s he lived in Germany for a spell and joined the Hitler Youth.[169] Rowland had a long-standing feud with the British establishment, which he sometimes disdained while still embracing its conventions of ownership and its institutions. He made his first fortune not in Britain but in the colony of Southern Rhodesia, where his good looks and upper-class accent charmed the local white elite. Rowland was long associated with British intelligence, even though there is little substantive proof. It was thanks to the former MI5 man Sir Joseph Ball that he was hired by Lonrho. It is speculated that Ball might have been his controller when he was detained on the Isle of Man during the war. In addition, one of the members of his board, until at least 1973, had been an MI6 agent.[170]

Rowland was on good terms with African heads of state, including Libya's Muammer Gaddafi, Zambia's Kenneth Kaunda, and Jomo Kenyatta and Daniel Arap Moi of Kenya. His privileged relationship with the Malawian autocrat Hastings Banda is said to have aided Lonrho in large-scale transfer pricing, effectively a massive under-payment of taxes, which was common practice in Lonrho's African business empire.[171] A similar allegation was made about Lonmin in South Africa under the leadership of its CEO Ian Farmer before the Marikana massacre of 2012.[172]

Rowland had easy access to the CIA chief, Bill Casey, Mossad's deputy chief, David Kimche, and the Middle Eastern arms dealer Adnan Kashoggi.[173] Ronald Reagan's assistant secretary for African affairs, Chester Crocker, a major player in southern African politics through his policy of 'constructive engagement' towards Pretoria, trusted Rowland because of his unfettered access to African heads of state and reassuring penchant for clandestine diplomacy, guaranteed by the invisibility of any staff.[174] Rowland ticked all the boxes for the perfect spy.

The Conservative prime minister Edward Heath dubbed Rowland's boardroom behaviour 'the unpleasant and unacceptable face of capitalism', thus sealing his perennial 'outsider' status in the British press. This belied the fact that he was the consummate insider trader, enjoying access to powerful networks of influence across the world. His was the face of capitalism that seamlessly conflated business and politics in a manner that has become ordinary in most countries today, despite its deeply corrosive effect on integrity in public life.

It should therefore be no surprise that his personal fortune peaked during Margaret Thatcher's doggedly pro-market prime minister-ship. This was thanks to the Lonrho chairman Sir Edward du Cann, who was instrumental in getting Thatcher elected leader of the Conservative Party in 1975.[175] Du Cann was also key in lobbying Thatcher to meet with Rowland and persuaded her private secretary to 'insert documents supporting Lonrho into the Prime Minister's red boxes at the end of a working day'.[176] According to du Cann, 'Margaret regarded Tiny as extraordinary'.[177] While this didn't always translate into policy, it enabled Rowland to bypass Whitehall's foreign affairs mandarins, who were more sceptical of him. The British establishment treated him with contempt only because he exemplified some of the worst elements both of their past colonial entitlement and their future embrace of unregulated hyper-profit, without any of the usual dissembling and diplomatic cover-speak.

In South Africa Rowland befriended Prime Minister John Vorster, Harry Oppenheimer and the ANC leader Oliver Tambo. He even offered to assist the ANC government-in-waiting to buy a newspaper in 1993, long before the pillaging Gupta brothers captured the political scene and the state in South Africa.[178] For this and other services, he was awarded the Star of South Africa by President Mandela in 1996. Did Mandela know the true extent of Rowland's links to the apartheid military machine? While Mandela may have been privately briefed about the networks nurtured by the chameleon–like Rowland in the old South Africa, the public had no inkling of his decades-long association with South African Military Intelligence. These top-secret documents have remained hidden in the dusty SADF archive in downtown Pretoria – until now. They provide an extraordinary insight into African politics in the 1970s and 1980s, South Africa's growing relationship with senior members of various African governments, and the role of private brokers such as Lonrho, who actively sought to profit from these developments. It was a mutually beneficial relationship with the most significant military power in southern Africa, which ended with Rowland's empire sinking its first platinum mineshaft on the Highveld.

To do business, Tiny Rowland always preferred to deal directly with heads of state, jetting with his Gulfstream between countries and continents with pit stops long enough to squeeze flesh with senior politicians and security men, exchange information and conclude deals. However, he also had to rely on local agents. In South Africa his bagman was the cardiologist Dr Marquard de Villiers, who controlled Lonrho's diverse interests in South Africa and Mozambique from his Pretoria medical practice. De Villiers, who moved easily between Lonrho's corporate headquarters and the world of the apartheid military and intelligence, described his motive for engaging in business on behalf of Lonrho as being driven by a 'strong sense of social responsibility'.[179]

Given what can be gleaned from declassified Military Intelligence records, he was most likely also driven by a strong sense of profit. An old golf buddy of BJ Vorster and part of the Pretoria elite, he could provide Rowland with direct access to the white oligarchs.[180] He first met Rowland, while in England to watch his son play golf for Oxford University, through an introduction from a Lonrho board member.[181] The pair immediately hit it off and played a behind-the-scenes role in facilitating the first meeting between Zambian President Kenneth Kaunda and Vorster. This ensured Rowland direct access to Vorster, whom he subsequently visited on a number of occasions at his holiday home.[182]

An 'unconventional corporate diplomat'

The *Financial Mail* described Rowland as an unconventional corporate diplomat.[183] He was as comfortable in boardrooms and state houses as he was at defence headquarters. In one of the first recorded meetings between Rowland and South African Military Intelligence in 1975, Rowland briefed the South Africans on a meeting he had had with the number two in the US State Department, Joseph Sisco,[184] a meeting that Henry Kissinger also joined. The purpose of the meeting was primarily to discuss Angola and the role of UNITA. Kissinger argued that South Africa, which by that time had invaded Angola, must act quickly and on a large scale, keeping the matter under cover as it had done until then. South Africa had to ensure the takeover of Angola. In return, the US would try to buy time and offer the Portuguese government an $80 million loan to delay their withdrawal from the former colony until January 1976. The South Africans reported that Rowland had no problem in gaining access to Sisco, who had asked him to work for the Americans. They felt that he had easier access to Sisco than their own diplomats; and his intelligence from Kissinger, including the proposal to bribe the Portuguese, made him even more interesting.[185]

The South Africans, who still seemed to be assessing Rowland at this juncture, described him as knowing everything about South Africa's military operations and as a man who knew every head of state in Africa and in Arab countries.[186] Military Intelligence also noted that Rowland had good contacts in Saudi Arabia, including the head of security services there, and Rowland reported that the Saudis were wholly supportive of the South Africans. Rowland also claimed that the former secretary of the Organisation of African Unity (OAU) was in his service. This provided access to valuable sources at the OAU, underscoring Rowland's value to South Africa in Africa.[187] The South Africans, however, were under no illusion that Rowland's primary motive remained profit, as Military Intelligence believed that he would 'stab [white] South Africa in the back if in his own interests'.[188] As an example of this, Rowland had already put out feelers to SWAPO in the event that Namibia, just like Zimbabwe, would obtain its independence.[189]

Military Intelligence records also reveal a transcription of an audiocassette recording of comments by Marquard de Villiers concerning meetings he had had, likely with or on behalf of Tiny Rowland, with various politicians. UNITA required money, medical supplies and weaponry, according to De Villiers's informer Jorge Sangumbe, who was described as Savimbi's number two. De Villiers was also informed that the Chinese government had assisted in providing weapons to UNITA, which had taken six or seven months to arrive overland from the Tanzanian port of Dar es Salaam. The reason for the delay was that Mozambique President Samora Machel had pressured his counterpart Julius Nyerere to block the release of weapons for UNITA, given his own support for the MPLA in Angola.[190]

Spies and red eyes

But it was not just behind-the-scenes information that South Africa got from its relationship with Rowland and Lonrho: they got arms as well.

The first recorded instance of Lonhro's involvement in supplying weapons to South Africa came in 1978, a year after the UN embargo. It is found in a Military Intelligence interview with De Villiers in which Lonrho offered to assist in supplying South Africa with weapons and weapons systems, using the covert capacity at its disposal. Two possible types of equipment on offer were gears produced by the German truck manufacturer Magirus Deutz and steel for the production of armoured vehicles and artillery.[191] By the mid-1980s the offer to assist with weapons procurement became more tangible and sinister. Rowland arranged for De Villiers to meet with the Israeli spy David Kimche, who at that stage was director general of Israeli Foreign Affairs after a stint as deputy head of Mossad. Kimche could assist in providing Rowland with 'Red Eyes' (US Stinger surface-to-air missiles) should South African-backed UNITA require them.[192]

Lonrho could also offer useful intelligence. The South Africans noted that De Villiers provided information about foreign military activity, such as East German Stasi officers in Zimbabwe, and the location of newly arrived MiG fighters in Zambia.[193] While Lonrho had its ear to the ground in Zimbabwe, the motive was always its usefulness as leverage and in maximising profit. One example is that Rowland, through his intelligence sources, must have had direct insight into Robert Mugabe's notorious Fifth Brigade, which was responsible for massacring up to 30,000 people during the infamous Matabeleland massacres of 1983–87 known as the Gukurahundi.[194] According to a briefing given by De Villiers to South African Military Intelligence in 1981, well before the massacres, Rowland's German-born pilot had informed him that the Fifth Brigade was being trained by 110 North Koreans.[195]

Rowland did, in any event, attempt to cover up efforts to shed light on the massacre by his own newspaper, *The Observer*. Donald Trelford, the editor of the paper, travelled to Zimbabwe in April 1984 to write about the killings. Mugabe reported to Trelford chillingly that 'the situation in Matabeleland is one that requires a change. The people must be reoriented.'[196] The morning after *The Observer* editor had published his insight into the ongoing massacres, Rowland released a letter of apology to Mugabe, describing the investigative report as 'discourteous, disingenuous and wrong'. He also threatened to dismiss his editor.[197] Rowland eventually disposed of *The Observer* following a finding by independent directors that he had meddled in editorial affairs. De Villiers, upon enquiry by Military Intelligence, spun his boss's decision as 'an opportunity to show his loyalty to Mrs Thatcher and protect his financial interests in Zimbabwe at the same time'.[198]

While Rowland wanted to be regarded as the aloof proprietor of *The Observer*, he could not help himself in meddling in editorial content when it conflicted with his business empire in Africa. In 1982 the Swazi king asked Rowland, given his own personal interests in Swaziland, to support his government in ongoing land negotiations with South Africa.[199] At the same time, *The Observer* carried an article highly critical of the proposed Swazi–South Africa land transactions, authored by the renowned South African liberal journalist Allister Sparks.[200] Rowland turned to South African Military Intelligence for assistance in getting rid of Sparks and asked them to provide him with any information they had collected of his conduct while he had been the editor of the *Rand Daily Mail*, which was famously critical of the apartheid regime. Following the meeting, a note from Military Intelligence indicated that the chief of staff intelligence was in agreement that Rowland should be provided with information about Sparks.[201]

In another meeting in 1978 De Villiers met General Van der Westhuizen, the chief of Military Intelligence, and his senior officials. De Villiers was no doubt aware of the power struggle between PW Botha's Military Intelligence and Vorster's dreaded intelligence chief, Hendrik van den Bergh. He made it clear that his preference was to work with the military as opposed to Van den Bergh's BOSS, which he regarded as unprofessional and as having been infiltrated.[202] On behalf of Lonrho, he offered to broker a clandestine meeting between Prime Minister PW Botha and Zambian President Kaunda along the lines of the one he and Rowland had arranged between Vorster and Kaunda in collaboration with Van den Bergh.[203] De Villiers made it clear that nothing he did took place without Rowland's knowledge or co-operation. The prize that De Villiers was after was a meeting with PW Botha, which would please his boss. In return, he offered not only the Kaunda meeting but leverage he had with various African heads of state and leaders, including Jonas Savimbi, to whom he provided financial support.[204] Military Intelligence seemed to be convinced of the value of associating with Lonrho, noting that the relationship would have to be managed very carefully.[205]

Within months, Tiny Rowland received the chief of staff intelligence at his English country estate in Buckinghamshire. Rowland reported on feedback from Kenneth Kaunda, as well as his ongoing support for Jonas Savimbi and the UNITA rebels. Rowland claimed that he had personally spent £1.5 million in support of UNITA since 1956. He lamented the lack of tangible support for Savimbi from African countries such as South Africa. The South Africans undertook to play their part, which included the provision of aircraft and security personnel for Savimbi when travelling abroad, as well as the use of its contacts to polish his international image. Rowland was also keen to assist the South Africans in busting sanctions in return for profit, and claimed that he was in a position to procure the controlling shares in a new North Sea oilfield in the event that South Africa would provide the capital for drilling. This in turn would guarantee oil-poor South Africa a controlling interest in the oil production.[206]

Rowland used his new-found relationship with Military Intelligence to claim an amount of £50,000 for transporting Savimbi between his bolthole in the Moroccan city of Rabat and Grootfontein in Namibia in February 1980.[207] This was paid by the South African spooks into Lonhro's bank account in the UK.[208]

Later the same year, Rowland requested a follow-up meeting with the Military Intelligence chief in Madrid.[209] The reason for the meeting was unclear, but Rowland arrived with De Villiers and his pilot, and asked that he and Van der Westhuizen be seated separately as he meant to talk business. The South African's opening gambit was that Rowland must make a decision: their co-operation would be all or nothing. Rowland countered by asking how on earth the South Africans could tape record a meeting they had had with Kaunda. He expected something of this nature from National Intelligence, but not the military. The South African explanation was that they had only taped part of the conversation in which Kaunda had spoken poorly of Jonas Savimbi in order to prove to Savimbi that he could not trust Kaunda.[210] While Rowland undertook never to mention this to Kaunda, he regarded it as a high-risk strategy.

With the air cleared on these issues, it was agreed that Rowland, the Military Intelligence chief and Savimbi should soon meet, as Savimbi was frustrated with his relationship with Pretoria. He had told Rowland that the South Africans didn't give him any money and 'treat him like a Bantustan'.[211] With De Villiers sitting at a separate table, Rowland turned to the Military Intelligence chief and asked if De Villiers, his South African employee, worked for them. The South Africans confirmed that he in fact did not, nor had he done so in the past.[212]

Shortly after the Madrid meeting, the head of the Military Intelligence special tasks unit met De Villiers at his consulting rooms, possibly under the cover of a check-up. The two men discussed ties that Lonrho was helping to broker between the head of Saudi intelligence services, Sheikh Kamal Adham, and Jonas Savimbi. Adham, on behalf of the Saudis, wished to hand UNITA $1 million as well as military equipment, including the Milan guided missile. There was a catch, however: the Saudis had previously sent equipment via Morocco to UNITA which went missing. This time they requested of De Villiers that he involve the trustworthy South Africans in arranging channels and methods of delivery.[213]

Rowland and De Villiers repeatedly expressed their fear that the South Africans might abandon UNITA, whom they were clearly backing with the prospect of future access to Angolan oil and diamond reserves. While Rowland would at times use the West to support his allies in Africa, he was equally adept at using his African allies to put pressure on the West and, at the same time, help set the agenda from behind the scenes. For example, he met with Kenyan leader Daniel Arap Moi and lobbied him to lead the call that any future elections in Angola had to be free and fair, thereby suggesting that past elections in which Savimbi had been defeated might not have been so. Moi agreed to raise these issues at the Organisation of African Unity and gather support from Zaire, Zambia and Nigeria, and in turn raise the issue with Ronald Reagan at a meeting at the White House. The South Africans were advised by Lonrho to support this call but allow the US to play the lead role in doing so.[214]

In late 1981 Savimbi travelled to Washington DC to meet with senior US officials in the newly installed Reagan administration. Rowland travelled to Rabat, where Savimbi stopped over en route back to Angola, to get a first-hand account of these meetings. He then relayed the information to De Villiers for the ears of South African Military Intelligence. Savimbi basked in the publicity he had received in the US, where he had met with the chief of the National Security Council, General Hague, on two occasions and with Chester

Crocker on three. Present in at least one meeting was Paul Wolfowitz, future president of the World Bank. A clear highlight had been a day-long briefing provided by CIA officials in which Savimbi was told that South Africa was the United States' friend and ally, regardless of what they were sometimes required to say in public. Hague apparently told Savimbi that there would be 'no settlement in South West Africa which is contrary to their [South Africa's] interests. We'll get rid of the Cubans or bleed them.' Savimbi was also told that the US had no interest in repealing the Clark Amendment, which banned the US from providing military assistance to Angola, as this provided convenient cover for clandestine operations.[215]

Not only did Lonrho help support Savimbi in his relations with the US, but Rowland had for some time sought greater support from Margaret Thatcher. On 18 January 1982 De Villiers called Military Intelligence's director of special tasks from Rowland's office in London to share 'good news': on the previous day Rowland had met Thatcher for lunch at her invitation, and she had given her personal support to 'us' [Pretoria and Lonrho] in support of Savimbi, and would send a person on that day to General Hague in Washington DC to inform him of her support.[216] Thatcher indicated that she had never been given the facts concerning Savimbi and the importance of UNITA, which De Villiers remarked was probably the work of her foreign secretary, Lord Carrington.[217] Rowland flew to Rabat immediately after the meeting to inform Savimbi of the developments and returned to London the next morning.[218]

Within weeks Rowland was back in Pretoria. When Military Intelligence officials arrived to meet him at his hotel, he stayed at the dinner table with his pilot and sent De Villiers to talk to them in the hotel lounge.[219] Rowland was clearly upset. The South Africans had not arranged for him to meet the South African minister of defence, Magnus Malan, with whom any 'bum of a leader or farmers' association could schedule a meeting'.[220] Rowland felt slighted. While the South Africans spent millions on making their case overseas, he was doing so free of charge for South Africa through his media interests in Zambia, Uganda, Kenya and the United Kingdom. One of the reasons Rowland was upset was that Kaunda had asked Rowland to relay a verbal message directly and only to Magnus Malan. This petulant behaviour did not, however, prove an obstacle to his long-term relationship with Pretoria.[221]

During this period, Rowland was also involved in an intricate game of double-cross. He was helping to broker contact between the US government and UNITA at the highest level, while loyally reporting back to Pretoria on these negotiations. In January 1983 Rowland met Chester Crocker at his request in the UK, and proposed a meeting between himself and Savimbi at an American air force base in Iceland, with Rowland managing Savimbi's transport from Angola. The South African military felt that the clandestine trip could place Savimbi's life in danger and advised him not to travel to Iceland, thereby also sabotaging the American's bilateral engagement with Savimbi.[222]

Rowland eventually managed to arrange a meeting between Savimbi and a group of top US State Department officials.[223] The group arrived in northern Namibia together with Rowland on his jet, from where they would be taken in an SADF helicopter to meet Savimbi. The Americans were clear that they refused to meet Savimbi in Angola as it would create political problems for them back home. The South African Military Intelligence pointed out the duplicity, given that a CIA official had been stationed in Savimbi's headquarters in Jamba the previous year. Rowland was asked repeatedly by the Americans to confirm that they would not enter Angola, to which Rowland responded, 'We are lucky it is just off the border', indicating a 1 cm distance with his fingers.[224]

According to Military Intelligence, the US group knowingly or unknowingly entered Angolan airspace to meet Savimbi on 14 and 15 August 1983.[225] The Americans were met with great fanfare by UNITA supporters in Angola and with waving US flags. One American official, following a speech by Savimbi, referred to their relationship as that of 'allies'. After what Rowland regarded as a successful meeting, the group flew on to South Africa, landing at Wonderboom military airport, where they jointly met with the South African Military Intelligence chiefs. The Americans clearly left Angola impressed by UNITA and said that while 'they could not help Savimbi militarily, they expect South Africa to continue doing so … South Africa assists militarily and they assist in international politics.'[226] The Americans also expressed concern about a weapons build-up in Angola and jibed that South African military must speak to the Israelis about counter-measures against SAM-8 missile systems, using South African special forces or other methods. They alluded to the fact that they would provide the necessary information to the Israelis for release to the South Africans.[227]

While Rowland looked forward to cashing in eventually on his Angolan investment, Lonrho's presence in Mozambique was already bearing fruit. The Nkomati Peace Accord between South Africa and Mozambique buoyed his investments in gas and the tourism sector, such as the purchase of Maputo's prestigious Polana Hotel in 1984. De Villiers reported that the golden era of communism had passed and South Africa now had to court the ruling party, FRELIMO. What would be in this for Lonrho? They would act as a broker between the South African and Mozambican governments in a new 'anti-sanctions relationship', ensuring the supply of oil, computers and other commodities, and working closely with the Mozambican state-owned enterprise SOCIMA.[228]

By April 1985 Rowland and De Villiers were offering tantalising contacts to Military Intelligence: John Garang, leader of the Sudan People's Liberation Army, and the Libyan leader, Muammar Gaddafi. Kenyan President Daniel Arap Moi had also agreed to meet the head of South African Military Intelligence. Rowland proposed a one-day meeting in which he would collect the South African securocrats in his jet in the morning, travel to meet Moi at his farm away from prying eyes, and return to Pretoria the same evening.[229]

It is easy to dismiss Tiny Rowland as some sort of rogue, an anomaly in the British way of doing things. Robin Renwick, the former UK ambassador to South Africa, is of this view: 'One company that wasn't above improper relations was Tiny Rowland and Lonrho ... He had a corrupt relationship with some African leaders. It is unthinkable that he would have done what he did in Africa in the UK, if he had acted in that manner in Britain he would have gone straight to prison.'[230] Such a view is profoundly misplaced. Rowland was no sidebar or swashbuckling businessman. He was a sanctions buster who paid his tax in Britain from a fortune made in largely poor African countries. Craig Williamson told me that he met Rowland and recalls him flying into Waterkloof military airport just outside Pretoria. He believes that Rowland 'was a businessman, in it for himself'.[231] A former senior Armscor employee describes Rowland's role in illicit weapons procurement as 'a good channel for us [South Africa] during the sanctions period'.[232] The final characterisation worth noting is by the UNISA emeritus law professor André Thomashausen, who was close to the National Party establishment in the 1980s. He met Rowland in the company of Pik Botha at the time and recalls their interaction: 'I asked him how he got so successful and he said that he had an effective distribution arm in Africa. He loved Africa. I don't think he had an ideology other than profit. As for Lonhro, it was probably a front for UK intelligence.'[233]

Is it not possible that Rowland was all three: British businessman, friend of apartheid and English spy? He certainly acted like a spy in the service of the apartheid regime when it suited him. He was also both corrupt and in the service of many governments and political agendas. One of those was without doubt the UK and another was South Africa.

Amery and Rowland: Two sides of the same pound coin

Tiny Rowland, with a foothold on the British Isles and at home aboard a jet crisscrossing the equator, paved the way for Britain's involvement in new forms of imperialism in its old African stomping ground. Unlike Julian Amery, he did not seek to preserve white power as an avenue for his own profit making. Instead, he recognised the importance of clandestine dealings with whoever controlled the land that surrounded his mineshafts and other business interests. It mattered little whether they were kleptocrats, white oligarchs or black nationalists.

Both Amery and Rowland represent the underbelly of British politics and its private sectors, which dabble in the dark arts of intelligence and covert military dealings. Rowland's major insight, which has proven correct, is that cash and power networks would in future supplant 'kith and kin'. The result: the spectre of fairness, a threat to the ruling class, would once again be boxed in. These networks were mostly subterranean. As we have shown, they relied on Rowland's rendezvous with Military Intelligence in Pretoria. Amery can easily be dismissed as an old British patrician who was happiest when lounging about Harry Oppenheimer's pool. He was far more menacing than that. His politics were right wing and his intelligence connections, through Le Cercle, were an important source of support for Pretoria.

The connections that both these men had with apartheid South Africa are illuminating. They represent two sides of the same coin of the British establishment, seeking to bolster apartheid for its own pecuniary and other ends.

The sum of all the relationships in this chapter exposes the hypocrisy of the British government. Despite statements made by politicians at the time against the policies of apartheid, this chapter shows the range of powerful friends the apartheid regime could rely on for its own survival. Politicians such as Margaret Thatcher argued against sanctions because it was not in the interests of black South Africans. However, many senior members of the British establishment continued to support the flow of money – and in some instances, weapons – in support of the apartheid regime. This was duplicity of the first order.

The United Kingdom
Kith, kin and kindred spirits

Secret Networks

Lord Julian Amery was firmly entrenched in the British Conservative establishment. His legacy would be his role in building and shaping the international neoconservative pro-apartheid secret organisation Le Cercle, while nurturing business links in South Africa.

Sanctions Busters

Maverick businessman Tiny Rowland, the driving force behind Lonrho for 30 years, was a key source of intelligence to the apartheid military. He used wide-ranging contacts throughout Africa and in Europe to access information sought by Pretoria. Jetting across southern Africa, Rowland's plane often carried weapons as well.

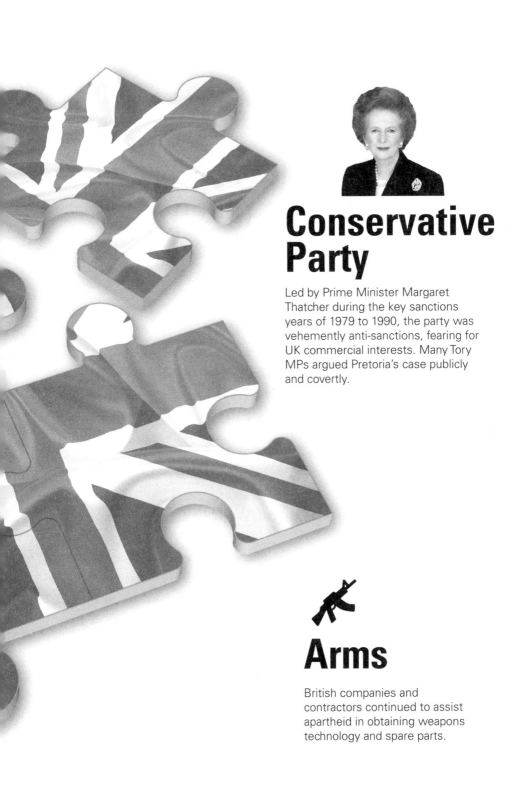

Conservative Party

Led by Prime Minister Margaret Thatcher during the key sanctions years of 1979 to 1990, the party was vehemently anti-sanctions, fearing for UK commercial interests. Many Tory MPs argued Pretoria's case publicly and covertly.

Arms

British companies and contractors continued to assist apartheid in obtaining weapons technology and spare parts.

CHAPTER 10

The People's Republic
of China (PRC)

*'The Chinese people have always been staunchly supporting
the just struggle of the South African people and are sincerely
pleased to see their victory.'*

– JIANG ZEMIN, CHINESE STATE PRESIDENT,
CONGRATULATING PRESIDENT NELSON MANDELA
ON HIS ELECTION (1994)[1]

The Great Wall?

The Chinese embassy in Pretoria covers almost an entire city block
and sits across from the entrance to the Presidential Guest House.
It is an imposing compound, as aesthetically unappealing as the
American embassy down the road, yet its size and location suggest a
relationship between the two countries that is expected to be eternal.
After only 20 years of full diplomatic and economic ties, China is
today one of South Africa's main trading partners, benefiting from
raw materials, investing in the country's banks and pumping cash
into the economy through the lucrative share that Naspers owns

in China's communications behemoth Tencent. Everyone in power benefits from this situation, from the billionaires behind the once strongly Afrikaner nationalist company Naspers to the ANC National Executive Council members who are sent on sponsored trips to study the Chinese system of governance.

Officially there were no diplomatic or trade relations between China and Pretoria during apartheid. The staunchly pro-Western and anti-communist Pretoria government treated Beijing with the contempt it otherwise reserved for the Soviet Union. The feeling was mutual. Apartheid South Africa instead recognised the legitimacy of Taiwan (the Republic of China/RoC) and not mainland China (the People's Republic of China/PRC). South Africa and China had chosen sides in the Cold War and there was no way the distance could be bridged.

The same applied to the struggle for the country's liberation. In the 1950s there had been initial contact between top ANC leaders and their counterparts in Beijing. However, during the 1960s and 1970s, as a result of the Sino–Soviet conflict China backed the Pan Africanist Congress (PAC), not least because of the support that the ANC enjoyed from the Soviet Union.[2] However, in 1975 Oliver Tambo travelled to China. The major turning point came about in 1982 following a meeting in Lusaka between Premier Zhao Ziyang and Tambo, which allowed for the restoration of party-to-party relations,[3] with regularised contact and even limited Chinese financial assistance to the South African Communist Party.[4]

According to the official version, 'China was never a supporter of the apartheid regime.'[5] The truth suggests that this understanding of the historical relationship between the two countries is far too simplistic, and ignores embarrassing details that all parties probably consider best buried. Were it not for archives and informants, we too might not have been any the wiser about the role that China played in supporting apartheid, despite its position as a permanent member of the UN Security Council and ally of the liberation movements. Indeed, as the pressure grew on the West to cut its military ties with Pretoria, so the bond between Red China and South Africa seemed to strengthen.

The Silk Road

According to Zhong Weiyun, director general of the Department of African Affairs of the Chinese Communist Party's Central Committee, writing in 2008 with Xu Sujiang, China was consistently committed to comprehensive sanctions against apartheid.[6] This position only changed, according to the authors, from 1989 to 1991 'when the Chinese government readjusted its trade policy towards South Africa. In 1989 the government allowed overseas branches of central state-owned companies to have unofficial indirect trade ties with South African companies established in another country.'[7] Direct non-governmental trade with South Africa was only permitted starting in 1991 and China resumed economic trade co-operation in 1993 when the UN announced the lifting of economic sanctions against South Africa.[8]

There is, however, significant contrary evidence to suggest that China worked closely with the apartheid regime in busting sanctions. As far back as 1982 *Africa Confidential* claimed that a South African delegation had travelled to Beijing 'to arrange the transfer of sophisticated South African technology sorely needed for the development of Chinese minerals'.[9] It reported that South Africa would, in turn, receive a steady supply of Chinese tungsten, much of which China had for years sold directly to the Soviet Union.[10]

In 1987, at the time that the ANC Secretary General Alfred Nzo and the SACP chairman, Joe Slovo, visited China, *Africa Confidential* reported:

> It is possible that the Chinese government also has channels of communication with the South African government. There have been intermittent reports of trade between the two countries, mostly via Hong Kong, most recently involving the alleged sale of Chinese maize to South Africa in March 1985. The Chinese aim seems to be to have workable relations with the ANC, although China has also pronounced itself against a violent transition in South Africa.[11]

Three Buddhas: this is the gift that the apartheid spy Craig Williamson claimed to have received as mementos of his first interaction with Communist China on home soil. 'I was the first politician [as a member of PW Botha's President's Council] to host the first delegation of Mainland China (PRC) officials to South Africa in 1988,' he claims.[12] 'It was a covert trip and I still have the three Buddhas they gave me. My people were horrified that these were "communists" that they were meeting. They also met with the Defence Intelligence.'[13] A letter found in PW Botha's archive confirms this. Marked 'top secret', Botha's minister for trade and industry, Danie Steyn, wrote to inform Botha of new trade relations that were developing with China in 1988. The new trade fell under Steyn's sanctions-busting section, known as 'Unconventional Trade'.[14] The South African state president had personally authorised the visas for an 'unofficial' delegation from China who visited South Africa on a secret trip with the permission of their government. The outcome of the encounter was described by Steyn as lucrative for South Africa.

The secret trip to Pretoria was led by a four-person delegation representing Beijing: Zhengu Yu (Chinese government), Rene FC Yu (a middleman based in Hong Kong), Ms PP Li (secretary) and Billy MK Wong (representing a Chinese front company in Hong Kong). The delegation participated in numerous meetings over a 13-day period from 29 May to 10 June 1988. Some of the positive outcomes for South Africa included the sharing of technology with China for the cooling of power stations; a joint venture to produce steel pipes in China; the sale to China of vanadium, iron ore, coal and maize; an underground communications system for mines valued at R30 million; and an order for 20,000 litres of brandy and fruit juice.[15] It was agreed that a further meeting would take place between members of the Department of Unconventional Trade and Chinese officials in the 'near future'. At the recommendation of the Chinese delegation, arrangements were made to appoint Rene Yu in Hong Kong as a consultant to the South African trade representative to deal with Chinese matters.[16]

At the same time, the South African Department of Foreign Affairs, through its own sanctions-busting unit headed by Marc Burger, was also in the process of developing ties with China in the late 1980s. According to Burger, Chinese officials were complicit in subverting the trade embargo, possibly with the sanction of top officials. He sketches the example of covert trade using various middlemen and outright fraud.[17] A South African government front company in the Levant (probably Turkey or Israel) would place an order for 200,000 tonnes of a mineral (iron ore or coal) from a Latin American mining company with South African links. A European associate would then in turn secure an order from China for 400,000 tonnes of the same mineral.

Burger's people, through a shipping front company, would then charter a large vessel that would set sail for China, with 200,000 tonnes of the mineral in its hull, heading east across the Atlantic and round the southern tip of Africa. The ship would then make an 'unplanned' stop for engine repairs at South Africa's minerals export harbour at Richard's Bay, where another 200,000 tonnes of the same mineral were loaded with falsified documentation to hide the South African origin. 'If the rest of the journey is fairly typical, the vessel might discharge some of her cargo at Singapore or Hong Kong. At one of these ports, Chinese employees who were proficient with trade documentation would board and accompany the vessel to the PRC port(s)', at which point the Chinese officials would expedite the discharge of the minerals.[18] All of this would no doubt come at a cost, given that South African minerals needed to be sold cheaply (a burden carried by South African workers no doubt) and various officials needed to be bribed along the way.[19]

It is arguable that the opening of China's economy to the world in the 1980s and its mercantile orientation inclined the country to trade with apartheid South Africa. But this explanation is insufficient. The real driver of the increased trade relations between South Africa and China was, simply, guns.

China arms apartheid

Hansa: 'The one that refreshes'

Hansa was the codename used by the South African Defence Force (SADF) for China from at least the early 1980s. It is marked in stencil on brown 'top secret' A4 folders retrieved from the SADF archives. Military codewords give us an insight into the thinking of the men who assigned these monikers. A sober mind, with an interest in world affairs, might associate Hansa with the Hanseatic League of trading guilds which dominated northern European cities between 1400 and 1800. But a more prosaic explanation can be found in the well-stocked Military Intelligence pubs with their state-subsidised supply of Hansa Pilsener, a beer which in the 1980s had the tagline 'The one that refreshes'.

For much of the 1980s, China was 'the one that refreshed' the apartheid regime's arms supply. According to the retired Military Intelligence chief, Chris Thirion, apartheid's

> predominant need for weapons in the late 1970s into the 1980s was to arm and support UNITA in Angola and RENAMO in Mozambique. It was not plausible to do this with South African weapons or those explicitly procured for the SADF [as they could be traced back to Pretoria] and the requirements went up significantly as the war escalated. As such, to provide for Angola and Mozambique, the SADF and Military Intelligence procured AK-47s from the Soviets, and landmines, mortars and sub-machine guns from the Chinese.[20]

While Armscor was officially in charge of all procurement of weapons and weapons systems, the military did a lot of procuring themselves, and received crucial assistance from Military Intelligence to facilitate the transactions.[21] One of the reasons for this was that Armscor was, at times, inflexible and did not have the necessary military experience to determine what to purchase, and in what quantity, and struggled to assess the quality of the goods acquired and their relative adaptability.[22]

It was also a way to keep some of the most clandestine procurements off the books.

In April 1984, the SADF chief of staff intelligence and a small party travelled to Hong Kong as part of an Asian tour to promote military relations with various Asian countries, including the island state of Taiwan. The stop-over in Hong Kong involved a clandestine meeting with Johnny Wang, who was acting as go-between for Beijing and Pretoria. Wang was quite possibly representing a Chinese arms company in its dealings with the SADF.[23] More specifically the documents suggest that he was acting on behalf of one of China's largest state-owned military manufacturers, Norinco. Norinco, an industrial behemoth that continues to play a large role in the Chinese military–industrial complex, was essentially Armscor's equivalent in China. Wang reported that all was going well with their office in Hong Kong, then still a British protectorate. However, he suspected that the office next door had been rented out and 'he believes that this is to monitor Norinco', requiring the office to be relocated.[24] Although no indication was given of who the spies might be, the likely candidates are Britain, the United States or Taiwan.

Wang also raised the need to resolve political problems, referring to South Africa's domestic politics, in order to allow business relations to flow between the countries. In this context the reports noted that the chief of staff intelligence was required to travel via Europe to get to China, which no doubt created logistical problems and a far lengthier trip. The South African intelligence chief pointed out to Wang that China 'must not place conditions on trade – if so, then South Africa could also tell China to stop all its support for SWAPO'. Wang responded by saying that there were differing opinions in China as to the question of contact with South Africa.[25]

At a supper later that evening a man named Lee, who represented the Chinese government, joined them. The South Africans pushed the point that Jonas Savimbi (codename Spyker) and his UNITA forces would prevail in Angola and that China must quickly choose sides as it had been a mistake to recognise the MPLA government at independence. Wang's response was that support for the MPLA was a short-term solution that the Chinese were forced to follow. In a subtle hint to the SADF officials that they should abandon their alliance with Taiwan, Lee added that the Chinese prime minister Deng Xiaoping's vision of 'All Chinese under one roof' would be achieved in the 1980s.[26] Neither of the predictions came about. Savimbi lived out his last days on the run in the Angolan bush, while Taiwan and China continue to coexist under two roofs.

This exchange sums up many of the contradictions between these 'enemies', who were simultaneously dealing in weapons. The SADF was killing SWAPO fighters whom China was supporting, all the while building its armoury from purchases from China. South Africa supported China's arch-enemy Taiwan, while China returned the favour by supporting South Africa's nemesis in Luanda. Yet, unofficially peace was being brokered over supper in Hong Kong during negotiations to buy weapons of war. The reference to the different schools of thought in Beijing also suggests that this relationship was not a one-off affair but constituted a pattern of behaviour that must have been the cause of intense debate among top ideologues in the Communist Party's Africa Department, just as it was among the Broederbond in South Africa.

The discussion between the two countries wasn't only focused on small arms. China wanted to buy South Africa's most sophisticated piece of artillery, the G5 howitzer. The design of the cannon was based on technology supplied by a Canadian-American sanctions buster, Gerald Bull. Bull and the Chinese were also in discussion at the time about the procurement of his 'super-gun' technology in a deal before it went sour. Wang reported to the SADF that 'They were swindled by Mr Bull with the G5 blueprints'.[27] This seemed to be the reason why Beijing turned to Pretoria: they wanted to test Armscor's product with an eye to procurement. Wang indicated that he was optimistic about the G5 deal and the two parties discussed how to carry out armour-plating tests. Given that Chinese officials could be photographed in South Africa, and that transporting all the parts to

China posed a logistical problem, Wang believed that Pakistan could help arrange a flight to enable South Africa to bring the equipment to China. Alternatively, Wang proposed that the tests be carried out in West Germany.[28]

The documents also confirm that by 1984 Armscor had established an office in Hong Kong from which it could trade with the region.

Mobutu, man in the middle

A key conduit for the transfer of Chinese weapons destined for UNITA forces in Angola, but paid for by the South African government, was Zaire.[29] The choice was obvious: the kleptocrat Mobutu Sese Seko was close to Washington and Paris, and was also an ally of Savimbi. In March 1983, the first plans were made by the SADF Directorate of Foreign Relations for a trip to Zaire to facilitate the procurement of weapons from China. The purpose of the visit was the 'signing of Hansa related contracts' and obtaining letters of accreditation and documentation from Zaire. According to an SADF memo, 'The Hansa purchases of weapons and ammunition are being undertaken with a Zairean end user certificate and the PRC has demanded the letter of accreditation'. To this end, Colonel Pretorius and Mr Otto of the Armscor Technical Council in Paris were appointed by Zaire to act on its behalf through an Armscor front company, Adam Export, and conclude a contract with Norinco.[30] Registered in Geneva, Adam Export listed its directors as Henry Paul Duvillier and Steven Hoogendijk.[31]

Meetings took place with Alain-André Atundu Liongo (refered to as Mr Atundu), the deputy head of Zairean intelligence, on 24 February 1983, after which he reported back to President Mobutu. That evening, Atundu informed SADF's Colonel Pretorius of the president's views on a number of issues, including the letters of accreditation. Mobutu had given orders to Atundu to issue the letters as proposed by the SADF, and the memo notes that 'this matter was therefore successfully concluded and provides much room for future business with the People's Republic of China'.[32] The exchange was also useful in further cementing ties between the SADF and Mobutu, who requested a meeting with the SADF chief of staff intelligence in the near future.

Colonel Pretorius proposed a return trip to Kinshasa in May 1983 to meet again with Atundu. The purpose of the meeting was to finalise a trip to Zaire by the SADF chief of staff intelligence. In addition, the Armscor Technical Council in Paris asked that Zaire should be urgently contacted in order to issue end-user certificates for importing ±R5 million worth of pistols and shotguns. While no reference was made to the supplier, it is likely that it was a Chinese firm like Norinco.[33]

A shopping list for the Chinese market

On 24 February 1984, Major DJ Kotze of the SADF Directorate of Foreign Relations travelled to Kinshasa on a two-day trip. He carried a teleprinter (a precursor to email, used by the SADF) and top-secret documents that the defence force was requested to ensure were not opened by customs upon his return to South Africa.[34] A series of secret cables between Kinshasa and Pretoria discussed an end-user certificate for a major purchase of weapons from Norinco by the Armscor front company Adam Export. The fiction was that Adam Export was acting as an agent for Zaire. Zaire, in turn, provided end-user certificates against payments made by Armscor through one of its secret accounts at Kredietbank Luxembourg. Norinco was represented in correspondence by its president, which suggests that figures at the very top of China's military establishment, and probably some of its most senior politicians, had sanctioned these deals.[35] They too must have known of Armscor's intimate relationship with Kredietbank Luxembourg.

The South Africans intended to present a shopping list of weapons to the Chinese. This included machine guns (such as AK-47s), landmines, mortars, rocket launchers and missiles, as well as 20,000 rounds of 20 mm ammunition. Most notably, they wanted to buy 200 bombs weighing 250 kg each and a further 200 bombs weighing 200 kg each.[36]

As a first step in the procurement the SADF managed to secure a letter of accreditation from Zaire officials for Adam Export, in return for payment for the favour. A total of just over $2.5 million was paid into an account with Kredietbank Luxembourg in order to facilitate this arrangement and was signed by Admiral Lomponda, the Zairean state secretary for defence.[37] The likely beneficiary of this facilitation fee was the Zairean government or its senior officials. It is evident that permission for these types of transactions was required from Mobutu's office, which did not preclude his taking a cut of this deal. However, shortly after payment was made the Zaireans had not yet provided the end-user certificates, and the South Africans expressed concern about the reliability of their counterparts in Zaire.[38]

At this stage, the South Africans provided more details of the weapons they urgently required from the Chinese including 74,000 kg of bombs and 45,000 rounds of high-explosive incendiary shells capable of piercing armour.[39] While it can be assumed that the majority of weapons were required to arm UNITA, the SADF also provided the Zairean military with weapons from the same order. These could be used in support of UNITA by the Zairean military, and some no doubt found their way to other bloody conflicts on the continent. On 6 September 1984, Armscor supplied a quote to the SADF for its 'Zaire gift', which largely mirrored the order of high-incendiary shells from Norinco.[40] Everybody got to feast on the same carcass.

Turning Chinese guns into Congolese ploughshares

China, South Africa and Zaire had to go to enormous lengths in conspiring to hide their burgeoning arms trade. Fortunately for the SADF, they had Zairean intelligence on their side. In 1985 Like Nkapa, the head of Zaire's Special Intelligence Service, agreed to deny that any ships had docked in Zaire and offloaded military cargo if he was asked.[41] With this, the so-called Operation Kauka could be rolled out, involving the transport of 282,000 kg of Chinese weapons from

Shanghai with a value of almost $5 million. The Danish-registered *Vinderslevholm* was hired to transport the weapons between the three countries, using what would become a well-worn channel for embargo busting.[42] The plan was to offload the cargo at Zaire's main port of Matadi. It would then be loaded into containers and innocuously re-exported as 'coffee'. A Zairean agent, Zaire Containers, along with clearing agents, was hired and tasked with delivering 32 empty containers for the export of the 'coffee'.[43]

Richard Steyl of Armscor sent one of his agents, José Pedro, to manage the transhipment, which would cost Armscor approximately $220,000, to be paid through a special channel created by the Armscor office in Paris. This covert operation was signed off by President Mobutu Sese Seko on 27 April 1985. SADF officials noted that the success of the project depended on Mobutu's personal involvement. Mobutu, for example, waived all customs-related landing costs. The mission carried his personal seal of approval, as it almost certainly had of the South African head of state and of senior Chinese officials.[44]

One of the additional recommendations made by SADF officials was that the vessel *Vinderslevholm* could be bought by the SADF and used repeatedly in future to deliver weapons for Pretoria, manned with a newly selected crew and operating between Shanghai and Matadi.[45] In the 1980s the port of Matadi was frequently used for the delivery of Chinese weapons destined for South Africa or for onward passage to UNITA, RENAMO or other allies. A 1985 investigation by the journalists Colm Foy and Christine Abdelkrim came close to exposing these links, although they seem not to have identified the role of the *Vinderslevholm*. According to their research, the scheme involved the Danish shipping company Svendborg Enterprises, owned by Jørgen Jensen. Svendborg operated a ship that had by 1984 made at least three trips from Shanghai via Matadi to South African harbours.[46]

While Operation Kauka was under way, it became apparent that the original plan to repackage the weapons as coffee destined for Maputo was no longer possible because of logistical difficulties in Zaire. As a result, an alternative arrangement had to be found – and quickly: the slow boat from China was due to arrive any day. It was decided that the weapons would be offloaded, taken to a warehouse and placed in new containers in the name of a Pretoria-based front company, Rust Enterprises, destined for Maputo. A Rust Enterprises invoice dated 10 May 1985 listed the camouflaged cargo as 16,500 cook sets, 5,000 ploughs, 2,000 bicycles and 26 trucks, with a total value of $4.7 million.[47]

The cargo eventually reached Matadi on 10 May 1985, and the operation was immediately beset with logistical problems. Many of the key actors were not fully informed of the nature of the cargo; warehouses were not available to store the containers during the transhipment period; and there was a concern that they would not be ready for collection when the onward-bound ship arrived. A payment of a further $40,000 to Zaire Containers seemed to clear up many of these logistical difficulties, but the scheme remained precarious.[48]

The final spanner in the works risked not only upsetting the whole deal, but causing a major international incident. On the evening of 15 May 1985, as the material was to be transferred between containers, a Russian ship docked directly in front of the store containing the Chinese weapons. It too proceeded to offload goods onto trucks and forced the South Africans to keep the door to their warehouse firmly shut as the Russian captain and his crew went about their business. The Russian sailors passed within 20 metres of the Chinese bombs on a sweltering tropical evening, some with cigarettes in hand, blissfully unaware of what lay nearby. If the Russians had found out about the deal and blown the whistle, it could have spelt disaster for the deal and had major repercussions for both the Chinese and South African governments. In South Africa it had the potential to do serious damage to PW Botha and his regime.

Following an evening of negotiation with local officials, the Russian ship departed, none the wiser, and the dock was closed. With the coast now clear, the 32 empty containers were brought into the warehouse and rapidly loaded with weapons over two days. In an act of apparent petulance, the *Vinderslevholm* and its crew had left the harbour without offloading the rope needed to secure the cargo in the new containers. SADF officials had to find a replacement rope, which was purchased from a nearby ship, in order to secure 26 cannons in 13 containers.[49] The cargo of Chinese weapons did not reach Maputo but was instead offloaded in Durban, South Africa. Thus criminal bureaucratic alchemy transmuted swords into ploughshares, napalm into bicycles – and none would be the wiser.

Sharing the bounty

The Chinese weapons bought by the SADF were primarily used to fuel conflict in southern Africa. They contributed to a flood of Chinese and Eastern bloc armaments, which appear to have been more freely available than one would have expected. Indeed, the SADF was even willing to export its surplus stock of weapons to other conflict regions across the globe, as it had no reason to doubt that it could be easily resupplied.

In November 1983 the chief of staff intelligence sent a memo to the chief of the SADF noting that 'Armscor recently received an enquiry from Singapore regarding the procurement of certain communist weapons'.[50] Stuart Pretorius of the Armscor Asia division confirmed that Armscor could provide the following weapons for Singapore: 3,000 AK-47s; 3 million bullets; 50 RGP-7s (anti-tank rocket-propelled grenade launchers); and 1,000 rounds of RPG-7 ammo. The total cost of these weapons was $1,375,800.[51] The SADF was concerned that this sale should not be allowed to endanger the defence stockpile but noted that their replacement 'can be done without any difficulty through the project HANSA [from the PRC]'. The document added that 'Armscor therefore requests the SADF to make these weapons available as tangible proof of our cooperation with Singapore. The weapons will be purchased by the Singapore Intelligence service who we have been in contact with regarding the requirement. It appears that they want to use the weapons in support of resistance organisations in Cambodia and/or Afghanistan. The DMI can gain an intelligence advantage through its willingness to make the weapons available.'[52] Both the chief of the SADF and the chief of staff intelligence signed off their approval of this request.[53] The most likely recipients of these weapons were Mujahideen fighters countering the Russian occupation in Afghanistan or guerrilla groups in Cambodia that enjoyed Chinese support.[54]

The Mujahideen, once funded and armed as a useful bulwark against the Soviets, would morph into al-Qaeda and, eventually, what we know today as ISIS. Support for these groups has cast a long shadow over the world today. The SADF, in turn, traded its Chinese stockpile for intelligence and cash with other countries. They would soon again call on China to restock their supplies. Gradually the relationship was reinforced as it became more complex and lucrative for all concerned.

Shooting for the stars

The covert defence relationship between the SADF and China went from strength to strength in the second half of the 1980s. As we have seen in Chapter 8, South Africa passed US missile technology that it had clandestinely obtained on to China. A 1986 SADF annual report of special projects reflected on the smooth progress made with the procurement of arms and ammunition from the PRC, and envisaged the continuation of arms deals, which were considered a vital element of the burgeoning relationship with China. Answer was also awaited from the Chinese about a proposed visit by South African Military Intelligence to China. Such a trip would form the basis of formalising intelligence co-operation between the two countries.[55]

As part of the arms trade between China and South Africa, a senior member of Norinco asked to visit South Africa in May 1986 in order to have discussions with Armscor. He also requested the issuing of a third-country passport for him by South Africa – photographs were already in possession of Military Intelligence to facilitate this. In return, the PRC invited Armscor officials from its research and marketing department to visit armaments factories in Mongolia.[56] The relationship thus steadily intensified through direct contact between the militaries and their powerful state-owned arms companies. An Armscor financial report for 1988–9 reports a payment of over R22 million to Norinco for the delivery of 'goods' between September and November 1989. The purpose of the procurement was Project Scraper, which focused on highly sensitive projects, including the procurement of intelligence and clandestine support for foreign resistance movements.[57] In the same year the SADF Directorate of Foreign Relations budgeted for 'special contact under Project Hansa' to the amount of R25,000. This was likely to be for a meeting in South Africa, China or Hong Kong between the new allies.[58]

Towards the end of apartheid in 1988, the increasing contact between South Africa and China led to high-tech military collaboration. PW Botha was informed of the collaboration by his minister of economic affairs and technology, Danie Steyn. The Centre for Scientific and Industrial Research (CSIR), controlled by the South African state, invited China to co-operate in the development of its nascent satellite technology. The collaboration included the proposed joint procurement of strategic goods and follow-up visits between the two countries.[59] This was a major step: the relationship had shifted from mutually beneficial trade to strategic and sensitive collaboration. For South Africa, such satellite technology not only had the potential to provide a means of monitoring its neighbours, but was also an important step in the development of a programme to design long-range ballistic missiles and the longer-term goal of developing intercontinental ballistic missiles (ICBMs). This capacity to fire nuclear warheads at any city in Africa, or eventually Europe, India or the United States, would have provided PW Botha with his ultimate deterrent against external threats to white domination. It would have given South African nuclear weapons a potentially wider reach by extending the range capability beyond the 1,400 km that had been achieved through collaboration with the Israelis in the Jericho II missile project in 1989.

According to a report in the London *Sunday Times* published in 1993, 'South Africa reached a clandestine $2 billion deal with China to give the apartheid regime the capability of sending a nuclear weapon deep into black Africa, according to senior military sources. The secret treaty, made in the late 1980s, gave Pretoria access to Peking's long-range missile technology, allowing it to develop the capability of launching ballistic nuclear weapons and sending its own satellites into space.'[60] The South Africans also worked closely with Israel in the development of its long-range RSA-1, RSA-2 and RSA-3 missiles. The RSA-3 could, for example, send a satellite into space and deliver a nuclear weapon's payload to neighbouring countries such as Angola.[61] The RSA-4 was then still in a development phase: based on the Israeli Shavit missile, with possible added Chinese know-how, it would have had the capacity to send nuclear weapons hurtling directly towards New York or Moscow.[62] It was the development of this technology that the American authorities were able to scupper in 1993 through financial inducements paid to Pretoria.

In addition to the claims that China may have helped South Africa develop missiles to deliver nuclear weapons, there has long been speculation about China's delivery of low-enriched uranium to South Africa in 1981 through a third party. Nic von Wielligh, who helped both develop and decommission South Africa's nuclear weapons arsenal, confirmed that China did indeed supply such uranium.[63] He stated that South Africa received approximately 88 tonnes of low enriched uranium, which could only have come from two countries, France or China. Neither countries were signatories to the Non-Proliferation Treaty at the time and thus were not required to disclose to whom they sold such material.[64] Von Wielligh was present when the International Atomic Energy Association (IAEA) inspected some of the cylinders containing this material. The IAEA official concluded, based on the inscription on the cylinders and a test of the material, that it was undeniably of Chinese origin. He apparently remarked, 'You can see for yourself where the stuff came from.'[65] China had not only helped arm apartheid, but enabled it to acquire its deadliest weapon.

In silence, nobody loses face

When the ANC came to power, the Mandela administration gently dispensed with South Africa's ties with Taiwan and finally recognised only the government of China. This move reflected China's growing economic importance in the world. But in the pomp and ceremony of embassy openings and reciprocal trips by successive South African presidents to China and vice versa, nobody has ever officially spoken a word about how China helped the apartheid government to procure arms.

This must surely be a source of great displeasure for all involved, the Chinese Communist Party leadership, the anti-communist National Party supporters and the current ANC government. China, the most important partner in the BRICS economic and political project, does not have a squeaky-clean record when it comes to collaboration with apartheid. The evidence no doubt lies strewn on battlefields across southern Africa.

It is apparent that all five members of the UN Security Council, the Big Five entrusted with the power of veto to keep world peace, facilitated conflict and racial oppression in South Africa. They did not act alone. In the next chapters, we turn to the network of states that acted in tandem with the big powers in support of apartheid South Africa.

On the Silk Road
China, arms & apartheid

Pretoria, China and Zaire: The SADF needs a range of machine guns, mortars and high-calibre bombs. Armscor's offices in Paris and Hong Kong are instructed to find and buy the weapons. **Chinese** state-owned arms company Norinco, likely with approval from the Chinese Communist Party, agrees to supply the weapons to Pretoria. **Zaire's** intelligence officials agree to assist.

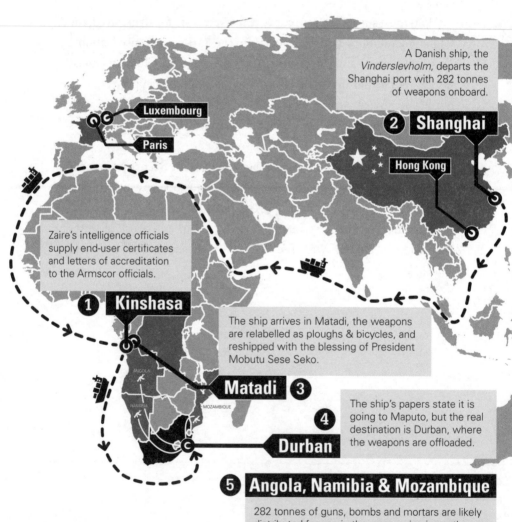

A Danish ship, the *Vinderslevholm*, departs the Shanghai port with 282 tonnes of weapons onboard.

Luxembourg

Paris

2 **Shanghai**

Hong Kong

Zaire's intelligence officials supply end-user certificates and letters of accreditation to the Armscor officials.

1 **Kinshasa**

The ship arrives in Matadi, the weapons are relabelled as ploughs & bicycles, and reshipped with the blessing of President Mobutu Sese Seko.

ANGOLA

NAMIBIA

MOZAMBIQUE

Matadi **3**

4

Durban

The ship's papers state it is going to Maputo, but the real destination is Durban, where the weapons are offloaded.

5 **Angola, Namibia & Mozambique**

282 tonnes of guns, bombs and mortars are likely distributed for use in the wars raging in southern Africa. More was likely to follow.

Proxies, Players and Pariahs

'*We have a laager with open doors.*'
– PW Botha, September 1986

CHAPTER 11

Proxies and Other Players

*'We are probably no better, but certainly no worse than the
rest of the world.'*

– PW Botha, August 1986

The permanent five members of the United Nations Security Council
failed to enforce the arms embargo against apartheid. As the previous
five chapters have shown in many instances, these countries wilfully
violated the embargo or encouraged their agents to do so. Such
behaviour trickled down throughout the international system. Pretoria
could call on the support of dozens of states across the globe that
acted as clandestine supporters providing weapons and intelligence
and participating in covert trade. There was an extensive network of
embargo-busting allies. The most obvious are the four other pariah
states – all outsiders in the international system, for different reasons.
We return to them in the next chapter.

In this chapter we focus on the network of proxies and other
players, states that largely operated in the Western powers' field
of influence. They were conduits for covert relations with the big
powers or ran sanctions-busting efforts for their own interests. They
supplied transit points for shipping arms, exchanged intelligence and

false documents, and provided the other covert activities required to facilitate arms embargo busting. These countries engaged in this for profit, political gain and, occasionally, out of ideological sympathy. Intelligence was an important conduit for these relations between deep state networks.

These countries were a mix of dictatorships and democracies ruled by chancellors, presidents and kleptocrats who openly condemned Pretoria, while their governments and private sector cultivated dirty business ties. In a number of instances we can reveal for the first time the nature of these clandestine relations. The countries identified in this chapter are case studies of what was probably a far larger phenomenon. They are drawn from Africa, Asia and Europe and provide a unique insight into the countries and corporations that were eager to show solidarity and, if necessary, break the law to assist Pretoria. Secrecy provided the perfect cover.

A super-gun: Proxies in practice

In the late 1970s the South African Defence Force (SADF) was in the market for a super-gun. They wanted a mobile cannon that could shoot projectiles up to 50 kilometres into the Angolan bush, far into the front line of their Cuban and Angolan opponents. With the development of the G5 and G6 motorised 155 mm howitzer cannon, Armscor became one of the world leaders in artillery manufacture. The company described this as one of its 'most outstanding achievements', an example of home-built military excellence, which became a major revenue earner as countries around the world lined up to use the new super-gun in wars of their own.[1] As with so many of Armscor's 'achievements', it came with a great deal of help from friends abroad, embargo busting to boot. In the development of the G5 cannon, Pretoria had the assistance of everyone, from US intelligence to a Caribbean island and the king of Spain.

The man behind the initial development of the G5 was the

eccentric Canadian weapons developer, Gerald Bull. His lasting passion was the unrealised development of a super-gun, with a barrel that was 52 m long and 40 cm wide, which could launch shells across the world and satellites into space.[2] The US government, at the height of its Cold War ambitions, invested in this process and granted Bull and his Space Research Corporation (SRC) great leeway for research and testing on the Quebec–Vermont border of the United States and Canada.

In the mid-1970s, as Pretoria was being desperately outgunned in Angola by Soviet artillery, the South Africans turned to the Americans for help. Through the CIA's representative in Pretoria, Lieutenant Colonel John Clancey, Armscor was put in touch with a CIA fixer, Jack Frost, who in turn arranged contact with Gerald Bull and his closest associate, Luis Palacio. Bull and the SRC were in need of cash, and Pretoria needed bigger guns. A deal was struck. In 1976, in exchange for a $10 million Armscor investment (resulting in 19.9% ownership in the company),[3] the SRC would ship containers of the 155 mm shells and guns to South Africa for replication. In addition, Armscor's engineers would be welcomed to SRC facilities in Canada and Belgium for training and assistance.[4] Crucially, Frost alerted the US State Department to the scheme, possibly for reasons of conscience, but the government unremarkably failed to act on the whistleblower's report.[5]

This clandestine supply worked effortlessly. Bull had previously used his relationship with the government of the Caribbean island of Antigua, where the SRC operated and tested shells for the US military, to bypass any prying eyes. In Antigua the shipment of weapons was collected by a German-registered ship, the *Tugelaland*, which was the property of a New York company owned by the South African government.[6] The ship, now laden with weapons, was meant, according to official documents, to travel to Barbados, but it changed course and set sail for Durban.

This guise worked well until a careless ship's captain let slip to a dockworker the real destination of the guns (painted yellow to disguise them as Caterpillar tractor parts). Subsequent investigation in Canada by the Trudeau government and international protest, at the time of the arms embargo in 1977, led to the closure of the supply channel. A convenient replacement was found with the assistance of the SRC employee Luis Palacio, who had Spanish friends in high places – so high in fact that Armscor employees were granted a private audience with King Juan Carlos. He agreed that Spain would act as conduit for this weapons trade in exchange for Armscor's assistance in obtaining manufacturing rights for Spain.[7]

As the provision of weapons to South Africa became obvious to law enforcement in the United States and Canada, Bull's options started to run out. The US Department of Justice launched an investigation and Bull was sentenced to a year in prison, while the SRC was fined $105,000. This lenient sentence represented a willingness on the Americans' part to grant a plea bargain for fear that 'possible US government authorization of SRC shipments to South Africa' would be revealed.[8]

By this time, the South Africans had been provided the skills, technology and know-how they needed, and could proceed without Bull and manufacture upgrades of the cannon at home. PW Botha proudly announced the 'home-grown' G5 cannon and dismissed all talk that the technology had been imported.[9] The US Congress, for its part, was not unaware of American complicity in the deal. A report by the congressional Africa subcommittee commented that 'it is probable that a US Defense Consultant who was assisting the CIA's covert action programme in Angola … planned with South African government officials shipment of US-origin arms to South Africa for use in Angola. At the very least this episode suggests serious negligence on the part of the Agency. At most, there is a possibility that elements of the CIA purposively evaded US policy.'[10]

The CIA had an interest in supporting the South African military in Angola. But there would be other knock-on benefits down the line. The former spy Craig Williamson told me that during the 1980s South Africa used the Comoros Islands as a transhipment point in supplying the Iraqi army of Saddam Hussein with 155 mm shells for use in its war with Iran, and that 'Saddam was shooting these at a rate of knots'.[11] He added that 'the US was pissed off with Iran and was aware that South Africa was playing this role'.[12] However, the security services of Israel, a key South African ally at the time, saw Iraq as a bigger threat than Iran and were unhappy with the situation. In the end, 'the USA was the "bigger dog" and given that they approved the supply of South African weapons to Iraq and Saddam Hussein, we continued despite Israeli protestations'.[13]

One of the reasons for this was also financial – Armscor needed a return on its investment as it was in serious economic difficulties and there was talk of retrenching almost five thousand Armscor employees in 1983 if a deal, such as the sale of the G5 to Iraq, did not come through.[14] Following an initial heavy investment to procure the technology, Armscor now proceeded to export the G5 into conflict zones, turning it into a prize cash cow. Soon, South Africa was reportedly supplying the G5 gun not only to Iraq, but also to Iran.[15] There is nothing more profitable than arming both sides of a war. This was a vital coup for the South Africans, who were feeling the pinch of the oil embargo and relied on barter trade with oil-rich nations such as Iran and Iraq.[16] As we have seen in Chapter 10, even China was interested in buying these weapons directly from source.

Gerald Bull continued to nurture his ambition of designing a true super-gun to fire satellites into space and he even worked for Saddam Hussein's ballistic missile programme. In 1990 Bull was murdered by an assassin who shot him five times as he entered his apartment in Brussels. Although never definitely proved, it has been largely suspected that the assassination was the work of Israeli intelligence, displeased with his continued collaboration with the Iraqis on the eve of the first Gulf War.[17]

Europe: A covert union

West Germany

During the 1980s, West Germany had strong trading links with South Africa, being one of the top exporters to South Africa and one of the top five importers of South African goods.[18] West German banks were among the leading private creditors to South Africa, and in the early 1980s they managed 63% of all major loans by international banks to the country.[19] An estimated 400 West German companies were active in apartheid South Africa, and those with a significant presence included the industrial giants Siemens, Daimler-Benz and BMW. As a major international weapons producer, Germany also kept a keen eye on the lucrative South African market.

Key to this long-standing relationship were members of the political elite who encouraged close ties with Pretoria. Chief among them in the 1980s were the conservative politicians Helmut Kohl and Franz Josef Strauss. Kohl was chancellor of Germany from 1982 to 1998 and chair of the conservative Christian Democratic Union (CDU) for almost a decade longer. The driving force behind the reunification of Germany in 1990, his reputation was tainted by a CDU party-funding scandal which was exposed after he was voted out of office. It soon became apparent that under Kohl's leadership the CDU had set up a relatively complex money-laundering scheme, including secret accounts and separate 'civic' organisations to act as middlemen – all to collect illegal donations and avoid paying tax on these.[20]

Kohl's primary political rival was the Bavarian politician Franz Josef Strauss, the leader of the Christian Social Union (CSU), which was also the CDU's coalition partner in government. Minister president of Bavaria from 1978 until his death in 1988, Strauss is remembered today as the 'colourful' conservative who 'stood out in the colourless world of present-day German politics as a fighter who played politics with the same passion he devoted to hunting, flying and drinking'.[21]

Compared with Strauss, Kohl was more careful about distancing himself from Pretoria. During his 1984 European tour, PW Botha was received by Kohl. But when the chancellor's office realised almost too late the negative media coverage that would ensue, at the last minute Kohl ordered that the couch upon which he usually hosted international leaders be removed from his office – opting to stand and declining the mandatory political handshake with Botha. In marked contrast, Strauss, who visited South Africa every two years between the mid-1960s and the mid-1980s, conspicuously offered Botha a warm welcome during the same visit.[22] During one of his trips to South Africa in 1983, Strauss told a German diplomat accompanying him that while he rejected 'petty apartheid', he did not support equal rights for black South Africans in a one-man one-vote system, as this would, he said, lead to South Africa's 'downfall'.[23]

In the early evening of 8 June 1983 Strauss welcomed the head of South African Military Intelligence into his office. In the mood for an informal conversation, he immediately served his guests large stone tankards of Bavarian beer.[24] In this exchange, Strauss was critical of the liberal minister of foreign affairs, Hans-Dietrich Genscher, whom he regarded as being 'obsessed with the United Nations'.[25] He also informed his guests that, despite their reported rivalry, he helped school Helmut Kohl in African affairs in a weekly two-hour briefing. Claims by the South Africans that they could 'roll the Communists back in southern Africa' received his whole-hearted approval. Not hiding his racism, Strauss added, 'when the USSR suffers further setbacks [in Southern Africa], the blacks' "black mentality" will change. However, we must prove to the blacks that we are on their side.'[26]

The third partner in Kohl's centre-right coalition was the liberal Free Democratic Party (FDP). The party's minister, Genscher, unlike Kohl and Strauss, was a thorn in the side of attempts to bust the arms embargo. As a result PW Botha sought to exclude him from high-level meetings with German politicians. Genscher's attitude to apartheid was a cause of much irritation to Pretoria. To counter his 'negative' influence, efforts were made to place pressure on him through allies in Germany. According to his reminiscences, the South African diplomat Donald Sole relied on top-level German businessmen such as the Daimler-Benz chairman, Joachim Zahn, to do his lobby work.[27] Before a controversial issue related to South Africa was submitted to Genscher, Sole would ask Zahn to call Genscher and mention that something sensitive was on its way to him. In so doing, he would 'head off any anti-apartheid proposition' submitted to Genscher, who was always conscious of his party's close links to the private sector.[28]

German U-boats

In 1999 Howaldtswerke-Deutsche Werft (HDW)[29] and Ingenieurkontor Lübeck (IKL), today trading as a subsidiary of ThyssenKrupp, were two of the three companies (together with Ferrostaal) in a German consortium that won the bid to supply the South African Navy with new submarines. This process was highly skewed in their favour and formed part of the controversial arms deal of Thabo Mbeki's government. It is little known, however, that both HDW and IKL were controversially linked to the sale of blueprints and technology to equip the apartheid military with new submarines during the mid-1980s, a subject to which we now turn.

A peculiar coincidence between the sanctions-busting deal and the arms deal is that both involved a South African Navy captain, Jeremy Mathers. In the post-apartheid deal, Mathers acted as a consultant for the German bidder Ferrostaal. At that point very recently retired from the navy, Mathers was hired by Ferrostaal to provide information on the navy's requirements. Controversially, Mathers's substantial communication included a 'success fee' in the event that the deal was awarded to Ferrostaal.[30] A decade prior, in 1984, Mathers was the navy's project manager for Project Tamboeryn, which involved the successful acquisition of submarine blueprints from West Germany.[31]

Helmut Kohl, as West German chancellor, controversially agreed to a deal to supply submarine plans to the South African military: the Germans would supply the know-how and the South Africans would build the vessels in Durban and Cape Town. In June 1984, ten days after a meeting between PW Botha and Kohl in Bonn, a contract for DM116 million sealed the arrangement.[32] This deal, initiated in 1982 and exposed in 1986, was secretly concluded through middlemen in Turkey and Israel. It would grow to include not just submarine blueprints, but also expertise and electronic components for the submarines and other strike craft – ultimately resulting in a contract worth DM423 million (R3.5 billion in today's value).[33]

How Kohl and Botha brokered this agreement is worth recounting.

In Kohl, PW Botha found his match. When the German chancellor met Botha in Bonn on 5 June 1984, with hundreds of protesters outside the building, he started the conversation by saying that 'it would not help to hide behind the diplomatic niceties. The Prime Minister [Botha] did not look a diplomat to him. He was exactly as he had imagined him to be.'[34] The two men met without their ministers of foreign affairs present and were ready to talk business, which Botha described as 'personal matters'.[35]

Botha got straight to the point. The South African government was ready to facilitate the investment of German businesses in South Africa. He added that 'it was important that certain specialized know-how be made available to the South African authorities'.[36] According to Botha, 'everything had been arranged between IKL/HDW and the South African shipbuilder'. Botha stressed the seriousness of the matter and appealed to Kohl to make a positive decision as soon as possible. Kohl responded that 'he would take care of the matter personally'. Kohl first asked whether it was speedboats South Africa needed. Botha was clear: South Africa would build its own U-boats using the specialised know-how it had acquired. Kohl promised Botha that 'he would look into the matter and write to the Prime Minister personally'.[37]

Experts in naval ship-building, HDW and IKL provided the all-important submarine plans, while the German electronics companies Siemens and Zeiss provided expertise for the equipment required by the vessels.[38] In addition, 'Two Krupps subsidiaries supplied torpedoes and sonar, and MBB, a company closely associated with Franz Josef Strauss's CSU, was contracted to supply a simulator for training crews.'[39] Strauss was also a strong lobbyist for the deal, and internal memos from HDW described him as the 'constant pressing force in the background'. As the coalition partner in Kohl's government, Strauss had unique political leverage with which he could support both the German arms industry and his friends in Pretoria. Together, the German companies provided the necessary expertise and assistance to build four submarines and to equip them and the South African strike command vessel, the *Drakensberg*, with sophisticated technology. They were required for the type of commando and sabotage raids that the SADF regularly carried out in Mozambique and Angola in the 1980s.[40]

According to General Bertus Steenkamp, who was stationed in Germany as military attaché at the time, he on occasion collected the blueprints in the port city of Lübeck and subsequently ensured their delivery via diplomatic bag to Pretoria.[41] He believes that Armscor had already made progress in constructing the facilities needed to build the submarines in Durban before the plan was exposed in 1986.[42]

Owing to the public exposure, after significant pressure from the German Green Party, the South Africans and Germans needed to develop alternative delivery and payment plans. The answer was found in Germany's NATO ally Turkey (which was itself involved at the same time in negotiations to build a deep-water port for South African sanctions-busting operations). Providing the submarine plans to Turkey was no problem, and the onward supply to South Africa was then negotiated by Turkish and South African military officials in Mauritius.[43]

The scandal became the subject of a lengthy public inquiry in Germany, largely thanks to the German Green Party and the Social Democrats.[44] South African military correspondence shows that when 'friends of South Africa with good contact to members of the committee' required information to support South Africa's case, they were secretly assisted by the South African military.[45] The German parties' parliamentary efforts were also bedevilled by excessive secrecy on the side of the government. Ultimately, the supplier companies got off lightly. Following a criminal investigation into their activities, the Kiel state prosecutor dropped the investigation and the corporations were instead fined less than 1% of the value of the contract for a tax offence.[46] In a candid admission of the sanctions-busting problem, a spokesperson for Kohl's economic ministry said 'there are some companies that will always find a loophole, some that have no morality'.[47]

As South Africa moved towards a democracy and the end of the Angolan War, the submarines were no longer required and the plans were shelved despite a hefty financial investment. Within a decade the German companies were again bidding for the sale of submarines to a new democratic administration.

Arms 'made in Germany'

During the embargo period, South Africa had no shortage of offers of weapons from German arms companies and middlemen. For example, immediately after the imposition of the arms embargo, the chair of the far right-wing National Democratic Party of Germany, Adolf von Thadden, approached the South African embassy in Bonn in October 1977 with an offer of ammunition for long-range rocket launchers.[48] The South African diplomats felt that, even for them, his politics were distasteful, and they were not willing to do any business with him.[49] Managing these offers and the military mission in Bonn was not without complications.

As an indication of the delicacy of South African–German military relations at the time, when the South Africans were looking to replace a long-standing military attaché in 1981, they were informed that the Germans would not favour a new appointment. The Ministry of Foreign Affairs, led by Hans-Dietrich Genscher, which largely drove these concerns, was conscious of the political embarrassment that might ensue. However, during a visit to Bonn, the South African chief of staff of Military Intelligence was told by his German counterpart that the Germans would support the covert appointment of a military attaché.[50] What followed was three years of delicate and protracted correspondence between Bonn and Pretoria.

By 1984, the existing South African military attaché, Commander Bitzker, expressed the wish to return home. There seemed little possibility of a resolution to the problem that now faced both governments. As long as he stayed in Bonn, the Germans were unlikely to disaccredit him, but the moment he returned permanently to Pretoria they would refuse to accredit a replacement. In January 1984, the South African chief of staff intelligence was in Bonn again and met his counterpart, General Söder, and agreed to a *modus vivendi*, or covert solution to the problem. The military attaché would not resign his post, but would rather return to South Africa and then travel back to Bonn from time to time. This neat solution would be a cover for a civilian official who would be secretly placed in the South African embassy to continue all the normal military liaison tasks of his predecessor.[51]

This fiction, set up with the approval of the German government, continued throughout the rest of the 1980s. A secret report from 1988 shows that exchanges between the military intelligence services of both countries happened every three months and that when material had to be handed over to the Germans, it would take place away from prying eyes at the German Ministry of Defence.[52] The South African contacts in the German Chancellery also gave their nod to this scheme. Remarkably, the state secretary, the Chancellery and, later, the German Ministry of Foreign Affairs all eventually agreed that this clandestine solution was a fair compromise.[53]

Despite the arms embargo, large German corporations continued to supply equipment and weapons to the South African military.[54] The electronics giant Siemens was a sought-after supplier for the proposed submarine deal and welcomed SADF officials to their Munich headquarters in 1984 to test equipment.[55] Krauss-Maffei, the Munich-based producer of the Leopard tank, also worked closely with the SADF and Armscor, and at one point in the mid-1980s South

African Military Intelligence reported that the Armscor project team procuring tank equipment and technology 'practically has free access to Krauss-Maffei's facilities'.[56]

The German arms behemoth Thyssen also welcomed Armscor and the South African Navy in July 1986 to discuss an offer of TR-1700 submarines, at the time among the fastest diesel-electric submarines in the world. Dr Werner Bartels, a member of Thyssen's executive board, was the go-between in this deal with the South African minister of defence.[57] At Bartels's request, naval officials, including Captain Jeremy Mathers, travelled to Germany on a top-secret visit to meet him in August 1986.[58]

Records reveal that there also was a steady flow of dozens of senior German military officers to South Africa.[59] One of the surprising guests in October 1989 was Bernd Wilz, the government's spokesperson on defence at the time and a future German minister of defence in Kohl's cabinet from 1992 to 1998. Wilz was described as a good contact of the South African embassy, 'and has often stood up for the RSA in Germany'.[60] The visit was organised by the South African Department of Foreign Affairs but had an almost purely military agenda, with Wilz requesting to meet senior SADF officials, including Magnus Malan and the chief of the SADF, General Jannie Geldenhuys.[61] Wilz also expressed a desire to view South African armaments technology and tour the Simonstown naval base.[62] The visit had a distinctly clandestine character: the SADF described Wilz's decision to travel to South Africa as coming with 'considerable political risk to himself, should it become public knowledge. His visit to the RSA and the SADF in particular should be handled with the necessary confidentiality.'[63]

One of the areas in which the German military was particularly helpful was in the provision of NATO codes, used by members of the alliance to integrate their equipment and weapons systems. Access by the South Africans made it far easier to procure weapons from Western suppliers and ensured a behind-the-scenes alignment with the alliance. A number of visits overseas by South Africans emphasised the importance of obtaining updated NATO codification data from Germany, which was one of the only NATO countries said to be willing to supply these.[64]

By the early 1990s, dozens of German middlemen and arms manufacturers were knocking on the South African embassy's door to sell all manner of weapons as the Cold War market began to lose its importance. These included fraudulent offers, such as the mysterious bogus chemical known as red mercury, which was on sale for $136,000/kg.[65] On the more serious side, Thyssen Rheinstahl Technik offered to sell naval frigates at half-price. The source was the Argentinian navy, which it appears was under financial strain at the time, possibly to repay their German supplier, and South Africa was invited to purchase the frigates on the cheap at $100 million each.[66] In 1999, Thyssen was one of the lead suppliers in the German Frigate Consortium's (GFC) sale of fighter vessels to the South African Navy, and was implicated in this corrupt multi-billion-dollar deal.

German spies

At the same time that the German Ministry of Foreign Affairs showed an unwillingness to accredit a new military attaché, the relationship between South African Military Intelligence and their counterparts in the West German Federal Intelligence Services, the BND, strengthened. From late 1982 a South African military intelligence official was deployed covertly to Munich, where his primary task was liaison with the BND.[67]

In June 1983, Norbert Klusak, the deputy president of the BND, led a delegation of seven officers to a meeting in downtown Pretoria.[68] Klusak had travelled to South Africa the previous month, as a guest of South African Military Intelligence: they discussed the exchange of tradecraft 'to intensify the co-operation of both services'.[69] For the June 1983 meeting, the aim of which was to identify areas of future co-operation, the South African delegation was led by the chief of staff intelligence, PW van der Westhuizen. The South African officials felt that there was a need for closer collaboration than that provided by the existing annual intelligence conferences held between the services. The BND agreed to hold seminars supplying information on new equipment and covert collection techniques, and the South African military agreed in turn to allow the Germans the 'opportunity to interrogate Russians/East Germans if captured in South West Africa'. The BND indicated that it would welcome such an opportunity.[70] Another issue discussed was closer collaboration in counter-intelligence operations, and there was in principle agreement that South Africa could use West Germany as a base for covert intelligence operations, as long as the BND was informed.[71]

A little more than a year later, a delegation of Military Intelligence, SADF and Armscor officials travelled to meet Klusak and his team in Germany.[72] In the exchange of information, the SADF noted that no requests that they made were denied by the BND, and that a large amount of sensitive technical information had been obtained and shared, including information about Soviet missiles. The BND offered the South Africans a reward of $2 million should they be able to 'import a Soviet MI-24 helicopter or SU-22 aircraft from Angola'.[73] Such exchanges of military material had been happening for a number of years.[74] The BND also offered to purchase a Soviet MiG-23 fighter jet for $25 million, which both agencies could jointly evaluate in South Africa. As the BND was short of funds, they asked the South Africans to stump up half the amount.[75]

In June 1984, a group of seven South African military officials travelled to Germany for a two-week training course (codenamed SK201), provided by the BND. This was the second such course offered, and 'it was clear that SK201 undertook great effort and a measure of risk in presenting this training to military intelligence'.[76] The Germans also informed the South Africans that they wished to distance themselves from the shoddy official treatment that PW Botha had received earlier that month on his visit to Bonn, and that the head of the BND had also expressed his displeasure concerning this.[77]

Top-level contact between South African Military Intelligence and the BND continued throughout the 1980s, with regular intelligence conferences, despite increasing reluctance on the part of the military to approve overt collaboration or official visits by military personnel to South Africa because of pressure from the Anti-Apartheid Movement.[78] In 1988 the German military intelligence head, Brigadier General Bautzmann, informed the head of the SADF that 'with the current political climate in the FRG, it would be impossible for any Senior Officer (excluding those serving in the BND) to visit the RSA'.[79]

With much contact then happening in secret, the BND provided assistance in the procurement of sensitive German arms. When the South African military attempted to buy sophisticated reconnaissance cameras for their fighter jets, they approached the German company Zeiss. Following an initial rebuff, a decision was taken to travel in January 1988 to Germany to meet the head of the BND, Dr Hans-Georg Wieck, with whom Military Intelligence 'had a very good working relationship especially after his visit to South Africa during 1987'.[80] The South Africans noted that 'Dr Wieck's involvement can assist negotiations and limit the risks'.[81] It is unclear if Zeiss delivered the goods, but the documents show the potential role entrusted to the BND as a go-between when negotiating with arms manufacturers.

As the 1980s wore on, military intelligence ties came to define the important deep state relations that existed between Germany and South Africa.

Belgium
Trading shotguns and flamethrowers
Belgium, as we have seen in Chapter 5, was central to Armscor's arms money machine. Kredietbank in Belgium and its Luxembourg subsidiary enabled Armscor to move billions of rands around the world to pay for weapons and technology procured from a wide range of sources. Nonetheless, this was not the only arms connection between South Africa and Belgium – arms and intelligence were traded bilaterally as well.

Belgium has been described by the investigative journalist Walter de Bock as an 'arms bazaar' 'at the crossroads of NATO, the European community ... We have a very developed business concentration, multinational companies and being at the crossroads of international exports – it is a very privileged transit zone, in fact it is such a small country that is ... no more than a transit zone for a greater part of the economy.'[82]

While this opportunity wasn't lost on Pretoria, Belgian officials were also keen not to lose out on the lucrative South African trade, despite arms sanctions. Accordingly, an official from the Belgian embassy in Pretoria drew his minister's attention to Armscor's growing procurement budget in 1978.[83] This was just as the UN mandatory arms embargo began to take effect. He reported that the trade counsellor in the embassy believed that 'he would make himself guilty of a dereliction of duty if he did not inform [Brussels] ... fully of all the business opportunities that exist. How this information will be used and to what extent is not in the competency or in the responsibility of this embassy.'[84] This diplomatic doublespeak is a reminder that Belgium, with its own domestic arms business, remained interested in opportunities in South Africa.

Trade opportunities aside, many of the 23,000 Belgian citizens living in South Africa in the 1980s served in the SADF, using South African-manufactured R1 rifles produced by Armscor, which were copies of the Belgian FN rifle.[85]

One of the more disturbing files we found in the SADF archive concerned a failed arms deal to purchase over 20,000 flamethrowers.[86] Who was the military intending to smoke out and set alight with 20,000 flamethrowers? Nobody carries a flamethrower, which ejects a long stream of burning liquid fuel, without knowing that they may well roast another human being alive. This is the reason that all armies are prohibited from using them as a result of the 1980 Geneva Convention on Certain Conventional Weapons (which entered into force in 1983).[87] While this deal didn't violate the Convention in legal terms, it was in violation of the spirit of the Convention as well as of the arms embargo.

Who would provide the weapons? This was the Zimbabwean

weapons smuggler, John Bredenkamp, and his Antwerp-based company, Casalee.[88] Bredenkamp is a notorious figure in the world of clandestine deals in southern Africa. He is said to have made his first fortune as one of Rhodesia's chief sanctions busters, moving at least one commodity that we know of, tobacco, offshore.[89] Bredenkamp, a Rhodesian, emigrated to the Netherlands in 1968. From 1976, he was linked to the Rhodesian firm Intabex, which illegally imported Rhodesian tobacco to Europe via Antwerp. Bredenkamp worked at Intabex together with Nicholas McKisack, who was sent to Antwerp by the Smith regime to facilitate clandestine tobacco imports. The Belgian government never put a stop to this, despite demands by the UN secretary general, Kurt Waldheim.[90]

In 1976 Bredenkamp and McKisack established the firm Casalee, which was involved in arms sanctions busting for Pretoria.[91] By the mid-1980s Bredenkamp was back in Zimbabwe as a close ally of Robert Mugabe, helping to prop up that regime by becoming involved in that country's resource-plundering war in the Congo between 1998 and 2003.[92] While Bredenkamp has admitted to his role in Rhodesian sanctions busting, he has denied involvement as an important broker for the British arms company BAE in the post-apartheid arms deal.[93]

In mid-1982 Armscor agents approached Bredenkamp and the Casalee subsidiary Nuoria Trading to procure flamethrowers. The minutes of an Armscor meeting show that Bredenkamp (codenamed Peptic) and other representatives of his company met Armscor officials to discuss the deal.[94] Bredenkamp had spent $100,000 on acquiring fraudulent end-user certificates from Nigeria and Zimbabwe for the export of the flamethrowers, which were manufactured by the Belgian arms company PRB. However, the deal hit a major snag: the airplane that had been chartered at a cost of $174,000 was prevented from flying from Egypt to pick up its cargo in Belgium. It appeared that bad management – an unpaid bill in Cairo – had scuppered the deal.[95] The cargo was moved from the airport back to the arms company, but Belgian authorities smelt a rat: why was a Nigerian transport plane not used to transport the weapons if that was where they were headed? The deal was stymied, and it was agreed that the Nigerian authorities were to be asked to put pressure on the Belgian arms company to ensure that the weapons could be released.[96] An SADF internal audit document shows that further plans to export the weapons in early 1983 were halted when the Belgian authorities were asked by their UK allies to review all weapons exports 'southwards' for fear that they might fall into the hands of the Argentinian army during the Falklands War, which was then raging.[97]

Belgium: Trading intelligence

In March 1991, as the stop-start South African political negotiations process was under way, Belgian and South African military intelligence services were busy exchanging pleasantries. Major General R van Calster, Belgium's chief of Intelligence and Security Services, the SGRS, wrote to his counterpart, Lieutenant General Badenhorst of South African Military Intelligence. He hoped that the South African negotiation process would 'normalise' secret intelligence contacts between the countries. 'The recent development, and the way that they are perceived by the responsible authorities in my country, gives me the opportunity to anticipate further official consolidation and even extension of the longstanding but up to now confidential relations between our services.'[98]

Documents from the SADF archive reveal that a cordial relationship existed between the military intelligence agencies of both countries throughout the arms embargo period. While successive Belgian heads of state railed against apartheid, the military intelligence services continued their work largely undisturbed in the shadows. In September 1985 Major General J de Mild, the head of the SGRS, wrote to Lieutenant General van der Westhuizen, who was about to leave Military Intelligence for the State Security Council.[99] He noted: 'The military intelligence will certainly miss you ... I wish to also thank you for the excellent relationship which has been established with your service.'[100] This was written in the same month that

Belgium announced that it would no longer accredit a South African military attaché. It seems South African Military Intelligence was unperturbed by this decision and simply moved its relationship with Belgian intelligence deeper underground.[101]

General Mild's deputy head, Colonel Moreau, expressed his gratitude to the South Africans, writing: 'I remain very indebted to you for the excellent collaboration and interesting exchange between our services and more personally the kind invitation to visit your beautiful country. It was a sojourn that my wife and I will never forget.'[102] The relationship with Moreau appears to have been long-standing: he hosted a top delegation from the SADF at an intelligence conference between the two countries in Belgium in 1984. Major General H Roux, chief of the SADF, wrote to Moureau after that trip to thank him for a successful meeting and added 'a special word of thanks to you and Mrs Moreau for the very personal attention paid to us at home during our interesting visit to Brugge'.[103] Thus, at the height of the arms embargo, the Belgian intelligence top brass received their South African counterparts at home for supper.

How much intelligence material was exchanged? The SADF archive does not provide any of the details. However, a cable from the South African ambassador stationed in Brussels and sent to Pretoria in June 1977, just after the UN embargo was implemented, provides insight into how this took place. It reflects the contents of a letter between the South African military attaché (MA) and the head of Military Intelligence in Pretoria. 'Belgian intelligence refuse to make copies of documents available to MA, but are willing to circumvent the ban, so doc[ument]s to be left under supervision for half an hour with MA, and notes can be made on subjects and matters of interest,' the cable noted. '[Belgian] Intelligence will then make a summary of the issues available to the MA.'[104] Such trickery, also employed by British security (see Chapter 9), could allow the Belgians to wipe their hands of the matter if it was ever exposed in the media.

Switzerland

In 1993, on the eve of South Africa's first democratic elections, the South African government purchased a Pilatus trainer jet from the Swiss arms company Oerlikon-Bührle. This transaction was coloured by allegations of corruption at the time, but was never properly investigated. The ANC at first objected to the sale, but eventually warmed to it, giving the go-ahead despite the continuing arms boycott. The South African embassy in Bern remarked that it had been informed by its contacts that the Swiss business community was jubilant about the sale: 'the fact that South Africa decided on the Pilatus airplane is regarded as a reward to Switzerland for their support over many years to South Africa during difficult times'.[105]

In Chapter 4 we saw that Switzerland was a first port of call for South Africa's moneymen seeking the continued flow of capital to South Africa. Bankers like Bruno Saager and Fritz Leutwiler used their power as senior members of the powerful and secretive Swiss banking sector to smooth the way for apartheid's representatives. This relationship was built on gold and the promise of mutual profit. Yet it was not the only basis for the relationship between Switzerland and apartheid. Placed strategically in Europe, and one of the largest per capita arms suppliers in the world,[106] Switzerland was also an important ally of apartheid when it came to obtaining intelligence and weapons technology.

The Swiss historian Peter Hug has written a thousand-page study of Swiss–South African military and nuclear relations during apartheid. He believes that political, military and arms industry relations between the two countries were at their peak during the 1980s. Hug's findings are almost exclusively based on declassified documents made available by both South African and Swiss authorities, as he undertook his research as part of a Swiss government-sanctioned project. Switzerland largely broke the embargo using a range of illegal and semi-legal transactions. Its contacts with South Africa extended to intelligence co-operation and the exchange of information, and directly contributed to the close links in the arms trade in favour of the South African government. Hug also shows that prominent Swiss companies delivered important components that assisted the South African government in its uranium enrichment programme, as part of the development of nuclear weapons.[107]

One of the reasons for the growing military contact was that Switzerland was one of the few countries in Europe that allowed the presence of an official South African military attaché.[108] Intelligence contact between the countries was formalised in 1977, and thereafter senior heads of both intelligence services paid regular visits and attended annual intelligence conferences, the venue alternating between the two countries.[109]

One of the most important supporters of the arms trade with apartheid was Dr Dieter Bührle and his company, Oerlikon–Bührle, now part of the German arms company Rheinmetall. Bührle's father was infamous for supplying weapons to both Nazi and Allied forces during the Second World War, and he was also close to Hermann Goering.[110] His son Dieter, then one of Switzerland's wealthiest people, was given a suspended sentence and a fine in 1970 for his involvement in the unauthorised supply of weapons to a number of countries, chief of which was apartheid South Africa.[111] Despite this, his trade with South Africa continued through licences provided to South African weapons manufacturers, including Armscor subsidiaries. Bührle's office was also an important port of call for South African military officials visiting Switzerland in the 1980s.[112]

As a sign of appreciation to Oerlikon–Bührle, PW Botha conferred South Africa's highest award on both Dieter Bührle and his chief sales representative, Gabriel Lebedinsky, in 1978. Following their return to Switzerland, both men wrote to thank Botha, with Bührle seeing the award as recognition of the fact that he was 'a true friend of your country and your government'.[113] Lebedinsky believed himself committed to the weapons trade with South Africa: '[it] means for me an obligation for the future as well'.[114]

Switzerland was useful in addition as a transit point for making contact with arms suppliers and trading in weapons. The financial capital of Zurich was host to most of these meetings.[115] One of Armscor's primary contacts was Dr Hansjakob Hugelshofer, who was both a sanctions buster for Armscor and involved in the uranium trade with South Africa. The South African embassy noted that he would travel by train to Bern, to hand-deliver or take receipt of documents from Armscor.[116] Hugelshofer was also the representative of the German tank company Krauss-Maffei in Switzerland, which at the time was involved in sales to South Africa, possibly through Hugelshofer himself.[117]

Spain

Both South African military and civilian intelligence exchanged material with their Spanish counterparts. The civilian National Intelligence Service (NIS) had an agent in the South African embassy who would regularly exchange intelligence with the Spanish intelligence agency.[118] The military intelligence agencies of the two countries also collaborated, and in the words of a Spanish naval captain writing to South African Military Intelligence in 1985, 'our exchange of information is mutually beneficial'.[119] The presence of both military and civilian intelligence agents was not limited to Spain. Records show that the South African embassy in Portugal also hosted agents from both agencies, who were active in Lisbon.[120] Military reports from Spain show that Armscor was involved in 'smuggling' in Spain in 1980.[121]

Military intelligence was also a potential go-between for proposed barter arrangements. From 1980 to 1981, the SADF and Armscor were drawn into a proposal to sell coal to the Spanish company Carboex, in exchange for sensitive, possibly military, material. In June 1981, it was reported that the prominent Spanish businessman José Sierra López, then chairman of the minerals company Carboex, asked an intermediary to inform the South African embassy to renew negotiations for the delivery of coal to Spain.[122] López, who today is the chairman of Rio Tinto's Spanish subsidiary, Emed Tartessus,[123] gave the South Africans the tip that the Spanish government was keen to discuss the import of South African coal. In exchange, he let it be known that the delivery 'of certain sensitive materials to South Africa' might be a quid pro quo for such trade.[124]

At about the same time, the military received an intriguing business plan from a Spanish entrepreneur, Antonio Garcia Lopez, proposing to establish a joint front company with Armscor, in order to 'unite Spanish and South African interests'.[125] The company, Austral OF Technology, would have a 60% South African ownership through Armscor, but would operate as a nominally Spanish company although domiciled in one of the Caribbean tax havens. Armscor would manage its investment through one of its offshore companies and thereby ensure that this nominally 'Spanish' company could illegally claim export credit guarantee benefits from the Spanish government.[126] There is no confirmation that the company was set up, other than a report from Military Intelligence that López had met with members of Armscor.[127]

Italy

Military Intelligence agents operating from the South African embassy were active in Italy (unimaginatively codenamed Monza) in the 1980s. From a handful of documents available in the SADF's archive, it appears that they focused their activities on covert propaganda campaigns, meddling in Italian politics, and more benign public diplomacy.

One of the more revealing documents shows that Military Intelligence considered funding an Italian political party in April 1989. In a letter to the chief of staff intelligence, Ivor Little, the embassy's first secretary, said that the founders of a new political party 'have hinted that they would not object to receiving covert funding in return for using their influence. Perhaps you might care to discuss this with your own friends when they call on you in the near future.'[128] Somewhat inexplicably, the supporting documents, which included the prospectus of the new party, are missing from the file. However, a likely candidate is the Lega Nord (North League), a right-wing political party established in 1989. The Lega Nord, which had a strong anti-immigrant stance, received up to 10% of national support in the polls during the 1990s, and eventually assisted the scandal-prone Silvio Berlusconi to form a government on several occasions.

This was not the only occasion on which South Africa considered funding local domestic politics in other countries. As we have seen, funds were made available to US politicians, and requests were also made by French politicians. In another instance, the South African ambassador to Portugal in 1980 proposed funding the centre-right governing party through a secret channel, in return for a quid pro quo, such as the provision of weapons and equipment.[129]

The other notable leg of the Italian operations was a covert attempt to place pro-SADF articles in leading Italian defence publications. Italy, as one of Europe's largest arms producers, remained an important source of weapons for South Africa, and attempts were made to influence the senior security officials who read these magazines. The documents show that two Italian journalists (both still active in this field of work) undertook to place pro-South African military articles in several prominent publications, including *Panaroma Difesa* and *Diana Armi*.[130] Vincenco Fenili and Luca Poggiali were said to be 'keen to act as comops agents for the SADF and UNITA'.[131] In 1988, Fenili and his wife undertook a trip to the South African battlefront and were reported to have had 'nothing but praise for the South African Air Force', and were 'fired up with enthusiasm'. The report went on to note that 'we can thus look forward to a good return on our financial investment in this couple'.[132] A measure of the return on investment was that Fenili and Poggiali published a total of 18 articles in defence publications, focusing on different arms of the South African military, between December 1988 and mid-1989.[133]

South African and Italian military intelligence enjoyed well-established contacts from at least 1983 onwards. In 1983 the head of South African Military Intelligence, Lieutenant General PW van der Westhuizen, wrote to his Italian counterpart at SISMI to thank him for receiving him in Rome, and lauded him for his 'decision to personally visit Southern Africa in order to see for yourself what the real situation is'.[134] These ties were important, as the Italian government took a decision in 1986 to stop accepting military attachés from South Africa. The links between the intelligence agencies meant that the contacts could continue on a clandestine basis.

The two agencies also engaged in a prolific exchange of visitors. While inter-defence force visits between the two countries were not allowed, three visits to South Africa, including an intelligence conference, were planned by officials from SISMI in 1988–9. With regard to weapons transfers, the report noted that 'visits to suppliers are a dangerous and embarrassing business and should be left to Armscor or else carried out extremely carefully in a covert manner. Factories are carefully watched for a SA connection.'[135] Despite this, Italy remained an important supplier of aircraft equipment. Armscor's authorised history notes that, despite the arms embargo, the delivery of components by the Italian aircraft manufacturer Aermacchi continued 'without problems'.[136]

Befriending Asian tigers

Singapore's GDP per capita has increased a hundredfold in the past 50 years and is now the fourth highest in the world.[137] This remarkable surge in wealth and growth in the tiny city-state is largely due to its being a crucial strategic port for access to Asia more broadly, and to its immediate neighbours in Indonesia and Malaysia. During the 1980s, under the authoritarian leadership of Lee Kuan Yew, the country prospered as a financial hub and trading centre. This gateway to Asia made it an attractive ally in apartheid's covert sanctions-busting operations.

Military ties between the two countries developed in the late 1970s, and Armscor used Singapore extensively as a covert go-between to procure weapons from other countries. Armscor also supplied Singapore with weapons for re-export to the Eastern bloc and Iraq in the early 1980s.[138] Indicative of Armscor's access to Singapore's political leadership was a meeting between the chairman of Armscor, PG Marais, and Goh Keng Swee, the senior deputy prime minister of Singapore, in 1982.[139] Subsequently, PW Botha personally invited Swee to South Africa with the promise that 'I can assure you that your presence here will be treated with the appropriate discretion'.[140] Goh Keng Swee was an influential politician and had been a cabinet minister, his responsibilities including defence, since independence in 1965. He visited South Africa in July 1983, and met with top government officials, the Reserve Bank, as well as the head of Armscor and the minister of defence.[141]

The political contacts between the regimes were only a backdrop to the more important and enduring contact that existed at the highest level between the countries' military intelligence agencies. This relationship was not only the basis for the exchange of information during apartheid, but a conduit for the clandestine exchange of weapons. Contact with the South African military began to intensify in 1982 following a visit by a Singaporean delegation to South Africa, who handed Military Intelligence a shopping list of Eastern bloc weapons they wished to purchase.[142] Within months, the chiefs of the South African and Singaporean intelligence services met in Hong Kong. They agreed to exchange intelligence and co-operate in the arms trade through their respective military attachés in Taipei. Shortly thereafter, they met in Singapore, where initial discussions concerning weapons trade took place.[143]

In Singapore, the South Africans developed an important ally in the head of the secretive Security and Intelligence Division (SID), Eddie Teo. Teo, current chairman of Singapore's Public Service Commission, is a respected public servant who headed both the country's internal and external intelligence departments during the 1980s. Following a significant sale of Eastern Bloc weapons to Singapore by Armscor in 1984 (including 3,000 AK-47s and three million rounds of ammunition, as detailed in chapter 10), Teo visited South Africa in April 1984. The secret payment to Armscor for these weapons was made from the Singaporean development bank via banks in Luxembourg.[144] At the 1984 meeting, it was agreed that the two intelligence services would come together in an annual conference.[145] The SADF also arranged for Teo to meet Jonas Savimbi, who he described as 'a sure winner for your country'.[146] Intelligence conferences between the countries continued throughout the 1980s, and Teo paid a further visit to Pretoria in 1988.

Singapore was not the only valuable point of entry in South East Asia. The ties developed in Singapore resulted in Eddie Teo facilitating contact between South African Military Intelligence and the head of the Thai army, General Chavalit, a future Thai prime minister. Chavalit welcomed South African Military Intelligence officers to his country in 1984.[147]

Despite Indonesia's strong anti-apartheid position within the Non-Aligned Movement, the first official contacts between the South African chief of staff intelligence and a group of Indonesian military officials under the leadership of General Benny Moerdani took place in a London hotel in 1980.[148] According to Moerdani, President Suharto had given him 'carte blanche' to speak to the South Africans. The two intelligence services immediately agreed to start exchanging information; this would take place through their respective contact people based in Washington DC. Moerdani, who was appointed the chief of the Indonesian military in 1983, also indicated his eagerness to visit South Africa and its Sasol plants. He speculated that, given their common interest in weapons, the two countries could procure weapons together and thereby gain a bulk discount.[149]

Military Intelligence was also the recipient of fraudulent Indonesian end-user certificates, which it was strongly suggested had been approved by President Suharto.[150] Suharto also approved the covert import of South African goods, and it was intimated to Military Intelligence that his son would handle the Indonesian side of this arrangement, thereby enabling him to draw considerable personal benefit.[151] Little record exists of the relationship during the 1980s, other than that by 1987 the first delegation of Indonesian officials arrived in South Africa for meetings with Armscor and, later that year, South African Military Intelligence in turn paid its first visit to Jakarta.[152]

The Africa network

Many African countries had a complicated relationship with South Africa during the 1980s. On the one hand, they paid a great financial price in showing their opposition to apartheid and rallied international support behind the cause of the liberation movements and for more stringent sanctions measures. However, many of the same countries were also reliant on South Africa for overt trade and clandestine support for both their civil and military needs. For example, Zaire relied on South African ports for 57% of its imports and almost half of its copper exports. De Beers, through its local subsidiary, was also the primary diamond mining company active in Zaire at the time.[153] The Malawian President Hastings Banda, a vocal ally of Pretoria, was critical of what he saw as African duplicity, 'those who maintain a clear conscience by voting resolutions against Pretoria, but who fill their stomachs with South African meat'.[154]

When President Omar Bongo of Gabon called for South African Airways to be denied landing rights in his country, he ignored the fact that a South African company was at the time helping to build a landing strip in Libreville that could accommodate wide-bodied aircraft, including 'phantom' South African flights.[155] Morocco was a South African ally in North Africa, and Kenya from time to time provided fraudulent end-user certificates, enabling the import of weapons by the SADF.[156] In Mauritius, Military Intelligence fostered ties with the opposition politician and cabinet member, Sir Gaëtan Duval. These were so close that a cryptography machine, to facilitate secret communication, was set up in his office in 1984.[157]

In the Ivory Coast, Félix Houphouët-Boigny, 'the father of Françafrique', served as that country's first post-independence

president for 33 years until his death in 1993. He was the darling
of pro-market advocates, who pointed to the prosperity of the
Ivory Coast economy in the 1960s and 1970s, when Boigny relaxed
capital controls and encouraged foreign investment.[158] Although
his relationship with French President François Mitterrand was less
warm than with his Gaullist predecessors, it is unsurprising that
Houphouët-Boigny became a key middleman in the relationship
between France and apartheid South Africa. Relations between the
two countries dated back to 1968, when Jean Mauricheau-Beaupré,
a pillar of Foccart's Françafrique, established contact.[159] Following a
nearly two-decades-long lull in the relationship, Beaupré informed
South African Military Intelligence in 1986 that Houphouët-
Boigny was ready to re-establish contact at head-of-state level.[160]
Military Intelligence returned to Houphouët-Boigny's palace in
July 1987 (and again in February 1988),[161] where they were warmly
welcomed. Within months Houphouët-Boigny received the chief
of South Africa's Military Intelligence in Abidjan in April 1986.[162]
Houphouët-Boigny was a strong supporter of PW Botha's so-
called reform efforts and also of UNITA's Jonas Savimbi, which
was another reason for the contact he was keen to foster with the
South Africans.

In addition to trade links, various African countries became
important proxies in the supply of intelligence to the South African
security forces. Such contacts sometimes bordered on the farcical:
the South African security police agent Vic McPherson, when based
in Malawi, operated under the cover of a sports clothes manufacturer
which he unimaginatively named Blue Line Enterprises.[163] A fan of
Marlene Dietrich, he called himself Klaus Dietrich and became a
feature of the social scene at the Capital Hotel in Lilongwe, where he
played the trumpet.[164] However, by day McPherson used his presence
to plot gruesome activities such as an attempt in the mid-1980s to
blow up the entire ANC leadership during a conference at Arusha
in Tanzania. The plan was only called off at the last moment by
Magnus Malan, when somebody sensibly pointed out that Pretoria

had just started negotiations with the same people they intended to murder.[165]

Zaire and Central Africa

Mobutu Sese Seko, president of Zaire (now the Democratic Republic of Congo) for 31 years, was the archetypal kleptocrat. Backed by Western powers, particularly senior intelligence and political figures in the United States, France and Belgium, Mobutu systematically looted Zaire's wealth, accumulating a fortune estimated at $5 billion. Wearing what would become a 'trademark leopard-skin cap and wooden walking stick, carved with the figure of an eagle at the top', and ensconced in his extravagant palace in Gbadolite (dubbed the 'Versailles of the jungle'), Mobutu did not tolerate dissent and used his security forces to maintain order through violence.[166] He had come to power through a CIA-encouraged coup in 1961, which resulted in the overthrow and murder of Patrice Lumumba. The CIA would continue their longstanding relationship with Mobutu, which included using Zaire's troops to launch an attempt to capture Luanda, the Angolan capital, in 1975.[167] In the 1980s, Reagan called Mobutu 'a voice of good sense and good will'.[168]

Mobutu's relationship with the CIA is well documented; his relationship with apartheid's leaders is less so. Beyond a marriage of convenience as allies in the war in Angola, Mobutu and his securocrats nurtured a close and extensive relationship with the apartheid military. Military Intelligence was able to build important listening stations in Zaire, in exchange for weapons, training and funding from Pretoria. In addition, as we saw in Chapter 10, Zaire became a central node for the transit of weapons bought illegally by the apartheid regime. Remarkably, the relationship developed to such an extent that Mobutu clearly had the ear of PW Botha, and used this to lobby for the release of Nelson Mandela.

Zaire was an opponent of apartheid, at least on the surface. In early 1977, as the UN debated arms sanctions against apartheid, Africa's largest country sent a clear message to the world during a meeting of the UN in New York. 'The Security Council should also adopt resolutions inviting states to enact legislation not only banning the sale of arms to South Africa but also banning any transfer of capital to that country, because lending money to South Africa when one knows that that money is going to be used to perpetuate apartheid is even more criminal, if anything, than financing trade in drugs.'[169]

But the country had a more complicated relationship with Pretoria than appeared at first glance. Within a day of the statement to the UN, Kinshasa cabled the SADF with a list of weapons it required as urgent military aid from Pretoria. It included 1,300 napalm bombs, rockets, cannon ammunition, and maintenance for ten of the country's fighter aircraft.[170] The SADF responded favourably to this request, despite its own budget constraints.

The first clandestine contact between Mobutu Sese Seko, his security chiefs and South African Military Intelligence took place in early 1980. Mobutu was joined by, among others, Pie Roger Nkema Liloo (commonly known as Nkema), the head of the foreign department of Zaire's security police, the CND.[171] Pretoria had established regular contact with the CND via Paris. The focus of the discussions was on political developments in southern Africa. Mobutu agreed to send Nkema as his representative to visit South Africa and South West Africa, as a guest of Military Intelligence, as long as this took place covertly, with Nkema pretending to be a journalist.[172]

By October of the same year, Nkema proposed that South African Military Intelligence should place an officer under cover in Zaire to facilitate contact between the two countries. He also suggested a courier system for the frequent exchange of intelligence material.[173] At around this time, Military Intelligence was increasingly active in Central Africa, and had direct contact with President Omar Bongo in Gabon and the government of Obiang Nguema Mbasogo in Equatorial Guinea. Zaire was an important transit point for Safair flights carrying South African military personnel, technical specialists and equipment through Africa.[174] Bongo was particularly interested in procuring six South African Impala fighter jets and SA-7 missiles, which the South

Africans sought to deliver using Zairean end-user certificates.[175] Bongo was briefed by South Africa's chief of staff intelligence on at least one occasion in January 1982, when his weapons requirements were also discussed.[176]

In addition, Zaire was also used, with Mobutu's knowledge and approval, as a covert refuelling stop for the delivery of weapons to Hissène Habré in Chad in February 1982, months before the brutal dictator seized power in a CIA-backed coup.[177] A Senegalese court in 2016 found him guilty, during his eight-year rule, of rape, sexual slavery, torture and the killing of 40,000 people. Once Habré was installed in N'Djamena, he continued to seek military support to counter a Libyan-led challenge to his authority. Zaire, which played an important role in providing support, asked South African Military Intelligence to assist in providing further bombs, missiles, ammunition and spare parts. Apparently US intelligence was prepared to provide a supply of spares, but only on payment of cash.[178] The South Africans informed the Zaireans through an agent in Washington DC that they were eager to assist to a limited extent.[179]

Following a two-year hiatus, the head of South Africa's Military Intelligence returned to Kinshasa in January 1983 to meet Mobutu.[180] During the hour-long audience, they exchanged opinions on the conflict in Angola and regional political dynamics. Towards the end of the conversation, the South Africans revealed the real intention of their visit. They needed Mobutu's help. Jonas Savimbi's UNITA forces urgently required weapons and military equipment of Soviet origin, given that his troops were most familiar with these, which South Africa did not possess. South African intelligence was ready to buy the weapons, but needed Zaire to provide the necessary end-user certificates to help camouflage this illicit trade.[181]

When Mobutu was informed that the supplier country was China, he was at first hesitant because of his good relationship with that country. He was quickly put at ease when told that the Chinese knew that the weapons were intended for UNITA, and had previously supplied the rebel group with 300 tonnes.[182] Mobutu was satisfied and immediately ordered his secretary of defence to issue the necessary certificates. As we have seen in Chapter 10, Zaire became an important channel for the supply of weapons from the Chinese state-owned arms company Norinco both to UNITA and the SADF. Documents show that this channel was used throughout the 1980s.[183] In 1988 Zaire, under the signature of the presidency, provided South Africa with a fraudulent end-user certificate for the purchase of 1.3 million rounds of ammunition, 43,000 mortar rounds, 100,000 grenades, 35,000 rockets and 20,000 AK-47 rifles, among other things.[184]

As the two countries' military collaboration gained pace, Zaire's defence force and intelligence increasingly turned to the SADF and Military Intelligence to provide them with weapons and equipment needed to restock their military supplies, given their own involvement in supporting Habré's regime in Chad.[185] In the light of Zaire's usefulness in supplying end-user certificates, South African Military Intelligence undertook to offer R2 million in cash to help Zaire procure spare parts and weapons for its own needs. Furthermore, the South Africans would make crucial repairs to its air force fleet, against payment from Zaire.[186]

In the mid-1980s the Zairean Air Force general Kikunda Ombala offered to buy weapons ostensibly for Zaire, which the air force would then relabel and ship onwards to South Africa.[187] In the same manner, he proposed to use a well-known Aérospatiale front company, GICERS, based in Switzerland, to help camouflage South African purchases. Kikunda raised these issues with South African Military Intelligence in the presence of Aérospatiale's representative in Kinshasa.[188]

The countries' ties grew consistently stronger. In early 1984 the Zairean secretary of defence, Admiral Lomponda, accompanied by the head of the air force and the deputy chief of Zairean intelligence, Alain-André Atundu Liongo, visited South Africa, where they met with Magnus Malan and participated in extensive discussions with the South African military.[189] By May 1984, South African diplomats and National Intelligence agents travelled to Kinshasa to prepare for a planned meeting between Mobutu and PW Botha that month in Lubumbashi.[190]

In 1985, as the South African presence in Central Africa became entrenched, Military Intelligence was eager to establish an intelligence listening post in either Gabon or Zaire, where it had good relations with both heads of state. This facility would allow them to monitor communications in the region, as they were already doing in Malawi and the Comoros.[191] Kinshasa was eventually selected as the host for such a facility in Central West Africa. By that year, the intelligence agencies of the two countries had a classified direct telex connection, and had agreed that they would both host undercover intelligence agents in their countries.[192]

Another turning point in 1985 was the appointment of Honoré Ngbanda as the head of Zaire intelligence. The appointment of the former Zaire ambassador to Israel, who was regarded as very pro-Israel, was seen as a positive move by the South Africans.[193] The links between military intelligence in both countries were formalised in a 1986 agreement between the heads of the two services.[194] Examples of this co-operation were annual intelligence conferences and assistance from the SADF in the establishment of Zaire's own counter-intelligence capacity.[195]

Just a year after his appointment, in 1986, Ngbanda visited South Africa where he met PW Botha and his minister of defence, Magnus Malan, and had lunch with members of the State Security Council.[196] At the end of the meeting, which discussed collaboration and international terror threats, Ngbanda was presented with a Krugerrand by PW Botha.[197] The visit was important to the SADF, as discussions focused on ensuring the continued supply of end-user certificates from Zaire, as well as on deepening existing intelligence contacts. Ngbanda also used the opportunity to discuss South African assistance and hand PW Botha a personal message from Mobutu.[198] When Ngbanda met the chief of South African intelligence later that year, relations had developed to such an extent that while on a sightseeing tour on the Congo River, he proposed that the SADF,

UNITA and Zaire should establish a formal three-way alliance.[199] There is little to suggest that this was ever concluded, but South African collaboration with Mobutu's intelligence and military services continued into the 1990s in the training of his special forces, the provision of basic goods, and the collection of intelligence.[200]

In December 1988, an agreement regarding the withdrawal of South African and Cuban troops from Angola was signed at UN headquarters. During the negotiations, Pretoria had refused to release Nelson Mandela. However, in the same month that the agreement was signed, *Africa Confidential* reported on a meeting between PW Botha and Mobutu at the latter's palace in Gbadolite which had occurred just two months previously.[201] According to this report, Botha and Mobutu discussed a plan for Mobutu to fly to South Africa in early 1989, and return to Zaire with Mandela.[202] This would likely have been a useful solution to Pretoria and a boost to Mobutu's reputation. As the report notes, it is highly unlikely that Mandela, who had long refused release on Botha's terms, would have agreed.[203]

At the end of the Cold War, like many other proxies, Mobutu became more an embarrassment than an asset to his Western allies. In 1997, increasingly isolated, he was overthrown by a coalition of forces led by Laurent Kabila. In the following year, peace negotiations between the warring factions in Zaire, led by President Mandela, took place on board the South African Navy vessel *Outeniqua* off the coast of Pointe-Noire. So much had changed that not even Mobutu's old military allies in South Africa could come to his rescue. He fled the country and died of cancer in November 1997.

Seychelles

The 115 islands that make up the Seychelles are an idyllic tropical holiday destination. To the super-wealthy, it is also a tax haven. Yet to the apartheid state it was a weak state, compromised by links to the criminal underworld, and thus ripe for use in the global sanctions-busting networks. The first significant attempt to alter the islands' politics was a coup led by 'Mad Mike' Hoare, and organised by South

African Military Intelligence, in 1981. This failed, but a decade later, more insidious and covert projects were put in place to use the islands to the benefit of the regime. The historian Stephen Ellis, who has written extensively about the role of the Seychelles in these networks, provides useful background to this story.

A key player in Pretoria's network was Giovanni Mario Ricci, an Italian businessman who found his niche in the Seychelles in the late 1970s (see Chapter 3). Trading under his surname (GMR), he became an indispensable friend of both the Seychellois political elite and a range of shady international business and government interests. Ricci, a convicted fraudster, was already middle-aged when he settled in the Seychelles in the mid-1970s.[204] The islands, governed by a president who came to office through a coup, were a strategically important site for both superpowers in the Cold War, as well as for South Africa's attempts to project its power on the rest of the region. As a result, several regional and global powers competed here for influence, making the islands a target for external manipulation and destabilisation, including foreign-backed coup plots.

According to his partner and business associate, the apartheid spy Craig Williamson, who worked in GMR in 1986–87, Ricci was 'very flamboyant and played a similar role to [oil sanctions buster] John Deuss. He had serious contacts in the European financial sector and especially Italy.'[205] Soon after his arrival in the Seychelles, Ricci became a friend and financial adviser of President René, as well as financier of the single political party and of the government itself. Ellis describes how in 1978 Ricci was granted the sole rights to incorporate and administer offshore companies in the Seychelles, through a new entity called the Seychelles Trust Company. It started as a joint venture with the Seychelles government, but was fully privatised by 1981, making it the first private offshore registration company in the world. Ricci also got diplomatic status in Seychelles, apparently on the mistaken assumption that he was a representative of the Vatican. (His status was as emissary of an entity called the Sovereign Order of the Coptic Catholic Knights of Malta, which, though bearing a resemblance to the Knights of Malta order of the Catholic Church, turned out to be a commercial company registered in New York).[206]

Through all of this, Ricci became a natural go-between for foreigners wishing to cultivate influence or financial interests with the Seychellois political elite. As Ellis writes, 'Although having no official government position, he was diplomat, unofficial head of security, businessman and financial advisor to President René all rolled into one.'[207] Ricci soon became, as it were, a big fish in shallow tropical waters. He appears to have become an especially important intermediary for South Africa following that country's botched attempt in 1981 to effect a coup in the Seychelles, in which six operatives were captured and put on trial. In the aftermath of this embarrassing international event, South Africa had to negotiate for the return of its operatives, and it is quite likely that Ricci was the person to whom they turned.[208]

Ricci, using his base in the Seychelles, was also an important oil sanctions buster. After the Suez Canal was closed in 1967 as a result of the Six-Day War between Egypt and Israel, the Seychelles resumed its place in the key oil trade route down the east coast of Africa.[209] Craig Williamson confirmed in an interview with me that 'I ran a lot of oil through Seychelles for South Africa. However, it didn't all arrive in South Africa.'[210] According to Williamson, who worked with Ricci in GMR as a sanctions buster, he provided intelligence services to the Seychelles government, which were funded by GMR.[211]

When I asked Williamson why he chose to assist the apartheid regime in this manner, he said:

> We did it because it was fun. It was great to be in the know. People who read the newspaper don't have a clue what is really going on. Government then was run like a military operation and required military discipline. We would caucus in Magnus Malan's office together with Ters Ehlers [PW Botha's private secretary]. There were no debates even in the NP party caucus about directives. The caucus was told 'this is policy'.[212]

Williamson describes GMR as 'just one little cog in the wheel'.[213] However, its role as a sanctions-busting vehicle must have generated a fair amount of profit. When Ricci moved to South Africa in the late 1980s, he was said to be a billionaire.[214]

Comoros

Vehemently anti-communist, Bob Denard was a soldier of fortune who had fought for the French in Algeria and then as a mercenary in conflicts from the Congo to Rhodesia. He was widely believed to have operated at least with the knowledge of, but more likely under the direction of, the French DGSE and Jacques Foccart, as part of the Françafrique network.[215] After his 2006 trial for a final coup attempt in the Comoros (he led at least four over two decades), he described the support he received from the French establishment: 'Subsequent officials at the Elysée had provided money and passports.'[216] When asked during one trial whether he had had a green light from the government for his plots, he said, 'No, not exactly; just an amber light, meaning that there was no opposition.'[217] Craig Williamson was unequivocal: 'Bob Denard was definitely a French asset [agent]. He shot the president of the Comoros after an argument about money.'[218]

In 1975 Denard led a coup to oust Ahmed Abdallah, the first post-independence president of the Comoros. Despite this, Denard brought Abdallah back to power in 1978 and would lead the 'Presidential Guard' for the next 11 years, acting as the de facto ruler of the island. In this period, Denard and Abdallah drew the Comoros closer and closer to apartheid South Africa. The relationship was beneficial to South Africa in various ways. Air Comores provided a cover for South African commercial flights, which were limited by a civil aviation boycott. But perhaps most importantly, the Comoros acted as a forward base for intelligence gathering and a staging area from which to arm militants in Mozambique.[219] Ultimately, the Comoros was deeply integrated into South African military and political strategy at a variety of levels.[220]

French and South African interests in the Comoros coexisted with various levels of tension over time. The French were unhappy with South Africa's continued use of the Comoros to arm RENAMO, and were also unimpressed by South Africa's attempts to gain economic advantage through hotel chains on the islands.[221] Despite this, the French clearly tolerated the relationship and the sanctions-busting advantages that it offered South Africa. Both France and South Africa had an intelligence listening station in the Comoros by 1980, and agreed to collaborate in the collection of signals and in code-breaking in order to avoid duplication.[222] Of course, the South Africans had to pay for the advantages they enjoyed, and they funded Denard throughout the 1980s.

Craig Williamson confirms that 'the Comoros was generally used as a military End User Certificate (EUC) paper trail'.[223] Sometimes, despite the best intention to be discreet, a single mistake from one's hosts in Comoros could blow one's cover. Williamson recounts an occasion when 'I travelled to the Comoros in the 1980s as an undercover agent. When I arrived I was picked up by mercenaries on the tarmac and driven straight past immigration. Nobody would talk to me at the hotel excepting a drunk NGO worker at the bar. My cover was blown!'[224] Williamson got a small taste of what others truly thought of his associations even if they didn't know who he really was.

The proxies and players we have discussed in this chapter played a significant role in supporting the apartheid state. In Europe, Asia and Africa arms companies, security services and middlemen worked closely with Pretoria. What is apparent is that towards the end of the 1980s, as the pressure on South Africa continued to mount, far greater reliance was placed on covert intelligence networks. The role of these intelligence agencies in establishing contacts in the arms industry and in providing weapons and information is not to be underestimated. In the shadows, rules no longer apply, and none of the documents we have examined suggest that any of the proxies'

intelligence agencies came under any significant pressure to cut ties with Pretoria. Covert collaboration by the proxies showed that the myth of apartheid isolation was just that. Pretoria could rely on both obvious and unlikely allies to assist in busting the arms embargo it faced.

We turn to the world's pariah states next and investigate a similar pattern of behaviour.

Proxies, Players and Pariahs
The secret alliances

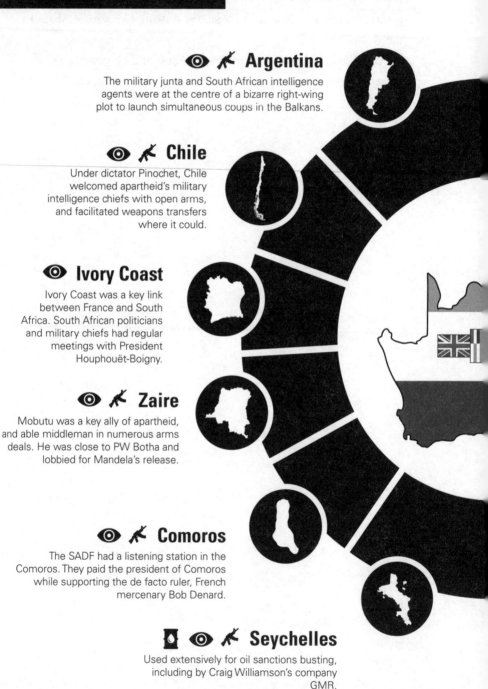

👁 🔫 Argentina
The military junta and South African intelligence agents were at the centre of a bizarre right-wing plot to launch simultaneous coups in the Balkans.

👁 🔫 Chile
Under dictator Pinochet, Chile welcomed apartheid's military intelligence chiefs with open arms, and facilitated weapons transfers where it could.

👁 Ivory Coast
Ivory Coast was a key link between France and South Africa. South African politicians and military chiefs had regular meetings with President Houphouët-Boigny.

👁 🔫 Zaire
Mobutu was a key ally of apartheid, and able middleman in numerous arms deals. He was close to PW Botha and lobbied for Mandela's release.

👁 🔫 Comoros
The SADF had a listening station in the Comoros. They paid the president of Comoros while supporting the de facto ruler, French mercenary Bob Denard.

⧗ 👁 🔫 Seychelles
Used extensively for oil sanctions busting, including by Craig Williamson's company GMR.

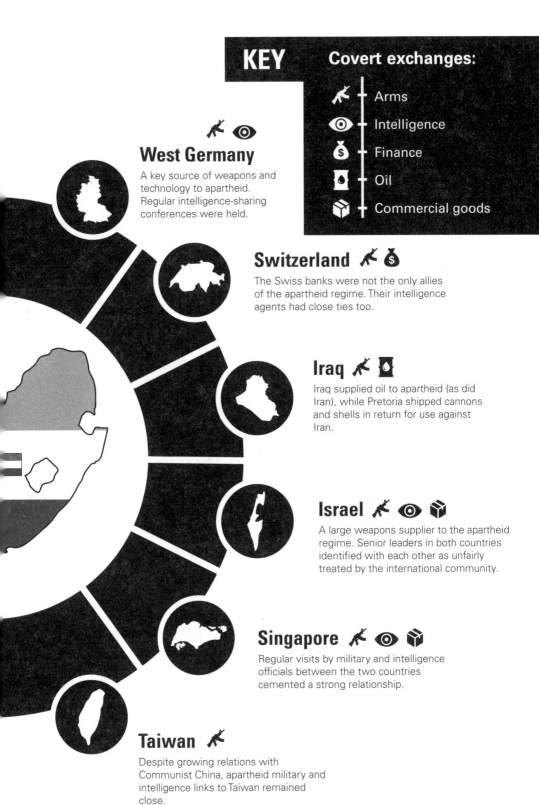

KEY — Covert exchanges:

- Arms
- Intelligence
- Finance
- Oil
- Commercial goods

West Germany

A key source of weapons and technology to apartheid. Regular intelligence-sharing conferences were held.

Switzerland

The Swiss banks were not the only allies of the apartheid regime. Their intelligence agents had close ties too.

Iraq

Iraq supplied oil to apartheid (as did Iran), while Pretoria shipped cannons and shells in return for use against Iran.

Israel

A large weapons supplier to the apartheid regime. Senior leaders in both countries identified with each other as unfairly treated by the international community.

Singapore

Regular visits by military and intelligence officials between the two countries cemented a strong relationship.

Taiwan

Despite growing relations with Communist China, apartheid military and intelligence links to Taiwan remained close.

CHAPTER 12

Pariahs

'We were the most unpopular country in the world – and hardly a week went by without some or other manifestation of the UN's comprehensive anti-South African campaign. Israel limped in a poor second and Chile third.'

– SOUTH AFRICAN DIPLOMAT TO THE UNITED NATIONS[1]

As thick as thieves

The apartheid state embraced its outsider status. The regime saw itself as misunderstood, a victim of bullies and a bastion of Christian anti-communist values in a rough neighbourhood. Such victimhood became a necessary defence used to rally domestic support.

There were few countries willing to collaborate openly with the apartheid security establishment. As we have seen, for the majority of countries there was a fair amount of hypocrisy involved in their covert relations with Pretoria. However robust the ego of the apartheid state, it needed friends, and in the 1970s and 1980s the regime found them in countries such as Argentina, Chile, Taiwan (Republic of China) and Israel. What all five countries had in common was that they were treated as outsiders by other countries. The term 'pariah state' is not only a pejorative term. It refers to the way in which the rest of the world viewed many of these countries at the time. They were isolated for different reasons: Taiwan because of China's claim on the island; Israel because of its policy towards Palestine and Palestinians and conflict with its neighbours; and Argentina and Chile because of their right-wing governments and state-sanctioned death squads.

None of these five countries had a glowing human rights record at the time. This alone did not make them pariahs. Such a description is reserved for smaller countries that develop a significant siege mentality over time.[2] As Noam Chomsky has pointed out, the United States was, during its invasion of Iraq in 2003, a prime candidate for pariah status.[3] However, the big nuclear powers, with their own appalling human rights records, are never accorded this title.

All these countries had a relatively open security collaboration with South Africa – this was a well-known fact at the time. However, we are still developing an understanding of the nuts and bolts of these relationships. The visits by generals, contact between intelligence agencies, and the extent of clandestine military collaboration at the time have not yet been fully uncovered. The archives and the work of other researchers provide an important insight into the covert relations between these four pariahs from very different regions of the world. These allies were as thick as thieves.

Argentina

In the 1970s and 1980s, the military junta in Argentina oversaw a reign of terror. Brought to power in the 1976 coup that ousted Isabel Péron, the military junta that ruled from Buenos Aires was intent on crushing leftist resistance throughout the country. Human rights groups estimate that up to 30,000 people were 'disappeared' by the dictatorship between 1976 and 1983. This was a period of misery and fear for Argentinians, characterised by torture and death camps. The end of the junta came only after the generals were defeated in their war with the United Kingdom over their claim to the Falklands/

Malvinas Islands. However, the activities of the junta are still felt today as Argentine courts continue to prosecute many of those involved in the disappearances, torture and extrajudicial executions that occurred in this period.[4]

The junta didn't act alone. It received support from its key ally in the Western hemisphere, the United States. Declassified US State Department documents have shown that the US secretary of state, Henry Kissinger, encouraged the military dictatorship. In a meeting with Argentina's foreign minister, Admiral Guzzetti, Kissinger said, 'I have an old-fashioned view that friends ought to be supported ... We read about human rights problems but not the context. The quicker you succeed the better ... We won't cause you unnecessary difficulties.'[5] This support is unsurprising given the role of the United States and Argentina in supporting right-wing regimes in the 'dirty wars' throughout South America. Argentina's military stepped into the breach for the CIA when the latter was constrained by the more liberal presidency of Jimmy Carter.[6]

In South Africa, the dictatorship opened up new opportunities for collaboration across the South Atlantic. Armscor launched a vigorous marketing effort in Argentina, and Armscor and its Atlas Aircraft Corporation became important suppliers to the Argentine Air Force.[7] In the year before the Falklands War, more than 20 Latin American generals visited South Africa, including a number of Argentinians. At the time, the US was a supporter of a proposed South Atlantic Treaty Organisation (SATO), intended to supplement NATO, and made up of South Africa, Argentina and Uruguay.[8] The former spy Craig Williamson recalls that some of the ties between South Africa and Argentina were cemented by an Argentinian naval general, responsible for torture in his country and subsequently sent on a diplomatic posting to Pretoria.[9]

An example of the close relationship between the countries is that on the eve of the ten-week Falklands War of 1982, South Africa and Israel were the only countries reportedly willing to supply weapons and spare parts to the Argentinian military.[10] However, South Africa came under pressure from London not to supply any sophisticated weaponry to Argentina that could give them the upper hand against British forces. To boost their existing stockpile, the Argentinians were at the time shopping around for Exocet missiles, a number of which were successfully fired at, and sank, British warships. Craig Williamson describes this period as a 'most difficult time for us politically ... The Argentinians wanted the Exocet missile. Even though the relationship between South Africa and Argentina was very close ... there is a hierarchy of relations, and the UK was more important.'[11]

One aspect of this relationship, secret until now, was proposed coup plots jointly hatched by the Argentinian and South African militaries in support of armed groups in Central America and Southern Europe. Never carried out, they are a mark of hubris and naïvety, but if successful they might have changed the course of the Cold War in the 1980s.

In the shadow of the Olympics

At the beginning of the 1980s, South Africa and Argentina were drawn into a bizarre plan to organise three coups on two continents in the space of six months. Egged on by a group of questionable middlemen and convicted criminals, the intelligence agencies of both countries seriously considered supporting these coups. They were intended to overthrow the governments of Haiti, Albania and Yugoslavia. The Albanian government of Enver Hoxha and the Yugoslav government of Josip Tito both had lukewarm relations with the Soviet Union during the Cold War but lay all the same within Moscow's sphere of influence; an attack on them would no doubt have provoked the ire of the Russian bear.

The backdrop to the coup plots would be the 1980 Moscow Summer Olympic Games. The calculation was that the Soviet empire, focused on logistical arrangements for millions of tourists, would be hard pressed to mount an effective response. An added benefit was that with so much attention directed on Moscow, this would be the perfect opportunity to humiliate the Soviet Union. For both avowed anti-communist regimes, the prospect of these fantastical plans was too appealing to pass up. Distance did not discourage the antipodean allies. The world was their playground and they were not even discouraged by the prospect of supporting the violent overthrow of governments in the backyard of the world's two superpowers. According to archival documents, the coup plotters actively sought the support of powerful Catholic leaders in the Vatican as well as the Muslim-dominated states of Saudi Arabia and Qatar.

Recently declassified South African Military Intelligence documents suggest that the go-between in this affair was a retired US diplomat, Stephen A Koczak, who was treated with some seriousness by the parties, despite the fanciful nature of this proposed adventure. Koczak was a former US diplomat to Hungary (declared persona non grata by the Hungarians in 1949), Berlin and Israel.[12] He resigned from the State Department in the 1960s and unsuccessfully contested both the Democratic and Republican presidential primaries three times between 1984 and 1992.

How Koczak gained such access to Argentinian and South African intelligence is unclear. However, if the audacious plan had been carried out, there is little doubt that it could have brought the world closer to the brink of an international conflict.

To set the international coup plot in motion, the first target was the government of Haitian President Jean-Claude 'Baby Doc' Duvalier. The Haitian coup was planned for late December 1979. Duvalier, a dynastic ruler and kleptocrat,[13] was earmarked for replacement by a well-off Haitian banker, Clemard Charles.[14] The politically aspirant Charles, who later stood charged of a bank scam in the United States, had just been released from a Haitian prison after serving a ten-year term for opposing Duvalier.[15] According to military intelligence documents, Charles had undertaken, once installed as new Haitian president, to cut ties with Fidel Castro's Cuba, work with South Africa and recognise the bantustan of Transkei.[16] These would all have been attractive propositions to Pretoria at the time.

A crucial element of the Haitian operation, according to Charles, would be to capture and imprison both President Duvalier and his mother, the supposed power behind the throne, in an attempt to recoup $500 million that Duvalier was alleged to have hidden in Swiss bank accounts.[17] Charles said he had all the necessary account numbers, and only required access to Duvalier, whom it can be assumed he intended to force to repatriate the cash to Haiti. By November 1979 Charles claimed to have raised $1.5 million for his coup plot from US private institutions and requested an additional contribution of $1 million from the South African military.[18]

The significance of the Haitian coup was that it would support the two subsequent coup plots in southern Europe. Charles, once in power, would provide logistical support in the form of ships to transport the coup plotters to the Mediterranean. As soon as the battle commenced, he would recognise the coup plotters' claims in Yugoslavia and Albania.[19]

South African Military Intelligence, without any explanation in the documents, decided not to support the Haitian initiative but offered instead to provide assistance to Charles, only if his proposed coup was successful.[20] Perhaps the South Africans wanted to test his seriousness or they were wary of irritating the United States in its own backyard.

The records show that the Haitian coup attempt was in any event scuttled at the end of 1979. This was due to 'indiscreet actions and lack of security', involving two ex-CIA men and two civilians (including a South African) who were in the process of buying $35,000 of weapons from South Africa and shipping them clandestinely to the Dominican Republic for the coup.[21] It transpired that the ex-CIA agents had bungled the operation, and it was further compromised by an advertisement calling for the overthrow of 'Baby Doc' Duvalier, which was placed in the *New York Times* and signed by one of the coup plotters. Fatally, the coup plotters had signalled their intentions too soon in advance. The government of 'Baby Doc' protested to the US authorities and it was only a matter of time before the plot was exposed.[22]

Despite this, the South Africans and Argentinians still saw a prospect for coup attempts in Albania and Yugoslavia. These were scheduled to take place between mid–July and early August 1980 to coincide with the Moscow Summer Olympics. Koczak, the American go-between, arrived in Pretoria on 21 November 1979 to discuss the plans. South Africa was a transit stop between Rome, where he suggested he had been in contact with Vatican officials, and Argentina, where he was to meet with local security officials.[23] The chief of the SADF, Magnus Malan, approved travel for a Military Intelligence officer, Colonel Knoetze, to join Koczak in his deliberations with his Argentinian counterparts in December 1979.[24]

According to Koczak, the project had the support of the Argentinian Army, Air Force, Navy and intelligence services, who had agreed to train 1,500 Croatian soldiers for this operation.[25] The Croats, a Yugoslav minority, would focus their efforts on winning control of an area of the country today known as Croatia.[26] Once trained, the Croat militia would be transported by ship to Yugoslavia under the guise of returning migrant workers. The harbours, which were controlled by Croat naval officers, would be captured with their assistance, and they relied upon Croats working in Yugoslav air bases to sabotage military aircraft.[27] This would effectively cripple any major military effort to counter the coup.

Simultaneously, plans were afoot to stoke a revolution in the neighbouring state of Albania. The exiled Albanian king Leka proposed to lead a force of Albanian fighters, who he claimed could take control of all the country's border posts within 14 days.[28] The plan was that the Albanian coup would only be rolled out three or four days after power had been seized in Croatia, as the Croat forces would send ships to back the Albanian fighters.[29] King Leka was at that point in exile in Rhodesia (now Zimbabwe), and after that country's first democratic elections, he moved to South Africa where he was granted diplomatic status. In November 1979, Leka travelled to Saudi Arabia and Qatar to gain both the blessing and financial support of these kingdoms.[30] The reason for this was also strategic, given the large ethnic Muslim population in Albania.[31]

An added advantage from Military Intelligence's perspective was potential support for this operation from within the Vatican and for the development of strong future ties with the Vatican.[32] A top-secret memo from the military attaché in Washington indicated that if the Vatican approved of the coup, the pope would keep a discreet distance from the affair and rely instead on the involvement of a trusted cardinal or archbishop.[33] The coup plotters also regarded the election of the Polish Pope John Paul II as of strategic value. Given his anti-communist stance, they felt that he would be inclined to support the plot. One of the clerics on whom the plotters placed some hope was the conservative Croat Cardinal Franjo Šeper, who they thought could provide support for their plot from within the Vatican.[34] The Vatican's support was so crucial to the entire enterprise that the Argentinian security officials had reportedly identified two Argentinian Catholic priests to receive and transmit any possible message of support from the Pope. Failing this, neither the Argentinians nor the South Africans would support the initiative.[35]

The Argentinians viewed the potential support of the Vatican as an affirmation that 'the Vatican is committed to eliminate liberal elements in the Catholic Church in western countries, and any accommodation of Marxists in left leaning countries'.[36] They no doubt saw the rise of liberation theology in Latin America as a direct threat to their authoritarian rule, and regarded Vatican involvement in the proposed coup as an opportunity to challenge this.

The chief of South African Military Intelligence in turn identified two specific advantages in supporting this operation. The first would be access to the Vatican's intelligence service, and, secondly, should the revolt fail, that it might force the Soviet Union to shift its attention back from Africa to Europe.[37] By this calculation the Soviets might withdraw support from Angola, where South Africa was backing the UNITA rebels, and thereby smooth the way for greater South African control of the region.

Assistance from South Africa would be required in the form of finance and the training of the Croat troops. The Argentinians had agreed to train 1,500 Croat soldiers in preparation for the coup and an equal number of Albanian soldiers.[38] However, as not all of these soldiers could be clandestinely incorporated into the Argentinian defence force without notice, it was proposed that some of the training should covertly take place in South Africa. To prevent any embarrassment for their hosts, it was proposed that Croat and Albanian soldiers need not be told they were being shipped to South Africa for training, but rather that a 'fictitious site in Latin America can be named'.[39] How they intended to keep up the disguise is never revealed.

According to Koczak, he was hopeful that financing would be shared equally by Saudi Arabia and the Croats and Albanians. However, as they were still awaiting confirmation from the Saudis, he turned to South Africa to provide an 'advance line of credit'.[40] As with the Haitian coup, the plotters were looking to South Africa to bankroll the effort.

None of the three coups ever took place. The South African and Argentinian officials may have questioned the seriousness of the plotters (although the documents don't suggest this). They might also have been dissuaded by other friendly Western intelligence agencies – after all, neither Albania nor Yugoslavia was a hardline pro-Moscow supporter. Added to the mix was the fact that the Yugoslav leader, Tito, died in May 1980, which may have changed matters. In addition, over 60 countries withdrew from or boycotted the Moscow Summer Olympics, led by the United States, following the Soviet invasion of Afghanistan the previous year. Even if the coup had taken place, it might have packed much less punch in this context.

Despite this, the rollicking tale of the coup plot is significant, as it shows the willingness of Argentinian and South African intelligence officials to co-operate, even to the extent of organising coups in the northern hemisphere. It reveals too the level of trust enjoyed between the militaries of these countries, their bravado in hatching such plans, and their naïvety in imagining that they could be successful.

While the entire enterprise may seem a little far-fetched, secret defence documents show that this was not the only instance in which South Africa was approached to assist with organising a coup in the 1980s. The apartheid government's support for a military coup in Seychelles in 1981 is a well-recorded fact. But Military Intelligence was approached on at least two other separate occasions to assist in attempted coups in Iran (1982) and Madagascar (1988). Records show that both requests were turned down.

The Iranian coup plotters, a group of former top security officials in the government of the Shah of Iran, led by General Bahram Aryana, were taken seriously up to a point and were invited to send a senior delegation to Pretoria at South African government expense.[41] According to secret documents, the United States had indicated that it had no objections to South African participation in this coup.[42] However, the request was ultimately rejected, primarily it seems because Israeli intelligence dissuaded the SADF from becoming involved.[43]

Chile

'Close to perfect' was how a US Defense memorandum described the CIA-backed coup that brought Augusto Pinochet to power in Chile in 1973, deposing the democratically elected President Salvador Allende.[44] In fact, President Nixon had promised $10 million or 'more if necessary' to ensure that Allende didn't assume the presidency, and supported the idea of a coup immediately if he did. Pinochet's power grab was announced through hundreds of extrajudicial executions and his rule would be defined by repression and torture.[45] He was to be president of Chile for 17 years, after which he retained power as head of the military and then as a 'senator for life'. His eventual exit from the presidency took place in 1990, within a year of PW Botha's demise.

Pinochet's pals

Pinochet and his generals were not only the friends of the United States and their right-wing neighbours in Argentina. They developed a very close relationship with apartheid South Africa and its military officials, and from 1981 the two militaries hosted an annual bilateral intelligence conference.[46]

Military officials from both countries were also keen to pin medals on each other's lapels. Both the South African minister of defence, Magnus Malan, and the head of the Chilean Air Force received their counterpart country's highest awards.[47] South African ambassadors to Chile in the 1980s were all retired top generals, signalling the primacy of the military connection.[48] These contacts also had embargo busting on the agenda. In September 1987, the chief of the South African Air Force, Denis Earp, met with his Chilean counterpart and Augusto Pinochet in the presidential palace in Santiago. According to the Chilean Air Force head, General Fernando Matthei, they discussed 'the possibilities of dealing jointly with all the shared problems that we face over embargoes'.[49]

Armscor was eager to sell its weapons in Latin America. Chile's premier arms fair, the Feria Internacional del Aire (FIDA), was an important staging post for South Africa to market its weapons on friendly Chilean soil. In 1988 two South African Navy ships, a missile strike craft and a replenishment vessel, arrived heavily laden with South African armaments in Santiago to attend that year's FIDA. Leading the South African representation was the SADF, Armscor and 20 private South African military manufacturers. Armscor's general manager, Fred Bell, was quoted at the time as saying, 'Chile is our main port of entry into Latin America.'[50]

This was in addition to Amscor's collaboration with the Chilean arms manufacturer Carlos Cardoen, whose Cardoen Industries factory in northern Chile was visited by General Magnus Malan in early 1989. At the time Cardoen confirmed a co-production agreement with Armscor in making South Africa's G5 155 mm artillery gun.[51] Cardoen is today known in Chile as a philanthropist and wine farmer;[52] during the Cold War, however, his company was a major producer of deadly cluster bombs (which were banned in 2010 after the UN Convention on Cluster Munitions came into force). One of his biggest clients at the time was Saddam Hussein's Iraq, which bought up to $200 million worth of these bombs.[53]

In 1986 Adriaan Vlok, deputy minister of defence and of law and order, travelled to Chile to participate in the FIDA arms fair, and met numerous high-ranking officials. Accompanied by a delegation from Armscor, he visited military shipyards and cocktail functions offered by Armscor.[54] I interviewed Vlok, who subsequently as minister of police under PW Botha was implicated in serious human rights violations. Over the past decade Vlok has become an active proponent of reconciliation (he is known to wash the feet of those he harmed during apartheid), largely as a reflection of his Christian faith. I asked him about his impressions and whether he questioned the activities of the Chilean regime. In his words, 'I didn't know what happened there. They rolled out a red carpet for us. I never even knew what had happened there. They were one of the few friends we had.'[55] I then asked Vlok if he ever wondered why Chile, with its appalling human rights record, was one of Pretoria's few friends. He looked a little startled by the question. 'No, I never asked such questions. I am not that type of person.'[56]

In contrast, declassified documents show that the South African Military Intelligence chief, Dries Putter, was under no illusion as to whom he was dealing with; he described the Chilean government as at best 'an enlightened dictatorship'.[57] He noted that the Chilean army was engaged in rolling out pro-Pinochet propaganda in a crucial forthcoming referendum in October 1988 in which the electorate would ultimately reject an attempt by Pinochet to extend his rule by a further term.[58]

The negative outcome of that referendum for Pinochet motivated the South African ambassador to Chile, General PW van der Westhuizen, to consider the impact of a future, more progressive, left-oriented government on South Africa's relationship with Chile. The embassy came to the conclusion that in the event 'the so called skunk status of the two countries is left out of the equation', there was very little in common between Chile and South Africa or ties that would bind them together.[59] Located far away from one another, the countries did not share the same strategic interests 'other than strong anti-communism and the problem of Cuban-supported terrorism'.[60] He went on to add that even in the area of trade, the two countries were largely competitors.[61]

Despite this, the two regimes opportunistically collaborated in the area of arms and intelligence. An example is a March 1988 visit by a South African Air Force (SAAF) electronic warfare team to Chile. The Chilean Air Force had developed an advanced electronic reconnaissance system with American assistance, but they needed Russian equipment to test its effectiveness.[62] Helpfully, the SAAF had captured Russian radar and the Chilean Air Force proposed to test their equipment on board South African aircraft flights in the operational areas in Namibia and Angola. The South African chief of staff intelligence suggested that 'this is a golden opportunity to expose the SAAF to the best American technology currently available outside America'.[63]

General Chris Thirion, a former senior South African Military Intelligence official, explained in an interview to me that he had a 'very good relationship' with the head of Chilean Military Intelligence.[64] According to him, at one point in the Angolan War, the SADF could intercept all of the Cuban MiG fighter jet pilots' communications, but did not have a suitably efficient system to translate those intercepts into English. Attempts to use civilian Spanish speakers as translators were apparently unsuccessful because of concerns around secrecy and because they did not understand the Spanish-speaking Cuban fighter pilots.[65] Thirion used his connections and struck a deal with Chile for them to provide a number of their own pilots to do the translations for the South Africans. He says that they were based on the border between Namibia and Angola, and this approach 'proved to be very successful'.[66]

As popular resistance in South Africa gathered momentum, the South African and Chilean militaries sought collaboration in dealing with civilian urban unrest and revolt. The Chilean counterpart of the South African security police was the paramilitary Carabineros. The SADF's military attaché in Santiago reported that he was asked to give talks about the South African police with such frequency that South Africa should consider posting a police attaché to the country.[67] The head of the Carabineros, Rodolfo Stange Oelckers, was invited to South Africa by Magnus Malan in 1986 on Armscor's ticket, to make contact with the SADF, the police and Armscor.[68] Oelckers was a close ally of Pinochet and was later accused of human rights abuses committed during the junta.

Taiwan

As we have seen in Chapter 10, the apartheid regime cultivated a close, clandestine relationship with China, which included regular weapons trade, despite its stated opposition to the communist state. Officially, though, it enjoyed far better military and intelligence ties with China's foe, Taiwan, throughout the 1970s and 1980s. The apartheid state was one of the few countries to continue recognition of the island as an independent state. One reason is that the international community marginalised both Taiwan and South Africa from the 1970s. UN Resolution 2758 formally recognised Beijing as the 'only legitimate representative of China to the United Nations', essentially expelling Taiwan from the UN.[69] During the 1980s military, economic and intelligence ties were strengthened between the two pariah nations. This led the apartheid regime to confer the title of 'honorary whites' on Taiwanese nationals visiting South Africa from the early 1980s (as well as on Japanese and Koreans), thus excluding them from some of the harsher racist policies of the time.

Once again, the archives provide important slivers of material describing the nature of this relationship. These reflect the exchanges between the political and military elites of the two countries. At an executive level PW Botha paid an official visit to Taiwan in October 1980 as prime minister.[70] In return the vice-premier of Taiwan, Chiu Chuang-huan, visited South Africa in 1983.[71] Ties at a military level were also improved. In May 1981, PW Botha was congratulated on his successful re-election by General Wang Sheng, in effect the second-in-command of the Taiwanese military at the time.[72] 'I am very glad to have learnt ... that the National Party under your leadership won an overwhelming victory in the South African parliament election. I believe that the RSA under your intelligent leadership will go forward with continued success and prosperity.'[73]

During this time, regular exchanges included the joint training of fighter pilots[74] and prominent participation by top SADF officials in Taiwanese military parades.[75] In November 1986, the commander-in-chief of Taiwan's armed forces, General Wen Ha-hsiung, paid a visit to South Africa. He noted to the chief of the SADF, 'I feel especially honoured for the medal conferred on me.'[76]

As from 1982, top Taiwanese and South African intelligence officials met at the annual Republic of China–Republic of South Africa (ROC-RSA) intelligence exchange conference.[77] These were hosted in both countries and were often followed by warm letters of appreciation from intelligence and military chiefs.[78] In October 1986, the chief of the SADF, Jannie Geldenhuys, was hosted by the head of the Taiwanese defence force. This included a trip to the Kinmen islands, a small disputed territory just two kilometres off the coast of mainland China. Geldenhuys noted that 'with the buildup of USSR conventional weaponry in our neighbouring states, we have much to learn from your situation on Kinmen, opposing the Communist threat from the mainland'.[79]

However, the military relationship seems to have been more about style than substance. In August 1988, Captain PC Potgieter, the SADF Naval and Air Force attaché in Taipei, reported on his two-year tour of duty. He stressed the importance of US relations with Taiwan and the impact of this on Taiwan's relationship with South Africa and the SADF.[80] Any opportunity for co-operation, he argued, was moderated by US interests. He noted that Taiwan's reliance on US weaponry and training meant that any request by the SADF or Armscor for intelligence or technology was avoided or delayed in view of sensitivities about how 'an important third party' (the United States) would react.[81] Although defence technological agreements were already in place between Taiwan and South Africa, with meetings taking place every nine months, he was of the impression that there had been no significant exchange of weapons during the previous two years. Therefore, 'Taiwan cannot be described as a South African supporter in this sense'.[82]

An instance of US pressure on Taiwan in this regard was recalled by Chris Thirion. South Africa had a 'very good relationship with the Taiwanese'. They tried to use this relationship to test a new drone that the South Africans had developed in a state-of-the-art (US-built) wind tunnel in Taiwan. This was given the OK by the Taiwanese, but at the last minute the Taiwanese demurred and said it was not possible. Thirion suggests that this was at the behest of the Americans.[83] The development of drone technology was crucial for the SADF at the time because of the surveillance capabilities it provided on ANC safe houses in Mozambique.[84] Ultimately, he says the South Africans 'got lucky' in developing their drone capacity. A South African merchant navy ship sailing in the Far East contacted Military Intelligence to alert them to a 'small plane' which they had spotted just below the surface of the ocean. Following the instructions of Military Intelligence, the sailors brought the craft on board, and upon arrival in South Africa it was discovered that they had found a high-tech drone at sea. Based on its performance, they could upgrade their own technology, without Taiwanese assistance.[85]

Trade with Taipei

South African–Taiwanese trade ties were probably more fruitful during apartheid than any tangible benefit derived from military contact. Just at the time that foreign firms were disinvesting from South Africa, Taiwan was one of the largest new foreign investors, according to the CIA. In 1988, a CIA internal report indicated that Taiwan contributed 21 of the 41 foreign firms that had been granted permission to set up large factories in South Africa.[86] Taiwanese businesses, particularly in the garment industry, invested heavily in building clothing factories in bantustans such as the Ciskei. One Taiwanese trade official, based in Johannesburg, when quizzed by the *Boston Globe* about the political wisdom of investing in South Africa, quipped in 1988, 'We, too, know what it is like to be isolated. So while we do not approve apartheid … we must still consider South Africa our good friend.'[87]

Trade also increased. Taiwanese imports from South Africa grew a staggering 146% between 1983 and 1986, increasing from $236 million to $510 million.[88] The following year, the CIA reported that 'total trade between South Africa and Taiwan increased by more than 45 percent in 1987'.[89] In addition, the CIA reported that Taiwan was being used as a conduit for the export of South African goods that were subject to sanctions. The report noted that 'West German imports of steel from Taiwan in 1987 increased 20-fold in value and more than 50-fold in volume over the totals for 1986'.[90] This suggests that Taiwan was an important conduit for embargoed South African commercial goods, even if its value as an arms sanctions buster was questionable.

Israel

The relationship between Israel and South Africa during the final decade of apartheid still remains shrouded in some mystery. Records of the collaboration between the two regimes are still by and large strictly under lock and key in Pretoria. The author Sasha Polakow-Suransky, following an intervention from Defence Minister Mosiuoa Lekota, achieved some success in this regard a decade ago. His findings were published in his 2010 book, *The Unspoken Alliance*, on Israel's secret relationship with apartheid South Africa. However, as an official in the Foreign Affairs archive told me, after the book was published access by researchers was unofficially blocked. 'There was hell to pay for that,' he said to me with a wry smile as he reflected on rumours about the Israeli government's response to the release of archival records. At the Department of Defence, almost all access to information requests pertaining to Israel were denied. Public access to any material that relates to Israel seems to be taboo. This may be music to the ears of the Mossad station chief in South Africa, but is anathema to information activists.

What we know has been gleaned from fragments of archival records and important research by others. Despite the unwillingness of officials to release material on relations between Tel Aviv and Pretoria during apartheid, what we know leaves little room for doubt that the two were the most important allies in the network of proxies and pariahs. Both countries saw themselves as victims despite the injustices their security establishments meted out to the people they treated as subjects. The two states, isolated by their neighbours, strongly militaristic and deeply devout to similar biblical texts, were from the late 1970s governed by conservatives who became firm friends.

Ties that bind

The exchange of weapons between the two countries began in earnest in 1970 when French arms dealers representing the firm Dassault approached the South Africans, urging them to order 50 Mirage jets and to consider re-exporting them to Israel. This covert channel would allow French arms companies to sell weapons to Tel Aviv, despite a breakdown in government relations between France and Israel following the Six-Day War.[91] Armscor historians identify the role of French arms companies, seeking alternative go-betweens, as a primary reason for the burgeoning arms trade between Israel and South Africa.[92] As military ties blossomed in the 1980s, it became Israel's turn to assist in upgrading the South African Air Force's fleet of fighter jets. The last Mirage jets had been supplied by France more than a decade previously. Although Chapter 6 has shown that the French were more than willing to bust the embargo to provide spares for these craft, along with a range of other weaponry, South Africa was in need of a more fundamental overhaul. At the height of the conflict in Angola, Cuban and Russian MiGs were proving a handful for the South African forces. In return for a huge injection of cash to the Israeli Aircraft Industry (IAI), Israeli experts ultimately upgraded prototypes of the Cheetah with state-of-the-art weaponry, electronics and navigation, based largely on the Kfir fighter jet.[93]

In the early 1970s, a South African military delegation travelled to Israel to scope out the possibilities of greater collaboration. They enthused that 'there was not a country to be found from whom South Africa could learn as much about technology as Israel'.[94] This prompted a flood of South African military visitors to Israel, who began to search for the technology and equipment they could get, particularly from the large state-owned Israeli Military Industries (IMI) and Israeli Aircraft Industries (IAI).[95]

However, the real surge in purchases came after 1973, following the Yom Kippur War. Two factors were important in this regard. The first was that Israel, under the leadership of the defence minister, Shimon Peres, decided that arms production was a route out of Israel's economic woes and that self-sufficiency was key.[96] They would sell to any government and regime in need, and it just so happened that this period coincided with a booming military budget in South Africa.[97] As Armscor's historians put it: 'the Israeli economy was in a bad state because of the incessant wars against Arab countries … Israel had a fairly large amount of surplus armaments which South Africa could use, the Israelis were keen to carry on trade with South Africa. Both countries would derive benefits from such trade.'[98]

The scene was set for closer ties. First, Shimon Peres visited South Africa in 1974 for a secret meeting with his counterparts. This paved the way for Peres and PW Botha to meet in Geneva the following year and sign the Israel–South Africa Agreement (ISSA); this security pact saw biannual meetings take place between the countries' security and intelligence officials.[99]

In 1975, Israeli and South African defence officials would meet and negotiate the purchase of tanks, missile boats and fighter jet engines and the development of the Jericho missile. By 1975, South Africa accounted for the bulk of Israel's arms exports, predominantly as a result of an order for 200 tank engines for $84 million and what must have been a staggeringly large purchase of ammunition from IMI totalling over $100 million.[100]

It was not just individual purchases that were negotiated during these meetings. They laid the groundwork for long-term collaboration on the development of new weapons, including tanks, light arms and missiles. According to Armscor, 'The exclusive nature of the cooperation made it very special. From the start it was agreed that no party would make manufacturing licences or rights and skills in respect of defence or armaments available to other organisations or countries without the approval of the other party.'[101]

On a political level, ties began to strengthen, and in 1976 Prime Minister BJ Vorster, who during the Second World War had been a Nazi sympathiser, paid Israel a state visit and famously laid a wreath bearing the South African flag's colours at the Holocaust memorial at Yad Vashem.[102] The big political breakthrough came about in 1977 with the election of the conservative Likud Party under the leadership of Menachem Begin. This introduced an ideological element to the relationship which until then had been largely based on profit. A far greater shared self-image of an isolated minority under siege by 'terrorists' took shape and, as we will see, 'it was the defence establishments – not the diplomatic corps – that managed the alliance'.[103]

Armscor sets up shop in Tel Aviv

South African and Israeli arms traders were keen from the start to formalise their relationship and points of contact. An important step was the establishment of an Armscor office, initially with only one official representative, based in the South African consulate in Tel Aviv. With the movement of Armscor and SADF staff to Israel for periods ranging from a few months to a year or two, it was decided in 1975 to establish an Armscor office on the ninth floor of the building occupied by the South African consulate.[104] This arrangement, as we have seen, was similar to Armscor's office in the South African embassy in Paris, allowing sanctions busting to take place under the cover of diplomacy.

The South African consul general liaised closely with senior Israeli military officials, including Colonel Zvi Reuter, the chief external relations officer of the Israeli Defence Force (IDF).[105] He agreed that Armscor's representative, Mr Jagoe, should co-ordinate all Armscor's projects from within the consulate and would officially be listed as 'consul for scientific affairs'.[106] The IDF undertook to brief its ministries responsible for scientific matters, 'in order to ensure that the cover is as secure as possible'.[107] The Israelis were at pains to stress the need for Jagoe to have proper standing as a member of the consulate-general, with an official passport. One of the reasons for this was that with diplomatic status, unlike that of a private concern, the military censor could extend his protection to Armscor.[108]

The South African Air Force general Pierre Steyn moved to Israel with his family between 1975 and 1978. He told me that he was employed as a so-called cultural attaché while based at the Herzlia and Lod air force base. He recalls great camaraderie at the time; his children attended the American school and learnt Hebrew.[109] According to Steyn, 'The Americans didn't want anything to do with us. They allowed Israel to act as a proxy.'[110]

Despite the attempts at creating a cover, the South African military presence left an inevitable footprint. As Sasha Polakow-Suransky explains:

In 1981, there were twenty South African students attending the American School in Tel Aviv, but only four of them belonged to parents appearing on the South African embassy's diplomatic list; the rest were the sons and daughters of South African defense officials working clandestinely in Israel. Teachers and other parents were becoming suspicious about the unusually large South African contingent at the school and Armscor officials were afraid that their covert mission in Israel – and the extent of the military ties between the two countries – might be exposed.[111]

The presence of such a heavy military contingent and the obvious need for innocuous cover stories sometimes had comical consequences, which led the Tel Aviv mission to ask that new staff from Pretoria should preferably not have school-going children:

The SADF mission cabled headquarters complaining that it was hard to keep cover stories intact while learning Hebrew in an Ulpan (language school) because it was difficult for children to conceal their parents' true identity in a classroom setting. South Africa's naval attaché was pretending to be an underwater researcher but had no idea who the prominent Israeli oceanographers were; his predecessor, posing as a computer engineer, was caught off guard when asked to help a friend's school-going son with math problems, which he could not solve.[112]

This issue remained a challenge to the SADF until the early 1990s, when an embassy official noted in a top-secret memo that 'the large South African presence here is very noticeable … South African children are by way of example the largest single group in the American school. There are more South African children than American children in the school.' He added that everywhere in shopping centres, Afrikaans could be heard, and in the neighbourhood of Herzliya Pituah, a wealthy beachfront district, a number of houses were occupied by South Africans.[113]

While we don't know the total number of South African defence personnel in Israel, during the second half of the 1980s Military Intelligence had at least five officials based in the Tel Aviv consulate. These were in addition to the military attachés, Air Force officers and the large contingent of Armscor officials.[114]

Clandestine travel by military officials to Israel also presented unique problems. A report following a successful trip to procure large-screen displays for the military in 1987 reads like a handbook for South African spies from the 1980s. Firstly, Air Force personnel would travel to Israel under an alias and develop a civilian identity that included manufactured company details, business cards, a 'front home address', and knowledge of their civilian job. All care had to be taken to ensure that flight bookings and traveller's cheques could not be traced back to the South African government. The officials recognised that they could not disguise South African accents, but a substantial clothing allowance would apparently deal with the problem of what was referred to as 'typical SA clothing'.[115] As part of the ruse, the new clothing, presumably bought in South Africa, had to be worn for three weeks prior to departure from Johannesburg and for a minimum of three weeks after return, to ensure a lived-in look.

Booming business

From 1977 (the year the UN arms embargo came into effect) into the 1980s, South Africa was Israel's largest weapons customer.[116] Arms sales to South Africa boomed from $70 million to over $1 billion from 1973 to 1981.[117] This provided much-needed foreign currency for the Israeli state in return for the procurement of technology, ships, aircraft and, ultimately, co-operation in the development of nuclear weapons. In 1977 South African Air Force personnel were in Israel working on plans for a fortified base while Naschem (an Armscor subsidiary) was receiving training on bomb-making. That same year, Armscor negotiated a $400 million contract for the purchase of ammunition with IMI – a vital inflow of cash to Israel and a vast supply of ammunition for the SADF to let loose in southern Africa.[118]

Israeli arms manufacturers would also regularly approach Armscor to sell their wares. As one Armscor official revealed to me, defence companies such as Tadiran,[119] an Israeli conglomerate that manufactured everything from drones to sophisticated electronics, would travel to Pretoria to offer weapons for sale to Armscor.[120] Israeli arms companies, collaborating with Israeli intelligence, were willing to bust the embargo. Craig Williamson told me that Israeli companies working in the armaments sector, such as Israeli Aircraft Industries (IAI), exported weapons to a third country that 'may or may not be Indonesia', and then Indonesia would allow the re-export of the weapons to South Africa.[121] 'We procured spares from the Indonesians with the help of the Israeli Air Force,' he says. 'There was a Mossad guy I worked with.'[122]

The countries also collaborated in the exchange of intelligence. Such reliance on Israeli weapons in particular could have presented a risk to the South Africans if anyone in the Israeli establishment succeeded in disclosing these ties. There were regular trips by Armscor and military personnel to Israel. In 1977, General Constand Viljoen visited the occupied territories to learn how Israel controlled the movement of Palestinians.[123]

Apart from Israel's reliance on her largest export customer, the South Africans also noted that the Israelis were old hands at secret arms deals. 'Since the Israelis do have a good deal of experience in operating a covert arms trade, it is ... not foreseen ... that the military cooperation between the two countries will drastically alter unless something untoward happens.'[124] One conduit for such covert deals was coal-for-guns bartering between the two countries. Despite the size of the Israeli military–industrial sector, the country was cash poor on various occasions in the 1980s. On one occasion, in preparation for a trip to Pretoria of the director general of Israel's Ministry of Defence in 1981, the chairman of Armscor wrote to Magnus Malan that the Israelis had an expectation that the South African Ministry of Defence would place pressure on its minister of finance to undertake 'further loans', in addition to existing agreements between the two countries.[125] The South African military rejected the idea of a further 'big loan' on this occasion, as it needed any additional cash from the finance ministry for its own needs.[126]

Where cash was in short supply, the countries turned to barter trade. As weapons were provided to Israel by the US, guns were sometimes in oversupply and provided an important source of leverage in international trade negotiations. In May 1985 the South African consulate in Tel Aviv was approached by an unnamed representative of the Israeli government to explore the possibility of bartering Israeli weapons in exchange for South African coal.[127] With South Africa having increasingly to disguise its international coal exports, this no doubt was an attractive proposition. It meant that South African coal exports to Israel, $100 million in 1985, could increase threefold.[128]

In a letter to the chairman of Armscor, the chief of the SADF revealed that Israel was not in a position to pay for the coal in cash. In the event of barter, it was proposed that 'the South African government would pay SA coalmines money that would have been paid for Israeli products'.[129] This also meant that valuable foreign exchange would remain in South Africa, and in addition it would stymie similar barter propositions from coal-producing countries such as Australia. The military hawks, looking for an argument with which to convince the cabinet, argued that this transaction could prevent the loss of between $100 million and $300 million in foreign exchange. Importantly, the SADF confirmed that to make a fair trade, Israel should only be allowed to offer weapons in return.[130]

No wishy-washy

The relationship between Israel and South Africa relied on an intersection of ideological interests, military collaboration, profit and their mutual pariah status. However, fundamental to the longevity were personal relations between the most senior political leaders. An illuminating example is an exchange between a South African diplomat and the Israeli minister of defence, Ezer Weizman, in 1978. The diplomat had the unenviable task of delivering to Weizman an undiplomatic rebuke, not at all uncommon, from Prime Minister PW Botha.[131] In addition to his position as head of state, Botha was also at the time minister of defence, a capacity in which he had no doubt nurtured a relationship with Weizman. They had met as early as 1972 in Pretoria to ratify an agreement on mutual military assistance.[132] A further meeting between the two men in 1978 led to an additional agreement, that each country would supply the other with weapons from its own stockpile in the case of shortages during times of war.[133] Weizman, a former soldier and head of the IDF, known as a blunt-talking maverick, would later become president of Israel from 1993 to 2000, when he kept alive the ailing Oslo peace process. His family was considered the closest thing to royalty in Israel: his uncle, Chaim Weizmann, was the first president of the country.

The South African diplomat, referred to only as Jacobs, met Weizman in his office in December 1978. The conversation between Weizman (W) and Jacobs (J) is recorded below:[134]

W: I hope you have good news.

J: No sir, I'm afraid not.

W: We are used to it. I am prepared for the worst.

J: I have been instructed by Prime Minister Botha to convey a message verbally to you. I have received it in Afrikaans and I am giving my own translation, which I think is not too bad.

What followed was a five-point tirade from Botha, accusing Israel of disloyalty and siding with South Africa's enemies. Botha ended by stressing that both countries are fighting the same enemy and that Israel should not at inopportune times increase the pressure on South Africa. He concluded: 'the cooperation between Israel and South Africa as a whole may be detrimentally affected by Israel's voluntarily participation in political and psychological pressure on us'. Weizman reportedly listened attentively, eyes closed, changing his sitting position a few times.

W: I am sorry to receive this message. I accept it and will pass it on to the Prime Minister and [Moshe] Dayan [minister of foreign affairs]. I will talk to the Prime Minister [Menachem Begin] when he comes back from Scandinavia and will answer then. I accept the message as from a friend that is hurt. I like Mr Botha very much. I came to like him better last time when we met and appreciate his straightforward and blunt way. He does not wishy-washy around … saying this is our excuse. We are also pinched in a political sense. We are definitely fighting the same enemies. We are now in a situation where big decisions have to be made [in Israel]. Please convey my respect and esteemed friendship to Mr Botha. I will do my utmost to restore relations. I highly respect the South African Prime Minister and like his straightforward way. In fact, I won a bet on him that he will become the Prime Minister.

How are things otherwise?

J: We are fine. At present, we are taking leave of our Air Force attaché, Cmdt Steyn [possibly General Pierre Steyn who retired from the military as secretary of defence in the Mandela administration].

W: Are we in for a party? (*Enthusiastically*)

J: I can assure you that the Israeli Air Force are giving him a good farewell. Further on the local scene [Israel] everything is fine …

J: You might consider meeting Mr Botha again.

W: Yes of course. Where shall we meet? Here? There?[135]

Israeli officials made a regular appearance in Pretoria. However, this also meant that their hosts had to turn on the 'charm'. In February the Air Force general Tienie Groenewald found that when he picked up the Israeli Air Force head, David Ivry, and the intelligence chief, Oded Erez, they were reluctant to talk. Groenewald, whose aim was to kickstart the project to upgrade South Africa's Mirage aircraft, needed a way to loosen up his guests. His solution was to begin the trip by co-opting a military helicopter, handing the Israelis some rifles and taking them for a hunt on a farm in Hoedspruit. According to Groenewald, after shooting a zebra and being invited to fly the helicopter back, David Ivry was much more talkative.[136]

Love letters: Ariel Sharon, Magnus Malan and 'mutual military interests'

The Israeli prime minister Ariel Sharon has long been a controversial figure. A career soldier, considered a brilliant strategist by some, but one with a history of insubordination, he brought to both his military and political life a leadership style that would rightly be termed reckless, were it not-so-often rewarded with success. His place at the centre of almost every key military moment in Israel's history earned him the title of war hero, while his leadership of two massacres of civilians (one of 69 people in a village in the West Bank in 1953, another of as many as 3,000 in a Lebanese refugee camp in 1982) earned him the moniker of the 'Butcher'. He was instrumental in the development of the Israeli policy of swift, violent reprisals for any attack on Jewish life. His subsequent political record is similarly controversial. As minister of housing in the 1990s he received another epithet, the 'Bulldozer', before ending his career as prime minister in the 2000s.

There has been little reflection on Sharon's place in the relationship between Israel and South Africa during the final decades of apartheid rule. Sharon played a key role in maintaining ties with Pretoria, going further than most Israelis in publicly asserting South Africa's urgent need to be allowed access to more and better weaponry. There was a clear sense of parallels between the struggles of the apartheid and Israeli states, and although many Israelis were at pains to maintain their ideological distance, Sharon was not among them.

A surprising measure of the controversy of Sharon's legacy was foreshadowed in a 1982 document, from the office of the chief of the SADF to the South African defence minister, Magnus Malan, providing him with a CV and character assessment of his new Israeli counterpart.[137] 'Sharon's behaviour should be carefully weighed. On the one hand, he is an impulsive politician apt to make drastic, far-reaching decisions on the spur of the moment. On the other hand, his reputation in dealings with other countries is highly impressive … The Americans not only have great respect for him, but seem to

479

like dealing with him … Furthermore, it is clear that [Prime Minister Menachem] Begin trusts him to handle virtually all highly sensitive matters.'[138] The note provides guidelines for interacting with Sharon: 'A policy of "do not beat around the bush" seems to be his preference. Creating false hope/expectations that later turn out to be unfeasible could be counterproductive.'[139]

The South African approach seems to have paid off and Sharon, like others in the Israeli military establishment, developed close ties with apartheid securocrats. During a secret visit in 1981, Sharon spoke to South African forces along the border of Angola.[140] South African troops had by then repeatedly invaded and commenced occupation of part of Angola, in support of the CIA-backed UNITA rebel movement. Sometime shortly afterwards, Sharon visited Washington and, according to a report by the *New York Times*, '[he], in company with many American and NATO military analysts, reported that South Africa needed more modern weapons if it was to fight successfully against Soviet-supplied troops'.[141]

While a vast amount of money was wasted on weapons that were never used during the Cold War, various southern African countries experienced real conflict. In August and September 1981, just as Sharon took office as Israeli minister of defence, the SADF invaded Angola in what it termed Operation Protea. This was by far the biggest battle in the war between South Africa and Angola, resulting in massive bloodshed: almost a thousand Angolan and SWAPO soldiers were killed while ten SADF soldiers died. To achieve this, the regime in Pretoria mobilised 142 aircraft, including Unmanned Aerial Vehicles (UAVs) used for reconnaissance.[142] These drones were developed in South Africa but based on similar craft purchased from the Israeli Aircraft Industries (IAI).[143] Some reports suggest that this was the first use of modern drones in military conflict.[144] The IAI Scout drone was subsequently deployed by the Israeli military during the 1982 Lebanon War.

Following the Lebanon War, the Israeli government established a commission of inquiry which found that Sharon, as minister of defence, bore 'personal responsibility' for the massacre by Lebanese militias of Palestinian civilians in the refugee camps of Sabra and Shatila. The commission recommended that he resign, which Sharon did with great reluctance on 14 February 1983.[145] Magnus Malan wrote a letter to Sharon two weeks later, expressing 'regret of the circumstances under which you vacated the Defence portfolio and wish to thank you for the friendly and understanding way in which you have conducted matters of mutual interest between ourselves and our respective Defence Forces'.[146] Sharon responded, thanking Malan for his letter and making the point that 'I am sure that the understanding between our countries will develop for our mutual interest'.[147]

The nuclear option

South Africa's and Israel's nuclear connection dates back to the 1960s, before the countries developed their military alliance. At that time South Africa provided Israel with 500 tonnes of uranium for its nuclear weapons capacity, with the assistance of France.[148] However, it was not until the mid-1970s, in the context of a growing military relationship between the nations and the increasing appeal to the apartheid regime of a nuclear deterrent, that collaboration for the purposes of acquiring nuclear weapons was first discussed. Sasha Polakow–Suransky lays out what he sees as the trail of this relationship. According to his reading of declassified South African defence records, the Israelis made their first offer of the Jericho missile system, a 300-mile-range missile capable of delivering a nuclear bomb, in 1975. The deal was attractive to the South Africans, who were at the early stages of developing their own nuclear arsenal. The project (named 'Chalet') was discussed at two further meetings between PW Botha and Shimon Peres, at one of which Botha enquired whether the Jericho 'came with the correct payload' – presumably, says Suransky, he meant nuclear warheads. This first foray into collaboration was ultimately aborted owing to the nascent state of South Africa's nuclear programme and the high cost.[149] In response to Polakow-Suransky's revelations, Shimon Peres's spokesperson denied that there had ever been discussion about an exchange of nuclear weapons between the countries. According to him, 'Israel did not conduct any negotiations for the sale of nuclear weapons to South Africa and none of the aforementioned documents are original signed Israeli documents that confirm the existence of such talks of such negotiations'.[150]

However, this denial should not detract from the fact that an exchange of materials crucial to the development of nuclear weapons did take place. An important role in the relationship was played by Air Force pilot Jan Blaauw and the cabinet minister Fanie Botha. Botha was a senior minister and later National Party leader in the Transvaal. Both men were involved in the 1976 agreement between Israel and South Africa for 500 tonnes of uranium in exchange for 30 grams of tritium.[151] Tritium is a radioactive substance required to increase the explosive power of thermonuclear weapons.

Much has been made over the past few decades of alleged nuclear weapons tests carried out by South Africa and Israel in the South Atlantic in the late 1970s and subsequently in the Kalahari. A file of handwritten notes by Magnus Malan of discussions with PW Botha and Ariel Sharon on 23 November 1981 may shed a little light on the issues.[152] Issues raised at the meeting focused, unsurprisingly, on defence and nuclear weapons. Firstly, future arrangements between the two countries would take place by written agreement, not under camouflage.[153] Malan noted that both he and Sharon recognised the sensitivity around proposed nuclear tests, of which there was a 'willingness', but agreed that these should take place underground as 'air, sea will become known'.[154] The issue of nuclear explosions and tests was also discussed between Sharon and PW Botha. The notes finally suggested that a decision had been taken about a satellite.[155] These cryptic clues do not provide a definitive answer about the extent of nuclear tests that might have taken place, but they do show that discussions on this issue took place at the highest level between the two governments.

In addition to testing nuclear weapons, the military wanted to develop a system that had the potential to deliver nuclear and other warheads over a long range. Missile testing took place in both Israel and

South Africa from the late 1970s and throughout the 1980s. As tests and collaboration accelerated in the 1980s, Israeli and South African engineers and nuclear scientists were required to travel extensively between the countries. Several Israeli scientists were enticed to South Africa to work at Pelindaba.[156] At one point, South African diplomats working in Tel Aviv and Pretoria were concerned that not enough was being done to obscure the nature of the nuclear collaboration and raised the extensive travel requirements as a security threat.[157]

The nuclear relationship began to intensify in 1984 when both Israel and South Africa were set on developing the Jericho 2 missile with a firing range of 900 miles. In order to test the missile, South Africa made available its secret Overberg missile testing facility near Cape Town in the Kogelberg biosphere. Over the next five years, Polakow-Suransky's research shows that 75 highly skilled Israelis travelled to the Overberg facility and 200 South Africans made the return journey, despite new stringent arms sanctions placed on South Africa by the Israeli government in 1987. The project culminated in July 1989 when a US satellite picked up a trail identical to that of the Jericho 2 over the seaside town of Arniston close to Africa's most southern tip.[158] Despite Israeli and South African denials, it was hard to erase such evidence of the fact that the South Africans had launched an intermediate-range missile, developed with assistance from their Israeli allies.

The end of an era

By late 1990, it was evident that the 'new South Africa' would prevail. Both Israel and South Africa began to re-evaluate their future relationship. A top-secret South African Foreign Affairs memo in October that year set out some of these challenges.[159] Military ties between the two countries remained strong, with as many as 5,000 Israelis employed as a result of South Africa's appetite for their weapons. The Armscor officials in Israel still maintained that this relationship was critical, although with new markets beginning to open up, this was about to change.

According to the report, the embassy was informed by a senior Kuwaiti journalist that Arab countries were aware of nuclear collaboration between South Africa and Israel, which would prove a major stumbling block to future relationships as long as this was ongoing. The letter also lamented that South Africa's relationship with Israel was upsetting Israel's primary ally, the United States. At the same time, 'South Africa is constantly pressurized to provide financial support to Israel … South Africa must pay but receives little in return, and this sword which is always being held above our heads can disappear together with the Armscor connection.'[160] The diplomat noted that if Nelson Mandela and others had a say in the 'new South Africa', South Africa's relationship with the Arab countries would change dramatically. He added that continued military collaboration with Israel could create the impression that whites were pro-Israel and anti-Arab. 'This could be detrimental to whites in the new South Africa.'[161]

By mid-1993, with democratic elections agreed to, the SADF was looking to wind up aspects of its covert relationship with Israel. In preparation for a trip by General Pierre Steyn to Israel, Military Intelligence wanted to be sure it could allay Israeli fears by giving guarantees that 'Israeli military secrets known to the SADF could be kept safe after the transition'.[162] Foreign Affairs officials informed their South African military counterparts that this could not be guaranteed once a new government came to power. Military Intelligence concluded that 'it would be wise to inform appropriate leaders in the ANC of the nature of these projects and attempt to "get them on board" before they made this discovery of their own accord'.[163] According to the Foreign Affairs officials, Military Intelligence 'seems to accept that their special relationship is nearing its end'.[164]

The last apartheid-era annual meeting between the chairman of Armscor and the Israeli minister of defence took place on 24 June 1993.[165] The Israeli prime minister and minister of defence, Yitzhak Rabin, who was assassinated two years later, received the chairman of Armscor, Tielman de Waal. Rabin emphasised the excellent military relationship between the countries and welcomed positive future changes in South Africa. Armscor's top brass confirmed to Rabin that they had discussed current projects, presumably those with Israel, with the ANC and it looked as if these were acceptable: in his words, they were engaged in 'managing the transition while developing new relations'.[166] A sign of how things were changing was that Rabin said he would like to build up his relationship with the ANC, but that the South African Department of Foreign Affairs had asked him to hold back on any overtures.[167] Armscor agreed that this would be a step in the right direction, but suggested that they needed to go about this in a careful manner.[168] The two countries recognised that in a new political dispensation nothing would remain the same in their very close military relationship. It was understood that this would inevitably be wound down, but they agreed that the secrets should remain under lock and key.

Old friendships that fade away

Pariah states were, with good reason, the most obvious choice of allies for the apartheid state. However, as we have seen elsewhere, they were only one important part of a much more complex puzzle.

The only glue that bound South Africa and this group of countries together was their status as pariahs. The nature of these covert relations ranged from fanciful coups to police training and the development of long-range missiles and nuclear weapons tests. These were, after all, allies of convenience and, with a change in government in all these countries, relations would eventually unravel.

Nelson Mandela's government would swap ties with Taiwan for China, today one of South Africa's firmest friends. Argentina and Chile would witness fundamental changes in government. Israel, while still on friendly terms with Pretoria, has had a lukewarm relationship with the ANC, given the latter's historical alignment with the Palestinian cause. The old ties between these states have been allowed to fade away. But locked in the archives are many more stories of past clandestine relations between these states deserving of revelation.

The Long Shadow

'There is a strange atmosphere in the land, as if people have
no faith in the future, and consequently want, as soon as
possible, to make as much money as possible. By the time
they are discovered, so they reason, the whole affair
will have collapsed anyway.'

– JUDGE VICTOR HIEMSTRA, 1989

CHAPTER 13

The Long Shadow

The ever-present past

A president, a billionaire and bounty hunters

The lawyers, with great skill, ensnared the archbishop. As Desmond Tutu left from early Friday morning Mass in December 2012, I watched as they waited for the right moment to engage the anti-apartheid cleric. A fixer facilitated the briefest of introductions. After being told that these were good guys, Tutu sounded pleasantries, 'You must bring back the apartheid money,' and gave his generous mischievous laugh as he shuffled off.

If Desmond Tutu had been fully briefed about his well-wishers' intentions, his smile might have been far less generous. Some in this party like myself had stumbled onto this scene after being told that we would discuss a stunning reparations claim. However, it was soon evident to me that this was little more than an attempt to make money for some very wealthy people – off the back of legal claims on behalf of people of questionable character.

Chief among these is Jorge Pinhol, who was represented by the lawyers trying to draw Tutu into their scheme. Pinhol is a Portuguese former racing-car driver and arms middleman. A commodities trader, he was drawn into the murky world of arms trading from the late

1970s. A serial embargo buster, he claims to have supplied weapons to the Rhodesian military, working closely with a senior representative of Rhodesian military intelligence.[1] During the 1980s Pinhol ferried arms from Israel to Iran and claims he had 'made good contacts particularly with the Israeli security, but met with security persons from other countries, including the Americans'.[2] The arms business was good to Pinhol and by the mid-1980s he had accumulated $5 million in offshore bank accounts controlled by his companies Beverly Securities Incorporated/Limited (BSI/BSL) in Switzerland and Liechtenstein.[3]

Starting in 1985, he developed close ties with the Armscor office in Paris, whose officials first asked him to provide them with fraudulent end-user certificates for weapons sales.[4] Very soon, Pinhol was in the business of supplying clandestine arms to South Africa and recalls several meetings in Pretoria and across Europe with some of Armscor's top leadership at the time.[5] To add to the intrigue he also claims he was keeping tabs on his clients at Armscor on behalf of Israeli intelligence.[6]

By far the most important business deal between Armscor and Pinhol was negotiated in 1986–87 as part of Project Adenia. Pinhol claims he created a Portuguese clandestine channel that Armscor used to illicitly import 50 Super Puma helicopters (in disassembled kit form) and spare parts from France. This channel was created with the assistance of the Portuguese military, with which he had good contacts.[7] Signed affidavits by four retired Portuguese generals confirm the role of Pinhol in establishing this 'channel', of which they carried personal knowledge at the time. The Portuguese Air Force imported the unassembled helicopter kits but ensured that they made their way to South Africa. In return the Portuguese Air Force was given helicopter kits and spares at Armscor's expense to upgrade its own fleet of Puma helicopters.[8]

In return, Pinhol claims he signed an agreement that guaranteed him a 10% commission fee on the $3 billion deal, which was camouflaged by the channel he had helped create.[9] According to him, the money was never paid for his commission as Armscor officials, sensing the forthcoming change in government and the end of the embargo, lost interest in him. He alleges that this was especially true after they secured the support of the Portuguese Air Force generals for their new channel.[10]

In court papers he claims that he is therefore owed a $300 million fee (escalating to $500 million with interest) for facilitating a massive apartheid-era arms sanctions-busting deal. This involved the French arms manufacturer Aérospatiale, a group of Portuguese generals, Armscor (and, by extension, the South African government) and its chief sanctions-busting bank, Kredietbank Luxembourg (KBL).

In making his claims Pinhol has been involved in a legal dispute over the past 25 years that is yet to yield him any significant pay-off. However, he is assisted by a small group of international lawyers funded since about 2006 by a generous Canadian billionaire, John Risley.[11] Acting as a venture capitalist 'investor', Risley has sustained Pinhol's legal campaign to the amount of, I am told, a few million dollars. It would be a curious alignment of characters, were it not for a shared interest in fast cars and profit. If the claim is successful Pinhol, his lawyers and Risley (as the wealthy investor) stand to make a small fortune of up to R5 billion. At one point Pinhol's lawyers told me that they would be prepared to settle with Armscor at $300 million.

Who will stump up the cash for this apartheid-era sanctions-busting claim? The state-owned arms procurement corporation, Armscor. This means that the claim, if successful, will have to be authorised and financed by the Treasury. Effectively, the apartheid sanctions buster is trying to force a payment out of the pockets of every South African citizen. This is a deeply unjust proposition, an additional apartheid tax to fund an avaricious adventurer.

Pinhol's claim represents one of many aspects of the long shadow of our past. Similar deals have been kept secret for many years and are ripe for manipulation by parties and individuals who continue to operate in the shadows. Even the name of President Jacob Zuma has been mentioned as a party with an interest in resolving this matter.

◎

The background to this claim takes us back to the height of the sanctions period in 1985. As we have seen in Chapter 6, the South African Air Force relied heavily on French-designed fighter jets and helicopters (or modifications of these). Good relations with the French arms industry, through the Armscor office in Paris, were therefore essential to ensure continuity of supply and access to updated technology. Through Project Adenia, the military initially intended to purchase 66 French Super Puma S2 helicopters from France.[12] Once converted into the 'home-grown' Oryx, they would feature prominently in sea rescue operations. Most notably, four of these helicopters were used to carry the new South African flag over the Union Buildings moments after Nelson Mandela was sworn in as the first state president of a democratic South Africa.

The procurement of the helicopters was one of the most lucrative sanctions-busting deals undertaken by the military and is thought to have cost as much as $3 billion at the time. What Project Adenia reveals is not only the porousness of the arms blockade but the deep complicity of European banks, defence corporations, military officials and politicians in enabling the embargo to be broken. The Armscor Paris office co-ordinated these efforts, and KBL in turn is alleged to have helped move the cash through its bank accounts.[13] This represents an archetypal example of the architecture and complicity described in Chapter 5, and evidenced in other chapters.

According to declassified SADF documents, there were two suppliers in the deal. One was the state-owned French arms manufacturer Aérospatiale, which designed the helicopters and today is part of the Airbus group of companies. The other is Turbomeca (today Safran Helicopter Engines), which produced the engines. Both corporations were willing accomplices and are thought to have stepped into the breach after the United States refused permission to sell its Black Hawk helicopters to South Africa.[14] Secret SADF documents confirm the role of the two companies as the two primary contractors, which worked closely with the Armscor office in Paris in setting up the deal.[15]

A number of visits were undertaken by SADF officials to Paris to plan the shipment of the helicopter frames, which would be reassembled in South Africa and, with modifications made by the Armscor subsidiary Atlas Aircraft, become the Oryx.[16] By September 1986 SADF officials reported that they were in the process of preparing the orders for delivery together with ground equipment, spare parts and components required to support the Puma S2.[17] They confirm that Aérospatiale in France undertook the development of the new aircraft. In addition, Turbomeca, the engine supplier, had submitted new plans for future logistical support.[18] Given security concerns, it was decided that only one or two foreign experts should travel to South Africa during the test phase of the aircraft, and instead South African Air Force personnel would travel to France for some of the test flights, visiting the Aérospatiale headquarters in Marseilles and Turbomeca in Biarritz.[19] The SADF officials noted in October 1986, after a visit to complete the ground tests on the helicopters, that 'Aérospatiale is extremely concerned about security during this period and therefore do not wish to receive any South African personnel while the aircraft is in plain sight'.[20]

At this point we turn to Pinhol's evidence, as submitted in various courts, to understand how he and his companies allegedly came to play the role of middlemen. This was done by creating a 'safe', long-term and 'credible channel' through Portugal which Armscor could use to import the helicopters.[21] The Puma helicopters were officially marked for shipment to the Portuguese Air Force from Aérospatiale. However, once in Portugal they were discreetly redirected to South Africa.[22]

We have affidavits from four Armscor officials, three of whom worked at the Armscor office in Paris, confirming that Pinhol negotiated the deal with the Armscor. They provide damning detailed evidence in support of his claim. They also confirm that the bankers in this deal were Kredietbank (see Chapter 5) and its group of banks, including KBL, which Pinhol visited in the company of an Armscor official.[23]

Pinhol's legal claim of non-payment has wound its way through various courts from South Africa to Paris and Brussels. The matter is now being heard in a Portuguese court. Pinhol has either withdrawn his claims (on one occasion for fear of his life) or has lost in court on various technical grounds such as jurisdiction. Armscor, Kredietbank and Aérospatiale have in turn vigorously contested Pinhol's claim.

Importantly, there has been no denial of the role played by the banks in Belgium and Luxembourg. Their defence against any claims Pinhol has tried to make against them is that he was involved in illegality. In court proceedings in Brussels in 2010, the banks claimed that, given the illegality of the procurement and the blatant breach of the 1977 UN arms embargo, it was not an interest that could be enforced by a court. The Brussels court agreed and said that Pinhol and his companies 'were not ignorant, obviously, of the fact that they were breaching [UN arms embargo] resolution 418 by performing the role of intermediaries in the sale of this military material. Under these circumstances, the reason behind this legal action should be qualified as illicit.'[24] The banks, in other words, didn't contest their alleged involvement in the sanctions-busting scheme. Instead they argued that Pinhol as a sanctions buster could make no claim against them because *he* was acting illicitly. Read differently, this was a tacit admission by the banks that they were indeed part of his scheme.

The proceedings in the Lisbon civil court against Armscor are ongoing. Armscor suffered a setback in 2014 when it was ordered to pay €1.3 million as a fine for bringing an 'unfounded appeal' linked to this matter.[25] As the next step in the ongoing legal battle, the Portuguese court has now asked to examine various witnesses in South Africa. This process is known as a rogatory commission and a preliminary rogatory hearing was held in Pretoria in March 2015, chaired by a Portuguese advocate. One of the people who testified in support of Pinhol, in a three-hour marathon session, was the former South African minister of foreign affairs, Pik Botha. In an interview with me, Botha described Pinhol as 'my old friend'.[26] At the time of writing I was informed that the commission would soon take place, but as such hearings cannot be accessed on the court roll, details are hard to come by. Most worrying from a public interest perspective is the possibility of a very hefty settlement being reached by Armscor in secret with the sanctions buster, away from prying eyes.

I have purposely kept a discreet distance from this matter. Our interest has been in the arms money machine, a significant example of the systemic abuse of power. However, Pinhol's pursuit of profit deserves attention. His case has been poorly reported in the media and many of the journalists have not asked the simple question: Is it appropriate for an apartheid-era sanctions buster to be rewarded for such crimes?

There have been a few attempts to pull me into this scheme given my interest and work in uncovering the machinations of the modern-day deep state. For example, in late 2012 one of the lawyers suggested I should join their team. I declined. To my surprise he let drop into the conversation the remark, 'A young man like you would do well in politics; however, that would require the necessary resources. There may be a mutually advantageous situation.'

Having passed up the offer, I have followed the matter from some distance. The lawyers at one point suggested that their case might change into a potential general 'reparations claim' against foreign corporations that supported apartheid. They said this claim would be worth tens of billions, all for the South African people. Of course, they too would profit from such an enterprise.

They have informed me about meetings with the leadership of political parties whom they were trying to woo into supporting their efforts. They have also drawn South African lawyers into supporting this initiative. According to Pinhol's lawyers, this network of connections include politicians, political parties, lawyers and civil society organisations. This is not to suggest that any of this contact is illicit. Pinhol's team has built a circle of influence, much like any campaign, regardless of how distasteful it might seem to some observers.

The most damning evidence stems from the leaked minutes of a meeting between Pinhol's lawyers (who drafted the minutes) and Armscor in Portugal on 1 and 2 September 2010. The meeting had been called to start discussions about a potential arbitration process between Pinhol and Armscor to explore the idea of a settlement, focused on a ballpark figure. Armscor's team of lawyers at the meeting was led by Wim Cilliers of the Pretoria law firm Gildenhuys Malatji and the head of Armscor's legal team, Meshack Teffo. Pinhol's legal team included his Swiss-based lead attorney, David Lawson, and William Humphreys.

The most noteworthy addition to Pinhol's team is a South African 'media consultant', Liesl Göttert, who has been described as a 'BSI/BSL consultant'. Göttert's association with Jacob Zuma dates back to when she interviewed him during his rape trial for a documentary she was then making. In 2006 she described Zuma as one of her clients; when questioned about the kind of person she was representing, she stated that she would go as far as acting on behalf of Adolf Hitler.[27]

What was Göttert doing at that meeting? Her appearance is concerning for the following reasons: Firstly, why was she as the only non-lawyer present in a meeting with lawyers to discuss a possible settlement? Secondly, why was a self-proclaimed representative of Zuma acting directly in a matter when the state was already represented by Armscor? Thirdly, why was such a representative of Zuma sitting on the side of an apartheid-era sanctions buster when negotiating with the South African state? If true, this could suggest that President Zuma, allegedly acting through an emissary, has attempted to insert himself in the deal.

Returning to the minutes, they show that prior to the start of the meeting Armscor's lawyers informed David Lawson that 'Armscor would not accept the attendance at the Lisbon meeting of Ms Göttert, based on instructions received from the Chairman of Armscor [Popo

Molefe]'.[28] Lawson proposed a 'pre-meeting' at which there would be discussion of the procedural issues raised by Armscor, without Göttert in attendance.[29] At the pre-meeting Armscor's attorneys held firm, despite representations by Humphreys in support of Göttert's presence. Humphreys went further with a suprising claim: 'Ms Göttert had been asked to attend the meeting, and noted that prior to accepting to do so, she had sought and received the agreement of the RSA [Republic of South Africa] President [Zuma] for whom she also acts.' [30]

When the legal teams convened for a second day of meetings on 2 September, the lead attorneys for either side (Lawson for Pinhol and Wim Cilliers and José da Silva for Armscor) are reported to have stepped outside for a private meeting with Göttert. This was so she could 'inform them personally of her overnight discussions with the RSA President'.[31] In the short separate meeting, Göttert requested Cilliers to confirm to her personally that she was not welcome to attend the Lisbon meeting with the parties' representatives.[32] She then confirmed to the three men that 'she had spoken to the RSA President who asked her to attend any part of the Lisbon meeting at which settlement of the Lisbon Court matter would be discussed'.[33] Armscor's lawyers indicated that their client's view had remained unchanged and that

> they could not accept that she attend any part of the Lisbon meeting. Ms Göttert replied that she regretted that position being taken, which she would have to report back to the RSA President. She said that under such circumstances she would not attend the Lisbon meeting, although she believed it would be in everyone's interest if she would do so as she had been requested and agreed to do, at the direction of the RSA President.[34]

If Göttert was misrepresenting Zuma, this would have been an incredibly risky move. It would only have taken Armscor a call to the South African Ministry of Defence to establish the truth, and

Göttert upon her return could have faced very serious charges of misrepresenting the president.

From these meetings it is clear that Armscor was prepared to allow the matter to go to full arbitration, suggesting that they wished to find a settlement and believed that Pinhol had a 'genuine' claim in this matter.[35] This proposed settlement sought from Armscor appears at that stage to have been but a little piece in a bigger puzzle. Pinhol's lawyers described the Armscor issue as a 'small commercial matter' which would enable them to launch a far bigger reparations case against the Luxembourg-based KBL for its role in apartheid-era sanctions busting. For this to succeed, they wanted Armscor's support, including access to its archives, as the size of the claim would no doubt be significantly higher as a result. In return for its co-operation they offered Armscor a 'discounted settlement arrangement'.[36] This was ultimately rejected by Armscor.

It is evident from a reading of the minutes that the claimants had their eye on a far bigger prize. While we can only speculate on the motive for President Zuma's seeming attempt at an intervention in a matter being negotiated by a state party, it does on the face of it appear highly irregular. The lack of public access to such secret meetings is an indication of the potential for the public interest to be skewed in favour of the rich and powerful – including former apartheid-era sanctions busters.

There is one further twist in this tale concerning Pinhol's legal team and the prospects of a reparations claim. In January 2017 a copy of an interim report by the Public Protector's Office was leaked to the media. It focused on the findings made, in a tardy manner, by the former protector, Thuli Madonsela, of an investigation into a loan (known as a 'lifeboat') given to ABSA's predecessor, Bankorp, by the South African Reserve Bank in the early 1990s. A long-standing matter of contention has been whether ABSA was given preferential treatment in this deal and whether it paid back interest on the loan to the Reserve Bank. The matter has already been investigated by the Special Investigation Unit in the late 1990s and again by a Reserve Bank-commissioned panel headed by Judge Dennis Davis.

However, there have been continued claims that ABSA still owes the Reserve Bank an amount of R2 billion in interest payments. The source of these claims is, in part, a 1997 report produced by a UK-based private investigations company called Ciex. The company is headed by a former top British MI6 spook, Michael Oatley. He approached the South African government to investigate apartheid plunder and identified up to R26 billion he believed could be clawed back from ABSA and from transactions related to the arms embargo.

The Ciex report has done the rounds since about 2010 when Advocate Paul Hoffman wrote to the Public Protector and asked her to investigate the matter. However, a cursory glance at the document reveals little: it is a proposal from a group of bounty hunters to help the democratic government identify apartheid-era plunder, which was eventually turned down by the Mandela administration. As the Serjeant at the Bar legal column in the *Mail & Guardian* observed, 'the CIEX document reads more like a sales document than a serious investigation'.[37]

The Ciex report has since been sprung upon in particular by a splinter group that robustly lobbies for President Jacob Zuma, Black First Land First (BFLF). The group, which seems always ready to defend those implicated in scandal, such as the influential Gupta family, argues that a force it has termed 'white monopoly capital' is the most serious threat to economic liberation in South Africa. However, BFLF reserves its most trenchant criticism for anyone who stands in opposition to President Zuma; in so doing it appears as yet another group wishing to preserve a particular status quo. BFLF is the most vocal group that publicly supports the Ciex report and its claims. They have made it their biggest issue while consistently arguing against any attempt to hold others implicated in corruption to account. One cannot but form the impression that this is a political device to defend the political fortunes of Jacob Zuma and undermine his detractors and potential rivals.

Challenging monopolies of power and wealth is an important element of democratic practice, but the Ciex report is a straw man and unhelpful in this task. It risks shifting public debate to the point where we rely more on polemics and less on evidence to win the argument concerning accountability for past crimes. To ensure justice we require a competent public investigation agency, free from political interference, to investigate and prosecute these issues. This is hard to imagine in the current political climate, but it is another reminder of why we desperately need such independent capacity within the state. Were such an investigation to be undertaken, the public archives would provide a rich source of information and would not require the service of foreign consultants to access.

Michael Oatley told me that he had personally met Jacob Zuma in 2008 before his election as president to discuss the Ciex report with him. Zuma was apparently reluctant to pursue the matter. However, according to Oatley, Zuma 'did suggest that if there is clear evidence it can be handled in a "delicate manner"'.[38] Oatley gave no indication of what this meant.

However, Oatley's interests extend beyond just Ciex. In closing the loop, it is worth noting that he has also collaborated with Jorge Pinhol, the arms sanctions buster. When I interviewed Oatley in 2013, he described Pinhol as an old client who is 'agreeable but lacking in gravity'.[39] In addition, Oatley has for a number of years worked with the media consultant Liesl Göttert. In January 2017, the pro-Zuma blogger Pinky Khoabane reported that Göttert and Oatley had jointly met Zuma to lobby him on the Ciex report. According to comments attributed to Göttert in the report, the duo's engagement with Zuma included 'endless briefings starting with Mr Oatley and myself at the kitchen table and in his dining room in Forest Town, Johannesburg [Zuma's private residence]'.[40]

◎

The activities of this small group of people matter deeply, as they exemplify what happens when we do not deal with past crimes. It allows people who claim benefit from sanctions busting to continue to make claims on the democratic state. It invites intrigue and sinister dealings involving bounty hunters and alleged secret emissaries for the president. It also serves to obfuscate far greater crimes, many of which are detailed in this book, that are hidden from public view as a result. The less we know about our past, the greater the opportunity for it to be manipulated for personal and narrow political gain. It is a toxic affair that undermines the public's interests.

Holding the future to account

If this book had been written two decades ago, it would have ended with a well-worn argument that history should not be allowed to repeat itself. But history has done so. However, this should not diminish the need for us to ensure that we deal with the past as a prerequisite for ensuring that those involved in future economic crimes are held to account.

The most significant economic crime that occurred after the end of apartheid was the multibillion-dollar arms deal in the late 1990s. Shortly after the country's transition to democracy, the arms deal became the scandal that has shaped South African politics for the past two decades. It is not the size of the deal that matters as much as the lasting legacy. It introduced democratic South Africa to politicians who quickly mastered the art of the bald-faced lie.

Of all the politicians implicated in corruption in the arms deal, President Jacob Zuma has the most to lose. He is deeply implicated in malfeasance in the deal and potentially faces charges that come with a stiff prison sentence. His supporters have worked tirelessly to ensure that he avoids prosecution. This includes the chronic undermining of the capacity of the criminal justice system to do its work.

However, the arms deal did not happen in a vacuum. The primary players and beneficiaries in the deal were European arms companies. As we have seen, many of these companies were active participants in the supply of sophisticated weaponry to the apartheid regime. They knowingly broke international sanctions as they sought to make a profit from collaboration with the apartheid state. As we have also seen, some of the middlemen implicated in corruption in the arms deal plied a similar trade when busting oil and arms sanctions during the 1980s.

This network of politicians, arms companies, intelligence agencies and middlemen that operated in cahoots with the apartheid regime reorganised itself after 1994. With the passage of time it changed, but its modus operandi has remained the same: when in doubt, break the law. Yet we still struggle as a country to face this aspect of our past. It is as if, were we to do so, we would have to recognise the ugly fact that too many people have chosen to look away from such crimes for so long that they feel the sting of complicity for their inaction.

There are at least three ways in which the narrative of apartheid economic crime should be dealt with, which I set out below.

Free the secrets

A reason for denying access to information is often hinged on a mix of political conservatism and bureaucratic inefficiency that sees government departments acting in a manner that is errant and contrary to the rule of law. While undertaking research for this book we have experienced both.

In certain instances our partners, the South African History Archive and Lawyers for Human Rights, have had to go to court to ensure that documents were released; almost four years later some of these matters are only now winding their way towards an outcome. Far greater transparency and access to information are required to enable research to take place so that the public can make informed opinions. It would also help us to better understand our present and ensure that criminal practices such as corruption do not continue to shape our future. A nation that has a full understanding of its past is better placed to avoid repeating the same mistakes.

However, as this book attests, there is an incredible volume of material that is accessible to researchers as long as they are willing to persist. Though it was a hard slog, ultimately we worked in over two dozen archives, each of which yielded new and important information. There is a wealth of material awaiting a new generation of researchers in South Africa's archives. This is part of our national heritage and it must be maintained and preserved, and access must be opened to all. In an era of fake news, the only way to challenge lies is to dig deeper and ensure that the stories we tell are based on evidence that can win arguments and public support. The archives are a fundamental resource in our understanding of our recent past.

Fundamentally, the apartheid archive must be made free from the constraints of continued secrecy. These are the records of our nation's past and its pain. Far too much of this remains secret. Civil society should support a call for the proactive public release of the 'apartheid archive', rather than having to acquire access through a cumbersome request process. This material should be made available online for the public.

Many of the restrictions on access to information should be lifted, across the board, and universities in particular need to be encouraged to promote the use of these resources among students. We need a new generation to scour the hundreds of metres of National Party archives that remain unsorted at the University of the Free State. Far more students from across the country should access the liberation movement archives of the ANC at Fort Hare. State archives such as those of the Department of Defence should be packed with young researchers – it would be a tragedy if these are the preserve of only aged military historians. We have to continue to tell our own story as a young nation, and that requires us to dig deep into our past, beyond the point of discomfort.

Unmask the deep state

What this book has set out to show is how networks of deep state actors operate in subverting the rule of law. The term 'deep state' is wilfully misrepresented by the supporters of Donald Trump. They see it as a backlash against their brand of conservatism. The origins of the deep state lie in secretive military networks, including bureaucrats, politicians and organised criminals in countries such as Turkey where, starting in the 1950s, they acted covertly and killed many people as a backlash against secularism and democracy.[41] When the interests of banks, intelligence agencies, arms companies and politicians intersect, there is an appetite to undermine the rule of law. The apartheid regime drew on these networks for its support, and they became accomplices in economic crime when aiding and abetting a crime against humanity.

If these networks had been better policed, it is probable that the apartheid regime would have been forced much sooner to make fundamental concessions leading to a new non-racist, non-sexist democratic constitutional order. However, as we have seen, a major impediment was that the United Nations Security Council members, tasked then as they are now with policing the international system, failed South Africa. Despite the efforts of ordinary citizens, it was the Permanent Five that not only did not properly police the embargo, but actively broke it when it was in their interests to do so. China, France, Russia, the United Kingdom and the United States are nuclear and economic powers who continue to hold great sway in this world forum. However, we should ask the question whether it isn't time to ensure that this body is reformed and made far more democratic.

There is also no doubt that the struggle is global in nature. As we have seen, apartheid South Africa relied on allies not only in the Permanent Five group of countries but among proxies, players and pariahs as well. The influence of these networks persists in many countries. They are supported by the global arms trade, which is a wasteful enterprise, highly dependent on public subsidies, a drain on the economy in most countries, and with disastrous impact across the globe. Far more must urgently be done to tackle corruption and economic crime in this sector, which is as prevalent now as it was in the 1980s. The arms industry, when one considers the manner in which it operates, is not a force for innovation or global stability. It represents in fact a threat to international peace.

There is a renewed appetite for right-wing populism across the globe, from the United States, to Europe, the Philippines, India and Russia. As we have seen in the 1980s, it is precisely these forces that are most likely to subvert the democratic state in favour of the markets and their private interests. Any politician who emerges from the swamp and then promises to drain it is deserving of mistrust. Equally, we must learn from apartheid's dirty tricks of funding foreign politicians and using paid lobbyists and secret networks to do its dirty work at arm's length. This practice has reared its head following allegations that Vladimir Putin's government attempted to influence the 2016 US presidential election outcome. Some feel little pity given the record of the United States in doing the same, yet we should universally condemn such practices as attempts that threaten democracy across the globe.

In South Africa, the deep state is making a slow comeback. As corruption and state capture become entrenched, elite groups within the state are increasingly turning to the use of the state security apparatus to protect their interests. The most prominent among these is the State Security Agency. While it sometimes seems to lurch from one scandal to another, it should not be the focus of ridicule but of concern. This is an incredibly powerful instrument in the hands of men and women who may wish to undermine our constitutional freedoms. The apartheid regime of the 1980s is an example of what awaits ordinary citizens when securocrats are allowed to run amok. Our lodestar must remain the Constitution, and its greatest defence lies in the struggle of ordinary citizens against political and economic injustice. The law and the struggle for openness, fairness and justice are the most potent antidote we have to the deep state and the persistence of networks of corruption.

Challenge impunity

Until we understand grand corruption in South Africa today as continuity from our past, we cannot hope to root it out. In no small part, the massive incidence of economic crime that plagues our democracy today is a result of our failure to dismantle the criminal networks that thrived under apartheid. This is another kind of 'unfinished business' of the transition: the ghosts of our tortured past will continue to haunt us until they are exorcised fully and publicly.

There can be no doubt that economic crimes are integral to oppression and conflict, and that there are significant potential benefits that can accrue by actively tackling them during a transition. We must also recognise that transition is a process, often lengthy, and never the outcome of just one moment. Thus, despite a path being politically impossible at one point, it may not be precluded at another. The establishment of a new commission to examine economic crimes under the Argentinian military junta of over 30 years ago is testimony to this.

South Africa's transition in fact brings these issues into sharp focus. The relative invisibility of economic crimes and violations that resulted from the South African Truth and Reconciliation Commission's (TRC) focus on torture and physical violence is something that continues to compromise those seeking economic and social justice in South Africa's ongoing transition. The narrative constructed by the TRC obscures this part of the country's history by presenting victims of apartheid as those who suffered physical violence. At a fundamental level, our memories are now filled with testimonies of the horrors of torture and detention, not of those who had their houses destroyed and land stolen or were forced to work for large corporations for little pay.

On the other side of the coin, we know of the police operative Eugene de Kock as the quintessential perpetrator of apartheid's crimes. However, we know comparatively little of the corruption and sanctions busting that funded apartheid's police state, and that facilitated the mass theft of money from the public purse. In addition, those responsible for economic crimes have never faced prosecution or sanction in South Africa, encouraging a culture of impunity and allowing networks of corruption to survive and draw in new politicians and businessmen. Particularly for these individual and corporate interests, the 'South African transition' was actually just business as usual.

These factors fundamentally undermine the process of transition to a more just society. At a very basic level, the economic and social rights enshrined in South Africa's Constitution have less meaning when there is no attempt to identify and return the billions of rands stolen both before and since the transition. In addition, we are unable to shake off a racialised view of corruption and economic crime, which is supported by the perception that they are something new in our society. Corruption is not a phenomenon that is the result of a black-led government. White compatriots should be the first to volunteer such an admission.

The current struggle against corruption in South Africa is undermined by a basic lack of appreciation of the nature of that corruption and the criminal networks that facilitate it – namely, that they are continuities of a profoundly corrupt system that predates the first democratic election.

What is equally clear is that changing these things is not impossible – we do not need to consider South Africa's transition as ending with the report of the TRC. The work of civil society in documenting economic crimes committed under apartheid provides a solid basis for instigating criminal investigations and proceedings against individuals and corporations for their role in those crimes. This would help achieve accountability and, combined with the dissemination of the documentation, would contribute to a shift in the nation's understanding of South Africa's past, as well as its understanding of the present. It would also help to disrupt criminal networks that continue to corrupt South African politics today.

The identification and return of money stolen through these crimes could contribute towards a broader and further-reaching reparations programme. New hearings and community meetings could help develop a better understanding of how individuals and communities suffered as a result of economic crimes and structural violence. An

507

active civil society that is concerned with social justice exists in South Africa and is well placed to facilitate these kinds of processes.

The very wealthy need to show real contrition for these acts, which have been to their benefit. This cannot be relegated to a simple act of charity but must constitute a significant portion of their private wealth to fund philanthropic causes that promote social justice and human rights. Some might balk at this suggestion but the super-rich in particular need to repatriate far more of their wealth and invest it in South Africa's future. They and their children can no longer look away and pretend as if the source of the luxury with which they surround themselves is untainted. Their connection to South Africa cannot only be nostalgic. They must be challenged to do far more than is the case right now.

While some of the remedies lie in transitional justice processes and philanthropic funds, others lie in the simple issue of justice. Based on the evidence we have accumulated, it is evident that murders were committed to cover up sanctions-busting activities. The assassination of Dulcie September is one example. We must demand the right to truth about who was behind these murders. This is not only necessary justice for the surviving family and friends, but would be a powerful signal that impunity for gross violations of human rights will not be tolerated.

There are promising signals that justice is possible. In a watershed judgment of May 2016, the South Gauteng High Court found for the first time that almost 500,000 miners could bring a class action claim against the country's gold mines. This after almost a century during which far too little precaution was taken to prevent workers from contracting silicosis and TB, which in many instances have shortened their lives. The judgment is important in terms of our understanding of corporate accountability and of profit-taking at human expense. After approximately a decade of legal battles, it also underscores the almost impossible task of holding private interests to account for damages suffered by the public.[42]

International banks, as we have seen, grew fat and lazy off the profits from the apartheid state and then raked in more money when they refused to absolve the apartheid debt after 1994. For those banks operating in tax havens where they move about the money of wealthy investors who refuse to pay tax, this was just another illegitimate income stream. Apartheid and the 2008 global financial crisis, from which many banks profited, are stark reminders of the human consequences of malfeasance in the financial sector. Should they be allowed to continue to escape accountability for this?

In 2008 the International Commission of Jurists released a report that emphasised that corporations 'should be held responsible for assisting in gross violations of human rights when they "enable," "make easier" or "improve the efficiency" of the commission of those crimes'.[43] An additional requirement for complicity in the case of banks, it is argued, is that the lender had to have known or could not have not known about the criminal activities of the borrower.[44]

Based on this criterion, the banks that supported the arms money machine deserve the most attention. If the banks had not acted as willing accomplices in the schemes of Armscor and its international network of arms traders and middlemen, the war in Angola might have been significantly curtailed. What happened in practice, however, was that the bankers in countries such as Belgium and Luxembourg sat back and watched the profits roll in, all the while helping Armscor to construct an international system of money laundering.

As the book shows, the extent of involvement of the banks was massive. Such complicity can no longer be rewarded with silence. These powerful actors must be held to account for this past injustice. This is not only in the interests of the people of South Africa, but in the interests of citizens of all countries. As long as banks believe they can operate outside the law in tax havens, they will continue to help finance wars and create a financial system that facilitates the flow of cash for guns. The link between the international finance sector and human rights abuses must receive more public attention in view of the consequences suffered by ordinary people.

Such abuse of power cannot be treated as an uncomfortable fact to be dealt with by future generations. It deserves our attention right now. We must open the secrets that reveal new evidence, organise as citizens along non-sectarian lines, and seek to hold those who profited from injustice to account.

Acknowledgements

This book reflects a significant collective undertaking. For every sceptic and naysayer there have been many more people who have provided support, advice and encouragement. On many occasions over the past five years, this task seemed impossible. Documents were not forthcoming, clues were endless, and for nearly three years we ran a parallel campaign to support efforts for justice in the arms deal corruption in the midst of a cover-up. The perseverance of many people paid off, and I am deeply appreciative of the support of every person and institution that helped make this book possible.

I have been immensely fortunate to work with a small team of talented researchers for whom the search has been a shared passion. Michael Marchant has been an outstanding lead researcher who has tackled this project with an inexhaustible supply of effort, dedication and patience – after this, other secrets await opening. Anine Kriegler and Murray Hunter, who were part of the research at an early stage, contributed their wit, enthusiasm and insight in equal measure. I am also grateful to Bradley Petersen and Naomi Marshak, who joined the Open Secrets team as interns. You have all been stellar colleagues to work with; even when the adventure took us into dusty archives, dead-ends and parts unknown, you kept the faith.

The project started under the wing of the Open Society Foundation for South Africa (OSF-SA) who awarded me a fellowship. I extend my thanks to the board of OSF-SA and colleagues for their support from inception.

After more than a year the Open Secrets project moved to the Institute for Justice and Reconciliation, which has been a partner for the past three years. Many thanks to Jan Hofmeyr and his colleagues Pamella Vutula, Wendy Mpatsi and Anyway Chingwete for their support and the IJR finance team led by Renee Choto. Thanks also to IJR management and board for hosting us and trusting us to get on with the task at hand.

We have been fortunate that a small group of funders have been committed to the project and shared our vision. They are the Open Society Foundation Human Rights Initiative, OSF-SA, Bertha Foundation, Claude Leon Foundation and Heinrich Böll Foundation. A small travel grant was also provided by the Oppenheimer Fund.

The manuscript has benefited from the hard work of a team of experts who have all helped ensure its improvement. While I take responsibility for errors and omissions, many of the improvements are thanks to the patience of a skilled group of people all led by my South African publisher Bridget Impey, a true ally, from Jacana Media. My thanks to her entire team of colleagues who have assisted in rallying support for this project and worked long hours to ensure that we get this big book just right. This book has finally made its way into the world, beyond Southern Africa, thanks to Michael Dwyer and his colleagues at Hurst Publishers in the UK and Oxford University Press in the USA. I am grateful for their support – and also to my agent David Godwin for making this important introduction.

My friend Paul Holden, a meticulous researcher and formidable opponent of graft and greed, reviewed the draft chapters. I have relied on the careful copyediting of Russell Martin, who was patient to a fault even after I attempted to push back against his skilled red pen. Zanele Mbuyisa is the media lawyer we had wished for. She believes in fairness and the right to free expression in equal measure, and I am grateful for her feedback, advice and assurance. Gaelen Pinnock from Scarlet

Studio, a designer, photographer and architect, is responsible for the magnificent infographics – the treasure maps that accompany the text.

Accessing research material for this project from public (state) archives in South Africa was made possible through our collaboration with the South African History Archive (SAHA) in Johannesburg. Thanks to Catherine Kennedy, Toerien van Wyk, Kathryn Johnson and our team of supporters at SAHA who carefully managed 50 freedom of information requests to eight government departments. You are all tenacious believers in the right to know.

When SAHA needed to use the law to take on errant government institutions that denied access to documents, we could turn to a formidable *pro bono* legal team who support the right to truth. Thanks to Prashianne Hansraj and David Cote and Lawyers for Human Rights in Gauteng. In addition, we drew on the wise counsel of a caring group of advocates in Geoff Budlender, Nasreen Rajab-Budlender, Nyoko Muvangua, Hermione Cronje, Lebogang Kutumela and Frances Hobden.

Accessing the documents was made easier by the staff in the two dozen archives we visited. We were guided by their advice and appreciate their willingness to carry and cart hundreds of boxes that fed our voracious appetite for documents. The archives consulted include the Archive for Contemporary Affairs at the University of the Free State; Armscor Archive; Belgian Foreign Affairs Archive; Belgian National Archives; BStU (Stasi) Archive in Berlin; the Company and Intellectual Property Commission at the Department of Trade and Industry; Department of Defence Force Archive in Pretoria; Department of International Relations and Cooperation Archive in Pretoria; German Ministry of Foreign Affairs Archive in Berlin; International Institute of Social History in Amsterdam; Liberation Movement Archive at the University of Fort Hare; the National Archive in Pretoria; the National Library in Cape Town and Pretoria; the National Security Archive at George Washington University in Washington DC; Shipping Research Bureau Archive in Amsterdam; South African History Archive in Johannesburg; Swiss

Federal Archive in Bern; Times Media Archive in Johannesburg; University of Cape Town Archives; the University of Cambridge Archives; University of Leuven Archives and the Kadoc Archive; United Kingdom National Archive at Kew; University of Oxford Archives; and the University of the Witwatersrand Historical Papers. We also received documentation, in response to access to information requests, from the Department of Justice (TRC Archive), National Treasury, Office of the Auditor General of South Africa and the South African Police Service. In addition Danie Steyn, David Klatzow and Maggie Davey gave us access to their private papers.

I would like to thank the numerous individuals who gave generously of their time and provided valuable insight and first-hand experience in over a hundred interviews. Some may disagree with my analysis but I appreciate their willingness to share their experiences.

Over the past few years a number of wise friends and colleagues generously gave of their advice and support which strengthened our arguments and resolve. They include Andrew Feinstein, Angela Mutukudi, Barbara Hogan, Basetsana Molebatsi, Bonita Meyersfeld, Charles Abrahams, Chris Gevers, Dumisa Ntsebeza, Fatima Hassan, Frank Dutton, Geoff Budlender, Howard Varney, Jonny Steinberg, Paul Holden, Piers Pigou, Stefaans Brümmer and the late Stephen Ellis.

During my travels many friends and family hosted me in their homes and on their couches and provided a hot meal and much support in Amsterdam, Berlin, Brussels, Cape Town, Johannesburg, London, New York and Paris.

A special word of thanks to friends and comrades at the Right2Know Campaign, who provided a frenetic, inspiring environment in Community House in which to write and work. You and many other partners in civil society are a reminder that another world is indeed possible.

Finally, to my friends and family – and those of my colleagues – your love and support has made this possible. Thank you.

Hennie van Vuuren

Cape Town, September 2018

Endnotes

Introduction

1   As recounted to Patti Waldmeir by Roelf Meyer (then deputy minister in De Klerk's cabinet) in Patti Waldmeir, *Anatomy of a Miracle: The End of Apartheid and the Birth of a New South Africa*, Rutgers University Press, New Jersey, 1997, p. 134.

2   Anthony Turton, *Shaking Hands with Billy: The Private Memoirs of Anthony Richard Turton*, Just Done Productions, Durban, 2010, p. 342.

3   Terry Bell with Dumisa Ntsebeza, *Unfinished Business: South Africa, Apartheid and Truth*, Verso Books, London, 2003, p. 9.

4   Adam Withnall, 'All the world's most unequal countries revealed in one chart', *The Independent* (London), 23 November 2016.

5   Larry Elliott, 'World's richest people have same wealth as poorest 50%', *The Guardian*, 16 January 2017.

6   First letter from Nelson Mandela to Hendrik Verwoerd, 20 April 1961, O'Malley Archive, Nelson Mandela Centre of Memory, Johannesburg.

7   John Dugard, *Introductory Note: Convention on the Suppression and Punishment of the Crime of Apartheid*, United National Online Library, New York, 30 November 1973. Audiovisual Library of International Law, United Nations Office of Legal Affairs, 2016. See www.legal.un.org/avl/ha/cspca/cspca.html.

8   Songezo Zibi, *Raising the Bar: Hope and Renewal in South Africa*. Picador Africa, Johannesburg, 2014.

9   Hannah Arendt, *The Origins of Totalitarianism*, Harcourt, New York, 1976.

Chapter 1

1   Ivor Wilkins and Hans Strydom, *The Super-Afrikaners: Inside the Afrikaner Broederbond*, Jonathan Ball Publishers, Johannesburg and Cape Town, 2012, pp. 46–47.

2   Ibid., p. xvii. Those that did resign, like anti-apartheid cleric Beyers Naudé, would suffer the castigation that followed. In 1980 investigative

515

journalists like Hennie Serfontein (author of *Brotherhood of Power*) and Hans Strydom and Ivor Wilkins (authors of *The Super-Afrikaners*) finally exposed the secret identity of members of the Broederbond.

3   Wilkins and Strydom, *The Super-Afrikaners*, pp. xxvii–xxviii.
4   Vorster's police were vicious in the manner in which they dealt with dissenters and imprisoned thousands of people. His minister of justice, Jimmy Kruger, in justifying the use of live ammunition against protesters in Soweto, cruelly argued that black people had to be made 'tame to the gun'.
5   As quoted in James Sanders, *Apartheid's Friends: The Rise and Fall of South Africa's Secret Service*, John Murray, London, 2006, p. 36.
6   Dan O'Meara, *Forty Lost Years*, Ravan Press, Johannesburg, 1996, pp. 206–207.
7   Ibid., p. 220.
8   Ibid., p. 217.
9   Ibid., p. 222.
10 Ibid., p. 225.
11 Ibid., p. 267.
12 Phillip Frankel, *Pretoria's Praetorians*, Cambridge University Press, Cambridge, 1985, pp. 34–35, cited in Paul Holden and Hennie van Vuuren, *The Devil in the Detail: How the Arms Deal Changed Everything*, Jonathan Ball Publishers, Cape Town, 2011, p. 20.
13 Holden and Van Vuuren, *The Devil in the Detail*, p. 26.
14 Interview with Abdul Minty, Pretoria, 24 June 2016.
15 The war started with the encouragement of the United States.
16 Holden and Van Vuuren, *The Devil in the Detail*, p. 27.
17 Ibid., p. 28.
18 At its absurdist height, the South African media were banned from reporting on the country's involvement in the war in Angola – precisely at the time it was splashed over front pages of newspapers across the globe.
19 As Jacob Dlamini reminds us in his book *Askari*, apartheid relied to a large extent on collaboration. Dlamini argues that South Africa was a hybrid between the large-scale collaboration and surveillance found in the former Soviet Union and Eastern Europe and the small band of military men who committed crimes in Latin America.
20 From 1984 onwards three houses of parliament (for whites, coloureds and Indians) and the parliaments of the nominally independent bantustans would debate policy.
21 Christi van der Westhuizen, *White Power and the Rise and Fall of the National Party*, Zebra Press, Cape Town, 2007, p. 123.
22 William Cobbett, 'Apartheid's army and the arms embargo', in *War and Society: The Militarisation of South Africa*, ed. Jacklyn Cock and Laurie Nathan, David Philip, Cape Town, 1989, p. 223.
23 UN, *Transnational Corporations in South Africa and Namibia: UN Public Hearings, vol. I: Reports of the Panel of Eminent Persons of the Secretary General, 1986*, United Nations Centre on Transnational Corporations, New York, 1986, p. 255.
24 Ibid., p. 256.

25 Interview with Abdul Minty, Pretoria, 24 June 2016.

26 Holden and Van Vuuren, *The Devil in the Detail*, p. 24.

27 The CIA World Factbook, *South Africa Defying International Embargoes*, available at www.photius.com/countries/south_africa/nationaly_security /south_africa_national_security_defying_internationa~2507.html.

28 LJ van der Westhuizen and JH le Roux, *Armscor: The Leading Edge*, unpublished, University of the Free State, Institute for Contemporary History, 1997, p. 375.

29 Interview with Danie (DW) Steyn, Pretoria, 18 February 2016.

30 Ibid.

31 See the 2016/2017 National Budget as released by National Treasury: www.treasury.gov.za/documents/national%20budget/2016/review/ FullReview.pdf.

32 Review by the Auditor General of the Secret Funds for the Period 1960– 1994, Report to the Truth and Reconciliation Commission, 17 July 1998.

33 Ibid.

34 Ibid.

35 Section 11A of the Armaments Development and Production Act, 1968, Open Secrets Collection.

36 Auditor General of South Africa, Review by the Auditor-General of Secret Funds, as submitted to the Truth and Reconciliation Commission, 7 August 1998.

37 Ibid.

38 Ibid.

39 Ibid.

40 Interview with Wally van Heerden, Pretoria, 6 June 2016. (Van Heerden audited secret projects for the AG in the 1980s.)

41 Interview with Joop de Loor, Somerset West, 26 May 2016.

42 Ibid.

43 Helen Suzman, *In No Uncertain Terms: A South African Memoir*, Knopf, New York, 1993, p. 278.

44 Interview with Joop de Loor, Somerset West, 26 May 2016.

45 Interview with Barend du Plessis, Pretoria, 6 June 2016.

46 Ibid.

47 Ibid.

48 Ibid.

49 Ibid.

50 Interview with Wally van Heerden, Pretoria, 6 June 2016.

51 Ibid.

52 Ibid.

53 Interview with Jan van Schalkwyk, Pretoria, 6 June 2016.

54 Ibid.

55 Ibid.

56 It's also important to note that projects differ from operations. The latter are usually military manoeuvres – hence operational – and are generally time-bound, e.g. Operation Savannah was a major incursion by SADF forces into Angola. In certain instances projects would run over many years to enable the delivery of material or in-house R&D.

57 Minutes of Cabinet Meeting, 8 March 1989, University of the Free State, Archive for Contemporary Affairs (PV 734, K/S 19, 1989 (vervolg), FW de Klerk).

58 Ibid.

59 Andrew Feinstein, *The Shadow World: Inside the Global Arms Trade*, Jonathan Ball Publishers, Cape Town, 2012, p. xxii.

60 Commission of Inquiry into Alleged Arms Transactions Between Armscor and One Eli Wazan and Other Related Matters (Cameron Commission), First Report to President Nelson Mandela, 15 June 1995, p. 25.

61 Magnus Malan, *My Life with the SA Defence Force*, Protea Book House, Pretoria, 2006, pp. 227–228.

62 Ibid., p. 237.

63 Ibid.

64 Niël Barnard, *Secret Revolution: Memoirs of a Spy Boss*, Tafelberg, Cape Town, 2015 p. 46.

65 Interview with former Armscor official, name withheld, November 2015 (Number 1).

66 Interview with former Armscor official, name withheld, November 2015 (Number 2).

67 Ibid.

68 Interview with former Armscor official, name withheld, June 2016 (Number 3).

69 Ibid.

70 Ibid.

71 Ibid.

72 Interview with former Armscor official, name withheld, November 2015 (Number 1).

73 Ibid.

74 Interview with former Armscor official, name withheld, June 2016 (Number 3).

75 Hermann Giliomee, *The Last Afrikaner Leaders: A Supreme Test of Power*, Tafelberg, Cape Town, 2012, p. 135.

76 Eschel Rhoodie, *The Real Information Scandal*, Orbis SA, Johannesburg, 1983, p. 725.

77 Allister Sparks, *The Sword and the Pen*, Jonathan Ball Publishers, Cape Town, 2016, pp. 368–369.

78 Ibid., pp. 385–386.

79 Ibid., p. 364.

80 Amir Oren, 'Did Milchan and Packer push Netanyahu to pick their buddy to head the Mossad?', *Haaretz*, 20 January 2017.

81 Meir Doron and Joseph Gelman, *Confidential: The Life of Secret Agent Turned Hollywood Tycoon: Arnon Milchan*, Gefen Publishing, New York, 2011, p. 126.

82 Interview with Mervyn Rees, Amanzimtoti, 14 March 2013.

83 Ibid.

84 Ibid.

85 Sparks, *The Sword and the Pen*, p. 357.

86 John Matisonn, *God, Spies and Lies*, Missing Ink, Cape Town, 2015, p. 180.

87 Interview with Vic McPherson, telephonic, 31 December 2016.

88 Interview with Vic McPherson, email, 8 January 2017.

89 Ibid.

90 Interview with Craig Williamson, WhatsApp, 21 January 2017.

91 Ibid.

92 Ibid.

93 Interview with John Matisonn, telephonic, 31 January 2017.

94 Truth and Reconciliation Commission of South Africa Report, vol. 4, 29 October 1998, p. 184.

95 Interview with Terry and Barbara Bell, Cape Town, 2 January 2017.

96 Ibid.

97 Ibid.

98 Ibid.

99 Sparks, *The Sword and the Pen*, p. 375.

100 O'Meara, *Forty Lost Years*, p. 242.

101 Frans Esterhuyse, 'Info probe "full of blunders"', *Saturday Star*, 1 October 1989.

102 Sanders, *Apartheid's Friends*, pp. 108–109.

103 Report of Commission of Enquiry into the Information Scandal, Appointed on 3 November 1978, University of the Free State, Archive for Contemporary Affairs (PV 476, 1/59/2/2, 1978, Piet Koornhof).

104 Letter from RPB Erasmus to PW Botha, 31 March 1980, University of the Free State, Archive for Contemporary Affairs (PV 203, A1/2/5, 1980 March–1980 April, PW Botha).

105 Telegraph from RPB Erasmus to PW Botha, 27 February 1982, University of the Free State, Archive for Contemporary Affairs (PV 203, A1/2/20, 1982, PW Botha).

106 Interview with John Matisonn, telephonic, 31 January 2017.

107 O'Meara, *Forty Lost Years*, p. 257.

108 Matisonn, *God, Spies and Lies*, pp. 178–179.

109 Interview with John Matisonn, email, 31 January 2017.

110 Wilkins and Strydom, *The Super-Afrikaners*, p. xxxv.

111 Interview with John Matisonn, email, 31 January 2017.

112 Interview with Joop de Loor, Somerset West, 26 May 2016.

113 Ibid.

114 Ibid.

115 Sparks, *The Sword and the Pen*, p. 368.

116 Statement to the Truth and Reconcilliation Commission by Liza Grundlingh (Smit) and Robert Smit (children of Robert and Jeanne Smit), August 1997.

117 Ibid.

118 South Africa Police Investigative Diary, Murder of Robert and Jean Cora Smit, pp. 1–6.

119 Ibid.

120 Mervyn Rees and Chris Day, *Muldergate*, Macmillan, Johannesburg, 1980, p. 13.

121 Sanders, *Apartheid's Friends*, p. 104.

122 South Africa Police Investigative Diary, Murder of Robert and Jean Cora

Smit, pp. 27–29.
123 Robert Smit, Election Manifesto, Springs 1977 (Times Media Archive).
124 South Africa Police Investigative Diary, Murder of Robert and Jean Cora Smit, p. 114.
125 Sanders, *Apartheid's Friends*, p. 89.
126 Sparks, *The Sword and the Pen*, pp. 399–400.
127 Robert Smit, Election Manifesto, Springs 1977 (Times Media Archive).
128 'Kenners sê banke sal nie boikot', *Die Transvaler*, 6 October 1977.
129 Ibid.
130 South Africa Police Investigative Diary, Murder of Robert and Jean Cora Smit, pp. 45–46.
131 Ibid., p. 73.
132 Ibid., pp. 74–75.
133 Ibid.
134 Statement to the Truth and Reconciliation Commission by Liza Grundlingh (Smit) and Robert Smit (children of Robert and Jeanne Smit), August 1997.
135 Ibid.
136 Ibid.
137 Ibid.
138 Ibid.
139 Brian Bunting, *The Rise of the South African Reich*, Penguin, London, 1969.
140 See www.fin24.com/Finweek/Archive/Focus-on-SantamFocus-on-Santam-20050920-5.
141 Shipping Research Bureau, *Embargo: Apartheid's Oil Secrets Revealed*, ed. Richard Hengeveld and Jaap Rodenburg, Amsterdam University Press, Amsterdam, 1995.
142 Statement to the Truth and Reconciliation Commission by Liza Grundlingh (Smit) and Robert Smit (children of Robert and Jeanne Smit), August 1997.
143 Wilkins and Strydom, *The Super-Afrikaners*.
144 Van der Westhuizen and Le Roux, *Armscor*.
145 Trimester Report for June to September 1980 by the Financial Planning Department of Armscor, October 1980, DOD/SANDF (CSF, GP 3, Box 933, HSF 521/4/1/2, Krygkor, 1, 17/04/1979–28/02/1985).
146 Letter from Dr CHJ van Aswegen to Magnus Malan, 7 June 1982, DOD/SANDF (MVV, GP 5, Box 88, 65/4, Krygkor: Beleid, 5, 24/03/1981–08/07/1992).
147 Ebbe Dommisse, *Anton Rupert: A Biography*, Tafelberg, Cape Town, 2007 (ebook version).
148 Statement to the Truth and Reconciliation Commission by Liza Grundlingh (Smit) and Robert Smit (children of Robert and Jeanne Smit), August 1997.
149 Ibid.
150 Ibid.
151 Interview with Pik Botha, Pretoria, 26 January 2016.
152 Interview with Joop de Loor, Somerset West, 26 May 2016.

153 Sanders, *Apartheid's Friends*, p. 86.
154 Ibid.
155 Ibid., p. 90.
156 Statement to the Truth and Reconciliation Commission by Liza Grundlingh (Smit) and Robert Smit (children of Robert and Jeanne Smit), August 1997.
157 Sanders, *Apartheid's Friends*, p. 88.
158 Ibid.

Chapter 2

1 SABC, 'TRC Special Report', Episode 74, Part 3, 16 November 1997.
2 Truth and Reconciliation Commission Report, vol. 6, section 2, chapter 5, 'Reparations and the business sector'.
3 Nicoli Nattrass, 'The Truth and Reconciliation Commission on business and apartheid: A critical evaluation', *African Affairs*, 98 (1999), pp. 373–391.
4 Truth and Reconciliation Commission Report, vol. 4, 1998, p. 49.
5 Dan O'Meara, *Forty Lost Years*, Ravan Press, Johannesburg, 1996, p. 294.
6 Christi van der Westhuizen, *White Power and the Rise and Fall of the National Party*, Zebra Press, Cape Town, 2007, p. 123.
7 National Supplies Procurement Amendment Act, No. 89 of 1974.
8 James P McWilliams, *Armscor: South Africa's Arms Merchant*, Brassey's, London, 1989, p. 6.
9 O'Meara, *Forty Lost Years*, p. 226.
10 Kenneth Grundy, *The Militarisation of South African Politics*, Oxford University Press, Oxford, 1988, p. 9.
11 Graeme Simpson, 'The politics and economics of the armaments industry in South Africa', in *War and Society: The Militarisation of South Africa*, ed. Jacklyn Cock and Laurie Nathan, David Philip, Cape Town, 1990.
12 Truth and Reconciliation Commission Report, vol. 4, 1998, p. 49.
13 Submission to the TRC Business Hearings by the Centre for Conflict Resolution, University of Cape Town, October 1997, SAHA FOIP Collection, AL2878, A2.2.14.4.
14 Truth and Reconciliation Commission Report, vol. 4, 1998, p. 36.
15 Simpson, 'The politics and economics of the armaments industry in South Africa'.
16 Ibid.
17 Ibid.
18 Ibid.
19 Ibid.
20 Letter from PW Botha to Dr Anton Rupert, 12 March 1980, University of the Free State, Archive for Contemporary Affairs (PV 203, A1/2/5, 1980 March – 1980 April, PW Botha).
21 Letter from Dr Anton Rupert to PW Botha, 17 March 1980, University of the Free State, Archive for Contemporary Affairs (PV 203, A1/2/5, 1980 March – 1980 April, PW Botha).
22 List of Individuals to Be Invited to Serve as Members of the Defence Advisory Council, March 1980, University of the Free State, Archive for

Contemporary Affairs (PV 203, PS 6/22/2, 1980–1981, PW Botha).

23 Interview with Basil Hersov, Johannesburg, 9 December 2015.

24 Magnus Malan, *My Life with the SA Defence Force*, Protea Book House, Pretoria, 2006, pp. 227–228.

25 Section 15A(1)(b) of the Companies Act, No. 61 of 1973.

26 KG Mockler, 'Section 15A(1)(b) of the Companies Act', SAICA Circular, July 1991.

27 Interview with Barend du Plessis, Pretoria, 6 June 2016.

28 Sundeep Tucker, 'ISS buys US research group IRRC', *Financial Times*, 14 July 2005.

29 Sven Lunsche, 'Disclosure of pay looms for SA directors', *Sunday Times*, 1 January 1995.

30 '150 secret companies don't give information', *Rand Daily Mail*, 22 March 1984.

31 Ibid.

32 The CIPC has records indicating use of the exemption from 1985 until 1994. News articles suggest that Rembrandt was using it long before this, from at least 1980.

33 'A cagey blue-chip', *Financial Mail*, 12 September 1980.

34 Ibid.

35 Anglo American Annual Reports, 1984–1994, accessed at the South African National Library.

36 Interview with Joop de Loor, Somerset West, 26 May 2016.

37 Ibid.

38 Ibid.

39 Interview with Basil Hersov, Johannesburg, 9 December 2015.

40 Campaigning organisations such as My Vote Counts (MVC) continue to tirelessly call for the regulation of private funding to political parties. See www.myvotecounts.org.za.

41 Kathy Whitehead, 'Zuma calls on business to fund the ANC', *News24*, 11 January 2015.

42 For example, we found no proof of direct funding by Anglo American or De Beers to the NP. However, a 1982 minute of the NP's fundraising committee in the Transvaal, chaired by Schoeman and with De Klerk in attendance, notes the need to follow up with various business people, including Gavin Relly, then chairman of Anglo American.

43 The reasons for this are manifold and include the fact that the democratic electorate has grown by a factor of 10, as well as the over-commercialisation of party politics.

44 This dynamic is not reflected in South African politics alone. A useful example of this is the cost of US presidential campaigns. In 2016, Hillary Clinton alone raised $1.2 billion, more than ten times more than *both* presidential candidates spent in the 1980 campaign. See Bill Allison, Mira Rojanasakul, Brittany Harris and Cedric Sam, 'Tracking the 2016 presidential money race', Bloomberg, 9 December 2016.

45 Other companies and individuals identified as NP donors include AECI (1988); Perskor (1989); Jan Pickard of Picbel (1984); the SA Sugar Millers' Association (1984); property tycoon Brian Stocks (1989); Oceana

Fishing Group (1983); and LTA from 1983 to 1989.

46 Correspondence between FW de Klerk and T Vosloo (Nasionale Pers), 17 August – 5 September 1989, University of the Free State, Archive for Contemporary Affairs (PV 734, 4/1/5/2 Vol. 2, 1989–1990, FW de Klerk).

47 Ibid.

48 Ibid.

49 Letter from Hendrik Schoeman (Schoeman Boerdery) to Johann Rupert (Rembrandt), 11 August 1989, University of the Free State, Archive for Contemporary Affairs (PV 734, 4/1/5/2 Vol. 1, 1989, FW de Klerk).

50 As at 11 February 2017. See http://www.forbes.com/profile/christoffel-wiese.

51 Letter from Kent Durr to FW de Klerk, 25 August 1989, University of the Free State, Archive for Contemporary Affairs (PV 734, 4/1/5/2 Vol. 2, 1989–1990, FW de Klerk).

52 Ibid.

53 Letter from FW de Klerk to Christo Wiese (Pepkor), 8 November 1989, University of the Free State, Archive for Contemporary Affairs (PV 734, 4/1/5/2 Vol. 2, 1989–1990, FW de Klerk).

54 Letter from PT van der Merwe to PW Botha, 12 May 1976, University of the Free State, Archive for Contemporary Affairs (PV 203, MV 1/4/81, May 1976, PW Botha).

55 Letter from Jan Marais to Cmdt E Lamprecht, 20 April 1979, University of the Free State, Archive for Contemporary Affairs (PV 203, C3/15/1, 1979–1980, PW Botha).

56 Kevin Maguire, 'Isaac Kaye', *The Guardian*, 13 April 2002.

57 Letter from Dr FJ du Plessis (Sanlam) to PW Botha, 2 September 1983, University of the Free State, Archive for Contemporary Affairs (PV 203, A1/2/27, 1983, PW Botha).

58 Letter from PW Botha to Dr FJ du Plessis (Sanlam), 14 September 1983, University of the Free State, Archive for Contemporary Affairs (PV 203, A1/2/27, 1983, PW Botha).

59 Letter from Dr FJ du Plessis (Sanlam) to PW Botha, 12 November 1984, University of the Free State, Archive for Contemporary Affairs (PV 203, A1/2/38, 1984 December – 1985 January, PW Botha).

60 Ibid.

61 Letter from TL de Beer (Gencor) to PW Botha, 20 March 1981, University of the Free State, Archive for Contemporary Affairs (PV 203, C3/15/2, 1981–1982, PW Botha).

62 Letter from FW de Klerk to Mr TL de Beer (Gencor), 25 October 1988, University of the Free State, Archive for Contemporary Affairs (PV 734, 4/A/5/1 Vol. 1, 1987–1988, FW de Klerk).

63 Record of Income to the Federale Raad, 20 August 1987, University of the Free State, Archive for Contemporary Affairs (PV 203, PS2/3/4, 1986–1988, PW Botha).

64 Niël Barnard, *Secret Revolution: Memoires of a Spy Boss*, Tafelberg, Cape Town, 2015.

65 Letter from PW Botha to B Troskie, 16 September 1983, University of

the Free State, Archive for Contemporary Affairs (PV 203, C3/15/3, 1983–1984, PW Botha).

66 Letter from HJ van Wijk to DE Cooper (Barlow Rand), 6 October 1988, University of the Free State, Archive for Contemporary Affairs (PV 734, 4/A/5/1 Vol. 1, 1987–1988, FW de Klerk).

67 Record of Income to the Federale Raad, 20 August 1987, University of the Free State, Archive for Contemporary Affairs (PV 203, PS2/3/4, 1986–1988, PW Botha).

68 Letter from WP Venter (Altech) to FW de Klerk, 22 September 1982, University of the Free State, Archive for Contemporary Affairs (PV 203, C3/15/2, 1981–1982, PW Botha).

69 Minutes of meeting of the National Party Finance Committee of the Transvaal, 17 October 1985, DW Steyn Private Papers.

70 Financial Report for Federale Raad, 24 September 1981, University of the Free State, Archive for Contemporary Affairs (PV 203, PS2/3/2, 1981–1983, PW Botha).

71 Letter from B Slome (Tedelex) to PW Botha, 25 June 1984, University of the Free State, Archive for Contemporary Affairs (PV 203, C3/15/3, 1983–1984, PW Botha).

72 Ibid.

73 Record of Income to the Federale Raad, 20 August 1987, University of the Free State, Archive for Contemporary Affairs (PV 203, PS2/3/4, 1986–1988, PW Botha).

74 Letter from PW Botha to L Shill, 21 April 1983, University of the Free State, Archive for Contemporary Affairs (PV 203, C3/15/3, 1983–1984, PW Botha).

75 Letter from B Lubner (PGSI) to PW Botha, 23 June 1982, University of the Free State, Archive for Contemporary Affairs (PV 203, C3/15/2, 1981–1982, PW Botha).

76 Interview with Bertie Lubner, Johannesburg, 27 January 2016.

77 According to the archives, Hersov did turn down one request for funding. In 1982 he and his business partner Clive Menell turned down a request from the NP for funding, on the ground that 'they are not well disposed towards the National Party', according to one NP fundraiser.

78 Interview with Basil Hersov, Johannesburg, 9 December 2015.

79 Handwritten letter from Basil Hersov (Anglovaal Group) to PW Botha, 31 October 1983, University of the Free State, Archive for Contemporary Affairs (PV 203, C3/15/3, 1983–1984, PW Botha).

80 Minutes, NP of Transvaal Executive Management, Pretoria, 9 August 1984, DW Steyn Private Papers.

81 Minutes, NP of Transvaal Executive Management, Pretoria, 18 October 1984, DW Steyn Private Papers.

82 Minutes, NP of Transvaal Executive Management, Pretoria, 1 August 1988, DW Steyn Private Papers.

83 Letter from Minister Danie Steyn to Dyason, Odendaal and Van Eeden Attorneys, 23 January 1985, DW Steyn Private Papers.

84 Minutes, NP of Transvaal Executive Management, Pretoria, 1 August 1988, DW Steyn Private Papers.

85 CIPC Records, Projek Republiek, accessed 18 April 2016.
86 Gerhardus Willem Koornhof profile, available at anccaucus.org.za.
87 Minutes, NP of Transvaal Executive Management, Pretoria, 1 August 1988, DW Steyn Private Papers.
88 Renier Schoeman profile on *Who's Who Southern Africa*, www.whoswho.co.za.
89 Jenna Etheridge, 'Naspers apologises for its role in apartheid', *News24*, 25 July 2015.
90 Gareth van Zyl, 'Naspers market cap hits R1 trillion', *Fin24 Tech*, 31 May 2016.
91 Sibusiso Tshabalala, 'What's missing? Naspers' late half-apology for apartheid', *The Journalist*, July 2015, www.thejournalist.org.za.
92 Karin Brynard, 'The media and the TRC: My individual yes', *Rhodes Journalism Review*, November 1997, p. 33.
93 John Matisonn, *God, Spies and Lies*, Missing Ink, Cape Town, 2015, p. 308.
94 O'Meara, *Forty Lost Years*, p. 257.
95 Minutes, NP of Transvaal Executive Management, Pretoria, 18 October 1984, DW Steyn Private Papers.
96 Letter from WD Beukes (*Die Burger*) to PW Botha, 25 February 1980, University of the Free State, Archive for Contemporary Affairs (PV 203, A1/2/4, 1980 January – 1980 February, PW Botha).
97 Letter from PW Botha to WD Beukes (*Die Burger*), 27 February 1980, University of the Free State, Archive for Contemporary Affairs (PV 203, A1/2/4, 1980 January – 1980 February, PW Botha).
98 Letter from PW Botha to PJ Cillié (Nasionale Pers), 9 October 1981, University of the Free State, Archive for Contemporary Affairs (PV 203, A1/2/14, 1981 October – 1981 November, PW Botha).
99 Letter from PW Botha to PJ Cillié (Nasionale Pers), 9 October 1981, University of the Free State: Archive for Contemporary Affairs (PV 203, A1/2/14, 1981 October – 1981 November, PW Botha).
100 Letter from PJ Cillié (Nasionale Pers) to PW Botha, 30 October 1981, University of the Free State, Archive for Contemporary Affairs (PV 203, A1/2/14, 1981 October – 1981 November, PW Botha).
101 Dene Smuts, *Patriots and Parasites*, Quiver Tree Publications, Cape Town, 2016, p. 35.
102 Letter from PW Botha to Dr W van Heerden (Perskor), 11 September 1985, University of the Free State, Archive for Contemporary Affairs (PV 203, B1/10, 1985 October, PW Botha).
103 Letter from PW Botha to Dr W van Heerden (Perskor), 8 October 1985, University of the Free State, Archive for Contemporary Affairs (PV 203, B1/10, 1985 October, PW Botha).
104 Letter from Dr WJ de Klerk (*Rapport*) to PW Botha, 1 September 1983, University of the Free State, Archive for Contemporary Affairs (PV 203, A1/2/27, 1983, PW Botha).
105 Letter from WJ de Klerk (*Rapport*) to PW Botha, 18 September 1984, University of the Free State, Archive for Contemporary Affairs (PV 203, A1/2/35, 1986 September, PW Botha).

106 Handwritten Letter from PJ Cillié (Nasionale Pers) to PW Botha, 26 September 1984, University of the Free State, Archive for Contemporary Affairs (PV 203, A1/2/35, 1986 September, PW Botha).

107 Letter from Ton Vosloo (Nasionale Pers) to PW Botha, 31 October 1984, University of the Free State, Archive for Contemporary Affairs (PV 203, PS 6/6/3, 1985, PW Botha).

108 Letter from PJ Cillié (Nasionale Pers) to PW Botha, 23 January 1985, University of the Free State, Archive for Contemporary Affairs (PV 203, A1/2/38, 1984 December – 1985 January, PW Botha).

109 Document on Project RBC Sent from Ton Vosloo (Nasionale Pers) to PW Botha, 25 April 1984, University of the Free State, Archive for Contemporary Affairs (PV 203, B1/6, 1985 June–July, PW Botha)

110 Letter from Ton Vosloo (Nasionale Pers) to PW Botha, 4 July 1985, University of the Free State, Archive for Contemporary Affairs (PV 203, B1/6, 1985 June–July, PW Botha)

111 Report on the Awarding of the Contract for Subscription Television, 14 March 1985, University of the Free State, Archive for Contemporary Affairs (PV 203, PS 6/6/3, 1985, PW Botha).

112 Report on Meeting between PW Botha and Members of Government with Ton Vosloo (Nasionale Pers), 15 June 1987, University of the Free State, Archive for Contemporary Affairs (PV 203, PS 14/2/1, 1986–1987, PW Botha).

113 'Joernaliste se taak is dringend, sê Ton Vosloo by hulde', *Netwerk 24*, 4 October 2015.

114 Andrew Meldrum, 'Anton Rupert', *The Guardian*, 23 January 2006.

115 SAPA article on Anton Rupert Speech at Detroit Economic Club, 1966, University of the Free State, Archive for Contemporary Affairs (PV 476, 1/26/1, 1966; 1980, Piet Koornhof).

116 Ibid.

117 Interview with Bertie Lubner, Johannesburg, 27 January 2016.

118 Ibid.

119 Ibid.

120 Ibid.

121 Ibid.

122 Ibid.

123 Interview with Basil Hersov, Johannesburg, 9 December 2015.

124 Ibid.

125 Ibid.

126 Ibid.

127 Ibid.

128 Interview with Tony Bloom, London, 30 May 2015.

129 Ibid.

130 Ibid.

131 Ron Nixon, *Selling Apartheid*, Jacana Media, Johannesburg, 2015, p. 29.

132 'The anti-apartheid movement, what kind of history?', SA History Online, Anti-Apartheid Movement Collection, available at www.sahistory. org.za/.

133 Nixon, *Selling Apartheid*, pp. 29–30.

134   Ibid., p. 77.
135   Interview with Basil Hersov, Johannesburg, 9 December 2015.
136   Ibid.
137   Ibid.
138   Ibid.
139   Interview with Bertie Lubner, Johannesburg, 27 January 2016.
140   Ibid.
141   Ibid.

Chapter 3
1   Interview with Pik Botha, Pretoria, 26 January 2016.
2   Marc Burger, *Not the Whole Truth*, Kindle edition, 2013.
3   Interview with Pik Botha, Pretoria, 26 January 2016.
4   Ibid.
5   Ibid.
6   Interview with Joop de Loor, Somerset West, 26 May 2016.
7   See www.goodreads.com/book/show/18958408-not-the-whole-truth.
8   Burger, *Not the Whole Truth*.
9   Interview with Alexandra Burger, Cape Town, 15 July 2016.
10   Burger, *Not the Whole Truth*.
11   Ibid.
12   Marc Burger, 'Written contribution to the book "Verwoerd to Mandela"',
     University of Stellenbosch.
13   See www.encyclopedia-titanica.org/titanic-victim/emil-taussig.html.
14   Burger, 'Written contribution to the book "Verwoerd to Mandela"'.
15   Report of the Khan Commission, First Interim Report, 17 October 1991.
16   'Prinz zu Sayn-Wittgenstein gestorben', *Der Spiegel*, 25 February 2010.
17   Burger, 'Written contribution to the book "Verwoerd to Mandela"'.
18   Ibid.
19   Interview with Alexandra Burger, Cape Town, 15 July 2016.
20   Burger, 'Written contribution to the book "Verwoerd to Mandela"'.
21   Interview with Tom Wheeler, Johannesburg, 23 February 2015.
22   Ibid.
23   Ibid.
24   Burger, *Not the Whole Truth*.
25   Ibid.
26   Ibid.
27   Burger, 'Written contribution to the book "Verwoerd to Mandela"'.
28   Report of the Khan Commission, Second Interim Report, Undated [after
     October 1991].
29   Annual Report on Special Projects, 15 April 1986, DOD/SANDF (DI
     Directorate Foreign Relations, GP 38, Box 178, DBB(SK) 501/8/2,
     Jaarverslae, 1, 15/05/1985–15/04/1986).
30   See www.en.wikipedia.org/wiki/Rauf_Denkta%C5%9F.
31   Annual Report on Special Projects, 15 April 1986, DOD/SANDF (DI
     Directorate Foreign Relations, GP 38, Box 178, DBB(SK) 501/8/2,
     Jaarverslae, 1, 15/05/1985–15/04/1986).
32   Richard Hengeveld and Jaap Rodenburg, *Embargo: Apartheid's Oil Secrets*

Revealed, Amsterdam University Press, Amsterdam, 1995, p. 270.

33   Michael Kranish, 'Oil may be key in Iran dealings: US probes role of Pretoria, Saudis', *Boston Globe*, 22 March 1987.

34   Ibid.

35   Ibid.

36   Sietse Bosgra, 'From Jan van Riebeeck to solidarity with the struggle: The Netherlands, South Africa and apartheid', in *The Road to Democracy in South Africa*, vol. 3, *International Solidarity*, Part 1, ed. SADET, Unisa Press, Pretoria, 2008, pp. 578–580.

37   Ibid., p. 580.

38   Hengeveld and Rodenburg, *Embargo*, pp. 115–116.

39   Interview with Kobus van Zyl, Cape Town, 22 November 2013.

40   Ibid.

41   Interview with Kobus van Zyl, Cape Town, 10 May 2016.

42   Ibid.

43   Hennie van Vuuren, 'Apartheid Grand Corruption', Institute of Security Studies, Cape Town, 2006.

44   Tom de Quaastniet and Paul Aarts, 'Putting money over mouth, profit over principle', in *Embargo*, ed. Hengeveld and Rodenburg, p. 271.

45   Ibid., p. 273.

46   Interview with Kobus van Zyl, Cape Town, 10 May 2016.

47   Ibid.

48   Ibid.

49   Ibid.

50   De Quaastniet and Aarts, 'Putting money over mouth, profit over principle', p. 278.

51   Ibid., p. 274.

52   Ibid., p. 275.

53   Ibid., p. 277.

54   Interview with Danie Steyn, Pretoria, 18 February 2016.

55   Der Bundesbeauftragte für die Unterlagen des Staatssicherheitsdienstes der ehemaligen Deutschen Demokratischen Republik, Computer Technology_FRG in Namibia_Hungary Oil, MfS HA VIII 9062 (Stasi Archives, Berlin).

56   RT Naylor, *Patriots and Profiteers: On Economic Warfare, Embargo Busting and State-Sponsored Crime*, McClelland & Stewart, Toronto, 1999, p. 204.

57   Ibid., p. 204.

58   Kranish, 'Oil may be key in Iran dealings'.

59   Ibid.

60   Ibid.

61   Ibid.

62   Ibid.

63   Ibid.

64   Ibid.

65   Ibid.

66   Ibid.

67   Ibid.

68   Van Vuuren, 'Apartheid grand corruption'.

69 See www.statista.com/statistics/262858/change-in-opec-crude-oil-prices-since-1960/; and www.inflationdata.com/Inflation/Inflation_Rate/Historical_Oil_Prices_Table.asp.

70 Interview with Kobus van Zyl, Cape Town, 10 May 2016.

71 Ibid.

72 Memorandum to the Minister of Mineral and Energy Affairs on Crude Oil Procurement, 3 June 1991, South African History Archive, Kobus van Zyl Collection, AL3157, B2.15.

73 Stephen Ellis, 'Africa and international corruption: The strange case of South Africa and Seychelles', *African Affairs*, 95 (1996), p. 186.

74 This section on Rich draws from Murray Hunter, 'Marc Rich: Apartheid's most important sanctions buster', *Daily Maverik*, 19 July 2013.

75 Daniel Ammann, *King of Oil: The Secret Lives of Marc Rich*, St Martin's Press, New York, 2009, p. 193.

76 Ibid., p. 195.

77 A Craig Copetas, *Metal Men: Marc Rich and the 10-Billion-Dollar Scam*, Putnam & Sons, New York and London, 1995, p. 198.

78 Martin van der Weyer, 'The world is better off without Marc Rich – but his heirs still control the price of almost everything', *The Spectator*, 6 July 2013.

79 Kevin Maguire and David Pallister, 'Top Tory at centre of sanctions busting claim', *The Guardian*, 4 May 2001.

80 Steve LeVine, 'Legendary tycoon John Deuss's latest exploit is cutting a money-laundering deal with Dutch prosecutors', *Quartz*, 1 August 2013.

81 Ibid.

82 Steve LeVine, *The Oil and the Glory: The Pursuit of Empire and Fortune on the Caspian Sea*, Random House, New York, 2007, p. 135.

83 Ibid., p. 160.

84 At the time, Player enjoyed a close association with members of the apartheid political elite with whom he played golf, including Prime Minister BJ Vorster. The sale of the house is mentioned in Hengeveld and Rodenburg, *Embargo*, p. 147.

85 Ibid., p. 147.

86 Ibid., p. 148.

87 Interview with Danie Steyn, Pretoria, 18 February 2016.

88 Memorandum to the Minister of Mineral and Energy Affairs on Crude Oil Procurement, 3 June 1991, South African History Archive, Kobus van Zyl Collection, AL3157, B2.15.

89 Draft minutes of crude pricing meeting held at SFF on 30 November 1992, AL3157, SJ van Zyl Collection, SAHA.

90 Ibid.

91 Hengeveld and Rodenburg, *Embargo*, p. 160.

92 Ibid., p. 89.

93 Martie Retief-Meiring, *Elita and Her Life with FW de Klerk*, Tafelberg, Cape Town, 2008, p. 41.

94 Ibid., p. 56.

95 Sam Sole and Stefaans Brümmer, 'Mbeki, Chippy and the Greek

lobbyist', *Mail & Guardian*, 9 February 2007.

96 Ibid.

97 Ibid.

98 Ibid.

99 Interview with Kobus van Zyl, Cape Town, 10 May 2016.

100 Ibid. 'Oil tanker springs leak off South Africa,' 5 October 1989, UPI Archives.

101 Interview with Kobus van Zyl, Cape Town, 22 November 2013.

102 Ibid.

103 This was confirmed in a statement issued by the Presidency in 2007. See Evelyn Groenink, Sam Sole and Stefaans Brümmer, 'Arms deal: "Ministers got millions"', *Mail & Guardian*, 14 December 2007.

104 Paul Holden and Hennie van Vuuren, *The Devil in the Detail: How the Arms Deal Changed Everything*, Jonathan Ball Publishers, Cape Town, 2011, p. 227.

105 Ibid., p. 227.

106 Interview with Vic McPherson, Cape Town, 17 February 2016.

107 Report of the Board of Inquiry into the Loss of South African Airways Boeing 747 244B Combi Aircraft 'Helderberg' in the Indian Ocean on November 28th 1987, Presented to the Minister of Transport and Public Works, 14 May 1990.

108 Mark Young, 'The Helderberg disaster: Was this the cause of the crash?', *Politicsweb*, 1 October 2014.

109 Report of the Board of Inquiry into the Loss of South African Airways Boeing 747 244B Combi Aircraft 'Helderberg' in the Indian Ocean on November 28th 1987, Presented to the Minister of Transport and Public Works, 14 May 1990.

110 The SADF's confirmation came in the form of a one-line letter signed by General Jannie Geldenhuys on 17 May 1989, David Klatzow's Private Papers.

111 Armscor's response was two lines, 30 May 1989, David Klatzow's Private Papers.

112 Report of the Board of Inquiry into the Loss of South African Airways Boeing 747 244B Combi Aircraft 'Helderberg' in the Indian Ocean on November 28th 1987, Presented to the Minister of Transport and Public Works, 14 May 1990.

113 Both affidavits were found in David Klatzow's Private Papers.

114 Truth and Reconciliation Commission, vol. 2, chapter 6, Special investigation into the Helderberg crash, pp. 503–509.

115 Ibid., pp. 506–509.

116 Ibid., pp. 507–508.

117 Summary of CSI and Director of Foreign Relations Visits to Asia, April 1984, DOD/SANDF (DI Directorate Foreign Relations, GP 38, Box 105, DBB/SK/311/1/26, Hulpverlening and Samewerking met ander Lande/Regerings: Taiwan, 1, 18/03/1981–07/08/1995).

118 It is important to note that such rocket fuel is different from a wild theory that did the rounds in the media in the 1990s that the *Helderberg* was carrying a mysterious combustible chemical called 'Red Mercury'. This

so-called super-weapon has since been proven to be a fictitious substance sold by conmen to gullible customers across the globe and there is no known connection to the *Helderberg*.

119 Ministry of Transport, Media Release, 'Latest reports on the Helderberg air disaster', 11 October 2002, David Klatzow Private Papers.
120 Preliminary Report: Helderberg Plane Disaster, from Advocate Welch and Mr MB Whale to Dullah Omar, 8 October 2001, David Klatzow's Private Papers.
121 Correspondence from Advocate Welch to Dullah Omar, Undated, David Klatzow's Private Papers.
122 Preliminary Report: Helderberg Plane Disaster, from Advocate Welch and Mr MB Whale to Dullah Omar, 8 October 2001, David Klatzow's Private Papers.
123 Ibid.
124 Interview with Geordie Osler, Johannesburg, 14 April 2014.
125 Truth and Reconciliation Commission, Special Hearing, In Camera, Helderberg Hearing, Day 2, 2 June 1998, p. 191.
126 Ibid.
127 Email from John Hare to Hennie van Vuuren, 13 July 2016.
128 Ibid.
129 Phillip de Bruyn, 'Krygkor konneksie', *Beeld*, 24 May 2000.
130 Interview with Kobus van Zyl, Cape Town, 10 May 2016.
131 Interview with Geordie Osler, Johannesburg, 14 April 2014.
132 Ibid.
133 Interview with Kobus van Zyl, Cape Town, 10 May 2016.
134 Affidavit of Willem Bothma, 17 September 2014, David Klatzow's Private Papers.
135 Ray White, 'Alleged cause of Helderberg plane exposed', *Eye Witness News*, 2014.
136 Lukas Meyer, 'SAL man vertel van wapens', *Rapport*, 4 June 2000.
137 Telegram from MANA to Armscor, via Ambassador, 1 March 1977, DIRCO (Correspondence, 9/56/8, Vol. 2, 15/11/71–8/4/81, Defence Purchases).
138 State Security Council Meeting Minutes, 3 February 1987, DOD/ SANDF (Inspector General, GP 2, Box 429, IG/SAW 521/2/2/30, Staatsveiligheidsraad, 3, 7/11/86–18/03/87).
139 Jonathan Rosenthal and Richard Stovin-Bradford, 'Weapons flown in SA cargo', *The Star* Business Report, 7 August 1988.

Chapter 4

1 See www.tackletaxhavens.com/more-stuff/quotes/.
2 See www.swissinfo.ch/eng/apartheid-dealings_swiss-lift-restrictions-on-south-africa-archives/38828730.
3 Céline Zünd, 'Apartheid, des archives si embarrassantes', *Le Temps*, 14 December 2013.
4 Ibid.
5 Interview with Peter Hug, Bern, 4 July 2013.
6 Ibid.

7   Zünd, 'Apartheid, des archives si embarrassantes'.
8   Interview with Peter Hug, Bern, 4 July 2013.
9   See www.swissinfo.ch/eng/apartheid-dealings_swiss-lift-restrictions-on-south-africa-archives/38828730.
10 See www.khulumani.net/khulumani/statements/item/826-joint-press-release-us-circuit-court-dismisses-apartheid-litigation.html.
11 See www.swissinfo.ch/eng/apartheid-dealings_swiss-lift-restrictions-on-south-africa-archives/38828730.
12 Ibid.
13 Daniel Mariani, 'Bunkers for all', www.swissinfo.ch/eng/bunkers-for-all/995143.
14 Letter from F Kappelar, Swiss Envoy in Pretoria, to GP Jooste, SA Department of External Affairs, 6 May 1960, Federal Archives of Switzerland (E2200.178#2000/44#41*, 244.0, 8, Sitzverlegung schweizerischer Firmen, 1960–1982).
15 Memorandum to South Africa from Switzerland, on Relocating Swiss Corporations to South Africa in Times of War or Crisis, 6 May 1960, Federal Archives of Switzerland (E2200.178#2000/44#41*, 244.0, 8, Sitzverlegung schweizerischer Firmen, 1960–1982).
16 Correspondence from the Swiss Department of Foreign Affairs to the Mission in Pretoria, 4 February 1960, Federal Archives of Switzerland (E2200.178#2000/44#41*, 244.0, 8, Sitzverlegung schweizerischer Firmen, 1960–1982).
17 Ibid.
18 Ibid.
19 Correspondence to Minister R Kohli, Secretary General of Political Department in Swiss Department of Foreign Affairs, 5 May 1960, Federal Archives of Switzerland (E2200.178#2000/44#41*, 244.0, 8, Sitzverlegung schweizerischer Firmen, 1960–1982).
20 Memorandum on the 'Emergency Agreement for the South African Trust Fund', Sent to the Swiss Embassy in Pretoria, 11 November 1982, Federal Archives of Switzerland (E2200.178#2000/44#41*, 244.0, 8, Sitzverlegung schweizerischer Firmen, 1960–1982).
21 Confidential Memorandum from UBS to the Swiss Union Trust for South Africa, 30 November 1982, Federal Archives of Switzerland (E2200.178#2000/44#41*, 244.0, 8, Sitzverlegung schweizerischer Firmen, 1960–1982).
22 Letter from Francois EP Jeannerat (UBS) to Ambassador CH Bruggmann, Swiss Embassy Pretoria, 9 December 1982, Federal Archives of Switzerland (E2200.178#2000/44#41*, 244.0, 8, Sitzverlegung schweizerischer Firmen, 1960–1982).
23 Interview with Barend du Plessis, Pretoria, 6 June 2016.
24 Interview with Joop de Loor, Cape Town, 26 June 2016.
25 RW Johnson, *How Long Will South Africa Survive?*, Macmillan, Johannesburg, 1977, p. 81.
26 Ibid., p. 70.
27 Ibid., p. 71.
28 Ibid., p. 77.

29 Ibid., p. 81.
30 Georg Kreis, *Switzerland and South Africa 1948–1994*, International Academic Publishers, Bern, 2007, p. 318.
31 World Gold Commission briefing document, May 27 1988, World Council of Churches Archive.
32 Sandra Bott, 'South African gold at the heart of the competition between the Zurich and London gold markets', in *The Global Gold Market and the International Monetary System from the Late 19th Century to the Present*, ed. Sandra Bott, Palgrave Macmillan, New York, 2013, pp. 109–110.
33 Ibid., p. 113.
34 Ibid.
35 Kreis, *Switzerland and South Africa*, p. 319.
36 Ibid., p. 106.
37 Ibid., p. 320.
38 Ibid., p. 321.
39 Bott, 'South African Gold', p. 126.
40 Johnson, *How Long Will South Africa Survive?*, p. 72.
41 Bott, 'South African Gold', pp. 131–134.
42 Kreis, *Switzerland and South Africa*, p. 323.
43 Bott, 'South African Gold', p. 133.
44 Mascha Madörin, *Gold Gier*, Action Group on Switzerland as a Financial Centre and the Third World, Bern, 1989, p. 60, quoted in Kreis, *Switzerland and South Africa*, p. 326.
45 Ibid.
46 Kreis, *Switzerland and South Africa*, p. 324.
47 Interview with Joop de Loor, Cape Town, 26 June 2016.
48 Ibid.
49 Christina Stucky, 'Switzerland's part in aiding South Africa', *Sunday Independent*, 21 February 1999.
50 Sebastien Guex and Bouda Etemad, *Economic Relations between Switzerland and South Africa: 1945–1990*, Research Summary PNR42+, FNSNF, Bern.
51 Ibid.
52 Kreis, *Switzerland and South Africa*, p. 349. As well as Memorandum from the Swiss Anti-Apartheid Movement, 7 June 1985, World Council of Churches Archive.
53 Mascha Madörin and Gottfried Wellmer, *Apartheid Debt: The Role of Swiss and German Finance*, 1997, South African History Archive (AL3021, Yasmin Sooka Collection).
54 Paper by Dr Bettina Hürni on Swiss banks and South Africa, August 1983, DIRCO (Switzerland, 1/49/2, Vol 3A, 23/12/80–12/6/84, Switzerland Relations with SA).
55 A number of letters of authorisation for such loans are to be found in the Swiss Federal Archives. An example is the letter from the Swiss Federal Department of Foreign Affairs to the Swiss Embassy Pretoria, Approving a Loan from Credit Suisse to ESCOM, 13 December 1983, Federal Archives of Switzerland (File Reference: 521.61).
56 Memorandum from the Swiss Anti-Apartheid Movement, 7 June 1985,

World Council of Churches Archive.

57 Ibid.

58 Urs Sekinger, Mascha Madörin and Martina Egli, *Collaboration with the Apartheid Regime*, Switzerland-South Africa Research Group, Bern, 1985, p. 6. See also Peter Hug, *Mit der Apartheid-Regierung gegen den Kommunismus: Die militärischen, rüstungsindustriellen und nuklearen Beziehungen der Schweiz zu Südafrika und die Apartheid-Debatte*, Schweizerischen Nationalfonds zur Förderung der wissenschaftlichen Forschung, Bern, 2005.

59 Interview with Barend du Plessis, Pretoria, 6 June 2016.

60 Switzerland Bern Embassy reps, DIRCO Archive, Switzerland Bern (4/2/75, 1/7/77–30/10/96).

61 Switzerland – relations with SA (2 volumes), DIRCO Archive, Switzerland (1/49/3, Vol. 5, 10/5/84–20/9/84).

62 Kreis, *Switzerland and South Africa*, pp. 455–456.

63 Clipping from *Business Day*, 10 October 1988, Federal Archives of Switzerland (E2200.178#2000/45#42*, 342.1, 5, Regierung, Aussenministerium, 1977–1988).

64 Ibid.

65 See Ebbe Dommisse, *Anton Rupert: A Biography*, Tafelberg, Cape Town, 2005.

66 Memorandum from the President's Deputy Special Assistant for National Security Affairs (Kaysen) to President Kennedy, Kennedy Library, National Security Files, Kaysen Series, Balance of Payments, General, 7/1/62–7/15/62. Confidential. Available at www.history.state.gov/historicaldocuments/frus1961-63v09/d56#fn-source.

67 Kreis, *Switzerland and South Africa*, p. 337.

68 Sandra Bott, *La Suisse et l'Afrique du Sud, 1945–1990: Commerce, Finance et Achats d'Or Durant l'Apartheid*, Chronos Verlag, Zurich, 2013, p. 97.

69 Ibid., p. 128.

70 List of Overseas Guests Attending Receptions at Fleur du Cap and The Tuynhuys, April 1975, KADOC – Archief André Vlerick (Diverse engagementen en persoonlijke stukken, Zuid-Afrika, 9.1.1.3, Reis naar Zuid-Afrika n.a.v. inhuldiging president N. Diederichs, April 1975).

71 'Dr Nico, had nie geheime rekening', *Die Volksblad*, 9 September 1980.

72 Hennie van Vuuren, *Apartheid Grand Corruption Report*, Institute for Security Studies, Cape Town, 2006.

73 Ibid.

74 Ibid.

75 'Disclosure now' (editorial), *Financial Mail*, Johannesburg, 12 September 1980.

76 Richard Leonard, *South Africa at War: White Power and the Crisis in Southern Africa*, Lawrence Hill, Newport, 1983.

77 Dommisse, *Anton Rupert*, p. 188.

78 Rupert's biography describes the manner in which the boards of his non-South African businesses were dominated by individuals from those countries. As can be expected, many of these men were also influential players in their own countries. See Dommisse, *Anton Rupert*.

79 'Rothmans International Limited', *Financial Times* (London), 12 September 1972; Dommisse, *Anton Rupert*, p. 271.

80 Dommisse, *Anton Rupert*, p. 290.

81 Ibid., p. 295.

82 Interview with Joop de Loor, Cape Town, 26 June 2016.

83 Ibid.

84 Interview with Barend du Plessis, Pretoria, 6 June 2016.

85 Ibid.

86 'The 300 richest people in 2015', Bilanz, 2015, www.bilanz.ch/300-Reichste-live?rid=3227&row_pos=275&page=list&sel_jahr=v13.

87 David Henry, 'Nikolaus Senn, former Union Bank of Switzerland CEO, dies at 88', www.bloomberg.com/news/articles/2014-11-05/nikolaus-senn-former-union-bank-of-switzerland-ceo-dies-at-88.

88 Letter from Nikolaus Senn and Robert Holzach, Vice-President Directors of UBS, to the South African Minister of Finance, 2 April 1970, (NAP) TES FER 231/3 FER 231/3/1/9429, as quoted in Bott, *La Suisse et l'Afrique du Sud*, p. 296.

89 Interview with Barend du Plessis, Pretoria, 6 June 2016.

90 Dommisse, *Anton Rupert*, p. 418.

91 Ibid., p. 418.

92 'Bank investors jeer bishop on S. Africa', *St Louis Post*, 16 April 1989.

93 Christina Stucky, 'Switzerland's part in aiding South Africa', *Sunday Independent*, 21 February 1999.

94 Kreis, *Switzerland and South Africa*, p. 225.

95 Stucky, 'Switzerland's part in aiding South Africa'.

96 Interview with Barend du Plessis, Pretoria, 6 June 2016.

97 Daniel Bradlow, 'Debt development and human rights: Lessons from South Africa', *Michigan Journal of International Law*, 1991.

98 Ibid.

99 'The favoured one', *Economic and Political Weekly*, 20, 42 (19 October 1985), pp. 1761–1762.

100 Interview with Barend du Plessis, Pretoria, 6 June 2016.

101 Ibid.

102 'Swiss expert faces tough bank talks', *New York Times*, 30 September 1985.

103 See www.hls-dhs-dss.ch/textes/d/D29589.php.

104 Considered the meeting place of central bankers.

105 'The fighting Swiss', *Financial Times* (London), 9 March 1987.

106 Obituary, *New York Times*, 6 June 1997.

107 Obituary, *The Economist*, London, 12 June 1997.

108 Ibid.

109 'The favoured one', *Economic and Political Weekly*, pp. 1761–1762.

110 Ibid.

111 Pieter Wolvaardt, Tom Wheeler and Werner Scholtz, *From Verwoerd to Mandela: South African Diplomats Remember*, vol. 3, Brenthurst Foundation, 2010, p. 345.

112 Hugh Murray, 'Fritz Leutwiler', *Leadership*, no.1, Johannesburg, 1986.

113 Ibid.

114 Swiss National Bank, Fritz Leutwiler profile, www.snb.ch/en/mmr/
reference/hist_bios_dm_leutwiler/source/hist_bios_dm_leutwiler.
en.pdf.

115 CP Birch, Koeberg, an Industry Perspective, Symposium on Nuclear
Technology in Southern Africa, CSIR, Johannesburg, 1990.

116 'Leutwiler will head Pretoria debt talks', *Wall Street Journal*, 27
September 1985.

117 'Swiss expert faces tough bank talks', *New York Times*, 30 September
1985.

118 'Debt mediator indicates he won't press Pretoria for political changes',
Wall Street Journal, 13 January 1986.

119 Murray, 'Fritz Leutwiler'.

120 Kreis, *Switzerland and South Africa*, pp. 356–360.

121 Peter Montagnon, 'South Africa and banks reach broad agreement',
Financial Times (London), 21 February 1986.

122 'A deal for all seasons', *Business Day*, 21 February 1986.

123 'The fighting Swiss', *Financial Times*.

124 Jeff Rubin, 'Challenging apartheid's foreign debt', April 1997,
www.citeseerx.ist.psu.edu/viewdoc/summary?doi=10.1.1.516.2114.

125 Howard Preece in *Finance Week*, 27 March 1987, quoted in Rubin,
'Challenging apartheid's foreign debt', p. 14.

126 Marc Burger, *Not the Whole Truth*, Kindle edition, 2013.

127 Letter from TR Gibbon, Armscor, to Brigadier A Savides, 6 July 1988,
DOD/SANDF (Verslae, Box 280, AMI/520/3/4, Visits: Overseas SAW
Krygkor pers, 56, 19/08/88–07/09/88).

128 Ibid.

129 Memorandum from CSL to CSI, 11 August 1988, DOD/SANDF
(Verslae, Box 280, AMI/520/3/4, Visits: Overseas SAW Krygkor pers, 56,
19/08/88–07/09/88).

130 Chris Lang, Nick Hildyard, Kate Geary and Matthew Granger, *Dams
Incorporated*, Swedish Society for Nature Conservation, Corner House,
February 2000, p. 118.

131 Ibid., p. 22.

132 Ibid., p. 118.

133 Vishnu Padayachee, 'Private International Banks, the Debt Crisis and the
Apartheid State 1982–1985', *African Affairs*, Vol. 87, No. 348 (July 1988),
pp. 361–376.

134 Dustin N Sharp, 'The significance of human rights for the debt of
countries in transition', in *Making Sovereign Financing and Human Rights
Work*, ed. Juan Pablo Bohoslavsky and Jernej Cernic, Hart Publishing,
Oxford, 2014, pp. 47–59.

135 Patrick Bond, *Elite Transition: From Apartheid to Neoliberalism in South
Africa*, University of Natal Press, Scottsville, 2000.

136 Vishnu Padayachee, 'Private international banks, the debt crisis and the
apartheid state: 1982–1985', *African Affairs*, 1988, pp. 361–376.

137 'A warm welcome from the lenders', *Euromoney Magazine*, June 1984,
World Council of Churches Archive.

138 Ibid.

139 Note on the Visit of Nicolaas Diederichs to Switzerland, Sent to
     President Furgler, 28 January 1977, Federal Archives of Switzerland
     (E2001E-01#1988/16, B.15.50.4.Afr.S, Sudafrika – Aufenthalt und
     Empfang fremder Personlichkeiten, 1976–1978).

Chapter 5

1 Clipping from *Humo* magazine titled 'The Belgian elite: Rich but
   upstanding', 1985, KADOC, Archief Walter de Bock (Banken en
   Bedrijven, Banken, Bedrijven, Belgie, 2.20, 4).

2 André Mommen, 'Een Vlaams sprookje', *De Nieuwe Maand*, January
   1986, KADOC, Archief Walter de Bock (Banken en Bedrijven, Banken,
   Bedrijven, Belgie, 2.20, 4).

3 Ludwig Verduyn, *Het KBLux dossier*, Uitgeverij Van Halewyck, Leuven,
   2011, p. 40.

4 Ibid., p. 48.

5 'The Belgian elite', *Humo* magazine.

6 Ibid.

7 Terry Gourvish (ed.), *Business and Politics in Europe: 1900–1970*,
   Cambridge University Press, Cambridge, 2003.

8 See www.vlerick.com/en/about-Vlerick/logo-and-boilerplate.

9 Linda Anderson, 'Belgian school receives €50 m gift', *Financial Times*, 18
   June 2006.

10 Report on Meeting of the Commissie Rechtvaardigheid en Vrede, 12
    November 1979, KADOC, Archief André Vlerick (Diverse engagementen
    en persoonlijke stukken, Zuid-Afrika, 9.1.2.4, Toespraak Vlerick over
    Protea voor Algemene Vergadering Commissie Rechtvaardigheid en Vrede,
    18 Oktober 1979, Notities, briefwisseling, verslag van de vergadering).

11 Banque Paribas director Leon Rochtus was elected as Protea's secretary.
    Leon Rochtus, like Vlerick, had a long-standing relationship with the
    apartheid regime. Known as 'black Leon' because of his Nazi sympathies
    and his financial links to the extreme right, including the Vlaams Bloc
    (VB), Rochtus was a South African honorary consul in Antwerp from
    1975 until his death in 1997. He, like Vlerick, was awarded the Order of
    Good Hope by the FW de Klerk government in 1992. In 1995, he is said
    to have made an emotional submission to the TRC in South Africa. This
    enabled him to retain his title of honorary consul despite the election
    of a democratic government. Following his death in 1997, he received
    a glowing obituary in a South African government-funded publication
    Beelden, written by Ambassador Joubert and Minister of Foreign Affairs
    Alfred Nzo: 'Mr Rochtus was an exceptional man for South Africa, since
    he fulfilled the role of Honorary Consul in an admirable way. He received
    in 1992 the Order of Good Hope for his excellent record of service.'

12 Clipping from *De Morgen* on John Bredenkamp, 3 December 1981,
    KADOC, Archief Walter de Bock (Centraal en Zuidelijk Afrika, Zuid-
    Afrika, 5.06, 1, 1981–1988).

13 Clipping from *Knack* magazine titled 'Protea beklim die berg', 26 October
    1977, KADOC, Archief Walter de Bock (Centraal en Zuidelijk Afrika,
    Zuid-Afrika, 5.06, 1, 1981–1988).

14 Ibid.

15 Clipping from *Het Laatste Nieuws*, 9 December 1977, KADOC, Archief Walter de Bock (Centraal en Zuidelijk Afrika, Zuid-Afrika, 5.06, 1, 1981–1988).

16 Walter de Bock, Jef Coeck, Paul Goossens and Maurice Mthombeni, *Suikerbossie: België en Zuidelijk Afrika*, Manteau, Brussels, January 1978, Open Secrets Collection, pp. 109–110.

17 Clipping from *Knack* magazine, 6 January 1982, KADOC, Archief Walter de Bock (Centraal en Zuidelijk Afrika, Zuid-Afrika, 5.06, 1, 1981–1988).

18 Newsletter distributed by Protea, 1987, KADOC, Archief Walter de Bock (Centraal en Zuidelijk Afrika, Zuid-Afrika, 5.07, 1, 1985–2002).

19 Eurosa members included the Association de la Communauté Franco-Africaine (ACFA), Association Belge–Sud-africaine (ABSA), Deutsch-Südafrikanische Gesellschaft (DSAG) and Protea.

20 Its formal founding took place in Paris on 9 June 1979 and the former prime minister of France, Antoine Pinay (of the secret organisation Le Cercle, which will be the subject of more attention in Chapter 9), was the honorary chair of the union.

21 Report on the Meeting of the Executive Committee of Eurosa, 26 February 1980, KADOC, Archief André Vlerick (Diverse engagementen en persoonlijke stukken, Zuid-Afrika, 9.1.1.8, Protea/Eurosa, 1979–1982).

22 Minutes of Eurosa Board Meeting, 14 July 1980, KADOC, Archief André Vlerick (Diverse engagementen en persoonlijke stukken, Zuid-Afrika, 9.1.1.8, Protea/Eurosa, 1979–1982).

23 Letter from André Vlerick to SA Ambassador, Brussels, 13 March 1980, KADOC, Archief André Vlerick (Diverse engagementen en persoonlijke stukken, Zuid-Afrika, 9.1.1.8, Protea/Eurosa, 1979–1982).

24 Letter from Albert van Oppens to Johan Lotter, 31 July 1980, KADOC, Archief André Vlerick (Diverse engagementen en persoonlijke stukken, Zuid-Afrika, 9.1.1.8, Protea/Eurosa, 1979–1982).

25 André Vlerick took numerous trips to South Africa. His diaries and personal archives at the University of Leuven record trips in 1970, 1975, 1979, 1982, 1983 and 1986. All these trips included meeting with high-ranking officials (the minister of finance or state president) and senior business (Anglo and Rembrandt) and political leaders (Broederbond chairman). He flitted between five-star hotels, visited the bantustan of Bophuthatswana, and gold mines. Townships such as Khayelitsha in Cape Town were 'observed' from a helicopter.

26 Invitation to Dr and Mrs Vlerick to attend the inauguration of Nico Diederichs, 19 April 1975, KADOC, Archief André Vlerick (Diverse engagementen en persoonlijke stukken, Zuid-Afrika, 9.1.1.3, Reis naar Zuid-Afrika n.a.v. inhuldiging president N. Diederichs, April 1975).

27 They were joined by plutocrats and some of the wealthiest families in the world. As a guest of Prime Minister BJ Vorster, Vlerick was one of a number of prominent foreign visitors at the Rupert family home Fleur du Cap and at Tuynhuys for the inauguration. Other guests included the wealthy French Bettencourts and the former French minister of foreign

affairs. Kredietbank was represented by Vlerick as well as its honorary chairman Professor Fernand Collin, as well as the chair, Dr Luc Wauters. Other notable bankers included the top management of Deutsche Bank, Dresdner Bank, Swiss Credit Bank, Commerzbank, UBS (Bruno Saager), Banque de l'Indochine, Berliner Handels-Gesellschaft and Frankfurter Bank, Hambros Bank (C Hambro, chairman), and Banque de Paris et des Pays-Bas. It was a relatively small affair and the Vlericks were accorded pride of place among the top-ranking dignitaries. See invitation to Dr and Mrs Vlerick to attend the inauguration of Nico Diederichs, 19 April 1975, KADOC, Archief André Vlerick (April 1975).

28 Letter from WC Dempsey to PW Botha, 20 September 1983, University of the Free State, Archive for Contemporary Affairs (PV 203, A1/2/27, 1983, PW Botha).

29 Aloïs van de Voorde, *André Vlerick: Een Minister-Manager; Een Politieke Bibliografie; Van Vlaamse Streekeconomie tot Financiën*, Lannoo, Tielt, 1996.

30 'SA vereer Belg met hoogste orde', *Beeld*, 14 December 1987.

31 Hugo Cijsels, 'Baron André Vlerick: Apartheidsprofessor gelauwerd door Zuid-Afrika', 3 March 1988, Open Secrets Collection.

32 Verduyn, *Het KBLux dossier*, p. 92.

33 Ibid., p. 117.

34 Ibid., p. 46.

35 'Almanij vertrouwt in financiële roeping', January 1984, KADOC, Archief Walter de Bock (Banken en Bedrijven, Banken, Bedrijven, Belgie, 2.20, 4).

36 Interview with Joop de Loor, Somerset West, 26 May 2016.

37 Mommen, 'Een Vlaams sprookje'.

38 Interview with Ludwig Verduyn, Brussels, May 2015.

39 Verduyn, *Het KBLux dossier*, p. 120.

40 Interview with Ludwig Verduyn, Brussels, May 2015.

41 Verduyn, *Het KBLux dossier*, p. 122.

42 According to Mommen, Almanij split its holdings into three pools. Pool 1 included Kredietbank (42.39%), which in turn controlled Credit General (63.26%), the Walloonian counterpart of the Flemish Kredietbank. Pool 2 focused on investment and contained Belgian companies such as Investco (64.64%), which was involved in venture capital and was directed by André Vlerick. Investco soon started providing finance not only to small businesses, the traditional clients of Kredietbank, but also to multinationals. Investco also placed money in a number of large US and Canadian multinationals in the 1950s, including Goodyear and Boeing. Pool 3 contained the international and merchant investment banking wing, centred around Kredietbank Luxembourg (49.22%), which in turn controlled the Kredietbank Suisse (81.66%), run by Vlerick's trusted adviser, Jean Blondeel.

43 'Almanij vertrouwt in financiële roeping'.

44 Verduyn, *Het KBLux dossier*, p. 124.

45 Ibid.

46 Mommen, 'Een Vlaams sprookje'.

47 Ibid.

48 Report by Ambassador WC Dempsey, 2 November 1982, DIRCO (Luxembourg, 4/2/103, Brussels, Luxembourg and Paris).
49 Ibid.
50 Ibid.
51 Verduyn, *Het KBLux dossier*, p. 11.
52 Ibid., p. 21.
53 Verduyn, *Het KBLux dossier*, p. 169.
54 Christopher Connelly, 'Apartheid rock, the Rolling Stones', *Rolling Stone*, 10 June 1982.
55 Report on Compagnie Financière de l'Union des Industries SA, February 1961, KADOC, Archief André Vlerick (Beheerder van maatschappijen, Kredietbank NV, 5.1.8, KBL Documentatie).
56 KBL 1974 Annual Report, 1974, KADOC, Archief André Vlerick (Beheerder van maatschappijen, Kredietbank NV, 5.1.7.5, Establishment of an office or branch of Kredietbank Luxembourg in the Far East, 1979).
57 'Belgische banken "steen in de muur van apartheid"', 6 June 1984, KADOC, Archief Walter de Bock (Centraal en Zuidelijk Afrika, Zuid-Afrika, 5.06, 1, 1981–1988).
58 Eva Militz, 'Bank loans to South Africa mid-1982 to end 1984', April 1985, World Council of Churches Programme to Combat Racism, World Council of Churches Archive.
59 'Belgische banken "steen in de muur van apartheid"'.
60 Ibid.
61 Ibid.
62 Militz, 'Bank loans to South Africa mid-1982 to end 1984'.
63 Clipping from *De Morgen*, 2 April 1988, KADOC, Archief Walter de Bock (Personen and Instellingen, Biographies, 1.64).
64 OFOR Revision Bancaire SA Report on Kredietbank (Suisse) SA and Their Revision of the 1981 Annual Accounts, June 1982, Federal Archives of Switzerland (E6521B#1991/210#943*, B.06/07, Kredietbank (Suisse) SA: Reglemente und Statuten, 1970–1984).
65 Ibid.
66 'In search of money morals', *De Standaard*, 18 January 1980, KADOC, Archief Walter de Bock (Centraal en Zuidelijk Afrika, Zuid-Afrika, 5.06, 1, 1981–1988).
67 Ibid.
68 'Generale zal leningen aan Zuid-Afrika niet stoppen', *De Standaard*, 13 January 1978, Open Secrets Collection.
69 Interview with Mark Pieth, Cape Town, October 2013.
70 See the Armaments Act, Government Gazette, Cape Town, 3 July 1968.
71 Application made by BSL/BSI against Armscor to the Lisbon Civil Court, 3 November 2008, Open Secrets Collection; and Expert Legal Opinion by Prof. Mark Pieth, 2 August 2007, Open Secrets Collection.
72 Armscor Trimester Report, 2 October 1980, DOD/SANDF (CSF, GP 3, Box 933, HSF 521/4/1/2, Krygkor, 1, 17/04/1979–28/02/1985).
73 Email correspondence from Ms Gertie Lindemans, Historical Archives, KBC Group, Brussels.
74 Follow-up Statements by 'A' (Daniel Loubser) and 'B' (Martin Steynberg)

– Loubser's comments, 1 October 2006, Open Secrets Collection.

75 Sworn Statement by Mr Martin Steynberg, 20 April 2001, Open Secrets Collection.

76 Supplementary Statement by Mr Martin Steynberg, 8 April 2006, Open Secrets Collection.

77 Ibid.

78 Sworn Statement by Mr Martin Steynberg, 20 April 2001, Open Secrets Collection.

79 Follow-up Statements by 'A' (Daniel Loubser) and 'B' (Martin Steynberg) – Steynberg's comments, 1 October 2006, Open Secrets Collection.

80 Follow-up Statements by 'A' (Daniel Loubser) and 'B' (Martin Steynberg) – Loubser's comments, 1 October 2006, Open Secrets Collection.

81 Supplementary Statement by Mr Martin Steynberg, 8 April 2006, Open Secrets Collection.

82 Follow-up Statements by 'A' (Daniel Loubser) and 'B' (Martin Steynberg) – Loubser's comments, 1 October 2006, Open Secrets Collection.

83 Ibid.

84 Signed Statement by Mr Tonie de Klerk, 2 February 1996, Open Secrets Collection.

85 Supplementary Statement by Mr Martin Steynberg, 8 April 2006, Open Secrets Collection.

86 Ibid.

87 Ibid.

88 Sworn Statement by Mr Martin Steynberg, 20 April 2001, Open Secrets Collection.

89 Ibid.

90 'Krygkor baas ná 11-jaar uit tuig', *Die Transvaler*, 12 May 1979.

91 'PW Botha gets top award', *Rand Daily Mail*, 6 November 1979.

92 LJ van der Westhuizen and JH le Roux, *Armscor: The Leading Edge*, unpublished, University of the Free State, Institute for Contemporary History, 1997.

93 Memorandum from CS OPS to CSADF, 20 July 1977, DOD/SANDF (DI: DBB, GP 22, 41, AMI/520/3/4, Oorseese Besoek, 09/11/87–07/01/88).

94 Letter from Armscor to CSADF, 1 November 1977, DOD/SANDF (CS OPS, GP 5, Box 134, CS OPS/311/1/ 11/1, Projek Pynappel, 1, 30/08/70–18/02/86).

95 'Arms: SA is "most advanced"', *The Star*, 22 November 1978.

96 Letter from PW Botha to LW Dekker, 1 June 1979, University of the Free State, Archive for Contemporary Affairs (PV 203, A1/2/2, 1979 July–October, PW Botha).

97 Letter from LW Dekker to PW Botha, 26 July 1979, University of the Free State, Archive for Contemporary Affairs (PV 203, A1/2/2, 1979 July–October, PW Botha).

98 The State Trust Board, Act 88 of 1979, *Government Gazette*, 19 June 1979.

99 Letter from LW Dekker to PW Botha, 26 July 1979, University of the Free State, Archive for Contemporary Affairs (PV 203, A1/2/2, 1979

July–October, PW Botha).

100 Note on Letter from LW Dekker to PW Botha, 26 July 1979, University of the Free State, Archive for Contemporary Affairs (PV 203, A1/2/2, 1979 July–October, PW Botha).

101 KBL had a representative there from at least 1978; their 1978 annual report lists KBL representative in Johannesburg as Jurie J Visagie, one of ten offices outside Luxembourg.

102 Telephone conversation, Leendert Dekker, August 2016.

103 Ibid.

104 Ibid.

105 Ibid.

106 Follow-up Statements by 'A' (Daniel Loubser) and 'B' (Martin Steynberg) – Steynberg's comments, 1 October 2006, Open Secrets Collection.

107 Supplementary Statement by Mr Martin Steynberg, 8 April 2006, Open Secrets Collection.

108 Sworn Statement by Mr Martin Steynberg, 20 April 2001, Open Secrets Collection.

109 Ibid.

110 Sworn Statement by Mr Nicolaas Palm, 14 May 1998, Open Secrets Collection.

111 Follow-up Statements by 'A' (Daniel Loubser) and 'B' (Martin Steynberg) – Loubser's comments, 1 October 2006, Open Secrets Collection.

112 Follow-up Statements by 'A' (Daniel Loubser) and 'B' (Martin Steynberg) – Steynberg's comments, 1 October 2006, Open Secrets Collection.

113 Follow-up Statements by 'A' (Daniel Loubser) and 'B' (Martin Steynberg) – Loubser's comments, 1 October 2006, Open Secrets Collection.

114 Supplementary Statement by Mr Martin Steynberg, 8 April 2006, Open Secrets Collection.

115 Follow-up Statements by 'A' (Daniel Loubser) and 'B' (Martin Steynberg) – Loubser's comments, 1 October 2006, Open Secrets Collection.

116 Ibid.

117 Supplementary Statement by Mr Martin Steynberg, 8 April 2006, Open Secrets Collection.

118 Ibid.

119 Follow-up Statements by 'A' (Daniel Loubser) and 'B' (Martin Steynberg) – Loubser's comments, 1 October 2006, Open Secrets Collection.

120 Sworn Affidavit by Mr Daniel Loubser, 23 March 1998, Open Secrets Collection.

121 Ibid.

122 Supplementary Statement by Mr Martin Steynberg, 8 April 2006, Open Secrets Collection.

123 Sworn Statement by Mr Martin Steynberg, 20 April 2001, Open Secrets Collection.

124 Supplementary Statement by Mr Martin Steynberg, 8 April 2006, Open Secrets Collection.

125 Ibid.

126 Follow-up Statements by 'A' (Daniel Loubser) and 'B' (Martin Steynberg) – Steynberg's comments, 1 October 2006, Open Secrets Collection.

127 Ibid.
128 Expert Witness Statement by Philippe Mortge, 30 May 2007, Open Secrets Collection.
129 Supplementary Statement by Mr Martin Steynberg, 8 April 2006, Open Secrets Collection.
130 Sworn Statement by Mr Martin Steynberg, 20 April 2001, Open Secrets Collection.
131 Follow-up Statements by 'A' (Daniel Loubser) and 'B' (Martin Steynberg) – Steynberg's comments, 1 October 2006, Open Secrets Collection.
132 Report by Ambassador WC Dempsey, 2 November 1982, DIRCO (Luxembourg, 4/2/103, Brussels, Luxembourg and Paris).
133 Follow-up Statements by 'A' (Daniel Loubser) and 'B' (Martin Steynberg) – Loubser's comments, 1 October 2006, Open Secrets Collection.
134 Follow-up Statements by 'A' (Daniel Loubser) and 'B' (Martin Steynberg) – Steynberg's comments, 1 October 2006, Open Secrets Collection.
135 Supplementary Statement by Mr Martin Steynberg, 8 April 2006, Open Secrets Collection.
136 Follow-up Statements by 'A' (Daniel Loubser) and 'B' (Martin Steynberg) – Steynberg's comments, 1 October 2006, Open Secrets Collection.
137 Paul Holden, Expert Opinion, April 2014.
138 Ibid.
139 Roberto Cicciomessere, 'Iraq Weapons: A bribe of state', Radio Radicale Italy, 30 October 1987.
140 Memorandum from Director of Foreign Relations to CSI, 2 March 1983, DOD/SANDF (DI, GP 31, Box 4, DBB/SK/311/1/30, Ops Zaire, 1, 08/01/1980–11/05/1983).
141 Export Invoice for Payment to Be Made to Kredietbank Luxembourg, 25 February 1984, DOD/SANDF (DI, GP 31, Box 4, DBB/SK 311/1/30 Gallery, Ops Zaire: Gallery, 3, 27/02/1984–18/01/1985).
142 Handwritten List of Weapons and Their Prices Signed by Col. Pretorius, 19 March 1984, DOD/SANDF (DI, GP 31, Box 4, DBB/SK 311/1/30 Gallery, Ops Zaire: Gallery, 3, 27/02/1984–18/01/1985).
143 Bank records indicating front companies and their purpose, n.d., Open Secrets Collection.
144 Armscor Board Meeting Agenda, 2 October 1980, DOD/SANDF (CSF, GP 3, Box 933, HSF 521/4/1/2, Krygkor, 1, 17/04/1979–28/02/1985).
145 Armscor Trimester Report, 7 October 1980, DOD/SANDF (CSF, GP 3, Box 933, HSF 521/4/1/2, Krygkor, 1, 17/04/1979–28/02/1985).
146 Ibid.
147 Announcement of Lockheed Corporation Bonding Facility Being Managed by KBL, 4 February 1978, KADOC, Archief Walter de Bock (Banken en Bedrijven, Banken, Bedrijven, Belgie, 2.20, 4).
148 Interview with Joop de Loor, Somerset West, 26 May 2016.
149 Expert Witness Statement by Philippe Mortge, 30 May 2007, Open Secrets Collection.
150 Ibid.
151 Ibid.
152 Ibid.

153 Ibid.

154 Expert Legal Opinion by Prof. Mark Pieth, 2 August 2007, Open Secrets Collection.

155 Ibid.

156 Ibid.

157 Ibid.

158 Expert Witness Statement by Mr Christian Weyer, 7 March 2007, Open Secrets Collection.

159 Ibid.

160 Philippe Vlerick, Executive Profile, Bloomberg.

Chapter 6

1 Attributed by Jean-Pierre Raffarin to Jacques Chirac when speaking to Silvio Berlusconi about the invasion of Iraq in 2003: 8pm News, TF1, 11 March 2007.

2 Dulcie Evonne September, *South African History Online*, www.sahistory.org.za/people/dulcie-evonne-september.

3 Letter from Commissioner of South African Police to the Secretary of Justice, Pretoria, 14 February 1969, as released to the South African History Archive by the South African National Archive in 2013.

4 Letter from the Magistrate of Wynberg, Cape Town, to Miss D.E. September, 19 December 1973, as released to the South African History Archive by the South African National Archive in 2013.

5 Sahra Ryklief, 'An inconvenient person: Remembering Dulcie September', *GroundUp*, 1 September 2016.

6 Dulcie September's Report on President's Visit to Paris, 20 June 1986, University of Fort Hare, ANC Archive (French Mission, Box 22, Folder 39, Report on the President's Visit to Paris, 1986).

7 September was adept in managing changing political circumstances. On one day she was organising opposition to loans by Swiss bankers to the apartheid regime; next she was in Swiss supermarkets loading a trolley of South African goods and then declining to purchase the wine, marmalade and Cape fruit. She was juggling the roles of organiser, activist, fundraiser and investigator. Regular protests were organised at the South African embassy and against visits to France by the likes of PW Botha. In response the South African ambassador wanted the French foreign minister to shut down the ANC's office.

8 Interview with Jacqueline Derens, Paris, 22 July 2013.

9 Telegram from Paris to Pretoria, 11 June 1982, DIRCO (France, 1/30/3, Vol. 14, 6/5/82–10/6/83, France Relations with SA).

10 Her notes also included reference to an Australian-based banking operation, Nugan Hand, allegedly a front for the CIA operating from Australia that was exposed in the early 1980s. In January 1985 she was investigating reports which had surfaced in the Danish media concerning the shipment of 2,000 tonnes of weapons from Bordeaux to Durban in 1981–2. Danish authorities were investigating the involvement of the vessel *Tinemaru*, which we believe was linked to Danish shipper Jørgen Jensen (see more detail in Chapter 7). Were these pieces of a puzzle that

she was assembling? At the time she was petitioning Mitterrand to reject the credentials of the South African ambassador and calling on the French government to enforce sanctions.

11 Dulcie September's handwritten notes for a speech to commemorate Walter Sisulu's 75th birthday, May 1987, University of the Witwatersrand, Historical Papers.

12 Records of Threats Made against ANC and Known Suspicious Incidents in Paris, 15 November 1985, University of Fort Hare, ANC Archive (French Mission, Box 6, Folder 114, Minister of External Relations Correspondence 1984–1992).

13 Ibid.

14 Telex from Dulcie September to Z Pallo Jordan, 8 February 1988, University of Fort Hare, ANC Archive (French Mission, Telexes, Box 65, Folder 7, Telexes, 8 January–30 June 1988).

15 Maggie Davey, 2009 Ruth First Lecture, 24 August 2009.

16 Dulcie Evonne September, *South African History Online*. In South Africa, MK attempted to hit back. A bomb was detonated at night, avoiding fatalities, outside a branch of the French Bank not far from the seat of parliament in Cape Town. MK operative Shirley Gunn, who helped lead the operation, concedes that the message was lost on the public. A camera-savvy cabinet minister arrived on the scene to claim to the media that given the proximity this should be read as a terrorist attack on parliament and by extension on white 'democracy'.

17 ANC Submission to the TRC, August 1996, www.justice.gov.za/trc/hrvtrans/submit/anctruth.htm.

18 Interview with Craig Williamson, Johannesburg, 29 January 2016.

19 His tenure in Paris, just short of three years, was a period of what seems to have been purposely missed opportunities. One example of this was a plaintive letter from a number of trade union and solidarity organisations sent to ANC President Oliver Tambo in July 1988. It detailed attempts to inject energy into solidarity actions with the ANC, which were met with tacit rejection by Smith.

20 Clipping from *Le Monde*, 6 April 1988, University of Fort Hare, ANC Archive (French Mission, Box 18, Folder 32, Assassination of Dulcie September, Newspaper Clippings/Cuttings 1988 French Language).

21 Robin Renwick, *Mission to South Africa: Diary of a Revolution*, Jonathan Ball Publishers, Johannesburg, 2015, p. 75.

22 Report on Murder of Dulcie September, TRC Investigation, n.d., as provided by Department of Justice and Constitutional Development, 28 July 2016.

23 Truth and Reconciliation Commission of South Africa Report, vol. 2, 29 October 1998, pp. 119–121.

24 Ibid.

25 Interview with Jan-Åke Kjellberg, electronic, 5 May 2015.

26 Ibid.

27 Interview with source (military) 2015/2016.

28 Ibid.

29 Ibid.

30 Ibid.
31 Ibid.
32 Interview with Craig Williamson, Johannesburg, 29 January 2016.
33 Interview with source (military), 2015/2016.
34 Interview with Vic McPherson, Cape Town, 15 February 2016.
35 Ibid.
36 Interview with Craig Williamson, Johannesburg, 29 January 2016.
37 Interview with Breyten Breytenbach, Cape Town, 10 February 2016.
38 *Special Investigation*, Dulcie September, Canal +, April 2011, www.youtube.com/watch?v=9XAWQckoF2A.
39 Ibid.
40 Interview with Vic McPherson, Pretoria, 20 May 2016.
41 Stephan Hofstatter, Mzilikazi waAfrika, Piet Rampedi and André Jurgens, 'Exposed: How arms dealer Thales bankrolled Zuma', *Sunday Times*, 28 September 2014.
42 Ibid.
43 Ibid.
44 Ibid.
45 Jacques Chirac, *Life in Politics*, Palgrave Macmillan, London, 2013, pp. 213–14.
46 Ibid.
47 'Paris – Ambassade Afrique du Sud – Oeuf Centre d'Etudes', www.astudejaoublie.blogspot.co.za/2013/10/paris-ambassade-afrique-du-sud-loeuf.html.
48 Interview with Abdul Minty, Pretoria, 24 June 2016.
49 Interview with Glenn Babb, Cape Town, 16 September 2014.
50 LJ van der Westhuizen and JH le Roux, *Armscor: The Leading Edge*, unpublished, University of the Free State, Institute for Contemporary History, 1997, p. 237.
51 Ibid., p. 239.
52 Report by CS OPS, 20 July 1977, DOD/SANDF (DI: DBB, GP 22, 41, AMI/520/3/4, Oorseese Besoek, 09/11/87–07/01/88).
53 Van der Westhuizen and Le Roux, *Armscor*, pp. 239–240.
54 Memorandum from Manager of Personnel Administration, Armscor, to DG Foreign Affairs, 22 October 1985, DIRCO (Paris, 4/2/7, Vol. 9, Brussels, Luxembourg and Paris).
55 Ibid.
56 'Transcript of comments by Dr Marc Burger on South Africa's relations with France', diplomatic memoirs *From Verwoerd to Mandela: A trilogy*, original contributions, 2011, Stellenbosch University Library and Information Service/JS Gericke Library Africana.
57 Documents on Appointment of Mr Mark Allen Verwey of Armscor to Paris, 17 September 1985, DIRCO (Paris, 4/2/7, Vol. 9, Brussels, Luxembourg and Paris).
58 Ibid.
59 Memorandum to DG DFA, 11 September 1981, DIRCO (Foreign Representation, 4/2/7/3, Vol. 2, 12/9/68–6/1/83, Paris Military Attaché).

60 Documents on Appointment of Trevor Gerald Shaefer of Armscor to Paris, 15 September 1986, DIRCO (Paris, 4/2/7, Vol. 9, Brussels, Luxembourg and Paris).

61 Messages from Paris Ambassador to Van Niekerk, 24 June 1981, DIRCO (Foreign Representation, 4/2/7/3, Vol. 2, 12/9/68–6/1/83, Paris Military Attaché).

62 Each one of the forms uses standard wording to describe the suitability of the Armscor officials. For example, Mark Verwey, who was to be transferred in 1985 and is thought to still work at Armscor as a senior manager, is described as follows: 'he has proved himself to be a person upon which we can rely. He has the ability to adapt to foreign environments, to get along with others, and acquiesce to discipline.'

63 Budget for DI Operations in Paris, 1989/1990, 29 January 1988, DOD/ SANDF (DI, GP 25, Box 128, AMI 504/3/1 (89/90), Begroting 89/90, 2, 29/01/1988–02/02/1988).

64 'Transcript of comments by Dr Marc Burger on South Africa's relations with France', diplomatic memoirs *From Verwoerd to Mandela*.

65 Charles de Gaulle, in *La France et son armée*, 1938, as quoted in www. wikiquote.org/wiki/Charles_de_Gaulle.

66 Itinerary of PW Botha's Visit to Thomson-CSF in France, June 1969, University of the Free State, Archive for Contemporary Affairs (PV 203, 1/W1/4, 1969 June, PW Botha).

67 Ibid.

68 Ibid.

69 Letter from G Cauvin (Thomson-CSF) to PW Botha, 28 June 1976, University of the Free State, Archive for Contemporary Affairs (PV 203, MV 1/4/82, 1976 June–1976 July, PW Botha).

70 In the folklore of Afrikanerdom, the arrival of 200 Huguenots from France and Wallonia in 1688 remains powerful. In the first half of the 20th century both black and white South African soldiers lost their lives in liberating France and other parts of Europe in two world wars. Importantly, France was one of the few powers that openly supported the Boer side during the South African War against the combined forces of the British empire.

71 Victor Moukambi, 'Relations between the South African Defence Force and France, 1960–1990' (DPhil, University of Stellenbosch, 2008), p. 19.

72 Report on the Operation of the Mandatory United Nations Arms Embargo against South Africa, 28 July 1988, Oxford University, Anti-Apartheid Movement Archive (MSS AAM 1550, O.4.4, Military and Nuclear Collaboration, Background papers on the arms embargo and South African militarisation, 1970s–1990s).

73 MA dissertation by Dominique Hudson at the University of Southampton, 1989, University of Fort Hare, ANC Archive (French Mission, IV, Box 57, Folder 106, Dissertation – French Policies by Dominique Hudson, 1989).

74 Moukambi, 'Relations between the South African Defence Force and France', p. 88.

75 Van der Westhuizen and Le Roux, *Armscor*, pp. 208–209.

76 Interview with PW Botha, cited in ibid., p. 210.
77 Interview with HJ Samuels, cited in ibid., p. 210.
78 Interview with Stephen Ellis, Cape Town, 9 October 2013.
79 Interview with Glenn Babb, Cape Town, 16 September 2014.
80 Interview with Pierre Steyn, Pretoria, 11 November 2015.
81 Moukambi, 'Relations between the South African Defence Force and France', p. 110.
82 Ibid., p. 112.
83 Ibid., p. 113.
84 Van der Westhuizen and Le Roux, *Armscor*, p. 230.
85 Letter from Alain Gomez to DW Steyn, 10 February 1987, DW Steyn Private Papers.
86 Janice McCormick and Nan Stone, 'From national champion to global competitor: An interview with Thomson's Alain Gomez', *Harvard Business Review* (May–June 1990).
87 Report from CSADF to CSI, 17 August 1988, DOD/SANDF (DI, GP 24, Box 284, AMI 520/3/4/18, Besoeke, bewegings, persone, vliegtuie. Besoeke aan die buiteland. SAW Krygor personeel: Chile, 10, 10/08/1988–25/10/1988).
88 Interview with Fritz Louw, 8 September 2005, as cited in Hennie van Vuuren, 'Apartheid grand corruption', Institute for Security Studies, 2006.
89 Ibid.
90 Moukambi, 'Relations between the South African Defence Force and France', p. 110.
91 Ibid., p. 114.
92 Interview with anonymous ex-Armscor official, 2015.
93 Moukambi, 'Relations between the South African Defence Force and France', p. 118.
94 Ibid., p. 124.
95 Ibid., p. 126.
96 Ibid., p. 156.
97 Ibid., p. 156.
98 Ibid., p. 130.
99 Van der Westhuizen and Le Roux, *Armscor*, pp. 233–234.
100 Moukambi, 'Relations between the South African Defence Force and France', p. 132.
101 Letter from Piet Koornhof to Olivier Giscard d'Estaing, 8 December 1977, University of the Free State, Archive for Contemporary Affairs (PV 476, PK1/7/1/2, 1975–1977, Piet Koornhof).
102 Report by CS OPS, 20 July 1977, DOD/SANDF (DI: DBB, GP 22, 41, AMI/520/3/4, Oorseese Besoek, 09/11/87–07/01/88).
103 Ibid.
104 Ibid.
105 Debevoise and Plimpton LLP, Ferrostaal Final Report, Compliance Investigation, 13 April 2011.
106 Memorandum from CS OPS to CSADF, 20 July 1977, DOD/SANDF (DI: DBB, GP 22, 41, AMI/520/3/4, Oorseese Besoek, 09/11/87–07/01/88).

107 Correspondence by Director of Financial Administration on Daphne
     Submarines, 18 March 1980, DOD/SANDF (CSF, GP 3, Box 936,
     505/5/3/8/5/1, Kontrak: Aankoop Franse Duikbote, 1, 31/01/1974–
     14/07/1987).
108 Documents with Costs for Simonstown Submarine Base and Aircraft
     Parts, 1977, University of the Free State, Archive for Contemporary
     Affairs (PV 203, 1/W1/9, 1977–1982, PW Botha).
109 They were of course not alone as the cost charged to South Africa for a
     valve head for a fuel system, supplied by British company Plessey, also
     increased by 4,800% in one year.
110 Interview with Chris Thirion, Pretoria, 11 December 2015.
111 Ibid.
112 Minutes of Cabinet Meeting, 12 May 1981, University of the Free State,
     Archive for Contemporary Affairs (PV 203, K/S 8, 1981, PW Botha).
113 Minutes of Cabinet Meeting, 26 May 1981, University of the Free State,
     Archive for Contemporary Affairs (PV 203, K/S 8, 1981, PW Botha).
114 Letter from Dr Etienne Rousseau, Chairman of Federale Volksbeleggings
     Beperk, to RF Botha, MFA, 15 June 1981, DIRCO (France, 1/30/3, Vol.
     13, 16/6/81–28/4/82, France Relations with SA).
115 Ibid.
116 Ibid.
117 Letter from Basil Landau to Piet Koornhof, 24 September 1982,
     University of the Free State, Archive for Contemporary Affairs (PV 476,
     5/1/15, 1982, Piet Koornhof).
118 Letter from Paris Embassy to DG DFA, 13 July 1981, DIRCO (Guests
     of the Government, 22/3/48, Vol. 6, 24/10/80–30/9/83, Minister
     Horwood).
119 MA dissertation by Dominique Hudson at the University of
     Southampton, 1989, p. 34.
120 Ibid.
121 Ibid., p. 44.
122 Ibid., p. 128.
123 Bruce Stephenson, 'Not one rifle for SA, says France', *Rand Daily Mail*,
     24 August 1981, in DIRCO (France, 1/30/3, Vol. 13, 16/6/81–28/4/82,
     France Relations with SA).
124 Report from CSAAF to MA Paris, 14 May 1985, DOD/SANDF (DI,
     GP 13, Box 63, 520/3/4/3/1, Besoeke aan die Buiteland: Farnborough, 1,
     09/06/77–27/09/84).
125 Report for CSADF, 7 May 1985, DOD/SANDF (DI, GP 13, Box 63,
     520/3/4/3/1, Besoeke aan die Buiteland: Farnborough, 1, 09/06/77–
     27/09/84).
126 Minutes of Meeting between Aerospatiale and Armscor, 16 April 1986,
     Open Secrets Collection.
127 Ibid.
128 Ibid.
129 Ibid.
130 'Western Europe: Government Policies Toward South Africa', CIA
     Directorate of Intelligence Report, 31 July 1986, available at cia.gov.

131 Correspondence from CSAAF to CSADF and CSI, 30 August 1988, DOD/SANDF (Verslae, Box 280, AMI/520/3/4, Visits: Overseas SAW Krygkor pers, 56, 19/08/88–07/09/88).

132 See www.wikiqiuote.org/wiki/Charles_de _Gaulle.

133 Douglas Porch, *The French Secret Services: From the Dreyfus Affair to the Gulf War*, Oxford University Press, Oxford, 1997, p. 451.

134 Memorandum from CSI to CSADF, 18 August 1988, DOD/SANDF (Verslae, Box 280, AMI/520/3/4, Visits: Overseas SAW Krygkor pers, 56, 19/08/88–07/09/88).

135 Memorandum from Director of Covert Intelligence to Director of Finance, 2 February 1988, DOD/SANDF (DI, GP 25, Box 128, AMI 504/3/1 (89/90), Begroting 89/90, 2, 29/01/1988–02/02/1988).

136 In February 2016 I spoke briefly with author Breyten Breytenbach, a French and South African citizen who spent many years in exile in Paris, about his view of the role of French intelligence. Breytenbach suggested that the French intelligence relationship with South Africa was by no means unvarying. According to Craig Williamson, Breytenbach's arrest in South Africa may in fact have been the result of a tip-off from French intelligence. However, Breytenbach points out that when arriving by plane in France after his imprisonment, the pilot asked the other passengers to remain seated to allow a DGSE official on board, who kissed him on both cheeks and welcomed him to France. He does go on to say that there was a history of collaboration, giving the example of his brother Jan Breytenbach, a commander in the SADF's feared 32 Battalion. He recounts that he bumped into his brother in Paris in the 1980s in the company of an unidentified woman who he thought might be his brother's lover. It turned out that Jan was in Paris on secret military business and the woman was an agent as well. They subsequently got drunk at his flat and his brother said: 'Come, call the police, I'm on your turf now.' Both recognised the unlikelihood of any state sanction from French authorities.

137 Report from Director of Special Tasks to CSI, 8 April 1980, DOD/SANDF (DI Directorate Foreign Relations, GP 38, Box 80, DBB/SK/311/1/11, Hulpverlening en Samewerking met Frankryk, 2, 01/04/1980–03/07/1995).

138 Ibid.

139 Ibid.

140 Memorandum from Director of Foreign Relations to CSI, 9 July 1984, DOD/SANDF (DI Directorate Foreign Relations, GP 38, Box 177, DBB/SK/311/6/3, Burgerlike instansies individue, 2, 13/06/1984–28/01/1986).

141 Ibid.

142 An indication of the close relations between France, South Africa and UNITA is an urgent message from Savimbi to French Admiral La Coste, who headed the renamed foreign secret service, the DGSE. The message was transmitted from Angola via Pretoria and the South African embassy in Paris, to the French spy chief. The message read: 'Unita is prepared to undertake negotiations for the exchange of Czech citizens captured in Angola for, amongst others, the [release] of French doctors who are being

held in Afghanistan.' The Angolan rebels were looking to trade favours in a complex game of geopolitics involving at least five countries in three continents.

143 Eddie Koch and Mungo Soggot, 'Oelschig's role in Bisho probed', *Mail & Guardian*, 16 September 1996. General Marius Oelschig is today a budding self-published writer living in the small town of Okotoks in Alberta, Canada. One of his recent books is a tale that proffers advice to children on how to deal with bullies.

144 Report on Meeting between DGSE and CSADF, 21 July 1987, DOD/ SANDF (DI Onder-Afdeling Inligting Operasies, Gp 26, Box 13, AMI/IO/311/1/69, Hulpverlening en samewerking met Ivoorkus, 1, 04/08/86–18/05/90).

145 Ibid.

146 Ibid.

147 Ibid.

148 Stephen Smith and Antoine Glaser, *Ces Messieurs Afrique: Le Paris-Village du Continent Noir*, Calmann-Lévy, Paris, 1992.

149 Smith and Glaser, *Ces messieurs Afrique*.

150 Email correspondence between Professor Stephen Smith and Hennie van Vuuren, 14 October 2015.

151 Memorandum from 'Lily' to 'Voyager', 14 March 1989, DOD/ SANDF (DI Onder-Afdeling Inligting Operasies, GP 26, Box 13, AMI/IO/311/1/11, Hulpverlening en samewerking met Frankryk, 3, 12/09/88–22/08/89).

152 Ibid.

153 Smith and Glaser, *Ces Messieurs Afrique*, p. 227.

154 Ibid., p. 229.

155 Ibid., p. 229.

156 Ibid., p. 230.

157 Ibid.

158 Documents on Appointment of Mr Mark Allen Verwey of Armscor to Paris, 17 September 1985, DIRCO (Paris, 4/2/7, Vol. 9, Brussels, Luxembourg and Paris).

159 The party was renamed in 2002 the UMP, which supported the election of both Jacques Chirac and Nicolas Sarkozy as French presidents between 2002 and 2012.

160 Smith and Glaser, *Ces messieurs Afrique*, pp. 230–231.

161 Extract from *Le Canard Enchaîné*, 6 April 1988, University of Fort Hare, ANC Archive (French Mission, Box 18, Folder 32, Assassination of Dulcie September, Newspaper Clippings/Cuttings 1988 French Language).

162 Smith and Glaser, *Ces Messieurs Afrique*.

163 *Indian Ocean Newsletter*, 9 July 1988, Maggie Davey Private Papers.

164 Jean-Yves Ollivier, *Ni vu ni connu*, Fayard, Paris, February 2014.

165 Smith and Glaser, *Ces Messieurs Afrique*.

166 Ibid., p. 223.

167 Ibid.

168 Ibid., p. 222.

169 'Congo: Missiles and clan warfare', *Africa Confidential*, 30 (1989).
170 Report on Meeting between DGSE and CSADF, 21 July 1987, DOD/
      SANDF (DI Onder-Afdeling Inligting Operasies, Gp 26, Box 13,
      AMI/IO/311/1/69, Hulpverlening en samewerking met Ivoorkus, 1,
      04/08/86–18/05/90).
171 Ibid.
172 Report on Meeting between CSADF and Mr Foccart, 22 July 1987,
      DOD/SANDF (DI Onder-Afdeling Inligting Operasies, Gp 26, Box 13,
      AMI/IO/311/1/69, Hulpverlening en samewerking met Ivoorkus, 1,
      04/08/86–18/05/90).
173 Smith and Glaser, *Ces Messieurs Afrique*.
174 Ibid.
175 Report on Meeting between CSADF and Mr Foccart, 22 July 1987,
      DOD/SANDF (DI Onder-Afdeling Inligting Operasies, Gp 26, Box 13,
      AMI/IO/311/1/69, Hulpverlening en samewerking met Ivoorkus, 1,
      04/08/86–18/05/90).
176 Porch, *The French Secret Services*, pp. 452–453.
177 Report on Meeting between CSADF and Mr Foccart, 22 July 1987,
      DOD/SANDF (DI Onder-Afdeling Inligting Operasies, Gp 26, Box 13,
      AMI/IO/311/1/69, Hulpverlening en samewerking met Ivoorkus, 1,
      04/08/86–18/05/90).
178 Report on Meeting between CSADF and Mr Roussin and Mr Ollivier,
      22 July 1987, DOD/SANDF (DI Onder-Afdeling Inligting Operasies,
      Gp 26, Box 13, AMI/IO/311/1/69, Hulpverlening en samewerking met
      Ivoorkus, 1, 04/08/86–18/05/90).
179 Ibid.
180 Ibid.
181 Ibid.
182 Report on Meeting between Director Intelligence Operations and Mr
      Roussin, 24 July 1987, DOD/SANDF (DI Onder-Afdeling Inligting
      Operasies, Gp 26, Box 13, AMI/IO/311/1/69, Hulpverlening en
      samewerking met Ivoorkus, 1, 04/08/86–18/05/90).
183 Smith and Glaser, *Ces messieurs Afrique*.
184 See www.plotforpeace.com.
185 Report on Meeting between Director Intelligence Operations and Mr
      Roussin, 24 July 1987, DOD/SANDF (DI Onder-Afdeling Inligting
      Operasies, Gp 26, Box 13, AMI/IO/311/1/69, Hulpverlening en
      samewerking met Ivoorkus, 1, 04/08/86–18/05/90).
186 Report on Meeting between Director Intelligence Operations and Mr
      Roussin, 24 July 1987, DOD/SANDF (DI Onder-Afdeling Inligting
      Operasies, Gp 26, Box 13, AMI/IO/311/1/69, Hulpverlening en
      samewerking met Ivoorkus, 1, 04/08/86–18/05/90).
187 Extract from *Le Canard Enchaîné*, 6 April 1988, University of Fort Hare,
      ANC Archive.
188 Itinerary of FW de Klerk's Visit to Europe, May 1990, University of the
      Free State, Archive for Contemporary Affairs (PV 734, B2 Vol. 24, 1990,
      FW de Klerk).
189 Memorandum from 'Snuffy' to 'Dreamer', 24 August 1988, DOD/

SANDF (DI Onder-Afdeling Inligting Operasies, GP 26, Box 13, AMI/IO/311/1/11, Hulpverlening en samewerking met Frankryk, 3, 12/09/88–22/08/89).

190   Ibid.

191   Correspondence from 'Lily' and 'Greedy' to DMI and CSADF, 29 March 1989, DOD/SANDF (DI Onder-Afdeling Inligting Operasies, GP 26, Box 13, AMI/IO/311/1, Hulpverlening en samewerking met lande en regerings, 2, 12/09/88–07/03/90).

192   Report on Meeting between Brigadier Oelschig and General Mermet, 21 June 1988, DOD/SANDF (DI Onder-Afdeling Inligting Operasies, GP 26, Box 13, AMI/IO/311/1/11, Hulpverlening en samewerking met Frankryk, 3, 12/09/88–22/08/89).

Chapter 7

1   Pieter-Dirk Uys, *PW Botha in His Own Words*, Penguin, Cape Town, 1987.

2   Interview with Armscor official (identity withheld at his request), June 2014.

3   Irina Filatova and Apollon Davidson, *The Hidden Thread: Russia and South Africa in the Soviet Era*, Jonathan Ball Publisher, Cape Town, 2013, p. 246.

4   Briefing Paper on Dr Igor S Glagolev, April 1980, United Kingdom National Archive (FCO 105/456, 1980, UK/SA Talks on the Communist Threat).

5   Report on Meeting between DGSE and CSADF, 23 July 1987, DOD/SANDF (DI Onder-Afdeling Inligting Operasies, Gp 26, Box 13, AMI/IO/311/1/69, Hulpverlening en samewerking met Ivoorkus, 1, 04/08/86–18/05/90).

6   Interview with Chris Thirion, Pretoria, 11 December 2015.

7   Ibid.

8   Ibid.

9   Knut Royce, 'Arms deal bilks Pretoria for $26M', *Newsday Washington*, 14 June 1987.

10   Jose de Coroba, 'A farewell to arms: How a mystery ship keeps making waves', *Wall Street Journal*, 9 March 1988.

11   Georges Starckmann, *Noir Canon*, Pierre Belfond, Paris, 1992.

12   Ibid.

13   Ibid.

14   LJ van der Westhuizen and JH le Roux, *Armscor: The Leading Edge*, unpublished, University of the Free State, Institute for Contemporary History, 1997.

15   Telegram from Ambassador to DFA, for Armscor, 24 June 1977, DIRCO (Defence, 9/56/8, Vol 2, 15/11/71–8/4/81, Defence Purchases).

16   Memorandum from Director of Foreign Relations to CSI, 4 May 1984, DOD/SANDF (DI Directorate Foreign Relations, GP 38, Box 129, DBB/SK/311/1/42, Hulp & Samewerking: Mauritius, 1, 15/02/1980–06/06/1980).

17   See www.ddr-wissen.de/wiki/ddr.pl?IMES_GmbH.

18 Starckmann, *Noir Canon*.
19 Ibid.
20 Der Bundesbeauftragte für die Unterlagen des Staatssicherheitsdienstes der ehemaligen Deutschen Demokratischen Republik. Danish Arms to SA, MfS HA III, 9549 (Stasi Archives, Berlin).
21 Ibid.
22 See www.stiften.dk/doedsfald/joergen-jensen-0#.
23 Der Bundesbeauftragte für die Unterlagen des Staatssicherheitsdienstes der ehemaligen Deutschen Demokratischen Republik. Danish Arms to SA, MfS HA III, 9549 (Stasi Archives, Berlin).
24 Starckmann, *Noir Canon*.
25 Ibid.
26 Ibid.
27 Ibid.
28 Ibid.
29 Ibid.
30 See Open Corporates database: www.opencorporates.com/companies/gg?q=TIT.
31 Starckmann, *Noir Canon*.
32 Ibid.
33 Ibid.
34 Ibid.
35 De Coroba, 'A farewell to arms'.
36 Starckmann, *Noir Canon*.
37 Ibid.
38 Ibid.
39 Ibid.
40 Ibid.
41 Royce, 'Arms deal bilks Pretoria for $26M'.
42 Ibid.
43 Ibid.
44 De Coroba, 'A farewell to arms'.
45 Ibid.
46 Ibid.
47 Memorandum from David Laux to Oliver North, 29 August 1986, George Washington University, National Security Archive, Iran–Contra Collection.
48 Van der Westhuizen and Le Roux, *Armscor*.
49 Theresa Papenfus, *Pik Botha and His Times*, Litera, Pretoria, 2010.
50 Ibid.
51 John Maré, Contribution to *From Verwoerd to Mandela*, Stellenbosch Library.
52 Letter from DW Steyn to PW Botha, 23 June 1988, University of the Free State, Archive for Contemporary Affairs (PV 203, PS 12/82/3, 1987–1988, PW Botha).
53 Ibid.
54 Ibid.
55 Landesverwaltung Fürstenturm Liechtenstein, Vaduz, Firmenindex. See

www.oera.li/webservices/HRG/HRG.asmx/getHRGHTML?chnr=0001
026604&amt=690&toBeModified=0&validOnly=11000&lang=&sort=0.

56 See www.en.wikipedia.org/wiki/Stasi.

57 Ibid.

58 Der Bundesbeauftragte für die Unterlagen des Staatssicherheitsdienstes
der ehemaligen Deutschen Demokratischen Republik, GDR-FRG Arms
Sanctions Busting, Deutrans, MfS-HA VI 8812 (Stasi Archives, Berlin).

59 Ibid.

60 Der Bundesbeauftragte für die Unterlagen des Staatssicherheitsdienstes
der ehemaligen Deutschen Demokratischen Republik, Austria Consul-
General Trade_Eastern Bloc, MfS HA XVIII 7468 (Stasi Archives,
Berlin).

61 Ibid.

62 Der Bundesbeauftragte für die Unterlagen des Staatssicherheitsdienstes
der ehemaligen Deutschen Demokratischen Republik, GDR SA Trade
Deals, MfS HA XVIII 13348 (Stasi Archives, Berlin).

63 Ibid.

64 Ibid.

65 Der Bundesbeauftragte für die Unterlagen des Staatssicherheitsdienstes
der ehemaligen Deutschen Demokratischen Republik Zimbabwe,
Computer Sanctions Busting_GDR, MfS HA XVIII 385 (Stasi Archives,
Berlin).

66 Ibid.

67 Der Bundesbeauftragte für die Unterlagen des Staatssicherheitsdienstes
der ehemaligen Deutschen Demokratischen Republik. Computer
Technology_FRG in Nambia_Hungary Oil, MfS HA VIII 9062 (Stasi
Archives, Berlin).

68 Ibid.

69 'Waffenhandel: Heiße Achse', *Der Spiegel*, 22 December 1980, www.
spiegel.de/spiegel/print/d-14338318.html.

70 'Todor Zhivkov, Bulgarian communist dictator dies at 86', *Washington
Post*, 7 August 1998.

71 'Waffenhandel: Heiße Achse', *Der Spiegel*, 22 December 1980

72 Ibid.

73 Stefaans Brümmer and Rehana Rossouw, 'Danish arms smuggler could be
charged', *Mail & Guardian*, 29 March 1996.

74 See www.fyens.dk/svendborg/Han-havde-haabet-at-gense-Sv.

75 Telegram from MANA Brussels to Armscor, 8 March 1977 (Defence,
9/56/8, Vol. 2, 15/11/71–8/4/81, Defence Purchases).

76 Letter from Kiril Shterev, Bulgarian Ambassador to the UK, to Robert
Hughes, 5 June 1984, Oxford University, Anti-Apartheid Movement
Archive (MSS AAM 1495, O.4, Military and Nuclear Collaboration,
Correspondence and Memoranda, 1982–1987).

77 Interview with Armscor official (identity withheld at his request), June
2014.

78 Ibid.

79 Interview with Tom Wheeler, Johannesburg, 23 February 2015.

80 Filatova and Davidson, *The Hidden Thread*, pp. 242–243.

81 David Pallister, Sarah Stewart and Ian Lepper, *South Africa Inc.: The Oppenheimer Empire*, Media House Publications, Johannesburg, 1987, pp. 102–103.
82 Filatova and Davidson, *The Hidden Thread*, p. 242.
83 Ibid., p. 459.
84 'Soviet Minerals to SA'. *Africa Confidential*, 28 (1987).
85 Ibid.
86 Ibid.
87 Pallister, Stewart and Lepper, *South Africa Inc.*, pp. 102–103.
88 Ibid.
89 Ibid.
90 Ibid.
91 Filatova and Davidson, *The Hidden Thread*, p. 242.
92 Ibid., p. 258.
93 CIA Archive, USSR–South Africa Trade CIA 1971, www.cia.gov.
94 Filatova and Davidson, *The Hidden Thread*, p. 242.
95 Marc Burger, *Not the Whole Truth*, Willem Albert Marc Burger, Johannesburg, 2013.
96 Ibid.
97 Vladimir Shubin and Marina Traikova, 'There is no threat from the Eastern bloc', in SADET, *The Road to Democracy in South Africa*, vol. 3, *International Solidarity*, Part 2, South African Democracy Education Trust, Johannesburg, 2008.
98 Ibid.
99 Ibid.
100 Filatova and Davidson, *The Hidden Thread*, p. 412.
101 Ibid.
102 Ibid., pp. 244–245.
103 Interview with Chris Thirion, Pretoria, 15 April 2016.
104 Handwritten notes by Magnus Malan, 1981, University of the Free State, Archive for Contemporary Affairs (PV 634, 5/1/1, 1989, Magnus Malan).
105 Interview with former Armscor official (identity withheld at his request), November 2015.
106 See https://en.wikipedia.org/wiki/Omsk.
107 Interview with former Armscor official (identity withheld at his request), November 2015.
108 Paul Holden and Hennie van Vuuren, *The Devil in the Detail: How the Arms Deal Changed Everything*, Jonathan Ball, Cape Town, 2011, p. 115.
109 Ibid.
110 Ibid.

Chapter 8

1 Ronald Reagan, Transcript of talk by Ronald Reagan on South Africa and apartheid, *New York Times*, 23 July 1986.
2 Pieter-Dirk Uys, *PW Botha in His Own Words*, Penguin, Cape Town, 1987.
3 Alan I Abramowitz and Jeffrey A Segal, *Senate Elections*, University of Michigan Press, Ann Arbor, 1992.

4 Minority Rights Group International, 'The Maya of Guatemala', Report 94/3, 1994.

5 Letter and Memorandum from Washington Ambassador to DG DFA, 7 November 1985, DIRCO (USA, 1/33/3/6, Vol. 1, 26/03/84–07/02/90, US Agents Acting on Behalf of SA Government).

6 Ibid.

7 Ibid.

8 The purpose of FARA is not only to monitor but to help regulate the activities of foreign lobbyists and their impact on US policy. It had been set up in the late 1930s to monitor the activities of the many pro-Nazi Germany lobbyists in the US.

9 Memorandum from Patrick Evans to DG DFA, 28 February 1986, DIRCO (USA, 1/33/3/6, Vol. 1, 26/03/84–07/02/90, US Agents Acting on Behalf of SA Government).

10 Letter and Memorandum from Washington Ambassador to DG DFA, 7 November 1985, DIRCO (USA, 1/33/3/6, Vol. 1, 26/03/84–07/02/90, US Agents Acting on Behalf of SA Government).

11 Letter from A Jaquet to Mr Becker, 30 January 1986, DIRCO (USA, 1/33/3/6, Vol. 1, 26/03/84–07/02/90, US Agents Acting on Behalf of SA Government).

12 Correspondence from Washington to Pretoria, 2 April 1986, DIRCO (USA, 1/33/3/6, Vol. 1, 26/03/84–07/02/90, US Agent Acting on Behalf of SA Government).

13 Letter from Washington Ambassador to DG DFA, 7 January 1986, DIRCO (USA, 1/33/3/6, Vol. 1, 24/12/79–26/4/84, US Lobbyists for RSA).

14 Letter from A Jaquet to Mr Becker, 30 January 1986, DIRCO (USA, 1/33/3/6, Vol. 1, 26/03/84–07/02/90, US Agents Acting on Behalf of SA Government).

15 Correspondence from Washington to Pretoria, 2 April 1986, DIRCO (USA, 1/33/3/6, Vol. 1, 26/03/84–07/02/90, US Agents Acting on Behalf of SA Government).

16 Correspondence marked Attention Burger, from Washington to Pretoria, 4 February 1986, DIRCO (USA, 1/33/3/6, Vol. 1, 26/03/84–07/02/90, US Agents Acting on Behalf of SA Government).

17 Correspondence from Washington to Pretoria, 25 March 1986, DIRCO (USA, 1/33/3/6, Vol. 1, 26/03/84–07/02/90, US Agents Acting on Behalf of SA Government).

18 Ibid.

19 Correspondence from Washington to Pretoria, 2 April 1986, DIRCO (USA, 1/33/3/6, Vol. 1, 26/03/84–07/02/90, US Agents Acting on Behalf of SA Government).

20 Correspondence from Pretoria to Washington, 19 February 1986, DIRCO (USA, 1/33/3/6, Vol. 1, 26/03/84–07/02/90, US Agents Acting on Behalf of SA Government).

21 Correspondence from Pretoria to Washington and Cape Town, 2 April 1986, DIRCO (USA, 1/33/3/6, Vol. 1, 26/03/84–07/02/90, US Agents Acting on Behalf of SA Government).

22 Telephonic interview with Richard Stone, USA, 15 May 2014.
23 Ibid.
24 Ibid.
25 Interview with Basil Hersov, Johannesburg, 9 December 2015.
26 Ibid.
27 Interview with Bertie Lubner, Johannesburg, 27 January 2016.
28 Ibid.
29 Sanford Ungar, 'South Africa's lobbyists', *New York Times*, 13 October 1985.
30 The journalist Sanford Ungar cites Eschel Rhoodie as the source of this information in his article, 'South Africa's lobbyists'.
31 Ibid.
32 James Adams, *The Unnatural Alliance: Israel and South Africa*, Quartet Books, London, 1984.
33 Letter from John McGoff to Jan Marais, 5 December 1974, University of the Free State, Archive for Contemporary Affairs (PV 476, 1/1/8/1, 1972–1983, Piet Koornhof).
34 Marais in turn forwarded the letter to Piet Koornhof, then minister of immigration. There is much to suggest that apartheid propaganda practices abroad were slowly starting to inform the National Party's practice in clandestinely subverting public opinion at home. Within a year of McGoff's letter the Department of Information had successfully established an English-language mouthpiece newspaper, *The Citizen*, which would later be exposed as a government front in the Information Scandal.
35 Letter from Herbert Beukes to The Hague, 17 April 1986, DIRCO (USA, 1/33/3/6, Vol. 1, 26/03/84–07/02/90, US Agents Acting on Behalf of SA Government).
36 These figures are drawn and collated from the reports of FARA to Congress in this time period; www.fara.org.
37 Ibid.
38 Interview with Tom Wheeler, Johannesburg, 23 February 2015.
39 Interview with Craig Williamson, Johannesburg, 29 January 2016.
40 See www.en.wikipedia.org/wiki/Larry_McDonald.
41 List of Consultants from Washington to Pretoria, 14 February 1987, DIRCO (USA, 1/33/3/6, Vol. 3, 01/12/85–26/03/90, US Agents Acting on Behalf of SA Government).
42 Ibid.
43 Correspondence from Washington to Pretoria, 21 November 1979, DIRCO (USA, 1/33/3/6, Vol. 1, 24/12/79–26/4/84, US Lobbyists for RSA).
44 Letter from Ambassador Donald Sole to George A Smathers, 1 April 1980, DIRCO (USA, 1/33/3/6, Vol. 1, 24/12/79–26/4/84, US Lobbyists for RSA).
45 Correspondence from Washington to Pretoria, 21 November 1979, DIRCO (USA, 1/33/3/6, Vol. 1, 24/12/79–26/4/84, US Lobbyists for RSA).
46 Memorandum from Head: Overseas Countries to DG DFA, 13 March

1981, DIRCO (USA, 1/33/3/6, Vol. 1, 24/12/79–26/4/84, US Lobbyists for RSA).

47 Correspondence from RF Botha to DG DFA, 11 February 1981, DIRCO (USA, 1/33/3/6, Vol. 1, 24/12/79–26/4/84, US Lobbyists for RSA).

48 Report from Smathers, Symington and Herlong to Ambassador Donald Sole, 10 November 1981, DIRCO (USA, 1/33/3/6, Vol. 1, 24/12/79–26/4/84, US Lobbyists for RSA).

49 Report by John P Sears Law Offices, 7 May 1986, DIRCO (USA, 1/33/3/6, Vol. 1, 26/03/84–07/02/90, US Agents Acting on Behalf of SA Government).

50 Correspondence from A Jaquet to Mr van Niekerk, 6 September 1985, DIRCO (USA, 1/33/3/6, Vol. 1, 02/05/84–30/11/85, US Lobbyists for RSA).

51 List of US Consultants Used, 20 August 1986, DIRCO (USA, 1/33/3/6, Vol. 1, 26/03/84–07/02/90, US Agents Acting on Behalf of SA Government).

52 Letter from Washington Ambassador to DG DFA, 10 July 1986, DIRCO (USA, 1/33/3/6, Vol. 1, 26/03/84–07/02/90, US Agents Acting on Behalf of SA Government).

53 Ron Nixon, *Selling Apartheid*, Jacana Media, Johannesburg, 2015, pp. 157–162.

54 Correspondence from DFA Department in the USA to DFA, January 1989, DIRCO (USA, 1/33/3/6, Vol. 1, 26/03/84–07/02/90, US Agents Acting on Behalf of SA Government).

55 Ibid.

56 Ibid.

57 Ibid.

58 Correspondence from Washington to Pretoria, 9 December 1985, DIRCO (USA, 1/33/3/6, Vol. 1, 26/03/84–07/02/90, US Agents Acting on Behalf of SA Government).

59 Letter from Washington Ambassador to DG DFA, 13 February 1986, DIRCO (USA, 1/33/3/6, Vol. 1, 26/03/84–07/02/90, US Agents Acting on Behalf of SA Government).

60 Ibid.

61 Ibid.

62 Ibid.

63 Correspondence from Adjunct Director Special Projects to DG Foreign Affairs, 6 January 1987, DIRCO (USA, 1/33/3/6, Vol. 1, 26/03/84–07/02/90, US Agents Acting on Behalf of SA Government).

64 Ibid.

65 Ibid.

66 Letter from Washington Ambassador to DG DFA, 10 July 1986, DIRCO (USA, 1/33/3/6, Vol. 1, 26/03/84–07/02/90, US Agents Acting on Behalf of SA Government).

67 Letter from South African Consul-General to Ambassador in Washington, 25 October 1985, DIRCO (Finance, 28/27/4/5/3, Vol. 1, 19/06/85–16/2/86, Disinvestment Campaign Counter Arguments – Lobbyists and Consultants).

68 Ibid.
69 See www.americanloons.blogspot.co.za/2015/04/1342-david-balsiger.
    html.
70 Report by National Citizens Action Network, 23 November 1988, DIRCO
    (USA, 1/33/3/6, Vol. 1, 26/03/84–07/02/90, US Agents Acting on).
71 Handwritten Letter from Steph Erasmus, DMI, 2 December 1988,
    DIRCO (USA, 1/33/3/6, Vol. 1, 26/03/84–07/02/90, US Agents Acting
    on)
72 Ibid.
73 Richard Leonard, *Apartheid Whitewash: South Africa Propaganda in the
    United States*, The Africa Fund, Washington DC, December 1988.
74 Report by National Citizens Action Network, 23 November 1988, DIRCO
    (USA, 1/33/3/6, Vol. 1, 26/03/84–07/02/90, US Agents Acting on).
75 Ibid.
76 Nixon, *Selling Apartheid*.
77 Ibid.
78 Ian Mayes, 'T-shirt test', *The Guardian*, 6 October 2001.
79 See www.espac.org/profile/profile.asp.
80 Invitation to an International Freedom Foundation Fringe Meeting at the
    UK Conservative Party Conference, 6 October 1992, Oxford University,
    Anti-Apartheid Movement Archive (MSS AAM 887, G4, Britain, British
    Organisations, International Freedom Foundation, 1988–1994).
81 Letter from Howard Phillips to Nico van Rensburg, 6 August
    1985, DIRCO (Finance, 28/27/4/5/3, Vol. 1, 19/06/85–16/2/86,
    Disinvestment Campaign Counter Arguments – Lobbyists and
    Consultants).
82 Ibid.
83 Emily Langer, 'Howard J Phillips, conservative activist and three-time
    presidential candidate, dies at 72', *Washington Post*, 24 April 2013.
84 Article by US Conservative Caucus Against Sanctions on South Africa,
    June 1985, DIRCO (Finance, 28/27/4/5/3, Vol. 1, 19/06/85–16/2/86,
    Disinvestment Campaign Counter Arguments – Lobbyists and
    Consultants).
85 Letter from Washington Embassy to Dr AWM Burger, DFA, 13 February
    1986, DIRCO (USA, 1/33/3/6, Vol. 1, 26/03/84–07/02/90, US Agents
    Acting on Behalf of SA Government).
86 Ibid.
87 Interview with Craig Williamson, Johannesburg, 29 January 2016.
88 President Trump's inaugural address, www.npr.org/2017/01/20/
    510629447/watch-live-president-trumps-inauguration-ceremony.
89 Ryan Lizza, 'Roger Stone versus the "deep state"', *New Yorker*, 20
    January 2017.
90 Ibid.
91 Jacob Weisberg, 'How Trump adviser Roger Stone became Washington's
    sleaziest political operator', www.slate.com, 20 January 2017.
92 Lizza, 'Roger Stone'.
93 Kenneth P Vogel, 'Paul Manafort's wild and lucrative Philippine
    adventure', *Politico*, 10 June 2016.

94 Jack Anderson and Dale van Atta, 'Mobutu in search of an image boost', *Washington Post*, 25 September 1989.

95 Robert Kolker, 'Paul Manafort is back', *Bloomberg Business Week*, 28 November 2016.

96 Nixon, *Selling Apartheid*, p. 181.

97 Ibid., p. 182.

98 Ibid.

99 David Smith, 'Trump chair Paul Manafort: "Mercenary" lobbyist and valuable asset', *The Guardian*, 31 May 2016.

100 Weisberg, 'How Trump adviser Roger Stone became Washington's sleaziest political operator'.

101 Eddie Koch, 'How SA agents offered Kemp a campaign jet', *Mail & Guardian*, 16 August 1996.

102 Ibid.

103 Ibid.

104 Interview with Craig Williamson, WhatsApp, 21 January 2017.

105 Dele Olojede, 'Papers show Kemp aide sought help from S. Africa', *Newsday* (Buffalo, NY), 23 July 1995.

106 Interview with Craig Williamson, WhatsApp, 21 January 2017.

107 Ibid.

108 See YouTube, 'Senator Daniel Inouye on the shadow government', www.youtube.com/watch?v=EbFphX5zb8w.

109 James Sanders, 'How the CIA trapped Mandela', *The Times*, 15 May 2016

110 Ibid.

111 Stephen Ellis, 'Africa and international corruption: The strange case of the Seychelles', *African Affairs*, 95, 379 (1996), p. 188.

112 Ibid.

113 Ibid.

114 Ibid.

115 Anthony Sampson, *Mandela: The Authorised Biography*, HarperCollins, London, 2000, p. 321 as quoted in James Sanders, *Apartheid's Friends: The Rise and Fall of South Africa's Secret Service*, John Murray, London, 2006.

116 Sanders, *Apartheid's Friends*.

117 Interview with Craig Williamson, Johannesburg, 29 January 2016.

118 Ibid.

119 Ibid.

120 Memorandum from Director of Foreign Relations on Discussion with 'Citric', 15 March 1983, DOD/SANDF (DI Directorate Foreign Relations, GP 38, Box 112, ST 311/1/29, Hulpverlening en Samewerking: VSA, 1, 21/09/1981–03/07/1995).

121 Ibid.

122 Ibid.

123 Ibid.

124 Ibid.

125 Correspondence from Director of Foreign Relations to Director of MI, 25 March 1983, DOD/SANDF (DI Directorate Foreign Relations, GP 38, Box 112, ST 311/1/29, Hulpverlening en Samewerking: VSA, 1, 21/09/1981–03/07/1995).

126 Memorandum from Portugal on Meeting with USA Assistant MA, 5 February 1988, DOD/SANDF (DI, GP 24, Box 133, MI/203/2/7, Eie Militêre Attachés, Portugal, 21, 07/05/1987–15/02/1988).
127 Budget for Visits to South Africa for 1988/1989, February 1988, DOD/SANDF (DI, GP 25, Box 128, AMI 504/3/1 (89/90), Begroting 89/90, 2, 29/01/1988–02/02/1988).
128 David Stout, 'Theodore Shackley, enigmatic CIA official, dies at 75', *New York Times*, 14 December 2002.
129 Ibid.
130 Memorandum from Director of Special Tasks on USA Interest in SA, 5 February 1982, DOD/SANDF (DI Directorate Foreign Relations, GP 38, Box 112, ST 311/1/29, Hulpverlening en Samewerking: VSA, 1, 21/09/1981–03/07/1995).
131 Ibid.
132 Ibid.
133 RT Naylor, *Patriots and Profiteers: On Economic Warfare, Embargo Busting and State-Sponsored Crime*, McClelland & Stewart, Toronto, 1999, p. 204.
134 Theodore Draper, *A Very Thin Line: The Iran–Contra Affairs*, Touchstone, New York, 1991.
135 Ibid.
136 Interview with Craig Williamson, Johannesburg, 29 January 2016.
137 Interview with Stephen Ellis, Cape Town, 9 October 2013.
138 Emerson produced a number of strident pieces of investigative journalism. However, from the mid-1990s his work started to lurch rightwards and by 2015 he was a commentator on Fox News making clearly Islamophobic statements. The publication of this book predates these events and it received good reviews, including by the *New York Times*, when first published in 1988.
139 Steven Emerson, *Secret Warriors*, GP Putnam & Sons, New York, 1988.
140 Ibid., p. 222.
141 See www.flysafair.co.za/about-us.
142 Michael Kranish, 'Oil may be key in Iran dealings: US probes role of Pretoria, Saudis', *Boston Globe*, 22 March 1987.
143 Ibid.
144 Jonathan Marshall, Peter Scott and Jane Hunter, *The Iran–Contra Connection: Secret Teams and Covert Operations in the Reagan Era*, South End Press, Boston, 1987, pp. 12–13.
145 Ibid.
146 Report of the Congressional Committees investigating the Iran–Contra affair, www.archive.org/stream/reportofcongress24unit/reportofcongress24unit_djvu.txt.
147 Alan A Block, 'The origins of Iran–Contra: Lessons from the Durrani Affair', *Crime Law and Social Change*, 2000, pp. 53–84.
148 Ibid.
149 Ibid.
150 'Two men arrested at Intercontinental Airport in May 1981', www.upi.com.

151 'Guns for Africa', *Financial Mail*, 12 June 1981.

152 Letter from PG Marais to Magnus Malan, 5 July 1982, DOD/ SANDF (MVV, GP 5, Box 88, 65/4, Krygkor: Beleid, 5, 24/03/1981– 08/07/1992).

153 DB Sole, Notes on the Meeting between Minister RF Botha and President R Reagan, DIRCO (as provided by Sizwe Mpofu-Walsh), 15 May 1981, Washington DC.

154 Ibid.

155 Ibid.

156 Ibid.

157 LJ van der Westhuizen and JH le Roux, *Armscor: The Leading Edge*, unpublished, University of the Free State, Institute for Contemporary History, 1997.

158 Ibid.

159 Research Report on Military Exports to South Africa by National Action/ Research on the Military-Industrial Complex, January 1984, Oxford University, Anti-Apartheid Movement Archive (MSS AAM 1512, O.4.3, Military and Nuclear Collaboration, General Files, Military Collaboration between the United States and South Africa, 1977–1984).

160 Armscor informed us that full details of contracts concluded before 1990 cannot be provided as these are stored on software which Armscor officials insist they no longer have the technical ability to access (given changes in computer technology).

161 Records released to SAHA in 2015 following a PAIA request submitted in 2013, in consultation with Open Secrets, ref: SAH2013_ARM0002.

162 See SIPRI Arms Transfers Database, www.sipri.org/databases/ armstransfers; and Research Report on Military Exports to South Africa by National Action/Research on the Military-Industrial Complex, January 1984, Oxford University, Anti-Apartheid Movement Archive (MSS AAM 1512, O.4.3, Military and Nuclear Collaboration, General Files, Military collaboration between the United States and South Africa, 1977–1984).

163 DB Sole, 'This Above All: Reminiscences of a South African Diplomat', 1989, University of the Free State, Archive for Contemporary Affairs (PV 862, DB Sole).

164 Message from MA Paris to Director of Special Tasks, 25 February 1981, DOD/SANDF (DI Directorate Foreign Relations, GP 38, Box 112, ST 311/1/29, Hulpverlening en Samewerking: VSA, 1, 21/09/1981– 03/07/1995).

165 Ibid.

166 Memorandum from Director of Foreign Relations to CSI, 14 May 1984, DOD/SANDF (DI Directorate Foreign Relations, GP 38, Box 177, DBB/SK/311/6/3, Burgerlike Instansies Individue, 2, 13/06/1984– 28/01/1986).

167 Ibid.

168 The *Washington Times*, less influential than the *Washington Post*, was the only other significant newspaper in the US capital at the time. The newspaper was owned by the Unification Church of the United States,

well known for its mass South Korean weddings and its ardent support for right-wing anti-communist causes.

169 See hwww.en.wikipedia.org/wiki/Mil_Mi-24.

170 Interview with Craig Williamson, Johannesburg, 29 January 2016.

171 Correspondence from CSAA to CSI and CSADF, 15 September 1982, DOD/SANDF (CS OPS, GP 3, Box 309, HS OPS/311 1/29, Hulpverlening en Samewerking met ander Lande/Regerings: VSA, 4, 27/08/82–02/05/85).

172 List of Weapons Desired by US Department of Defense, 9 August 1982, DOD/SANDF (CS OPS, GP 3, Box 309, HS OPS/311 1/29, Hulpverlening en Samewerking met ander Lande/Regerings: VSA, 4, 27/08/82–02/05/85).

173 Interview with Vic McPherson, Pretoria, 20 May 2016.

174 Ibid.

175 Ibid.

176 Telefax from JA de Kock to Armscor Security, 22 August 1989, DOD/SANDF (DI, GP 25, Box 138, AMI 520/3/4/2, Besoeke/Bewegings van persone, vliegtuie, vaartuie. Besoeke aan die Buiteland: SAW Krygkor lede VK, 10, 02/05/89–16/10/89).

177 See www.mide.com/pages/about-us.

178 Telefax from JA de Kock to Armscor Security, 22 August 1989, DOD/SANDF (DI, GP 25, Box 138, AMI 520/3/4/2, Besoeke/Bewegings van persone, vliegtuie, vaartuie. Besoeke aan die Buiteland: SAW Krygkor lede VK, 10, 02/05/89–16/10/89).

179 Martha Susanna van Wyk, 'The 1977 United States arms embargo against South Africa: Institution and implementation to 1997', University of Pretoria, 2005.

180 Ibid.

181 Ibid.

182 Ibid.

183 Ibid.

184 'Executive is sentenced in arms-sale scheme', *New York Times* Company News, 11 June 1992.

185 Edward Pound and Andy Pasztor, 'Shadowy trail: American arms dealer was amazing success, or so Ferranti believed – British concern paid millions for James Guerin's deals, but did contracts exist? The South African connection', *Wall Street Journal*, 23 January 1990.

186 Richard Knight, 'Inman raised the right issue, the news media; South Africa link', Letter to the *New York Times*, 28 January 1994.

187 Ibid.

188 Ibid.

189 James Bamford, *NSA: Die Anatomie des mächtigsten Geheimdienstes der Welt*, Bertelsman, Munich, 2001, p. 377 as cited in Peter Hug, *Mit der Apartheidregierung gegen den Kommunismus: Die militärischen, rüstungsindustriellen und nuklearen Beziehungen der Schweiz zu Südafrika und die Apartheid-Debatte der Uno, 1948–1994* (Final Report to the Swiss National Fund for the Advancement of Scientific Research, National Research Programme, NFP 42+, 'Relations Switzerland-South Africa', 2005), p. 558.

190 Ibid.
191 Van der Westhuizen and Le Roux, *Armscor*.
192 Mark Fazlollah, 'A Lancaster firm, the CIA and illegal arms deals', *Philadelphia Inquirer*, 13 September 1991.
193 Bamford, *NSA: Die Anatomie des mächtigsten Geheimdienstes der Welt*, p. 377.
194 Fazlollah, 'A Lancaster firm, the CIA and illegal arms deals'.
195 Ibid.
196 Clipping from the *Financial Times*, 24 May 1991, University of Fort Hare, ANC Archive (London Mission, Press Cuttings, Box 54, Folder 74, Missiles: USA, Israel, SA 1991).
197 Ibid.
198 Ibid.
199 Ibid.
200 Fazlollah, 'A Lancaster firm, the CIA and illegal arms deals'.
201 Letter from RJ Petersen, Armscor, to Director Counter-Intelligence, 22 March 1990, DOD/SANDF (DI, GP 25, Box 110, APD/W/311/5/1, Hulpverlening en samewerking met statutêre liggame: Krygkor, 6, 8/11/89–10/9/90).
202 Ibid.

Chapter 9

1 Susan Williams, *Who Killed Hammarskjold?: The UN, the Cold War and White Supremacy in Africa*, Oxford University Press, New York, 2014, p. 139.
2 Leo Amery was an active member in the pro-Empire 'Secret Society'. This unimaginatively named society was a covert network of Anglo-Saxon men led by the British high commissioner in South Africa, Alfred Milner, and based on the vision of another colonial reprobate, Cecil John Rhodes. Leo Amery's participation in conspiratorial enterprises and his abiding appreciation for the riches of South Africa would be passed on to his son Julian. See Robin Brown, *The Secret Society: Cecil John Rhodes's Plan for a New World Order*, Penguin Random House, Cape Town, 2015.
3 Steve Lohr, 'World class fraud: How BCCI pulled it off – a special report; At the end of a twisted trail, piggy bank for a favored few', *New York Times*, 12 August 1991.
4 Stephen Ellis, 'Africa and international corruption: The strange case of South Africa and Seychelles', *African Affairs*, 95, No. 379 (April 1996).
5 See Cindy Perman, 'This ex-undercover agent infiltrated Pablo Escobar's cartel as a money launderer', CNBC, 15 July 2016.
6 As recorded in a series of correspondence between Amery and BCCI, documents located in the Julian Amery Collection at the Winston Churchill Archives Centre, Cambridge University.
7 Macmillan, who had proclaimed that the 'winds of change' were sweeping through Africa, was also Amery's father-in-law.
8 Monday Club Newsletter, January 1972, Oxford University, Conservative Party Archive (Think Tanks, The Monday Club, Monday News, Pub 149/4, 1972).

9 Monday Club Pamphlet, July 1965, Oxford University, Conservative Party Archive (Think Tanks, The Monday Club, Pamphlets, Pub 117/11, 1965).

10 Monday Club Pamphlet, 1974, Oxford University, Conservative Party Archive (Think Tanks, The Monday Club, Pamphlets, Pub 117/38, 1974).

11 Letter from George Younger to Julian Amery, 28 April 1988, Cambridge University Archives, Julian Amery Collection, Correspondence, General Correspondence, AMEJ 2/1/146, 01/1988–09/1988.

12 Ibid.

13 Letter from US Embassy Oman to Julian Amery, 11 May 1988, Cambridge University Archives, Julian Amery Collection, Correspondence, General Correspondence, AMEJ 2/1/146, 01/1988–09/1988.

14 Ibid.

15 Ibid.

16 The association continued until at least 1991, when Oman hosted a meeting of the secretive Le Cercle group, then under Amery's chairmanship.

17 See www.theguardian.com/uk-news/2016/sep/08/britains-secret-wars-oman.

18 After leaving his post at Oman, Montgomery has worked as a lobbyist in the US law and lobbying firm of Baker Donelson (one of the notable former partners of the firm was Howard Baker). Montgomery, according to the firm's website, still undertakes work in the Middle East. See www.bakerdonelson.com/george-c-montgomery/.

19 Johannes Großmann, *Die Internationale der Konservativen: Transnationale Elitenzirkel und private Außenpolitik in Westeuropa seit 1945*, Oldenbourg Verlag, Munich, 2014, p. 552.

20 Letter from the South African Prime Minister's office to Julian Amery, 25 May 1978, Cambridge University Archives, Julian Amery Collection, Correspondence, General Correspondence, AMEJ 2/1/89, 05/1978–08/1978.

21 Monday Club Pamphlet, December 1983, Oxford University, Conservative Party Archive (Think Tanks, The Monday Club, Pamphlets, Pub 117/48, 1983).

22 Cambridge University Archives, Julian Amery Collection, Correspondence, General Correspondence, AMEJ 2/1/89, 05/1978–08/1978.

23 Letter from Magnus Malan to Julian Amery, 8 October 1989, Cambridge University Archives, Julian Amery Collection, Correspondence, General Correspondence, AMEJ 2/1/151, 06/1989–06/1990.

24 Letter from Julian Amery to Patrick Macnab, 31 May 1990, Cambridge University Archives, Julian Amery Collection, Correspondence, General Correspondence, AMEJ 2/1/151, 06/1989–06/1990.

25 Letter from Julian Amery to Harry Oppenheimer, 30 October 1981, Cambridge University Archives, Julian Amery Collection, Correspondence, General Correspondence, AMEJ 2/1/109, 11/1981–12/1981.

26 Report on Issues in Southern Africa by Julian Amery for Margaret Thatcher, 12 November 1981, Cambridge University Archives, Julian Amery Collection, Correspondence, General Correspondence, AMEJ 2/1/109, 11/1981–12/1981.

27 Julian Amery Diary Extracts from 6–17 January 1986, January 1986, Cambridge University Archives, Julian Amery Collection (Diaries, Diaries, Typescript diary, AMEJ 4/1/22, Jan 1986 Trip to South Africa).

28 Ibid.

29 Ibid.

30 Ibid.

31 Ibid.

32 Oppenheimer and Amery were on very friendly terms, frequently corresponding through handwritten notes; and Oppenheimer helped Amery to publish his 1,000-page tome of his father Leo's diaries.

33 Julian Amery Diary Extracts from 6–17 January 1986, January 1986, Cambridge University Archives, Julian Amery Collection (Diaries, Diaries, Typescript diary, AMEJ 4/1/22, Jan 1986 Trip to South Africa).

34 Ibid.

35 Ibid.

36 Ibid.

37 Ibid.

38 Julian Borger, 'The Conservative Party's uncomfortable relationship with Nelson Mandela', *The Guardian*, 6 December 2013.

39 Julian Amery Diary Extracts from 19–30 January 1987, January 1987, Cambridge University Archives, Julian Amery Collection (Diaries, Diaries, Typescript diary, AMEJ 4/1/22, Jan 1987 Trip to South Africa).

40 Ibid.

41 Ibid.

42 Ibid.

43 The Khan Committee – Advisory Committee on Special Projects, Third Interim Report, 4 November 1991.

44 Letter from Julian Amery to Frank Steele, 8 November 1991, Cambridge University Archives, Julian Amery Collection (Public and Political, General Political, AMEJ 1/10/55, Cercle).

45 Letter from AE van Niekerk to Julian Amery, 12 October 1992, Cambridge University Archives, Julian Amery Collection (Public and Political, General Political, AMEJ 1/10/56, Cercle).

46 Overview of Le Cercle by Julian Amery, 13 November 1991, Cambridge University Archives, Julian Amery Collection (Public and Political, General Political, AMEJ 1/10/53, Cercle).

47 Adrian Hänni, 'A global crusade against communism: The Cercle in the Second Cold War', in *Transnational Dimensions of Cold War Anticommunism: Actions, Networks, Transfers*, ed. Giles Scott-Smith, Luc van Dongen and Stephanie Roulin. Palgrave Macmillan Transnational History Series, New York, 2014, pp. 161–174.

48 Ibid.

49 Ibid.

50 Ibid.

51 Brian Crozier, Obituary, *The Telegraph*, 8 August 2012.
52 Brain Crozier, *Free Agent: The Unseen War 1941–1991*, Harper Collins, London, 1993, pp. 184–186.
53 Ibid., p. 183.
54 Brian Crozier, Obituary, *The Telegraph*, 8 August 2012.
55 According to David Teacher, the ISC was replicated in the United States with the establishment of the Washington Institute for the Study of Conflict (WISC), which relied on an important network of former high-ranking US intelligence agents and foreign policy wonks.
56 David Teacher, *Rogue Agents: The Cercle Pinay Complex: 1951–1991*, Second Revision, December 2008.
57 Ibid.
58 Großmann: *Die Internationale der Konservativen*, p. 494.
59 'A secret shield for the Lady', *The Times* (London), 28 June 1993, p. 12.
60 Hänni, 'A global crusade against communism', pp. 161–174.
61 The Mujahideen was represented in Le Cercle by Fatima Gailani, the daughter of Mujahideen leader Said Ahmed Gailani. See Hänni, 'A global crusade against communism'.
62 Ibid.
63 The German political foundations were particularly generous and hosted a total of seven Le Cercle meetings between 1977 and 1986. The funds were provided by two German political foundations with links to mother parties: the Konrad Adenauer Foundation (KAS), linked to Helmut Kohl's Christian Democratic Union (CDU); and the Hanns Seidel Foundation (HSS), close to his coalition partner Franz Josef Strauss's Christian Social Union (CSU).
64 Letter from Geneva Mission to Brand Fourie, DFA, 5 November 1974, DIRCO (The Cercle, 126/75, Vol. 1, 5/11/74–20/2/86, Secretive Global Policy Forum).
65 Letter from Geneva Mission to Brand Fourie, DFA, 17 December 1974, DIRCO (The Cercle, 126/75, Vol. 1, 5/11/74–20/2/86, Secretive Global Policy Forum).
66 Letter from J van Dalsen to HLT Taswell, 8 February 1974, DIRCO (The Cercle, 126/75, Vol. 1, 5/11/74–20/2/86, Secretive Global Policy Forum).
67 Letter from HLT Taswell to J van Dalen, DFA, 14 June 1977, DIRCO (The Cercle, 126/75, Vol. 1, 5/11/74–20/2/86, Secretive Global Policy Forum).
68 Letter from Geneva Mission to Brand Fourie, DFA, 17 December 1974, DIRCO (The Cercle, 126/75, Vol. 1, 5/11/74–20/2/86, Secretive Global Policy Forum).
69 Letter from DB Sole, Washington Ambassador, to Brand Fourie, DFA, 4 December 1978, DIRCO (The Cercle, 126/75, Vol. 1, 5/11/74–20/2/86, Secretive Global Policy Forum).
70 Programme and Participant List of Meeting of Pinay Group, 1978, 4 December 1978, DIRCO (The Cercle, 126/75, Vol. 1, 5/11/74–20/2/86, Secretive Global Policy Forum).
71 Bella was a member of the right-wing Catholic order Opus Dei, which

also had strong links to Franco's regime.

72 Telegram from Madrid Embassy to DG DFA, 2 December 1980, DIRCO (The Cercle, 126/75, Vol. 1, 5/11/74–20/2/86, Secretive Global Policy Forum).

73 Ibid.

74 Programme and Participants of Cercle Meeting in Munich, 13 July 1984, DIRCO (The Cercle, 126/75 Vol. 2, 7/6/83–3/4/85, Secretive Global Policy Forum).

75 Ibid.

76 DB Sole, 'This Above All: Reminiscences of a South African Diplomat', 1989, University of the Free State, Archive for Contemporary Affairs (PV 862, DB Sole).

77 Letter from Julian Amery to Richard Nixon, 10 May 1991, Cambridge University Archives, Julian Amery Collection (Correspondence, General Correspondence, AMEJ 2/1/154, 01/1991–12/1991).

78 Letter from Cape Town to Ambassador Van Dalsen, Paris, 18 May 1983, DIRCO (The Cercle, 126/75, Vol. 1, 5/11/74–0/2/86, Secretive Global Policy Forum).

79 Ibid.

80 Telegram from Paris to Pretoria, 3 January 1984, DIRCO (The Cercle, 126/75 Vol. 2, 7/6/83–23/4/85, Secretive Global Policy Forum).

81 Telegram from Paris to Pretoria, 25 June 1984, DIRCO (The Cercle, 126/75 Vol. 2, 7/6/83–23/4/85, Secretive Global Policy Forum).

82 Relly declined the invitation by Strauss due to short notice and the documentation sheds no light as to whether Hersov accepted the invitation, given the 10 days' notice.

83 Interview with Basil Hersov, Johannesburg, 9 December 2015.

84 List of Members of Le Cercle and Their Addresses, February 1992, Cambridge University Archives, Julian Amery Collection (Public and Political, General Political, AMEJ 1/10/53, Cercle).

85 Großmann: *Die Internationale der Konservativen*, p. 543.

86 Programme for Le Cercle Meeting in Somerset West, March 1991, Cambridge University Archives, Julian Amery Collection (Correspondence, General Correspondence, AMEJ 2/1/154, 01/1991–12/1991).

87 Ibid.

88 List of Participants at Le Cercle Meeting in Amman, May 1996, Cambridge University Archives, Julian Amery Collection (Public and Political, General Political, AMEJ 1/10/56, Cercle).

89 Notes on the Meetings between Oliver Tambo and British Businessmen, 24 October 1985, Oxford University, Anthony Sampson Collection (MS Sampson dep. 53, B.4, Meetings between ANC and Business Leaders, 1985–1987).

90 Andy McSmith, 'Margaret Thatcher branded ANC "terrorist" while urging Nelson Mandela's release', *The Independent*, 2014.

91 Interview with Pik Botha, Pretoria, 26 January 2016.

92 Report on Meeting between Margaret Thatcher and Pik Botha, 12 November 1980, United Kingdom National Archive (FCO 105/471,

1980, Ministerial Visits from SA to UK).

93   Report on Meeting between Lord Carrington (FCO) and Pik Botha, 12 November 1980, United Kingdom National Archive (FCO 105/471, 1980, Ministerial Visits from SA to UK).

94   Ibid.

95   Programme of Margaret Thatcher's Visit to SA, March 1973, United Kingdom National Archive (FCO 105/191, Possible Meetings Between PW Botha and Other Heads of Government).

96   Denis Thatcher's uncle in Durban was a businessmen and Denis Thatcher is said to have had extensive South African business interests. See Terry Bell and Dumisa Ntsebeza, *Unfinished Business: South Africa, Apartheid and Truth*, Verso, London, 2003.

97   Alan Travis, 'Margaret Thatcher made no case for Mandela's release', *The Guardian*, 3 January 2014.

98   Letter from BL Barder to Mr Aspin, 5 October 1979, United Kingdom National Archive (FCO 105/191, Possible Meetings Between PW Botha and Other Heads of Government).

99   The UK consulate in Cape Town was informed to take the line that, should Hunt's presence become public, attention should be drawn to Prudential's offices in Cape Town and Johannesburg where he had scheduled meetings, and that his meeting with Botha should be described as a 'courtesy call for an informal chat'. See ibid.

100   Correspondence from BL Barder to Mr Watkins, 11 March 1980, United Kingdom National Archive (FCO 105/455, 1980, UK/South Africa Talks on the Communist Threat).

101   Letter from Michael Alexander to George Walden, 31 March 1980, United Kingdom National Archive (FCO 105/455, 1980, UK/South Africa Talks on the Communist Threat).

102   Telegram from Cape Town Embassy to FCO, 10 April 1980, United Kingdom National Archive (FCO 105/456, 1980, UK/SA Talks on the Communist Threat).

103   Letter from PW Botha to Dr Jack Penn, 14 October 1983, University of the Free State, Archive for Contemporary Affairs (PV 203, A1/2/27, 1983, PW Botha).

104   Letter from Richard Dorman to Simon Hemans (FCO), 2 May 1980, United Kingdom National Archive (FCO 105/514, Diplomatic Bag Services to UK).

105   Borger, 'The Conservative Party's uncomfortable relationship with Nelson Mandela'.

106   Ibid.

107   Extract from Minutes of Meeting of the Ministerial Group on Southern Africa, 11 April 1978, United Kingdom National Archive (Defence, 1978, Possible Measures Against SA).

108   Extract and Annexes from Minutes of Meeting of the Ministerial Group on Southern Africa, 11 July 1978, United Kingdom National Archive (Defence, 1978, Possible Measures Against SA).

109   Ibid.

110   Ibid.

111 Letter from Mary Dickson (FCO) to RL Collins, 3 June 1980, United Kingdom National Archive (BT 241/3139, 3/1/80–6/8/80, South Africa Sanctions).

112 Correspondence from RL Collins to Mr Clarke, 2 January 1980, United Kingdom National Archive (BT 241/3139, 3/1/80–6/8/80, South Africa Sanctions).

113 Interview with Robin Renwick, Cape Town, 11 February 2015.

114 Telegram from the Consul-General Johannesburg to the Cape Town Embassy, 8 September 1981, United Kingdom National Archive (FCO 105/492, 1980, UK Economic Links with SA).

115 Ibid.

116 Note by the Bank of England on City Links with SA, January 1980, United Kingdom National Archive (FCO 105/492, 1980, UK Economic Links with SA).

117 It was renamed First National Bank. Barclays subsequently re-entered the South African market 20 years later to purchase ABSA, Africa's biggest bank.

118 Letter from John Browne to Piet Koornhof, 25 April 1986, University of the Free State, Archive for Contemporary Affairs (PV 476, P1/1/19, 1986, Piet Koornhof).

119 Ibid.

120 Notes on the Meetings between Oliver Tambo and British Businessmen, 24 October 1985, Oxford University, Anthony Sampson Collection (MS Sampson dep. 53, B.4, Meetings between ANC and Business Leaders, 1985–1987).

121 Ibid.

122 Special Report by SSC, 24 August 1983, DOD/SANDF (INSAM, Box 49, 10/83, Rio Tinto Zinc (RTZ): Verbintenis met SWAPO, 24/08/83).

123 Ibid.

124 Minutes of Meeting of the Cabinet Committee on Sanctions, 28 January 1987, University of the Free State, Archive for Contemporary Affairs (PV 734, K/S 49, 1986–1990, FW de Klerk).

125 Annexure to Minutes of Meeting of the Cabinet Committee on Sanctions, 20 May 1987, University of the Free State, Archive for Contemporary Affairs (PV 734, K/S 49, 1986–1990, FW de Klerk).

126 UK Anti-Apartheid Movement Submission to the South African Truth and Reconciliation Commission, 10 November 1997, Oxford University, Anti-Apartheid Movement Archive (AAM Archives Committee).

127 Hugh Purcell, *A Very Private Celebrity: The Nine Lives of John Freeman* (Biteback Publishing, London, 2015.

128 Interview with Vic McPherson, Pretoria, 19 May 2016.

129 Ibid.

130 Ibid.

131 Ibid.

132 Thomas Harding, 'Tory MP "tipped off MI5 about IRA meeting"', *The Telegraph*, 5 December 2002.

133 Interview with Andrew Hunter, Telephonic, 13 January 2017.

134 Ibid.

135 Ibid.

136 Ibid.

137 Interview with Vic McPherson, Pretoria, 19 May 2016.

138 Correspondence from MA London to CSADF, 18 May 1987, DOD/ SANDF (CSI/DI, GP 18, Box 3, 203/2/1, Insameling van Inligting. Eie MA: Verenigde Koningkryk, 23, 04/08/86).

139 Minutes of UK Cabinet Meeting, 27 October 1977, United Kingdom National Archive (CAB/128/62/12, 27/10/1977, Cabinet Meeting).

140 Brief on Possible Measures against SA for the UK Secretary of State for Defence, 11 April 1978, United Kingdom National Archive (Defence, 1978, Possible Measures Against SA).

141 Letter from John Gilbert to Ted Rowlands, 1978, United Kingdom National Archive (Defence, 1978, Possible Measures Against SA).

142 MOD Working Paper on the Arms Embargo against SA, 5 August 1977, United Kingdom National Archive (DEFE 68/205, Economic Links with Africa and SA Arms Embargo (MOD)).

143 Interview with General Pierre Steyn, Pretoria, 11 November 2015.

144 Notes on Meeting between Mr Jordaan (South African Embassy Paris) and the UK MOD, 27 April 1978, United Kingdom National Archive (Defence, 1978, Possible Measures Against SA).

145 LJ van der Westhuizen and JH le Roux, *Armscor: The Leading Edge*, unpubished, University of the Free State, Institute for Contemporary History, 1997, pp. 202–204.

146 James Sanders, *Apartheid's Friends: The Rise and Fall of South Africa's Secret Service*, John Murray, London, 2006, p. 172.

147 Correspondence from AD Sprake to DM Day, 30 September 1980, United Kingdom National Archive (BT 241/3138, South African Sanctions).

148 Interview with Armscor employee, name withheld, 2016.

149 Ibid.

150 Interview with Robin Renwick, Cape Town, 11 February 2015.

151 Ibid.

152 Correspondence from Jim Spicer to Ian Gow, 2 February 1981, United Kingdom National Archive (PREM 19/565, Cabinet Memos).

153 Correspondence from Michael Alexander to Francis Richards, 20 February 1981, United Kingdom National Archive (PREM 19/565, Cabinet Memos).

154 Correspondence from Roderic Lyne to Michael Alexander, 13 March 1981, United Kingdom National Archive (PREM 19/565, Cabinet Memos).

155 Correspondence from MA London to CSADF, 16 October 1986, DOD/ SANDF (CSI/DI, GP 18, Box 3, 203/2/1, Insameling van Inligting. Eie MA: Verenigde Koningkryk, 23, 04/08/86).

156 UK Anti-Apartheid Movement Submission to the South African Truth and Reconciliation Commission, 10 November 1997, Oxford University, Anti-Apartheid Movement Archive (AAM Archives Committee).

157 Letter from Coventry Four to Mr FJ Bell, Armscor, 4 June 1984, DOD/ SANDF (MVV, GP 5, Box 105, 65/4, Krygkor: Beleid, 8, 02/07/1984–

25/03/1985).

158 Letter from Magnus Malan to PW Botha, 18 July 1984, DOD/
     SANDF (MVV, GP 5, Box 105, 65/4, Krygkor: Beleid, 8, 02/07/1984–
     25/03/1985).

159 Van der Westhuizen and Le Roux, *Armscor*, pp. 203–204.

160 'Arms and the man', *Financial Mail*, 5 May 1989.

161 Ian Cobain, 'Northern Ireland shootings: One night of carnage, 18 years
     of silence', *The Guardian*, 15 October 2012.

162 'Arms and the man', *Financial Mail*, 5 May 1989.

163 Minutes of Cabinet Meeting, 3 May 1989, University of the Free State,
     Archive for Contemporary Affairs (PV 734, K/S 19, 1989 (vervolg), FW
     de Klerk).

164 James Adams, 'Loyalists may be victims of missile "sting"', *Sunday Times*
     (Johannesburg), 30 April 1989.

165 Fax from MA Santiago to Director of Military Intelligence, 25 May 1989,
     DOD/SANDF (DI, GP 24, Box 136, MI/203/2/12, Insameling van
     Inligting, Eie Militêre Attachés, Chile, 13, 17/02/1988–15/09/1989).

166 Ibid.

167 As told by Zambian Minister Vernon Mwaanga in Tom Bower, *Tiny
     Rowland: A Rebel Tycoon*, Mandarin, London, 1994, p. xiii.

168 Clipping from the *Financial Times*, 12 February 1987, Oxford University,
     Anti-Apartheid Movement Archive (MSS AAM 1645, O.6.1.d, Other
     Economic Campaigns, Companies, Lonrho plc, 1986–1987).

169 Bower, *Tiny Rowland*, p. xi.

170 Nick Davies, 'Tiny Rowland: Portrait of the bastard as a rebel', *The
     Guardian*, August 1990.

171 Bower, *Tiny Rowland*, p. 366.

172 Investigative journalism unit AmaBhungane has shown that hundreds
     of millions of dollars flowed to a company in tax-free Bermuda for
     'marketing fees'. This practice of 'transfer pricing' may not be outright
     illegal but in the words of an official at the South African Revenue
     Services, 'increasingly a lot of it is becoming morally reprehensible'. See
     Craig McKune, 'Questions Lonmin must answer', AmaBhungane, 16
     October 2014.

173 'Lonhro and the Tiny factor', *Africa Confidential*, 30, 2 (20 January 1989).

174 Bower, *Tiny Rowland*, p. 411.

175 'Lonhro and the Tiny factor'.

176 Bower, *Tiny Rowland*, p. 365.

177 Ibid., p. 364.

178 Gareth van Onselen, 'The ANC's own newspaper', *Business Day*, 2 April
     2014.

179 *Financial Mail*, 15 February 1985 (found in DOD/SADF archive).

180 Marquard, together with famed cardiologist Chris Barnard and
     industrialist Anton Rupert, was one of the only non-government officials
     listed as attending State President Nico Diederichs's inauguration
     reception at Fleur du Cap in 1975 as per the official programme for the
     event.

181 His son Etienne de Villiers was, at the time of writing, a prominent

Cape Town businessman and past president of Walt Disney Television International. He got his first big break by joining Sol Kerzner's business empire in the 1980s.

182 Bower, *Tiny Rowland*, p. 273.

183 *Financial Mail*, 15 February 1985 (found in DOD/SADF archive).

184 The document erroneously refers to Joseph Cisho. Searches could not trace any such official and it was likely a typo by the South African Military Intelligence official. This is confirmed by the fact that Joseph Sisco was US undersecretary of state in 1975.

185 Report on Meeting between Tiny Rowland and US State Department, 19 October 1975, DOD/SANDF (DI Directorate Foreign Relations, GP 38, Box 177, ST 311/10/1/2, Lonrho, 1, 30/10/1975–22/05/1980).

186 Ibid.

187 Ibid.

188 Memorandum from Director of MI to CSI, 24 February 1981, DOD/ SANDF (DI Directorate Foreign Relations, GP 38, Box 177, ST 311/10/1/2, Lonrho, 2, 23/01/1980–21/01/1982).

189 Ibid.

190 Transcription of a Tape Recording of Marquard de Villiers, 1975, DOD/SANDF (DI Directorate Foreign Relations, GP 38, Box 177, ST 311/10/1/2, Lonrho, 1, 30/10/1975–22/05/1980).

191 Memorandum on Meeting with Marquard de Villiers, 30 September 1978, DOD/SANDF (DI Directorate Foreign Relations, GP 38, Box 177, ST 311/10/1/2, Lonrho, 1, 30/10/1975–22/05/1980).

192 Memorandum from DBB to CSI, May 1984, DOD/SANDF (DI Directorate Foreign Relations, GP 38, Box 177, DBB/SK/311/10/1/2, Lohnro, 3, 22/02/82–14/05/85).

193 Memorandum on Liaison with Marquard de Villiers from Director of Special Tasks to Director of Covert Intelligence, 16 October 1981, DOD/SANDF (DI Directorate Foreign Relations, GP 38, Box 177, ST 311/10/1/2, Lonrho, 2, 23/01/1980–21/01/1982).

194 The massacre was aimed primarily at so-called dissidents aligned to Joshua Nkomo's Zimbabwe African People's Union (ZAPU). Rowland had backed and bankrolled Nkomo during the liberation struggle, but by the early 1980s had to make amends with his political foe Robert Mugabe in order to consolidate Lonrho's business position in a free Zimbabwe. See Bower, *Tiny Rowland*.

195 Memorandum on Liaison with Marquard de Villiers from Director of Special Tasks to Director of Covert Intelligence, 16 October 1981, DOD/SANDF (DI Directorate Foreign Relations, GP 38, Box 177, ST 311/10/1/2, Lonrho, 2, 23/01/1980–21/01/1982).

196 Donald Trelford, 'The patter of Tiny's feet', *The Guardian*, 12 March 2000.

197 Ibid.

198 Memorandum from DBB to CSI, 13 April 1984, DOD/SANDF (DI Directorate Foreign Relations, GP 38, Box 177, DBB/SK/311/10/1/2, Lohnro, 3, 22/02/82–14/05/85).

199 Handwritten Memorandum from CSI, 21 July 1982, DOD/SANDF (DI

Directorate Foreign Relations, GP 38, Box 177, DBB/SK/311/10/1/2, Lohnro, 3, 22/02/82–14/05/85).

200 Ibid.
201 Ibid.
202 Report of Meeting between Marquard de Villiers and General Van der Westhuizen, 5 October 1978, DOD/SANDF (DI Directorate Foreign Relations, GP 38, Box 177, ST 311/10/1/2, Lonrho, 1, 30/10/1975–22/05/1980).
203 Ibid.
204 Ibid.
205 Ibid.
206 Report from Director of Special Tasks to CSI, 8 April 1980, DOD/SANDF (DI Directorate Foreign Relations, GP 38, Box 80, DBB/SK/311/1/11, Hulpverlening en Samewerking met Frankryk, 2, 01/04/1980–03/07/1995).
207 Memorandum on Operation Silwer from CSI to CSADF, September 1980, DOD/SANDF (DI Directorate Foreign Relations, GP 38, Box 177, ST 311/10/1/2, Lonrho, 2, 23/01/1980–21/01/1982).
208 Request for Authorization to Transfer Funds to Britain, from CSADF to the SARB, 13 November 1980, DOD/SANDF (DI Directorate Foreign Relations, GP 38, Box 177, ST 311/10/1/2, Lonrho, 2, 23/01/1980–21/01/1982).
209 Memorandum on Talks with Tiny Rowland by Director of Special Tasks, 19 September 1980, DOD/SANDF (DI Directorate Foreign Relations, GP 38, Box 177, ST 311/10/1/2, Lonrho, 2, 23/01/1980–21/01/1982).
210 Ibid.
211 Ibid.
212 Ibid.
213 Memorandum on Liaison with Marquard de Villiers from Director of Special Tasks, 5 November 1980, DOD/SANDF (DI Directorate Foreign Relations, GP 38, Box 177, ST 311/10/1/2, Lonrho, 2, 23/01/1980–21/01/1982).
214 Memorandum on Liaison with Marquard de Villiers from Director of Special Tasks to CSI, 8 January 1981, DOD/SANDF (DI Directorate Foreign Relations, GP 38, Box 177, ST 311/10/1/2, Lonrho, 2, 23/01/1980–21/01/1982).
215 Memorandum on Liaison with Marquard de Villers from Director of Special Tasks to CSI and Neels van Tonder, 7 January 1982, DOD/SANDF (DI Directorate Foreign Relations, GP 38, Box 177, ST 311/10/1/2, Lonrho, 2, 23/01/1980–21/01/1982).
216 Memorandum on Liaison with Lonrho from Director of Special Tasks to CSI, January 1982, DOD/SANDF (DI Directorate Foreign Relations, GP 38, Box 177, ST 311/10/1/2, Lonrho, 2, 23/01/1980–21/01/1982).
217 Ibid.
218 Ibid.
219 Memorandum on Marquard de Villiers from Director of Special Tasks to CSI, 9 February 1982, DOD/SANDF (DI Directorate Foreign Relations, GP 38, Box 177, ST 311/10/1/2, Lonrho, 2, 23/01/1980–21/01/1982).

220 Ibid.
221 Ibid.
222 Correspondence from DBB to CSI, 3 March 1983, DOD/SANDF (DI Directorate Foreign Relations, GP 38, Box 177, DBB/SK/311/10/1/2, Lohnro, 3, 22/02/82–14/05/85).
223 Memorandum from CSI to CSADF, 18 August 1983, DOD/SANDF (DI Directorate Foreign Relations, GP 38, Box 177, DBB/SK/311/10/1/2, Lohnro, 3, 22/02/82–14/05/85).
224 Ibid.
225 Ibid.
226 Ibid.
227 Ibid.
228 Memorandum from DBB to CSI, 13 April 1984, DOD/SANDF (DI Directorate Foreign Relations, GP 38, Box 177, DBB/SK/311/10/1/2, Lohnro, 3, 22/02/82–14/05/85).
229 Memorandum from Head of Army Staff Intelligence to DBB, 1 May 1985, DOD/SANDF (DI Directorate Foreign Relations, GP 38, Box 177, DBB/SK/311/10/1/2, Lohnro, 3, 22/02/82–14/05/85)
230 Interview with Robin Renwick, Cape Town, 11 February 2015.
231 Interview with Craig Williamson, Johannesburg, 29 January 2016.
232 Interview with former Armscor employee, identity withheld, 2015.
233 Interview with André Thomashausen, Pretoria, 27 January 2016.

Chapter 10

1 Quoted in Zhong Weiyun and Xu Sujiang, 'China's support for and solidarity with South Africa's liberation struggle', in SADET, *The Road to Democracy in South Africa*, vol. 3, *International Solidarity*, Part 2, South African Democracy Education Trust, Johannesburg, 2008.
2 Sven Grimm, Yejoo Kim and Ross Anthony, 'South African relations with China and Taiwan', Centre for Chinese Studies, February 2014.
3 At around the same time it became apparent that China had started to shift its support to the pro-Namibian independence movement SWAPO as well. SWAPO was closely aligned with the ANC.
4 Chris Alden and Yu-shan Wu, 'South Africa and China: The making of a partnership', SAIIA, Occasional Paper 199, August 2014.
5 Grimm, Kim and Ross, 'South African relations with China and Taiwan', p. 5.
6 Zhong and Xu, 'China's support for and solidarity with South Africa's liberation struggle'.
7 Ibid.
8 Ibid.
9 'China: The South African connection', *Africa Confidential*, 23, 14 (7 July 1982).
10 Ibid.
11 'China: African affairs', *Africa Confidential*, 2, 3 (4 February 1987).
12 Interview with Craig Williamson, Johannesburg, 29 January 2016.
13 Ibid.
14 Letter from DW Steyn to PW Botha, 23 June 1988, University of the

Free State, Archive for Contemporary Affairs (PV 203, PS 12/82/3, 1987–1988, PW Botha).

15 Ibid.

16 Ibid.

17 Marc Burger, *Not the Whole Truth*, privately published, Johannesburg, 2013.

18 Ibid.

19 This manner of sanctions busting was confirmed in a 1984 meeting between a Chinese agent and the SADF in Hong Kong. During the meeting, it was revealed that China and Brazil had just concluded a large contract for the supply of iron, but that China would require more iron ore than the contract with the Brazilians could provide, suggesting that South Africa could clandestinely top up the difference. Reference is also made in the meeting to a previous shipment of iron ore from South Africa that went smoothly but was possibly monitored by the US and Taiwan.

20 Interview with Chris Thirion, Pretoria, 11 December 2015.

21 Ibid.

22 Ibid.

23 Summary of CSI and Director of Foreign Relations Visits to Asia, April 1984, DOD/SANDF (DI Directorate Foreign Relations, GP 38, Box 105, DBB/SK/311/1/26, Hulpverlening and Samewerking met ander Lande/Regerings: Taiwan, 1, 18/03/1981–07/08/1995).

24 Ibid.

25 Ibid.

26 Ibid.

27 Ibid.

28 Ibid.

29 Memorandum from Director of Foreign Relations to CSI, 2 March 1983, DOD/SANDF (DI, GP 31, Box 4, DBB/SK/311/1/30, Ops Zaire, 1, 08/01/1980–11/05/1983).

30 Memorandum from Director of Foreign Relations to CSI, 2 March 1983, DOD/SANDF (DI, GP 31, Box 4, DBB/SK/311/1/30, Ops Zaire, 1, 08/01/1980–11/05/1983).

31 Telegram from 'Harold' to 'Ali Samba', February 1984, DOD/SANDF (DI, GP 31, Box 4, DBB/SK 311/1/30 Gallery, Ops Zaire: Gallery, 3, 27/02/1984–18/01/1985).

32 Memorandum from Director of Foreign Relations to CSI, 2 March 1983, DOD/SANDF (DI, GP 31, Box 4, DBB/SK/311/1/30, Ops Zaire, 1, 08/01/1980–11/05/1983).

33 Memorandum from Director of Foreign Relations to CSI, 9 May 1983, DOD/SANDF (DI, GP 31, Box 4, DBB/SK/311/1/30, Ops Zaire, 1, 08/01/1980–11/05/1983).

34 Memorandum from Director of Foreign Relations to Director of Counter Intelligence, 23 February 1984, DOD/SANDF (DI, GP 31, Box 4, DBB/SK 311/1/30 Gallery, Ops Zaire: Gallery, 3, 27/02/1984–18/01/1985).

35 Telegram from 'Harold' to 'Ali Samba', February 1984, DOD/SANDF (DI, GP 31, Box 4, DBB/SK 311/1/30 Gallery, Ops Zaire: Gallery, 3, 27/02/1984–18/01/1985).

36 Ibid.
37 Export Invoice for Payment to Be Made to Kredietbank Luxembourg, 25 February 1984, DOD/SANDF (DI, GP 31, Box 4, DBB/SK 311/1/30 Gallery, Ops Zaire: Gallery, 3, 27/02/1984–18/01/1985).
38 Memorandum from Director of Foreign Relations to CSI, 5 March 1984, DOD/SANDF (DI, GP 31, Box 4, DBB/SK 311/1/30 Gallery, Ops Zaire: Gallery, 3, 27/02/1984–18/01/1985).
39 Handwritten List of Weapons and Their Prices Signed by Col. Pretorius, 19 March 1984, DOD/SANDF (DI, GP 31, Box 4, DBB/SK 311/1/30 Gallery, Ops Zaire: Gallery, 3, 27/02/1984–18/01/1985).
40 Armscor Quotation for Ammunition and Rockets, 6 September 1984, DOD/SANDF (DI, GP 31, Box 4, DBB/SK 311/1/30 Gallery, Ops Zaire: Gallery, 3, 27/02/1984–18/01/1985).
41 Memorandum from Major DJ Kotze to Director of Foreign Relations, 5 March 1985, DOD/SANDF (DI, GP 31, Box 5, DBB(SK)/311/1/30 Gallery, Ops Zaire: Gallery, 4, 18/01/1985–30/07/1985).
42 According to documents, at least six such shipments took place at the time.
43 Summary of Operation Kauka, 27 April 1985, DOD/SANDF (DI, GP 31, Box 5, DBB(SK)/311/1/30 Gallery, Ops Zaire: Gallery, 4, 18/01/1985–30/07/1985).
44 Ibid.
45 Ibid.
46 Colm Foy and Christine Abdelkrim, 'Arms to South Africa: The new triangle and the Chinese connection', *AfricaAsia*, February 1985.
47 Memorandum from Col. DR Muller to Brigadier JJJ van Rensburg, 23 May 1985, DOD/SANDF (DI, GP 31, Box 5, DBB(SK)/311/1/30 Gallery, Ops Zaire: Gallery, 4, 18/01/1985–30/07/1985).
48 Ibid.
49 Ibid.
50 Memorandum on Cooperation with Singapore from CSI to CSADF, 30 November 1983, DOD/SANDF (DI Directorate Foreign Relations, GP 38, Box 169, DBB/SK/311/1/121 IBEX, Singapore, 3, 30/11/1983–18/05/1984).
51 Correspondence from Stuart Pretorius, Armscor, to Hattingh Pretorius, 23 November 1983, DOD/SANDF (DI Directorate Foreign Relations, GP 38, Box 169, DBB/SK/311/1/121 IBEX, Singapore, 3, 30/11/1983–18/05/1984).
52 Memorandum on Cooperation with Singapore from CSI to CSADF, 30 November 1983, DOD/SANDF (DI Directorate Foreign Relations, GP 38, Box 169, DBB/SK/311/1/121 IBEX, Singapore, 3, 30/11/1983–18/05/1984).
53 Ibid.
54 The Cambodian conflict in the 1980s, following the genocide of almost 25% of the population in the 1970s, resulted in the displacement of over 600,000 people and the loss of tens of thousands of lives. Armscor, Singapore and Norinco all directly or indirectly contributed to this conflict.

55 Annual Report on Special Projects, 15 April 1986, DOD/SANDF (DI Directorate Foreign Relations, GP 38, Box 178, DBB(SK) 501/8/2, Jaarverslae, 1, 15/05/1985–15/04/1986).

56 Ibid.

57 Memorandum from AJ van Wyk, Armscor, to CSI, 15 March 1990, DOD/SANDF (DI, GP 25, Box 110, APD/W/311/5/1, Hulpverlening en samewerking met statutêre liggame: Krygkor, 6, 8/11/89–10/9/90).

58 Summary of CSI and Director of Foreign Relations Visits to Asia, April 1984, DOD/SANDF (DI Directorate Foreign Relations, GP 38, Box 105, DBB/SK/311/1/26, Hulpverlening and Samewerking met ander Lande/Regerings: Taiwan, 1, 18/03/1981–07/08/1995).

59 Letter from DW Steyn to PW Botha, 23 June 1988, University of the Free State, Archive for Contemporary Affairs (PV 203, PS 12/82/3, 1987–1988, PW Botha).

60 Richard Ellis, 'Secret deal with China extended range of nuclear firepower', *Sunday Times*, 28 March 1993.

61 Nic von Wielligh, *Die bom: Suid-Afrika se kernwapenprogram*, Litera, Pretoria, 2014, p. 186.

62 Ibid.

63 Ibid., p. 251

64 Ibid., p. 252.

65 Ibid., p. 251.

Chapter 11

1   LJ van der Westhuizen and JH le Roux, *Armscor: The Leading Edge*, unpublished, University of the Free State, Institute for Contemporary History, 1997, p. 134.

2   Magnus Malan, *My Life with the SA Defence Force*, Protea Book House, Pretoria, 2006, p. 233.

3   Report from PG Marais (Armscor) to PW Botha, 21 April 1980, University of the Free State, Archive for Contemporary Affairs (PV 203, PS4/1/10, 1981, PW Botha).

4   William Lowther, *Iraq and the Super-Gun: Gerald Bull, the True Story of Saddam Hussein's Dr Doom*, Pan Books, London, 1992.

5   Sam Hemmingway and William Scott Malone, 'CIA knew Space Research Corporation was ready to sell advance artillery shells to S. Africa', *Burlington Free Press* (Vermont), 6 January 1980.

6   Van der Westhuizen and Le Roux, *Armscor*, pp. 308–310.

7   Ibid., pp. 308–310.

8   Lowther, *Iraq and the Super-Gun*, p. 140.

9   Ibid.

10 Ibid., p. 141.

11 Interview with Craig Williamson, Johannesburg, 29 January 2016.

12 Ibid.

13 Ibid.

14 Message from Pretoria to Bonn, 24 November 1982, DIRCO (Armaments, 32/7, Vol. 1, 4/1/71–12/9/85, Export of Arms from SA).

15 Lowther, *Iraq and the Super-Gun*, p. 170.

16 Ibid., p. 170.
17 William Park, 'The tragic tale of Saddam Hussein's super-gun', *BBC Future*, 18 March 2016.
18 Memorandum on Cooperation between South Africa and West Germany, 26 September 1983, German Ministry of Foreign Affairs Archive Berlin (File 232, No. 320.15/18).
19 Paper by Jürgen Ostrowsky for UN Public Hearings on Activities of Transnational Corporations in SA and Namibia, 20 September 1985, University of Fort Hare, ANC Archive (German Mission, Subject Files, Box 19, Folder 132, German Military Collaboration with SA 1981–1985).
20 Gerd Langguth, 'The scandal that helped Merkel become chancellor', *Der Spiegel*, 7 August 2009.
21 Serge Schmemann, 'Franz Josef Strauss is dead at 73', *New York Times*, 4 October 1988.
22 James Markham, 'Europeans give Botha a frosty visit', *New York Times*, 10 June 1984.
23 Report from German Embassy Pretoria to Foreign Ministry Bonn, 12 November 1983, West German Foreign Affairs Archive, Berlin (Box. 320, No. 138.148).
24 Summary of Meeting between PW van der Westhuizen and Franz Josef Strauss, 14 June 1983, DOD/SANDF (DI Directorate Foreign Relations, GP 38, Box 177, DBB/SK 311/6/3/7, Joseph Strauss, 1, 14/06/1983–23/08/1983).
25 Ibid.
26 Ibid.
27 Extracts from DB Sole, 'This above all: Reminiscences of a South African diplomat', 1989, p. 279, University of the Free State, Archive for Contemporary Affairs (PV 862, DB Sole).
28 Ibid.
29 HDW was jointly owned by the West German federal government and the government of the state Schleswig-Holstein.
30 Ferrostaal Final Report, Compliance Investigation, Debevoise & Plimpton LLP, 13 April 2011.
31 Report by CSAN, 28 September 1984, DOD/SANDF (DI, GP 13, Box 64, 520/3/4/4, Besoeke aan die Buiteland: Duitsland, 5, 05/07/84–25/05/85).
32 'West Germany/South Africa: Secret ships deal goes ahead', *Africa Confidential*, 29, 6 (18 March 1988).
33 Ibid.
34 Report on the Meeting between PW Botha and Chancellor Helmut Kohl in Bonn, 5 June 1984, University of the Free State, Archive for Contemporary Affairs (PV 203, PS 12/27/1, 1984, PW Botha).
35 Ibid.
36 Ibid.
37 Ibid.
38 'West Germany/South Africa: Secret ships deal goes ahead', *Africa Confidential*.
39 Ibid.

40 Ibid.

41 Hilton Hamman, Hilton, *Days of the Generals*, Zebra, Cape Town, 2001, p. 162.

42 Ibid., p. 163.

43 'West Germany/South Africa: Secret ships deal goes ahead', *Africa Confidential*.

44 Report by AAM, 10 November 1989, University of Fort Hare, ANC Archive (German Mission, Subject Files, Box 36, Folder 245, SA–German Submarine Deal).

45 Telegram from MLVA Bonn to Armscor, 26 November 1986, DOD/SANDF (CSI/DI, GP 18, Box 5, 203/2/4, Insameling van Inligting. Eie MA: Wes-Duitsland, 14, 24/06/86–15/04/87).

46 Paper by Reinhard Kramer (German Green Party), 7 July 1990, University of Fort Hare, ANC Archive (German Mission, Subject Files, Box 36, Folder 245, SA–German Submarine Deal).

47 Clipping from *Independent on Sunday*, 'Germany crashes the sanctions barrier', 30 December 1990, University of Fort Hare, ANC Archive (German Mission, Subject Files, Box 19, Folder 131, German Economic Collaboration with SA 1981–1985).

48 Letter from SA Consulate-General to Bonn Ambassador, 13 October 1977, DIRCO (Defence, 9/56/5, West Germany Defence Purchases).

49 Ibid.

50 Letter from CSADF to DG DFA, 5 March 1981, DIRCO (Foreign Representation, 4/2/2/8, Vol. 2, 21/7/72–13/8/81, Bonn Military Attaché).

51 Letter from CSADF to DG DFA, 29 February 1984, DIRCO (Foreign Representation, 4/2/2/8, Vol. 3, 24/9/82–20/8/84, Bonn Military Attaché).

52 Intelligence Review of FRG Political Attitudes to SA, 28 February 1988, DOD/SANDF (DI, GP 24, Box 282, AMI/520/3/4/4, Besoeke aan Buiteland. SAW–Krygkor lede. Duitsland, 7, 01/07/1986–29/07/1988).

53 Telegram from Bonn to Pretoria, 2 August 1984, DIRCO (Foreign Representation, 4/2/2/8, Vol. 3, 24/9/82–20/8/84, Bonn Military Attaché).

54 For example, the company LITEF, a subsidiary of a US corporation based in Freiburg close to the Black Forest, was in 1984 a registered Armscor supplier of navigational systems for submarines. They also hosted visits by Armscor officials. LITEF is today a subsidiary of the US arms manufacturer Northrop Grumman. See Memorandum from CSI to CSADF, 5 March 1985, DOD/SANDF (DI, GP 13, Box 64, 520/3/4/4, Besoeke aan die Buiteland: Duitsland, 5, 05/07/84–25/05/85).

55 Letter from CSAA to CSI, 2 November 1984, DOD/SANDF (DI, GP 13, Box 64, 520/3/4/4, Besoeke aan die Buiteland: Duitsland, 5, 05/07/84–25/05/85).

56 Memorandum from CSI to CSADF, 4 November 1986, DOD/SANDF (DI, GP 24, Box 282, AMI/520/3/4/4, Besoeke aan Buiteland. SAW–Krygkor lede. Duitsland, 7, 01/07/1986–29/07/1988).

57 Proposal from CSAN to CSI, 31 July 1986, DOD/SANDF (DI, GP 24,

Box 282, AMI/520/3/4/4, Besoeke aan Buiteland. SAW–Krygkor lede. Duitsland, 7, 01/07/1986–29/07/1988).

58 Ibid.

59 Correspondence from 'Sulky' to 'Greedy', 30 March 1989, DOD/ SANDF (DI, GP 30, Box 520, AMI/520/2/5/4, Visitors to RSA: Germany, 3, 29/07/88–15/10/92).

60 Correspondence from 'Moneylist' to 'Outpost', 28 September 1989, DOD/SANDF (DI, GP 30, Box 520, AMI/520/2/5/4, Visitors to RSA: Germany, 3, 29/07/88–15/10/92).

61 Ibid.

62 Ibid.

63 Ibid.

64 Correspondence from EV Schmidt, Bonn Embassy, to CSL, 28 July 1988, DOD/SANDF (DI, GP 24, Box 282, AMI/520/3/4/4, Besoeke aan Buiteland. SAW–Krygkor lede. Duitsland, 7, 01/07/1986–29/07/1988).

65 Offer of Mercury Red Standard 20.2 from Dexim, 31 January 1990, DOD/SANDF (DI Directorate Foreign Relations, GP 37, Box 220, S/402/2/1, Aanbiedinge deur Buitelands Instansies, 5, 06/11/1989– 15/12/1992).

66 Correspondence from First Secretary Bonn to CSL, 11 March 1992, DOD/SANDF (DI Directorate Foreign Relations, GP 37, Box 220, S/402/2/1, Aanbiedinge deur Buitelands Instansies, 5, 06/11/1989– 15/12/1992).

67 Memorandum from CSI to CSADF, 26 November 1982, DOD/SANDF (DI Directorate Foreign Relations, GP 38, Box 78, DBB/SK/311/1/10, Hulpverlening and Samewerking met ander Lande/Regerings: Duitsland, 1, 26/11/1982–30/06/1995).

68 Minutes of BND/MID Conference, 7 June 1983, DOD/SANDF (DI, GP 42, Box 36, AFD INL/311/1/10, Hulpverlening and Samewerking: Duitsland, 1, 13/06/1977–11/03/1996).

69 Letter from Vice-President of BND to CSI, 6 May 1983, DOD/SANDF (DI, GP 38, Box 79, DBB/SK/311/1/10/1, Werksdokument, 07/06/1983).

70 Minutes of BND/MID Conference, 7 June 1983, DOD/SANDF (DI, GP 42, Box 36, AFD INL/311/1/10, Hulpverlening and Samewerking: Duitsland, 1, 13/06/1977–11/03/1996).

71 Ibid.

72 Memorandum from PC Smit, DFI, to CSI, 27 November 1984, DOD/ SANDF (DI, GP 13, Box 64, 520/3/4/4, Besoeke aan die Buiteland: Duitsland, 5, 05/07/84–25/05/85).

73 Ibid.

74 Letter from CSADF to DFA, 15 December 1982, DIRCO (Defence, 9/56/5, West Germany Defence Purchases).

75 Memorandum from PC Smit, DFI, to CSI, 27 November 1984, DOD/ SANDF (DI, GP 13, Box 64, 520/3/4/4, Besoeke aan die Buiteland: Duitsland, 5, 05/07/84–25/05/85).

76 Report on an Evaluation Course for MID and 'SK201' in Munich, 9 July 1984, DOD/SANDF (DI Directorate Foreign Relations, GP 38, Box

78, DBB/SK/311/1/10, Hulpverlening and Samewerking met ander Lande/Regerings: Duitsland, 1, 26/11/1982–30/06/1995).

77 Ibid.

78 Intelligence Review of SA–Federal Republic of Germany Relations, 8 April 1988, DOD/SANDF (DI, GP 24, Box 131, MI/203/2/4/1, Maandverslae: Bonn, 7, 25/03/1987–08/04/1988).

79 Letter from George Bautzmann to CSADF, 25 July 1988, DOD/SANDF (DI, GP 30, Box 520, AMI/520/2/5/4, Visitors to RSA: Germany, 3, 29/07/88–15/10/92).

80 Memorandum from CSI to CSADF, 12 January 1988, DOD/SANDF (DI, GP 24, Box 282, AMI/520/3/4/4, Besoeke aan Buiteland. SAW–Krygkor lede. Duitsland, 7, 01/07/1986–29/07/1988).

81 Ibid.

82 Transcript of Interview with Walter de Bock on the Arms Trade, KADOC, Archief Walter de Bock (Wapenhandel, Wapenhandel met Irak en Iran (incl. Gerald Bull, Eur. Wapenkartel), 7.13, 3, 1992–1994).

83 Report from Mr G van Denbos, Belgian Embassy Pretoria, to Minister H de Bruyne, Belgian Minister of Foreign Affairs, 1 August 1978, Belgian Foreign Affairs Archive (17.509/1978, File Number 18884 XIII/1, Correspondence Pretoria Cape Town, 01/08/1978).

84 Ibid.

85 'Belgen dienen in Leger Zuid-Afrika', 1985, KADOC, Archief Walter de Bock (Centraal en Zuidelijk Afrika, Zuid-Afrika, 5.06, 1, 1981–1988).

86 Armscor Report on Fruitless Expenditure on Flamethrowers, 3 May 1983, DOD/SANDF (IG, GP 2, Box 344, HSAW/IG(DIO) 506/4/3/6952-5, Purchase of flamethrowers from Belgium, 1, 22/04/1981–30/11/1984).

87 See www.en.wikipedia.org/wiki/Convention_on_Certain_Conventional_Weapons, accessed 13 November 2016.

88 Armscor Report on Fruitless Expenditure on Flamethrowers, 3 May 1983, DOD/SANDF (IG, GP 2, Box 344, HSAW/IG(DIO) 506/4/3/6952-5, Purchase of flamethrowers from Belgium, 1, 22/04/1981–30/11/1984).

89 Paul Holden and Hennie van Vuuren, *The Devil in the Detail: How the Arms Deal Changed Everything*, Jonathan Ball Publishers, Cape Town, 2011, p. 192.

90 Clipping from *De Morgen* on John Bredenkamp, 3 December 1981, Kadoc, Archief Walter de Bock (Centraal en Zuidelijk Afrika, Zuid-Afrika, 5.06, 1, 1981–1988).

91 Ibid.

92 See www.en.wikipedia.org/wiki/John_Bredenkamp, accessed 13 November 2016.

93 Holden and Van Vuuren, *The Devil in the Detail*.

94 Report by Armscor about Meeting with Peptic, 30 June 1982, DOD/SANDF (IG, GP 2, Box 344, HSAW/IG(DIO) 506/4/3/6952-5, Purchase of flamethrowers from Belgium, 1, 22/04/1981–30/11/1984).

95 Ibid.

96 Ibid.

97 Armscor Report on Fruitless Expenditure on Flamethrowers, 3 May 1983, DOD/SANDF (IG, GP 2, Box 344, HSAW/IG(DIO) 506/4/3/6952-5,

Purchase of flamethrowers from Belgium, 1, 22/04/1981–30/11/1984).

98 Letter from R van Calster, Chief of Intelligence Brussels, to CSI, 29 March 1991, DOD/SANDF (DI Directorate Foreign Relations, GP 38, Box 182, AMI/513/11/15, Belgium, 1, 22/06/83–29/11/96).

99 Letter from General Major J de Mild, Brussels, to Lieutenant General WP van der Westhuizen, SSC, 26 September 1985, DOD/SANDF (DI Directorate Foreign Relations, GP 38, Box 182, AMI/513/11/15, Belgium, 1, 22/06/83–29/11/96).

100 Ibid.

101 Clipping from *Beeld* titled 'SA attaché sy status kwyt', 14 September 1985, DIRCO (Foreign Representation, 4/2/3/4, Vol. 2, 8/1/71 14/9/85, Brussels Military Attaché).

102 Letter from Colonel Moreau, Brussels, to Lieutenant General WP van der Westhuizen, SSC, 1985, DOD/SANDF (DI Directorate Foreign Relations, GP 38, Box 182, AMI/513/11/15, Belgium, 1, 22/06/83–29/11/96).

103 Letters of thanks by Major General Le Roux to Belgian Military Officials, 4 June 1984, DOD/SANDF (DI Directorate Foreign Relations, GP 38, Box 182, AMI/513/11/15, Belgium, 1, 22/06/83–29/11/96).

104 Telegram from Ambassador to DFA, for SADF, 16 June 1977, DIRCO (Defence, 9/56/8, Vol. 2, 15/11/71–8/4/81, Defence Purchases).

105 Military Intelligence Correspondence, 21 January 1993, DOD/SANDF (Military Intelligence Division, Chief of Staff Intelligence, GP 24, Box 92, AMI/520/2/5/12, Besoeke, bewegings van persone, vliegtuie, vaartuie. Besoeke aan RSA, 3).

106 Data from Stockholm International Peace Institute, quoted in PRI's *The World and Global Post*, 'Peace-loving Sweden and Switzerland are among top arms exporters per capita in the world', 23 May 2014.

107 Peter Hug, *Mit der Apartheid-Regierung gegen den Kommunismus: Die Militärischen, Rüstungsindustriellen und Nuklearen Beziehungen der Schweiz zu Südafrika und die Apartheid-Debatte*, Schweizerischen Nationalfonds zur Förderung der wissenschaftlichen Forschung, Bern, 2005, p. 852.

108 Ibid., p. 561.

109 Ibid., p. 579.

110 Miodrag Certic and Mia Certic, 'A Swiss merchant of death's Nazi friends and suspicious masterpieces: A famous manufacturer of anti-aircraft guns collected hundreds of paintings in Nazi-occupied Paris with some help from Hermann Göring. Now what happens to them?', *Daily Beast*, New York, 17 May 2015.

111 Phil Davison, 'Dieter Bührle: Controversial arms dealer', *The Independent*, 2013.

112 Hug, *Mit der Apartheid-Regierung gegen den Kommunismus*.

113 Letter from Dr D Bührle to PW Botha, 19 December 1978, University of the Free State, Archive for Contemporary Affairs (PV 203, 1/W1/9, 1977–1982, PW Botha).

114 Letter from Gabriel Lebedinsky to PW Botha, 19 December 1978, University of the Free State: Archive for Contemporary Affairs (PV 203, 1/W1/9, 1977–1982, PW Botha).

115 Memorandum from MLA Bern on Armscor Offices and Personnel Abroad, 17 November 1986, DOD/SANDF (DI, GP 30, Box 244, 202/10/19, Switzerland, 1, 03/10/1977–07/08/1989).

116 Ibid.

117 Hug, *Mit der Apartheid-Regierung gegen den Kommunismus*, p. 644.

118 Memorandum from SF Grobbelaar to 'Dreamer', 25 January 1988, DOD/SANDF (DI, GP 24, Box 162, MI 203/5/SK211/B, Afdeling Militêre Inligting, 1, 01/02/1983–06/05/1989).

119 Letter from Francisco J Lopez de Arenosa (Spanish Navy Captain) to General Groenewald, 10 December 1985, DOD/SANDF (DI, GP 24, Box 162, MI 203/5/SK211/B, Afdeling Militêre Inligting, 1, 01/02/1983–06/05/1989).

120 Memorandum from Portugal to Col LJ Kemper, DBB, 13 July 1988, DOD/SANDF (DI, GP 24, Box 133, MI/203/2/7, Eie Miltêre Attachés, Portugal, 23, 03/06/1988–13/08/1988).

121 Brief from the Defence Attaché Madrid to Directorate Foreign Relations, 27 June 1979, DOD/SANDF (DI, GP 42, Box 37, AFD INL/311/1/24, Hulpverlening/samewerking met ander Lande/Regerings, Spanje, 1, 13/04/1978–19/02/1996).

122 Memorandum by DG DFA, 10 June 1981, DOD/SANDF (DI, GP 42, Box 37, AFD INL/311/1/24, Hulpverlening/samewerking met ander Lande/Regerings, Spanje, 1, 13/04/1978–19/02/1996).

123 See www.bloomberg.com/profiles/people/17434897-jose-nicolas-sierra-lopez.

124 Memorandum by DG DFA, 10 June 1981, DOD/SANDF (DI, GP 42, Box 37, AFD INL/311/1/24, Hulpverlening/samewerking met ander Lande/Regerings, Spanje, 1, 13/04/1978–19/02/1996).

125 Correspondence from Mr Garcia Lopez to CWH du Toit, 29 June 1981, DOD/SANDF (DI, GP 42, Box 37, AFD INL/311/1/24, Hulpverlening/samewerking met ander Lande/Regerings, Spanje, 1, 13/04/1978–19/02/1996).

126 Ibid.

127 Ibid.

128 Correspondence from Ivor Little to CSI, 14 April 1989, DOD/SANDF (DI, GP 24, Box 131, AMI/IO/203/2/5/1, Eie Militêre Attachés: Rome, 1, 11/02/1987–19/05/1989).

129 Message from Malan to Mr AA Mare, 12 June 1980, DIRCO (Portugal, 1/14/3, Vol. 8, 5/9/79–21/7/80, Portugal Relations with SA).

130 Translation of COMOPS Plan by Dr Luca Poggiali, 5 June 1987, DOD/SANDF (DI, GP 24, Box 131, AMI/IO/203/2/5/1, Eie Militêre Attachés: Rome, 1, 11/02/1987–19/05/1989).

131 Ibid.

132 Correspondence from Ivor Little to CSAAF, 6 September 1988, DOD/SANDF (DI, GP 24, Box 131, AMI/IO/203/2/5/1, Eie Militêre Attachés: Rome, 1, 11/02/1987–19/05/1989).

133 Visit Report from Ivor Little to CSAAF and CSI, 28 November 1988, DOD/SANDF (DI, GP 24, Box 131, AMI/IO/203/2/5/1, Eie Militêre Attachés: Rome, 1, 11/02/1987–19/05/1989).

134 Letter from Lt General PW van der Westhuizen to Lt General Ninetto Lugaresi, October 1983, DOD/SANDF (DI Directorate Foreign Relations, GP 38, Box 182, AMI/513/11/12, AMI/513/11/12, 1, 30/10/1981–26/11/1992).

135 Report by Ivor Little, 18 March 1988, DOD/SANDF (DI, GP 24, Box 131, MI/203/2/5, Insameling van Inligting. Eie Militêre Attachés: Monza, 16, 27/08/1987–23/03/1988).

136 Van der Westhuizen and Le Roux, *Armscor*, p. 253.

137 World Bank Data, available at www.data.worldbank.org/indicator/NY.GDP.PCAP.CD?end=2015&locations=SG&start=1965&view=chart.

138 Van der Westhuizen and Le Roux, *Armscor*, pp. 358–359.

139 Letter from PW Botha to Dr Goh Keng Swee (Deputy Prime Minister Singapore), 4 November 1982, University of the Free State, Archive for Contemporary Affairs (PV 203, A1/6/6, 1982, PW Botha).

140 Ibid.

141 Handwritten Report on Contact with Singapore, DOD/SANDF (DI Directorate Foreign Relations, GP 38, Box 169, DBB/SK/311/1/121 IBEX, Singapore, 4, 18/05/1984–05/11/1987).

142 Ibid.

143 Ibid.

144 Telegram from A Steven to A Harvey, 5 June 1984, DOD/SANDF (DI Directorate Foreign Relations, GP 38, Box 169, DBB/SK/311/1/121 IBEX, Singapore, 4, 18/05/1984–05/11/1987.

145 Handwritten Report on Contact with Singapore, DOD/SANDF (DI Directorate Foreign Relations, GP 38, Box 169, DBB/SK/311/1/121 IBEX, Singapore, 4, 18/05/1984–05/11/1987).

146 Letter from Eddie Teo to Lt General PW van der Westhuizen, 23 April 1984, DOD/SANDF (DI Directorate Foreign Relations, GP 38, Box 169, DBB/SK/311/1/121 IBEX, Singapore, 4, 18/05/1984–05/11/1987).

147 Report on CSI and Director of Foreign Relations Visit to Asia, 14 August 1984, DOD/SANDF (DI Directorate Foreign Relations, GP 38, Box 169, DBB/SK/311/1/121 IBEX, Singapore, 4, 18/05/1984–05/11/1987).

148 Report from Director of Special Tasks to CSI, 8 April 1980, DOD/SANDF (DI Directorate Foreign Relations, GP 38, Box 80, DBB/SK/311/1/11, Hulpverlening en Samewerking met Frankryk, 2, 01/04/1980–03/07/1995).

149 Ibid.

150 Ibid.

151 Correspondence from Director of Special Tasks to CSI, 2 February 1981, DOD/SANDF (DI, GP 31, Box 4, DBB/SK/311/1/30, Ops Zaire, 1, 08/01/1980–11/05/1983).

152 Memorandum from CSI to CSADF, August 1987, DOD/SANDF (DI Directorate Foreign Relations, GP 38, Box 169, DBB/SK/311/1/121 IBEX, Singapore, 4, 18/05/1984–05/11/1987).

153 Report on SA Trade Relations with Africa by Laurent Zecchini, 7 August 1986, DOD/SANDF (DI, GP 31, Box 5, DBB(SK) 311/1/30 Gallery, Ops Zaire, Gallery, 6, 06/03/1986–30/07/1986).

154 Ibid.

155 Ibid.

156 Unsigned Kenyan End User Certificate for Ammunition from Austria, 1982, DOD/SANDF (DI, GP 31, Box 4, DBB/SK/311/1/30, Ops Zaire, 1, 08/01/1980–11/05/1983).

157 Visit Report from Director of Foreign Relations to CSI, 28 August 1984, DOD/SANDF (DI Directorate Foreign Relations, GP 38, Box 129, DBB/SK/311/1/42/1, Org in Mauritius, 1, 21/09/1981–11/12/1984).

158 Kenneth Noble, 'Felix Houphouet-Boigny, Ivory Coast's leader since freedom in 1960, is dead', *New York Times*, 8 December 1993.

159 Memorandum from Head Director Military Intelligence to CSI, 4 August 1986, DOD/SANDF (DI Onder-Afdeling Inligting Operasies, Gp 26, Box 13, AMI/IO/311/1/69, Hulpverlening en samewerking met Ivoorkus, 1, 04/08/86–18/05/90).

160 Ibid.

161 Report on Meeting between President Houphouët-Boigny and CSI, 20 February 1988, DOD/SANDF (DI Onder-Afdeling Inligting Operasies, Gp 26, Box 13, AMI/IO/311/1/69, Hulpverlening en samewerking met Ivoorkus, 1, 04/08/86–18/05/90).

162 Memorandum from CSI to CSADF, 30 June 1986, DOD/SANDF (DI, GP 31, Box 5, DBB(SK) 311/1/30 Gallery, Ops Zaire: Gallery, 6, 06/03/1986–30/07/1986).

163 Interview with Vic McPherson, Pretoria, 20 May 2016.

164 Ibid.

165 De Wet Potgieter, Interview with Vic McPherson, 9 February 2009, SAHA Collection, AL3283.

166 Howard French, 'Mobutu Sese Seko, 66, long-time dictator of Zaire, dies', *New York Times*, 8 September 1997.

167 Ibid.

168 David Smith, 'Mobutu Sese Seko's body to be returned to Democratic Republic of Congo', *The Guardian*, 25 October 2013.

169 Telegram from Permanent Representative New York to Secretary of DFA, 28 March 1977, DOD/SANDF (MVV, GP 5, Box 88, MV/56/28, Zaire, 1, 29/03/1977–19/10/1981).

170 Telegram to SADF Cape Town, 29 March 1977, DOD/SANDF (MVV, GP 5, Box 88, MV/56/28, Zaire, 1, 29/03/1977–19/10/1981).

171 Visit Report from Director of Special Tasks to CSI, 20 February 1980, DOD/SANDF (DI, GP 31, Box 4, DBB/SK/311/1/30, Ops Zaire, 1, 08/01/1980–11/05/1983).

172 Ibid.

173 Report on Visit to Zaire by Officer in Special Tasks, October 1980, DOD/SANDF (DI, GP 31, Box 4, DBB/SK/311/1/30, Ops Zaire, 1, 08/01/1980–11/05/1983).

174 Telegram from DS Hamman to MA Paris, January 1982, DOD/SANDF (DI, GP 31, Box 4, DBB/SK/311/1/30, Ops Zaire, 1, 08/01/1980–11/05/1983).

175 Memorandum from Col JC Bosch to Director of Special Tasks, 14 January 1982, DOD/SANDF (DI, GP 31, Box 4, DBB/SK/311/1/30, Ops Zaire, 1, 08/01/1980–11/05/1983).

176   Note from Col JC Bosch on CSI Talks with Gabon and Zaire, 26 January 1982, DOD/SANDF (DI, GP 31, Box 4, DBB/SK 311/1/30 Gallery, Ops Zaire: Gallery, 3, 27/02/1984–18/01/1985).

177   Memorandum from Director of Foreign Relations to CSI, 2 March 1983, DOD/SANDF (DI, GP 31, Box 4, DBB/SK/311/1/30, Ops Zaire, 1, 08/01/1980–11/05/1983).

178   Memorandum from CSI to CSADF, 22 July 1983, DOD/SANDF (DI, GP 31, Box 4, DBB(SK) 311/1/30 Gallery, Ops Zaire: Gallery, 2, 11/05/1983–27/02/1984).

179   Telegram from Brigadier DS Hamman to MA Washington, August 1983, DOD/SANDF (DI, GP 31, Box 4, DBB(SK) 311/1/30 Gallery, Ops Zaire: Gallery, 2, 11/05/1983–27/02/1984).

180   Visit Report from CSI to CSADF, 31 January 1983, DOD/SANDF (DI, GP 31, Box 4, DBB/SK/311/1/30, Ops Zaire, 1, 08/01/1980–11/05/1983).

181   Ibid.

182   Ibid.

183   Memorandum from Director of Foreign Relations to CSI, 12 December 1985, DOD/SANDF (DI, GP 31, Box 5, DBB(SK) 311/1/30 Gallery, Ops Zaire: Gallery, 5, 16/07/1985–06/03/1986).

184   Request for Weapons and Ammunition from Pretoria, August 1987, DOD/SANDF (DI, Gp 31, Box 6, DBB/SK/311/1/30, SAW Verteenwoordiger in Zaire – Minorco, 2, 01/07/1987–11/01/1988).

185   Report on Project Gallery from Director Foreign Relations to CSI, 31 August 1983, DOD/SANDF (DI, GP 31, Box 4, DBB(SK) 311/1/30 Gallery, Ops Zaire: Gallery, 2, 11/05/1983–27/02/1984).

186   Ibid.

187   Memorandum from Director of Foreign Relations, April 1985, DOD/SANDF (DI, GP 31, Box 5, DBB(SK)/311/1/30 Gallery, Ops Zaire: Gallery, 4, 18/01/1985–30/07/1985).

188   Ibid.

189   Memorandum from Col Pretorius to Director of Foreign Relations, 10 February 1984, DOD/SANDF (DI, GP 31, Box 4, DBB(SK) 311/1/30 Gallery, Ops Zaire: Gallery, 2, 11/05/1983–27/02/1984).

190   Memorandum from Major DJ Kotze to Director of Foreign Relations, 9 May 1984, DOD/SANDF (DI, GP 31, Box 4, DBB/SK 311/1/30 Gallery, Ops Zaire: Gallery, 3, 27/02/1984–18/01/1985).

191   Memorandum from CSI to CSADF, November 1985, DOD/SANDF (DI, GP 31, Box 5, DBB(SK) 311/1/30 Gallery, Ops Zaire: Gallery, 5, 16/07/1985–06/03/1986).

192   Memorandum from Major DJ Kotze to Director of Foreign Relations, 5 March 1985, DOD/SANDF (DI, GP 31, Box 5, DBB(SK)/311/1/30 Gallery, Ops Zaire: Gallery, 4, 18/01/1985–30/07/1985).

193   Ibid.

194   Cooperation Agreement between AND, Zaire, and Military Intelligence, South Africa, 1 April 1986, DOD/SANDF (DI, GP 31, Box 5, DBB(SK) 311/1/30 Gallery, Ops Zaire: Gallery, 6, 06/03/1986–30/07/1986).

195   Memorandum from Col JM Barnard to CSI, 4 September 1986, DOD/

SANDF (DI, GP 31, Box 5, DBB(SK) 311/1/30 Gallery, Ops Zaire: Gallery, 6, 06/03/1986–30/07/1986).

196 Memorandum from CSI to CSADF, June 1986, DOD/SANDF (DI, GP 31, Box 5, DBB(SK) 311/1/30 Gallery, Ops Zaire: Gallery, 6, 06/03/1986–30/07/1986).

197 Ibid.

198 Ibid.

199 Summary of Talks between CSADF, CSI and Mr N'gbanda (AND), June 1986, DOD/SANDF (DI, GP 31, Box 5, DBB(SK) 311/1/30 Gallery, Ops Zaire: Gallery, 6, 06/03/1986–30/07/1986).

200 Operation Instruction for Operation Colley, 12 June 1991, DOD/ SANDF (DI, GP 31, Box 4, DBB(SK) 311/1/30 Colley, Opleiding deur Spes Magte – Colley, 1, 27/03/1991–02/09/1991).

201 'South Africa: Forced out of the laager', *Africa Confidential*, 29, 24 (December 1988).

202 Ibid.

203 Ibid.

204 'Nat Superspy's shadowy boss', *Sunday Star*, 1987.

205 Interview with Craig Williamson, Johannesburg, 29 January 2016.

206 Stephen Ellis, 'Africa and international corruption: The strange case of South Africa and Seychelles', *African Affairs*, 95 (1996), p. 171.

207 Ibid.

208 Ibid., p. 173.

209 RT Naylor, *Patriots and Profiteers: On Economic Warfare, Embargo Busting and State-Sponsored Crime*, McClelland & Stewart Inc., Toronto, 1999, p. 147.

210 Interview with Craig Williamson, Johannesburg, 29 January 2016.

211 Ibid.

212 Ibid.

213 Ibid.

214 'The new Chiavelli', *Sunday Star*, 31 January 1987.

215 Bob Denard obituary, *The Economist*, 18 October 2007.

216 Ibid.

217 Ibid.

218 Interview with Craig Williamson, Johannesburg, 29 January 2016.

219 Andrew Terrill, 'The Comoro Islands in South African regional strategy', *Africa Today*, 33, 2/3, (1986), pp. 59–70.

220 Ibid.

221 Ibid.

222 Report from Director of Special Tasks to CSI, 8 April 1980, DOD/ SANDF (DI Directorate Foreign Relations, GP 38, Box 80, DBB/ SK/311/1/11, Hulpverlening en Samewerking met Frankryk, 2, 01/04/1980–03/07/1995).

223 Interview with Craig Williamson, Johannesburg, 29 January 2016.

224 Ibid.

Chapter 12

1 Dave Steward, 'From Verwoerd to Mandela', Stellenbosch Library papers.

2   Deon Geldenhuys, 'Pariah states in the post-Cold War world: A conceptual exploration in US–South Africa relations and the "pariah" states', South African Institute for International Affairs, Report No. 2, Johannesburg, 1997.

3   'U.S. is now a "pariah state", Chomsky says', *Daily Free Press*, Boston University, 24 March 2003.

4   Juan Pablo Bohoslavsky and Veerle Opgenhaffen, 'The past and present of corporate complicity: Financing the Argentinean dictatorship', *Harvard Human Rights Journal*, 23 (2010), pp. 159–203.

5   'Kissinger to Argentines on dirty war: The quicker you succeed the better', National Security Archive, George Washington University, 4 December 2003.

6   Maria Seoane, 'Secrets of the continental dirty war of the dictatorship', *Clarin*, 24 March 2006.

7   LJ van der Westhuizen and JH le Roux, *Armscor: The Leading Edge*, unpublished, University of the Free State, Institute for Contemporary History, 1997, pp. 362–364.

8   James Sanders, *Apartheid's Friends*, John Murray, London, 2006, p. 168.

9   Interview with Craig Williamson, Johannesburg, 29 January 2016.

10 James Adams, *The Unnatural Alliance: Israel and South Africa*, Quartet Books, London, 1984, pp. 103–104.

11 Interview with Craig Williamson, Johannesburg, 29 January 2016.

12 Scott J Higham, 'They, too, seek the presidency', *New York Times*, 30 September 1984.

13 Duvalier, who died in 2014, took over as president from his father 'Papa Doc' Duvalier. Between them their regimes are said to have been responsible for the murder of 30,000 Haitians. Baby Doc was named by Transparency International as one of the world's top ten kleptocrats and is alleged to have stolen between $300 and $800 million during his rule from 1971 to 1986. See Transparency International, *Global Corruption Report 2004*, Pluto Press, London, 2004, p. 13.

14 Correspondence from SSO Special Tasks to Directorate Intelligence, 28 November 1979, DOD/SANDF (DI Directorate Foreign Relations, GP 38, Box 154, DBB/SK/311/1/81/1, Yugoslavia, 1, 27/11/79–21/08/90).

15 Charles would also mount an unsuccessful challenge for president of Haiti in the 1987 elections. See Ronald Powers, 'Former candidate for Haitian presidency arrested in bank scam', Associated Press, 7 July 1989.

16 Correspondence from SSO Special Tasks to Directorate Intelligence, 28 November 1979, DOD/SANDF (DI Directorate Foreign Relations, GP 38, Box 154, DBB/SK/311/1/81/1, Yugoslavia, 1, 27/11/79–21/08/90).

17 Ibid.

18 Ibid.

19 Report on 'Opportunities in the Year 1980', 22 September 1979, DOD/SANDF (DI Directorate Foreign Relations, GP 38, Box 154, DBB/SK/311/1/81/1, Yugoslavia, 1, 27/11/79–21/08/90).

20 Correspondence from SSO Special Tasks to Directorate Intelligence, 28 November 1979, DOD/SANDF (DI Directorate Foreign Relations, GP 38, Box 154, DBB/SK/311/1/81/1, Yugoslavia, 1, 27/11/79–21/08/90).

21 Letter from MA Washington to CSI, 17 January 1980, DOD/SANDF
    (DI Directorate Foreign Relations, GP 38, Box 154, DBB/
    SK/311/1/81/1, Yugoslavia, 1, 27/11/79–21/08/90).
22 Ibid.
23 Correspondence from CSI to CSADF, 28 November 1979, DOD/
    SANDF (DI Directorate Foreign Relations, GP 38, Box 154, DBB/
    SK/311/1/81/1, Yugoslavia, 1, 27/11/79–21/08/90).
24 Only the name of one Argentinian official is revealed, Raoul Cavalini (but
    without any details of his rank or designation). See Correspondence from
    CSI to CSADF, 28 November 1979, DOD/SANDF (DI Directorate
    Foreign Relations, GP 38, Box 154, DBB/SK/311/1/81/1, Yugoslavia, 1,
    27/11/79–21/08/90).
25 Correspondence from SSO Special Tasks to Directorate Intelligence, 28
    November 1979, DOD/SANDF (DI Directorate Foreign Relations, GP
    38, Box 154, DBB/SK/311/1/81/1, Yugoslavia, 1, 27/11/79–21/08/90).
26 It is worth noting that there were strong historical ties between Croatian
    officials, who had supported the Nazi regime, and Argentina, where
    they fled through the 'rat lines' at the end of the Second World War.
    These fascists were absorbed into the 10,000-strong Croat community in
    Argentina, and may well have facilitated contact with the right-wing junta
    in Buenos Aires.
27 Correspondence from SSO Special Tasks to Directorate Intelligence, 28
    November 1979, DOD/SANDF (DI Directorate Foreign Relations, GP
    38, Box 154, DBB/SK/311/1/81/1, Yugoslavia, 1, 27/11/79–21/08/90).
28 Ibid.
29 Ibid.
30 Ibid.
31 Ibid.
32 Letter from MA Washington to CSI, 16 October 1979, DOD/SANDF
    (DI Directorate Foreign Relations, GP 38, Box 154, DBB/
    SK/311/1/81/1, Yugoslavia, 1, 27/11/79–21/08/90).
33 Letter from MA Washington to CSI, 1 November 1979, DOD/SANDF
    (DI Directorate Foreign Relations, GP 38, Box 154, DBB/
    SK/311/1/81/1, Yugoslavia, 1, 27/11/79–21/08/90).
34 Report on 'Opportunities in the Year 1980', 22 September 1979, DOD/
    SANDF (DI Directorate Foreign Relations, GP 38, Box 154, DBB/
    SK/311/1/81/1, Yugoslavia, 1, 27/11/79–21/08/90).
35 Correspondence from Director of Special Tasks to MA Washington, 6
    February 1980, DOD/SANDF (DI Directorate Foreign Relations, GP
    38, Box 154, DBB/SK/311/1/81/1, Yugoslavia, 1, 27/11/79–21/08/90).
36 Memorandum from Director of Military Intelligence to CSI, 4 October
    1979, DOD/SANDF (DI Directorate Foreign Relations, GP 38, Box 154,
    DBB/SK/311/1/81/1, Yugoslavia, 1, 27/11/79–21/08/90).
37 Ibid.
38 Report on 'Opportunities in the Year 1980', 22 September 1979, DOD/
    SANDF (DI Directorate Foreign Relations, GP 38, Box 154, DBB/
    SK/311/1/81/1, Yugoslavia, 1, 27/11/79–21/08/90).
39 Ibid.

40 Ibid.

41 Correspondence from Director of Special Tasks to CSI, 6 February 1981, DOD/SANDF (DI Directorate Foreign Relations, GP 38, Box 83, DBB/ SK/311/1/12/1, Organisasies in Iran, 1, 09/03/1980–11/05/1982).

42 Memorandum from Director of Special Tasks to CSI, 5 February 1982, DOD/SANDF (DI Directorate Foreign Relations, GP 38, Box 83, DBB/ SK/311/1/12/1, Organisasies in Iran, 1, 09/03/1980–11/05/1982).

43 Letter from DG NI to DG DFA and CSI, 6 March 1981, DOD/ SANDF (DI Directorate Foreign Relations, GP 38, Box 83, DBB/ SK/311/1/12/1, Organisasies in Iran, 1, 09/03/1980–11/05/1982).

44 'Chile and the United States: Declassified documents relating to the military coup', National Security Archive, George Washington University, 1998.

45 'Life under Pinochet – Isabelle Allende: "The day we buried our freedom"', Amnesty International, 11 September 2013.

46 Report on MI Visit to Chile by Admiral Putter, CSI, October 1988, DOD/SANDF (DI, GP 24, Box 284, AMI 520/3/4/18, Besoeke, bewegings, persone, vliegtuie. Besoeke aan die buiteland. SAW Krygkor personeel: Chile, 10, 10/08/1988–25/10/1988).

47 Extract from a paper titled 'The Chilean Connection', University of Fort Hare, ANC Archive (French Mission, Box 17, Folder 84, Israel–Chile– South Africa Axis 1988–1989).

48 Ibid.

49 Article from *El Mercurio* titled 'Chile and South Africa look for ways to overcome arms embargo', 17 September 1987, attached to memorandum from Mandi Msimang (ANC's UK representative) to ANC Secretary for International Affairs, 19 September 1989, University of Fort Hare, ANC Archive (Lusaka Mission, Correspondence, Box 3, Folder 21, ANC Mission).

50 'New SA arms on show', *The Argus*, 18 March 1988.

51 Press release by the World Campaign against Military and Nuclear Collaboration with SA, 7 March 1989, University of Fort Hare, ANC Archive (Belgium Mission, Box 2, Folder 12, ANC Statements/ Declarations 1990–1992).

52 Matt Moffett and Anthony Esposito, 'In Chile: A shot of atonement', *Wall Street Journal*, 5 March 2011.

53 Shirley Christian, 'Chilean arms maker helps fill a world demand', *New York Times*, 22 July 1987.

54 Letter from Adriaan Vlok to General Fernando Aubel, 16 May 1986, DOD/SANDF (DI, GP 38, Box 181, AMI/513/11/6, Chile, 2, 16/05/1986–11/08/1989).

55 Interview with Adriaan Vlok, Centurion, 28 January 2016.

56 Ibid.

57 Report on MI Visit to Chile by Admiral Putter, CSI, October 1988, DOD/SANDF (DI, GP 24, Box 284, AMI 520/3/4/18, Besoeke bewegings, persone, vliegtuie. Besoeke aan die buiteland. SAW Krygkor personeel: Chile, 10, 10/08/1988–25/10/1988).

58 Ibid.

59 Memorandum from the MA in Santiago to CSAAF and CSI, 22
    December 1988, DOD/SANDF (DI, GP 24, Box 136, MI/203/2/12,
    Insameling van Inligting. Eie Militêre Attachés. Chile, 13, 17/02/1988–
    15/09/1989).
60 Ibid.
61 Ibid.
62 Memorandum from CSI to CSADF, 11 February 1988, DOD/SANDF
    (DI, GP 24, Box 284, AMI 520/3/4/18, Besoeke, bewegings, persone,
    vliegtuie. Besoeke aan die buiteland. SAW Krygkor personeel: Chile, 9,
    08/12/1988–11/07/1988).
63 Ibid.
64 Interview with Chris Thirion, Pretoria, 11 December 2015.
65 Ibid.
66 Ibid.
67 Memorandum from MA Santiago to Director of Military Intelligence,
    20 October 1986, DOD/SANDF (DI, GP 24, Box 135, MI/203/2/12,
    Insameling van Inligting. Eie Militêre Attachés: Chile, 12, 10/10/1986–
    11/01/1988).
68 Letter from Magnus Malan to General Rodolfo Oelckers, 26 March
    1986, DOD/SANDF (DI, GP 38, Box 181, AMI/513/11/6, Chile, 1,
    25/06/1980–15/05/1986).
69 'Restoration of the lawful rights of the People's Republic of China in the
    United Nations', General Assembly, Twenty-Sixth Session, 25 October 1971.
70 Scrapbook with news excerpts of the visit of PW Botha and Mrs Botha
    to the Republic of China, October 1980, University of the Free State,
    Archive for Contemporary Affairs (PV 203, 11/1/3, 1980, PW Botha).
71 Telegram from Chiu Chuang-huan (Vice-Premier of China) to PW Botha,
    24 May 1983, University of the Free State, Archive for Contemporary
    Affairs (PV 203, A1/2/26, 1983 June–1985 August, PW Botha).
72 Letter from General Wang Sheng to PW Botha, 4 May 1981, University
    of the Free State, Archive for Contemporary Affairs (PV 203, A1/2/10,
    1981 May, PW Botha).
73 Ibid.
74 Letter from Hsing Yuan Yuan, Chinese Airforce Academy, to Brigadier
    General EE van Ravesteyn, 22 August 1988, DOD/SANDF (VERSLAE,
    Box 280, AMI/520/3/4, Visits: Overseas SAW Krygkor personeel, 56,
    19/08/88–07/09/88).
75 Memorandum from CSI to CSADF, 4 June 1988, DOD/SANDF
    (Verslae, Box 280, AMI/520/3/4, Visits: Overseas SAW Krygkor
    personeel, 56, 19/08/88–07/09/88).
76 Letter from Wen Ha-hsiung, General ROC Army, to General JJ
    Geldenhuys, CSADF, 26 December 1986, DOD/SANDF (DI
    Directorate Foreign Relations, GP 38, Box 183, AMI/513/11/19, ROC,
    2, 26/12/1986–20/08/1990).
77 Letter from Lt General Chao Chih-yuan to Lt General PW van der
    Westhuizen, CSI, 5 January 1984, DOD/SANDF (DI Directorate
    Foreign Relations, GP 38, Box 183, AMI/513/11/19, ROC, 1,
    25/05/1981–18/01/1987).

78 Letter from Col CY Kao to Lt General PW van der Westhuizen, CSI, 9 May 1983, DOD/SANDF (DI Directorate Foreign Relations, GP 38, Box 183, AMI/513/11/19, ROC, 1, 25/05/1981–18/01/1987).

79 Letter from General JJ Geldenhuys, CSADF, to General Hau Pei-tsun, 30 October 1986, DOD/SANDF (DI Directorate Foreign Relations, GP 38, Box 183, AMI/513/11/19, ROC, 1, 25/05/1981–18/01/1987).

80 Report from Capt PC Potgieter to the Director of Foreign Relations, 10 August 1988, DOD/SANDF (DI, GP 24, Box 285, AMI 520/3/4/25, Besoeke, bewegings, persone, vliegtuie, vaartuie. SAW Krygkor lede: ROC Taiwan, 8, 28/04/1988–09/12/1988).

81 Ibid.

82 Ibid.

83 Interview with Chris Thirion, Pretoria, 11 December 2015.

84 Ibid.

85 Ibid.

86 'South Africa: Sanctions update', Briefing document for CIA's Directorate of Intelligence, 5 May 1988, CIA CREST 25-year release programme.

87 Colin Nickerson, 'Asian companies find bonanza in S. African marketplace', *Boston Globe*, 22 May 1988.

88 Howard Witt, 'S. Africa sanctions not effective: Non-complying nations are picking up the trade slack', *Chicago Tribune*, 4 August 1988.

89 'South Africa: Sanctions update', Briefing document for CIA's Directorate of Intelligence, 5 May 1988, CIA CREST 25-year release programme.

90 Ibid.

91 Sasha Polakow-Suransky, *The Unspoken Alliance: Israel's Secret Relationship with Apartheid South Africa*, Jacana Media, Johannesburg, 2010, p. 57.

92 Van der Westhuizen and Le Roux, *Armscor*, pp. 240–241.

93 Polakow-Suransky, *The Unspoken Alliance*, p. 151.

94 Van der Westhuizen and Le Roux, *Armscor*, pp. 241–242.

95 Ibid., pp. 241–242.

96 Polakow-Suransky, *The Unspoken Alliance*, pp. 77–79.

97 Ibid., pp. 77–79.

98 Van der Westhuizen and Le Roux, *Armscor*, pp. 240–241.

99 Polakow-Suransky, *The Unspoken Alliance*, pp. 80–81.

100 Ibid., pp. 84–85.

101 Van der Westhuizen and Le Roux, *Armscor*, p. 245.

102 Polakow-Suransky, *The Unspoken Alliance*, p. 4.

103 Ibid., pp. 8–10.

104 Letter from Tel Aviv Consulate to DFA, 5 March 1975, DIRCO (Defence, 9/74, Vol. 1, Israel Military Cooperation).

105 Office Memorandum, Armaments Board Representation in Israel, 5 March 1975, DIRCO (Defence, 9/74, Vol. 1, Israel Military Cooperation).

106 Ibid.

107 Ibid.

108 Ibid.

109 Interview with Pierre Steyn, Pretoria, 11 November 2015.

110 Ibid.

111 SANDF, 'Telegram: Tel Aviv to Secextern Pretoria', 16 November 1981, AMI 105/11/16, vol. 3, 117, quoted in Sasha Polakow-Suransky, 'The atomic bond', South African Nuclear History Conference, Pretoria, December 2012.

112 SANDF, 'Telegram: Hopper to CSADF 2', 31 March 1981, AMI 105/11/16, vol. 3, 7, quoted in Polakow-Suransky, 'The atomic bond', South African Nuclear History Conference, Pretoria, December 2012.

113 Letter from Tel Aviv Embassy to Derek Auret, 10 October 1990, DIRCO (Defence, 9/74, Vol 2, 10/10/90–10/10/90, Israel Military Cooperation).

114 Five Year Budget for Pilgrim, October 1987, DOD/SANDF (DI, GP 25, Box 128, AMI 504/3/1 (89/90), Begroting 89/90, 4, 04/03/1988–20/05/1988).

115 Report by Col PJ Roos on Project Acantha, 19 March 1987, DOD/SANDF (Verslae, Box 244, 87/215, Visit Report – Project Acantha, 08/02/87–23/02/87).

116 Polakow-Suransky, *The Unspoken Alliance*.

117 Ibid., pp. 77–79.

118 Ibid., pp. 102–103.

119 Tadiran Electronic Industries was the largest private firm engaged in defence production, notably communications, electronic warfare, and command and control systems, as well as the pilotless reconnaissance aircraft (UAVs) of which Israel had become a leading manufacturer. See www.wikipedia.org/wiki/Defense_industry_of_Israel.

120 Interview with Armscor official, name withheld, Pretoria, 2014.

121 Interview with Craig Williamson, Johannesburg, 29 January 2016.

122 Ibid.

123 Polakow-Suransky, *The Unspoken Alliance*, pp. 102–103.

124 Extract from Annual Report Israel, 1975/1976, DIRCO (Defence, 9/74, Vol. 1, Israel Military Cooperation).

125 Letter from PG Marais to Magnus Malan, 13 August 1981, DOD/SANDF (MVV, GP 5, Box 88, 65/4, Krygkor: Beleid, 5, 24/03/1981–08/07/1992).

126 Ibid.

127 Memorandum from CS OPS to CSADF, May 1985, DOD/SANDF (CS OPS, GP 3, Box 308, CS OPS/311 1/13, Hulpverlening en Samewerking met ander Lande/Regerings: Israel, 1, 02/08/83–25/07/85).

128 Ibid.

129 Memorandum from CSADF to Chairman of Armscor, May 1985, DOD/SANDF (CS OPS, GP 3, Box 308, CS OPS/311 1/13, Hulpverlening en Samewerking met ander Lande/Regerings: Israel, 1, 02/08/83–25/07/85).

130 Memorandum from CS OPS to CSADF, May 1985, DOD/SANDF (CS OPS, GP 3, Box 308, CS OPS/311 1/13, Hulpverlening en Samewerking met ander Lande/Regerings: Israel, 1, 02/08/83–25/07/85).

131 Correspondence between PW Botha and Israeli Defence Minister Weizman, 7 December 1978, DIRCO (Defence, 9/74, Vol. 1, Israel Military Cooperation).

132 Gordon Thomas, *Gideon's Spies: The Inside Story of Israel's Legendary*

Secret Service, St Martin's Griffin, New York, 2014.

133 Ari Ben-Menashe, *Profits of War: Inside the Secret US–Israeli Arms Network*, Sheridan Square Publishers, New York, 1992.

134 Correspondence between PW Botha and Israeli Defence Minister Weizman, 7 December 1978, DIRCO (Defence, 9/74, Vol. 1, Israel Military Cooperation).

135 Ibid.

136 Polakow-Suransky, *The Unspoken Alliance*, p. 143.

137 CV of Ariel Sharon sent from CSADF to MoD, 30 June 1982, DOD/SANDF (MVV, GP 5, Box 103, MV/56/17, Israel, 3, 13/03/1980–1983)

138 Ibid.

139 Ibid.

140 'Itemised account of relationship between Israel and South Africa', *Southscan*, 2, 26 (16 March 1983).

141 Drew Middleton, 'South Africa needs more arms Israeli says', *New York Times*, 14 December 1981.

142 Leopold Scholtz, *The SADF in the Border War 1968–1989*, Tafelberg, Cape Town, 2013.

143 See the South African Air Force Museum website, www.saafmuseum.org/drone/267-kentron-champion.

144 See Steven Zaloga, *Unmanned Aerial Vehicles: Robotic Air Warfare 1917–2007*, Bloomsburg, London, 2011, p. 22, quoted in Wikipedia, Israel–South Africa relations.

145 See www.en.wikipedia.org/wiki/Sabra_and_Shatila_massacre.

146 Letter from Gen. Magnus Malan, Minister of Defence, South Africa, to Major General Ariel Sharon, Tel Aviv, 2 March 1983, MV/MS/56/17.

147 Letter from Ariel Sharon to Magnus Malan, 20 April 1983, DOD/SANDF (MVV, GP 5, Box 103, MV/56/17, Israel, 3, 13/03/1980–1983).

148 Polakow-Suransky, *The Unspoken Alliance*, p. 151.

149 Ibid., pp. 82–83.

150 'Israel's Peres denies South African nuclear weapons deal', *BBC News*, 24 May 2010.

151 Polakow-Suransky, *The Unspoken Alliance*, p. 121.

152 Handwritten Notes by Magnus Malan, November 1982, University of the Free State, Archive for Contemporary Affairs (PV 634, 5/1/1, 1989, Magnus Malan).

153 Ibid.

154 Ibid.

155 Ibid.

156 Polakow-Suransky, *The Unspoken Alliance*.

157 Ibid.

158 Ibid., pp. 152–155.

159 Letter from Tel Aviv Embassy to Derek Auret, 10 October 1990, DIRCO (Defence, 9/74, Vol. 2, 10/10/90–10/10/90, Israel Military Cooperation).

160 Ibid.

161 Ibid.

162 Report from PLU Viljoen to Derek Auret, 8 June 1993, DIRCO (Defence,

9/74, Vol. 2, 9/8/74–21/3/94, Israel Military Cooperation).

163 Ibid.

164 Ibid.

165 Summary of Meeting between Armscor and Israeli Minister of Defence, 24 June 1993, DIRCO (Defence, 9/74, Vol. 2, 9/8/74–21/3/94, Israel Military Cooperation).

166 Ibid.

167 Ibid.

168 Ibid.

Chapter 13

1 Minutes of a meeting between DA Lawson and Jorge Pinhol, Sloane Club, London, 11 September 2006.

2 Ibid.

3 Ibid.

4 Statement by Jorge Manuel Correia Pinhol da Encarnação, dated 4 May 2007, Open Secrets Collection.

5 Ibid.

6 Ibid.

7 Pinhol and his father, Luís Pinhol, had excellent relations with senior officials of the Portuguese armed forces, namely with General Espadinha, who was at the time the chairman of OGMA, a logistical support and maintenance company of the Portuguese Air Force.

8 Expert Legal Opinion by Professor Mark Pieth, 2 August 2007, Open Secrets Collection.

9 Statement by Jorge Manuel Correia Pinhol da Encarnação, dated 4 May 2007, Open Secrets Collection.

10 Ibid.

11 Monstrous Hatchlings, *Noseweek*, Number 132, October 2010, Cape Town.

12 Expert Legal Opinion by Professor Mark Pieth, 2 August 2007, Open Secrets Collection.

13 Ibid.

14 'Helicopter deal with France', *Indian Ocean Newsletter*, 9 November 1985, p. 2.

15 Motivation for Visit to France for Project Adenia from CSAAF, 2 June 1986, DOD/SANDF (CSF, GP 3, Box 793, 302/6/A160, SAW Proj: Proj Adenia, 1, 22/07/1985).

16 Ibid.

17 Ibid.

18 Memorandum from CSAAF on Project Adenia, 15 September 1986, DOD/SANDF (CSF, GP 3, Box 793, 302/6/A160, SAW Proj: Proj Adenia, 1, 22/07/1985).

19 Ibid.

20 Memorandum from CSAAF on Project Kingsley, 2 October 1986, DOD/ SANDF (CSF, GP 3, Box 793, 302/6/A160, SAW Proj: Proj Adenia, 1, 22/07/1985).

21 Expert Legal Opinion by Professor Mark Pieth, 2 August 2007, Open

Secrets Collection.   22   Judgment of Brussels Commercial
Court, *Beverly Securities Limited* v *KBC
Bank and Others*, Case Number: RG
3000/08, 2 April 2010; Armscor internal
documents.

23   Statement by Jorge Manuel Correia Pinhol da Encarnação, 4 May 2007,
Open Secrets Collection.

24   Judgment of Brussels Commercial Court, *Beverly Securities Limited* v
KBC Bank and Others, Case Number: RG 3000/08, 2 April 2010.

25   David Lawson, quoted in Anton Ferreira, 'Sanctions buster demands
R4bn', *Sunday Times*, 7 December 2014.

26   Interview with Pik Botha, Pretoria, 26 January 2016.

27   Moshoeshoe Monare, 'I'm no PR prostitute, says Zuma's spin doctor',
The Star, 30 July 2006. Göttert is not without controversy and sang
the requiem hymn, 'Pie Jesu', at the funeral of the slain fraudster Brett
Kebble (see ibid.).

28   Confidential Internal Minutes of the Lisbon meetings on 1 & 2
September 2010 between representatives of BSL/BSI and Armscor at the
Miranda law firm.

29   Ibid.

30   Ibid.

31   Ibid.

32   Ibid.

33   Ibid.

34   Ibid.

35   Ibid.

36   Ibid.

37   Serjeant at the Bar, 'Protector's report thin on ABSA's liability', *Mail &
Guardian*, 27 January 2017.

38   Interview with Michael Oatley, telephonic, 19 April 2013.

39   Ibid.

40   Pinky Khoabane, 'Uncensored opinion: Zuma promised to pursue case of
apartheid looting – CIEX', 13 January 2017.

41   The term 'deep state' is derived from the Turkish *derin devlet*. See 'What
is the "deep state"?', *The Economist*, 9 March 2017.

42   Pete Lewis, 'Understanding the silicosis judgment', *GroundUp*, 16 May
2016.

43   Juan Pablo Bohoslavsky and Veerle Opgenhaffen, 'The past and present of
corporate complicity: Financing the Argentinean dictatorship', *Harvard
Human Rights Journal*, 23 (2010), pp. 159–203.

44   Ibid., p. 170.

Index

This is a subject and name index arranged alphabetically in word-by-word order, so that 'Armament Board' is filed before 'arms'. *See* and *see also* references guide the reader to the preferred or alternative access terms used.

The Long Shadow
in numbers

$300 million

the current claim by an apartheid-era arms sanctions buster against the SA government.

$0 publicly disclosed

money given to big political parties by private donors in 2016.

$24 billion

apartheid foreign debt paid off by democratic SA government.*

*Current value

$5.1 billion

SA tax money illicitly moved offshore annually.

783 fraud and corruption charges

related to the Arms Deal that could be again brought against President Jacob Zuma.

30%

of youth (15–24) not in employment, education or training.

56%

of children do not complete matric.

90%

of South Africa's wealth is in the hands of

10%

of its people.

SA WEALTH

SA POPULATION

11 million

South Africans go hungry every day.

An Atlas of Apartheid Allies

Hom
estab
of th
netw
Vléri
grou
playe

Margaret Thatcher's Conservative government was staunchly against sanctions. While Tory MP Julian Amery co-ordinated covert intelligence operations for Pretoria, the maverick Tiny Rowland took care of sanctions busting.

Belg

Canada

Pretoria's covert operatives worked with US conservative groups and Reagan acolytes in backroom deals for arms and intelligence, while pouring money into Washington's lobbying firms.

 **United Kingdom**

⊙ ⚔ **France**

⊙ ⚔ **USA**

Paris was the centre of Armscor's weapons trading activities across Europe. Senior French politicians and intelligence officials approved the flow of weapons technology and information to Pretoria.

⊙ ⚔ Portugal
📦 ⚔ Spain
⊙ ⚔ Morocco

Panama 💰

Key

The players:

 The Big Five
The five permanent members of the UN Security Council.

 Proxy
Over 30 countries that bust sanctions in their own interests while the Big Five turned a blind eye

 Pariah
South Africa, Argentina, Chile, Israel and Taiwan were all outsider countries and generally regarded as pariahs within the international system.

Mobutu and his intelligence chiefs were close allies of Pretoria. Many covert arms shipments came to South Africa via Zaire, and military intelligence established important listening stations in the country.

📦 ⊙ Togo
💰 Liberia
⊙ Ivory Coast
📦 ⊙ Equatorial Guinea
📦 Gabon

⊙ ⚔ **Zaire**

⊙ ⚔ **Angola**

Many of the weapons obtained through Armscor's illicit procurement were for the use of the South African military and their ally, Jonas Savimbi's UNITA, in the civil war in Angola.

Covert trade:

⊙ Intelligence

⚔ Arms

🛢 Oil

📦 Commercial goods

💰 Finance

Paraguay ⚔
Chile ⊙ ⚔
Argentina ⊙ ⚔